T0280593

Scaling Up Machine Learning

Parallel and Distributed Approaches

This book comprises a collection of representative approaches for scaling up machine learning and data mining methods on parallel and distributed computing platforms. Demand for parallelizing learning algorithms is highly task-specific: in some settings it is driven by the enormous dataset sizes, in others by model complexity or by real-time performance requirements. Making task-appropriate algorithm and platform choices for large-scale machine learning requires understanding the benefits, trade-offs, and constraints of the available options.

Solutions presented in the book cover a range of parallelization platforms from FPGAs and GPUs to multi-core systems and commodity clusters; concurrent programming frameworks that include CUDA, MPI, MapReduce, and DryadLINQ; and various learning settings: supervised, unsupervised, semi-supervised, and online learning. Extensive coverage of parallelization of boosted trees, support vector machines, spectral clustering, belief propagation, and other popular learning algorithms accompanied by deep dives into several applications make the book equally useful for researchers, students, and practitioners.

Dr. Ron Bekkerman is a computer engineer and scientist whose experience spans across disciplines from video processing to business intelligence. Currently a senior research scientist at LinkedIn, he previously worked for a number of major companies including Hewlett-Packard and Motorola. Ron's research interests lie primarily in the area of large-scale unsupervised learning. He is the corresponding author of several publications in top-tier venues, such as ICML, KDD, SIGIR, WWW, IJCAI, CVPR, EMNLP, and JMLR.

Dr. Mikhail Bilenko is a researcher in the Machine Learning Group at Microsoft Research. His research interests center on machine learning and data mining tasks that arise in the context of large behavioral and textual datasets. Mikhail's recent work has focused on learning algorithms that leverage user behavior to improve online advertising. His papers have been published in KDD, ICML, SIGIR, and WWW among other venues, and I have received best paper awards from SIGIR and KDD.

Dr. John Langford is a computer scientist working as a senior researcher at Yahoo! Research. Previously, he was affiliated with the Toyota Technological Institute and IBM T. J. Watson Research Center. John's work has been published in conferences and journals including ICML, COLT, NIPS, UAI, KDD, JMLR, and MLJ. He received the Pat Goldberg Memorial Best Paper Award, as well as best paper awards from ACM EC and WSDM. He is also the author of the popular machine learning weblog, hunch.net.

Scaling Up Machine Learning

Parallel and Distributed Approaches

Edited by

Ron Bekkerman

Mikhail Bilenko

John Langford

CAMBRIDGE
UNIVERSITY PRESS

CAMBRIDGE
UNIVERSITY PRESS

University Printing House, Cambridge CB2 8BS, United Kingdom

One Liberty Plaza, 20th Floor, New York, NY 10006, USA

477 Williamstown Road, Port Melbourne, VIC 3207, Australia

314-321, 3rd Floor, Plot 3, Splendor Forum, Jasola District Centre, New Delhi - 110025, India

79 Anson Road, #06-04/06, Singapore 079906

Cambridge University Press is part of the University of Cambridge.

It furthers the University's mission by disseminating knowledge in the pursuit of
education, learning and research at the highest international levels of excellence.

www.cambridge.org
Information on this title: www.cambridge.org/9781108461740

© Cambridge University Press 2012

First published 2012
First paperback edition 2018

A catalogue record for this publication is available from the British Library

Library of Congress Cataloging in Publication data
Scaling up machine learning : parallel and distributed approaches / [edited by]
Ron Bekkerman, Mikhail Bilenko, John Langford.
   p. cm.
Includes index.
ISBN 978-0-521-19224-8 (hardback)
1. Machine learning. 2. Data mining. 3. Parallel algorithms. 4. Parallel programs
(Computer programs) I. Bekkerman, Ron. II. Bilenko, Mikhail. III. Langford, John.
Q325.5.S28 2011
006.3′1–dc23   2011016323

ISBN 978-0-521-19224-8 Hardback
ISBN 978-1-108-46174-0 Paperback

Contents

Part Three   Alternative Learning Settings

Contributors

Polina Akselrod
Yale University, New Haven, CT, USA

Arthur Asuncion
University of California, Irvine, CA, USA

Hongjie Bai
Google Research, Beijing, China

Sugato Basu
Google Research, Mountain View, CA, USA

Roberto J. Bayardo
Google Research, Mountain View, CA, USA

Ron Bekkerman
LinkedIn Corporation, Mountain View, CA, USA

Mikhail Bilenko
Microsoft Research, Redmond, WA, USA

Jeff Bilmes
University of Washington, Seattle, WA, USA

Mihai Budiu
Microsoft Research, Mountain View, CA, USA

Christopher J. C. Burges
Microsoft Research, Redmond, WA, USA

Srihari Cadambi
NEC Labs America, Princeton, NJ, USA

Srimat Chakradhar
NEC Labs America, Princeton, NJ, USA

Edward Y. Chang
Google Research, Beijing, China

Wen-Yen Chen
University of California, Santa Barbara, CA, USA

Jike Chong
Parasians LLC, Sunnyvale, CA, USA

Adam Coates
Stanford University. Stanford, CA, USA

Eric Cosatto
NEC Labs America, Princeton, NJ, USA

Eugenio Culurciello
Yale University, New Haven, CT, USA

Igor Durdanovic
NEC Labs America, Princeton, NJ, USA

Clément Farabet
New York University, New York, NY, USA

Dennis Fetterly
Microsoft Research, Mountain View, CA, USA

Amol Ghoting
IBM Research, Yorktown Heights, NY, USA

Ekaterina Gonina
University of California, Berkeley, CA, USA

Joseph Gonzalez
Carnegie Mellon University, Pittsburgh, PA, USA

Hans Peter Graf
NEC Labs America, Princeton, NJ, USA

Carlos Guestrin
Carnegie Mellon University, Pittsburgh, PA, USA

Joshua S. Herbach
Google Inc., Mountain View, CA, USA

Daniel Hsu
Rutgers University, Piscataway, NJ, USA and University of Pennsylvania, Philadelphia, PA, USA

Meichun Hsu
HP Labs, Palo Alto, CA, USA

Michael Isard
Microsoft Research, Mountain View, CA, USA

Venkata Jakkula
NEC Labs America, Princeton, NJ, USA

Nikos Karampatziakis
Cornell University, Ithaca, NY, USA

Koray Kavukcuoglu
NEC Labs America, Princeton, NJ, USA

Kurt Keutzer
University of California, Berkeley, CA, USA

Jeremy Kubica
Google Inc., Pittsburgh, PA, USA

John Langford
Yahoo! Research, New York, NY, USA

Yann LeCun
New York University, New York, NY, USA

Jian Li
Google Research, Beijing, China

Chih-Jen Lin
National Taiwan University, Taipei, Taiwan

Nathan Liu
Hong Kong University of Science and Technology, Kowloon, Hong Kong

Yucheng Low
Carnegie Mellon University, Pittsburgh, PA, USA

Abhinandan Majumdar
NEC Labs America, Princeton, NJ, USA

Berin Martini
Yale University, New Haven, CT, USA

Frank McSherry
Microsoft Research, Mountain View, CA, USA

Ramesh Natarajan
IBM Research, Yorktown Heights, NY, USA

David Newman
University of California, Irvine, CA, USA

Andrew Y. Ng
Stanford University. Stanford, CA, USA

Biswanath Panda
Google Inc., Mountain View, CA, USA

Srinivasan Parthasarathy
Ohio State University, Columbus, OH, USA

Edwin Pednault
IBM Research, Yorktown Heights, NY, USA

Ian Porteous
Google Inc., Kirkland, WA, USA

Zhihuan Qiu
Google Research, Beijing, China

Rajat Raina
Facebook Inc., Palo Alto, CA, USA

Martin Scholz
HP Labs, Palo Alto, CA, USA

Sameer Singh
University of Massachusetts, Amherst,
MA, USA

Alex J. Smola
Yahoo! Research, Santa Clara, NY, USA

Padhraic Smyth
University of California, Irvine, CA,
USA

Yangqiu Song
Tsinghua University, Beijing, China

Daria Sorokina
Yandex Labs, Palo Alto, CA, USA

Amarnag Subramanya
Google Research, Mountain View, CA,
USA

Krysta M. Svore
Microsoft Research, Redmond, WA,
USA

Selcuk Talay
Yale University, New Haven, CT, USA

Shirish Tatikonda
IBM Research, San Jose, CA, USA

Scott Triglia
University of California, Irvine, CA,
USA

Hao Wang
Google Research, Beijing, China

Max Welling
University of California, Irvine, CA,
USA

Ren Wu
HP Labs, Palo Alto, CA, USA

Evan Xiang
Hong Kong University of Science and
Technology, Kowloon, Hong Kong

Qiang Yang
Hong Kong University of Science and
Technology, Kowloon, Hong Kong

Elad Yom-Tov
Yahoo! Research, New York, NY, USA

Kisun You
Seoul National University, Seoul, Korea

Yuan Yu
Microsoft Research, Mountain View,
CA, USA

Bin Zhang
HP Labs, Palo Alto, CA, USA

Kaihua Zhu
Google Research, Beijing, China

Preface

This book attempts to aggregate state-of-the-art research in parallel and distributed machine learning. We believe that parallelization provides a key pathway for scaling up machine learning to large datasets and complex methods. Although large-scale machine learning has been increasingly popular in both industrial and academic research communities, there has been no singular resource covering the variety of approaches recently proposed. We did our best to assemble the most representative contemporary studies in one volume. While each contributed chapter concentrates on a distinct approach and problem, together with their references they provide a comprehensive view of the field.

We believe that the book will be useful to the broad audience of researchers, practitioners, and anyone who wants to grasp the future of machine learning. To smooth the ramp-up for beginners, the first five chapters provide introductory material on machine learning algorithms and parallel computing platforms. Although the book gets deeply technical in some parts, the reader is assumed to have only basic prior knowledge of machine learning and parallel/distributed computing, along with college-level mathematical maturity. We hope that an engineering undergraduate who is familiar with the notion of a classifier and had some exposure to threads, MPI, or MapReduce will be able to understand the majority of the book's content. We also hope that a seasoned expert will find this book full of new, interesting ideas to inspire future research in the area.

We are deeply thankful to all chapter authors for significant investments of their time, talent, and creativity in preparing their contributions to this volume. We appreciate the efforts of our editors at Cambridge University Press: Heather Bergman, who initiated this project, and Lauren Cowles, who worked with us throughout the process, guiding the book to completion. We thank chapter reviewers who provided detailed, thoughtful feedback to chapter authors that was invaluable in shaping the book: David Andrzejewski, Yoav Artzi, Arthur Asuncion, Hongjie Bai, Sugato Basu, Andrew Bender, Mark Chapman, Wen-Yen Chen, Sulabh Choudhury, Adam Coates, Kamalika Das, Kevin Duh, Igor Durdanovic, Clément Farabet, Dennis Fetterly, Eric Garcia, Joseph Gonzalez, Isaac Greenbaum, Caden Howell, Ferris Jumah, Andrey Kolobov, Jeremy

Kubica, Bo Li, Luke McDowell, W. P. McNeill, Frank McSherry, Chris Meek, Xu Miao, Steena Monteiro, Miguel Osorio, Sindhu Vijaya Raghavan, Paul Rodrigues, Martin Scholz, Suhail Shergill, Sameer Singh, Tom Sommerville, Amarnag Subramanya, Narayanan Sundaram, Krysta Svore, Shirish Tatikonda, Amund Tveit, Jean Wu, Evan Xiang, Elad Yom-Tov, and Bin Zhang.

Ron Bekkerman would like to thank Martin Scholz for his personal involvement in this project since its initial stage. Ron is deeply grateful to his mother Faina, wife Anna, and daughter Naomi, for their endless love and support throughout all his ventures.

CHAPTER 1

Scaling Up Machine Learning: Introduction

Ron Bekkerman, Mikhail Bilenko, and John Langford

Distributed and parallel processing of very large datasets has been employed for decades in specialized, high-budget settings, such as financial and petroleum industry applications. Recent years have brought dramatic progress in usability, cost effectiveness, and diversity of parallel computing platforms, with their popularity growing for a broad set of data analysis and machine learning tasks.

The current rise in interest in scaling up machine learning applications can be partially attributed to the evolution of hardware architectures and programming frameworks that make it easy to exploit the types of parallelism realizable in many learning algorithms. A number of platforms make it convenient to implement concurrent processing of data instances or their features. This allows fairly straightforward parallelization of many learning algorithms that view input as an unordered batch of examples and aggregate isolated computations over each of them.

Increased attention to large-scale machine learning is also due to the spread of very large datasets across many modern applications. Such datasets are often accumulated on distributed storage platforms, motivating the development of learning algorithms that can be distributed appropriately. Finally, the proliferation of sensing devices that perform real-time inference based on high-dimensional, complex feature representations drives additional demand for utilizing parallelism in learning-centric applications. Examples of this trend include speech recognition and visual object detection becoming commonplace in autonomous robots and mobile devices.

The abundance of distributed platform choices provides a number of options for implementing machine learning algorithms to obtain efficiency gains or the capability to process very large datasets. These options include customizable integrated circuits (e.g., Field-Programmable Gate Arrays – FPGAs), custom processing units (e.g., general-purpose Graphics Processing Units – GPUs), multiprocessor and multicore parallelism, High-Performance Computing (HPC) clusters connected by fast local networks, and datacenter-scale virtual clusters that can be rented from commercial cloud computing providers. Aside from the multiple platform options, there exists a variety of programming frameworks in which algorithms can be implemented. Framework choices tend to be particularly diverse for distributed architectures, such as clusters of commodity PCs.

The wide range of platforms and frameworks for parallel and distributed computing presents both opportunities and challenges for machine learning scientists and engineers. Fully exploiting the available hardware resources requires adapting some algorithms and redesigning others to enable their concurrent execution. For any prediction model and learning algorithm, their structure, dataflow, and underlying task decomposition must be taken into account to determine the suitability of a particular infrastructure choice.

Chapters making up this volume form a representative set of state-of-the-art solutions that span the space of modern parallel computing platforms and frameworks for a variety of machine learning algorithms, tasks, and applications. Although it is infeasible to cover every existing approach for every platform, we believe that the presented set of techniques covers most commonly used methods, including the popular "top performers" (e.g., boosted decision trees and support vector machines) and common "baselines" (e.g., k-means clustering).

Because most chapters focus on a single choice of platform and/or framework, the rest of this introduction provides the reader with unifying context: a brief overview of machine learning basics and fundamental concepts in parallel and distributed computing, a summary of typical task and application scenarios that require scaling up learning, and thoughts on evaluating algorithm performance and platform trade-offs. Following these are an overview of the chapters and bibliography notes.

1.1 Machine Learning Basics

Machine learning focuses on constructing algorithms for making predictions from data. A machine learning task aims to identify (to *learn*) a function $f : \mathcal{X} \to \mathcal{Y}$ that maps input domain $\mathcal{X}$ (of data) onto output domain $\mathcal{Y}$ (of possible predictions). The function f is selected from a certain function class, which is different for each family of learning algorithms. Elements of $\mathcal{X}$ and $\mathcal{Y}$ are application-specific representations of data objects and predictions, respectively.

Two canonical machine learning settings are *supervised learning* and *unsupervised learning*. Supervised learning algorithms utilize *training data* to construct a prediction function f, which is subsequently applied to *test* instances. Typically, training data is provided in the form of *labeled examples* $(x, y) \in \mathcal{X} \times \mathcal{Y}$, where x is a data instance and y is the corresponding *ground truth* prediction for x.

The ultimate goal of supervised learning is to identify a function f that produces accurate predictions on test data. More formally, the goal is to minimize the prediction error (*loss*) function $l : \mathcal{Y} \times \mathcal{Y} \to \mathbb{R}$, which quantifies the difference between any $f(x)$ and y – the predicted output of x and its ground truth label. However, the loss cannot be minimized directly on test instances and their labels because they are typically unavailable at training time. Instead, supervised learning algorithms aim to construct predictive functions that *generalize* well to previously unseen data, as opposed to performing optimally just on the given training set, that is, *overfitting* the training data.

The most common supervised learning setting is *induction*, where it is assumed that each training and test example (x, y) is sampled from some unknown joint probability distribution P over $\mathcal{X} \times \mathcal{Y}$. The objective is to find f that minimizes *expected loss* $\mathbb{E}_{(x,y)\sim P} \, l(f(x), y)$. Because the joint distribution P is unknown, expected loss cannot be minimized in closed form; hence, learning algorithms approximate it based on training examples. Additional supervised learning settings include *semi-supervised learning* (where the input data consists of both labeled and unlabeled instances), *transfer learning*, and *online learning* (see Section 1.6.3).

Two classic supervised learning tasks are *classification* and *regression*. In classification, the output domain is a finite discrete set of categories (*classes*), $\mathcal{Y} = \{c_1, ..., c_k\}$, whereas in regression the output domain is the set of real numbers, $\mathcal{Y} = \mathbb{R}$. More complex output domains are explored within advanced learning frameworks, such as *structured learning* (Bakir et al., 2007).

The simplest classification scenario is *binary*, in which there are two classes. Let us consider a small example. Assume that the task is to learn a function that predicts whether an incoming email message is spam or not. A common way to represent textual messages is as large, sparse vectors, in which every entry corresponds to a vocabulary word, and non-zero entries represent words that are present in the message. The label can be represented as 1 for spam and -1 for nonspam. With this representation, it is common to learn a vector of weights w optimizing $f(x) = \text{sign}\left(\sum_i w_i x_i\right)$ so as to predict the label.

The most prominent example of unsupervised learning is *data clustering*. In clustering, the goal is to construct a function f that partitions an *unlabeled* dataset into $k = |\mathcal{Y}|$ clusters, with $\mathcal{Y}$ being the set of cluster indices. Data instances assigned to the same cluster should presumably be more similar to each other than to data instances assigned to any other cluster. There are many ways to define similarity between data instances; for example, for vector data, (inverted) Euclidean distance and cosine similarity are commonly used. Clustering quality is often measured against a dataset with existing class labels that are withheld during clustering: a quality measure penalizes f if it assigns instances of the same class to different clusters and instances of different classes to the same cluster.

We note that both supervised and unsupervised learning settings distinguish between *learning* and *inference* tasks, where learning refers to the process of identifying the prediction function f, while inference refers to computing $f(x)$ on a data instance x. For many learning algorithms, inference is a component of the learning process, as predictions of some interim candidate f' on the training data are used in the search for the optimal f. Depending on the application domain, scaling up may be required for either the learning or the inference algorithm, and chapters in this book present numerous examples of speeding up both.

1.2 Reasons for Scaling Up Machine Learning

There are a number of settings where a practitioner could find the scale of a machine learning task daunting for single-machine processing and consider employing parallelization. Such settings are characterized by:

1. **Large number of data instances:** In many domains, the number of potential training examples is extremely large, making single-machine processing infeasible.

2. **High input dimensionality:** In some applications, data instances are represented by a very large number of features. Machine learning algorithms may partition computation across the set of features, which allows scaling up to lengthy data representations.
3. **Model and algorithm complexity:** A number of high-accuracy learning algorithms either rely on complex, nonlinear models, or employ computationally expensive subroutines. In both cases, distributing the computation across multiple processing units can be the key enabler for learning on large datasets.
4. **Inference time constraints:** Applications that involve sensing, such as robot navigation or speech recognition, require predictions to be made in real time. Tight constraints on inference speed in such settings invite parallelization of inference algorithms.
5. **Prediction cascades:** Applications that require sequential, interdependent predictions have highly complex joint output spaces, and parallelization can significantly speed up inference in such settings.
6. **Model selection and parameter sweeps:** Tuning hyper-parameters of learning algorithms and statistical significance evaluation require multiple executions of learning and inference. Fortunately, these procedures belong to the category of so-called *embarrassingly parallelizable* applications, naturally suited for concurrent execution.

The following sections discuss each of these scenarios in more detail.

1.2.1 Large Number of Data Instances

Datasets that aggregate billions of events per day have become common in a number of domains, such as internet and finance, with each event being a potential input to a learning algorithm. Also, more and more devices include sensors continuously logging observations that can serve as training data. Each data instance may have, for example, thousands of non-zero features on average, resulting in datasets of 10^{12} instance–feature pairs per day. Even if each feature takes only 1 byte to store, datasets collected over time can easily reach hundreds of terabytes.

The preferred way to effectively process such datasets is to combine the distributed storage and bandwidth of a cluster of machines. Several computational frameworks have recently emerged to ease the use of large quantities of data, such as MapReduce and DryadLINQ, used in several chapters in this book. Such frameworks combine the ability to use high-capacity storage and execution platforms with programming via simple, naturally parallelizable language primitives.

1.2.2 High Input Dimensionality

Machine learning and data mining tasks involving natural language, images, or video can easily have input dimensionality of 10^6 or higher, far exceeding the comfortable scale of $10 - 1,000$ features considered common until recently. Although data in some of these domains is sparse, that is not always the case; sparsity is also lost in the parameter space of many algorithms. Parallelizing the computation across features can thus be an attractive pathway for scaling up computation to richer representations, or just for speeding up algorithms that naturally iterate over features, such as decision trees.

1.2.3 Model and Algorithm Complexity

Data in some domains has inherently nonlinear structure with respect to the basic features (e.g., pixels or words). Models that employ highly nonlinear representations, such as decision tree ensembles or multi-layer (deep) networks, can significantly outperform simpler algorithms in such applications. Although feature engineering can yield high accuracies with computationally cheap linear models in these domains, there is a growing interest in learning as automatically as possible from the base representation. A common characteristic of algorithms that attempt this is their substantial computational complexity. Although the training data may easily fit on one machine, the learning process may simply be too slow for a reasonable development cycle. This is also the case for some learning algorithms, the computational complexity of which is superlinear in the number of training examples.

For problems of this nature, parallel multinode or multicore implementations appear viable and have been employed successfully, allowing the use of complex algorithms and models for larger datasets. In addition, coprocessors such as GPUs have also been employed successfully for fast transformation of the original input space.

1.2.4 Inference Time Constraints

The primary means for reducing the testing time is via embarrassingly parallel replication. This approach works well for settings where *throughput* is the primary concern – the number of evaluations to be done is very large. Consider, for example, evaluating 10^{10} emails per day in a spam filter, which is not expected to output results in real time, yet must not become backlogged.

Inference latency is generally a more stringent concern compared to throughput. Latency issues arise in any situation where systems are waiting for a prediction, and the overall application performance degrades rapidly with latency. For instance, this occurs for a car-driving robot making path planning decisions based on several sensors, or an online news provider that aims to improve user experience by selecting suggested stories using on-the-fly personalization.

Constraints on throughput and latency are not entirely compatible – for example, data pipelining trades throughput for latency. However, for both of them, utilizing highly parallelized hardware architectures such as GPUs or FPGAs has been found effective.

1.2.5 Prediction Cascades

Many real-world problems such as object tracking, speech recognition, and machine translation require performing a sequence of interdependent predictions, forming *prediction cascades*. If a cascade is viewed as a single inference task, it has a large joint output space, typically resulting in very high computational costs due to increased computational complexity. Interdependencies between the prediction tasks are typically tackled by stagewise parallelization of individual tasks, along with adaptive task management, as illustrated by the approach of Chapter 21 to speech recognition.

1.2.6 Model Selection and Parameter Sweeps

The practice of developing, tuning, and evaluating learning algorithms relies on workflow that is embarrassingly parallel: it requires no intercommunication between the tasks with independent executions on the same dataset. Two particular processes of this nature are parameter sweeps and statistical significance testing. In parameter sweeps, the learning algorithm is run multiple times on the same dataset with different settings, followed by evaluation on a validation set. During statistical significance testing procedures such as cross-validation or bootstrapping, training and testing is performed repeatedly on different dataset subsets, with results aggregated for subsequent measurement of statistical significance. Usefulness of parallel platforms is obvious for these tasks, as they can be easily performed concurrently without the need to parallelize actual learning and inference algorithms.

1.3 Key Concepts in Parallel and Distributed Computing

Performance gains attainable in machine learning applications by employing parallel and distributed systems are driven by concurrent execution of tasks that are otherwise performed serially. There are two major directions in which this concurrency is realized: *data parallelism* and *task parallelism*. Data parallelism refers to simultaneous processing of multiple inputs, whereas task parallelism is achieved when algorithm execution can be partitioned into segments, some of which are independent and hence can be executed concurrently.

1.3.1 Data Parallelism

Data parallelism refers to executing the same computation on multiple inputs concurrently. It is a natural fit for many machine learning applications and algorithms that accept input data as a batch of independent samples from an underlying distribution. Representation of these samples via an instance-by-feature matrix naturally suggests two orthogonal directions for achieving data parallelism. One is partitioning the matrix rowwise into subsets of instances that are then processed independently (e.g., when computing the update to the weights for logistic regression). The other is splitting it columnwise for algorithms that can decouple the computation across features (e.g., for identifying the split feature in decision tree construction).

The most basic example of data parallelism is encountered in embarrassingly parallel algorithms, where the computation is split into concurrent subtasks requiring no intercommunication, which run independently on separate data subsets. A related simple implementation of data parallelism occurs within the *master–slave communication model*: a master process distributes the data across slave processes that execute the same computation (see, e.g., Chapters 8 and 16).

Less obvious cases of data parallelism arise in algorithms where instances or features are not independent, but there exists a well-defined relational structure between them that can be represented as a graph. Data parallelism can then be achieved if the computation can be partitioned across instances based on this structure. Then, concurrent execution on different partitions is interlaced with exchange of information across them; approaches presented in Chapters 10 and 15 rely on this algorithmic pattern.

The foregoing examples illustrate coarse-grained data parallelism over subsets of instances or features that can be achieved via algorithm design. Fine-grained data parallelism, in contrast, refers to exploiting the capability of modern processor architectures that allow parallelizing vector and matrix computations in hardware. Standard libraries such as BLAS and LAPACK[1] provide routines that abstract out the execution of basic vector and matrix operations. Learning algorithms that can be represented as cascades of such operations can then leverage hardware-supported parallelism by making the corresponding API calls, dramatically simplifying the algorithms' implementation.

1.3.2 Task Parallelism

Unlike data parallelism defined by performing the same computation on multiple inputs simultaneously, task parallelism refers to segmenting the overall algorithm into parts, some of which can be executed concurrently. Fine-grained task parallelism for numerical computations can be performed automatically by many modern architectures (e.g., via pipelining) but can also be implemented semimanually on certain platforms, such as GPUs, potentially resulting in very significant efficiency gains, but requiring in-depth platform expertise. Coarse-grained task parallelism requires explicit encapsulation of each task in the algorithm's implementation as well as a scheduling service, which is typically provided by a programming framework.

The partitioning of an algorithm into tasks can be represented by a directed acyclic graph, with nodes corresponding to individual tasks, and edges representing inter-task dependencies. Dataflow between tasks occurs naturally along the graph edges. A prominent example of such a platform is MapReduce, a programming model for distributed computation introduced by Dean and Ghemawat (2004), on which several chapters in this book rely; see Chapter 2 for more details. Additional cross-task communication can be supported by platforms via point-to-point and broadcast messaging. The Message Passing Interface (MPI) introduced by Gropp et al. (1994) is an example of such messaging protocol that is widely supported across many platforms and programming languages. Several chapters in this book rely on it; see Section 4.4 of Chapter 4 for more details. Besides wide availability, MPI's popularity is due to its flexibility: it supports both point-to-point and collective communication, with synchronous and asynchronous mechanisms.

For many algorithms, scaling up can be most efficiently achieved by a mixture of data and task parallelism. Capability for hybrid parallelism is realized by most modern platforms: for example, it is exhibited both by the highly distributed DryadLINQ framework described in Chapter 3 and by computer vision algorithms implemented on GPUs and customized hardware as described in Chapters 18 and 19.

1.4 Platform Choices and Trade-Offs

Let us briefly summarize the key dimensions along which parallel and distributed platforms can be characterized. The classic taxonomy of parallel architectures proposed

---

[1] http://www.netlib.org/blas/ and http://www.netlib.org/lapack/.

by Flynn (1972) differentiates them by concurrency of algorithm execution (single vs. multiple instruction) and input processing (single vs. multiple data streams). Further distinctions can be made based on the configuration of shared memory and the organization of processing units. Modern parallel architectures are typically based on hybrid topologies where processing units are organized hierarchically, with multiple layers of shared memory. For example, GPUs typically have dozens of multiprocessors, each of which has multiple stream processors organized in "blocks". Individual blocks have access to relatively small locally shared memory and a much larger globally shared memory (with higher latency).

Unlike parallel architectures, distributed computing platforms typically have larger (physical) distances between processing units, resulting in higher latencies and lower bandwidth. Furthermore, individual processing units may be heterogeneous, and direct communication between them may be limited or nonexistent either via shared memory or via message passing, with the extreme case being one where all dataflow is limited to task boundaries, as is the case for MapReduce.

The overall variety of parallel and distributed platforms and frameworks that are now available for machine learning applications may seem overwhelming. However, the following observations capture the key differentiating aspects between the platforms:

- **Parallelism granularity:** Employing hardware-specific solutions – GPUs and FPGAs – allows very fine-grained data and task parallelism, where elementary numerical tasks (operations on vectors, matrices, and tensors) can be spread across multiple processing units with very high throughput achieved by pipelining. However, using this capability requires redefining the entire algorithm as a dataflow of such elementary tasks and eliminating bottlenecks. Moving up to parallelism across cores and processors in generic CPUs, the constraints on defining the algorithm as a sequence of finely tuned stages are relaxed, and parallelism is no longer limited to elementary numeric operations. With cluster- and datacenter-scale solutions, defining higher-granularity tasks becomes imperative because of increasing communication costs.
- **Degree of algorithm customization:** Depending on platform choice, the complexity of algorithm redesign required for enabling concurrency may vary from simply using a third-party solution for automatic parallelization of an existing imperative or declarative-style implementation, to having to completely re-create the algorithm, or even implement it directly in hardware. Generally, implementing learning algorithms on hardware-specific platforms (e.g., GPUs) requires significant expertise, hardware-aware task configuration, and avoiding certain commonplace software patterns such as branching. In contrast, higher-level parallel and distributed systems allow using multiple, commonplace programming languages extended by APIs that enable parallelism.
- **Ability to mix programming paradigms:** Declarative programming languages are becoming increasingly popular for large-scale data manipulation, borrowing from a variety of predecessors – from functional programming to SQL – to make parallel programming easier by expressing algorithms primarily as a mixture of logic and dataflow. Such languages are often hybridized with the classic imperative programming to provide maximum expressiveness. Examples of this trend include Microsoft's DryadLINQ,

Google's Sawzall and Pregel, and Apache Pig and Hive. Even in applications where such declarative-style languages are insufficient for expressing the learning algorithms, they are often used for computing the basic first- and second-order statistics that produce highly predictive features for many learning tasks.

- **Dataset scale-out:** Applications that process datasets too large to fit in memory commonly rely on distributed filesystems or shared-memory clusters. Parallel computing frameworks that are tightly coupled with distributed dataset storage allow optimizing task allocation during scheduling to maximize local dataflows. In contrast, scheduling in hardware-specific parallelism is decoupled from storage solutions used for very large datasets and hence requires crafting manual solutions to maximize throughput.
- **Offline vs online execution:** Distributed platforms typically assume that their user has higher tolerance for failures and latency compared to hardware-specific solutions. For example, an algorithm implemented via MapReduce and submitted to a virtual cluster typically has no guarantees on completion time. In contrast, GPU-based algorithms can assume dedicated use of the platform, which may be preferable for real-time applications.

Finally, we should note that there is a growing trend for hybridization of the multiple parallelization levels: for example, it is now possible to rent clusters comprising multicore nodes with attached GPUs from commercial cloud computing providers. Given a particular application at hand, the choice of the platform and programming framework should be guided by the criteria just given to identify an appropriate solution.

1.5 Thinking about Performance

The term "performance" is deeply ambiguous for parallel learning algorithms, as it includes both predictive accuracy and computational speed, each of which can be measured by a number of metrics. The variety of learning problems addressed in the chapters of this book makes the presented approaches generally incomparable in terms of predictive performance: the algorithms are designed to optimize different objectives in different settings. Even in those cases where the same problem is addressed, such as binary classification or clustering, differences in application domains and evaluation methodology typically lead to incomparability in accuracy results. As a consequence of this, it is not possible to provide a meaningful quantitative summary of relative accuracy across the chapters in the book, although it should be understood in every case that the authors strove to create effective algorithms.

Classical analysis of algorithms' complexity is based on O-notation (or its brethren) to bound and quantify computational costs. This approach meets difficulties with many machine learning algorithms, as they often include optimization-based termination conditions for which no formal analysis exists. For example, a typical early stopping algorithm may terminate when predictive error measured on a holdout test set begins to rise – something that is difficult to analyze because the core algorithm does not have access to this test set by design.

Nevertheless, individual subroutines within learning algorithms do often have clear computational complexities. When examining algorithms and considering their application to a given domain, we suggest asking the following questions:

1. What is the computational complexity of the algorithm or of its subroutine? Is it linear (i.e., $O(\text{input size})$)? Or superlinear? In general, there is a qualitative difference between algorithms scaling as $O(\text{input size})$ and others scaling as $O(\text{input size}^{\alpha})$ for $\alpha \geq 2$. For all practical purposes, algorithms with cubic and higher complexities are not applicable to real-world tasks of the modern scale.
2. What is the bandwidth requirement for the algorithm? This is particularly important for any algorithm distributed over a cluster of computers, but is also relevant for parallel algorithms that use shared memory or disk resources. This question comes in two flavors: What is the aggregate bandwidth used? And what is the maximum bandwidth of any node? Answers of the form $O(\text{input size})$, $O(\text{instances})$, and $O(\text{parameters})$ can all arise naturally depending on how the data is organized and the algorithm proceeds. These answers can have a very substantial impact on running time, as the input dataset may be, say, 10^{14} bytes in size, yet have only 10^{10} examples and 10^{8} parameters.

Key metrics used for analyzing computational performance of parallel algorithms are speedup, efficiency, and scalability:

*   *Speedup* is the ratio of solution time for the sequential algorithms versus its parallel counterpart.
*   *Efficiency* measures the ratio of speedup to the number of processors.
*   *Scalability* tracks efficiency as a function of an increasing number of processors.

For reasons explained earlier, these measures can be nontrivial to evaluate analytically for machine learning algorithms, and generally should be considered in conjunction with accuracy comparisons. However, these measures are highly informative in empirical studies. From a practical standpoint, given the differences in hardware employed for parallel and sequential implementations, viewing these metrics as functions of costs (hardware and implementation) is important for fair comparisons.

Empirical evaluation of computational costs for different algorithms should be ideally performed by comparing them on the same datasets. As with predictive performance, this may not be done for the work presented in subsequent chapters, given the dramatic differences in tasks, application domains, underlying frameworks, and implementations for the different methods. However, it is possible to consider the general *feature throughput* of the methods presented in different chapters, defined as $\frac{\text{running time}}{\text{input size}}$. Based on the results reported across chapters, well-designed parallelized methods are capable of obtaining high efficiency across the different platforms and tasks.

1.6 Organization of the Book

Chapters in this book span a range of computing platforms, learning algorithms, prediction problems, and application domains, describing a variety of parallelization techniques to scale up machine learning. The book is organized in four parts. The

Table 1.1. *Chapter summary.*

Chapter	Platform	Parallelization Framework	Learning Setting	Algorithms/ Applications
2	Cluster	MapReduce	Clustering, classification	k-Means, decision tree ensembles
3	Cluster	DryadLINQ	Multiple	k-Means, decision trees, SVD
4	Cluster	MPI	Multiple	Kernel k-means, decision trees, frequent pattern mining
5	GPU	CUDA	Clustering, regression	k-Means, regression k-means
6	Cluster	MPI	Classification	SVM (IPM)
7	Cluster, multicore, FPGA	TCP, UDP, threads, HDL	Classification, regression	SVM (SMO)
8	Cluster	MPI	Ranking	LambdaMART, web search
9	Cluster	MPI	Regression, classification	Transform regression
10	Cluster	MPI	Inference	Loopy belief propagation
11	Cluster	MPI	Inference	MCMC
12	Cluster	MapReduce, MPI	Clustering	Spectral clustering
13	Cluster	MPI	Clustering	Information-theoretic clustering
14	Cluster	TCP, threads	Classification, regression	Online learning
15	Cluster, multicore	TCP, threads	Semi-supervised learning (SSL)	Graph-based SSL
16	Cluster	MPI	Transfer learning	Collaborative filtering
17	Cluster	MapReduce	Classification	Feature selection
18	GPU	CUDA	Classification	Object detection, feature extraction
19	FPGA	HDL	Classification	Object detection, feature extraction
20	Multicore	Threads, task queue	Pattern mining	Frequent subtree mining
21	Multicore, GPU	CUDA, task queue	Inference	Speech recognition

first part focuses on four distinct programming frameworks, on top of which a variety of learning algorithms have been successfully implemented. The second part focuses on individual learning algorithms, describing parallelized versions of several high-performing supervised and unsupervised methods. The third part is dedicated to task settings that differ from the classic supervised versus unsupervised dichotomy, such as online learning, semi-supervised learning, transfer learning, and feature selection. The final, fourth part describes several application settings where scaling up learning has been highly successful: computer vision, speech recognition, and frequent pattern mining. Table 1.1 contains a summary view of the chapters, prediction tasks considered, and specific algorithms and applications for each chapter.

1.6.1 Part I: Frameworks for Scaling Up Machine Learning

The first four chapters of the book describe programming frameworks that are well suited for parallelizing learning algorithms, as illustrated by in-depth examples of specific algorithms provided in each chapter. In particular, the implementation of k-means clustering in each chapter is a shared example that is illustrative of the similarities, differences, and capabilities of the frameworks.

Chapter 2, the first contributed chapter in the book, provides a brief introduction to MapReduce, an increasingly popular distributed computing framework, and discusses the pros and cons of scaling up learning algorithms using it. The chapter focuses on employing MapReduce to parallelize the training of decision tree ensembles, a class of algorithms that includes such popular methods as boosting and bagging. The presented approach, PLANET, distributes the tree construction process by concurrently expanding multiple nodes in each tree, leveraging the data partitioning naturally induced by the tree, and modulating between parallel and local execution when appropriate. PLANET achieves a two-orders-of-magnitude speedup on a 200 node MapReduce cluster on datasets that are not feasible to process on a single machine.

Chapter 3 introduces DryadLINQ, a declarative data-parallel programming language that compiles programs down to reliable distributed computations, executed by the Dryad cluster runtime. DryadLINQ presents the programmer with a high-level abstraction of the data, as a typed collection in .NET, and enables numerous useful software engineering tools such as type-safety, integration with the development environment, and interoperability with standard libraries, all of which help programmers to write their program correctly before they execute it. At the same time, the language is well matched to the underlying Dryad execution engine, capable of reliably and scalably executing the computation across large clusters of machines. Several examples demonstrate that relatively simple programs in DryadLINQ can result in very efficient distributed computations; for example, a version of k-means is implemented in only a dozen lines. Several other machine learning examples call attention to the ease of programming and demonstrate strong performance across multi-gigabyte datasets.

Chapter 4 describes the IBM Parallel Machine Learning Toolbox (PML) that provides a general MPI-based parallelization foundation well suited for machine learning algorithms. Given an algorithm at hand, PML represents it as a sequence of operators that obey the algebraic rules of commutativity and associativity. Intuitively, such operators correspond to algorithm steps during which training instances are exchangeable and can be partitioned in any way, making their processing easy to parallelize. Functionality provided by PML is particularly beneficial for algorithms that require multiple passes over data – as most machine learning algorithms do. The chapter describes how a number of popular learning algorithms can be represented as associative-commutative cascades and gets into the details of their implementations in PML. Chapter 9 from the second part of the book discusses *transform regression* as implemented in PML.

Chapter 5 provides a gentle introduction to Compute Unified Device Architecture (CUDA) programming on GPUs and illustrates its use in machine learning applications by describing implementations of k-means and regression k-means. The chapter offers important insights into redesigning learning algorithms to fit the CPU/GPU computation model, with a detailed discussion of *uniformly fine-grained* data/task parallelism in GPUs: parallel execution over vectors and matrices, with inputs pipelined to further increase efficiency. Experiments demonstrate two-orders-of-magnitude speedups over highly optimized, multi-threaded implementations of k-means and regression k-means on CPUs.

1.6.2 Part II: Supervised and Unsupervised Learning Algorithms

The second part of the book is dedicated to parallelization of popular supervised and unsupervised machine learning algorithms that cover key approaches in modern machine learning. The first two chapters describe different approaches to parallelizing the training of Support Vector Machines (SVMs): one showing how the Interior Point Method (IPM) can be effectively distributed using message passing, and another focusing on customized hardware design for the Sequential Minimal Optimization (SMO) algorithm that results in a dramatic speedup. Variants of boosted decision trees are covered by the next two chapters: first, an MPI-based parallelization of boosting for ranking, and second, transform regression that provides several enhancements to traditional boosting that significantly reduce the number of iterations. The subsequent two chapters are dedicated to graphical models: one describing parallelizing Belief Propagation (BP) in factor graphs, a workhorse of numerous graphical model algorithms, and another on distributed Markov Chain Monte Carlo (MCMC) inference in unsupervised topic models, an area of significant interest in recent years. This part of the book concludes with two chapters on clustering, describing fast implementations of two very different approaches: spectral clustering and information-theoretic co-clustering.

Chapter 6 is the first of the two parallel SVM chapters, presenting a two-stage approach, in which the first stage computes a kernel matrix approximation via parallelized Incomplete Cholesky Factorization (ICF). In the second stage, the Interior Point Method (IPM) is applied to the factorized matrix in parallel via a nontrivial rearrangement of the underlying computation. The method's scalability is achieved by partitioning the input data over the cluster nodes, with the factorization built up one row at a time. The approach achieves a two-orders-of-magnitude speedup on a 500-node cluster over a state-of-the-art baseline, LibSVM, and its MPI-based implementation has been released open-source.

Chapter 7 also considers parallelizing SVMs, focusing on the popular SMO algorithm as the underlying optimization method. This chapter is unique in the sense that it offers a hybrid high-level/low-level parallelization. At the high level, the instances are distributed across the nodes and SMO is executed on each node. To ensure that the optimization is going toward the global optimum, all locally optimal working sets are merged into the globally optimal working set in each SMO iteration. At the low level, specialized hardware (FPGA) is used to speed up the core kernel computation. The cluster implementation uses a custom-written TCP/UDP multicast-based communication interface and achieves a two-orders-of-magnitude speedup on a cluster of 48 dual-core nodes. The superlinear speedup is notable, illustrating that linearly increasing memory with efficient communication can significantly lighten the computational bottlenecks. The implementation of the method has been released open-source.

Chapter 8 covers LambdaMART, a boosted decision tree algorithm for learning to rank, an industry-defining task central to many information retrieval applications. The authors develop several distributed LambdaMART variants, one of which partitions features (rather than instances) across nodes and uses a master–slave structure to execute the algorithm. This approach achieves an order-of-magnitude speedup with an MPI-based implementation using 32 nodes and produces a learned model exactly equivalent to a sequential implementation. The chapter also describes experiments with instance-distributed approaches that approximate the sequential implementation.

Chapter 9 describes Transform Regression, a powerful classification and regression algorithm motivated by gradient boosting, but departing from it in several aspects that lead to dramatic speedups. Notably, transform regression uses prior trees' predictions as features in subsequent iterations, and employs linear regression in tree leaves. The algorithm is efficiently parallelized using the PML framework described in Chapter 4 and is shown to obtain high-accuracy models in fewer than 10 iterations, thus reducing the number of trees in the ensemble by two orders of magnitude, a gain that directly translates into corresponding speedups at inference time.

Chapter 10 focuses on approximate inference in probabilistic graphical models using loopy Belief Propagation (BP), a widely applied message-passing technique. The chapter provides a comparative analysis of several BP parallelization techniques and explores the role of message scheduling in efficient parallel inference. The culmination of the chapter is the Splash algorithm that sequentially propagates messages along spanning trees, yielding a provably optimal parallel BP algorithm. It is shown that the combination of dynamic scheduling and over-partitioning are essential for high-performance parallel inference. Experimental results in shared and distributed memory settings demonstrate that the Splash algorithm strongly outperforms alternative approaches, for example, achieving a 23-fold speedup on a 40-node distributed memory cluster, versus 14-fold for the next-best method.

Chapter 11 is dedicated to parallelizing learning in statistical latent variable models, such as topic models, which have been increasingly popular for identifying underlying structure in large data collections. The chapter focuses on distributing collapsed Gibbs sampling, a Markov Chain Monte Carlo (MCMC) technique, in the context of Latent Dirichlet Allocation (LDA) and Hierarchical Dirichlet Processes (HDP), two popular topic models, as well as for Bayesian networks in general, using Hidden Markov Models (HMMs) as an example. Scaling up to large datasets is achieved by distributing data instances and exchanging statistics across nodes, with synchronous and asynchronous variants considered. An MPI-based implementation over 1,024 processors is shown to achieve almost three-orders-of-magnitude speedups, with no loss in accuracy compared to baseline implementations, demonstrating that the approach successfully scales up topic models to multi-gigabyte text collections. The core algorithm is open source.

Chapter 12 is the first of two chapters dedicated to parallelization of clustering methods. It presents a parallel *spectral clustering* technique composed of three stages: sparsification of the affinity matrix, subsequent eigendecomposition, and obtaining final clusters via k-means using projected instances. It is shown that sparsification is vital for enabling the subsequent modules to run on large-scale datasets, and although it is the most expensive step, it can be distributed using MapReduce. The following steps, eigendecomposition and k-means, are parallelized using MPI. The chapter presents detailed complexity analysis and extensive experimental results on text and image datasets, showing near-linear overall speedups on clusters up to 256 machines. Interestingly, results indicate that matrix sparsification has the benefit of improving clustering accuracy.

Chapter 13 proposes a parallelization scheme for *co-clustering*, the task of simultaneously constructing a clustering of data instances and a clustering of their features. The proposed algorithm optimizes an information-theoretic objective and uses an elemental *sequential* subroutine that "shuffles" the data of two clusters. The shuffling is done in parallel over the set of clusters that is split into pairs. Two results are of interest here: a two-orders-of-magnitude speedup on a 400-core MPI cluster, and evidence that *sequential* co-clustering is substantially better at revealing underlying structure of the data than an easily parallelizable k-means-like co-clustering algorithm that optimizes the same objective.

1.6.3 Part III: Alternative Learning Settings

This part of the book looks beyond the traditional supervised and unsupervised learning formulations, with the first three chapters focusing on parallelizing online, semi-supervised, and transfer learning. The fourth chapter presents a MapReduce-based method for scaling up feature selection, an integral part of machine learning practice that is well known to improve both computational efficiency and predictive accuracy.

Chapter 14 focuses on the *online learning* setting, where training instances arrive in a stream, one after another, with learning performed on one example at a time. Theoretical results show that delayed updates can cause additional error, so the algorithms focus on minimizing delay in a distributed environment to achieve high-quality solutions. To achieve this, features are partitioned ("sharded") across cores and nodes, and various delay-tolerant learning algorithms are tested. Empirical results show that a multicore and multinode parallelized version yields a speedup of a factor of 6 on a cluster of nine machines while sometimes even improving predictive performance. The core algorithm is open source.

Chapter 15 considers *semi-supervised learning*, where training sets include large amounts of unlabeled data alongside the labeled examples. In particular, the authors focus on graph-based semi-supervised classification, where the data instances are represented by graph nodes, with edges connecting those that are similar. The chapter describes *measure propagation*, a top-performing semi-supervised classification algorithm, and develops a number of effective heuristics for speeding up its parallelization. The heuristics reorder graph nodes to maximize the locality of message passing and hence are applicable to the broad family of message-passing algorithms. The chapter addresses both multicore and distributed settings, obtaining 85% efficiency on a 1,000-core distributed computer for a dataset containing 120 million graph-node instances on a key task in the speech recognition pipeline.

Chapter 16 deals with *transfer learning*: a setting where two or more learning tasks are solved consequently or concurrently, taking advantage of learning across the tasks. It is typically assumed that inputs to the tasks have different distributions that share supports. The chapter introduces DisCo, a distributed transfer learning framework, where each task is learned on its own node concurrently with others, with knowledge transfer conducted over data instances that are shared across tasks. The chapter shows that the described parallelization method results in an order-of-magnitude speedup over a centralized implementation in the domains of recommender systems and text classification, with knowledge transfer improving accuracy of tasks over that obtained in isolation.

Chapter 17 is dedicated to distributed feature selection. The task of feature selection is motivated by the observation that predictive accuracy of many learning algorithms can be improved by extracting a subset of all features that provides an informative representation of data and excludes noise. Reducing the number of features also naturally decreases computational costs of learning and inference. The chapter focuses on Forward Feature Selection via Single Feature Optimization (SFO) specialized for logistic regression. Starting with an empty set of features, the method proceeds by iteratively selecting features that improve predictive performance, until no gains are obtained, with the remaining features discarded. A MapReduce implementation is described based on data instances partitioned over the nodes. In experiments, the algorithm achieves a speedup of approximately 16 on a 20-node cluster.

1.6.4 Part IV: Applications

The final part of the book presents several learning applications in distinct domains where scaling up is crucial to both computational efficiency and improving accuracy. The first two chapters focus on hardware-based approaches for speeding up inference in classic computer vision applications, object detection and recognition. In domains such as robotics and surveillance systems, model training is performed offline and can rely on extensive computing resources, whereas efficient inference is key to enabling real-time performance. The next chapter focuses on frequent subtree pattern mining, an unsupervised learning task that is important in many applications where data is naturally represented by trees. The final chapter in the book describes an exemplary case of deep-dive bottleneck analysis and pattern-driven design that lead to crucial inference speedups of a highly optimized speech recognition pipeline.

Chapter 18 describes two approaches to improving performance in vision tasks based on employing GPUs for efficient feature processing and induction. The first half of the chapter demonstrates that a combination of high-level features optimized for GPUs, synthetic expansion of training sets, and training using boosting distributed over a cluster yields significant accuracy gains on an object detection task. GPU-based detectors also enjoy a 100-fold speedup over their CPU implementation. In the second half, the chapter describes how Deep Belief Networks (DBNs) can be efficiently trained on GPUs to learn high-quality feature representations, avoiding the need for extensive human engineering traditionally required for inducing informative features in computer vision.

Chapter 19 shows how large parallel filter banks, commonly used for feature selection in vision tasks, can be effectively deployed via customized hardware implemented on FPGAs or ASICs (application-specific integrated circuits). Convolutional neural networks are tested, with their implementation using a data flow model enabling efficient parallelism. Comparisons with CPU and GPU implementations on standard computer vision benchmarks demonstrate that customized hardware leads to 100-fold gains in overall efficiency measured with respect to power consumption.

Chapter 20 considers the problem of mining frequent subtrees, an important task in a number of domains ranging from bioinformatics to mining logs of browsing behavior. Detecting frequently occurring subtrees is computationally challenging in cases where tree instances can be arbitrarily complex in structure and large in size. The chapter demonstrates how frequent subtree mining can be efficiently parallelized on multicore systems, providing insights into various design aspects including memory utilization and load balancing. The chapter's approach is based on adaptive parallelization: employing multiple levels of task granularity to maximize concurrency. Multi-resolution task parallelism leads to high utilization of system resources, as demonstrated by near-linear speedups on standard web log, XML, and Natural Language Processing (NLP) benchmark datasets.

Chapter 21 focuses on parallelizing the inference process for Automatic Speech Recognition (ASR). In ASR, obtaining inference efficiency is challenging because highly optimized modern ASR models involve irregular graph structures that lead to load balancing issues in highly parallel implementations. The chapter describes how careful bottleneck analysis helps exploit the richest sources of concurrency for efficient ASR implementation on both GPUs and multicore systems. The overall application architecture presented here effectively utilizes single-instruction multiple-data (SIMD) operations for execution efficiency and hardware-supported atomic instructions for synchronization efficiency. Compared to an optimized single-thread implementation, these techniques provide an order-of-magnitude speedup, achieving recognition speed more than trice faster than real time, empowering development of novel ASR-based applications that can be deployed in an increasing variety of usage scenarios.

1.7 Bibliographic Notes

The goal of this book is presenting a practical set of modern platforms and algorithms that are effective in learning applications deployed in large-scale settings. This collection is by no means an exhaustive anthology: compiling one would be impossible given the breadth of ongoing research in the area. However, the references in each chapter provide a comprehensive overview of related literature for the described method as well as alternative approaches. The remainder of this section surveys a broader set of background references, along with pointers to software packages and additional recent work.

Many modern machine learning techniques rely on formulating the training objective as an optimization problem, allowing the use of the large arsenal of previously developed mathematical programming algorithms. Distributed and parallel optimization algorithms have been a fruitful research area for decades, yielding a number of theoretical and practical advances. Censor and Zenios (1997) is a canonical reference in this area that covers the parallelization of several algorithm classes for linear and quadratic programming, which are centerpieces of many modern machine learning techniques.

Parallelization of algorithms to enable scaling up to large datasets has been an active research direction in the data mining community since early nineties. The monograph of Freitas and Lavington (1998) describes early work on parallel data mining from a database-centric perspective. A survey by Provost and Kolluri (1999) provides a structured overview of approaches for scaling up inductive learning algorithms, categorizing them into several groups that include parallelization and data partitioning. Two subsequent edited collections (Zaki and Ho, 2000; Kargupta and Chan, 2000) are representative of early research on parallel mining algorithms and include chapters that describe several prototype frameworks for concurrent mining of partitioned data collections.

In the statistical machine learning community, scaling up kernel-based methods (of which Support Vector Machines are the most prominent example) has been a topic of significant research interest due to the super-linear computational complexity of most training methods. The volume edited by Bottou et al. (2007) presents a comprehensive set of modern solutions in this area, which primarily focus on algorithmic aspects, but also include two parallel approaches, one of which is extended in Chapter 7 of the present book.

One parallelization framework that has been a subject of study in the distributed data mining community is Peer-To-Peer (P2P) networks, which are decentralized systems composed of nodes that are highly non-stationary (nodes often go offline), where communication is typically asynchronous and has high latency. These issues are counter-balanced by the potential for very high scalability of storage and computational resources. Designing machine learning methods for P2P settings is a subject of ongoing work (Datta et al., 2009; Bhaduri et al., 2008; Luo et al., 2007).

Two recently published textbooks (Lin and Dyer, 2010; Rajaraman and Ullman, 2010) may be useful companion references for readers of the present book who are primarily interested in algorithms implemented via MapReduce. Lin and Dyer (2010) offer a gentle introduction to MapReduce, with plentiful examples focused on text processing applications, whereas Rajaraman and Ullman (2010) describe a broad array of mining tasks on large datasets, covering MapReduce and parallel clustering in depth.

MapReduce and DryadLINQ presented in Chapters 1 and 3 are representative samples of an increasingly popular family of distributed platforms that combine three layers: a parallelization-friendly programming language, a task execution engine, and a distributed filesystem. *Hadoop*[2] is a prominent, widely used open-source member of this family, programmable via APIs for popular imperative languages such as Java or Python, as well as via specialized languages with a strong functional and declarative flavor, such as Apache Pig and Hive.[3] Another, related set of tools such as Aster Data[4] or Greenplum[5] provide a MapReduce API for distributed databases. Finally, MADlib[6] provides a library of learning tools on top of distributed databases, while Apache Mahout[7] is a nascent library of machine learning algorithms being developed

---

[2] http://hadoop.apache.org/.
[3] http://pig.apache.org/ and http://hive.apache.org/.
[4] http://www.asterdata.com/resources/mapreduce.php.
[5] http://www.greenplum.com.
[6] http://madlib.net.
[7] http://mahout.apache.org.

for Hadoop. In this book, PML (presented in Chapter 4) is an example of an off-the-shelf machine learning toolbox based on a general library of parallelization primitives especially suited for learning algorithms.

Since starting this project, a few other parallel learning algorithms of potential interest have been published. Readers of Chapter 11 may be interested in a new cluster parallel Latent Dirichlet Allocation algorithm (Smola and Narayanamurthy, 2010). Readers of Chapter 8 may be interested in a similar algorithm made to interoperate with the Hadoop file system (Ye et al., 2009).

References

Bakir, G., Hofmann, T., Schölkopf, B., Smola, A., Taskar, B., and Vishwanathan, S. V. N. (eds). 2007. *Predicting Structured Data*. Cambridge, MA: MIT Press.

Bhaduri, K., Wolff, R., Giannella, C., and Kargupta, H. 2008. Distributed Decision-Tree Induction in Peer-to-Peer Systems. *Statistical Analysis and Data Mining*, **1**, 85–103.

Bottou, L., Chapelle, O., DeCoste, D., and Weston, J. (eds). 2007. *Large-Scale Kernel Machines*. MIT Press.

Censor, Y., and Zenios, S. A. 1997. *Parallel Optimization: Theory, Algorithms, and Applications*. Oxford University Press.

Datta, S., Giannella, C. R., and Kargupta, H. 2009. Approximate Distributed K-Means Clustering over a Peer-to-Peer Network. *IEEE Transactions on Knowledge and Data Engineering*, **21**, 1372–1388.

Dean, Jeffrey, and Ghemawat, Sanjay. 2004. MapReduce: Simplified Data Processing on Large Clusters. In: *Sixth Symposium on Operating System Design and Implementation (OSDI-2004)*.

Flynn, M. J. 1972. Some Computer Organizations and Their Effectiveness. *IEEE Transactions on Computers*, **21**(9), 948–960.

Freitas, A. A., and Lavington, S. H. 1998. *Mining Very Large Databases with Parallel Processing*. Kluwer.

Gropp, W., Lusk, E., and Skjellum, A. 1994. *Using MPI: Portable Parallel Programming with the Message-Passing Interface*. MIT Press.

Kargupta, H., and Chan, P. (eds). 2000. *Advances in Distributed and Parallel Knowledge Discovery*. Cambridge, MA: AAAI/MIT Press.

Lin, J., and Dyer, C. 2010. *Data-Intensive Text Processing with MapReduce*. Morgan & Claypool.

Luo, P., Xiong, H., Lu, K., and Shi, Z. 2007. Distributed classification in peer-to-peer networks. Pages 968–976 of: *Proceedings of the 13th ACM SIGKDD International Conference on Knowledge Discovery and Data Mining*.

Provost, F., and Kolluri, V. 1999. A survey of methods for scaling up inductive algorithms. *Data Mining and Knowledge Discovery*, **3**(2), 131–169.

Rajaraman, A., and Ullman, J. D. 2010. *Mining of Massive Datasets*. http://infolab.stanford.edu/~ullman/mmds.html.

Smola, A. J., and Narayanamurthy, S. 2010. An Architecture for Parallel Topic Models. *Proceedings of the VLDB Endowment*, **3**(1), 703–710.

Ye, J., Chow, J.-H., Chen, J., and Zheng, Z. 2009. Stochastic Gradient Boosted Distributed Decision Trees. In: *CIKM '09 Proceeding of the 18th ACM Conference on Information and Knowledge Management*.

Zaki, M. J., and Ho, C.-T. (eds). 2000. *Large-scale Parallel Data Mining*. New York: Springer.

PART ONE

Frameworks for Scaling Up Machine Learning

MapReduce and Its Application to Massively Parallel Learning of Decision Tree Ensembles

Biswanath Panda, Joshua S. Herbach, Sugato Basu,
and Roberto J. Bayardo

In this chapter we look at leveraging the MapReduce distributed computing framework (Dean and Ghemawat, 2004) for parallelizing machine learning methods of wide interest, with a specific focus on learning ensembles of classification or regression trees. Building a production-ready implementation of a distributed learning algorithm can be a complex task. With the wide and growing availability of MapReduce-capable computing infrastructures, it is natural to ask whether such infrastructures may be of use in parallelizing common data mining tasks such as tree learning. For many data mining applications, MapReduce may offer scalability as well as ease of deployment in a production setting (for reasons explained later).

We initially give an overview of MapReduce and outline its application in a classic clustering algorithm, *k*-means. Subsequently, we focus on PLANET: a scalable distributed framework for learning tree models over large datasets. PLANET defines tree learning as a series of distributed computations and implements each one using the *MapReduce* model. We show how this framework supports scalable construction of classification and regression trees, as well as ensembles of such models. We discuss the benefits and challenges of using a MapReduce compute cluster for tree learning and demonstrate the scalability of this approach by applying it to a real-world learning task from the domain of computational advertising.

MapReduce is a simple model for distributed computing that abstracts away many of the difficulties in parallelizing data management operations across a cluster of commodity machines. By using MapReduce, one can alleviate, if not eliminate, many complexities such as data partitioning, scheduling tasks across many machines, handling machine failures, and performing inter-machine communication. These properties have motivated many companies to run MapReduce frameworks on their compute clusters for data analysis and other data management tasks. MapReduce has become in some sense an industry standard. For example, there are open-source implementations such as Hadoop that can be run either in-house or on cloud computing services such as Amazon EC2.[1]

---

[1] http://aws.amazon.com/ec2/.

Startups such as Cloudera[2] offer software and services to simplify Hadoop deployment, and companies including Google, IBM, and Yahoo! have granted several universities access to MapReduce clusters to advance parallel computing research.[3]

Despite the growing popularity of MapReduce, its application to standard data mining and machine learning tasks needs to be better studied. In this chapter we focus on one such task: tree learning. We believe that a tree learner capable of exploiting a MapReduce cluster can effectively address many scalability issues that arise in building tree models on massive datasets. Our choice of focusing on tree models is motivated primarily by their popularity. Tree models are used in many applications because they are interpretable, can model complex interactions, and can easily handle both numerical and categorical features. Recent studies have shown that tree models, when combined with ensemble techniques, provide excellent predictive performance across a wide variety of domains (Caruana et al., 2008; Caruana and Niculescu-Mizil, 2006). The effectiveness of boosted trees has also been separately validated by other researchers; for example, Gao et al. (2009) present an algorithm for model interpolation and ensembles using boosted trees that performs well on *web search ranking*, even when the test data is quite different from the training data.

This chapter describes our experiences with developing and deploying a MapReduce-based tree learner called PLANET, which stands for Parallel Learner for Assembling Numerous Ensemble Trees. The development of PLANET was motivated by a real application in sponsored search advertising, in which massive clickstreams are processed to develop a model that can predict the quality of user experience following the click on a sponsored search ad (Sculley et al., 2009). We show how PLANET effectively scales to large datasets, describe experiments that highlight the performance characteristics of PLANET, and demonstrate the benefits of various optimizations that we implemented within the system. We show that although MapReduce is not a panacea, it still provides a powerful basis on which scalable tree learning can be implemented.

2.1 Preliminaries

Let us first define some notation and terminology that we will use in the rest of the chapter. Let $\mathcal{X} = \{X_1, X_2, \ldots X_N\}$ be a set of features with domains $\mathbb{D}_{X_1}, \mathbb{D}_{X_2}, \ldots \mathbb{D}_{X_N}$ respectively. Let Y be the class label with domain $\mathbb{D}_Y$. Consider a dataset $D = \{(\mathbf{x}_i, y_i) | \mathbf{x}_i \in \mathbb{D}_{X_1} \times \mathbb{D}_{X_2} \times \ldots \mathbb{D}_{X_N}, y_i \in \mathbb{D}_Y\}$ sampled from an unknown distribution, where the ith data vector $\mathbf{x}_i$ has a class label y_i associated with it. Given the dataset D, the goal of supervised learning is to learn a function (or *model*) $F : \mathbb{D}_{X_1} \times \mathbb{D}_{X_2} \times \ldots \mathbb{D}_{X_N} \to \mathbb{D}_Y$ that minimizes the difference between the predicted and the true values of Y, on unseen data drawn from the same distribution as D. If $\mathbb{D}_Y$ is continuous, the learning problem is a regression problem; if $\mathbb{D}_Y$ is categorical, it is a classification problem. In contrast, in unsupervised learning (e.g., clustering), the goal is to learn a function

---

[2] www.cloudera.com/.

[3] For example, see www.youtube.com/watch?v=UBrDPRlplyo and www.nsf.gov/news/news_summ.jsp?cntn_id=111470.

$F : \mathbb{D}_{X_1} \times \mathbb{D}_{X_2} \times \ldots \mathbb{D}_{X_N} \times \mathbb{D}_Y$ that best approximates the joint distribution of X and Y in D. For notational simplicity, we will use Y both to denote a class label in supervised methods and to denote a cluster label in clustering.

Let $\mathcal{L}$ be a function that quantifies the disagreement between the value of the function $F(\mathbf{x}_i)$ (predicted label) and the actual class label y_i, for example, the squared difference between the actual label and the predicted label, known as the *squared loss*. A model that minimizes the net loss $\sum_{(\mathbf{x}_i, y_i) \in D} \mathcal{L}(F(\mathbf{x}_i), y_i)$ on the *training set D* may not generalize well when applied to unseen data (Vapnik, 1995). Generalization is attained through controlling model complexity by various methods, e.g., pruning and ensemble learning for tree models (Breiman, 2001). The learned model can be evaluated by measuring its net loss when applied to a holdout dataset.

2.1.1 MapReduce

MapReduce (Dean and Ghemawat, 2004) provides a framework for performing a two-phase distributed computation on large datasets, which in our case is a training dataset D. In the *Map* phase, the system partitions D into a set of disjoint units that are assigned to worker processes, known as *mappers*. Each mapper (in parallel with the others) scans through its assigned data and applies a user-specified map function to each record. The output of the map function is a set of key–value pairs that are collected by the *Shuffle* phase, which groups them by key. The master process redistributes the output of shuffle to a series of worker processes called *reducers*, which perform the *Reduce* phase. Each reducer applies a user-specified reduce function to all the values for a key and outputs the value of the reduce function. The collection of final values from all of the reducers is the final output of MapReduce.

MapReduce Example: Word Histogram

Let us demonstrate how MapReduce works through the following simple example. Given a collection of text documents, we would like to compute the word histogram in this collection, that is, the number of times each word occurs in all the documents. In the Map phase, the total set of documents is partitioned into subsets, each of which is given to an individual mapper. Each mapper goes through the subset of documents assigned to it and outputs a series of $\langle word_i, count_i \rangle$ values as the key–value pair, where $count_i$ is the number of times $word_i$ occurs among the documents seen by the mapper. Each reducer takes the values associated with the a particular key (in this case, a word) and aggregates the values (in this case, word counts) for each key. The output of the reducer phase gives us the counts per word across the entire document collection, which is the desired word histogram.

MapReduce Example: k-means Clustering

MapReduce can be used to efficiently solve supervised and unsupervised learning problems at scale. In the rest of the chapter, we focus on using MapReduce to learn ensembles of decision trees for classification and regression. In this section, we briefly describe how MapReduce can be used for k-means clustering, to show its efficiency in unsupervised learning.

The k-means clustering algorithm (MacQueen, 1967) is a widely used clustering method that applies iterative relocation of points to find a locally optimal partitioning of a dataset. In k-means, the total distance between each data point and a representative point (centroid) of the cluster to which it is assigned is minimized. Each iteration of k-means has two steps. In the cluster assignment step, k-means assigns each point to a cluster such that, of all the current cluster centroids, the point is closest to the centroid of that cluster. In the cluster re-estimation step, k-means re-estimates the new cluster centroids based on the reassignments of points to clusters in the previous step. The cluster re-assignment and centroid re-estimation steps proceed in iterations until a specified convergence criterion is reached, such as when the total distance between points and centroids does not change substantially from one iteration to another.

In the MapReduce implementation of k-means, each mapper in the Map phase is assigned a subset of points. For these points, the mapper does the cluster assignment step – it computes y_i, the index of the closest centroid for each point x_i, and also computes the relevant cluster aggregation statistics: S_j, the sum of all points seen by the mapper assigned to the jth cluster; and n_j, the number of points seen by the mapper assigned to the jth cluster. At the end of the Map phase, the cluster index and the corresponding cluster aggregation statistics (sum and counts) are output. The Map algorithm is shown in Algorithm 1.

Algorithm 1: k-means::Map

Input: Training data $x \in D$, number of clusters k, distance measure d

1: **If** first Map iteration **then**
2:     Initialize the k cluster centroids C randomly
3: **Else**
4:     Get the k cluster centroids C from the previous Reduce step
5: Set $S_j = 0$ and $n_j = 0$ for $j = \{1, \cdots, k\}$
6: **For each** $x_i \in D$ **do**
7:     $y_i = \arg\min_j d(x_i, c_j)$
8:     $S_{y_i} = S_{y_i} + x_i$
9:     $n_{y_i} = n_{y_i} + 1$
10: **For each** $j \in \{1, \cdots, k\}$ **do**
11:     Output($j, < S_j, n_j >$)

The reducer does the centroid re-estimation step – it combines the values for a given clusterid key by merging the cluster statistics. For each cluster j, the reducer gets a list of cluster statistics $[< S_j^l, n_j^l >]$, where l is an index over the list – the lth partial sum S_j^l in this list represents the sum of some points in cluster j seen by any particular mapper, whereas the lth number n_j^l in the list is the count of the number of points in that set. The reducer calculates the average of S_j^l to get the updated centroid c_j for cluster j. The Reduce algorithm is shown in Algorithm 2.

Algorithm 2: k-means::Reduce

Input: List of centroid statistics – partial sums and counts $[< S_j^l, n_j^l >]$ – for each
centroid $j \in \{1, \cdots, k\}$

1: **For each** $j \in \{1, \cdots, k\}$ **do**
2:     Let λ be the length of the list of centroid statistics
3:     $n_j = 0, S_j = 0$
4:     **For each** $l \in \{1, \cdots, \lambda\}$ **do**
5:         $n_j = n_j + n_j^l$
6:         $S_j = S_j + S_j^l$
7:     $\mathbf{c}_j = \frac{S_j}{n_j}$
8:     Output$(j, \mathbf{c}_j)$

The whole clustering is run by a Master, which is responsible for running the Map
(cluster assignment) and Reduce (centroid re-estimation) steps iteratively until k-means
converges.

2.1.2 Tree Models

Classification and regression trees are one of the oldest and most popular data mining
models (Duda et al., 2001). Tree models represent F by recursively partitioning the
data space $\mathbb{D}_{X_1} \times \mathbb{D}_{X_2} \times \ldots \mathbb{D}_{X_N}$ into non-overlapping regions, with a simple model in
each region.

Figure 2.1 shows an example tree model. Non-leaf nodes in the tree define region
boundaries in the data space. Each region boundary is represented as a predicate

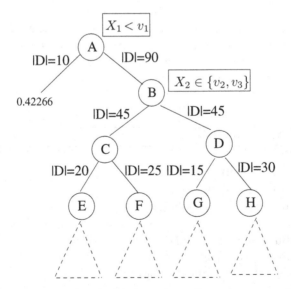

Figure 2.1 Example Tree. Note that the labels on the nodes (in boxes) are the split predicates,
whereas the labels on the edges are the sizes of the dataset in each branch (|D| denotes the
dataset size in that branch).

on a feature in $\mathcal{X}$. If the feature is numerical, the predicate is of the form $X < v$, $v \in \mathbb{D}_X$ (e.g., Node A in Figure 2.1). Categorical features have predicates of the form $X \in \{v_1, v_2, \ldots v_k\}$, $v_1 \in \mathbb{D}_X$, $v_2 \in \mathbb{D}_X$, $\ldots v_k \in \mathbb{D}_X$, (e.g., Node B in Figure 2.1). The path from the root to a leaf node in the tree defines a region. Leaf nodes (e.g., the left child of A in Figure 2.1) contain a region prediction that in most cases is a constant value or some simple function. To make predictions on an unknown $\mathbf{x}$, the tree is traversed to find the region containing $\mathbf{x}$. The region containing $\mathbf{x}$ is the path from the root to a leaf in the tree along which all non-leaf predicates are true when evaluated on $\mathbf{x}$. The prediction given by this leaf is used as the value for $F(\mathbf{x})$.

In our example tree model, predicate evaluations at non-leaf nodes have only two outcomes, leading to binary splits. Although tree models can have non-binary splits, for the sake of simplicity we focus only on binary splits for the remainder of this chapter. All our techniques also apply to tree algorithms with non-binary splits with straightforward modifications.

Tree models are popular because they are interpretable, capable of modeling complex classification and regression tasks, and handle both numerical and categorical domains. Caruana and Niculescu-Mizil (2006) show that tree models, when combined with ensemble learning methods such as bagging (Breiman, 1996), boosting (Freund and Schapire, 1996), and forests (Breiman, 2001), outperform many other popular learning methods in terms of prediction accuracy. A thorough discussion of tree models and different ensemble methods is beyond the scope of this chapter – see Rokach and Maimon (2008) for a good review.

2.1.3 Learning Tree Models

Previous work on learning tree models is extensive. For a given training dataset D, finding the optimal tree is known to be NP-Hard; thus most algorithms use a greedy top-down approach to construct the tree (Algorithm 3) (Duda et al., 2001). At the root of the tree, the entire training dataset D is examined to find the *best* split predicate for the root. The dataset is then partitioned along the split predicate and the process is repeated recursively on the partitions to build the child nodes.

Algorithm 3: InMemoryBuildNode

Input: Node n, Data D

1: $(n \rightarrow \text{split}, D_L, D_R) = \text{FindBestSplit}(D)$
2: **If** StoppingCriteria(D_L) **then**
3:    $n \rightarrow \text{left\_prediction} = \text{FindPrediction}(D_L)$
4: **Else**
5:    InMemoryBuildNode($n \rightarrow \text{left}, D_L$)
6: **If** StoppingCriteria(D_R) **then**
7:    $n \rightarrow \text{right\_prediction} = \text{FindPrediction}(D_R)$
8: **Else**
9:    InMemoryBuildNode($n \rightarrow \text{right}, D_R$)

Finding the best split predicate for a node (Line 3 of Algorithm 3) is the most important step in the greedy learning algorithm and has been the subject of much of the research in tree learning. Numerous techniques have been proposed for finding the right split at a node, depending on the particular learning problem. The main idea is to reduce the *impurity* (I) in a node. Loosely defined, the impurity at a node is a measure of the dissimilarity in the Y values of the training records D that are input to the node. The general strategy is to pick a predicate that maximizes $I(D) - (I(D_L) + I(D_R))$, where D_L and D_R are the datasets obtained after partitioning D on the chosen predicate. At each step, the algorithm greedily partitions the data space to progressively reduce region impurity. The process continues until all Y values in the input dataset D to a node are the same, at which point the algorithm has isolated a pure region (Lines 3 and 7). Some algorithms do not continue splitting until regions are completely pure and instead stop once the number of records in D falls below a predefined threshold.

Popular impurity measures are derived from measures such as entropy, Gini index, and variance (Rokach and Maimon, 2008), to name only a few. PLANET uses an impurity measure based on variance (*Var*) to evaluate the quality of a split. The higher the variance in the Y values of a node, the greater the node's impurity. Further details on the split criteria are discussed in Section 2.1.4. Although we focus concretely on variance as our split criterion for the remainder of this chapter, as long as a split metric can be computed on subsets of the training data and later aggregated, PLANET can be easily extended to support it.

Scalability Challenge

The greedy tree induction algorithm we have described is simple and works well in practice. However, it does not scale well to large training datasets. FindBestSplit requires a full scan of the node's input data, which can be large at higher levels of the tree. Large inputs that do not fit in main memory become a bottleneck because of the cost of scanning data from secondary storage. Even at lower levels of the tree where a node's input dataset D is typically much smaller than D, loading D into memory still requires reading and writing partitions of D to secondary storage multiple times.

Previous work has looked at the problem of building tree models from datasets that are too large to fit completely in main memory. Some of the known algorithms are disk-based approaches that use clever techniques to optimize the number of reads and writes to secondary storage during tree construction (e.g., Mehta, Agrawal, and Rissanen, 1996). Other algorithms scan the training data in parallel using specialized parallel architectures (e.g., Bradford, Fortes, and Bradford, 1999). We defer a detailed discussion of these approaches and how they compare to PLANET to Section 2.7. As we show in Section 2.7, some of the ideas used in PLANET have been proposed in the past; however, we are not aware of any efforts to build massively parallel tree models on commodity hardware using the MapReduce framework.

Post-pruning learned trees to prevent overfitting is also a well studied problem. However, with ensemble models (Section 2.4), post-pruning is not always needed. Because PLANET is primarily used for building ensemble models, we do not discuss post-pruning in this chapter.

2.1.4 Regression Trees

Regression trees are a special case of tree models where the output feature Y is continuous (Breiman, 2001). We focus primarily on regression trees within this chapter because most of our use cases require predictions on continuous outputs. Note that any regression tree learner also supports binary (0-1) classification tasks by modeling them as instances of logistic regression. The core operations of regression tree learning in Algorithm 3 are implemented as follows.

FindBestSplit(D): In a regression tree, D is split using the predicate that results in the largest reduction in variance. Let $Var(D)$ be the variance of the class label Y measured over all records in D. At each step the tree learning algorithm picks a split that maximizes

$$|D| \times Var(D) - (|D_L| \times Var(D_L) + |D_R| \times Var(D_R)), \qquad (2.1)$$

where $D_L \subset D$ and $D_R \subset D$ are the training records in the left and right subtree after splitting D by a predicate.

Regression trees use the following policy to determine the set of predicates whose split quality will be evaluated:

- For numerical domains, split predicates are of the form $X_i < v$, for some $v \in \mathbb{D}_{X_i}$. To find the best split, D is sorted along X_i, and a split point is considered between each adjacent pair of values for X_i in the sorted list.
- For categorical domains, split predicates are of the form $X_i \in \{v_1, v_2, \ldots v_k\}$, where $\{v_1, v_2, \ldots v_k\} \in \mathcal{P}(\mathbb{D}_{X_i})$, the power set of $\mathbb{D}_{X_i}$. Breiman et al. (1984) present an algorithm for finding the best split predicate for a categorical feature without evaluating all possible subsets of $\mathbb{D}_{X_i}$. The algorithm is based on the observation that the optimal split predicate is a subsequence in the list of values for X_i sorted by the average Y value.

StoppingCriteria(D): A node in the tree is not expanded if the number of records in D falls below a threshold. Alternatively, the user can also specify the maximum depth to which a tree should be built.

FindPrediction(D): The prediction at a leaf is simply the average of all the Y values in D.

2.2 Example of PLANET

The PLANET framework breaks up the process of constructing a tree model into a set of MapReduce tasks. Dependencies exist between the different tasks, and PLANET uses clever scheduling methods to efficiently execute and manage them. Before delving into the technical details of the framework, we begin with a detailed example of how tree induction proceeds in PLANET.

The example introduces the different components in PLANET, describes their roles, and provides a high-level overview of the entire system. To keep the example simple, we discuss only the construction of a single tree. The method extends naturally to ensembles of trees, as we discuss in Section 2.4.

Example Setup: Let us assume that we have a training dataset D^* with 100 records. Further assume that tree induction stops once the number of training records at a node falls below 10. Let the tree in Figure 2.1 be the model that will be learned if we run Algorithm 3 on a machine with sufficient memory. Our goal in this example is to demonstrate how PLANET constructs the tree in Figure 2.1 when there is a memory constraint limiting Algorithm 3 to operating on inputs of size 25 records or less.

2.2.1 Components

At the heart of PLANET is the *Controller*, a single machine that initiates, schedules, and controls the entire tree induction process. The Controller has access to a compute cluster on which it schedules MapReduce jobs. In order to control and coordinate tree construction, the Controller maintains the following:

- *ModelFile* (M): The Controller constructs a tree using a set of MapReduce jobs, each of which builds different parts of the tree. At any point, the model file contains the entire tree constructed so far.

Given the ModelFile (M), the Controller determines the nodes at which split predicates can be computed. In the example of Figure 2.1, if M has nodes A and B, then the Controller can compute splits for C and D. This information is stored in two queues.

- *MapReduceQueue* (MRQ): This queue contains nodes for which D is too large to fit in memory (i.e., > 25 in our example).
- *InMemoryQueue* (IMQ): This queue contains nodes for which D fits in memory (i.e., ≤ 25 in our example).

As tree induction proceeds, the Controller dequeues nodes off MRQ and IMQ and schedules MapReduce jobs to find split predicates at the nodes. Once a MapReduce job completes, the Controller updates M with the nodes and their split predicates and then updates MRQ and IMQ with new nodes at which split predicates can be computed. Each MapReduce job takes as input a set of nodes (N), the training data set (D^*), and the current state of the model (M). The Controller schedules two types of MapReduce jobs:

- Nodes in MRQ are processed using MR_EXPANDNODES, which for a given set of nodes N computes a candidate set of good split predicates for each node in N.
- Nodes in IMQ are processed using MR_INMEMORY. Recall that nodes in IMQ have input datasets D that are small enough to fit in memory. Therefore, given a set of nodes N, MR_INMEMORY completes tree induction at nodes in N using Algorithm 3.

We defer details of the MapReduce jobs to Section 2.3. In the remainder of this section, we tie the foregoing components together and walk through the example.

2.2.2 Walkthrough

When tree induction begins, M, MRQ, and IMQ are all empty. The only node the Controller can expand is the root (A). Finding the split for A requires a scan of the entire training dataset of 100 ($\geq$ 25) records. Because this set is too large to fit in memory, A is pushed onto MRQ and IMQ stays empty.

After initialization, the Controller dequeues A from MRQ and schedules a job MR_EXPANDNODES({A}, M, D^*). This job computes a set of good splits for node A along with some additional information about each split. Specifically, for each split we compute (1) the quality of the split (i.e., the reduction in impurity), (2) the predictions in the left and right branches, and (3) the number of training records in the left and right branches.

The split information computed by MR_EXPANDNODES gets sent back to the Controller, which selects the best split for node A. In this example, the best split has 10 records in the left branch and 90 records in the right. The selected split information for node A is then added into the ModelFile. The Controller next updates the queues with new nodes at which split predicates can be computed. The left branch of A has 10 records. This matches the stopping criteria, and hence no new nodes are added for this branch. For the right branch with 90 records ($\geq$ 25), node B can be expanded and is pushed onto MRQ.

Tree induction continues by dequeuing node B and scheduling MR_EXPAND NODES({B}, M, D^*). Note that for expanding node B, we need only the records that went down the right subtree of A, but to minimize bookkeeping, PLANET passes the entire training dataset to the MapReduce. As we describe in Section 2.3.3, MR_EXPANDNODES uses the current state of the ModelFile to determine the subset of D^* that will be input to B.

Once the Controller has received the results for the MapReduce on node B and updated M with the split for B, it can now expand both C and D. Both of these nodes get 45 records as input and are therefore pushed on to MRQ. The Controller can now schedule a single MR_EXPANDNODES({C, D}, M, D^*) job to find the best splits for both nodes C and D. Note that by expanding C and D in a single step, PLANET expands trees breadth first as opposed to the depth first process used by the in-memory Algorithm 3.

Once the Controller has the obtained the splits for C and D, it can schedule jobs to expand nodes E, F, G, and H. Of these, H uses 30 records, which still cannot fit in memory and hence get added to MRQ. The input sets to E, F, G are small enough to fit into memory, and hence tree induction at these nodes can be completed in-memory. The Controller pushes these nodes into the IMQ.

The Controller next schedules two MapReduce jobs simultaneously. MR_IN MEMORY({E,F,G}, M, D^*) completes tree induction at nodes E, F, and G because the input datasets to these nodes are small. MR_EXPANDNODES({H}, M, D^*) computes good splits for H. Once the InMemory job returns, tree induction for the subtrees rooted at E, F, and G is complete. The Controller updates MRQ and IMQ with the children of node H and continues tree induction. PLANET aggressively tries to maximize the number of nodes at which split predicates can be computed in parallel and schedules multiple MapReduce jobs simultaneously.

2.3 Technical Details

In this section, we discuss the technical details of PLANET's major components – the two critical MapReduces that handle splitting nodes and growing subtrees and the Controller that manages the entire tree induction process.

2.3.1 MR_Expand Nodes: Expanding a Single Node

MR_EXPANDNODES is the component that allows PLANET to train on datasets too large to fit in memory. Given a set of nodes (N), the training dataset (D^*), and the current model (M), this MapReduce job computes a set of good splits for each node in N.

Map Phase: The training dataset D^* is partitioned across a set of mappers. Each mapper loads into memory the current model (M) and the input nodes N. Note that the union of the input datasets to all nodes in N need not be equal to D^*. However, every MapReduce job scans the entire training dataset applying a Map function to every training record. We discuss this design decision in Section 2.3.3.

Pseudocode describing the algorithms that are executed by each mapper appear in Algorithms 4 and 5. Given a training record $(\mathbf{x}, y)$, a mapper first determines if the

---

Algorithm 4: MR_EXPANDNODES::Map

Input: NodeSet N, ModelFile M, Training record $(\mathbf{x}, y) \in D^*$

1:   $n = \text{TraverseTree}(M, \mathbf{x})$
2:   **If** $n \in N$ **then**
3:      $\text{agg\_tup}_n \leftarrow (y, y^2, 1)$
4:      **For each** $X \in \mathcal{X}$ **do**
5:        $v = \text{Value on } X \text{ in } \mathbf{x}$
6:        **If** X is numerical **then**
7:          **For each** Split point s of X s.t. $s < v$ **do**
8:            $T_{n,X}[s] \leftarrow \text{agg\_tup}_n$
9:        **Else**
10:         $T_{n,X}[v] \leftarrow \text{agg\_tup}_n$

Algorithm 5: MR_EXPANDNODES::Map_Finalize

Input: NodeSet N

1:   **For each** $n \in N$ **do**
2:      Output to all reducers$(n, \text{agg\_tup}_n)$
3:      **For each** $X \in \mathcal{X}$ **do**
4:        **If** X is numerical **then**
5:          **For each** Split point s of X **do**
6:            Output$((n, X, s), T_{n,X}[s])$
7:        **Else**
8:          **For each** $v \in T_{n,X}$ **do**
9:            Output$((n, X), (v, T_{n,X}[v]))$

record is part of the input dataset for any node in N by traversing the current model M with $(\mathbf{x}, y)$ (line 1, Algorithm 4). Once the input set to a node is determined, the next step is to evaluate possible splits for the node and select the best one.

Recall from Section 2.1.4 the method for finding the best split for a node n. For a numerical feature X, Equation 2.1 is computed between every adjacent pair of values for the feature that appears in the node's input dataset D. Performing this operation in a distributed setting would require us to sort D^* along each numerical feature and write out the results to secondary storage. These sorted records would then have to be partitioned carefully across mappers, keeping track of the range of values on each mapper. Distributed algorithms implementing such approaches are complex and end up using additional storage or network resources. PLANET makes a trade-off between finding the perfect split for a numerical feature and simple data partitioning. Splits are not evaluated between every pair of values of a feature. Rather, before tree induction we run a MapReduce on D^* and compute approximate equidepth histograms for every numerical feature (Manku, Rajagopalan, and Lindsay, 1999). When computing splits on a numerical feature, a single split point is considered from every histogram bucket of the feature.

On startup, each mapper loads the set of split points to be considered for each numerical feature. For each node $n \in N$ and feature X, the mapper maintains a table $T_{n,X}$ of key–value pairs. Keys for the table are the split points to be considered for X, and the values are tuples (agg_tup) of the form $\{\sum y, \sum y^2, \sum 1\}$. For a particular split point $s \in \mathbb{D}_X$ being considered for node n, the tuple $T_{n,X}[s]$ contains: (1) the sum of Y values for training records $(\mathbf{x}, y)$ that are input to n and have values for X that are less than s, (2) the sum of squares of these values, and (3) the number of training records that are input to n and have values of X less than s. Mappers scan subsets of D^* and compute agg_tups for all split points being considered for each node in N (lines 7, 8 in Algorithm 4). After processing all its input records, each mapper outputs keys of the form n, X, s and the corresponding $T_{n,X}[s]$ as values (line 6, Algorithm 5). Subsequently, a reduce function will aggregate the agg_tups with the same key to compute the quality of the split $X < s$ for node n.

For computing splits on a categorical feature X, Section 2.1.4 proposed computing Equation 2.1 for every subsequence of unique values of X sorted by the average Y. Each mapper performs this computation by maintaining a table $T_{n,X}$ of key, agg_tup pairs as described before. However, in this case keys correspond to unique values of X seen in the input records to node n. $T_{n,X}[v]$ maintains the same aggregate statistics as described earlier for all training records that are input to n and have an X value of v (line 10, Algorithm 4). After processing all input data, the mappers output keys of the form n, X and value $\langle v, T_{n,X}[v] \rangle$ (line 9, Algorithm 5). Note the difference in key–value pairs output for numerical and categorical features. Quality of a split on a numerical feature can be computed independently of other splits on that feature; hence, the split point s is part of the key. To run Breiman's algorithm, all values of a categorical feature need to be sorted by average Y value. Hence, the value v of an feature is not part of the key. A single reducer processes and sorts all the values of the feature to compute the best split on the feature.

In addition to the foregoing outputs, each mapper also maintains agg_tup$_n$ for each node $n \in N$ (line 3, Algorithm 4) and outputs them to all reducers (line 2, Algorithm 5).

Algorithm 6: MR_EXPANDNODES::Reduce

Input: Key k, Value Set V

1: **If** $k == n$ **then**
2:     // *Aggregate agg_tup$_n$'s from mappers by pre-sorting*
3:     agg_tup$_n$ = Aggregate(V)
4: **Else If** $k == n, X, s$ **then**
5:     // *Split on numerical feature*
6:     agg_tup$_{left}$ = Aggregate(V)
7:     agg_tup$_{right}$ = agg_tup$_n$ - agg_tup$_{left}$
8:     UpdateBestSplit($S[n]$,X,s,agg_tup$_{left}$, agg_tup$_{right}$)
9: **Else If** $k == n, X$ **then**
10:     // *Split on categorical feature*
11:     **For each** v,agg_tup $\in$ V **do**
12:         $T[v]$ ← agg_tup
13:     UpdateBestSplit($S[n]$,BreimanSplit(X,T,agg_tup$_n$))

These tuples are computed over all input records to their respective nodes and help reducers in computing split qualities.

Reduce Phase: The reduce phase, which works on the outputs from the mappers, performs aggregations and computes the quality of each split being considered for nodes in N. Each reducer maintains a table S indexed by nodes. $S[n]$ contains the best split seen by the reducer for node n.

The pseudocode executed on each reducer is outlined in Algorithm 6. A reducer processes three types of keys. The first is of the form n with a value list V of all the agg_tup$_n$ tuples output by the mappers. These agg_tups are aggregated to get a single agg_tup$_n$ with the $\{\sum y, \sum y^2, \sum 1\}$ values for all input records to node n (line 3, Algorithm 6). Reducers process keys in sorted order so that they process all keys of type n first. The other types of keys that a reducer processes belong to numerical and categorical features. The keys corresponding to categorical features are of the form n, X. Here the set V associated with each key is a set of pairs consisting of a categorical feature value v and an agg_tup. For each v, the agg_tups are aggregated to get $\{\sum y, \sum y^2, \sum 1\}$ over all input records to n where the value of X is v. Once aggregated, Breiman's algorithm is used to find the optimal split for X, and $S[n]$ is updated if the resulting split is better than any previous split for n (lines 11–13, Algorithm 6). For numerical features, keys are of the form n, X, s and V is again a list of agg_tups. Aggregating these into agg_tup$_{left}$ gives the $\{\sum y, \sum y^2, \sum 1\}$ values for all records input to n that fall in the left branch of $X < s$ (line 6, Algorithm 6). Using agg_tup$_n$ and agg_tup$_{left}$, it is straightforward to compute the *Var* based quality of the split $X < s$. If this split $X < s$ is better than the best split seen by the reducer for n so far, then $S[n]$ is updated to the current split (lines 7, 8, Algorithm 6).

Finally, each reducer outputs the best split $S[n]$ that it has seen for each node. In addition to the split quality and predicate, it also outputs the average Y value and number of the training records in the left and right branches of the split. The Controller

---

Algorithm 7: UpdateQueues

Input: DataSetSize $|D|$, Node n

1: **If** not StoppingCriteria($|D|$) **then**
2:     **If** $|D| <$ in_memory_threshold **then**
3:         IMQ.append(n)
4:     **Else**
5:         MRQ.append(n)

Algorithm 8: Schedule_MR_ExpandNode

Input: NodeSet N,Current Model M

1: CandidateGoodSplits = MR_EXPANDNODES(N,M,D^*)
2: **For each** $n \in N$ **do**
3:     $n \to$split,$n \to$l_pred, $n \to$r_pred,$|D_L|$,$|D_R|$ = FindBestSplit(n, CandidateGoodSplits)
4:     UpdateQueues($|D_L|$,$n \to$left)
5:     UpdateQueues($|D_R|$,$n \to$right)
6: *jobs_running* $--$

---

takes the splits produced by all the reducers and finds the best split for each node in N, then updates the ModelFile M with this information. The Controller updates the queues with the child nodes that should be expanded using information about the number of training records in each branch.

2.3.2 MR_InMemory: In Memory Tree Induction

As tree induction progresses, the size of the input dataset for many nodes becomes small enough to fit in memory. At any such point, rather than continuing tree induction using MR_EXPANDNODES, the Controller completes tree induction in-memory using a different MapReduce job called MR_InMemory. Like MR_EXPANDNODES, MR_InMemory partitions D^* across a set of mappers. The map function processes a training record $(\mathbf{x}, y)$ and traverses the tree in M to see if the $(\mathbf{x}, y)$ is input to some node $n \in N$. If such a node is found, then the map function outputs the node n as the key and $(\mathbf{x}, y)$ as the value. The reduce function receives as input a node n (as key) and the set of training records that are input to the node (as values). The reducer loads the training records for n into memory and completes subtree construction at n using Algorithm 3.

2.3.3 Controller Design

The example in Section 2.2 provides the intuition behind functionality of the Controller. Here we provide a more detailed look at its roles and implementation.

The main Controller thread (Algorithm 10) schedules jobs off of its queues until the queues are empty and none of the jobs it schedules remain running. Scheduled

---

Algorithm 9: Schedule_MR_InMemory

Input: NodeSet N,Current Model M

1: MR_InMemory(N,M,D)
2: *jobs_running* $--$

Algorithm 10: MainControllerThread

Input: Model M $= \emptyset$, MRQ$=\emptyset$, IMQ$=\emptyset$

1: MRQ.append(root)
2: **while** true **do**
3:    **while** MRQ not empty **do**
4:      **If** TryReserveClusterResources **then**
5:        *jobs_running* $++$
6:        NewThread(ScheduleMR_ExpandNode($\subseteq$MRQ,M))
7:    **while** IMQ not empty **do**
8:      **If** TryReserveClusterResources **then**
9:        *jobs_running* $++$
10:        NewThread(ScheduleMR_InMemory($\subseteq$IMQ,M))
11:    **If** *jobs_running*$==0$ && MRQ empty && IMQ empty **then**
12:      Exit

MapReduce jobs are launched in separate threads so that the Controller can send out multiple jobs in parallel. When an MR_ExpandNodes job returns, the queues are updated with the new nodes that can now be expanded (Algorithm 8). Note that when MR_InMemory finishes running on a set of nodes N (Algorithm 9), no updates are made to the queues because tree induction at nodes in N is complete.

Although the overall architecture of the Controller is fairly straightforward, we would like to highlight a few important design decisions. First, in our example in Section 2.2, recall that the Controller was able to remake the existing nodes from MRQ and IMQ and schedule MapReduce jobs. Therefore, it may seem that the Controller need not maintain queues and can schedule subsequent MapReduce jobs directly after processing the output of a MapReduce job. However, in practice this is not always possible. The memory limitations on a machine and the number of available machines on the cluster often prevent the Controller from scheduling MapReduce jobs for all nodes on a queue at once.

Second, when scheduling MapReduce jobs for a set of nodes, recall that the Controller does not determine the set of input records required by the nodes. Instead, it simply sends the entire training dataset D^* to every job. If the input to the set of nodes being expanded by a node is much smaller than D^*, then this implementation results in the Controller sending much unnecessary input for processing. On the other hand, this design keeps the overall system simple. In order to avoid sending unnecessary input, the Controller would need to write out the input training records for each node to storage. This in turn would require additional bookkeeping for the Controller when operating normally and would further complicate important systems such as the checkpointing mechanism (Section 2.5.3) and ensemble creation (Section 2.4). The amount of unnecessary information sent by our implementation is also mitigated by breadth-first tree construction. If we can expand all nodes at level $i + 1$ in one MapReduce job, then every training record is part of the input to some node that is being expanded. Finally, MapReduce frameworks are already optimized for scanning data efficiently in a distributed fashion – the additional cost of reading in a larger dataset can be mitigated by adding more mappers, if necessary.

2.4 Learning Ensembles

Until now we have described how the PLANET framework builds a single tree. Ensemble-based tree models have better predictive power when compared to single tree models (Caruana et al., 2008; Caruana and Niculescu-Mizil, 2006). Bagging (Breiman, 1996) and boosting (Friedman, 2001) are the two most popular tree ensemble learning methods. In this section we show how PLANET supports the construction of tree ensembles through these two techniques.

Boosting is an ensemble learning technique that uses a weighted combination of weak learners to form a highly accurate predictive model (Freund and Schapire, 1996). Our current boosting implementation uses the GBM algorithm proposed by Friedman (2001). In the GBM algorithm, every weak learner is a shallow tree (depth ≈ 2 or 3). Model construction proceeds as follows: Assume $k - 1$ weak learners (shallow trees) have been added to the model. Let F_{k-1} be the boosted model composed of those trees. Tree k is trained on a sample of D^* and residual predictions (z). For a given training record $(\mathbf{x}, y)$, the residual prediction for tree k is $z = y - F_{k-1}(\mathbf{x})$ for a regression problem and $z = y - \frac{1}{1+exp(-F_{k-1}(\mathbf{x}))}$ for a classification problem. The boosting process is initialized by setting F_0 as some aggregate defined over the Y values in the training dataset. Abstracting out the details, we need three main features in our framework to build boosted models:

- Building multiple trees: Extending the Controller to build multiple trees is straightforward. Because the Controller manages tree induction by reducing the process to repeated node expansion, the only change necessary for constructing a boosted model is to push the root node for tree k onto the MR after tree $k - 1$ is completed.
- Residual computation: Training trees on residuals is simple because the current model is sent to every MapReduce job in full. If the mapper decides to use a training record as input to a node, it can compute the current model's prediction and hence the residual.
- Sampling: Each tree is built on a sample of D^*. Mappers compute a hash of a training record's ID and the tree ID. Records hashing into a particular range are used for constructing the tree. This hash-based sampling guarantees that the same sample will be used for all nodes in a tree, but different samples of D^* will be used for different trees.

Building an ensemble model using bagging involves learning multiple trees over independent samples of the training data. Predictions from each tree in the model are computed and averaged to compute the final model prediction. PLANET supports bagging as follows: When tree induction begins at the root, nodes of all trees in the bagged model are pushed onto the MRQ. The Controller then continues tree induction over dataset samples as already described. In this scenario, at any point in time the queues will contain nodes belonging to many different trees instead of a single tree, thereby allowing the Controller to exploit greater parallelism.

2.5 Engineering Issues

In developing a production-capable deployment of PLANET, we encountered several unanticipated challenges. First, because MapReduce was not intended to be used for highly iterative procedures such as tree learning, we found that MapReduce startup and tear-down down costs were primary performance bottlenecks. Second, the cost of traversing models in order to determine split points in parallel turned out to be higher than we expected. Finally, even though MapReduce offers graceful handling of failures within a specific MapReduce computation, and because our computation spans multiple MapReduce phases, dealing with shared and unreliable commodity resources remained an issue that we had to address. We discuss our solutions to each of these issues within this section.

2.5.1 Forward Scheduling

Immediately after our initial attempt at deploying PLANET on a live MapReduce cluster, we noticed that an inordinate amount of time was spent in setting up and tearing down MapReduce jobs. Fixing latency due to tear-down time was a simple change to the logic in Algorithms 8 and 10. Instead of waiting for a MapReduce job to finish running on the cluster, the Controller ran a thread that would periodically check for the MapReduce's output files. Once the output files were available, the thread would load them and run the FindBestSplit and UpdateQueues logic described in Algorithm 8.

Addressing the latency caused by job set up was a more interesting challenge. Setup costs include time spent allocating machines for the job, launching a master to monitor the MapReduce job, and preparing and partitioning the input data for the MapReduce. To get around this problem, we implemented a simple trick of forward scheduling MapReduce jobs. Figure 2.2 illustrates the basic idea. Suppose the Controller has to run two MapReduce jobs to expand level i and $i + 1$ in the tree. According to our discussion, until now it would schedule Job-1 first and then Job-2 (upper part of

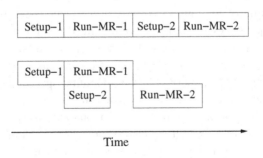

Time

Figure 2.2 Forward scheduling.

Figure 2.2). However, to eliminate the latency due to Setup-2, the Controller sets up Job-2 while Job-1 is still running (lower part of Figure 2.2).

To implement forward scheduling, the Controller runs a background thread that continuously keeps setting up one or more MapReduce jobs on the cluster. Once the jobs are set up, the mappers for the job wait on the Controller to send them a model file and the set of nodes to expand. When the Controller finds work on MRQ or IMQ, it sends the work information out to the waiting mappers for a job using a remote procedure call (RPC). With forward scheduling, lines 6 and 10 of Algorithm 10 now make RPCs rather than spawning off new threads, and the previous lines try to reserve one of the spawned MapReduces.

In practice, the Controller can forward-schedule multiple jobs at the same time depending on the number of MapReduce jobs it expects to be running in parallel. A possible downside of forward scheduling is that the forward scheduling of too many jobs can result in wasted resources, where machines are waiting to receive task specifications, or in some cases receive no tasks because tree induction may be complete. Depending on availability in the cluster and the expected tree depth and ensemble type, we tune the amount of forward scheduling in the Controller.

2.5.2 Fingerprinting

Another significant source of latency that we observed in our MapReduce jobs was the cost of traversing the model: an operation performed on every mapper to determine if the training record being processed is part of the input to any node being expanded in the job. After careful examination and profiling, we found that predicate evaluations at nodes that split on categorical features were a bottleneck because a single predicate evaluation required multiple string comparisons, and some of our features were long strings, e.g., URLs. To get around this, for a predicate of the form $X \in \{v_1, v_2, \ldots v_k\}$, we fingerprint the v_i's and store a hash set at the node. This simple optimization provided about 40% improvement in tree traversal costs.

2.5.3 Reliability

Deploying PLANET on a cluster of commodity machines presents a number of challenges not normally posed when running an application on a single machine. Because our clusters are shared resources, job failures due to preemption by other users are not uncommon. Similarly, job failures because of hardware issues occur occasionally. Because of the frequency of job failures, we require PLANET to have a mechanism for recovering from failures. Fortunately, the MapReduce framework provides us guarantees in terms of job completion. Therefore, we can reason about the system by considering the expansion of a set of nodes as an atomic operation, and when a single MapReduce fails, the Controller will simply restart the MapReduce again.

To handle the failure of the Controller, we annotate the model file with metadata marking the completion of each splitting task. Then, when the Controller fails, we start a new Controller that reads in the annotated model file generated during the failed run. Given the annotated model file, it is simple for the Controller to reconstruct the state of MRQ and IMQ prior to any jobs that were running when the Controller failed. With MRQ, IMQ, and M, the Controller can then continue with tree induction.

Monitoring turned out to be another issue in deploying PLANET. As developers and users of the system, we often needed to be able to monitor the progress of model construction in real time. To support such monitoring, we added a dashboard to PLANET to track its currently running tasks as well as the pending tasks in MRQ and IMQ. The dashboard collects training and validation error statistics and renders a plot of the error of the model as it grows (and offers a precision-recall curve when training a model for classification).

2.6 Experiments

In this section we demonstrate the performance of PLANET on a real-world learning task in computational advertising. In particular, we study the scalability of the system and the benefits obtained from the different extensions and optimizations proposed in the chapter.

2.6.1 Setup

We measure the performance of PLANET on the *bounce rate prediction problem* (Kaushik, 2007a,b). A click on a sponsored search advertisement is called a *bounce* if the click is immediately followed by the user returning to the search engine. Ads with high bounce rates are indicative of poor user experience and provide a strong signal of advertisement quality.

The training dataset (ADCORPUS) for predicting bounce rates is derived from all clicks on search ads from the Google search engine in a particular time period. Each record represents a click labeled with whether it was a bounce. A wide variety of features are considered for each click. These include the search query for the click, advertiser chosen keyword, advertisement text, estimated clickthrough rate of the ad clicked, a numeric similarity score between the ad and the landing page, and whether the advertiser keyword precisely matched the query. To improve generalization, we assigned the query and advertiser keywords into one of approximately 500 clusters, and used cluster properties as additional features. Overall, the dataset consisted of six categorical features varying in cardinality from 2 to 500, four numeric features, and 314 million records.

All of our experiments were performed on a MapReduce equipped cluster where each machine was configured to use 768MB of RAM and 1GB of hard drive space (peak utilization was < 200MB RAM and 50MB disk). Unless otherwise noted, each MapReduce job used 200 machines. A single MapReduce was never assigned more than four nodes for splitting, and at any time a maximum of three MapReduce jobs were scheduled on the cluster. Running time was measured as the total time between the cluster receiving a request to run PLANET and PLANET exiting with the learned model as output. In each experiment, the first run was ignored because of the additional one-time latency to stage PLANET on the cluster. To mitigate the effects of varying cluster conditions, all the running times have been averaged over multiple runs.

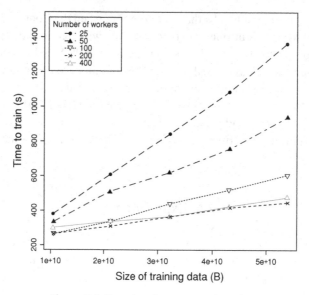

Figure 2.3 Running time versus data size.

To put the timing numbers that follow into perspective, we also recorded the time taken to train tree models in R using the GBM package (Ridgeway, 2006). This package requires the entire training data in memory, and hence we train on a sample of 10 million records (about 2GB). On a machine with 8GB RAM and sufficient disk, we trained 10 trees, each at depth between 1 and 10. Peak RAM utilization was 6GB (average was close to 5GB). The runtime for producing the different trees varied between 315 and 358 seconds (Figure 2.4).

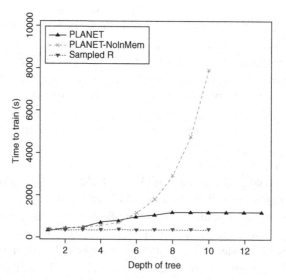

Figure 2.4 Running time versus tree depth. Note: The Sampled R curve was trained on 1/30 of the data used for the other curves.

2.6.2 Results

Scalability: Our first experiment measures the scalability of the PLANET framework. For this experiment, we randomly split the ADCORPUS into 5 roughly equal-sized groups and trained a single depth-3 classification tree, first on a single group, then two groups, and so on up to five groups. For each of these increasingly larger training datasets, we examined the effects of using between 50 and 600 machines. In this experiment, the Controller never scheduled more than two MapReduce jobs at a time and was configured to schedule MR_EXPANDNODES jobs only. In other words, we disabled the optimization to construct trees entirely in memory and limited forward scheduling to one job in order to evaluate the performance of the algorithm in a constrained (e.g., shared cluster) environment.

Figure 2.3 shows the results of this experiment. As expected, training time increases in proportion to the amount of training data. Similarly, adding more machines significantly decreases training time (ignoring the 400 machine curve for the moment). The most interesting observation in Figure 2.3 is the notion of marginal returns. When the dataset is large, adding more machine reduces costs proportionally, up to a point. For example, in our experiment, increasing the number of machines from 200 to 400 per MapReduce did not improve training time. Similarly, as the training set size decreases, the benefits of adding more machines also diminishes. In both these cases, after a certain point the overhead of adding new machines (networking overhead to watch the worker for failure, to schedule backup workers, to distribute data to the worker, and to collect results from the worker) dominate the benefits from each machine processing a smaller chunk of data. Empirically, it appears that for our dataset the optimal number of workers is under 400.

Benefits of MR_INMEMORY: Our next experiment highlights the benefits from in memory tree completion. Here, the Controller was configured to invoke MR_INMEMORY for nodes whose inputs contained 10M or fewer records. The reducers in MR_INMEMORY used the GBM package for tree construction and were configured with 8GB RAM in order to meet the memory requirements of the package. PLANET was used to train a single classification tree of varying depths on the entire ADCORPUS.

Figure 2.4 shows the results. PLANET-NoInMem plots the training time when MR_INMEMORY is not used by the Controller. In this case training time keeps increasing with tree depth as the number of MR_EXPANDNODES jobs keeps increasing. Note that even though we expand trees breadth first, the increase in training time is not linear in the depth. This happens because each MR_EXPANDNODES job is configured (based on memory constraints in the mappers) to expand four nodes only. At lower levels of the tree, a single MapReduce can no longer expand all nodes in a level, and hence we see a superlinear increase in training time. On the other hand, PLANET using a mix of MR_EXPANDNODES and MR_INMEMORY scales well and training time does not increase as significantly with tree depth.

As a reference point for the PLANET running times, we also provide the running time of Sampled-R in Figure 2.4, which shows the running time of the GBM in-memory algorithm on a 2GB sample of ADCORPUS.

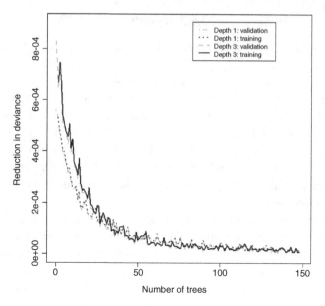

Figure 2.5 Error reduction as the number of trees increases.

Effect of Ensembles: The last experiment we report shows how error rates decrease in the bounce rate problem. Figure 2.5 shows the reduction in training and validation errors on a 90–10 split of the ADCORPUS. The figure plots the reduction in deviance as more trees are added to a boosted tree model. Two scenarios are shown – one in which the weak learners are depth one trees, and the other where the trees have depth three. For the depth-3 tree ensemble, the reduction in error is initially higher than with the depth-1 tree ensemble, as expected; however, the reduction asymptotes after about 100 trees for this dataset. The PLANET dashboard updates and displays such error graphs in real time. This enables users to manually intervene and stop model training when the error converges or overfitting begins.

2.7 Related Work

Scaling up tree learning algorithms to large datasets is an area of active research interest. There have been two main research directions taken by previous work: (1) centralized algorithms for large datasets on disk to avoid in-memory limitations and (2) parallel algorithms on specific parallel computing architectures. In applying the MapReduce framework to large-scale tree learning, PLANET borrows and builds on several ideas from these previous approaches.

Centralized Algorithms: Notable centralized algorithms for scaling decision tree learning to large datasets include SLIQ (Mehta et al., 1996), CLOUDS (Alsabti, Ranka, and Singh, 1998), RAINFOREST (Gehrke, Ramakrishnan, and Ganti, 1998), and BOAT (Gehrke et al., 1999). SLIQ uses strategies such as pre-sorting and feature lists in breadth-first tree-growing to enable learning from large training data on disk.

Although PLANET does not use pre-sorting or feature lists, it grows the tree breadth-first like SLIQ. The key insight in RAINFOREST is that the splitting decision at a tree node needs a compact data structure of sufficient statistics (referred to as AVC group in the RAINFOREST algorithm), which in most cases can be fit in-memory. PLANET similarly maintains sufficient statistics on mappers during MR_ExpandNodes. CLOUDS samples the split points for numeric features and uses an estimation step to find the best split point, resulting in lower computation and I/O cost compared to other tree learning algorithms such as C4.5. For efficient estimation of the best split, PLANET uses equidepth histograms of numerical features to estimate split points. Finally, BOAT uses statistical sampling to construct a tree based on a small subset of the whole data and then does corrections to the tree based on estimated differences compared to the actual tree learned on the whole data. In contrast, PLANET builds the tree from the whole data directly.

Parallel Algorithms: Numerous approaches for parallelizing tree learning have been proposed. Provost and Fayyad (1999) give an excellent survey of existing approaches, along with the motivations for large-scale tree learning. Bradford et al. (1999) discuss how the C4.5 decision tree induction algorithm can be effectively parallelized in the ccNUMA parallel computing platform. It also mentions other parallel implementations of decision trees, namely SLIQ, SPRINT, and ScalParC for message-passing systems, and SUBTREE, MWK, and MLC++ for symmetric multiprocessors (SMPs). Most of these algorithms have been developed for specific parallel computing architectures, many of which have specific advantages, such as shared memory to avoid replicating or communicating the whole dataset among the processors. In comparison, PLANET is based on the MapReduce platform that uses commodity hardware for massive-scale parallel computing.

For deciding the split points of features, SPRINT (Shafer, Agrawal, and Mehta, 1996) uses feature lists like SLIQ. Each processor is given a sublist of each feature list, corresponding to the instance indices in the data chunk sent to the processor. While computing good split points, each processor determines the gains over the instances assigned to that processor for each numerical feature and sends the master a portion of the statistics needed to determine the best split. However, this requires an all-to-all broadcast of instance IDs at the end. PLANET takes a simpler and more scalable approach – instead of considering all possible split points, it computes a representative subset of the splits using approximate histograms, after which the selection of the best split can be done using only one MapReduce job (details in Section 2.3.1).

ScalParC (Joshi, Karypis, and Kumar, 1998), which builds on SLIQ and SPRINT, also splits each feature list into multiple parts and assigns each part to a processor. However, rather than building the tree in a depth-first manner (as done by C4.5, MLC++, etc.), it does a breadth-first tree growth like SLIQ (and PLANET) to prevent possible load imbalance in a parallel computing framework.

Other notable techniques for parallel tree learning include (1) parallel decision tree learning on an SMP architecture based on feature scheduling among processors, including task pipelining and dynamic load balancing for speedup (Zaki, Ho, and Agrawal, 1999); (2) meta-learning schemes that train multiple trees in parallel along with a final arbiter tree that combines their predictions (Chan and Stolfo, 1993);

(3) distributed learning of trees by boosting, which operates over partitions of a large dataset that are exchanged among the processors (Lazarevic, 2001); (4) the SPIES algorithm, which combines the AVC-group idea of RAINFOREST with effective sampling of the training data to obtain a communication- and memory-efficient parallel tree learning method (Jin and Agrawal, 2003b); and (5) a distributed tree learning algorithm that uses only 20% of the communication cost to centralize the data, but achieves 80% of the accuracy of the centralized version (Giannella et al., 2004).

On the theoretical side Caragea, Silvescu, and Honavar (2004) formulated the problem of learning from distributed data and showed different algorithm settings for learning trees from distributed data, each of which is provably exact, that is, they give the same results as a tree learned using all the data in a centralized setting. Approximate algorithms for parallel learning of trees on streaming data have also been recently proposed (Ben-Haim and Yom-Tov, 2008; Jin and Agrawal, 2003a).

MapReduce in Machine Learning: In recent years, some learning algorithms have been implemented using the MapReduce framework. Chu et al. (2007) give an excellent overview of how different popular learning algorithms (e.g., locally weighted linear regression, naïve Bayes classification, Gaussian discriminative analysis, k-means, logistic regression, neural networks, principal component analysis, independent component analysis, expectation maximization, and support vector machines) can be effectively solved in the MapReduce framework. However, these algorithms have all been implemented using a shared-memory multiprocessor architecture. Our focus is on scaling learning algorithms (especially ensemble tree learning) to massive datasets using a MapReduce framework deployed on commodity hardware.

2.8 Conclusions

We have presented PLANET, a framework for large-scale tree learning using a MapReduce cluster. We are currently applying PLANET to problems within the sponsored search domain. Our experience is that the system scales well and performs reliably in this context, and we expect results would be similar in a variety of other domains involving large-scale learning problems. Our initial goal in building PLANET was to develop a scalable tree learner with accuracy comparable to a traditional in-memory algorithm, but capable of handling much more training data. We believe our experience in building and deploying PLANET provides lessons in using MapReduce for other nontrivial mining and data processing tasks. The strategies we developed for handling tree learning should be applicable to other problems requiring multiple iterations, each requiring one or more applications of MapReduce.

For future work, our short-term focus is to extend the functionality of PLANET in various ways to support more learning problems at Google. For example, we intend to support split metrics other than those based on variance. We also intend to investigate how intelligent sampling schemes might be used in conjunction with the scalability offered by PLANET. Other future plans include extending the implementation to handle multi-class classification and incremental learning.

Acknowledgments

We thank Ashish Agarwal, Puneet Chopra, Mayur Datar, Oystein Fledsberg, Rob Malkin, Gurmeet Singh Manku, Andrew Moore, Fernando Pereira, D. Sculley, and Diane Tang for their feedback and contributions to this work.

References

Alsabti, K., Ranka, S., and Singh, V. 1998. *CLOUDS: A Decision Tree Classier for Large Datasets.* Technical Reports, University of Florida.

Ben-Haim, Y., and Yom-Tov, E. 2008. A Streaming Parallel Decision Tree Algorithm. In: *Large Scale Learning Challenge Workshop at the International Conference on Machine Learning (ICML).*

Bradford, J. P., Fortes, J. A. B., and Bradford, J. 1999. *Characterization and Parallelization of Decision Tree Induction.* Technical Report, Purdue University.

Breiman, L. 1996. Bagging Predictors. *Machine Learning Journal,* **24**(2), 123–140.

Breiman, L. 2001. Random Forests. *Machine Learning Journal,* **45**(1), 5–32.

Breiman, L., Friedman, J. H., Olshen, R., and Stone, C. 1984. *Classification and Regression Trees.* Monterey, CA: Wadsworth and Brooks.

Caragea, D., Silvescu, A., and Honavar, V. 2004. A Framework for Learning from Distributed Data Using Sufficient Statistics and Its Application to Learning Decision Trees. *International Journal of Hybrid Intelligent Systems,* **1**(1–2), 80–89.

Caruana, R., and Niculescu-Mizil, A. 2006. An Empirical Comparison of Supervised Learning Algorithms. Pages 161–168 of: *International Conference on Machine Learning (ICML).*

Caruana, R., Karampatziakis, N., and Yessenalina, A. 2008. An Empirical Evaluation of Supervised Learning in High Dimensions. Pages 96–103 of: *International Conference on Machine Learning (ICML).*

Chan, P. K., and Stolfo, S. J. 1993. Toward Parallel and Distributed Learning by Meta-learning. Pages 227–240 of: *Workshop on Knowledge Discovery in Databases at the Conference of Association for the Advancement of Artificial Intelligence (AAAI).*

Chu, C.-T., Kim, S. K., Lin, Y.-A., Yu, Y., Bradski, G., Ng, A. Y., and Olukotun, K. 2007. MapReduce for Machine Learning on Multicore. Pages 281–288 of: *Advances in Neural Information Processing Systems (NIPS) 19.*

Dean, J., and Ghemawat, S. 2004. MapReduce: Simplified Data Processing on Large Clusters. In: *Symposium on Operating System Design and Implementation (OSDI).*

Duda, R. O., Hart, P. E., and Stork, D. G. 2001. *Pattern Classification,* 2nd ed. New York: Wiley.

Freund, Y., and Schapire, R. E. 1996. Experiments with a New Boosting Algorithm. Pages 148–156 of: *International Conference on Machine Learning (ICML).*

Friedman, J. H. 2001. Greedy Function Approximation: A Gradient Boosting Machine. *Annals of Statistics,* **29**(5), 1189–1232.

Gao, J., Wu, Q., Burges, C., Svore, K., Su, Y., Khan, N., Shah, S., and Zhou, H. 2009 (August). Model Adaptation via Model Interpolation and Boosting for Web Search Ranking. Pages 505–513 of: *Proceedings of the 2009 Conference on Empirical Methods in Natural Language Processing.*

Gehrke, J., Ramakrishnan, R., and Ganti, V. 1998. RainForest – A Framework for Fast Decision Tree Construction of Large Datasets. Pages 416–427 of: *International Conference on Very Large Data Bases (VLDB).*

Gehrke, J., Ganti, V., Ramakrishnan, R., and Loh, W.-Y. 1999. BOAT – Optimistic Decision Tree Construction. Pages 169–180 of: *International Conference on ACM Special Interest Group on Management of Data (SIGMOD).*

Giannella, C., Liu, K., Olsen, T., and Kargupta, H. 2004. Communication Efficient Construction of Decision Trees over Heterogeneously Distributed Data. Pages 67–74 of: *International Conference on Data Mining (ICDM)*.

Jin, R., and Agrawal, G. 2003a. Efficient Decision Tree Construction on Streaming Data. Pages 571–576 of: *SIGKDD Conference on Knowledge Discovery and Data Mining (KDD)*.

Jin, R., and Agrawal, G. 2003b. Communication and Memory Efficient Parallel Decision Tree Construction. Pages 119–129 of: *SIAM Conference on Data Mining (SDM)*.

Joshi, M. V., Karypis, G., and Kumar, V. 1998. ScalParC: A New Scalable and Efficient Parallel Classification Algorithm for Mining Large Datasets. Pages 573–579 of: *International Parallel Processing Symposium (IPPS)*.

Kaushik, A. 2007a (August). *Bounce Rate as Sexiest Web Metric Ever*. MarketingProfs. http://www .marketingprofs.com/7/bounce-rate-sexiest-web-metric-ever-kaushik.asp?sp=1.

Kaushik, A. 2007b (May). *Excellent Analytics Tip 11: Measure Effectiveness of Your Web Pages*. Occam's Razor (blog). www.kaushik.net/avinash/2007/05/excellent-analytics-tip-11-measure-effectiveness-of-your-web-pages.html.

Lazarevic, A. 2001. The Distributed Boosting Algorithm. Pages 311–316 of: *SIGKDD Conference on Knowledge Discovery and Data Mining (KDD)*.

MacQueen, J. B. 1967. Some Methods for Classification and Analysis of Multivariate Observations. Pages 281–297 of: Cam, L. M. Le, and Neyman, J. (eds), *Proceedings of the 5th Berkeley Symposium on Mathematical Statistics and Probability*, vol. 1. Berkeley: University of California Press.

Manku, G. S., Rajagopalan, S., and Lindsay, B. G. 1999. Random Sampling Techniques for Space Efficient Online Computation of Order Statistics of Large Datasets. Pages 251–262 of: *International Conference on ACM Special Interest Group on Management of Data (SIGMOD)*.

Mehta, M., Agrawal, R., and Rissanen, J. 1996. SLIQ: A Fast Scalable Classifier for Data Mining. Pages 18–32 of: *International Conference on Extending Data Base Technology (EDBT)*.

Provost, F., and Fayyad, U. 1999. A survey of methods for scaling up inductive algorithms. *Data Mining and Knowledge Discovery*, **3**, 131–169.

Ridgeway, G. 2006. *Generalized Boosted Models: A Guide to the GBM Package*. http://cran.r-project.org/web/packages/gbm.

Rokach, L., and Maimon, O. 2008. *Data Mining with Decision Trees: Theory and Applications*. World Scientific.

Sculley, D., Malkin, R., Basu, S., and Bayardo, R. J. 2009. Predicting Bounce Rates in Sponsored Search Advertisements. Pages 1325–1334 of: *SIGKDD Conference on Knowledge Discovery and Data Mining (KDD)*.

Shafer, J. C., Agrawal, R., and Mehta, M. 1996. SPRINT: A Scalable Parallel Classifier for Data Mining. Pages 544–555 of: *International Conference on Very Large Data Bases (VLDB)*.

Vapnik, V. N. 1995. *The Nature of Statistical Learning Theory*. Berlin: Springer.

Zaki, M. J., Ho, C.-T., and Agrawal, R. 1999. Parallel Classification for Data Mining on Shared-Memory Multiprocessors. Pages 198–205 of: *International Conference on Data Engineering (ICDE)*.

CHAPTER 3

Large-Scale Machine Learning Using DryadLINQ

Mihai Budiu, Dennis Fetterly, Michael Isard,
Frank McSherry, and Yuan Yu

This chapter describes DryadLINQ, a general-purpose system for large-scale data-parallel computing, and illustrates its use on a number of machine learning problems.

The main motivation behind the development of DryadLINQ was to make it easier for nonspecialists to write general-purpose, scalable programs that can operate on very large input datasets. In order to appeal to nonspecialists, we designed the programming interface to use a high level of abstraction that insulates the programmer from most of the detail and complexity of parallel and distributed execution. In order to support general-purpose computing, we embedded these high-level abstractions in .NET, giving developers access to full-featured programming languages with rich type systems and proven mechanisms (such as classes and libraries) for managing complex, long-lived, and geographically distributed software projects. In order to support scalability over very large data and compute clusters, the DryadLINQ compiler generates code for the Dryad runtime, a well-tested and highly efficient distributed execution engine.

As machine learning moves into the industrial mainstream and operates over diverse data types including documents, images, and graphs, it is increasingly appealing to move away from domain-specific languages like MATLAB and toward general-purpose languages that support rich types and standardized libraries. The examples in this chapter demonstrate that a general-purpose language such as C# supports effective, concise implementations of standard machine learning algorithms and that DryadLINQ efficiently scales these implementations to operate over hundreds of computers and very large datasets primarily limited by disk capacity.

3.1 Manipulating Datasets with LINQ

We use Language Integrated Queries, or LINQ (Microsoft, 2010), as our programming model for writing large-scale machine learning applications. LINQ adds high-level declarative data manipulation to many of the .NET programming languages, including C#, Visual Basic, and F#. This section provides a short introduction to LINQ.

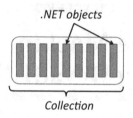

Figure 3.1 LINQ data model: collections of typed values.

LINQ comprises a set of operators to manipulate collections of .NET objects. The operators are integrated seamlessly in high-level .NET programming languages, giving developers direct access to all the .NET libraries as well the traditional language constructs such as loops, classes, and modules. The collections manipulated by LINQ operators can contain any .NET type, making it easy to compute with complex data such as vectors, matrices, and images. As shown in the rest of this chapter, many machine learning algorithms can be naturally and elegantly expressed using LINQ.

LINQ datasets are .NET collections. Technically, a .NET collection of values of type T is a data type that implements the predefined interface IEnumerable<T>. Many commonly used data structures such as arrays, lists, hash-tables, and sets are such collections. The elements of a collection can be any type, including nested collections. Figure 3.1 illustrates the abstract LINQ data model. We will see later that this model can be naturally extended to accommodate very large collections that span multiple computers. The IEnumerable interface provides access to an *iterator*, used to enumerate the elements of the collection. Programmers can use these iterators to scan over the datasets.

To simplify programming, LINQ provides a large set of operators to manipulate collections, drawn from common data-parallel programming patterns. All of these operators are *functional*: they transform input collections to completely new output collections, rather than update the existing collections in place. Although there are many primitive LINQ operators (and the users can easily add more), all of them can be seen as variants of the *seven* operators listed in Table 3.1. Readers familiar with the SQL database language will find these operators quite natural.

Table 3.1. *Essential LINQ operators.*

Operation	Meaning
Where	(Filter) Keep all values satisfying a given property.
Select	(Map) Apply a transformation to each value in the collection.
Aggregate	(Fold, Reduce) Combine all values in the collection to produce a single result (e.g., max).
GroupBy	Create a collection of collections, where the elements in each inner collection all have a common property (*key*).
OrderBy	(Sort) Order the elements in the collection according to some property (*key*).
SelectMany	(Flatten) Generate a collection for each element in the input (by applying a function), then concatenate the resulting collections.
Join	Combine the values from two collections when they have a common property.

Table 3.2. *Examples using LINQ operators on collection* C = {1,2,3,4,5}. Factors *is a user-defined function.*

Operation	Result
`C.Where(x => x > 3)`	(4,5)
`C.Select(x => x + 1)`	(2,3,4,5,6)
`C.Aggregate( (x,y) => x+y)`	15
`C.GroupBy(x => x % 2)`	((1,3,5), (2,4))
`C.OrderBy(x => -x)`	(5,4,3,2,1)
`C.Select(x => Factors(x))`	((1), (1, 2), (1, 3), (1, 2, 4), (1, 5))
`C.SelectMany(x => Factors(x))`	(1, 1, 2, 1, 3, 1, 2, 4, 1, 5)
`C.Join(C, x=>x, x=>x-4, (x, y)=>x+y)`	(6)

Most LINQ operators take as a parameter at least one *function* used to process the elements in the collection. These functions are most commonly *anonymous functions*, a convenient .NET shorthand written as `x => f(x)` for the function mapping a single variable x to a result $f(x)$. The anonymous function bodies can invoke user-defined methods or may simply consist of primitive .NET operations. For example, the anonymous function `x => x%2` computes the value of the input argument modulo 2. Anonymous functions with multiple inputs are written by parenthesizing the inputs together, as in `(x,y,z) => f(x,y,z)` for the case of three inputs.

To be concrete, Table 3.2 shows the result of applying some LINQ operators to the collection C = (1,2,3,4,5). The only example that may not be self-explanatory in Table 3.2 is Join, the only operation that we have shown that operates on two collections. Join receives three function arguments: (1) the first function argument (in our example `x=>x`) computes a *key* value for each element in the left collection; (2) the second function (`x=>x-4`) computes the key value for each element in the right collection; (3) finally, the third function `(x,y)=>x+y` reduces pairs of values, where x is from the first collection and y from the second collection. This function is invoked only for pairs of values that have matching keys. In our example, the only matching pair of values is 1 and 5, whose keys are both 1 (1 and respectively 5-4), and thus the result of the Join is a collection with a single element 1 + 5.

The final feature of LINQ we introduce is the IQueryable<T> interface, deriving from the IEnumerable<T> interface. An object of type IQueryable<T> represents a *query* (i.e., a computation) that can produce a collection with elements of type T. The queries are not evaluated until an element or aggregate is required from the collection.[1] Applying LINQ operators to an IQueryable object produces a new IQueryable object, describing the computation required to produce the new result.

Importantly, each IQueryable<T> can specify a *LINQ provider*, capable of examining the query and choosing from many different execution strategies. Many LINQ providers exist: PLINQ (Duffy, 2007) executes queries on a single computer using multiple CPU cores, and LINQ to SQL translates LINQ queries to SQL statements executed on a database engine. DryadLINQ (Yu et al., 2008) itself is simply a LINQ provider that executes the queries on a computer cluster.

---

[1] Queries are a form of *lazy evaluation* of code; this is encountered in other programming languages such as Haskell or Scheme.

3.2 *k*-Means in LINQ

We now show how to use LINQ to implement a basic machine-learning algorithm; in Section 3.3.4 we show how this program can be executed in a distributed fashion. *k*-means is a classical clustering algorithm that divides a collection of vectors into *k* clusters. The clusters are represented by their centroids; each vector belongs to the cluster with the nearest centroid. This is an iterative computation, which is performed until a termination criterion is reached.

LINQ collections can contain arbitrary types, and for our purposes we use a class `Vector` providing all the usual vector arithmetic operations (addition, scalar product, dot product, L2 norm, etc.). The `Vector` class could be predefined and imported from some shared library. We can then represent a collection of vectors using `IQueryable<Vector>`.

We first define a useful auxiliary function `NearestCenter` that computes the nearest neighbor of a vector from a set of vectors.

```
Vector NearestCenter(Vector point, IQueryable<Vector> centers)
{
    var nearest = centers.First();
    foreach (var center in centers)
        if ((point - center).Norm() < (point - nearest).Norm())
            nearest = center;

    return nearest;
}
```

The *k*-means algorithm is a simple iterative computation: each iteration groups the input vectors by their nearest center and averages each group to form the centers for the next iteration. The `KMeansStep` function below computes the updated centers from the input vectors and current centers. The LINQ code simply groups the input vectors using the nearest center as a key and uses aggregation to reduce each group to its average:

```
IQueryable<Vector> KMeansStep(IQueryable<Vector> vectors,
                              IQueryable<Vector> centers)
{
    return vectors.GroupBy(vector => NearestCenter(vector, centers))
                .Select(g => g.Aggregate((x,y) => x+y) / g.Count());
}
```

The *k*-means algorithm repeatedly invokes this step until a termination condition is met. The next example uses a fixed number of iterations, though more complex convergence criteria could be employed.

```
IQueryable<Vector> KMeans(IQueryable<Vector> vectors,
                          IQueryable<Vector> centers,
                          int iterations)
{
```

```
for (int i = 0; i < iterations; i++)
    centers = KMeansStep(vectors, centers);

return centers;
}
```

The result of the KMeans function is a single object with type IQueryable<Vector>, describing the computation necessary to produce the result from iterations steps of our iterative algorithm. Only when the user attempts to enumerate the result of KMeans will the query be executed and the iterations performed.

3.3 Running LINQ on a Cluster with DryadLINQ

In order to perform computations on very large datasets, we need to pool the resources of multiple computers. Fortunately, the computations expressed in LINQ are very easy to parallelize by distributing work to multiple computers. The software stack that we have built for this purpose is shown in Figure 3.2. In this text we particularly focus on two layers of this stack: Dryad and DryadLINQ. Layers such as Cluster storage and Cluster services, which provide a distributed file system and execution of processes on cluster machines, are important but their discription is outside the scope of this chapter.

3.3.1 Dryad

Dryad (Isard et al., 2007) is a software layer that coordinates the execution of multiple dependent programs (processes) running on a computer cluster. A Dryad job is a collection of processes that communicate with each other through unidirectional *channels*. Dryad allows the programmer to describe the computation as a directed acyclic multigraph, in which nodes represent processes and edges represent communication channels. The requirement that the graphs be acyclic may seem restrictive, but it enables Dryad to provide automatically fault-tolerance, without any knowledge of the application semantics. Moreover, we will see that many interesting algorithms can be expressed as acyclic graphs. Figure 3.3 shows a hypothetical example of a Dryad execution plan.

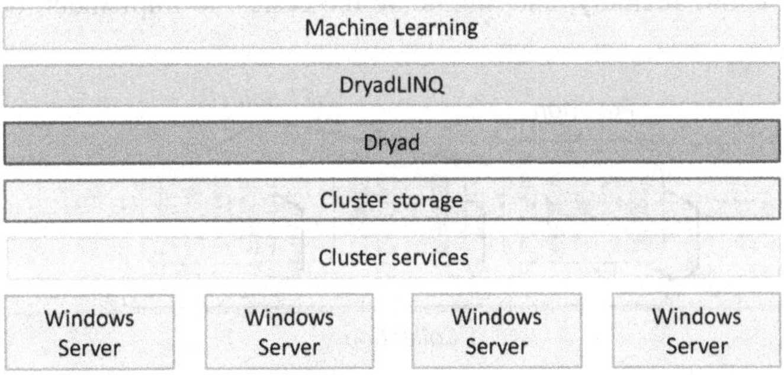

Figure 3.2 Software stack for executing LINQ programs on a cluster of computers.

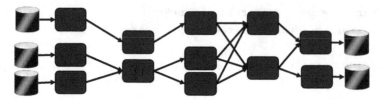

Figure 3.3 Example of a hypothetical Dryad job execution plan; the nodes are programs that execute, possibly on different computers, while the edges are channels transporting data between the processes. The input and output of the computation reside on the cluster storage medium.

Dryad handles the reliable execution of the graph on a cluster. Dryad schedules computations to computers, monitors their execution, collects and reports statistics, and handles transient failures in the cluster by re-executing failed or slow computations. Dryad jobs execute in a *shared-nothing* environment: there is no implicit shared memory or disk state between the various processes in a Dryad job; the only communication medium between processes is channels themselves.

3.3.2 DryadLINQ

We have introduced two essential ingredients for implementing large-scale cluster computation: a parallel language (LINQ) and an execution environment for clusters (Dryad). We now describe DryadLINQ, a compiler and runtime library that bridges the gap between these two layers. DryadLINQ translates programs written in LINQ into Dryad job execution plans (to be performed on a cluster by Dryad) and transparently returns the results to the host application.

DryadLINQ presents the same data model as LINQ to the programmers. But, in order to distribute the computation across multiple computers, DryadLINQ internally partitions the data into disjoint parts, as shown in Figure 3.4. The original collections become collections of partitions, the partitions being some (smaller) LINQ collections that reside on individual computers. (The partitions residing on the cluster storage medium can optionally be replicated on several computers each, for increased fault tolerance.)

DryadLINQ implements LINQ operators over partitioned collections. Figure 3.5 shows how this is done for some of the basic LINQ operators from Table 3.1. Operators such as `Select`, `SelectMany`, and `Where` are the easiest to implement, because they

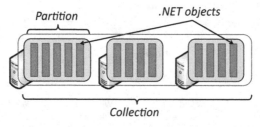

Figure 3.4 DryadLINQ data model: collections of typed values partitioned among several computers. Compare with Figure 3.1.

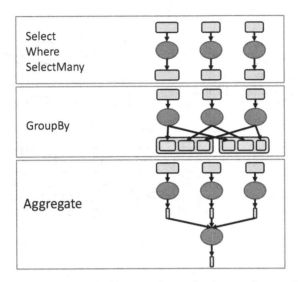

Figure 3.5 Dryad jobs generated by DryadLINQ for the simplest LINQ operators.

operate on individual elements; they can be applied to individual parts regardless of the partitioning scheme. The GroupBy requires records with the same key to be colocated, so it is implemented in two steps: (1) repartition the collection using a deterministic hash function applied to the grouping key; and (2) after repartitioning, all elements with the same key are present on the same computer, which can perform a standard LINQ GroupBy on the local data to produce the necessary collection of groups. Aggregation using an associative function can be done hierarchically: in a first phase, the data in each part is aggregated independently; in subsequent phases, subsets of intermediate results are combined, until in the last phase a single computer performs the final aggregation.

Figure 3.6 shows the translation for two of LINQ operators that generate binary collection operations. The first example results from the nested usage of collections (when an inner collection is used for all elements in the outer collection, as we see in Section 3.3.4): in the generated Dryad graph the inner collection is broadcast to all partitions of the outer collection.

The second example shows an implementation of the binary Join operator. Similar to GroupBy, it is implemented using deterministic hash function, ensuring that elements with matching keys end up in corresponding partitions.

The Dryad job execution plans generated by DryadLINQ are *composable*: the output of one graph can become the input of another one. In fact, this is exactly how complex LINQ queries are translated: each operator is translated to a graph independently, and the graphs are then concatenated. The graph generation phase is followed by a graph rewriting phase that performs optimizations and that can substantially alter the shape of the job execution plan. As a simple example, sequences of Select and Where operations can be pipelined and executed within a single vertex.

In general, during the computation, the collection elements must be moved between computers, so the in-memory data structures need to be *serialized* to a shared physical medium, either a disk or the network. DryadLINQ exploits its full knowledge of the types in the collections to automatically generate efficient serialization and

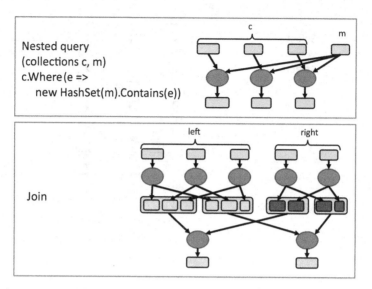

Figure 3.6 Dryad jobs generated by DryadLINQ for other LINQ operators.

de-serialization code. The user can always replace the default serialization routines with custom ones, but this is seldom needed. DryadLINQ also optionally compresses data before writing it to disk or transmitting it across the network.

3.3.3 MapReduce and DryadLINQ

Any MapReduce (Dean and Ghemawat, 2004) program can be easily translated into a DryadLINQ program. In consequence, any algorithm expressed using the MapReduce framework also can be implemented in DryadLINQ. The MapReduce approach requires the programmer to specify "map" and "reduce" functions, where the map function transforms each input record to a list of keyed intermediate records, and the reduce function transforms a group of intermediate records with the same key into a list of output records.[2]

```
IQueryable<R> MapReduce<S,T,R,K>(
       IQueryable<S> records,
       Func<S,IEnumerable<KeyValuePair<K,T>> mapper,
       Func<IGrouping<K,T>,IEnumerable<R>> reducer)
{
    return records.SelectMany(mapper)
                .GroupBy(temp => temp.Key, temp => temp.Value)
                .SelectMany(reducer);
}
```

---

[2] MapReduce as defined by Google specifies that a reducer will receive the records sorted on their keys; in our implementation, each reducer is only given all the records that have the same key. DryadLINQ is flexible enough to emulate the exact behavior of MapReduce as well, but we omit this implementation for simplicity.

There are some simple but noteworthy observations about using LINQ and DryadLINQ to implement MapReduce.

The LINQ version of MapReduce is strongly typed (the type of the elements in the input and output is known at compilation time), so more errors are caught at compilation time (this feature becomes very useful once programs become large). LINQ also provides complete integration with .NET libraries and existing integrated development environments; this immediately leverages the effort put into reusable libraries and development tools. Finally, because LINQ supports many providers, the computation can be immediately executed across a variety of LINQ providers, such as multicore PLINQ, LINQ to SQL, and DryadLINQ.

When using DryadLINQ, in particular, a few additional advantages emerge: Because of strong typing, DryadLINQ can generate very efficient serialization code for all objects involved, without the need to resort writing to manual serialization code, such as Protocol Buffers (Google, 2010). By using DryadLINQ to execute the MapReduce programs we inherit all of DryadLINQ's optimizations: computations are placed close to the data, multiple MapReduce programs can be composed, and optimizations can be applied across the MapReduce boundaries. MapReduce computations can even be mixed in with other LINQ computations that are difficult to express in MapReduce (e.g., Joins). Finally, the eager aggregation performed by DryadLINQ discussed in Section 3.3.4 is a generalization of the concept of *combiners* and *reducers* that MapReduce uses, but DryadLINQ can automatically infer the combiners and reducers in many cases (Yu, Gunda, and Isard, 2009).

3.3.4 *k*-means Clustering in DryadLINQ

The power of DryadLINQ is illustrated by how little the *k*-means program from Section 3.2 needs to change to be executed on a cluster of computers. To invoke DryadLINQ, one only needs to change the input collection of a query to be one of the partitioned collections shown in Figure 3.4.

Although using DryadLINQ is easy for the programmer, under the hood many optimizations concur to provide an efficient execution of the queries. Recall the core of our *k*-means iteration:

```
IQueryable<Vector> KMeansStep(IQueryable<Vector> vectors,
                              IQueryable<Vector> centers)
{
    return vectors.GroupBy(vector => NearestCenter(vector, centers))
              .Select(g => g.Aggregate((x,y) => x+y) / g.Count());
}
```

The GroupBy operation at the heart of the *k*-means aggregation collects a very large amount of data; even if the input vectors are initially spread over hundreds of balanced partitions, if half of them belong to a single cluster, it would seem that the runtime would need to bring them to a single computer in order to compute the average. (This is the problem of *data skew*, which is notoriously difficult to handle in a generic

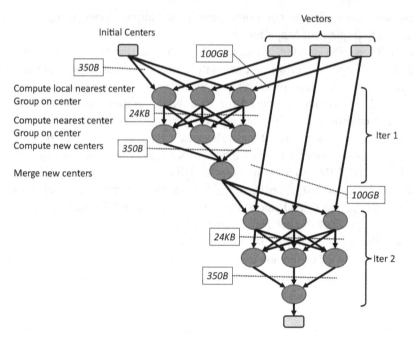

Figure 3.7 Dryad job execution plan generated for two iterations of the k-means algorithm on ten dimensional vectors, with $k = 10$. The vector data is split into three partitions. The boxes with dotted lines show the amount of data exchanged between stages for a 100GB set of vectors.

way.) Such a strategy would severely overload the machine computing the centroid for the large group. However, the DryadLINQ optimizer uses a robust *eager aggregation* algorithm to implement this particular computation (Yu, Gunda, and Isard, 2009). By inspecting the code for the centroid computation, DryadLINQ can infer that the computation of the average is associative and commutative. DryadLINQ thus generates a job execution plan that uses two-level aggregation (similar to the plan shown at the bottom of Figure 3.5): each machine builds local groups with the local data and only sends the aggregated information about these groups to the next stage; the next stage computes the actual centroid. DryadLINQ can often determine automatically whether a computation is associative and commutative; when this is unfeasible, the user can employ the C# annotation mechanism to tag functions. For example, we tagged the vector addition operation with the [Associative] attribute for this optimization to work in our case (not shown). Figure 3.7 shows the execution plan that is generated for this program.

The key selection function for the GroupBy operation uses the centroids from the previous iteration, by employing the nested pattern from Figure 3.6. DryadLINQ produces a plan that updates the centroids once and broadcasts the results once to each part, where they are reused. This optimization also allows us to chain multiple iterations of k-means together, without interrupting the computation on the cluster. This reduces the overhead for launching jobs on the cluster and allows DryadLINQ to optimize execution across iteration boundaries.

Measurements

For our measurements, we use a collection of random vectors with 10 dimensions each whose total size is 100GB. According to the execution plan shown in Figure 3.7, each vertex computes k pre-aggregated cluster centroids, each of the length of 10 doubles (one per dimension), which are then exchanged, aggregated, and rebroadcast to each of the vertices in the following iteration, independently of the number (or distribution) of vectors on each machine. The main bottleneck in data-parallel computations tends to be the data exchange, where the shared network fabric must support many point-to-point data transfers. The local operations are limited by the speed of reading data from the local disks and do only modest processing. Therefore, we present measurements just for the amount of data exchanged across the network. Figure 3.7 shows the amount of data read by each stage; the output of the first stage is only 24KB (we have used 31 partitions in this execution). The majority of the time is spent in the first stage of each iteration (computing local centers).

3.3.5 Decision Tree Induction in DryadLINQ

For our next DryadLINQ example, we consider the problem of computing a decision tree. We use a binary decision tree to classify records with the following structure:

```
class Record
{
    bool label;        // class the record belongs to
    bool[] attributes; // attributes to classify on
}
```

A decision tree is a tree of attribute choices, terminating in leaves with class labels on them. The tree is used to classify records by starting from the root, examining a specified attribute at each internal node, proceeding down the branch indicated by the attribute's value, and continuing recursively until a leaf (and class label) is reached. We represent a decision tree with a dictionary that maps tree node indices (integer values) to attribute indices in the `attribute` array: given a node index node in the tree, `tree[node]` is an index in the `attributes` array, indicating which attribute is tested by the node.

```
// compute index of node in (partial) tree reached by a record
int TreeWalk(Record record, Dictionary<int, int> tree)
{
    var node = 0;
    while (tree.ContainsKey(node))
        node = 2 * node + (record.attributes[tree[node]] ? 1 : 2);

    return node;
}
```

The most common algorithm to induce a decision tree starts from an empty tree and a set of labeled data records. The algorithm repeatedly extends the tree by grouping

records by their current location under the partial tree, and for each such group determining the attribute resulting in the greatest reduction in conditional entropy (of the
class label given the attribute value). For example, we might write:

```
records.GroupBy(record => TreeWalk(record, tree))
       .Select(group => FindBestAttribute(group));
```

Although this approach makes perfect sense in a single-computer setting, in the
data-parallel setting it has the defect that all of the input records must be reshuffled in
each iteration. Moreover, some machines can be overloaded when many records map
to a single node in the tree (e.g., during the first few levels of the tree) – the data skew
issue discussed in Section 3.3.4.

Instead, we consider an alternate "bottom-up" algorithm with a highly parallel
execution plan. We use (but do not show here) a function CondEntropy computing the
conditional entropy of a list of lists of counts.

```
IEnumerable<Pair<int, int>>
DecisionTreeLayer(IQueryable<Record> data,
    Dictionary <int, int> tree)
{
    // emit a quadruple for each attribute,
    var a = data.SelectMany(x => x.attrs.Select((y, i) => new
            {
                prefix = TreeWalk(x, tree),
                label = x.record.label,
                index = i,
                value = y
            }));

    // count distinct quadruples
    var b = a.GroupBy(x => x)
            .Select(g => new { g.Key, count = g.Count() });

    // compute conditional entropy for each attribute in each prefix
    var c = b.GroupBy(x => new { x.Key.prefix, x.Key.index })
            .Select(x => new
            {
                x.Key.prefix,
                x.Key.index,
                entropy = CondEntropy(x.GroupBy(x => x.value))
            });

    // group by prefix, return min-entropy attribute
    return c.GroupBy(x => x.prefix)
            .Select(g => g.OrderByDescending(y => y.entropy).First())
            .Select(x => new Pair<int, int>(x.prefix, x.index));
}
```

The computation proceeds in four steps:

1. The first step replaces each record with a collection of quadruples, one for each of the record's attributes. The quadruple contains the record's location in the current tree, the record's class label, the index of the corresponding attribute, and the attribute's value.
2. The second step aggregates all identical quadruples, counting the number of occurrences of each and performing the most significant data reduction in the computation.
3. The third step groups the counts from the second step, using the pair (tree prefix, attribute index) as the key, and then computes the entropy of these groups (which is the conditional entropy of this attribute).
4. Finally, the fourth step performs another grouping on the set identifier, selecting the attribute with the lowest conditional entropy (by using the `OrderBy` LINQ operator to sort the attributes and using the `First` LINQ operator to choose the one with minimum entropy). The result of this computation is list of set identifiers and optimal attribute index for each. This list can be used to attach a new layer of nodes to the decision tree.

The code presented computes a new level in the decision tree. To compute a full tree, we would write:

```
var records = PartitionedTable.Get<Record>(datafile);

var tree = new Dictionary<int, int>();
for (int i = 0; i < maxTreeDepth; i++)
    foreach (var result in DecisionTreeLayer(records, tree))
        tree.Add(result.Key, result.Value);
```

Each iteration through the loop invokes a query returning the list of attribute indices that are best for each of the leaves in the tree that we aim to extend. In principle, we could unroll the loop to a single DryadLINQ computation as we did with the k-means computation, using an `IQueryable<Pair<int,int>>` as the data structure for our tree, and simply feeding the result of one layer in as the tree for the next; however, we do not do this here. Instead, the `tree` variable is updated on the client computer (the one that produces the job to submit to the cluster), and retransmitted to the cluster by DryadLINQ with each iteration.

The plan generated for the decision tree layer is shown in Figure 3.8. One can view this plan as a sequence of MapReduce computations; in the resulting plan each "reduce" stage is fused with the following "map" stage. This plan also fundamentally benefits from DryadLINQ's eager aggregation; before any data exchange happens, each part is reduced to a collection of counts, no more than the $|sets| \times |labels| \times |attributes| \times |values|$. The number of records plays no role in the size of the aggregates. As the tree becomes deeper, the number of sets will increase, and there may come a point where it is more efficient to reshuffle the records rather than their resulting aggregates. However, the number of aggregates never exceeds the number of quadruples, which never exceeds the number of attributes present in the records.

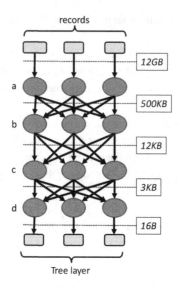

Figure 3.8 Dryad job execution plan generated for computing one layer of the decision tree, assuming that the records data is split into three partitions. The dotted lines show the amount of data that is crossing between layers when computing the second level of the tree for a 12 GB input set.

Measurements

As for the k-means algorithm, the volume of data transferred across the network by the decision tree induction code is largely independent of the volume of training data. Each group results in a number of aggregates bounded by the structure of the problem, rather than the number or distribution of records. We might see fewer aggregates if the records are concentrated properly (e.g., clustered by label, so that each part only produces half of the possible aggregates), but the performance on random data is a good worst-case evaluation.

We have used a 12GB input dataset for these measurements. Figure 3.8 shows the amount of data that crosses between computation stages; the second stage reads only 0.5MB, because of the local aggregation performed by DryadLINQ. The amount of data written by the last stage doubles for each successive tree layer computation.

3.3.6 Example: Singular Value Decomposition

The Singular Value Decomposition (SVD) lies at the heart of several large-scale data analyses: principal components analysis, collaborative filtering, image segmentation, and latent semantic indexing, among many others. The SVD of a $n \times m$ matrix A is a decomposition $A = U \Sigma V^T$ such that U and V are both orthonormal ($U^T U = V^T V = I$) and Σ is a diagonal matrix with non-negative entries.

Orthogonal Iteration is a common approach to computing the U and V matrices, in which candidates U and V are repeatedly updated to AV and $A^T U$, respectively, followed by re-orthonormalization of their columns. In fact, only one of the two iterates need be retained (we will keep V) because the other can be recomputed with one step. The process converges in the limit to the true factors, and convergence after any fixed number of iterations can be quite good; the error is exponentially small in the number of iterations, where the base of the exponent depends on the conditioning of the matrix.

We will represent a matrix as a collection of `Entry` objects, commonly reserved for sparse matrices but not overly inefficient for dense matrices.

```
struct Entry
{
    int row, col;
    double val;
}
```

Based on this representation, we can write several standard linear algebra operations using LINQ operations:

```
// aggregates matrix entries with the same coordinates into a
// single value
IQueryable<Entry> Canonicalize(IQueryable<Entry> a)
{
    return a.GroupBy(x => new { x.row, x.col }, x => x.val)
            .Select(g => new Entry(g.Key.row, g.Key.col, g.Sum()));
}

// multiplies matrices. best if one is pre-partitioned by join key
IQueryable<Entry> Multiply(IQueryable<Entry> a, IQueryable<Entry> b)
{
    return Canonicalize(a.Join(b,
        x => x.col,
        y => y.row,
        (x, y) => new Entry(x.row, y.col, x.val * y.val)));
}

IQueryable<Entry> Add(IQueryable<Entry> a, IQueryable<Entry> b)
{
    return Canonicalize(a.Concat(b));
}

IQueryable<Entry> Transpose(IQueryable<Entry> a)
{
    return a.Select(x => new Entry(x.col, x.row, x.val));
}
```

`Multiply` produces a substantial amount of intermediate data, but DryadLINQ's eager aggregation significantly reduces this volume before the data is exchanged across the network.

These operations are sufficient for us to repeatedly compute $A^T A V$, but they do not let us orthonormalize the columns of V. However, the $k \times k$ matrix $V^T V$ is quite small and contains enough information to produce (via Cholesky decomposition) a

$k \times k$ matrix L_V so that VL_V is orthonormal. We use DryadLINQ to compute $V^T V$ and return this value to the client computer where we compute L_V and introduce it into the computation.

The orthogonal iteration algorithm then looks like:

```
// Cholesky decomposition done on the local computer (not shown)
PartitionedTable<Entry> Cholesky(IQueryable<Entry> vtv);

// materialize a and a^T partitioned on columns
var a = a.HashPartition(x => x.col).ToPartitionedTable("a");
var at = Transpose(a).HashPartition(x => x.col)
                    .ToPartitionedTable<Entry>("at");

// run 100 orthogonal iteration steps
for (int iteration=0; iteration < 100; iteration++)
{
    v = Multiply(at, Multiply(a, v));

    // Perform Cholesky decomposition once every five iterations
    if (iteration % 5 == 0)
    {
        v = v.ToPartitionedTable("svd-" + iteration.ToString());
        v = Multiply(v, Cholesky(Multiply(Transpose(v), v)));
    }
}
```

Although it can also be written as a LINQ program, the body of the `Cholesky` function is not shown; it is executed on the client computer. On each loop iteration, DryadLINQ creates a query that "wraps around" the `for` loop, computing essentially $A^T \times A \times (V \times L_V)$. The orthonormalization step is required only for numerical stability and is executed only once every five iterations. A new DryadLINQ job is created and dispatched to the cluster once for every five iterations of the loop. Figure 3.9 shows the shape of the DryadLINQ job execution plan generated for this program.

Each loop iteration involves a `Join` of V with A, and with A^T. We use the `HashPartition` DryadLINQ-specific operator (an extension to basic LINQ) to give a hint to the system to pre-partition A using its columns as keys; as a consequence, the join against the rows of V does not move any of A's entries across the network; only entries corresponding to V, usually much smaller, are moved. Likewise, we keep a copy of A^T partitioned by its columns. Although keeping multiple copies of A may seem wasteful, the cost is paid in terms of cheap disk storage rather than a scarce resource such as memory.

Measurements

As we have noted, to extract optimum performance from the SVD algorithm, it is important to pre-partition the matrix data by row and column, avoiding full data

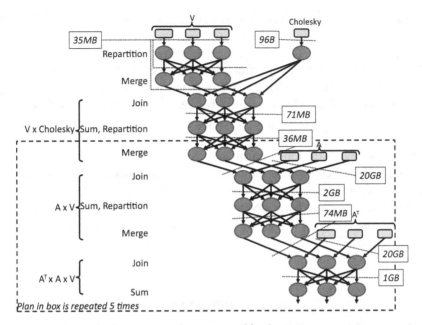

Figure 3.9 Partial Dryad job execution plan generated for the SVD computation, assuming that the matrices *V* and *A* are split into three partitions. The portion of the plan in the dotted box is repeated four more times. The dotted lines show the volume of data between computation stages for a 20GB *A* matrix.

exchanges in each iteration. As such, matrix structure can play a large role in the performance of the algorithm: matrices with block structure, partitioned accordingly, result in substantially fewer aggregates than matrices partitioned randomly. We evaluate our SVD algorithm on a random sparse matrix; we used a matrix *A* of 20GB. Figure 3.9 shows the volume of data that is crossing between stages; because *A* is rectangular, multiplication with *A* or A^T generates a different amount of intermediate data. Without the local aggregation feature of DryadLINQ, the result of a `Join` would be 72GB; the actual data exchanged in our implementation is 2GB. The final multiplication result is even smaller, at 74MB.

3.4 Lessons Learned

We have applied DryadLINQ to a large variety of data mining and machine learning problems, including decision trees, neural networks, linear regression, expectation maximization, probabilistic latent semantic indexing, probabilistic index maps, graphical models, and principal component analysis. We summarize here some of the lessons we have learned in this process.

3.4.1 Strengths

The main strength of DryadLINQ is the very powerful high-level language that integrates into a single source program both single-computer and cluster-level execution.

The seamless transition between the two environments allows one to build easily very complex applications using just Visual Studio as a tool for development and debugging.

When necessary, interoperation with other languages (and in particular with native code) is easily achieved using the standard .NET mechanisms for invoking unmanaged code. We sometimes have to rely on native code either for speed or for legacy reasons.

When writing very large programs, the richness of the datatypes manipulated by DryadLINQ and the strong typing of the language are particularly helpful. The strong typing enables DryadLINQ to automatically generate all the code for serializing the data moved between computers. For some projects the amount of serialization code can dwarf the actual analysis.

Because the output of DryadLINQ is also LINQ code, but running on individual partitions, we have been able to make use of other existing LINQ providers, such as PLINQ, which parallelizes the application across multiple cores, using effectively all the computers in the cluster.

3.4.2 Weaknesses

Although DryadLINQ is a great tool to program clusters, there is also a price to pay for the convenience that it provides. We discuss here several weaknesses that we have identified.

Efficiency: Managed code (C#) is not always as efficient as native code (C++); in particular, arithmetic and string operations can be up to twice as fast in native code.

Debugging: Debugging problems that occur when processing large data sets is not always easy. DryadLINQ provides some good tools for debugging, but the experience of debugging a cluster program remains more painful than debugging a single-computer program.

Transparency: Finally, although DryadLINQ does provide a high-level language to write cluster applications, one cannot just hide behind the language abstraction and hope to get efficient code. In most cases one needs to have some understanding of the operation of the compiler and particularly of the job execution plans generated (this is why we have shown the job execution plans for all our examples); this knowledge enables one to avoid egregious mistakes and to choose the queries that exhibit the best performance.

3.4.3 A Real Application

As an industrial-strength application of DryadLINQ, we have implemented (in collaboration with other researchers) several machine learning projects for Microsoft's Xbox Project Kinect. The goal of Kinect is to provide a natural interface to the Xbox gaming console by tracking the users' bodies and voices in real time; this transforms the user's body itself into a game controller. The visual input device for the Kinect system is a combination video + depth camera (measuring the color and distance to each pixel in the image), operating in real time at video frame rate. The output of the Kinect system, available to the application developers, is the 3D position of the body joints (a skeleton) of the players in the camera's field of view. The mapping between the input and output is computed by a collection of classifiers that operate in real time and aim to use as little as possible of the Xbox CPU.

One of these classifiers (Shotton et al., 2011) was trained from a massive dataset using supervised learning; the ground truth data used for the learning process is obtained from a motion capture device, similar to the ones used at movie studios for digitizing the movements of actors. The training is essentially performed on millions of pairs of video frames annotated with the correct joint positions.

Although the core algorithms are essentially simple, the actual implementation requires substantial tuning to perform efficiently, because of the immense amount of training data. For example, we cannot afford to explicitly materialize all the features used for training; instead, the features are represented implicitly and computed on demand. The data structures manipulated are multidimensional and sparse; a substantial amount of code deals with manipulating efficiently the distributed sparse representations; moreover, as the sparsity of the data structures changes dynamically during the training process (some dimensions become progressively denser), the underlying data representation is also changed dynamically.

The implementation of these algorithms has stretched the capabilities of DryadLINQ and uncovered several performance limitations that have in the meantime been fixed. For example, some of the objects represented become very large (several giga-bytes/object). There is a tension between obtaining good utilization for all cores (using PLINQ) and having enough RAM to keep all the required state in memory. This required us to change the algorithms performing data buffering and to override PLINQ's partitioning decisions.

To implement this application we have made use of several DryadLINQ features that we have not presented in this document, which allow us to tune the partitioning of the data and to control the granularity of state and the shape of the query plan. We make important use of .NET libraries, for example, to parse the video/image input format. We have also implemented (with very little effort) workflows of multiple jobs and checkpointing of workflows, which allows us to restart the computation pipelines mid-way.

Overall, DryadLINQ has been an invaluable tool for the Kinect training project; it allowed us to quickly prototype the algorithms and to execute them at scale on an essentially unreliable medium (at this scale, failures become frequent enough to make a simple-minded solution completely impractical).

3.4.4 Availability

Dryad, DryadLINQ, and the machine learning code from this chapter is available for download from the DryadLINQ project page: http://research.microsoft.com/dryadlinq/. A commercial implementation of DryadLINQ called *LINQ to HPC* is at this time available in Beta 2 at http://msdn.microsoft.com/en-us/library/hh378101.aspx.

References

Dean, J., and Ghemawat, S. 2004 (Dec.). MapReduce: Simplified Data Processing on Large Clusters. Pages 137–150 of: *Proceedings of the 6th Symposium on Operating Systems Design and Implementation (OSDI)*.

Duffy, J. 2007 (January). A Query Language for Data Parallel Programming. In: *Proceedings of the 2007 Workshop on Declarative Aspects of Multicore Programming.*

Google. 2010 (Accessed 27 August). *Protocol Buffers.* http://code.google.com/apis/protocolbuffers/.

Isard, M., Budiu, M., Yu, Y., Birrell, A., and Fetterly, D. 2007 (March). Dryad: Distributed Data-Parallel Programs from Sequential Building Blocks. Pages 59–72 of: *Proceedings of European Conference on Computer Systems (EuroSys).*

Microsoft. 2010 (Accessed 27 August). *The LINQ Project.* http://msdn.microsoft.com/netframework/future/linq/.

Shotton, J., Fitzgibbon, A., Cook, M., Sharp, T., Finocchio, M., Moore, R., Kipman, A., and Blake, A., Real-Time Human Pose Recognition in Parts from a Single Depth Image, In Computer Vision and Pattern Recognition (CVPR), 2011.

Yu, Y., Isard, M., Fetterly, D., Budiu, M., Erlingsson, Ú., Gunda, P. K., and Currey, J. 2008 (December 8–10). DryadLINQ: A System for General-Purpose Distributed Data-Parallel Computing Using a High-Level Language. In: *Proceedings of the 8th Symposium on Operating Systems Design and Implementation (OSDI).*

Yu, Y., Gunda, P. K., and Isard, M. 2009. Distributed Aggregation for Data-Parallel Computing: Interfaces and Implementations. Pages 247–260 of: *SOSP '09: Proceedings of the ACM SIGOPS 22nd Symposium on Operating Systems Principles.* New York: ACM.

CHAPTER 4

IBM Parallel Machine Learning Toolbox

Edwin Pednault, Elad Yom-Tov, and Amol Ghoting

In many ways, the objective of the IBM Parallel Machine Learning Toolbox (PML) is similar to that of Google's MapReduce programming model (Dean and Ghemawat, 2004) and the open source Hadoop system,[1] which is to provide Application Programming Interfaces (APIs) that enable programmers who have no prior experience in parallel and distributed systems to nevertheless implement parallel algorithms with relative ease. Like MapReduce and Hadoop, PML supports associative-commutative computations as its primary parallelization mechanism. Unlike MapReduce and Hadoop, PML fundamentally assumes that learning algorithms can be iterative in nature, requiring multiple passes over data. It also extends the associative-commutative computational model in various aspects, the most important of which are:

1. The ability to maintain the state of each worker node between iterations, making it possible, for example, to partition and distribute data structures across workers
2. Efficient distribution of data, including the ability for each worker to read a subset of the data, to sample the data, or to scan the entire dataset
3. Access to both sparse and dense datasets
4. Parallel merge operations using tree structures for efficient collection of worker results on very large clusters

In order to make these extensions to the computational model and still address ease of use, PML provides an object-oriented API in which algorithms are objects that implement a predefined set of interface methods. The PML infrastructure then uses these interface methods to distribute algorithm objects and their computations across multiple compute nodes. An object-oriented approach is employed to simplify the task of writing code to maintain, update, and distribute complex data structures in parallel environments.

Several parallel machine learning and data mining algorithms have already been implemented in PML, including Support Vector Machine (SVM) classifiers, linear

---

[1] http://hadoop.apache.org.

regression, transform regression, nearest neighbors classifiers, decision tree classifiers, k-means, fuzzy k-means, kernel k-means, principal component analysis (PCA), kernel PCA, and frequent pattern mining. Four of these algorithms are presented in this chapter to illustrate how algorithms are implemented using the PML API. A fifth algorithm, transform regression, is the subject of Chapter 9.

4.1 Data-Parallel Associative-Commutative Computation

Although the PML API supports an extended computational model, the key interface methods from the point of view of parallelization are still the ones that implement associative-commutative computations over data. The semantics of these key methods are inspired by the algebra of associative-commutative computation: namely, commutative monoids. A commutative monoid is an algebraic structure $\mathbf{M} = \langle M, \odot, e \rangle$ with a binary operator $\odot$ over domain M and an identity element e such that

$$\forall x, y \in M \; \exists z \in M \;\; z = x \odot y \tag{4.1}$$

$$\forall x, y, z \in M \;\; x \odot (y \odot z) = (x \odot y) \odot z \tag{4.2}$$

$$\forall x, y \in M \;\; x \odot y = y \odot x \tag{4.3}$$

$$\forall x \in M \;\; x \odot e = x. \tag{4.4}$$

The associative and commutative properties of the commutative monoid operator $\odot$ (Equations 4.2 and 4.3, respectively) enable a sequence of computations to be arbitrarily reordered and parallelized. For example, to compute $m_1 \odot \cdots \odot m_k$, the elements $m_1, \ldots, m_k$ of M can be partitioned across several processors, each processor can independently perform local operations on its partition, and these intermediate results can then be combined into a final overall computation. The computations would thus be carried out as

$$(m_1 \odot \cdots \odot m_{k_1}) \odot (m_{k_1+1} \odot \cdots \odot m_{k_2}) \odot \cdots \odot (m_{k_{p-1}+1} \odot \cdots \odot m_{k_p}).$$

To parallelize associative-commutative computations over a collection of data records $\mathbf{d}_1, \ldots, \mathbf{d}_k$, a function u is introduced to map data records to corresponding elements of M so that the computation to be performed is then given by $u(\mathbf{d}_1) \odot \cdots \odot u(\mathbf{d}_k)$. The calculation can then be carried out in parallel as

$$\big(u(\mathbf{d}_1) \odot \cdots \odot u(\mathbf{d}_{k_1}) \big) \odot \cdots \odot \big(u(\mathbf{d}_{k_{p-1}+1}) \odot \cdots \odot u(\mathbf{d}_{k_p}) \big).$$

For example, suppose we want to parallelize the centroid updating computation in the k-means algorithm. For a set of centroids $\mathbf{C} = \{\mathbf{c}_1, \ldots, \mathbf{c}_n\}$, the computation involves assigning each input data vector to the closest centroid, and for each centroid averaging the data vectors that are assigned to it. In this case, data structures are needed to accumulate the appropriate sums for the computation. The domain of the corresponding commutative monoid could therefore consist of tuples $\langle \mathbf{a}_1, \ldots, \mathbf{a}_n, k_1, \ldots, k_n \rangle$, where $\mathbf{a}_i$ is a vector that equals the sum of the data vectors assigned to centroid i, and k_i is a scalar that equals the number of data vectors assigned to centroid i. The identity element would then be

$$e = \langle \mathbf{0}, \ldots, \mathbf{0}, 0, \ldots, 0 \rangle. \tag{4.5}$$

The mapping function u would perform the nearest-neighbor assignment of data records to centroids and would be given by

$$u(\mathbf{d}) = \langle \mathbf{0}, \ldots, \mathbf{d}_j, \ldots, \mathbf{0}, 0, \ldots, 1, \ldots, 0 \rangle, \tag{4.6}$$

where

$$j = \arg\min_i \|\mathbf{c}_i - \mathbf{d}\|. \tag{4.7}$$

The commutative monoid operator $\odot$ would be responsible for calculating the sums and would be given by

$$x \odot y = \langle \mathbf{a}_1 + \mathbf{b}_1, \ldots, \mathbf{a}_n + \mathbf{b}_n, k_1 + l_1, \ldots, k_n + l_n \rangle, \tag{4.8}$$

where $x = \langle \mathbf{a}_1, \ldots, \mathbf{a}_n, k_1, \ldots, k_n \rangle$ and $y = \langle \mathbf{b}_1, \ldots, \mathbf{b}_n, l_1, \ldots, l_n \rangle$. Updated centroids would be calculated from the results of the commutative-monoid operations using the equation

$$\mathbf{c}_i = \frac{\mathbf{a}_i}{k_i}, \quad 1 \le i \le n. \tag{4.9}$$

As the k-means example illustrates, even relatively simple computations can involve data structures of some form. In this case, a simple tuple of vectors and scalars suffices. Many learning algorithms, on the other hand, require more sophisticated data structures, decision trees being a classic example. The complexity of data structures can sometimes present a challenge when parallelizing such algorithms. One of the benefits of the object-oriented approach that will now be introduced is that it enables the usual object-oriented programming practice of decomposing complex data structures and algorithms into component abstract data types and operations on them to likewise be applied to develop parallel learning algorithms.

4.2 API and Control Layer

To create an object-oriented API from the concept of commutative monoids, the elements of M can be viewed as objects in an object-oriented programming language. This approach is adopted in PML by defining a base class, `MLalgorithm`, that all learning algorithms must inherit, and by defining interface methods for this base class that algorithms must then implement.

Although interface methods to implement commutative monoid computations are necessary for parallelization and are therefore included in the API, they are not sufficient in and of themselves. For example, even in the simple case of the k-means algorithm, mechanisms are needed to pick an initial set of centroids (e.g., randomly), and to iteratively update centroids using Equation 4.9 based on the results of the commutative monoid computations defined by Equations 4.5–4.8. Additional methods are therefore introduced to provide a looping mechanism for iterative algorithms and to manage the distribution and collection of objects across compute nodes. Further API extensions are introduced in the next section to extend the computational model beyond pure associative-commutative computations over data.

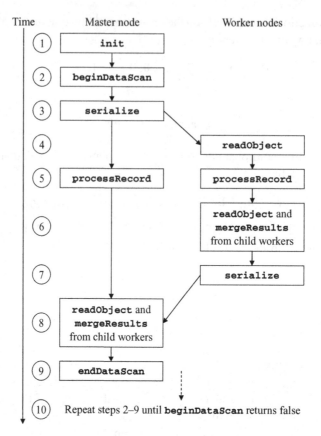

Figure 4.1 Interface methods for the MLalgorithm base class and the sequence in which they are called in the PML control flow.

Figure 4.1 illustrates the principal API methods for the MLalgorithm base class and the sequence in which they are called by the PML control layer. As illustrated, there are 10 basic steps in the PML control flow. These steps and the API methods that are invoked at each step are discussed in detail next. The API methods that are presented are an abstraction of those that appear in the actual implementation of PML in order to suppress details that are not relevant to the main concepts behind the design.

Step 1: On the master node, invoke the init method of the master algorithm object. The init method serves two purposes. One is to initialize the internal state of an algorithm object so that the object behaves as an identity element in a commutative monoid (i.e., $x.\text{init}() = e$). The other purpose is to provide a mechanism for passing configuration information into an algorithm, which in PML is specified via an XML document that is an input argument to the init method. For example, in the case of k-means clustering, the desired number of clusters k would be provided as configuration input to the k-means init method. Another configuration input might be a termination threshold ϵ on the minimum change in the location of a cluster centroid that must be observed in order for the algorithm to continue iterating over data.

Step 2: On the master node, invoke the `beginDataScan` method of the master algorithm object and terminate if `false` is returned. The `beginDataScan` method is used to set up a while-loop for iterating over input data. If a value of `true` is returned, the PML control layer performs a learning iteration defined by steps 3–9 in Figure 4.1; otherwise, learning terminates. To implement k-means, for example, one might first perform an initial iteration to randomly select k data records as centroids, with subsequent iterations recalculating the centroid locations until no centroid changes location by more than a termination threshold ϵ. The implementation of the `beginDataScan` method would then return `true` for the first two data iterations and would continue to return `true` for subsequent iterations as long as at least one centroid changes location by more than ϵ.

Step 3: On the master node, invoke the `serialize` method of the master algorithm object and broadcast the resulting output to the worker nodes. The `serialize` method outputs a byte-oriented representation (i.e., a serialization) of an algorithm object to an output stream so that the representation can be transmitted to other compute nodes. It is invoked on the master node at step 3 in order to communicate the state of the master algorithm object to each of the worker nodes. It is also invoked on worker nodes at step 7 to communicate the updated states of the worker objects back to the master node. An input argument to the `serialize` method indicates the direction of communication, which can affect the choice of information to include in the serialization. In particular, the information communicated from master to worker nodes must completely define the computation to be performed by the workers. For example, in the case of k-means, this would include the number and current locations of the centroids in order to assign data records to centroids. On the other hand, only updated information needs to be communicated back from worker nodes to the master. For example, in the case of k-means, this would include the updated accumulators for summing the data records assigned to each centroid, but it need not include the centroids themselves because the centroid locations are held constant during each data assignment iteration.

Step 4: On each worker node, receive the serialized object sent from the master node in Step 3 and reconstruct it using the `readObject` method. The standard approach used by the PML control layer to reconstruct (i.e., deserialize) an object is to first examine its serialized representation to identify the object's class type and to default-construct a new object of that type. The `readObject` method of the newly constructed object is then invoked with the remainder of the serialization passed as an argument in order to initialize the object's internal variables. As discussed later, a slightly modified deserialization approach is employed at step 4 for algorithms that require persistent-state workers. In the case of the k-means example, there is no need for worker nodes to maintain their states between iterations, so the standard deserialization approach would be employed.

Step 5: On the master node and on each worker node, perform all local commutative monoid operations by reading the data partition assigned to that compute node and by invoking the `processRecord` method on each data record in the partition. In PML, the master node acts as a worker node to perform computations on data. The `processRecord` method takes individual data records **d** as input and updates the state of an algorithm object accordingly. In terms of commutative monoids, the effect of the method is given by

$$x.\texttt{processRecord}(\mathbf{d}) = x \odot u(\mathbf{d}).$$

For example, in the second phase of the k-means algorithm wherein new centroid locations are calculated, the effect of the $\texttt{processRecord}$ method would be defined by Equations 4.6–4.8 and would be given by

$$\text{set } \mathbf{a}_j = \mathbf{a}_j + \mathbf{d}, \quad \text{set } k_j = k_j + 1,$$

where

$$j = \arg\min_i \|\mathbf{c}_i - \mathbf{d}\|.$$

Thus, at the end of step 5, the k-means algorithm objects on each compute node will contain the results of assigning each data record in that node's data partition to the closest centroid, and summing these data records based on their assigned centroids.

In the case of the first phase of the k-means algorithm, k data records need to be randomly selected as initial centroids. An efficient associative-commutative computation to perform the sampling can be obtained by making the following observations. One way to randomly select k data records would be to assign a pseudorandom number to each data record, sort the data records by their pseudo-random numbers, and select the top (or bottom) k records in the resulting list. One way to accomplish the sorting and selection would be to push the data records onto a priority queue using their pseudorandom numbers as priorities and to then pop k data records from the queue. Because we are interested only in the final k data records, an efficient algorithm can be obtained by modifying the logic of the priority queue to discard all data records that are guaranteed not to be included in the final k records. To make the computation associative-commutative, all we then need to do is use pseudorandom hash codes calculated from the data records as priorities instead of generating (noncommutative) sequences of pseudoran-dom numbers. The k-means $\texttt{processRecord}$ method could thus implement the following logic for the random centroid selection phase:

Set $p =$ pseudorandom hash code computed from data record $\mathbf{d}$
If priority queue size $< k$
    then push $\mathbf{d}$ onto priority queue with priority p
else if $p <$ highest priority in queue
    then pop highest priority and push $\mathbf{d}$ onto queue with priority p.

Thus, at the end of step 5, the k-means algorithm objects on the compute nodes would each contain a priority queue with k data records randomly selected from their associated data partitions (assuming at least k data records exist in each data partition).

Step 6: Parallelize the merging of results obtained in step 5 by performing the follow-ing: on each worker node, if it has not been assigned any child nodes, continue to step 7; otherwise, receive serialized algorithm objects sent from the child workers when they execute step 7, reconstruct those objects using the readObject method and incorporate the results using the mergeResults method. The purpose of step 6 is to achieve scalable merging of results for large numbers of worker nodes (e.g., the largest Blue Gene supercomputer installations contain more than 100,000 nodes). To achieve scalability, worker nodes are organized into a forest of trees. Workers with child nodes wait for serialized result objects to be sent from their child nodes. They then deserialize and use these child objects to update their own algorithm objects via the mergeResults method. The mergeResults method implements the commutative monoid operator $\odot$ so that the effect of the method is given by

$$x.\text{mergeResults}(y) = x \odot y.$$

Only after updating their own states based on the information passed to them by their child nodes do these worker nodes provide their parent nodes with updated serializations of their own algorithm objects. Nodes without children simply move on to step 7 to provide parent nodes with serializations of their results obtained in step 5. In this manner, a parallel mergeResults operation over n worker nodes requires only $O(\log n)$ time.

For example, during the second phase of the k-means algorithm in which new centroid locations are calculated, the effect of the mergeResults method would be given by Equation 4.8. Thus, at the end of step 6, the k-means algorithm objects at the root node of each merge tree would contain the results of the new-centroid calculations across the union of the data partitions for all worker nodes in that merge tree.

During the first phase of the k-means algorithm in which k data records are randomly selected as initial centroids, the effect of the mergeResults method would be to combine priority queues while discarding data records that are guaranteed not to be included in the final k records. The implementation of the mergeResults(y) method would thus execute the following logic during the random selection phase:

For each data record **d** with priority p in the priority queue of y do:
    If priority queue size $< k$
        then push **d** onto priority queue with priority p
    else if $p <$ highest priority in queue
        then pop highest priority and push **d** on queue with priority p.

At the end of step 6, the k-means algorithm objects at the root node of each merge tree would each contain a priority queue with k data records randomly selected from the union of the data partitions across all worker nodes in that merge tree (assuming at least k data records exist in the union of data partitions).

Step 7: On each worker node, invoke the serialize method of the worker algorithm object and send the resulting output to either the parent of the worker node in the corresponding merge tree if the worker is not a root node, or to the master node if the worker is a root node. The effect of step 7 is to communicate the intermediate and final results of the parallel merge process of step 6 to the appropriate compute nodes.

Step 8: On the master node, receive serialized algorithm objects sent from the root worker nodes in the merge trees when they execute step 7, reconstruct those objects using the `readObject` method, and incorporate the results into the master algorithm object using the `mergeResults` method. This step has the same effect as step 6, except that it is performed on the master node. At the end of step 8, the master algorithm object will hold the aggregate results from all of the worker nodes. In the case of the k-means example, in the first phase of the algorithm, the master object would contain a priority queue with k data records randomly selected from the complete input data (assuming at least k data records exist in the input data). In the second phase, the master object would contain the results of the new-centroid calculations on the entire input data.

Step 9: On the master node, invoke the `endDataScan` method of the master object. The purpose of this method is to perform post-data-scan processing and to set up for the next data iteration. In the case of the k-means example, in the first phase of the algorithm, the k randomly selected data records would become the current centroids and the processing phase would transition to the second phase. In the second phase, the locations of the centroids would be updated using Equation 4.9.

Step 10: Go to step 2. Steps 2–9 are repeated until the `beginDataScan` method returns `false`.

4.3 API Extensions for Distributed-State Algorithms

The interface methods and control flow presented in the previous section are sufficient to parallelize learning algorithms that perform associative-commutative computations on data. However, we have found it useful to further extend this framework to enable a broader class of algorithms to be efficiently parallelized.

The extensions presented in this section enable distributed-state algorithms to be parallelized in PML. An example would be algorithms that require kernel matrices to be calculated from data and to then be held in main memory for further operations. For large data, such matrices might be too large to fit in the main memory of a single processor, but for large clusters they could potentially fit in aggregate main memory by physically partitioning matrices across processors in a cluster. Another example would be graph mining algorithms for cases in which the graphs would have to be partitioned across processors in order to fit in aggregate main memory.

To support distributed-state computations, the computational framework introduced in the previous section must be extended in two respects. The first is that provisions must be made to allow distributed data structures to be persisted in main memory across worker nodes from one data iteration to the next; otherwise, efficient parallel computation would not be possible. Because, by design, such data structures would be contained within algorithm objects, the algorithm objects themselves would have to be persisted. Second, a mechanism is needed to share data across compute nodes in order to build and update distributed data structures.

To enable workers to persist their algorithm objects, an additional interface method, `requiresPersistentWorkers`, is introduced to the algorithm base class. If `requiresPersistentWorkers` returns `true`, the algorithm object is indicating that its workers should be persisted. In addition, a modification is made to the deserialization logic at step 4 in Figure 4.1. If a worker node is already holding an algorithm object of the type defined in the serialization sent by the master, and if the `requires-PersistentWorkers` method of the existing worker object returns `true`, then the `readObject` method is called directly to update object's internal variables based on the serialization without default-constructing a new object. In this manner, worker objects can remain persistent from one iteration to the next and receive updated state information from the master node.

With persistent worker objects, communications from master to workers can be greatly economized because master objects would only need to send updated state information to worker objects without redundantly sending information they already share. As previously discussed, an input argument to the `serialize` method indicates the direction of communication. In fact, this input is an enumeration type with possible values `InitWorkers`, `ReturnResults`, and `UpdateWorkers`, indicating not only the direction but the `Purpose` of the communication as well. Accordingly, if the `Purpose` argument to the `serialize` method is `UpdateWorkers`, then this is an indication to the `serialize` method to include only updated information in the serialization that is produced. The decision of whether to set the `Purpose` argument to `InitWorkers` or `UpdateWorkers` is made at step 3 in Figure 4.1. If the `requiresPersistentWorkers` method on the master object returns `true`, the `Purpose` argument will be given a value of `UpdateWorkers` on the second and subsequent data scans to indicate that only update information need be serialized. Otherwise, the `Purpose` argument will be given a value of `InitWorkers`. At step 7, the `Purpose` argument to the `serialize` method is always `ReturnResults`.

To enable data to be shared across compute nodes, an additional API method, `getDataRequirements`, is introduced to the `MLalgorithm` base class that allows algorithm objects to request not only input data associated with their own compute nodes, but also input data associated with other compute nodes. In the current version of PML, the `getDataRequirements` method can return either `WorkerPartition`, `AllData`, `OtherPartitions`, or `NoData` to request data from the object's own compute node, from all compute nodes, from all but their own nodes, and from no nodes, respectively. This method is invoked on the master and worker nodes at the start of each data scan at step 5 in Figure 4.1. The PML infrastructure then marshals the input data accordingly.

Examples of algorithms that exploit PML's ability to manage persistent worker objects and to share training data across compute nodes are presented in the following sections.

4.4 Control Layer Implementation and Optimizations

The PML control layer is implemented using MPI (message passing interface). Specifically, it uses an implementation of MPI known as the MPICH2 message-passing library for parallel programming, which is widely supported on several parallel platforms, ranging from shared-memory platforms (SMPs) to LAN-based clusters. It is especially suited to distributed-memory high-performance computing (HPC) platforms such as the IBM Blue Gene family.

MPI is a language-independent parallel programming interface. MPI's goals are high performance, scalability, and portability, and it remains the dominant model for high-performance computing on distributed memory systems. Most MPI implementations consist of a specific set of routines directly callable from C, C++, and from any language capable of interfacing with such libraries. The interface defines primitives for processes to perform point-to-point communication, collective communication, and collective file access.

Point-to-point communication, a common form of communication in parallel programs, involves two specific processes. A popular example is MPI_Send, which allows one specified process to send a message to a second specified process. These routines are particularly useful in patterned or irregular communication – for example, a master–slave architecture in which the master sends a new task to a slave whenever the previous task is completed.

Collective communication involves communication among all processes in a group that must be defined in a program. A popular example is the MPI_Bcast call that takes data from one node and broadcasts it to all processes in the group. A reverse operation is the MPI_Reduce call, which takes data from all processes in a group, performs an aggregation operation (such as a summation), and returns the result on one node. Other operations perform more sophisticated tasks, such as the MPI_Alltoall call, which rearranges n items of data from each process such that the nth node gets the nth item of data from each. MPI's collective file access routines provide an interface by which a group of processes can access a file at the same time, while minimizing the effects of contention.

The PML framework incorporates several performance optimizations for distributed-memory HPC platforms. The approach uses the MPI_Bcast operation to distribute the object to all the worker nodes. The optimized process for aggregating objects in parallel using the merge-tree based approach was presented earlier and is implemented using multiple point-to-point operations, because we cannot perform user-defined aggregations using MPI's reduction routines. In addition, the control layer incorporates several optimizations to improve I/O efficiency. Conceptually, the input data file is partitioned across the processing nodes such that each node receives roughly the same number of records, and during each data scan, the records in each partition are scanned and pushed to the algorithm objects. In practice, for improved I/O efficiency, the input data is transferred from the physical file in large blocks to in-memory file buffers on the nodes. MPI's collective file I/O primitives are used to ensure efficient and contention-free reading of a file. All record accesses in this block are then handled in memory, omitting repeated disk accesses. Furthermore, when a cluster has a large number of nodes, collective memory is often sufficient to store the entire data, obviating the need for subsequent disk accesses in following iterations of an algorithm. For algorithms where the nodes need to see more than their partition of the data (for which getDataRequirements returns OtherPartitions or AllData), when possible, the control layer maintains the data in collective memory, and the nodes access the data from remote memory to improve I/O efficiency. When the data does not fit in collective main memory, MPI's collective I/O primitives are used to read a block once and then efficiently distribute this block to all nodes using the network.

4.5 Parallel Kernel *k*-Means

Kernel-based algorithms define a (possibly) nonlinear transformation that maps data from their original space to high dimensional (and possibly infinite) space. This mapping is performed so that data can be more easily separable. In recent years, kernel-based variants of known learning methods have been shown to perform better using data transformed to this new space (Schölkopf and Smola, 2002).

In most cases, kernel-based algorithms do not explicitly compute the transformation of the data to the new (kernel) space. Instead, they rely on the fact that in many learning algorithms, only dot products between data points are used. Using appropriate choices for kernel functions, the dot product of data points in kernel space is equivalent to computing the kernel function of the dot product in the original space. This is sometimes known as the *kernel trick* (Schölkopf and Smola, 2002). Popular choices for kernel functions are:

1. Polynomial: $K(x_i, x_j) = (x_i \cdot x_j + 1)^d$
2. Radial basis function (RBF): $K(x_i, x_j) = exp\left(-g\left\|x_i - x_j\right\|^2\right)$
3. Hyperbolic tangent: $K(x_i, x_j) = tanh(ax_i \cdot x_j + b)$

Computing all pairs of dot products (the kernel matrix) is problematic for several reasons. Even for a modest number of data points (e.g., 100,000), this requires computing 10^{10} pairs and storing this number of data points on disk. This problem can be alleviated by computing and storing the matrix in a parallel or distributed environment, where each worker node is responsible for a subset of the data points. However, it is still costly to compute all pairs, and storage is prohibitively large beyond relatively modest data sizes.

In the following, we discuss the implementation of a kernel *k*-means algorithm that makes use of the parallel environment of PML, in conjunction with a sampling procedure. Together, these methods make it possible to compute the clustering of relatively large data on a modest computational environment.

First, we present the modification of the well-known *k*-means algorithm to the kernel *k*-means variant. Following the notation of Zhang and Rudnicky (2002), given N vectors $x_1, x_2, \ldots, x_N$, the kernel *k*-means algorithm attempts to partition these vectors into k clusters, $C_1, \ldots, C_k$. It can be shown (Zhang and Rudnicky, 2002) that the modification of the *k*-means algorithm to the kernel *k*-means variant requires transforming the basic algorithm to its variant as shown in Algorithm 11. As this pseudo-code shows, it is necessary to compute the full kernel matrix for the algorithm to proceed (line 3).

Computing the kernel matrix in a parallel environment can be efficiently performed through two scans of the data: First, each worker reads into memory a nonoverlapping subset of the data containing N/N_w vectors, where N_w is the number of worker nodes. This partition is maintained in memory for the second scan of the data, where each worker receives all vectors in the dataset. For each of these vectors, it computes the kernel value of the vector with every other vector in memory, thus forming a line of the complete kernel matrix. At the end of this process, the complete kernel matrix is

---

Algorithm 11: The Kernel k-means Algorithm

1: Assign each of the N points to a random cluster, forming clusters $C_1, \ldots, C_k$

2: **Repeat**

3:   For each cluster C_l compute $|C_l|$ and

$$g(C_l) = \frac{1}{|C_l|^2} \sum_{x_j \in C_l} \sum_{x_i \in C_l} K(x_i, x_j)$$

4:   Assign each data point x_i to the closest centroid l that satisfies:

$$f(x_i, C_l) + g(C_l) < f(x_i, C_j) + g(C_j) \forall j \neq l$$

where $f(x_i, C_l) = -\frac{2}{|C_l|} \sum_{x_j \in C_l} K(x_i, x_j)$

5: **Until** convergence

---

stored in memory, such that each worker node holds a slice of the kernel matrix, and together the workers hold the entire kernel matrix in memory.

However, as noted previously, even for moderately large datasets, computing and storing the kernel matrix is prohibitively expensive in both space and computational power. Therefore, in our implementation, we refrain from computing the full kernel matrix. Because both values needed for computing the assignment of a data point, $g(C_l)$ and $f(x_i, C_l)$, compare data points to all other data points in a cluster, we sample the data in the second iteration and compute the necessary values. This means that the full kernel matrix is never computed and therefore is not stored in memory.

The complete flow of the algorithm is shown in Figure 4.2. Referring to this figure, the master first initializes the algorithm (step 1) by randomly assigning each data point to a cluster. Then, each worker node reads a nonoverlapping subset of the data into memory (step 2). At the end of this iteration, the entire dataset is held in memory, distributed among the workers. The cluster similarities $g(C_l)$ and $f(x_i, C_l)$ are then initialized so that each worker maintains an estimate of $g(C_l)$ and a matrix $f(x_i, C_l)$ for every data point it holds in memory and every cluster (step 3). The main parts of the algorithm are steps 4 and 5. These steps are executed with the workers receiving a random sample of the entire data, at a predetermined rate (e.g., 10% of the data). For each data point received, the worker updates its local estimate of $g(C_l)$ and computes $f(x_i, C_l)$ for each data point in its memory, with every cluster. For example, if a data point currently assigned to cluster l is received at the worker, $g(C_l)$ will be updated using the new data point and all the data points in memory that are currently assigned to cluster l. A similar procedure will be carried out for $f(x_i, C_l)$. Once the data has been sampled, cluster assignments will be recomputed (step 5), and any reassignment will be communicated to the other workers via the master (step 6). The algorithm continues until the reassignment rate drops below a threshold.

4.6 Parallel Decision Tree

Decision trees are a simple yet effective classification technique. One of their main advantages is that they provide human-readable rules of classification. Decision trees

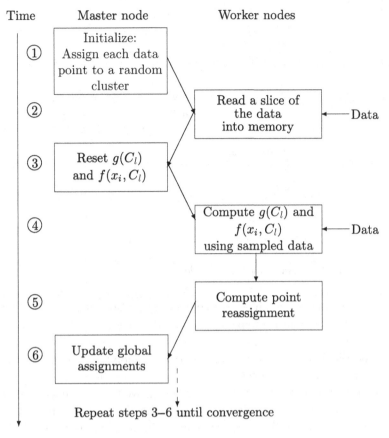

Figure 4.2 Implementation of Kernel *k*-means in PML.

have several drawbacks, especially when trained on large data, where the need to sort all numerical attributes becomes costly in terms of both running time and memory storage. The sorting is applied in the computation of the impurity gains. The attribute and point for which the gain is maximal constitute the node's decision rule. Various techniques for handling large data were proposed in the literature, taking one of two main approaches:

1. Performing pre-sorting of the data: This approach is used in SLIQ (Mehta, Agrawal, and Rissanen, 1996) and its successors SPRINT (Shafer, Agrawal, and Mehta, 1996) and ScalParC (Joshi, Karypis, and Kumar, 1998)
2. Replacing sorting by approximate representations of the data such as sampling and histogram building, which is used in BOAT (Gehrke et al., 1999), CLOUDS (AlSabti, Ranka, and Singh, 1998), and SPIES (Jin and Agrawal, 2003).

Although pre-sorting techniques are more accurate, they cannot accommodate very large datasets or infinite streaming data.

There are four main modes of data access in parallel decision tree algorithms. In horizontal parallelism, data is partitioned such that different workers see different examples. Vertical parallelism works by having different processors address different attributes. Task parallelism involves distribution of the tree nodes among the processors.

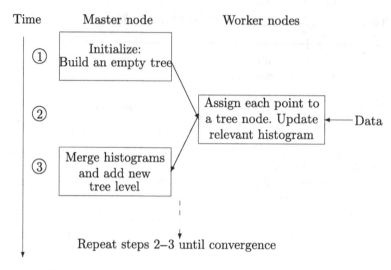

Figure 4.3 Implementation of decision tree learning in PML.

Finally, hybrid parallelism combines horizontal or vertical parallelism in the first stages of tree construction with task parallelism toward the end.

Like their serial counterparts, parallel decision trees overcome the sorting obstacle needed for deciding on the best splitting criterion by applying pre-sorting, distributed sorting, or approximations. In PML, decision trees are implemented using an approximation algorithm (For a more detailed description as well as experimental results, see Ben-Haim and Yom-Tov, 2010). The algorithm builds decision trees in a breadth-first mode, using horizontal parallelism. At the core of the algorithm is an online algorithm for building histograms from streaming data at the processors. These histograms are then used for making decisions on new tree nodes at the master processor.

Initially, the tree consists of only one node (see Figure 4.3). The tree is grown iteratively, such that in each iteration a new level of nodes is appended to the tree, that is, the tree's depth is incremented by 1. Using PML, each processor observes $1/N_w$ of the data but has a view of the complete classification tree built so far, which is sent at the beginning of each iteration from the master. Each example arriving at a worker is classified to a leaf node, where a histogram for each class is built. Once the data scan is complete, the histograms are merged and sent to the master, which makes the splitting decision for each terminal node of the tree and builds a new level to the tree where needed. This means that the master makes the splitting decisions based on histograms that were built from the entire data. If the node is already pure enough, the splitting is stopped and the node is assigned a label and a confidence level, both determined by the number of examples from each class that reached it. This building procedure is efficient in that it does not require holding the entire data in memory (only the histograms, which are fixed in their size, are kept in memory), and is provably as accurate as a single-node algorithm.

Figure 4.4 illustrates the speedups of the algorithm's multicore implementation over its sequential, single-core version. For this experiment, we utilized an 8-core Power5 PC with 16Gb RAM running Linux. The speedups were obtained on 100,000-instance subsets of two datasets used in the Pascal competition (Sonnenburg et al., 2008): the

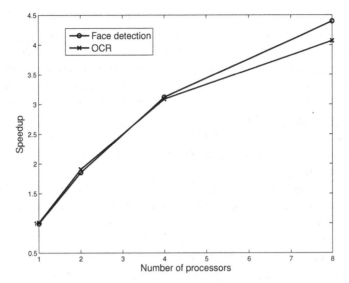

Figure 4.4 Speedup of the parallel decision tree algorithm for two datasets with 100,000 points each.

900-dimensional Face Detection dataset and the 1156-dimensional OCR dataset. As we can see on the plot, nearly optimal speedups are achieved on both datasets – as the number of cores goes from 1 to 4. However, the slope slightly decreases by the 8-core mark, most certainly due to the increasing communication cost.

4.7 Parallel Frequent Pattern Mining

Frequent pattern mining, also known as frequent itemset mining, is used to find groups of items (or values) that co-occur frequently in a transactional dataset. The frequent pattern mining problem was first formulated by Agrawal, Imielinski, and Swami (1993) for association rule mining. Briefly, the problem description is as follows. Let $I = \{i_1, i_2, .., i_n\}$ be a set of n items, and let $D = \{T_1, T_2, .., T_m\}$ be a set of m transactions, where each transaction T_i is a subset of I. An itemset $i \subseteq I$ of size k is known as a k-itemset. The support (also known as frequency) of i is $\sum_{j=1}^{m}(1 : i \subseteq T_j)$, or informally speaking, the number of transactions in D that have i as a subset. The frequent pattern mining problem is to find all $i \in D$ that have support greater than a user-supplied minimum value. Frequent pattern mining plays an important role in a range of data mining tasks. Examples include mining associations (Agrawal et al., 1993), correlations (Brin, Motwani, and Silverstein, 1997), causality (Silverstein et al., 1998), sequential patterns (Agrawal and Srikant, 1995), episodes (Mannila, Toivonen, and Verkamo, 1997), partial periodicity (Han, Dong, and Yin, 1999), and emerging patterns (Dong and Li, 1999).

Agrawal and Srikant (1994) presented *Apriori*, the first efficient algorithm to solve the frequent pattern mining problem. *Apriori* traverses the itemset search space in breadth-first order. Its efficiency stems from its use of the anti-monotone property: if a size k-itemset is not frequent, then any size $(k + 1)$-itemset containing it will not be frequent. The algorithm first finds all frequent 1-items in the dataset. It then iteratively finds all frequent k-itemsets by first generating a set of candidate k-itemsets using the frequent $(k-1)$-itemsets, then finding the frequency of all candidate k-itemsets, and finally pruning away the infrequent candidates. The frequencies for all candidate k-itemsets are obtained using one scan the dataset. For example, let A, B, C, and D be individual items (1-itemsets) that are frequent in a transaction database. Then, in the first iteration, AB, AC, AD, BC, BD, and CD are the candidate 2-itemsets. After counting, if 2-itemsets AB, AC, and AD were found to be frequent, then ABC, ABD, and ACD are the candidates in the second iteration. This process continues until we have no more candidates.

A number of other algorithms for frequent pattern mining exist today. Zaki et al. (1995) proposed *Eclat* and several other algorithms that use equivalence classes to partition the problem into independent subtasks. The *Apriori* algorithm stores the dataset in the *horizontal format*, that is, the dataset is represented as a list of transactions, where each transaction points to one or more items. Unlike *Apriori*, *Eclat* employs the *vertical data format*, in which the dataset is represented as a list of items, where each item points to all the transactions that contain this item (also known as a transaction-id list). The use of the vertical data format allows for fast support counting by set intersection. For example, the support count for itemset AB can be obtained by intersecting the transaction-id-lists for A and B.

Because of its efficiency, robustness, and guaranteed main memory footprint, the *Apriori* algorithm is widely used in frequent pattern implementations including those in commercial products such as IBM's InfoSphere Warehouse. Furthermore, *Apriori* is better suited to leverage data parallelism – *Eclat* is better suited to leverage task parallelism and requires a significantly larger main memory budget. Because of the aforementioned advantages, we considered *Apriori* for the parallelization of frequent pattern mining inside PML. There have been several research efforts on the parallelization of the *Apriori* algorithm. We mention only the most relevant work here. Agrawal and Shafer (1996) presented several *Apriori*-based parallel formulations for frequent pattern mining. They considered shared-nothing architectures. *Count Distribution (CD)* parallelizes the frequent itemset discovery process by replicating the candidate generation phase on all processors and parallelizing the counting process. Each iteration is followed by a global reduction operation to assimilate counts. *Data Distribution (DD)* partitions both the candidates and the data among the processors. However, this approach requires communication of locally stored transactions between processors, which is an expensive operation. We employed a hybrid strategy to most effectively utilize PML. Before presenting our parallel algorithm, we present a slightly modified *Apriori* algorithm. Its pseudo-code is given in Algorithm 12. This algorithm is very similar to the original *Apriori* algorithm except for the fact that it maintains the input dataset in the vertical format and finds the frequency of a candidate k-itemset by performing a join operation on the transaction-id lists of each individual item in the particular itemset.

We now discuss the parallel implementation of Algorithm 12 that makes use of the PML infrastructure. The control flow for the parallel implementation is provided in Figure 4.5. The algorithm is implemented as a class that extends the MLalgorithm interface and is parallelized as follows. First, the master initializes the object so that the getDataRequirements method returns WorkerPartition. The system then

---

Algorithm 12: The *Apriori* Algorithm

1: Find frequent 1-items (F_1) using a scan of the dataset
2: Remove infrequent items from the dataset and transform the dataset into its vertical format
3: $k = 2$
4: **Repeat**
5:     Generate all candidate k-itemsets (C_k) using frequent itemsets of size $k - 1$ (that is, F_{k-1})
6:     Find support counts for each itemset $i \in C_k$ by intersecting transaction-id-lists for all items in i
7:     Prune away infrequent itemsets from C_k to get F_k
8:     $k = k + 1$
9: **Until** C_k is empty

---

serializes this object and distributes it to all the worker nodes. Next, each worker node creates an instance of this object and delivers to it a portion of the transactional dataset (through the `processRecord` method) containing approximately $1/N_w$ of all transactions, where N_w is the number of worker nodes. Each object then transforms a

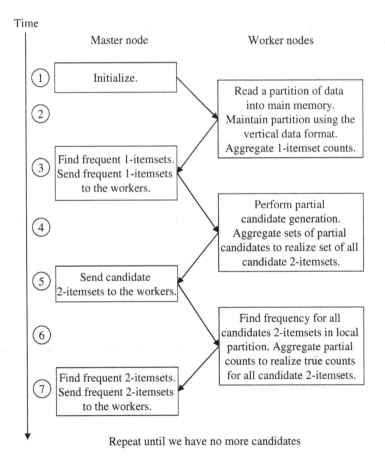

Repeat until we have no more candidates

Figure 4.5 Implementation of Frequent Pattern Mining in PML.

partition of the dataset into its equivalent vertical representation and maintains it in main memory. The worker nodes are required to maintain this transformed data in memory across all iterations by having the `requiresPersistentWorkers` method return true. If this data cannot be maintained in memory because of its size, it can be written to and read off the file system during each iteration. Next, using the `mergeResults` method, all copies of the object are aggregated so as to accumulate counts for all 1-*itemsets*. The aggregated object is then delivered to the master. At the master, the object then prunes away infrequent 1-*itemsets* in the `endDataScan` method. In the next iteration, the master sends a copy of the object containing all frequent 1-*itemsets* to the worker nodes. As candidate generation does not require a scan of the dataset, the `getDataRequirements` method returns `NoData`. At the worker node, the object then performs candidate generation for a group of itemsets with a certain prefix. This set of candidates is then aggregated using the `mergeResults` method and delivered to the master to realize the set of candidate 2-*itemsets*. In the following iteration, the master delivers all candidates to the worker nodes. At each worker node, a copy of the object finds frequency counts for all candidates in its local partition. These counts are then aggregated using the `mergeResults` method and the master receives an object with counts for all candidate 2-*itemsets*. The master then prunes away infrequent 2-*itemsets* in the `endDataScan` method and delivers the frequent 2-*itemsets* to the worker nodes in the following iteration for candidate generation. This process continues until we have no more candidates.

The main benefits of the presented parallelization scheme are as follows. First, the approach is memory efficient and does not create intermediate data other than the candidate itemsets. Second, the approach is highly scalable as it parallelizes both the frequency counting and the candidate generation phases.

4.8 Summary

This chapter presented the IBM Parallel Machine Learning (PML) toolbox, which makes it possible to apply machine learning and data mining algorithms to large datasets in reasonable computational time. PML is tuned for efficiently providing necessary services for machine learning algorithms on a parallel platform. The most important of these services are:

1. The ability to maintain the state of each worker node, making it possible, for example, to hold a kernel matrix distributed among workers
2. Efficient distribution of data, including the ability for each worker to read a subset of the data, to sample the data, or to scan the entire dataset
3. Access to both sparse and dense datasets
4. Using a tree structure for efficient collection of worker models even when a large number of these are at work

PML is the result of several years of research that spanned a series of projects. The first two projects (Apte et al., 1999; Natarajan and Pednault, 2001; Apte et al., 2001; Natarajan and Pednault, 2002; Apte et al., 2002) established the basic structure of the API. The third project, aimed at productizing the transform regression algorithm,

(Pednault, 2006; Dorneich et al., 2006) enabled the parallelization aspects of the API design to be refined, resulting in the design presented in Section 4.2. The transform regression algorithm is the subject of Chapter 9. The extensions to the API described in Section 4.3 were introduced as part of the PML project itself. The control layer was rewritten to use MPI for parallel communications in order to support persistent-state workers and efficient distribution of data, as well as to enable algorithms to run on the IBM Blue Gene line of supercomputers, on Linux clusters, and on other HPC platforms.

PML currently supports several state-of-the-art algorithms, as well as an API that enables programmers to utilize the services of PML for their algorithms by implementing several basic functions. These functions are then compiled and linked to PML for efficient execution. PML is freely available for download at www.alphaworks.ibm .com/tech/pml.

References

Agrawal, R., and Shafer, J. 1996. Parallel Mining of Association Rules. *IEEE Transactions on Knowledge and Data Engineering*.

Agrawal, R., and Srikant, R. 1994. Fast Algorithms for Mining Association Rules. In: *Proceedings of the International Conference on Very Large Data Bases (VLDB)*.

Agrawal, R., and Srikant, R. 1995. Mining Sequential Patterns. In: *Proceedings of the International Conference on Data Engineering (ICDE)*.

Agrawal, R., Imielinski, T., and Swami, A. 1993. Mining Association Rules between Sets of Items in Large Databases. In: *Proceedings of the International Conference on Management of Data (SIGMOD)*.

AlSabti, K., Ranka, S., and Singh, V. 1998 (August). CLOUDS: Classification for Large or Out-of-Core Datasets. In: *Conference on Knowledge Discovery and Data Mining*.

Apte, C., Grossman, E., Pednault, E., Rosen, B., Tipu, F., and White, B. 1999. Probabilistic Estimation Based Data Mining for Discovering Insurance Risks. *IEEE Intelligent Systems*, **14**(6), 49–58.

Apte, C., Bibelnieks, E., Natarajan, R., Pednault, E., Tipu, F., Campbell, D., and Nelson, B. 2001. Segmentation-Based Modeling for Advanced Targeted Marketing. Pages 408–413 of: *Proceedings of the Seventh ACM SIGKDD International Conference on Knowledge Discovery and Data Mining*. New York: ACM.

Apte, C., Natarajan, R., Pednault, E. P. D., and Tipu, F. 2002. A Probabilistic Estimation Framework for Predictive Modeling Analytics. *IBM Systems Journal*, **41**(3), 438–448.

Ben-Haim, Y., and Yom-Tov, E. 2010. A Streaming Parallel Decision Tree Algorithm. *Journal of Machine Learning Research*, **11**, 789–812.

Brin, S., Motwani, R., and Silverstein, C. 1997. Beyond Market Basket: Generalizing Association Rules to Correlations. In: *Proceedings of the International Conference on Management of Data (SIGMOD)*.

Dean, J., and Ghemawat, S. 2004. MapReduce: Simplified Data Processing on Large Clusters. In: *Proceedings of the Symposium on Operating System Design and Implementation*.

Dong, G., and Li, J. 1999. Efficient Mining of Emerging Patterns: Discovering Trends and Differences. In: *Proceedings of the International Conference on Knowledge Discovery and Data Mining (SIGKDD)*.

Dorneich, A., Natarajan, R., Pednault, E., and Tipu, F. 2006. Embedded Predictive Modeling in a Parallel Relational Database. Pages 569–574 of: *SAC '06: Proceedings of the 2006 ACM Symposium on Applied Computing*. New York: ACM.

Gehrke, J., Ganti, V., Ramakrishnan, R., and Loh, W.-Y. 1999 (June). BOAT – Optimistic Decision Tree Construction. Pages 169–180 of: *ACM SIGMOD International Conference on Management of Data*.

Han, J., Dong, G., and Yin, Y. 1999. Efficient Mining of Partial Periodic Patterns in Time Series Database. In: *Proceedings of the International Conference on Data Engineering (ICDE)*.

Jin, R., and Agrawal, G. 2003 (May). Communication and Memory Efficient Parallel Decision Tree Construction. In: *The 3rd SIAM International Conference on Data Mining*.

Joshi, M. V., Karypis, G., and Kumar, V. 1998 (March). ScalParC: A New Scalable and Efficient Parallel Classification Algorithm for Mining Large Datasets. Pages 573–579 of: *The 12th International Parallel Processing Symposium*.

Mannila, H., Toivonen, H., and Verkamo, A. 1997. Discovery of Frequent Episodes in Event Sequences. *Data Mining and Knowledge Discovery*.

Mehta, M., Agrawal, R., and Rissanen, J. 1996. SLIQ: A Fast Scalable Classifier for Data Mining. Pages 18–32 of: *The 5th International Conference on Extending Database Technology*.

Natarajan, R., and Pednault, E. 2001. Using Simulated Pseudo Data to Speed Up Statistical Predictive Modeling from Massive Data Sets. In: *First SIAM International Conference on Data Mining*.

Natarajan, R., and Pednault, E. 2002. Segmented Regression Estimators for Massive Data Sets. In: *Second SIAM International Conference on Data Mining*.

Pednault, E. P. D. 2006. Transform Regression and the Kolmogorov Superposition Theorem. In: *Proceedings of the Sixth SIAM International Conference on Data Mining*.

Schölkopf, B., and Smola, A. J. 2002. *Leaning with Kernels: Support Vector Machines, Regularization, Optimization, and Beyond*. Cambridge, MA: MIT Press.

Shafer, J., Agrawal, R., and Mehta, M. 1996. SPRINT: A Scalable Parallel Classifier for Data Mining. Pages 544–555 of: *The 22nd International Conference on Very Large Databases*.

Silverstein, C., Brin, S., Motwani, R., and Ullman, J. 1998. Scalable Techniques for Mining Causal Structures. In: *Proceedings of the International Conference on Very Large Data Bases (VLDB)*.

Sonnenburg, S., Franc, V., Yom-Tov, E., and Sebag, M. 2008. *Pascal Large Scale Learning Challenge*.

Zaki, M., Parthasarathy, S., Ogihara, M., and Li, W. 1995. New Algorithms for Fast Discovery of Association Rules. In: *Proceedings of the International Conference on Knowledge Discovery and Data Mining (SIGKDD)*.

Zhang, R., and Rudnicky, A. I. 2002. A Large Scale Clustering Scheme for Kernel k-Means. Page 40289 of: *Proceedings of the 16th International Conference on Pattern Recognition (ICPR'02) Volume 4*. Washington, DC: IEEE Computer Society.

CHAPTER 5

Uniformly Fine-Grained Data-Parallel Computing for Machine Learning Algorithms

Meichun Hsu, Ren Wu, and Bin Zhang

The graphics processing unit (GPU) of modern computers has evolved into a powerful, general-purpose, massively parallel numerical (co-)processor. The numerical computation in a number of machine learning algorithms fits well on the GPU. To help identify such algorithms, we present *uniformly fine-grained data-parallel computing* and illustrate it on two machine learning algorithms, clustering and regression clustering, on a GPU and central processing unit (CPU) mixed computing architecture. We discuss the key issues involved in a successful design of the algorithms, data structures, and computation partitioning between a CPU and a GPU. Performance gains on a CPU and GPU mixed architecture are compared with the performance of the regression clustering algorithm implemented completely on a CPU. Significant speedups are reported. A GPU and CPU mixed architecture also achieves better cost-performance and energy-performance ratios.

The computing power of the CPU has increased dramatically in the past few decades, supported by both miniaturization and increasing clock frequencies. More and more electronic gates were packed onto the same area of a silicon die as miniaturization continued. Hardware-supported parallel computing, pipelining for example, further increased the computing power of CPUs. Frequency increases speeded up CPUs even more directly. However, the long-predicted physical limit of the miniaturization process was finally hit a few years ago such that increasing the frequency was no longer feasible due to the accompanied nonlinear increase in power consumption, even though miniaturization still continues. This situation forced the industry to go in the direction of packing multiple CPU cores onto the same silicon die without increasing the clock frequency. Parallel computing emerged from an optional computational architecture for supercomputing into a mainstream choice for general computing now and in the future. As a result of this fundamental change in the computing architecture, algorithm design, data structure design, and programming strategies are all facing new challenges. This chapter presents a general design principle for a subclass of problems that can be solved by *uniformly fine-grained data-parallel algorithms*, which are defined in Section 5.2. This subclass of problems fits particularly well on GPUs.

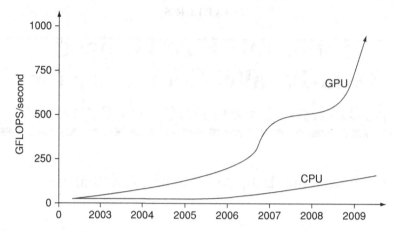

Figure 5.1 The performance increase of a GPU and a CPU. For more details, see the NVIDIA programming guide.

GPUs employed multicore parallel computing long before CPUs did, because of the nature of graphics computations. Some efforts were made to use GPU's special architecture for more general-purpose numerical computing; however, such efforts achieved mixed results, and the code written for the graphics interface to the GPU was often unintuitive to scientists. It was very difficult to program general-purpose numerical algorithms on a GPU because of its specialized architecture for graphics processing – numerical computations had to be shaped into "graphics operations" before they could be programmed through the graphics programming interface. In the past few years, however, the GPU has developed rapidly from a special GPU into a General-Purpose uniform multicore computing device (called GP-GPU), which has made the mapping of general-purpose numerical computing tasks onto the new GPU architecture much easier. An augmented C-language interface, NVIDIA's CUDA, is also available now for programming GPUs. These advances have made general-purpose computing on a GPU practical for generally-skilled programmers without knowledge of the graphics programming interface. The benefits of using a GP-GPU for numerical processing over CPU multicores are significant savings on both the hardware cost and power consumption per GFLOPS.[1]

Measured by the number of FLOPS, GPU performance has shown a significantly faster increase in the past few years (Figure 5.1) than that of CPUs. With hundreds of lightweight multiple-data and multiple-thread (MDMT) processors, the GPU offers much more computational power for general-purpose computing at both lower capital equipment cost and lower power consumption. A typical NVIDIA GPU sells for a few hundred dollars. When fully loaded, it uses about 300 W of power and can solve numerical problems about 40 or more times faster than a CPU (at 50 W) can.

This chapter explores a general design principle for GPU-based computing that we call *uniformly fine-grained data-parallel computing*. We illustrate this design principle by applying it to the design of two machine learning algorithms – clustering and regression clustering – on a GPU and CPU mixed computing architecture and present

---

[1] GFLOPS stands for Giga FLOating-point operations Per Second.

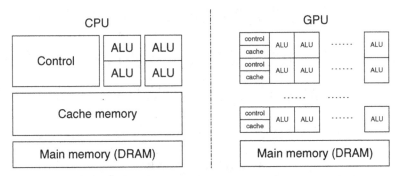

Figure 5.2 Comparing a GPU with a CPU. Each row on the right figure is a multiprocessor sharing the same program logic and the same cache memory.

performance comparisons. We believe that the design principle is applicable to many other classes of algorithms.

5.1 Overview of a GP-GPU

A GPU consists of a two-level hierarchical architecture: multiple multiprocessors, each of which has multiple lightweight data-parallel cores (Figure 5.2). The cores within the same multiprocessor share a small bank (16K to 32K) of low access-latency shared memory (cache). The cores in different multiprocessors communicate through the GPU's global memory, which has a much longer access latency (hundreds of clock cycles) than the shared memory has. The execution threads are organized in blocks (Figure 5.3); the threads within the same block are always executed on the same multiprocessor throughout their lifetime. Multiple blocks of threads can be loaded to the same multiprocessor and executed in a multiplexed fashion to hide the memory access latencies.

Each multiprocessor has a number of arithmetic logic units (ALUs). All ALUs in the same multiprocessor execute the same line of code synchronously. For example, the following if-else statement is allowed in the code:

If A is true **then**
    Do task 1;
Else
    Do task 2;

When A is true for a subset of processors in a multiprocessor, this subset of processors will execute the task 1 code; the remaining processors still have to go through the same clock cycles without doing any real work. When the *else* part of the statement is reached, the processors with condition A being false will execute the task 2 code, while the remaining processors will simply wait through the clock cycles. This example suggests that carefully designing the code to minimize the number of steps that have to be included into a conditional execution block is important to achieve higher utilization of the processors.

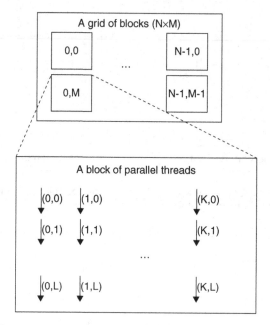

Figure 5.3 Computing threads are organized into blocks.

Computing threads on a GPU are organized into thread blocks with up to three-dimensional indices (thread IDs). Many thread blocks are organized into a thread grid (with block IDs), which is the unit of launch for execution (Figure 5.3). Enough thread blocks are necessary to keep all the multiprocessors busy. NVIDIA offers a CUDA Occupancy Calculator spreadsheet (NVIDIA, 2008) to help choose the right number of threads in a thread block and the right number of thread blocks. Threads are linked to data for data-parallel computing by mapping the block IDs and thread IDs to data indices.

The augmented C-programming interface from NVIDIA, CUDA, changed the path of programming a GPU for general-purpose computing. It made GPU programming accessible to C programmers without knowledge of the graphics programming interface. CUDA provides a set of function calls to help the programmer allocate GPU memory, copy data between CPU memory and GPU memory, organize parallel computing threads, and start execution of the threads on the GPU. In the same C program, CUDA allows the programmer to specify if a C function is to be executed on the CPU, GPU, or both. Even before CUDA, the graphics programming interface OpenGL (Wright et al., 2010) was a programming tool for GPU. If numerical computing is also associated with computer graphics, OpenGL is still an important tool to master. OpenCL (Open Computing Language; KhronosGroup, 2010) was initially developed by Apple Inc. It is now a new cross-vendor standard for heterogeneous computing that runs on the CUDA architecture. Using OpenCL, developers can harness the massive parallel computing power of NVIDIA GPU's to create compelling computing applications.

Details on GPU architecture and the CUDA programming interface, which are not the focus of this chapter, can be found in the cited CUDA manuals. In this chapter, our focus is on how to design a machine learning algorithm for a GPU.

5.2 Uniformly Fine-Grained Data-Parallel Computing on a GPU

Not all algorithms fit well on a GPU. We present a subclass of algorithms, which can be described as uniformly fine-grained data-parallel algorithms, that allow high-performance implementations on a GPU.

5.2.1 Data-Parallel Computing

Data parallelism is a very common parallel computing paradigm. Let $X = \{d_j\}_{j=0}^{J-1}$ be a partition of a dataset to which the computation procedure *proc* is applied in parallel. J computing threads $T = \{t_j\}_{j=0}^{J-1}$ are allocated, and data parallelism can be expressed as $thread_j : proc(d_j)$, which represents the jth computing thread executing the procedure *proc* on d_j. In this form, nothing is shared among different threads. Therefore, they can all go in parallel without blocking one another. Since some computing architectures, such as NVIDIA's GPUs, support broadcasting – synchronized reading by many threads from the same location of memory – shared parameters are allowed without concerns of losing performance, which can be expressed as $thread_j : p(shared\_read\_only\_parameters, d_j)$.

As an alternative, such parameters can also be embedded in the code as "constants" that all processors in the GPU can read concurrently without blocking. It is important to point out that different threads in this data-parallel computing structure share no variables that have write permissions. We call this property Share No Write Variables (SNWV).

Example 1: We look at a very simple summation task over N numbers: $S = \sum_{i=0}^{N-1} x_i$. It can be broken down into two steps, with the first step completely data parallel, using J auxiliary variables. We partition the dataset into J segments, assuming that J divides N (otherwise padding the data sequence with some zeros at the end), and perform the following two steps:

Step 1: Summation over each partition $S_j = \sum_{i=jM}^{(j+1)M-1} x_i$, where $M = N/J$ is the number of data values in the partition $d_j = \{x_i\}_{jM}^{(j+1)M-1}$, is done by a separate computing thread. Different threads share no written variables. This step is data parallel, satisfying SNWV.

Step 2: The outputs from all computing threads in step 1 are summed $S = \sum_{j=0}^{J-1} S_j$ to calculate the total summation.

The method in this extremely simple example is very general. We can follow the concept of *sufficient statistics* to create data-parallel computing segments satisfying SNWV for a general statistical estimator. The concept implies that, for the purpose of calculating an estimator, once the sufficient statistics is known, no further information from the sample data itself is needed. We first break the whole dataset into partitions, $X_1, X_2, \ldots, X_L$, and then calculate a set of sufficient statistics for S on each partition:

$\sigma_{1,1}, \ldots, \sigma_{1,m}$ on X_1,

$\sigma_{2,1}, \ldots, \sigma_{2,m}$ on X_2,

$\ldots$

$\sigma_{L,1}, \ldots, \sigma_{L,m}$ on X_L.

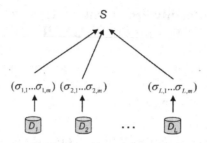

Figure 5.4 Distributed computing by communicating sufficient statistics.

All these sufficient statistics are collected to calculate S. No more information from each partition of data is needed other than the sufficient statistics. The diagram in Figure 5.4 shows the basic idea. However, this idea can be used either iteratively (Figure 5.5a), such as in k-means clustering, or recursively, forming a tree of computing tasks. Associated with this tree of computing tasks is a hierarchical partitioning of the dataset down to smaller and smaller sizes (Figure 5.5b). Obviously, iteration and recursion can be combined together.

Using the idea shown in Figure 5.5a, a number of clustering algorithms, including k-means, EM, and k-harmonic means, were implemented as distributed computing on remotely distributed datasets (Zhang, Hsu, and Forman, 2000). The authors show that the larger the dataset at each distributed location is, the more practical and economical it is to do distributed computing, because the cost of communicating the sufficient statistics per scan of the data remains a constant, independent of the number of data samples in the datasets.

In this chapter, following the same principle, we identify data-parallel segments of k-means and *regression k-means* for their implementation on GPUs. The same principle of communicating sufficient statistics is used by MapReduce. MapReduce has two phases of computation: the Map phase maps a computation to a distributed dataset on many computers and collects the computed results (sufficient statistics) from all processes, which are then "Reduced" to the final result.

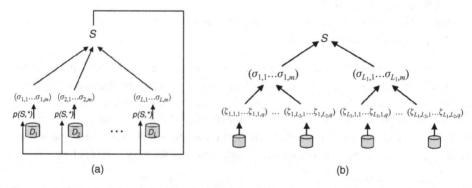

Figure 5.5 The principle of *distributed computing through communicating sufficient statistics* can be applied either iteratively (a) or recursively (b).

The recursive subdivision of data-parallel computing shown in Figure 5.5(b) is particularly important to the layout of computing tasks on a GPU because both GPU hardware and software platforms engage in multilevel integration.

At the hardware level:

- A GPU consists of a number of identical multiprocessors. They communicate only through the global memory they share.
- Each multiprocessor consists of a number of ALUs that share the same control unit and cache. Registers, cache, and shared memory among the ALUs in the multiprocessor are all from the same physical memory on the GPU chip.

At the software level:

- A block of threads, called a *thread block*, is executed on a multiprocessor. It typically has several times more execution threads than the number of ALUs in the multiprocessor. These threads are executed in warps in a time-sharing fashion.
- Multiple thread blocks can be assigned to the same multiprocessor (time sharing).
- All these thread blocks are organized into a grid as a unit of launch for execution.

At both hardware and software levels, we see a hierarchical subdivision down to the individual computing cores and individual computing threads. Figure 5.5(b) is a natural way to subdivide computing tasks for this architecture.

5.2.2 Uniformly Fine-Grained Data-Parallel Design

The highest utilization of the processors in a multiprocessor is achieved when all processors execute the same instruction. When different processors in a multiprocessor have to execute different branches of a conditional statement, some processors will be idling and utilization of the multiprocessor drops. *A coalesced and well-aligned memory access pattern in a program running on a GPU is crucial for achieving high utilization of memory bandwidth. Multiprocessing is used to trade off the latency of access to global memory on the GPU board. Scattered writes to memory hurt performance on GPUs most and should be avoided.* This condition limits the variety of algorithms that can run well on GPUs. In this section, we characterize the programs well suited for GPUs as *uniformly fine-grained data-parallel* algorithms. "Uniformity" refers to both the uniformity of executions that are truly data parallel with fewer branchings executed on the same multiprocessor and the uniformity of data partitioning over the array of processors. "Fine granularity" implies that parallelization is implemented at the lowest level. Instructions are executed on the multiprocessors at the same time while individual data access requests are made to the memory, so that each single memory access can keep all the processors busy. This will hide the memory access latency better. Having long, separated data access phases and computation phases is, in general, not a good design. It is better to streamline ("mingle") the computation into the data access so that the two run in parallel. To achieve this, fine-grained data-parallel computation is favored over coarse-grained separation of data access and computation phases.

Many computations on dense matrices and vectors are the best fit on GPUs, due to the natural uniformly fine-grained data parallelism in the algorithms on matrices and vectors. Before programming an algorithm on a GPU, discovering uniformly fine-grained data parallelism in the algorithm is very important for writing code with coalesced memory access patterns. This step often involves rewriting the existing algorithm so as to expose its fine-grained data-parallel structure to improve the performance of its implementation on a GPU.

On NVIDIA's GPUs, coalesced memory access significantly improves the performance of a program. A multiprocessor can read from up to B *contiguous* bytes (where B is currently 128) that are well-aligned with global memory blocks in one memory access cycle. Fine-grained data items help pack a compact contiguous memory block for coalesced access, which keeps the utilization of both memory bandwidth and processor cycles high. We use the same simple example to demonstrate this.

Uniformly fine-grained data parallelism means that the size of each data partition d_j in X is the same (uniform), the tasks to be performed on them are the same, and each task can access the data partition needed for its computation in as few memory access cycles as possible. Uniformity of the size of d_j helps (but does not guarantee to) design a common procedure *proc* for all threads so that their execution is truly synchronized without wasting cycles.

Example 2: We reexamine the same aggregation task in Example 1: $S = \sum_{i=0}^{N-1} x_i$. Suppose that we wish to design a uniformly fine-grained data-parallel program to perform this aggregation task. When the data is loaded into memory in its indexed ordering, as in Example 1, the cache lines of 128 bytes are filled by the byte streams from each $d_j = \{x_i\}_{jM}^{(j+1)M-1}$, which are not fine-grained. In this example, we choose the partitions at the individual data value level $d_j = \{x_j\}$ to satisfy the uniformly fine-grained requirement. Let thread $proc_m$ be a simple cumulation on data x_j, $proc_m(x_j) : s_m+ = x_j$. When the parallel threads concurrently make a data request, a 128-byte cache line is shared among a number of parallel threads. For example, if $x_1, x_2, \ldots, x_8$ are loaded in one cache line, the data requests from the parallel threads $proc_1, proc_2, \ldots, proc_8$ are all satisfied. Each thread loads only the smallest amount of data to be consumed immediately. Each cache line's load is completely consumed by the computing in the next step without risking any part of cache line's content to be overwritten before being used:

at time t_1: $proc_1(x_1), proc_2(x_2), \ldots, proc_M(x_M)$,
at time $t_{1+\delta}$: $proc_1(x_{M+1}), proc_2(x_{M+2}), \ldots, proc_M(x_{2M})$,
at time $t_{1+j\delta}$: $proc_1(x_{jM+1}), proc_2(x_{jM+2}), \ldots, proc_M(x_{(j+1)M})$

where $j = 0, \ldots, N/J$; δ is the amount of time to finish one line of work above. The advantage of such fine-grained data-parallel structure is to have coalesced memory access on the data items $x_1, x_2, \ldots, x_M$, and so on. Again, this example is very simple, but the fine-grained data-parallel idea demonstrated here goes beyond this simple example.

In Section 5.3, we use the k-means clustering algorithm to demonstrate the idea of uniformly fine-grained data-parallel computing with SNWVs.

5.3 The *k*-Means Clustering Algorithm

The *k*-means algorithm is one of the most popular clustering algorithms. Let $X = \{x_i | i = 1, \ldots, N\}$ be a dataset. We aim to find k clusters in the dataset by initializing k centroids $\{m_j | j = 1, \ldots, k\}$ of the clusters (randomly, for example) and iteratively refining the location of these centroids to find the clusters in a dataset. k is chosen by the practitioner.

The *k*-means Algorithm

Step 1: Initialize all centroids (randomly or based on some heuristic)

Step 2: Associate each data point with the nearest centroid. This step partitions the dataset into k disjoint subsets (*Voronoi Partition*)

Step 3: Calculate the centroids to maximize the objective function $\sum_{j=1}^{k}$ $\sum_{x \in S_j} ||x - m_j||^2$, which is the total squared distance from each data point to the nearest centroid

Repeat steps 2 and 3 until there are no more changes in the membership of the data points (proven to converge in a finite number of steps)

This algorithm guarantees convergence to only a local optimum of the objective function:

$$Obj_{KM}(X, M) = \sum_{j=1}^{k} \sum_{x \in S_j} ||x - m_j||^2, \tag{5.1}$$

where $S_j \subset X$ is the subset of x that are closer to m_j than to all other centroids.

The quality of the converged results, measured by the objective function in Equation 5.1, could be far from its global optimum. Several researchers have explored alternative initializations to achieve the convergence to a better local optimum (Pena, Lozano, and Larranaga, 1999; Bradley and Fayyad, 1998).

The time complexity per iteration for *k*-means is linear in the size of the dataset N, the number of clusters k, and the dimensionality of data X. The number of iterations it takes to converge is uaually insensitive to N.

5.3.1 Uniformly Fine-Grained Data Parallelism in *k*-means

A dataset is partitioned into blocks with the number of data points matching the thread block size, which is chosen on the basis of the recommendations from the NVIDIA's occupancy calculator. Different data blocks are treated as "distributed datasets," as shown in Figure 5.4. The "sufficient statistics" collected by each thread block on the partitioned datasets are further aggregated by the next segment of the program running either on the GPU or on the CPU, which corresponds to the calculation of S in Figure 5.4, the global cluster centroids in this case.

First, we need to look at the *k*-means algorithm as an SNWV parallel algorithm. More details can also be found in Zhang et al. (2000). In step 2 of the *k*-means algorithm, data's cluster membership is calculated from the data point's distances to

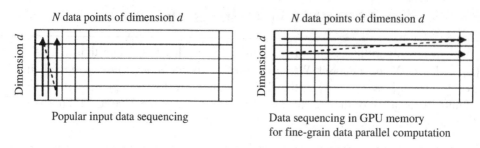

Figure 5.6 Data is arranged in GPU global memory so that when all threads in a thread block work on their assigned data value synchronously, these values are tightly packed into a continuous chunk of global memory, and even better if properly aligned with the 128-block boundaries. The small size (fine-grained) of the data item assigned to each thread in one synchronous computing step is good for coalesced memory access.

the centroids, and each data point goes with the centroid it is closest to. This step is data parallel and can be performed in an SNWV fashion. Each thread is responsible for evaluating the distances from a single data point to all the centroids, keeping track of the minimum distance and the corresponding centroid, and assigning the membership of the data points. The centroids are loaded to all the multiprocessors as read-only variables and shared by all the processors. The most expensive part of k-means is membership assignment. We made the membership assignment computation parallel on the GPU. The membership vector calculated on the GPU is transferred to the CPU in each iteration for the CPU to update the centroids.

Fine-grained data-parallel computation is achieved by arranging the data values of all threads in a thread block to work in a synchronized fashion close to each other (Figure 5.6). Input datasets are naturally given as rows of data; each row is one (multi-dimensional) data point. The input data should also be arranged in such a way that the data points that are accessed by all threads in a block in the same clock cycle are consecutive in memory.

Algorithm 12 shows the pseudocode for each thread to calculate the membership of the data points. This pseudocode is called in each iteration of k-means. Collectively over all threads, the output is the membership vector, which is transferred to the CPU's memory at the end of this pseudocode after all threads are done (and synchronized).

As shown in Figure 5.3, computing threads are organized hierarchically in grids and blocks.

We use the following notations in Algorithm 12:

gridDim – the total number of blocks in a grid
blockIdx – the index of a block inside its grid
blockDim – the total number of threads in a block
threadIdx – the index of a thread in its block
FLT_MAX – the maximum value of a floating point (hardware property)
i – data index
j – cluster index
dim – dimension index
cidx – the index of the closest centroid found so far

Algorithm 12: Assign Cluster Membership to Data Points

Input: Floating-point storage $data[.][.]$ for the transposed data array
Input: Floating-point storage $centroids[.][.]$ for the centroids
Input: Integer storage $membership[.]$ for the calculated membership of data points
Input: Integer parameters $data\_size, num\_dims, num\_clusters$
   $thread\_id \leftarrow blockDim * blockIdx + threadIdx$
   total number of threads $TN \leftarrow blockDim * gridDim$
   For $i = thread\_id$ to $data\_size - 1$ with step size TN **do**
      $min\_distance \leftarrow FLT\_MAX$
      $cidx \leftarrow 0$
      For $j = 0$ to $num\_clusters - 1$ **do**
        $distance \leftarrow 0$
        For $dim = 0$ to $num\_dims - 1$ **do**
           $distance \leftarrow distance + (data[dim][i] - centroids[j][dim])$
           If $dist < min\_distance$ **then**
           $min\_distance \leftarrow distance$
           $cidx \leftarrow j$
        $membership[i] \leftarrow cidx$
   Synchronize Threads

5.4 The *k*-Means Regression Clustering Algorithm

Regression clustering (RC) is a combination of clustering and regression. Clustering is an unsupervised learning method, while regression is a supervised learning method, which aims to fit all the training data with only single function. In contrast, RC allows multiple regression functions, each fitting part of the data. Regression clustering is performed in two steps: clustering and regression. Once clustering labels are assigned to the data points in the clustering step, a regression function is fit to the data in each cluster, in a supervised learning fashion. Each regression function is a cluster "centroid," representing all the data points that are best approximated by this function rather than other regression functions. Compared with the centroid-based *k*-means clustering, the centroids in *k*-means are replaced by more complex data models, regression functions, in RC. This gives an intuitive example of a more general concept of model-based clustering algorithms, which may use even more complex data models as the centroids of data clusters. In this chapter, however, we limit our scope to one particular model-based clustering – regression clustering.

RC has been studied under a number of different names, such as *clusterwise linear regression* by Spath (1981, 1982, 1985) and DeSarbo and Corn (1988), *cluster linear regression* by Hennig (1997), *regression clustering* by Zhang (2003), and others.

Given a training dataset $Z = \{< x_i, y_i > \in R^n \times R | i = 1, \ldots, N\}$, a family of functions $\Phi = \{f\}$, and a loss function $e() >= 0$, regression solves the following

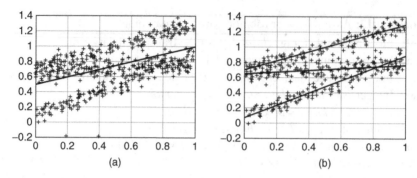

Figure 5.7 (a) A single function is regressed on all training data, which is a mixture of three different distributions. (b) Three regression functions, each regressed on a subset found by RC. The residue errors are much smaller.

minimization problem (Montgomery, Peck, and Vining, 2001):

$$f^{opt} = \arg\min_{f \in \Phi} \sum_{i=1}^{N} e(f(x_i), y_i) \tag{5.2}$$

Commonly, $\Phi = \{\sum_{l=1}^{m} \beta_l h(x, a_l) | \beta_l \in R, a_l \in R^n\}$ is a linear expansion of simple parametric functions h such as polynomials of degree up to m, Fourier series of bounded frequency, and neural networks. Usually, $e(f(x), y) = ||f(x) - y||_p$, with $p = 1, 2$ most widely used (Friedman, Hastie, and Tibshirani, 1998).

Regression in Equation 5.2 is not effective when the dataset contains a mixture of very different response characteristics, as shown in Figure 5.7a, it is much better to find the partitions in the data and learn a separate function on each partition, as shown in Figure 5.7b. This is the idea of RC. Regression provides a model for the clusters, whereas clustering partitions the data to achieve best fits of the models. The linkage between the two algorithms is a common objective function shared between the regression and the clustering.

RC algorithms can be viewed as replacing the k centroids in centroid-based clustering algorithms by a set of "data models" – in particular, a set of regression functions $M = \{f_1, \ldots, f_k\} \subset \Phi$. The objective function is similar to the k-means objective function, but the distance from a data point to a center is replaced by the residue regression error, such as $e(f(x), y) = ||f(x) - y||^2$,

$$d((x, y), M) = \min_{f \in M}(e(f(x), y)) \tag{5.3}$$

RC-k-means has the following steps:

Step 1: Initialize the regression functions.

Step 2: Associate each data point (x, y) with the regression function that provides the best approximation $\arg\min_j\{e(f_j(x), y)|j = 1, \ldots, k\}$. This step partitions the dataset into k partitions.

Step 3: Recalculate the regression function on each data partition that maximizes the objective function (see Equation 5.2).

Step 4: Repeat steps 2 and 3 until no more data points change their membership.

Comparing these steps with the steps of k-means, the only differences are that zero-dimensional centroids are replaced by regression functions and that the distance from a data point to a centroid is replaced by the residue error of a pair (x, y) approximated by a regression function.

5.4.1 Fine-Grained Data-Parallel Structures in *k*-means RC on a GPU

Like k-means clustering, k-means RC also has two phases in each iteration – membership calculation and calculating the new center-functions. The membership calculation step is performed similarly to the k-means: all k functions are loaded to the constant memory of all multiprocessors used as "parameters" to the common code executed by all threads. Each thread is responsible for calculating the cluster membership of one data point. The second step, calculating the new center-functions, is more complicated.

In the regression step, let us assume that we are doing a simple multivariate linear regression, with regression function $y = c_j^T x$, on the data in the jth cluster. The data points in each cluster are used to update the center-function they are associated with by a mean squared error (MSE) regression for the best fit to the data in the cluster. We take the jth cluster as an example here. Assuming that L_j data points are assigned into the jth cluster, we list the L_j data points in the jth cluster as follows:

$$A_j = \begin{bmatrix} x_{i_1} \\ x_{i_2} \\ \cdots \\ x_{i_{L_j}} \end{bmatrix}, b_j = \begin{bmatrix} y_{i_1} \\ y_{i_2} \\ \cdots \\ y_{i_{L_j}} \end{bmatrix}, \tag{5.4}$$

where the data vectors in the jth cluster are listed as rows in matrix A_j and the corresponding y-values are listed in vector b_j. The coefficients of the new center-function of the jth cluster are calculated as (see Allison, 1999, for a derivation)

$$c_j = (A_j^T A_j)^{-1} A_j^T b_j \tag{5.5}$$

When there are a large number of data points in the cluster, the computation of c_j is expensive. We carry out this computation in parallel on a GPU. To see the fine-grained data-parallel structure, we rewrite the matrix multiplication and the vector multiplication in Equation 5.5 as summations over the data points, respectively:

$$A_j^T A_j = \sum_{l=1}^{L_j} x_{i_l}^T * x_{i_l} \tag{5.6}$$

$$A_j^T b_j = \sum_{l=1}^{L_j} x_{i_l}^T * b_j \tag{5.7}$$

Equations 5.6 and 5.7 show the data-parallel structure of the computing tasks, and the work can be naturally partitioned by breaking up the long summation over 1 to L_j into many short summations. Following the distributed computing scheme in Figure 5.4, these summations are done in two phases over partitions of the data. This scheme helps break the work into many independent segments. The data in the jth cluster is segmented into many equally sized chunks so that each chunk of data is assigned to one block of threads running on a multiprocessor. Within one thread block, which is run on a single multiprocessor with shared memory (cache), fine-grained computation is applied to the calculation of $x_{i_l}^T * x_{i_l}$ and $x_{i_l}^T * b_j$, after x_{i_l} and b_j have been loaded into the shared memory.

5.5 Implementations and Performance Comparisons

In this section, we present our experimental results and performance comparisons. In order to compare the performance of a GPU implementation with that of a CPU-only implementation, we first must come up with a competitive CPU-only implementation. Since MineBench (Pisharath, 2005) has been used in a few related previous works (Che, 2007, 2008), we have used it as our baseline for performance comparison so as to align with previously published results. We also implemented our own CPU version of the k-means algorithm for more accurate comparisons (details in Section 5.5.1). Two machines used in our experiments are both HP XW8400 workstations with dual quad core Intel Xeon 5345 running at 2.33GHz, each equipped with an NVIDIA GeForce GTX 280, with 1GB onboard device memory; one machine has 4GB of memory running Windows XP, and the other has 20GB of memory running Windows XP x64. The GPU code was developed in CUDA using Microsoft Visual C++ 2005 environment/ editor.

Since our primary interest is in the performance acceleration ratios by GPUs, not the algorithm itself, we used randomly generated datasets. The maximum number of iterations is limited to 50 for all experiments, because for our purpose of speedup comparison, it is sufficient to measure the cost per iteration. The timing reported is the total wall clock time for all iterations, including the time for calculation and communication between the CPU and the GPU, but without the time for initializing the datasets. Both CPU and GPU versions result in identical centroids under identical initialization conditions. This confirms the algorithmic correctness of our GPU implementation.

5.5.1 CPU-Only Implementation of k-means

MineBench is a popular high-performance multi-threaded data-mining package, which includes k-means as one of its benchmark algorithms. It has been used in a few previous works as the baseline reference.

While focusing on exploring potential speedup achievable by a GPU over a CPU, we also bear in mind that the CPU has a lot of performance potential. Careful algorithm and data structure designs, various optimization techniques, the use of a CPU's SSE (Streaming SIMD Extensions) vector capabilities, and so on can usually help create a CPU implementation that outperforms a non-optimized version by a considerable margin.

Since we are interested in the performance difference betweenn the CPU-only version and the GPU-accelerated version, we have developed our own highly optimized k-means package on the CPU as well, trying to push the performance on the CPU

Table 5.1. *Performance comparison between MineBench and our optimized CPU implementation. N – number of data points; D – dimensionality; k – number of clusters; M – number of iterations run.*

Dataset				MineBench time(s)			Optimized time(s)			Speedups ($\times$)		
N	D	k	M	1c	4c	8c	1c	4c	8c	1c	4c	8c
2M	2	100	50	154	39	19	36	10	5	4.2	4.0	3.8
2M	2	400	50	563	142	71	118	30	16	4.8	4.7	4.6
2M	8	100	50	314	79	40	99	26	13	3.2	3.1	3.0
2M	8	400	50	1214	304	152	354	89	45	3.4	3.4	3.4
4M	2	100	50	308	78	39	73	20	10	4.2	4.0	3.7
4M	2	400	50	1128	283	142	236	60	30	4.8	4.7	4.7
4M	8	100	50	629	159	80	197	51	27	3.2	3.1	3.0
4M	8	400	50	2429	609	304	709	179	91	3.4	3.4	3.3

as much as possible. Our own optimized CPU code for k-means runs several times faster than MineBench. It provides a better CPU performance benchmark to judge more accurately the value of GPU accelerators. Table 5.1 shows the comparison between MineBench and our optimized CPU version, using 1 core, 4 cores, and 8 cores, respectively. It is shown that our optimized CPU implementation achieved about $3.8\times$ speedup over the MineBench implementation.

5.5.2 GPU-Accelerated k-means Algorithm

There are a few published works that have used GPUs for clustering, and in particular for the k-means clustering. A team at the University of Virginia, led by Professor Skadron, was one of the best to build an efficient GPU-based k-means implementation (Che, 2007, 2008). In their earlier work, an $8\times$ speedup was achieved on a G80 GPU versus MineBench running on a single-core Pentium 4. Subsequently, they fine-tuned their code and achieved much better performance. Their latest version showed about $72\times$ speedup on a GTX 260 GPU over a single-threaded CPU version on a Pentium 4 running MineBench, and about $35\times$ speedup over a four-thread CPU version running MineBench on a dual-core, hyper-threaded CPU.

In our previous papers (Wu, Zhang, and Hsu, 2009a,b), we report that our version is about 2–$4\times$ faster than that reported in Che (2007). For datasets smaller than the GPU's onboard memory, our results are shown in Table 5.2. In this table, "HPL CPU" refers to our optimized CPU-only implementations, whereas "HPL GPU" refers to our GPU-accelerated version. The speedup ratio of the GPU over CPU increases as the number of dimensions (D) and the number of clusters (k) increase, and for the set of parameters being experimented, we achieved an average of $190\times$ speedup over MineBench running on a single core, and $49\times$ speedup over our own optimized CPU implementations running on a single core.

Note that so far none of the published works has tackled the problem of clustering very large datasets that are too large to fit the GPU's onboard memory, which is usually a few gigabytes. For datasets larger than the size of the GPU's onboard memory, a streaming method can be used. Two (or more) data streams from the CPU to the GPU

Table 5.2. *Speedups compared with the CPU versions running on 1 CPU core (HPLC and HPLG are our own CPU and GPU implementations).*

Dataset				Time (s)			Speedups (×)	
N	D	k	M	MineBench	HPLC	HPLG	MineBench	HPLC
2M	2	100	50	154	36	1.45	106	25
2M	2	400	50	563	118	2.16	261	55
2M	8	100	50	314	99	2.48	127	40
2M	8	400	50	1214	354	4.53	268	78
4M	2	100	50	308	73	2.88	107	25
4M	2	400	50	1128	236	4.36	259	54
4M	8	100	50	629	197	4.95	127	40
4M	8	400	50	2429	709	9.03	269	79

can be deployed so that, while the GPU's processors are working on one batch of data transferred by a stream, another stream can work in parallel transferring another batch of data from the CPU to the GPU.

5.5.3 GPU-Accelerated *k*-means RC Algorithm

We are not aware of previously published results on the GPU-accelerated *k*-means regression clustering algorithm, so the comparison here is strictly between our own implementations. Since both *k*-means clustering algorithm and *k*-means RC algorithm have a similar structure and our CPU-only versions share most implementation optimizations as well, we can assume that our CPU version performs reasonably well.

Table 5.3 shows the performance comparison. The GPU-accelerated version offers more than $100\times$ performance over the CPU-only version running on a single core. It is clear that the GPU-accelerated version scales even better with larger datasets and larger number of clusters.

5.5.4 Issues Involved in Working with Real-World Data

One of the authors has applied both *k*-means and *k*-means RC to real-world data (Zhang, 2003, 2005). As long as the input data is in a dense matrix format, the most important

Table 5.3. *Performance of k-means RC algorithm.*

Dataset				Time (s)		
N	D	k	M	CPU	GPU	Speedups (×)
262144	4	100	50	59.4	0.95	62.5
262144	4	200	50	112	1.19	94
262144	4	400	50	216	1.67	129
524288	4	100	50	120	1.80	66.5
524288	4	200	50	224	2.22	101
524288	4	400	50	433	3.00	144
1048576	4	100	50	243	3.50	69.5
1048576	4	200	50	456	4.23	108
1048576	4	400	50	874	5.66	154

step is to discover the fine-grained data-parallel structure in the algorithm, which may require redesigning the algorithm to expose such parallelism and may also involve reorganizing the data in GPU memory for fine-grained coalesced memory access.

More utilities that make GPU programming easier are coming on the market. A utility software named Jacket (AccelerEyes, 2010) is a plug-on to MATLAB so that some matrix operations can be migrated to the GPU for higher performance. Users still write their program in a MATLAB programming environment. Only some matrix data structures can be processed on the GPU through the extensions to the MATLAB programming language defined in Jacket. The matrix operators defined in MATLAB are overloaded to cover the computations on the GPU. When using Jacket, the matrix orientations (rows and columns) need to be carefully chosen in a way that supports the fine-grained data-parallel computations.

Many GPU-related issues are not covered in this chapter. Complications arise when input data is in a sparse matrix format, which is often the case in text-mining applications. When data is in a sparse matrix format, its uniformity is lost. Different data points may have different non-zero attributes and may also have a different number of non-zero attributes. Data-processing commands are often conditional to an attribute being non-zero. Branching (if-else) statements are frequently used. This chapter does not cover such cases. Some work on applying a GPU to the computation on sparse matrices was published by Bell and Garland (2008).

5.6 Conclusions

Even though a number of parallel computing architectures are available, GP-GPU has advanced rapidly and has been applied to a variety of scientific computing algorithms. In this chapter, we provided an abstract paradigm and a general principle for designing high-performance parallel implementations of computing tasks on a GP-GPU. We illustrated this uniformly fine-grained data-parallel computing paradigm with efficient implementations of two classes of machine learning algorithms on a GP-GPU and compared their performance against CPU-based implementations. We have, through these examples, shown that the GP-GPU offers a flexible, general-purpose computing architecture that allows high-performance implementations of a fairly rich set of numerical scientific computing algorithms. Although the GPU provides significant speedups for intensive numerical computing at relatively low hardware cost and energy cost, the CPU is still the processor for executing the general logic of a program. It is not always clear at the beginning what should be put on the GPU and what should be put on the CPU. It may take some experimentation to find the best cut of the computing tasks between these two architectures.

References

AccelerEyes. 2010. *Jacket GPU Software for Matlab*. www.accelereyes.com.

Allison, P. D. 1999. *Multiple Regression: A Primer*. Thousand Oaks, CA: SAGE.

Bell, N., and Garland, M. 2008. *Efficient Sparse Matrix-Vector Multiplication on CUDA*. http://www .nvidia.com/object/nvidia research pub 001.html.

Bradley, P., and Fayyad, U. M. 1998. *Refining Initial Points for KM Clustering*. Technical Report MSR-TR-98-36.

Che, S. 2007. A Performance Study of General Purpose Application on Graphics Processors. *Workshop on GPGPU*, Boston.

Che, S. 2008. A Performance Study of General-Purpose Application on Graphics Processors Using CUDA. *Journal of Parallel and Distributed Computing*.

DeSarbo, W. S., and Corn, L. W. 1988. A Maximum Likelihood Methodology for Cluterwise Linear Regression. *Journal of Classification*.

Friedman, J., Hastie, T., and Tibshirani, R. 1998. Additive Logistic Regression: A Statistical View of Boosting. Technical Report, Department of Statistics, Sequoia Hall, Stanford Univerity.

Hennig, C. 1997. Datenanalyse mit Modellen Fur Cluster Linear Regression. *Dissertation, Institut Fur Mathmatsche Stochastik, Universitat Hamburg*.

KhronosGroup. 2010. OpenCL – *The Open Standard for Parallel Programming of Heterogeneous Systems*. http://www.khronos.org/opencl/.

Montgomery, D. C., Peck, E. A., and Vining, G. G. 2001. *Introduction to Linear Regression Analysis*, 3rd Edition. New York: Wiley.

NVIDIA. 2008. *CUDA Occupancy Calculator*. http://news.developer.nvidia.com/2007/03/cudaoccupancy.html.

Pena, J., Lozano, J., and Larranaga, P. 1999. An Empirical Comparison of Four Initialization Methods for the K-means Algorithm. *Pattern Recognition Letters*.

Pisharath, J. 2005. *NU-MineBench 2.0*. Technical Report CUCIS-2005-08-01, Northwestern University.

Spath, H. 1981. Correction to Algorithm 39: Clusterwise Linear Regression. *Computing*.

Spath, H. 1982. Algorithm 48: A Fast Algorithm for Clusterwise Linear Regression. *Computing*.

Spath, H. 1985. *Cluster Dissection and Analysis*. New York: Wiley.

Wright, R. S., Haemel, N., Sellers, G., and Lipchak, B. 2010. *OpenGL SuperBible: Comprehensive Tutorial and Reference*. Edwards Brothers.

Wu, R., Zhang, B., and Hsu, M. 2009a. Clustering Billions of Data Points Using GPUs. *ACM UCHPC09: Second Workshop on UnConventional High Performance Computing*.

Wu, R., Zhang, B., and Hsu, M. 2009b. *GPU-Accelerated Large Scale Analytics*. HP Labs Technical Report, HPL-2009-38. http://www.hpl.hp.com/techreports/2009/ HPL-2009-38.html.

Zhang, B. 2003. Regression clustering. *ICDM*.

Zhang, B. 2005. Center-based Clustering and Regression Clustering. *Encyclopedia of Data Warehousing and Mining*.

Zhang, B., Hsu, M., and Forman, G. 2000. Accurate Recasting of Parameter Estimation Algorithms Using Sufficient Statistics for Efficient Parallel Speed-up: Demonstrated for Center-based Data Clustering Algorithms. Pages 243–254 of: *Proceedings of PAKDD*.

PART TWO

Supervised and Unsupervised Learning Algorithms

CHAPTER 6

PSVM: Parallel Support Vector Machines with Incomplete Cholesky Factorization

Edward Y. Chang, Hongjie Bai, Kaihua Zhu,
Hao Wang, Jian Li, and Zhihuan Qiu

Support Vector Machines (SVMs) suffer from a widely recognized scalability problem in both memory use and computational time. To improve scalability, we have developed a parallel SVM algorithm (PSVM), which reduces memory use through performing a row-based, approximate matrix factorization and that loads only essential data to each machine to perform parallel computation. Let n denote the number of training instances, p the reduced matrix dimension after factorization (p is significantly smaller than n), and m the number of machines. PSVM reduces the memory use from $\mathcal{O}(n^2)$ to $\mathcal{O}(np/m)$ and improves computation time from $\mathcal{O}(n^3)$ to $\mathcal{O}(np^2/m)$. Empirical studies on up to 500 computers show PSVM to be effective. Open source code of PSVM was made available in Chang et al. (2007).

Support Vector Machines are a core machine learning technology that enjoy strong theoretical foundations and excellent empirical successes in many pattern recognition applications such as isolated handwritten digit recognition (Cortes and Vapnik, 1995), text categorization (Joachims, 1999), and information retrieval (Tong and Chang, 2001). In most of these cases, SVMs' generalization performance (i.e., accuracy in classifying previously unseen instances) either matches or is significantly better than that of competing methods. In this chapter, we discuss SVMs in a binary classification setting. Given a set of training data $\mathcal{X} = \{(\mathbf{x}_i, y_i) | \mathbf{x}_i \in \mathbb{R}^d\}_{i=1}^n$, where $\mathbf{x}_i$ is an observation vector, $y_i \in \{-1, 1\}$ is the class label of $\mathbf{x}_i$, and n is the size of $\mathcal{X}$, SVMs aim to search a hyperplane that maximizes the margin between the two classes of data in $\mathcal{X}$ (Figure 6.1a).

This problem can be formulated as the following quadratic optimization problem:

$$\min_{\mathbf{w}, b} \quad \mathcal{P}(\mathbf{w}) = \frac{1}{2} \|\mathbf{w}\|^2 \tag{6.1}$$

$$s.t. \quad y_i(\mathbf{w}^T \mathbf{x}_i + b) \geq 1,$$

where $\mathbf{w}$ is a weighting vector and b is a threshold. The decision function of SVMs is $f(\mathbf{x}) = \mathbf{w}^T \mathbf{x} + b$, where $\mathbf{w}$ and b are attained by solving $\mathcal{P}$ in Equation 6.1. However, in most cases, such a hyperplane may not exist because the data instances of the two

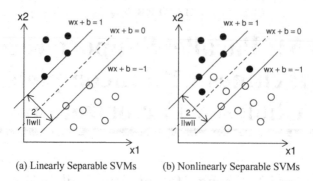

(a) Linearly Separable SVMs   (b) Nonlinearly Separable SVMs

Figure 6.1 SVMs: Finding the maximum-margin hyperplane.

classes are not linearly separable. Cortes and Vapnik (1995) suggested a modified maximum margin idea that allows for mislabeled examples (Figure 6.1b). It introduces slack variables ξ_i to measure the misclassification error, and the quadratic optimization formulation becomes

$$\min_{\mathbf{w},b,\boldsymbol{\xi}} \quad \mathcal{P}(\mathbf{w}, \boldsymbol{\xi}) = \frac{1}{2}\|\mathbf{w}\|^2 + C\sum_{i=1}^{n}\xi_i \tag{6.2}$$

$$s.t. \quad y_i(\mathbf{w}^T\mathbf{x}_i + b) \geq 1 - \xi_i, \quad \xi_i > 0,$$

where C is a regularization hyperparameter. In general it may be desirable to use different C values for different data instances. For simplicity, however, we assume that C is a positive scalar. The solution thus must achieve an optimal trade-off between increasing the margin and reducing training errors.

This maximum-margin hyperplane algorithm trains a linear classifier. Boser, Guyon, and Vapnik (1992) proposed to train nonlinear classifiers by applying the *kernel trick* (Aizerman, Braverman, and Rozonoer, 1964) to the data instances: each data point is mapped to a high-dimensional feature space called the *Reproducing Kernel Hilbert Space* through a basis function $\boldsymbol{\phi}(\cdot)$. The mapping can be nonlinear so that the training output is a linear hyperplane in the projected high-dimensional space, which may be nonlinear in the original space. The formulation thus becomes

$$\min_{\mathbf{w},b,\boldsymbol{\xi}} \quad \mathcal{P}(\mathbf{w}, \boldsymbol{\xi}) = \frac{1}{2}\|\mathbf{w}\|^2 + C\sum_{i=1}^{n}\xi_i \tag{6.3}$$

$$s.t. \quad y_i(\mathbf{w}^T\boldsymbol{\phi}(\mathbf{x}_i) + b) \geq 1 - \xi_i, \quad \xi_i > 0.$$

The optimization problem in Equation 6.3 is called the primal formulation of 2-norm SVMs with L_1 loss. It is difficult to solve $\mathcal{P}$ directly, partly because the explicit mapping via $\boldsymbol{\phi}(\cdot)$ can make the problem intractable and partly because the mapping function $\boldsymbol{\phi}(\cdot)$ is often unknown or very difficult to define given a large number of data instances. The work of Courant and Hilbert (1953) introduced the method of *Lagrangian multipliers* to transform the primal formulation into the dual one:

$$\min_{\boldsymbol{\alpha}} \quad \mathcal{D}(\boldsymbol{\alpha}) = \frac{1}{2}\boldsymbol{\alpha}^T\mathbf{Q}\boldsymbol{\alpha} - \boldsymbol{\alpha}^T\mathbf{1} \tag{6.4}$$

$$s.t. \quad \mathbf{0} \leq \boldsymbol{\alpha} \leq \mathbf{C}, \ \mathbf{y}^T\boldsymbol{\alpha} = 0,$$

where $\mathbf{Q}$, which is usually called the *kernel matrix* or *Hessian matrix*, is defined as $[\mathbf{Q}]_{ij} = y_i y_j \boldsymbol{\phi}^T(\mathbf{x}_i)\boldsymbol{\phi}(\mathbf{x}_j)$, and $\boldsymbol{\alpha} \in \mathbb{R}^n$ is the Lagrangian multiplier variable (or dual variable). The weighting vector $\mathbf{w}$ is related with $\boldsymbol{\alpha}$ in $\mathbf{w} = \sum_{i=1}^{n} \alpha_i \boldsymbol{\phi}(\mathbf{x}_i)$. In the solution, those points for which $\alpha_i > 0$ are called *support vectors*, and they lie on one of the two hyperplanes parallel to the decision boundary. The support vectors lie closest to the decision boundary and are the most critical instances of the training set. Even if all other training instances were to be removed and training were repeated, the same separating hyperplane would be produced by the training algorithm.

The dual formulation $\mathcal{D}(\boldsymbol{\alpha})$ requires an inner product of $\boldsymbol{\phi}(\mathbf{x}_i)$ and $\boldsymbol{\phi}(\mathbf{x}_j)$. SVMs utilize the kernel trick by specifying a kernel function to define the inner product $K(\mathbf{x}_i, \mathbf{x}_j) = \boldsymbol{\phi}^T(\mathbf{x}_i)\boldsymbol{\phi}(\mathbf{x}_j)$. This kernel trick eliminates the need to project instances $\boldsymbol{\phi}(\mathbf{x}_i)$ and $\boldsymbol{\phi}(\mathbf{x}_j)$ explicitly to a feature space, typically very high in dimensionality. Instead, the kernel function is performed in the d-dimensional input space. We thus can rewrite $[\mathbf{Q}]_{ij}$ as $y_i y_j K(\mathbf{x}_i, \mathbf{x}_j)$. There are several common choices for $K(\mathbf{x}_i, \mathbf{x}_j)$ such as

- Polynomial: $K(\mathbf{x}_i, \mathbf{x}_j) = (\mathbf{x}_i^T \mathbf{x}_j + 1)^d$; and
- Radial Basis: $K(\mathbf{x}_i, \mathbf{x}_j) = exp(-\gamma ||\mathbf{x}_i - \mathbf{x}_j||^2)$.

The best kernel to be employed is dataset dependent. The selection of a kernel and the setting of its parameters require to go through a cross-validation process (Devijver and Kittler, 1982).

The dual problem $\mathcal{D}(\boldsymbol{\alpha})$ is a convex quadratic programming (QP) problem with linear constraints, which can be solved via several approaches. Two widely adopted solutions are *Interior Point Method* (IPM) (Mehrotra, 1992) and *Sequential Minimal Optimization* (SMO) (Platt, 1998). For the IPM-based approach, the most effective solver is the primal-dual IPM (Mehrotra, 1992), which directly solves QP of Equation 6.4 and its dual form. The computational cost is $\mathcal{O}(n^3)$, and the memory usage is $\mathcal{O}(n^2)$. For the SMO-based approach, the solver decomposes the problem into a series of smaller tasks. The decomposition splits the data points into an inactive set and an active set. For each iteration, it chooses an active set and optimizes the problem by working on that set. This successfully reduces the memory use and the computational cost. However, the training speed of SMO on large datasets is still slow. For example, on a Pentium 2.8GHz machine with 8G RAM, the fastest algorithm is SVMLight (Joachims, 1998) with a finely tuned working-set size, which takes about 6 days to complete training on a 1-million binary-class dataset.

To further make large-scale dataset training practical and fast, parallelization on distributed computers is necessary. Although SMO-based algorithms are the preferred choice on a single computer, they are difficult to parallelize. During the training, although each iteration takes very little time, the fact that the kth iteration depends on the output of the $(k-1)$th iteration makes parallelization hard. In addition, the number of iterations it takes for the solver to converge is typically very large. In contrast, the IPM-based solver is more costly per iteration but takes many fewer iterations to converge. If the computation of each iteration can be effectively parallelized, the total computation time of IPM can beat SMO.

In this chapter, we propose a parallel SVM algorithm (PSVM) to reduce memory use and to parallelize both data loading and computation to trim the *copious* part of IPM. Given n training instances, each with d dimensions, PSVM first loads the training data in a round-robin fashion onto m machines. The memory requirement per machine is $\mathcal{O}(nd/m)$. Next, PSVM performs a parallel row-based Incomplete Cholesky Factorization (ICF) on the loaded data that tries to approximate the kernel matrix $\mathbf{Q} \in \mathbb{R}^{n \times n}$ by $\mathbf{H} \in \mathbb{R}^{n \times p}$, where $\mathbf{Q} \approx \mathbf{H}\mathbf{H}^T$. Parameter p is the column dimension of the factorized matrix. (Typically, p can be set to be about $\sqrt{n}$ without noticeably degrading training accuracy.) *Row-based* means that at the end of parallel ICF, each machine stores only some rows of the factorized matrix, which takes up space of $\mathcal{O}$ (np/m). PSVM reduces memory use of IPM from $\mathcal{O}(n^2)$ to $\mathcal{O}(np/m)$, where p/m is much smaller than n. PSVM then performs parallel IPM to solve the quadratic optimization problem in Equation 6.4. The computation time is improved to $\mathcal{O}$ (np^2/m), from $\mathcal{O}(n^3)$ of solving IPM directly and from about $\mathcal{O}(n^2)$ of a decomposition-based algorithm, e.g., SVMLight (Joachims, 1998), LIBSVM (Chang and Lin, 2001), and SMO (Platt, 1998).

PSVM is a practical, parallel approximate implementation to speed up SVM training on today's distributed computing infrastructures for dealing with Web-scale problems. What we do not claim is as follows: (1) We make no claim that PSVM is the sole solution to speed up SVMs. Algorithmic approaches such as Lee and Mangasarian (2001); Tsang, Kwok, and Cheung (2005); Joachims (2006); and Chu et al. (2006) can be more effective when memory is not a constraint or kernels are not used. (2) We do not claim that the algorithmic approach is the only avenue to speed up SVM training. Data-processing approaches such as Graf et al. (2005) can divide a serial algorithm (e.g., LIBSVM) into subtasks on subsets of training data to achieve good speedup. (Data-processing and algorithmic approaches complement each other and can be used together to handle large-scale training.)

6.1 Interior Point Method with Incomplete Cholesky Factorization

The Interior Point Method (IPM) is one of the state-of-the-art algorithms to solve convex optimization problems with inequality constraints, and the primal-dual IPM is one of the most efficient IPM methods. Whereas the detailed derivation could be found in Boyd (2004) or Mehrotra (1992), this section briefly reviews primal-dual IPM.

First, we take Equation 6.4 as a primal problem (it is the dual form of SVMs; however, it is treated as primal optimization problem here), and its dual form can be written as

$$\max_{\nu, \boldsymbol{\lambda}, \boldsymbol{\xi}} \quad \mathcal{D}'(\boldsymbol{\alpha}, \boldsymbol{\lambda}) = -\frac{1}{2}\boldsymbol{\alpha}^T \mathbf{Q}\boldsymbol{\alpha} - C \sum_{i=1}^{n} \lambda_i \qquad (6.5)$$

$$s.t. \quad -\mathbf{Q}\boldsymbol{\alpha} - \nu\mathbf{y} + \boldsymbol{\xi} - \boldsymbol{\lambda} = -\mathbf{1}$$

$$\boldsymbol{\xi} \geq 0, \boldsymbol{\lambda} \geq 0,$$

where $\boldsymbol{\lambda}$, $\boldsymbol{\xi}$ and ν are the dual variables in SVMs for constraints $\boldsymbol{\alpha} \leq \mathbf{C}$, $\boldsymbol{\alpha} \geq \mathbf{0}$ and $\mathbf{y}^T \boldsymbol{\alpha} = 0$, respectively.

The basic idea of the primal-dual IPM is to optimize variables $\boldsymbol{\alpha}$, $\boldsymbol{\lambda}$, $\boldsymbol{\xi}$, and ν concurrently. The algorithm applies Newton's method on each variable iteratively to gradually reach the optimal solution. The basic flow is depicted in Algorithm 13, where μ is a tuning parameter and the *surrogate gap*

$$\hat{\eta} = C \sum_{i=1}^{n} \lambda_i - \boldsymbol{\alpha}^T \boldsymbol{\lambda} + \boldsymbol{\alpha}^T \boldsymbol{\xi} \tag{6.6}$$

is used to compute t and check convergence. We omit the discussion on how to compute s here, as all the details could be found in Boyd (2004).

Algorithm 13: Interior Point Method

$\boldsymbol{\alpha} = 0, \nu = 0, \boldsymbol{\lambda} \geq \mathbf{0}, \boldsymbol{\xi} \geq \mathbf{0}$
Repeat
    Determine $t = 2n\mu/\hat{\eta}$
    Compute $\triangle\boldsymbol{\alpha}$, $\triangle\boldsymbol{\lambda}$, $\triangle\boldsymbol{\xi}$, and $\triangle\nu$ according to Equation (6.7)
    Determine step length $s > 0$ through backtracking line search and update
    $\boldsymbol{\alpha} = \boldsymbol{\alpha} + s\triangle\boldsymbol{\alpha}, \boldsymbol{\lambda} = \boldsymbol{\lambda} + s\triangle\boldsymbol{\lambda}, \boldsymbol{\xi} = \boldsymbol{\xi} + s\triangle\boldsymbol{\xi}, \nu = \nu + s\triangle\nu$
Until $\boldsymbol{\alpha}$ is primal feasible and $\boldsymbol{\lambda}, \boldsymbol{\xi}, \nu$ is dual feasible and the surrogate gap $\hat{\eta}$ is smaller than a threshold

---

Newton update, the core step of IPM, could be written as solving the following equation:

$$
\begin{pmatrix}
\mathbf{Q}_{nn} & \mathbf{I}_{nn} & -\mathbf{I}_{nn} & \mathbf{y}_n \\
-diag(\boldsymbol{\lambda})_{nn} & diag(\mathbf{C}-\boldsymbol{\alpha})_{nn} & \mathbf{0}_{nn} & \mathbf{0}_n \\
diag(\boldsymbol{\xi})_{nn} & \mathbf{0}_{nn} & diag(\boldsymbol{\alpha})_{nn} & \mathbf{0}_n \\
\mathbf{y}^T & \mathbf{0}_n^T & \mathbf{0}_n^T & 0
\end{pmatrix}
\begin{pmatrix}
\triangle\boldsymbol{\alpha} \\
\triangle\boldsymbol{\lambda} \\
\triangle\boldsymbol{\xi} \\
\triangle\nu
\end{pmatrix}
\tag{6.7}
$$
$$
= -\begin{pmatrix}
\mathbf{Q}\boldsymbol{\alpha} - \mathbf{1}_n + \nu\mathbf{y} + \boldsymbol{\lambda} - \boldsymbol{\xi} \\
\text{vec}(\lambda_i(C - \alpha_i) - \frac{1}{t}) \\
\text{vec}(\xi_i\alpha_i - \frac{1}{t}) \\
\mathbf{y}^T\boldsymbol{\alpha}
\end{pmatrix},
$$

where $diag(\mathbf{v})$ means generating an $n \times n$ square diagonal matrix whose diagonal element in the ith row is v_i; $\text{vec}(\alpha_i)$ means generating a vector with the ith component as α_i; I_{nn} is an identity matrix.

IPM boils down to solving the following equations in the Newton step iteratively:

$$\triangle\boldsymbol{\lambda} = -\boldsymbol{\lambda} + \text{vec}\left(\frac{1}{t(C - \alpha_i)}\right) + \text{diag}\left(\frac{\lambda_i}{C - \alpha_i}\right)\triangle\boldsymbol{\alpha} \tag{6.8}$$

$$\triangle\boldsymbol{\xi} = -\boldsymbol{\xi} + \text{vec}\left(\frac{1}{t\alpha_i}\right) - \text{diag}\left(\frac{\xi_i}{\alpha_i}\right)\triangle\boldsymbol{\alpha} \tag{6.9}$$

$$\triangle\nu = \frac{\mathbf{y}^T\boldsymbol{\Sigma}^{-1}\mathbf{z} + \mathbf{y}^T\boldsymbol{\alpha}}{\mathbf{y}^T\boldsymbol{\Sigma}^{-1}\mathbf{y}} \tag{6.10}$$

$$\mathbf{D} = \text{diag}\left(\frac{\xi_i}{\alpha_i} + \frac{\lambda_i}{C - \alpha_i}\right) \tag{6.11}$$

$$\triangle\boldsymbol{\alpha} = \boldsymbol{\Sigma}^{-1}(\mathbf{z} - \mathbf{y}\triangle\nu), \tag{6.12}$$

where Σ and z depend only on $[\alpha, \lambda, \xi, \nu]$ from the last iteration as follows:

$$\Sigma = Q + \text{diag} \left(\frac{\xi_i}{\alpha_i} + \frac{\lambda_i}{C - \alpha_i} \right) \tag{6.13}$$

$$z = -Q\alpha + 1_n - \nu y + \frac{1}{t} \text{vec} \left(\frac{1}{\alpha_i} - \frac{1}{C - \alpha_i} \right). \tag{6.14}$$

The computation bottleneck is on matrix inverse, which takes place on Σ for solving $\triangle \nu$ in Equation 6.10 and $\triangle \alpha$ in Equation 6.12. We mainly focus on this part because the other computations are trivial. Obviously, when the dataset size is large, it is virtually infeasible to compute inversion of an $n \times n$ matrix because of resource and time constraints. It is beneficial to employ matrix factorization to factorize Q. As Q is positive semi-definite, there always exists an exact Cholesky factor: a lower-triangular matrix G such that $G \in \mathbb{R}^{n*n}$ and $Q = GG^T$. If we truncate G to H ($H \in \mathbb{R}^{n*p}$ and $p \ll n$) by keeping only the most important p columns (i.e., minimizing $trace(Q - HH^T)$), this will become Incomplete Cholesky Factorization and $Q \approx HH^T$. In other words, H is somehow "close" to Q's exact Cholesky factor G.

If we factorize Q this way and D is an identity matrix, according to SMW (the *Sherman-Morrison-Woodbury formula*) (Golub and Loan, 1996), we can write Σ^{-1} as

$$\Sigma^{-1} = (D + Q)^{-1} \approx (D + HH^T)^{-1}$$
$$= D^{-1} - D^{-1}H(I + H^T D^{-1} H)^{-1} H^T D^{-1},$$

where $(I + H^T D^{-1} H)$ is a $p \times p$ matrix. As p is usually small, it is practically feasible to compute it. In the following section, we introduce the parallelization of the key steps of IPM to further speed it up.

6.2 PSVM Algorithm

The key steps of PSVM are parallel ICF (PICF) and parallel IPM (PIPM). Traditional column-based ICF (Fine and Scheinberg, 2001; Bach and Jordan, 2005) can reduce computational cost, but the initial memory requirement is $\mathcal{O}(np)$, and hence not practical for very large datasets. PSVM devises parallel row-based ICF (PICF) as its initial step, which loads training instances onto parallel machines and performs factorization simultaneously on these machines. Once PICF has loaded n training data on m machines and reduced the size of the kernel matrix through factorization, the rows of H are distributed across machines and IPM can be solved on parallel machines simultaneously. We present PICF first, and then describe how IPM takes advantage of PICF.

6.2.1 Parallel ICF

ICF can approximate Q ($Q \in \mathbb{R}^{n \times n}$) by a smaller matrix H ($H \in \mathbb{R}^{n \times p}$, $p \ll n$), i.e., $Q \approx HH^T$. ICF, together with the SMW, can greatly reduce the computational complexity in solving an $n \times n$ linear system. The work of Fine and Scheinberg (2001) provides a theoretical analysis of how ICF influences the optimization problem in Equation 6.4.

They proved that the error of the optimal objective value introduced by ICF is bounded by $C^2 l \epsilon / 2$, where C is the hyper-parameter of SVM, l is the number of support vectors, and ϵ is the bound of ICF approximation (i.e., $trace(\mathbf{Q} - \mathbf{HH}^T) < \epsilon$). Though ICF can introduce numeric error into the solution to an optimization problem, the goal of SVMs (or in general, a supervised learning task) is to minimize generalization error, not numeric error. Experimental results in Section 6.3 show that when p is set to $\sqrt{n}$, the degradation in generalization accuracy can be negligible.

Our row-based parallel ICF (PICF) works as follows: Let vector $\mathbf{v}$ be the diagonal of $\mathbf{Q}$, and suppose the pivots (the largest diagonal values) are $\{i_1, i_2, \ldots, i_k\}$. The kth iteration of ICF computes three equations:

$$\mathbf{H}(i_k, k) = \sqrt{\mathbf{v}(i_k)}, \tag{6.15}$$

$$\mathbf{H}(J_k, k) = (\mathbf{Q}(J_k, i_k) - \sum_{j=1}^{k-1} \mathbf{H}(J_k, j)\mathbf{H}(i_k, j))/\mathbf{H}(i_k, k), \tag{6.16}$$

$$\mathbf{v}(J_k) = \mathbf{v}(J_k) - \mathbf{H}(J_k, k)^2, \tag{6.17}$$

where J_k denotes the complement of $\{i_1, i_2, \ldots, i_k\}$ (i.e., suppose $\{i_1, i_2, \ldots, i_5\} = \{2, 5, 4, 3, 1\}$, then $J_1 = \{5, 4, 3, 1\}$ and $J_2 = \{4, 3, 1\}$). $\mathbf{H}(i_k, k)$ is the element that lies in the i_kth row and the kth column, and $\mathbf{H}(J_k, k)$ are the elements whose row index $\in J_k$ and whose column index is k. The algorithm iterates until the approximation of $\mathbf{Q}$ by $\mathbf{H}_k \mathbf{H}_k^T$ (measured by $trace(\mathbf{Q} - \mathbf{H}_k \mathbf{H}_k^T)$) ($\mathbf{H}_k$ is the first k columns of $\mathbf{H}$) is satisfactory, or the predefined maximum iterations (or say, the desired rank of the ICF matrix) p is reached.

As suggested by Golub and Loan (1996), a parallelized ICF algorithm can be obtained by constraining the parallelized Cholesky factorization algorithm to iterate at most p times. However, in Golub's algorithm, matrix $\mathbf{H}$ is distributed by columns in a round-robin way on m machines (hence we call it column-based parallelized ICF). Such a column-based approach is optimal for the single-machine setting, but cannot gain full benefit from parallelization for two major reasons:

1. Large memory requirement. All training data is needed for each machine to calculate $\mathbf{Q}(J_k, i_k)$. Therefore, each machine must be able to store a local copy of the training data.
2. Limited parallelizable computation. Only the inner product calculation

$$\sum_{j=1}^{k-1} \mathbf{H}(J_k, j)\mathbf{H}(i_k, j)$$

in Equation 6.16 can be parallelized. The calculation of pivot selection, the summation of local inner product result, column calculation in Equation 6.16, and the vector update in Equation 6.17 must be performed on one single machine.

To remedy these shortcomings of the column-based approach, we propose a row-based approach to parallelize ICF, which we summarize in Algorithm 14. Our row-based approach starts by initializing variables and loading training data onto m machines in a round-robin fashion (steps 1 to 5). The algorithm then performs the ICF main loop

---

Algorithm 14: Row-Based PICF

Input: n training instances; p: rank of ICF matrix H; m: number of machines

Output: H distributed on m machines

Variables:

$\mathbf{v}$: fraction of the diagonal vector of Q that resides in local machine

k: iteration number

$\mathbf{x}_i$: the ith training instance

M: machine index set, $M = \{0, 1, \ldots, m - 1\}$

I_c: row-index set on machine c ($c \in M$), $I_c = \{c, c + m, c + 2m, \ldots\}$

1: **For** $i = 0$ to $n - 1$ **do**
2:    Load $\mathbf{x}_i$ into machine $i\%m$
3: $k \leftarrow 0; H \leftarrow 0; \mathbf{v} \leftarrow$ the fraction of the diagonal vector of Q that resides in local machine. ($\mathbf{v}(i)(i \in I_m)$ can be obtained from $\mathbf{x}_i$)
4: Initialize *master* to be machine 0
5: **while** $k < p$ **do**
6:    Each machine $c \in M$ selects its local pivot value, which is the largest element in $\mathbf{v}$:

$$\mathbf{lpv}_{k,c} = \max_{i \in I_c} \mathbf{v}(i),$$

and records the local pivot index, the row index corresponds to $\mathbf{lpv}_{k,c}$:

$$\mathbf{lpi}_{k,c} = \arg \max_{i \in I_c} \mathbf{v}(i)$$

7:    Gather $\mathbf{lpv}_{k,c}$'s and $\mathbf{lpi}_{k,c}$'s ($c \in M$) to *master*
8:    The *master* selects the largest local pivot value as global pivot value $\mathbf{gpv}_k$ and records in i_k, row index corresponding to the global pivot value

$$\mathbf{gpv}_k = \max_{c \in M} \mathbf{lpv}_{k,c}.$$

9:    The *master* broadcasts $\mathbf{gpv}_k$ and i_k
10:   Change *master* to machine $i_k\%m$
11:   Calculate $H(i_k, k)$ according to Equation 6.15 on *master*
12:   The *master* broadcasts the pivot instance $\mathbf{x}_{i_k}$ and the pivot row $H(i_k, :)$. (Only the first $k + 1$ values of the pivot row need to be broadcast, because the remainder are zeros)
13:   Each machine $c \in M$ calculates its part of the kth column of H according to Equation 6.16
14:   Each machine $c \in M$ updates $\mathbf{v}$ according to Equation 6.17
15: $k \leftarrow k + 1$

---

until the termination criteria are satisfied (e.g., the rank of matrix $\mathbf{H}$ reaches p). In the main loop, PICF performs five tasks in each iteration k:

1. Distributedly find a pivot, which is the largest value in the diagonal $\mathbf{v}$ of matrix $\mathbf{Q}$ (steps 7 to 10). Notice that PICF computes only needed elements in $\mathbf{Q}$ from training data, and it does not store $\mathbf{Q}$.

2. Set the machine where the pivot resides as the *master* (step 11).
3. On the *master*, PICF calculates $\mathbf{H}(i_k, k)$ according to (Eq.6.15) (step 12).
4. The *master* then broadcasts the pivot instance $\mathbf{x}_{i_k}$ and the pivot row $\mathbf{H}(i_k, :)$ (step 13).
5. Distributedly compute Eqs.(6.16) and (6.17) (steps 14 and 15).

At the end of the algorithm, $\mathbf{H}$ is stored distributedly on m machines, ready for parallel IPM (presented in the next subsection). PICF enjoys three advantages: parallel memory use ($\mathcal{O}(np/m)$), parallel computation ($\mathcal{O}(p^2n/m)$), and low communication overhead ($\mathcal{O}(p^2 \log(m))$). On memory use, for instance, on a 1-million data set, storing $1M \times 1M \times 4B$ $\mathbf{Q}$ requires 4000GB storage. On 20 machines and setting $p = \sqrt{n}$, PICF can reduce the storage per machine to 200MB. On the communication overhead, its fraction of the entire computation time shrinks as the problem size grows. We verify this in the experimental section. This pattern permits a larger problem to be solved on more machines to take advantage of parallel memory use and computation.

Example

We use a simple example to explain how PICF works. Suppose we have three machines (or processors) and eight data instances. PICF first loads the data in a round-robin fashion on the three machines (numbered as #0, #1, and #2).

processor	data	row index
	label id : value [id : value $\cdots$]	
#0	-1 1:0.943578 2:0.397088	0
#1	-1 1:0.397835 2:0.097548	1
#2	1 1:0.821040 2:0.197176	2
#0	1 1:0.592864 2:0.452824	3
#1	1 1:0.743459 2:0.605765	4
#2	-1 1:0.406734 2:0.687923	5
#0	-1 1:0.398752 2:0.820476	6
#1	-1 1:0.592647 2:0.224432	7

Suppose the Laplacian kernel is used:

$$K(\mathbf{x}_i, \mathbf{x}_j) = e^{-\gamma \|\mathbf{x}_i - \mathbf{x}_j\|}, \tag{6.18}$$

and we set $\gamma = 1.000$. The first five columns of $Q_{ij} = y_i y_j K(\mathbf{x}_i, \mathbf{x}_j)$ is

$$Q = \begin{pmatrix} 1.000000 & 0.429436 & -0.724372 & -0.666010 & -0.664450 \\ 0.429436 & 1.000000 & -0.592839 & -0.576774 & -0.425776 \\ -0.724372 & -0.592839 & 1.000000 & 0.616422 & 0.614977 \\ -0.666010 & -0.576774 & 0.616422 & 1.000000 & 0.738203 \\ -0.664450 & -0.425776 & 0.614977 & 0.738203 & 1.000000 \\ 0.437063 & 0.549210 & -0.404520 & -0.656240 & -0.657781 \\ 0.379761 & 0.484884 & -0.351485 & -0.570202 & -0.571542 \\ 0.592392 & 0.724919 & -0.774414 & -0.795640 & -0.587344 \end{pmatrix}_{8 \times 5}$$

Note that the kernel matrix does not reside in memory; it is computed on demand according to Equation 6.18.

Iteration $k = 0$; PICF initializes $\mathbf{v}$, whose elements are all 1 at the start. The elements of $\mathbf{v}$ are stored on the same machines as their corresponding x_i.

processor   local diagonal vector v row index

$$\#0 \qquad v = \begin{pmatrix} 1.000000 \\ 1.000000 \\ 1.000000 \end{pmatrix} \qquad \begin{matrix} 0 \\ 3 \\ 6 \end{matrix}$$

processor   local diagonal vector v row index

$$\#1 \qquad v = \begin{pmatrix} 1.000000 \\ 1.000000 \\ 1.000000 \end{pmatrix} \qquad \begin{matrix} 1 \\ 4 \\ 7 \end{matrix}$$

processor   local diagonal vector v row index

$$\#2 \qquad v = \begin{pmatrix} 1.000000 \\ 1.000000 \end{pmatrix} \qquad \begin{matrix} 2 \\ 5 \end{matrix}$$

PICF next chooses the pivot. Each machine finds the maximum pivot and its index, and then broadcasts to the rest of the machines. Each machine then finds the largest value, and its corresponding index is the index of the global pivot. PICF sets the machine where the pivot resides as the *master* machine. In the first iteration, since all elements of $\mathbf{v}$ are one, the *master* can be set to machine #0. The global pivot value is 1, and its index 0.

Once the global pivot has been identified, PICF follows Equation 6.15 to compute $H(i_0, 0) = H(0, 0) = \sqrt{v(i_0)} = \sqrt{1} = 1$. The *master* broadcasts the pivot instance and the first $k + 1$ value (in iteration $k = 0$, the *master* broadcasts only one value) of the pivot row of H (the i_0th row of H). That is, the *master* broadcasts pivot instance $\mathbf{x}_0 = -1 \; 1 : 0.943578 \; 2 : 0.397088$ and 1.

Next, each machine can compute rows of the first column of H according to Equation 6.16. Take $H(4, 0)$ as an example, which is located at machine #1. $Q(4, 0)$ can be computed by the Laplacian kernel function using the broadcast pivot instance $\mathbf{x}_0$ and $\mathbf{x}_4$ on machine #1:

$$Q(4, 0) = y_4 y_0 K(x_4, x_0) = y_4 y_0 exp(-\gamma \|x_4 - x_0\|) = -0.664450.$$

$H(0, 0)$ can be obtained from the pivot row of H, which has been broadcast in the previous step. We thus get

$$H(4, 0) = (Q(4, 0) - \sum_{j=0}^{-1} H(4, j) H(0, j)) / H(0, 0) = Q(4, 0) / H(0, 0) = -0.664450.$$

Similarly, the other elements of the first column of H can be calculated on their machines. The result on machine #0 is as follows:

$$H_0 = \begin{pmatrix} 1.000000 & 0.000000 & 0.000000 & 0.000000 \\ 0.000000 & 0.000000 & 0.000000 & 0.000000 \\ 0.000000 & 0.000000 & 0.000000 & 0.000000 \end{pmatrix}$$

$$\downarrow$$

$$\begin{pmatrix} 1.000000 & 0.000000 & 0.000000 & 0.000000 \\ -0.666010 & 0.000000 & 0.000000 & 0.000000 \\ 0.379761 & 0.000000 & 0.000000 & 0.000000 \end{pmatrix}$$

The final step of the first iteration updates $\mathbf{v}$ distributedly according to Equation 6.17.

$$v = \begin{pmatrix} v(0) - H(0,0)^2 \\ v(3) - H(3,0)^2 \\ v(6) - H(6,0)^2 \end{pmatrix} = \begin{pmatrix} 1.000000 - 1.000000^2 \\ 1.000000 - (-0.666010)^2 \\ 1.000000 - 0.379761^2 \end{pmatrix} = \begin{pmatrix} 0.000000 \\ 0.556430 \\ 0.855782 \end{pmatrix}$$

Iteration $k = 1$: PICF again obtains local pivot values (the largest element of $\mathbf{v}$ on each machine, and their indexes.

#0	$localPivotValue_{1,0} = 0.855782$	$localPivotIndex_{1,0} = 6$
#1	$localPivotValue_{1,1} = 0.815585$	$localPivotIndex_{1,1} = 3$
#2	$localPivotValue_{1,2} = 0.808976$	$localPivotIndex_{1,2} = 5$

After the foregoing information has been broadcast and received, the global pivot value is identified as 0.855782, and the global pivot index $i_1 = 6$. The id of the *master* machine is $6\%3 = 0$. Next, PICF calculates $H(i_1, 1)$ on the *master* according to Equation 6.15:

$$H(6, 1) = \sqrt{v(i_6)} = \sqrt{0.855782} = 0.925085.$$

PICF then broadcasts the pivot instance $\mathbf{x}_6$, and the first $k + 1$ elements on the pivot row of H, which are 0.379761 and 0.925085. Each machine then computes the second column of H according to Equation 6.16. The result on machine #0 is as follows:

$$H_0 = \begin{pmatrix} 1.000000 & 0.000000 & 0.000000 & 0.000000 \\ -0.666010 & 0.000000 & 0.000000 & 0.000000 \\ 0.379761 & 0.000000 & 0.000000 & 0.000000 \end{pmatrix}$$

$$\downarrow$$

$$\begin{pmatrix} 1.000000 & 0.000000 & 0.000000 & 0.000000 \\ -0.666010 & -0.342972 & 0.000000 & 0.000000 \\ 0.379761 & 0.925085 & 0.000000 & 0.000000 \end{pmatrix}$$

In the final step of the second iteration, PICF updates $\mathbf{v}$ distributedly according to Equation 6.17.

$$v = \begin{pmatrix} v(0) - H(0,1)^2 \\ v(3) - H(3,1)^2 \\ v(6) - H(6,1)^2 \end{pmatrix} = \begin{pmatrix} 0.000000 - 0.000000^2 \\ 0.556430 - (-0.342972)^2 \\ 0.855782 - 0.925085^2 \end{pmatrix} = \begin{pmatrix} 0.000000 \\ 0.438801 \\ 0.000000 \end{pmatrix}$$

Iteration $k = 3$: We fast-forward to show the end result of the fourth and final iteration of this example. The ICF matrix is obtained as follows:

computer		ICF matrix H			row index
#0	1.000000	0.000000	0.000000	0.000000	0
#1	0.429436	0.347862	0.833413	0.000000	1
#2	-0.724372	-0.082584	-0.303618	0.147541	2
#0	-0.666010	-0.342972	-0.205731	0.260080	3
#1	-0.664450	-0.345060	-0.024483	0.662451	4
#2	0.437063	0.759837	0.116631	-0.154472	5
#0	0.379761	0.925085	0.000000	0.000000	6
#1	0.592392	0.247443	0.461294	-0.146505	7

6.2.2 Parallel IPM

Solving IPM can be both memory and computation intensive. Equation 6.13 shows that Σ depends on $\mathbf{Q}$, and we have shown that $\mathbf{Q}$ can be approximated through PICF by HH^T. Therefore, the bottleneck of the Newton step can be sped up from $\mathcal{O}(n^3)$ to $\mathcal{O}(p^2 n)$ and can be parallelized to $\mathcal{O}(p^2 n/m)$.

Parallel Data Loading

To minimize both storage and communication cost, PIPM stores data distributedly as follows:

- *Distribute matrix data.* $\mathbf{H}$ is distributedly stored at the end of PICF.
- *Distribute $n \times 1$ vector data.* All $n \times 1$ vectors are distributed in a round-robin fashion on m machines. These vectors are $\mathbf{z}$, $\boldsymbol{\alpha}$, $\boldsymbol{\xi}$, $\boldsymbol{\lambda}$, $\Delta\mathbf{z}$, $\Delta\boldsymbol{\alpha}$, $\Delta\boldsymbol{\xi}$, and $\Delta\boldsymbol{\lambda}$.
- *Replicate global scalar data.* Every machine caches a copy of global data including v, t, n, and Δv. Whenever a scalar is changed, a broadcast is required to maintain global consistency.

Parallel Computation of Δv

Rather than walking through all equations, we describe how PIPM solves Equation 6.10, where Σ^{-1} appears twice. An interesting observation is that parallelizing $\Sigma^{-1}\mathbf{z}$ (or $\Sigma^{-1}\mathbf{y}$) is simpler than parallelizing Σ^{-1}. Let us explain how parallelizing $\Sigma^{-1}\mathbf{z}$ works, and parallelizing $\Sigma^{-1}\mathbf{y}$ can follow suit.

According to SMW (the *Sherman-Morrison-Woodbury formula*) (Golub and Loan, 1996), we can write $\Sigma^{-1}\mathbf{z}$ as

$$\Sigma^{-1}\mathbf{z} = (\mathbf{D} + \mathbf{Q})^{-1}\mathbf{z} \approx (\mathbf{D} + \mathbf{HH}^T)^{-1}\mathbf{z}$$
$$= \mathbf{D}^{-1}\mathbf{z} - \mathbf{D}^{-1}\mathbf{H}(\mathbf{I} + \mathbf{H}^T\mathbf{D}^{-1}\mathbf{H})^{-1}\mathbf{H}^T\mathbf{D}^{-1}\mathbf{z}$$
$$= \mathbf{D}^{-1}\mathbf{z} - \mathbf{D}^{-1}\mathbf{H}(\mathbf{GG}^T)^{-1}\mathbf{H}^T\mathbf{D}^{-1}\mathbf{z}.$$

$\Sigma^{-1}\mathbf{z}$ can be computed in seven steps:

1. Compute $\mathbf{D}^{-1}\mathbf{z}$. $\mathbf{D}$ can be derived from locally stored vectors, following Equation 6.11. $\mathbf{D}^{-1}\mathbf{z}$ is an $n \times 1$ vector, and can be computed locally on each of the m machines.
2. Compute $\mathbf{t}_1 = \mathbf{H}^T\mathbf{D}^{-1}\mathbf{z}$. Every machine stores some rows of $\mathbf{H}$ and their corresponding part of $\mathbf{D}^{-1}\mathbf{z}$. This step can be computed locally on each machine. The results are sent to the *master* (which can be a randomly picked machine for all PIPM iterations) to aggregate into $\mathbf{t}_1$ for the next step.
3. Compute $(\mathbf{GG}^T)^{-1}\mathbf{t}_1$. This step is completed on the *master*, because it has all the required data. $\mathbf{G}$ can be obtained from $\mathbf{I} + \mathbf{H}^T\mathbf{D}^{-1}\mathbf{H}$ by Cholesky factorization. Computing $\mathbf{t}_2 = (\mathbf{GG}^T)^{-1}\mathbf{t}_1$ is equivalent to solving the linear equation system $\mathbf{t}_1 = (\mathbf{GG}^T)\mathbf{t}_2$. PIPM first solves $\mathbf{t}_1 = \mathbf{G}\mathbf{y}_0$, then $\mathbf{y}_0 = \mathbf{G}^T\mathbf{t}_2$. Once it has obtained $\mathbf{y}_0$, PIPM can solve $\mathbf{G}^T\mathbf{t}_2 = \mathbf{y}_0$ to obtain $\mathbf{t}_2$. The *master* then broadcasts $\mathbf{t}_2$ to all machines.
4. Compute $\mathbf{D}^{-1}\mathbf{H}\mathbf{t}_2$. All machines have a copy of $\mathbf{t}_2$ and can compute $\mathbf{D}^{-1}\mathbf{H}\mathbf{t}_2$ locally to solve for $\Sigma^{-1}\mathbf{z}$.
5. Compute $\mathbf{y}^T(\Sigma^{-1}\mathbf{z})$. We know that $\mathbf{t}_3 = \Sigma^{-1}\mathbf{z}$. Because $\mathbf{y}$ and $\mathbf{t}_3$ are distributed across all m machines, we have to sum up the local results to obtain $\mathbf{y}^T(\Sigma^{-1}\mathbf{z})$.

6. Compute $\mathbf{y}^T \boldsymbol{\Sigma}^{-1} \mathbf{y}$ similarly and $\mathbf{y}^T \boldsymbol{\alpha}$.

7. Compute $\Delta \nu$.

6.2.3 Computing b and Writing Back

When the IPM iteration stops, we have the value of $\boldsymbol{\alpha}$ and hence the classification function

$$f(x) = \sum_{i=1}^{N_s} \alpha_i y_i K(s_i, x) + b.$$

Here N_s is the number of support vectors and s_i are support vectors. In order to complete this classification function, b must be computed. According to the SVM model, given a support vector s, we obtain one of the two results for $f(s)$: $f(s) = +1$, if $y_s = +1$, or $f(s) = -1$, if $y_s = -1$.

In practice, we can select M, say $1,000$, support vectors and compute the average of the bs:

$$b = \frac{1}{M} \sum_{j=1}^{M} \left(y_{s_j} - \sum_{i=1}^{N_s} \alpha_i y_i K(s_i, s_j) \right).$$

Because the support vectors are distributed on m machines, PSVM collects them in parallel to compute b. For this purpose, we transform the preceding formula into the following:

$$b = \frac{1}{M} \sum_{j=1}^{M} y_{s_j} - \frac{1}{M} \sum_{i=1}^{N_s} \alpha_i y_i \sum_{j=1}^{M} K(s_i, s_j).$$

The M support vectors and their labels ys are first broadcast to all machines. All m machines then compute their local results. Finally, the local results are summed up by a reduce operation. When b has been computed, the last task of PSVM is to store the model file for later classification use.

6.3 Experiments

We conducted experiments on PSVM to evaluate its (1) class-prediction accuracy, (2) scalability on large datasets, and (3) overheads. The experiments were conducted on up to 500 machines at Google's data center. Not all machines are identically configured; however, each machine is configured with a CPU faster than 2GHz and memory larger than 4GB.

6.3.1 Class-Prediction Accuracy

PSVM employs PICF to approximate an $n \times n$ kernel matrix Q with an $n \times p$ matrix H. This experiment aimed to evaluate how the choice of p affects class-prediction accuracy. We set p of PSVM to n^t, where t ranges from 0.1 to 0.5 incremented by 0.1, and compared its class-prediction accuracy with that achieved by LIBSVM. The

Table 6.1. *Class-prediction accuracy with different p settings.*

Dataset	Samples (train/test)	LIBSVM	$p = n^{0.1}$	$p = n^{0.2}$	$p = n^{0.3}$	$p = n^{0.4}$	$p = n^{0.5}$
svmguide1	3,089/4,000	0.9608	0.6563	0.9	0.917	0.9495	0.9593
mushrooms	7,500/624	1	0.9904	0.9920	1	1	1
news20	18,000/1,996	0.7835	0.6949	0.6949	0.6969	0.7806	0.7811
Image	199,957/84,507	0.849	0.7293	0.7210	0.8041	0.8121	0.8258
CoverType	522,910/58,102	0.9769	0.9764	0.9762	0.9766	0.9761	0.9766
RCV1	781,265/23,149	0.9575	0.8527	0.8586	0.8616	0.9065	0.9264

first two columns of Table 6.1 enumerate the datasets[1] and their sizes with which we experimented. We used a radial basis function kernel and selected the best C and γ for LIBSVM and PSVM, respectively. For *CoverType* and *RCV1*, we loosed the terminate condition (set -e 1, default 0.001) and used shrink heuristics (set -h 1) to make LIBSVM terminate within several days. The table shows that when t is set to 0.5 (or $p = \sqrt{n}$), the class-prediction accuracy of PSVM approaches that of LIBSVM.

We compared only with LIBSVM because it is arguably the best open-source SVM implementation in both accuracy and speed. Another possible candidate is CVM (Tsang, Kwok, and Cheung, 2005). Our experimental result on the *CoverType* dataset outperforms the result reported by CVM on the same dataset in both accuracy and speed. Moreover, CVM's training time has been shown unpredictable by Loosli and Canu (2006), because the training time is sensitive to the selection of stop criteria and hyper-parameters.

6.3.2 Scalability

For scalability experiments, we used three large datasets. Table 6.2 reports the speedup of PSVM on up to $m = 500$ machines. Because when a dataset size is large, a single machine cannot store the factorized matrix H in its local memory, we cannot obtain the running time of PSVM on one machine. We thus used 10 machines as the baseline to measure the speedup of using more than 10 machines. To quantify speedup, we made an assumption that the speedup of using 10 machines is 10, compared to using one machine. This assumption is reasonable for our experiments, because PSVM does enjoy linear speedup when the number of machines is up to 30.

We trained PSVM three times for each dataset–m combination. The speedup reported in the table is the average of three runs with standard deviation provided in brackets. The observed variance in speedup was caused by the variance of machine loads, as all machines were shared with other tasks running on our data centers. We can observe in Table 6.2 that the larger the dataset is, the better the speedup is. Figures 6.2a, b, and c plot the speedup of *Image*, *CoverType*, and *RCV1*, respectively. All datasets enjoy

---

[1] The *RCV1* dataset is obtained from http://jmlr.csail.mit.edu/papers/volume5/lewis04a/lyrl2004_rcv1v2_README.htm. The *image* set is a binary-class image dataset consisting of 144 perceptual features. The others are obtained from www.csie.ntu.edu.tw/~cjlin/libsvmtools/datasets/. We separated the datasets into training/testing (see Table 6.1 for the splits) and performed cross validation.

Table 6.2. *Speedup (p is set to $\sqrt{n}$); LIBSVM training time is reported on the last row for reference.*

Machines	Image (200k) Time (s)		Speedup	CoverType (500k) Time (s)		Speedup	RCV1 (800k) Time (s)		Speedup
10	1,958	(9)	10*	16,818	(442)	10*	45,135	(1373)	10*
30	572	(8)	34.2	5,591	(10)	30.1	12,289	(98)	36.7
50	473	(14)	41.4	3,598	(60)	46.8	7,695	(92)	58.7
100	330	(47)	59.4	2,082	(29)	80.8	4,992	(34)	90.4
150	274	(40)	71.4	1,865	(93)	90.2	3,313	(59)	136.3
200	294	(41)	66.7	1,416	(24)	118.7	3,163	(69)	142.7
250	397	(78)	49.4	1,405	(115)	119.7	2,719	(203)	166.0
500	814	(123)	24.1	1,655	(34)	101.6	2,671	(193)	169.0
LIBSVM	4,334	NA	NA	28,149	NA	NA	184,199	NA	NA

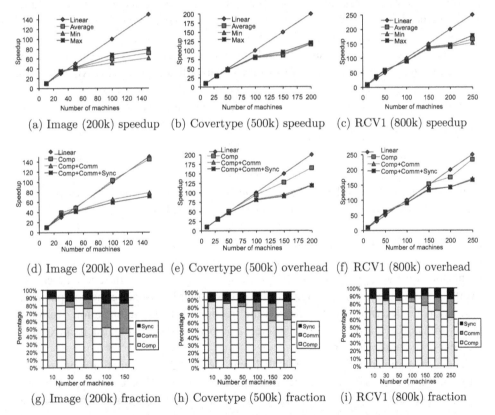

(a) Image (200k) speedup (b) Covertype (500k) speedup (c) RCV1 (800k) speedup

(d) Image (200k) overhead (e) Covertype (500k) overhead (f) RCV1 (800k) overhead

(g) Image (200k) fraction (h) Covertype (500k) fraction (i) RCV1 (800k) fraction

Figure 6.2 Speedup and Overheads of Three Datasets.

a linear speedup[2] when the number of machines is moderate. For instance, PSVM achieves linear speedup on *RCV1* when running on up to around 100 machines. PSVM scales well until around 250 machines. After that, adding more machines receives diminishing returns. This result led to our examination on the overheads of PSVM, presented next.

6.3.3 Overheads

PSVM cannot achieve linear speedup when the number of machines continues to increase beyond a data-size-dependent threshold. This is expected because of communication and synchronization overheads. Communication time is incurred when message passing takes place between machines. Synchronization overhead is incurred when the *master* machine waits for task completion on the slowest machine. (The *master* could wait forever if a child machine fails. We have implemented a check-point scheme to deal with this issue.)

The running time consists of three parts: computation (Comp), communication (Comm), and synchronization (Sync). Figures 6.2d, e, and f show how Comm and Sync overheads influence the speedup curves. In the figures, we draw on the top the computation only line (Comp), which approaches the linear speedup line. Computation speedup can become sublinear when adding machines beyond a threshold. This is because of the computation bottleneck of the unparallelizable step 12 in Algorithm 14 (whose computation time is $\mathcal{O}(p^2)$). When m is small, this bottleneck is insignificant in the total computation time. According to Amdahl's law, however, even a small fraction of unparallelizable computation can cap speedup. Fortunately, the larger the dataset is, the smaller this unparallelizable fraction is, which is $\mathcal{O}(m/n)$. Therefore, more machines (larger m) can be employed for larger datasets (larger n) to gain speedup.

When communication overhead or synchronization overhead is accounted for (the Comp + Comm line and the Comp + Comm + Sync line), the speedup deteriorates. Between the two overheads, the synchronization overhead does not affect speedup as much as the communication overhead does. Figures 6.2g, h, and i present the percentage of Comp, Comm, and Sync in total running time. The synchronization overhead maintains about the same percentage when m increases, whereas the percentage of communication overhead grows with m. As mentioned in Section 6.2.1, the communication overhead is $\mathcal{O}(p^2 \log(m))$, growing sub-linearly with m. But because the computation time per node decreases as m increases, the fraction of the communication overhead grows with m. Therefore, PSVM must select a proper m for a training task to maximize the benefit of parallelization.

The computation part is not completely linear; step 3 of Δv computation is performed only on the master. The computation complexity is $O(p^2)$. For CoverType dataset, this part takes about 150 seconds, whereas the total computation time is about 14,700

---

[2] We observed super-linear speedup when 30 machines were used for training *Image* and when up to 50 machines were used for *RCV1*. We believe that this super-linear speedup resulted from performance gain in the memory management system when the physical memory was not in contention with other processes running at the data center. This benefit was canceled by other overheads (explained in Section 6.3.3) when more machines were employed.

seconds for 10 machines and 890 seconds for 200 machines. The non-parallelizable part takes a larger percentage when more machines are utilized; therefore, the computation speedup curves lies under the linear curve.

The communication overhead can be estimated by $O(p^2 log(m))$. The optimal number of machines can be empirically determined as $m \approx 6 \times 10^{-4}n$. The training time can be estimated as $t(m) = K_1 np^2/m + K_2 p^2 log(m)$, where K_1 and K_2 are constants, and can be estimated using experiment by the least square method. The minimum training time (or the optimal number of machines) can be achieved by $t'(m) = 0$, that is, $m = K_1 n/K_2 \approx 6 \times 10^{-4}n$.

6.4 Conclusion

In this chapter, we have shown how SVMs can be parallelized to achieve scalable performance. PSVM distributively loads training data on parallel machines, reducing memory requirement through approximate factorization on the kernel matrix. PSVM solves IPM in parallel by cleverly arranging computation order. Through empirical studies, we have shown that PSVM does not sacrifice class-prediction accuracy significantly for scalability, and it scales well with training data size.

PSVM was made publicly available through Apache open source (Chang et al., 2007) and had been downloaded more than 2000 times by March 2011.

Acknowledgments

This work is partially supported by the National Science Foundation under Grant Number IIS-0535085.

References

Aizerman, M. A., Braverman, E. M., and Rozonoer, L. I. 1964. Theoretical Foundations of the Potential Function Method in Pattern Recognition Learning. *Automation and Remote Control*, **25**, 821–837.

Bach, F. R., and Jordan, M. I. 2005. Predictive Low-rank Decomposition for Kernel Methods. In: *Proceedings of the 22nd International Conference on Machine Learning*.

Boser, B. E., Guyon, I. M., and Vapnik, V. N. 1992. A Training Algorithm for Optimal Margin Classifiers. Pages 144–152 of: *COLT '92: Proceedings of the Fifth Annual Workshop on Computational Learning Theory*. New York: ACM.

Boyd, S. 2004. *Convex Optimization*. New York: Cambridge University Press.

Chang, C.-C., and Lin, C.-J. 2001. *LIBSVM: A Library for Support Vector Machines*. Software available at www.csie.ntu.edu.tw/~cjlin/libsvm.

Chang, E. Y., Zhu, K., Wang, H., Bai, H., Li, J., Qiu, Z., and Cui, H. 2007. Parallelizing Support Vector Machines on Distributed Computers. *Advances in Neural Information Processing Systems (NIPS)*, open source http://code.google.com/p/psvm/.

Chu, C.-T., Kim, S. K., Lin, Y.-A., Yu, Y., Bradski, G., Ng, A. Y., and Olukotun, K. 2006. Map Reduce for Machine Learning on Multicore. *NIPS*.

Cortes, C., and Vapnik, V. 1995. Support-Vector Networks. *Machine Learning*, **20**, 273–297.

Courant, R., and Hilbert, D. 1953. *Method of Mathematical Physics*. Vol. 1. New York: Interscience.

Devijver, P. A., and Kittler, J. 1982. *Pattern Recognition: A Statistical Approach*. London: Prentice Hall.

Fine, S., and Scheinberg, K. 2001. Efficient SVM Training Using Low-rank Kernel Representations. *Journal of Machine Learning Research*, **2**, 243–264.

Golub, G. H., and Loan, C. F. V. 1996. *Matrix Computations*. Baltimore: Johns Hopkins University Press.

Graf, H. P., Cosatto, E., Bottou, L., Durdanovic, I., and Vapnik, V. 2005. Parallel Support Vector Machines: The Cascade SVM. Pages 521–528 of: *Advances in Neural Information Processing Systems 17*.

Joachims, T. 1998. Making Large-Scale SVM Learning Practical. *Advances in Kernel Methods – Support Vector Learning*.

Joachims, T. 1999. Transductive Inference for Text Classification Using Support Vector Machines. *International Conference on Machine Learning*.

Joachims, T. 2006. Training Linear SVMs in Linear Time. *ACM KDD*, 217–226.

Lee, Y.-J., and Mangasarian, O. L. 2001, April. RSVM: Reduced Support Vector Machines. In: *First SIAM International Conference on Data Mining*.

Loosli, G., and Canu, S. 2006, June. *Comments on the Core Vector Machines: Fast SVM Training on Very Large Data Sets*. Technical Report.

Mehrotra, S. 1992. On the Implementation of a Primal-Dual Interior Point Method. *SIAM J. Optimization*, **2**, 575–601.

Platt, J. C. 1998. *Sequential Minimal Optimization: A Fast Algorithm for Training Support Vector Machines*. Technical Report. MSR-TR-98-14, Microsoft Research.

Tong, S., and Chang, E. Y. 2001. Support Vector Machine Active Learning for Image Retrieval. Pages 107–118 of: *ACM International Conference on Multimedia*.

Tsang, I. W., Kwok, J. T., and Cheung, P.-M. 2005. Core Vector Machines: Fast SVM Training on Very Large Data Sets. *Journal of Machine Learning Research*, **6**, 363–392.

CHAPTER 7

Massive SVM Parallelization Using Hardware Accelerators

Igor Durdanovic, Eric Cosatto, Hans Peter Graf,
Srihari Cadambi, Venkata Jakkula, Srimat Chakradhar,
and Abhinandan Majumdar

Support Vector Machines (SVMs) are some of the most widely used classification and regression algorithms for data analysis, pattern recognition, or cognitive tasks. Yet learning problems that can be solved by SVMs are limited in size because of high computational cost and excessive storage requirements. Many variations of the original SVM algorithm were introduced that scale better to large problems. They change the SVM framework quite drastically, such as apply optimizations other than the maximum margin, or introduce different error metrics for the cost function. Such algorithms may work for some applications, but they do not have the robustness and universality that make SVMs so popular.

The approach taken here is to maintain the SVM algorithm in its original form and scale it to large problems through parallelization. Computer performance cannot be improved anymore at the pace of the last few decades by increasing the clock frequencies. Today, significant accelerations are achieved mostly through parallel architectures, and multicore processors are commonplace nowadays. Mapping the SVM algorithm to multicore processors with shared-memory architectures is straightforward, yet this approach does not scale to a large number of processors. Here we investigate parallelization concepts that scale to hundreds and thousands of cores where, for example, cache coherence can no longer be maintained.

A number of SVM implementations on clusters or graphics processors (GPUs) have been proposed recently. A parallel optimization algorithm based on gradient projections has been demonstrated (see Zanghirati, and Zanni, 2003; Zanni, Serafini, and Zanghirati, 2006) that uses a spectral gradient method for fast convergence while maintaining the Karush-Kuhn-Tucker (KKT) constraints. The Cascade SVM (Graf et al., 2005) has been proposed for breaking a large problem into smaller optimizations that can be solved in parallel. The Spread-Kernel algorithm introduces a split of the data and intermediate results that can be distributed over a large number of processors and has demonstrated good scaling to several hundred processors (Durdanovic et al. 2007). Interior point (IP) algorithms are widely used for solving large QP problems, and parallelizations suited for solving SVMs have been proposed (D'Apuzzo and Marino, 2003). GPUs have become popular for scientific computing nowadays, and SVM

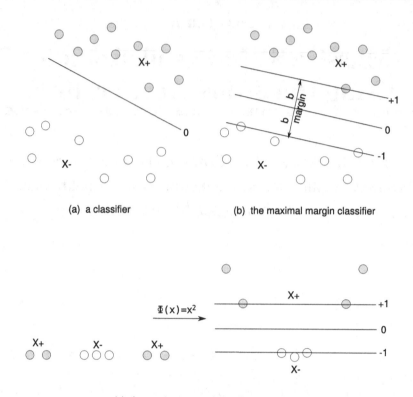

(a) a classifier   (b) the maximal margin classifier

(c) the maximum margin nonlinear classifier

Figure 7.1 Classifiers.

implementations on GPUs were demonstrated with very good performance (Catanzaro et al., 2008).

We describe here several of the parallelization concepts that were developed for SVMs (Durdanovic, Cosatto, and Graf 2007) and demonstrate an implementation with a field-programmable gate array (FPGA), where 128 cores operate in parallel. High performance is achieved with this architecture while maintaining power dissipation at a very low level. This makes it attractive for handheld and embedded applications where power dissipation is the main constraint. But power consumption is also becoming a major problem for server applications, and therefore this architecture looks attractive for data centers where large-scale data analysis is performed.

7.1 Problem Formulation

A classification problem is defined as finding a separating hyperplane $\mathbf{w}$ between two sets of points: X^+ for which the "labeling" function is $y(x_i) = y_i = +1$ and X^- for which $y(x_i) = y_i = -1$, where $x_i \in \mathcal{R}^d$. A classifier example (the task of geometrically separating two differently colored sets of vectors) is shown in Figure 7.1a.

An SVM classifier is defined as the maximum margin classifier between X^+ and X^- sets and is shown in Figure 7.1b. The term *support vectors* refers to the vectors of both classes that touch (or support) the margin planes. This results in the following quadratic optimization problem:

$$\min_{w,b,\xi} \frac{1}{2}\|\mathbf{w}\|^2 + C\sum \xi_i \ : \ y_i(\mathbf{w}\, x_i - b) \geq 1 - \xi_i,$$

with ξ_i being slack variables, allowing for soft errors, the penalty (sum) of which is controlled by the parameter C.

A nonlinear classifier is constructed by means of a nonlinear mapping function $\Phi(x)$. The separation is still a linear hyperplane (see Figure 7.1c) but now in the nonlinear space given by the function Φ (often of higher or even infinite dimensionality). Because the SVM only needs a dot product between two vectors, the dot product in the original (primal) space; $x_i \cdot x_j$, becomes $\Phi(x_i) \cdot \Phi(x_j)$ in the nonlinear space and is called a kernel function $K(x_i, x_j)$,[1] whereas the nonlinear space is referred to as the kernel space.

The dual SVM formulation – minimization of the objective function $W(\alpha)$ – is defined as:

$$W(\alpha) = \frac{1}{2}\left[\sum_{i=1}^{n} \alpha_i y_i \left[\sum_{j=1}^{n} \alpha_j y_j K(x_i, x_j) \right] \right] - \left[\sum_{i=1}^{n} \alpha_i \right]$$

$$\text{under constraints} : \ 0 \leq \alpha_i \leq C, \ \left[\sum_{i=1}^{n} \alpha_i y_i \right] = 0$$

Because we are going to use a gradient descent algorithm, it is beneficial to rewrite the objective function in terms of gradients:

$$G_i = \frac{\partial W(\alpha)}{\partial \alpha_i} = y_i \left[\sum_{j=1}^{n} \alpha_j y_j K(x_i, x_j) \right] - 1,$$

$$W(\alpha) = \frac{1}{2}\left[\sum_{i=1}^{n} \alpha_i (G_i - 1) \right]$$

7.1.1 Solving the Quadratic Optimization Problem

SVM implementations do not solve the QP problem (see Section 7.1) in one large optimization, because it tends to scale poorly, roughly with n^3, where n is the number of training samples. Rather, the training set is divided into smaller working and active sets, with n_w and n_a elements, respectively. The optimization is executed on a working set n_w, and after each optimization a new working set is selected from the n_a elements of the active set. Every now and then, the training data are tested, to see if they all meet the KKT constraints and the ones that do not are added to the active set. Often it is actually the other way around, that first all data are part of the active set and

---

[1] Most common kernel functions are linear: $K(x, y) = x \cdot y$, rbf: $K(x, y) = e^{-\gamma|x-y|^2}$, Laplacian: $K(x, y) = e^{-\gamma|x-y|}$, and so on. Kernel function parameters are often called *meta parameters*.

every so often the active set is checked, if any of the vectors can be set aside as likely candidates for not being support vectors. Various ways/heuristics of selecting the active and working sets have been developed, but this general structure is recognizable in most implementations.

In our implementation (MiLDe, see Section 7.4.1) we have opted for the simplest case of $n_w = 2$, which allows for the analytical solution (see 7.1.2), and $n_a = n$, avoiding memory fragmentation due to the caching of kernel columns of varying lengths.

7.1.2 Deriving SMO

Performing optimization on only two vectors (x_1, x_2) at a time is called SMO (Platt, 1999) or Sequential Minimal Optimization. We can analytically solve the partial gradient descent problem involving only two vectors and their coefficients (α_1 and α_2) while the rest of the α' coefficients remain constant:

$$\Delta W(\alpha) = W(\alpha_1 + d_1, \alpha_2 + d_2, \alpha') - W(\alpha_1, \alpha_2, \alpha')$$

$$\Delta W(\alpha) = \frac{d_1^2 K(x_1, x_1) + d_2^2 K(x_2, x_2) + 2y_1 y_2 d_1 d_2 K(x_1, x_2)}{2}$$

$$+ d_1 y_1 \left[\sum_{j=1}^{n} y_j \alpha_j K(x_1, x_j) \right] + d_2 y_2 \left[\sum_{j=1}^{n} y_j \alpha_j K(x_2, x_j) \right] - d_1 - d_2.$$

We have two cases to consider, case 1: $y_i \neq y_2$ meaning $d_1 = d_2$:

$$0 = \frac{\partial \Delta W(\alpha)}{\partial d_2} = d_2 \eta + y_1 \left[\sum_{j=1}^{n} y_j \alpha_j K(x_1, x_j) \right] + y_2 \left[\sum_{j=1}^{n} y_j \alpha_j K(x_2, x_j) \right] - 2$$

$$d_2 = -\frac{1}{\eta} \left[\left(y_1 \left[\sum_{j=1}^{n} y_j \alpha_j K(x_1, x_j) \right] - 1 \right) + \left(y_2 \left[\sum_{j=1}^{n} y_j \alpha_j K(x_2, x_j) \right] - 1 \right) \right]$$

$$d_2 = -\frac{G_1 + G_2}{\eta}$$

and the case 2: $y_i = y_2$ meaning $d_1 = -d_2$, which leads to the solution

$$d_2 = \frac{G_1 - G_2}{\eta},$$

where $\eta = K(x_1, x_1) + K(x_2, x_2) - 2K(x_1, x_2)$, and G_1 and G_2 are the partial gradients of $W(\alpha)$ as defined in Section 7.1.

The speed of convergence heavily depends on the selection of the two vectors – the working set.

7.1.3 Working Set Selection

There are many ways to select a working set; however, not all of them guarantee convergence. One that does is the first-order working set selection or *maximal violating pair* selection. However, because the objective function is quadratic, we can do even better by using the second-order working set selection. The only problem is, selecting the best second-order working set would require second-order inspection of all possible pairs. Hence, in practice, one uses first-order selection to select the first vector, whereas the second vector is selected (relative to the first) using the second-order selection. Although it is computationally more expensive (roughly twice as much as the first-order selection), in our experience, using the second-order selection results in about one-third of the iterations needed to reach the same convergence criteria as the first-order selection. We refer the reader to the Fan et al. (2005) article for mathematical derivations and detailed discussion on working set selections.

7.2 Implementation of the SMO Algorithm

Here (Algorithm 15) we present the SMO algorithm (as implemented in MiLDe) in the lo, hi parametrized form. In a sequential version, the algorithm works on the full dataset; hence, $lo = 1$ and $hi = n$ (lines 1,2). However, the algorithm is highly data independent and therefore embarrassingly parallel. It does not require shared memory and can be executed on multiple CPU(s)/core(s) as well as on a cluster of machines. When running in parallel, each CPU/core and/or machine in the cluster will work only on a subset of the data vectors indicated by the lo, hi parameters. The only thing we must take into consideration is merging of the locally found working sets into a global working set which adds an overhead of the parallelization.

Algorithm 15: SMO: Main Loop

1: $lo \Leftarrow 1$
2: $hi \Leftarrow n$
3: $\alpha_i \Leftarrow 0, \quad i = 1 \ldots n$
4: $G_i \Leftarrow -1, \quad i = lo \ldots hi$
5: **Repeat**
6:     $(i, j) \Leftarrow$ find working set(lo, hi)
7:     $(\Delta\alpha_i, \Delta\alpha_j) \Leftarrow$ compute delta alphas(i, j)
8:     $\alpha_i += \Delta\alpha_i$
9:     $\alpha_j += \Delta\alpha_j$
10:     $G_k += y_i y_k \Delta\alpha_i K(x_i, x_k), \quad k = lo \ldots hi$
11:     $G_k += y_j y_k \Delta\alpha_j K(x_j, x_k), \quad k = lo \ldots hi$
12: **Until** *converged*

The algorithm starts with a feasible solution (all α-s being 0 and all gradients being -1, lines 3,4) and then iterates until some stopping convergence criterion has been met. Figure 7.2 depicts the data access pattern for one iteration, where we highlighted the two gradients (G_i, G_j) and four (actually three because of symmetry $K_{i,j} = K_{j,i}$) kernel values $(K_{i,i}, K_{i,j}, K_{j,j})$ that are directly involved in the analytic computation of the two alphas (α_i, α_j). In each iteration we select two vectors (line 6), compute the analytic solution of the gradient descent (lines 7–9), and update the gradients (lines 10,11). Updating the gradients is the most costly part because it involves computing

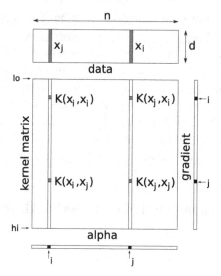

Figure 7.2 SVM/SMO algorithm – one iteration data access pattern.

two kernel columns and accessing all the training vectors in the process. The main loop repeats until the desired convergence criterion has been met.

The speed of convergence depends on the selection of the two vectors of the working set (Algorithm 16) on which the gradient descent will be performed; see Section 7.1.3. The first order working set selection is given in lines 2,3. The second-order selection (for the second vector only) is given in line 4.

Algorithm 16: SMO: Working Set Selection, First and Second Order

---

1: find working set(lo,hi) $\Leftarrow$

2: $i^{1^{st}} \Leftarrow \underset{k=lo...hi}{arg\,max} \begin{cases} -G_k & : y_k > 0 \;\&\; \alpha_k < C \\ +G_k & : y_k < 0 \;\&\; \alpha_k > 0 \end{cases}$

3: $j^{1^{st}} \Leftarrow \underset{k=lo...hi}{arg\,max} \begin{cases} +G_k & : y_k > 0 \;\&\; \alpha_k > 0 \\ -G_k & : y_k < 0 \;\&\; \alpha_k < C \end{cases}$

4: $j^{2^{nd}} \Leftarrow \underset{k=lo...hi}{arg\,max} \begin{cases} b_{i,k}^2/\eta & : y_k > 0 \;\&\; \alpha_k > 0 \;\&\; b > 0 \\ b_{i,k}^2/\eta & : y_k < 0 \;\&\; \alpha_k < C \;\&\; b > 0 \end{cases}$

5: $\qquad\qquad\qquad\qquad$ where: $\begin{aligned} b_{i,k} &= -y_i\,G_i + y_k\,G_k \\ \eta &= K(x_i, x_i) + K(x_k, x_k) - 2\,K(x_i, x_k) \end{aligned}$

We compute (Algorithm 17) the analytical solution (Section 7.1.2) for the gradient descent (lines 2–8), but then we must correct it to satisfy the box constraints (line 9).

7.3 Micro Parallelization: Related Work

The trend toward ever faster microprocessors has essentially come to a halt. The landscape has started to shift toward multicore and many-core architectures, the latter being championed by the GPUs. GPUs are many-core accelerators that have been

Algorithm 17: SMO: Analytical Solution
1: Compute delta alphas$(i, j) \Leftarrow$
2: $\eta \Leftarrow K(x_i, x_i) + K(x_j, x_j) - 2K(x_i, x_j)$
3: **If** $y_i = y_j$ **then**
4: $\quad \Delta\alpha_j \Leftarrow +(G_i - G_j)/\eta$
5: $\quad \Delta\alpha_i \Leftarrow -\Delta\alpha_j$
6: **Else**
7: $\quad \Delta\alpha_j \Leftarrow -(G_i + G_j)/\eta$
8: $\quad \Delta\alpha_i \Leftarrow +\Delta\alpha_j$
9: Box constraints$(\Delta\alpha_i, \Delta\alpha_j)$

increasingly employed for general-purpose, especially scientific workloads with impressive performance (Owens et al., 2007; Seiler et al., 2008). Other parallel chip architectures include Taylor et al. (2002), Diamond et al. (2008) and more recently, Kelm et al. (2009), all of which have been targeted to general-purpose workloads. Although we borrow ideas from many of these, and our system is also easy to program within the specific domain for which it has been designed, it is not general purpose. As key architectural differences, our design uses loosely coupled processor-off-chip memory channels; supports several custom data access patterns, both from off-chip and on-chip memories; and has on-chip smart memory blocks to perform computations in parallel with the processing elements. Being a programmable processor, we are more flexible than custom FPGA implementations of individual algorithms such as the designs of Zhuo and Prasanna (2005); Rousseaux et al. (2007). Our design maintains considerable internal state information and yet operates on streaming inputs and outputs. It combines elements of streaming and media architectures (Chatterji et al., 2003; Kapasi et al., 2003), such as banked off-chip memory and processor chain interconnection networks, with the internal smart memory blocks that hold state information. It also provides mechanisms to stall input and output streams when required by the smart memory blocks. We compare our work extensively to state-of-the-art multicore CPUs and also to GPUs.

7.4 Previous Parallelizations on Multicore Systems

In Durdanovic et al. (2007), we have analyzed the SVM/SMO algorithm on all levels:

Starting with the sequential algorithm, we have systematically replaced *naive* "for loops" with equivalent BLAS[2] function calls. This exposed all the data-independent aspects of the algorithm. For example: reordering vectors according to their labels allows us to simplify the gradient update loop (see Algorithm 15) by removing y_iy_j multiplication (or in/equality testing) from it. The gradient update loop now maps into a few efficient BLAS axpy function calls (Figure 7.3).

---

[2] Basic Linear Algebra Subroutines (See www.netlib.org/blas/faq.html) is a library of highly optimized (linear algebra) routines that has been in development for decades. There are many free and commercial versions available. We mainly use Intel's MKL (Math Kernel Library).

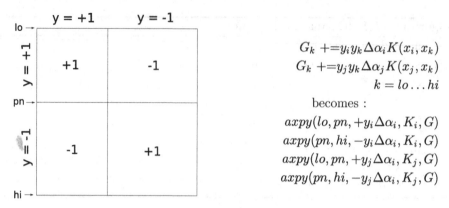

$$G_k \mathrel{+}= y_i y_k \Delta\alpha_i K(x_i, x_k)$$
$$G_k \mathrel{+}= y_j y_k \Delta\alpha_j K(x_j, x_k)$$
$$k = lo \ldots hi$$

becomes :

$$axpy(lo, pn, +y_i \Delta\alpha_i, K_i, G)$$
$$axpy(pn, hi, -y_i \Delta\alpha_i, K_i, G)$$
$$axpy(lo, pn, +y_j \Delta\alpha_i, K_j, G)$$
$$axpy(pn, hi, -y_j \Delta\alpha_i, K_j, G)$$

Figure 7.3 Data Reordering Effect.

We then proceeded to parallelize all the data-independent parts, starting at the CPU instruction level. Modern $\times 86$ (and x86_64) processors introduced extension instructions to the original x86 instruction set, in particular MMX[3] and SSE[4] instructions that execute in SIMD[5] fashion and allow us to hand-craft kernel functions for particular data types like pixels, thus computing four or more identical multiply-accumulate operations simultaneously.[6]

Next we employed multi-threading[7] to make maximal use of modern multicore architectures. We noticed, however, that the memory subsystem is often unable to keep pace with the multicore processors: whereas on the dual-core CPUs we achieve $1.9\times$ speedup, on the quadcore CPUs we achieve only $3\times$ speedup.

Our work culminated in the spread-kernel algorithm that runs with a super-linear speedup on a cluster. We have been able to solve a 4M MNIST problem[8] (see Section 7.6.1) in 18 hours on a 48 dual-core Athlon (1.5GHz, 2MB) cluster.

The linear component of the speedup comes from linearly increasing the computing power when we add nodes into the parallel supercomputer (combined equivalent of a machine with a 150GHz CPU). The nonlinear component, the super-linear speedup, comes from linearly increasing the amount of memory (combined equivalent of a machine with 96GB of RAM) available for caching the kernel computation, thus avoiding re-computing more and more of the kernel matrix.

We have implemented our own I/O library that utilizes the underlying network depending on its capabilities: half-duplex TCP/IP, full-duplex TCP/IP, and reliable UDP/MULTICAST. Less capable networks incur higher I/O costs (log time for one-to-all messages) compared to more capable networks (constant time for one-to-all messages).

---

[3] MMX – MultiMedia eXtension instructions.
[4] SSE – Streaming SIMD Extensions.
[5] SIMD is the Single Instruction Multiple Data mode of execution.
[6] Intel's MKL automatically uses SIMD instructions.
[7] Modern BLAS implementations such as MKL are multi-threaded as well.
[8] Because our sequential version is capable of solving the standard 60K MNIST odd-versus-even problem in two minutes, we needed a much larger dataset in order to test the parallel version.

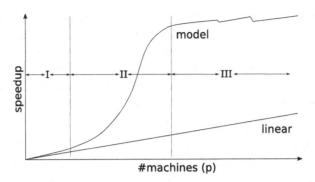

Figure 7.4 Spread-Kernel Speedup Model.

We have rigorously analyzed the parallel algorithm and developed a precise theoretical model of the speedup and the parallelization overhead. Figure 7.4 depicts three cases: In region **I**, the problem size is too large for the cluster and only a linear speedup is achieved. As we increase the number of machines in the cluster – region **II** – the cluster (memorywise) starts to "match" the size of the problem: the active portion of the kernel matrix can be effectively cached and reused. Eventually, adding more and more machines, the problem becomes too small for the cluster, and the active portion of the kernel matrix is completely cached, at which point the logarithmic costs of the parallelization overhead become noticeable – as depicted in region **III**. The theoretical model has been validated experimentally (Figure 7.5).

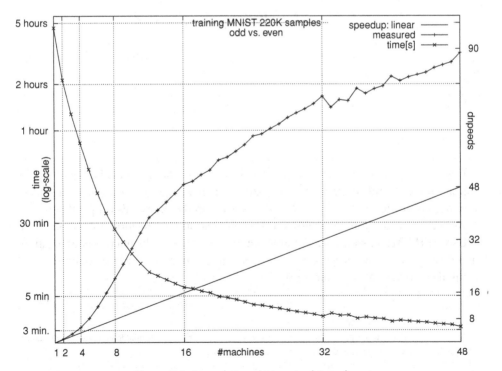

Figure 7.5 Spread-Kernel Measured Speedup.

Our method does not pose any restriction either on the kernel or on the variant of the SVM problem that is being solved: support vector classification, support vector regression, or support vector data description.

It is worth noting the orthogonality and independence of each level of parallelization, their effects being compounded to a large extent when used simultaneously, resulting in very fast implementations even on standard ×86 architectures. For example, the two-class 60K MNIST odd-versus-even problem can be solved in about 2 minutes on a dual-core 2.2GHz Opteron machine, using these parallelizations, compared to the several hours it takes with a sequentially implemented SVM algorithm (e.g., LIBSVM[9]).

7.4.1 MiLDe

All our work is incorporated into MiLDe (Machine Learning and Development Environment[10]), consisting of C/C++ back-end libraries and a front-end using the Lua scripting language. This implementation of the SVM/SMO algorithm can be used for single-label per-class classification, multilabel-per class classification, epsilon regression, and data description (minimal enclosing ball) problems; it also provides general math capabilities: vectors; matrices; tensors; and a plethora of common linear algebra (via interfaces to BLAS and LAPACK[11]), signal processing, and classical statistics algorithms. Using the kernel trick, many linear algebra algorithms can be made to work in the kernel space, greatly extending the range of potential applications.

7.5 Micro Parallelization: Revisited

The analysis of the SVM/SMO algorithm (see Figure 7.2) reveals the following complexities (per iteration) of each component of the algorithm:

$O(n)$ find working set
$O(n*d)$ compute kernel column(s)
$O(n)$ update gradients

When the dimensionality of the data d is large, computation of the kernel columns dominates the overall computation. In particular, machine vision deals with image pattern classification problems, which often have d in the thousands (of pixels).

We have already implemented micro-parallelization (see Section 7.4) on modern CPUs via SIMD extension instructions (Figure 7.6). However, the micro-parallelization support by general purpose processors is very limited, allowing for only four multiply-accumulate operations simultaneously.

---

[9] www.csie.ntu.edu.tw/~cjlin/libsvm.

[10] MiLDe is a in-house-developed software. A Linux (source code) version is available at www.nec-labs.com/research/machine/ml_website/main/software.php?project=milde.

[11] LAPACK is a Linear Algebra Package, a library of higher level linear algebra functions; see www.netlib.org/lapack/faq.html.

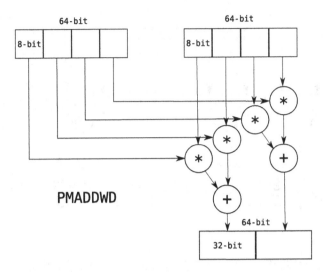

Figure 7.6 ×86 Vector Extension Instruction(s).

Working with high-dimensional data such as images opens up the possibility of massive micro-parallelization, supported by a dedicated hardware accelerators capable of performing hundred(s) of multiply-accumulate operations at a time (Figure 7.7).

Unlike the MMX/SSE version that is able to perform only four multiply-accumulate operations simultaneously, here we are dealing with hundreds of multiply-accumulate units. The matrix (data) is streamed into the accelerator one vector at a time (see long arrows in Figure 7.7) from the off-chip memory,[12] while the other vector (see short arrows) is stored locally in the on-chip memory. Components of both vectors are multiplied and summed up into the dot product of the two vectors.

However, we must point out that for a hardware accelerator to be successful, massive computational abilities of a custom processor must be accompanied by an equally massive memory bandwidth in order to sustain the computation. Accelerators of this type must be applied on problems that are of a sufficiently high dimension: $d >$ number of PEs (processing elements or DSPs), or the accelerator will be underutilized.

7.6 Massively Parallel Hardware Accelerator

Our goal was to create and test a hardware accelerator that can be plugged into a variety of machines (desktops and laptops), to which we commonly refer as the HOST (see Figure 7.11) and speed up the most computationally intensive part(s) of the algorithm, in particular the computation of the kernel columns.

The HOST machine runs the SVM/SMO algorithm while off-loading the computation of the (linear) kernel to the hardware accelerator. The accelerator computes the

---

[12] "Off-chip" here refers to the memory system that is local to the co-processor. During training we assume/require that all the data fit into the co-processor memory. During testing, we assume/require that all support vectors fit into the co-processor memory, while the testing vectors (ideally) are streamed in a (semi) batch fashion; see Section 7.6.3.

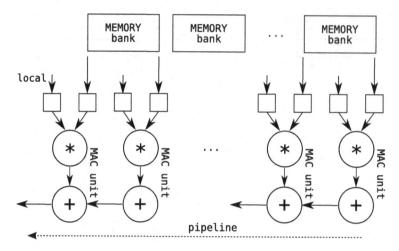

Figure 7.7 Massive Parallel Hardware Acceleration.

linear kernel column[13] and DMA[14]-transfers the resulting vector to the HOST, which computes the real (nonlinear) kernel (rbf, Laplacian, etc.) on top of it. In order to maximize utilization of both the HOST CPU(s) and the hardware accelerator, the resulting vector is computed and transferred in chunks, allowing us to overlap the HOST (nonlinear) computation with the accelerator (linear) computation.

We created a prototype of massively parallel hardware accelerator using the off-the-shelf AlphaData Virtex-5 FPGA board.[15] The board has four independent DDR2 banks capable of streaming 8.5 GB/s and 2 SDRAM banks, which we use for results. The architecture of the accelerator can be seen in Figure 7.8.

7.6.1 Datasets

We used two datasets for our experiments with the hardware accelerator. The first was the MNIST dataset (Figure 7.9), consisting of handwritten digits (10 classes, used in two-class setting as odd vs. even) at a resolution of 784 pixels, containing 60K training and 10K test vectors. For our experiments with the accelerator card, we used both the standard 60K and an expanded (limited by the available memory of the accelerator card) dataset with 2 million samples.[16] In our experiments we used RBF with kernel $\gamma = \frac{0.02}{256^2}$, $C = 10$.

The other dataset was NORB (Figure 7.10), containing images of five different object classes (used in two-class setting as classes 0, 1 vs. classes 2, 3, 4) at a resolution

---

[13] Computation of a linear kernel column is a vector-matrix product. BLAS provides gemv (generalized matrix vector) functions that work on floating-point data. However, when dealing with image pattern recognition problems, our native data type is often a single-byte (gray-scale) pixel. Hence, we designed a `pixel-gemv` function for the hardware accelerator that works well on the pixel data.

[14] DMA or Direct Memory Access is the ability of the hardware to transfer data into/from memory without involvement of the CPU.

[15] The particular board used was ADM-XRC-5T2; see www.alpha-data.com/products.php?product=adm-xrc-5t2. The card was successfully used in Linux and Windows environments.

[16] Datasets are available at http://ml.nec-labs.com/download/data/milde/.

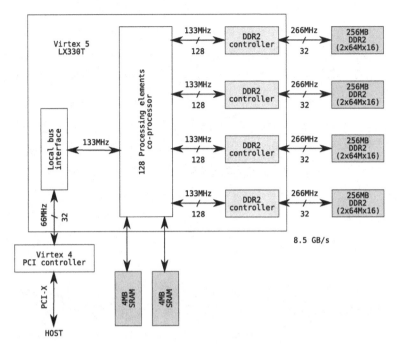

Figure 7.8 Hardware Accelerator Prototype.

of 5184 pixels, consisting of 48560 training and 48560 test vectors. We used RBF kernel with $\gamma = \frac{0.024}{256^2}$, $C = 100$ in our experiments.

We also used the Forest (cover-type) dataset (consisting of 522K training and 58K test vectors in two-class setting as class 2 versus the rest) with RBF kernel $\gamma = 4.1 \times 10^{-5}$, $C = 50$ and the ADULT dataset (consisting of 32K training and 16K test vectors) with RBF kernel $\gamma = 0.033$, $C = 3$ to validate reduced numerical precision. However, they were not used in the experiments with the hardware accelerator, because

Figure 7.9 MNIST ($d = 784$) Dataset.

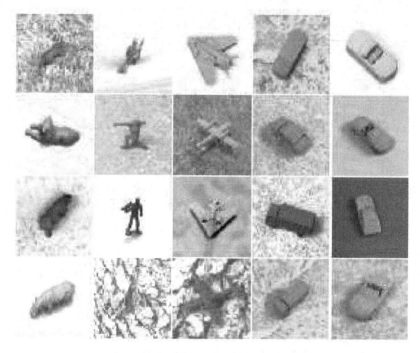

Figure 7.10 NORB ($d = 5184$) Dataset.

the FPGA was programmed to perform numerical computations on a different (pixel) data type that was incompatible with Forest (mixed floating-point and bit-set) and ADULT (bit-set) data types.

7.6.2 Numerical Precision

In order to minimize I/O overhead caused by the DMA transfer between the HOST and the hardware accelerator, we decided to truncate the fixed-point value of the computed linear kernel vectors to only 16 bits (a more detailed timing analysis is presented in Section 7.7). We expected minimal effects of such numerical truncation, which was confirmed with multiple experiments. Table 7.1 summarizes the effects that the kernel truncation has on the classifier precision – expressed as the F-score – on various datasets. We used an RBF kernel, which is a dot-product based kernel, hence consisting

Table 7.1. *The effect of (linear, dot-product) truncation in RBF kernel on the overall precision.*

	F-score:	
kernel:	float 32-bit	fixed 16-bit
ADULT	77.58%	77.63%
FOREST	98.29%	98.28%
MNIST	99.11%	99.11%
NORB	93.34%	93.26%

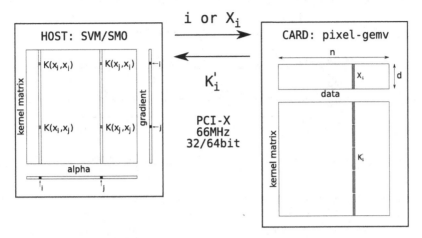

Figure 7.11 The functional layout of the HOST and the accelerator.

of a linear part, the dot product, which can be off-loaded to FPGA, and a nonlinear part, the exponential, that is computed by the HOST.

The second optimization was done to (functionally) *increase* the available memory bandwidth. Because the memory bandwidth is fixed by the available hardware at 8.5 GB/s, doubling the data rate really meant reducing or truncating the data – pixel values – from 8-bit to 4-bit. The effect of this numerical compromise is data dependent. Tasks that consist of nearly binary images (such as MNIST) are not affected by the quantization at all. Tasks that use the full dynamic range of gray-scale images (such as NORB) experience a small loss of precision. The truncation of the data was necessary to increase the memory bandwidth and sustain the massive computational power of 128 DSP units. The effects of the data truncation on various datasets are expressed in terms of the F score in Table 7.2.

7.6.3 HOST – Accelerator Timing

We report here results for a particular HOST (dual 2.2GHz Opteron with 12GB RAM) and an FPGA (PCI-X) accelerator card. During training, all the training vectors are pre-loaded onto FPGA memory, and the only I/O from the HOST to the accelerator sends the index of the vectors for which the linear kernel column is to be computed. The only I/O from the accelerator to the HOST sends the computed kernel column back to the HOST. Note: in this setup, offloading the kernel computation and the data to an accelerator card leaves the HOST with more memory to use for caching of the

Table 7.2. *The effect of data truncation on the precision.*

	F-score:		
kernel:	float 32-bit	fixed 16-bit	
data:	8-bit		4-bit
MNIST	99.11%	99.11%	99.11%
NORB	93.34%	93.26%	92.78%

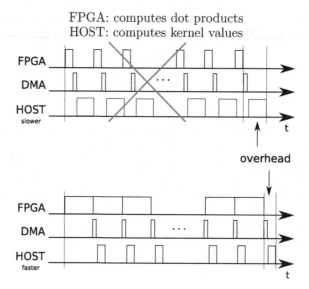

Figure 7.12 FPGA and HOST: Chunk Size Timing.

kernel columns, which might produce an additional improvement in the speed of the algorithm, as demonstrated by the super-linear speedup in Durdanovic, Cosatto, and Graf (2007).

In order to overlap HOST and FPGA computation, the computed linear kernel column is not sent all at once, but in chunks. In that way, HOST can compute the real kernel on one chunk while the FPGA is computing the next chunk. The timing analysis in Figure 7.12 reveals two cases:

1. HOST (computation) is slower than the FPGA. That happens only for tasks with vectors of a very small dimension. In such cases, FPGA accelerator is underutilized (there is not enough work per vector to utilize 128 processing elements) and we are better off computing the vector-matrix operation on the HOST itself, avoiding the high I/O costs compared to the amount of computation. Alternatively, we could port the whole SVM algorithm to the accelerator, thus avoiding I/O costs altogether.
2. FPGA (computation) is slower than the HOST. That is usually the case with images, where the data dimension is in the thousands of pixels (MNIST $d = 784$, NORB $d = 5184$).

The timing (see Figure 7.12) reveals that the cost of chunking is the overhead of the last chunk. This overhead is usually just a few percentages (the last chunk versus all the chunks) for a large dataset, but can be significant in the case of smaller datasets (small number of chunks). Therefore, it is desirable to minimize this overhead. The overhead consists of the DMA chunk transfer time and the time HOST needs to compute the real kernel. Both parts have fixed (DMA setup time, thread synchronization) and dynamic costs (DMA transfer itself, thread-computation of the kernel), or more formally:

$$T_{overhead}(c) = T_{dma}(c) + T_{HOST}(c)$$
$$T_{dma}(c) = T_{dma-setup} + T_{dma-transfer}(c)$$
$$T_{HOST}(c) = T_{thread-sync} + T_{thread-compute}(c)$$

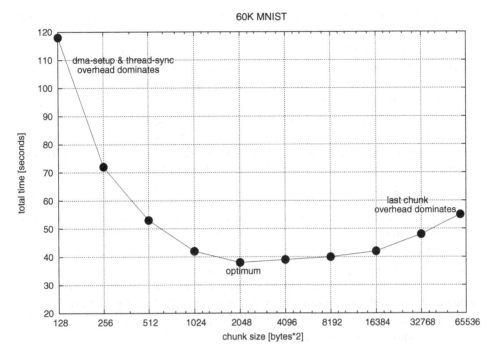

Figure 7.13 FPGA and HOST: Chunk Size Optimization.

Figure 7.13 shows the nonlinear relation between chunk sizes and the overall computation (training) time for the MNIST (60K vectors) data set. Note: the same computation on the HOST alone takes about 120 seconds. For 2M vectors, the HOST computation takes about 88 hours, whereas the HOST + accelerator requires about 28 hours.

Accelerator Speedup

The accelerator we developed does fixed-point vector-matrix product very fast by unrolling (parallelizing) the dot product between vectors. As such, its performance is strongly bound by the memory bandwidth available for streaming the matrix into the processing elements. The assumptions are that all the data (matrix) fits into the internal accelerator memory, and that the dimensionality of the vectors is sufficiently large to utilize all processing elements.

Because the acceleration is strongly bound by the available memory bandwidth, the only way we can increase the number of operations is via the ability to reduce data representation from 8 to 4 bits and/or compute more than one vector-matrix product (for different vectors, but the same matrix) at a time.

This is achieved in two ways:

- Double clocking – the co-processor can easily run at twice the speed of the data streaming to it. If we pre-load a second vector onto the co-processor, it can compute two columns at the same time.

- Double data computation – because our data is stored as nibbles, we are wasting the DSP ability to do a much wider multiplication-accumulation[17] by feeding it only a pair of nibbles at a time. Instead, we can feed it two pairs of nibbles – *properly zero separated*. For example: given three vectors $x = [x_1, x_2, x_3, x_4]$, $y = [y_1, y_2, y_3, y_4]$, and $z = [z_1, z_2, z_3, z_4]$, where x is streaming from the memory, and y and z are pre-loaded vectors, computation of $dot(x, y) = x_1 y_1 + x_2 y_2 + x_3 y_3 + x_4 y_4$ and $dot(x, z) = x_1 z_1 + x_2 z_2 + x_3 z_3 + x_4 z_4$ can be performed simultaneously if computed as $x_1(y_1 * C + z_1) + x_2(y_2 * C + z_2) + x_3(y_3 * C + z_3) + x_4(y_4 * C + z_4)$. Note that generating $(y_i * C + z_i)$ does not require any computation; it is a simple re-packing of the data during pre-loading of the vectors, where y_i is properly shifted and zero separated from z_i as $y_i 00 \ldots 00 z_i$.

During the training we can compute only one kernel column at a time if we use the second-order working set selection, two if we use the first-order selection. Classification is slightly different: all the support vectors are pre-loaded onto the FPGA memory (similar to the training), but the testing vectors are streamed from the HOST while the computed linear kernel values are streamed back. Such a setup (see Figure 7.11) is more suitable for (semi) batch testing than for the testing of individual vectors. In particular, during testing, if multiple test vectors are available, we can use the double clocking and the double data computation to compute two or four kernel columns in the time it would take to compute one.

We have to note that both the double clocking and the double data computation, although having no effects on the computation time, have a large impact on the I/O because two (or four) vectors have to be transferred where previously we only had to transfer one. This soon leads to the saturation of the PCI bus.

7.6.4 Other Parallelization

A hardware accelerator providing massive micro parallelization of the vector-matrix is orthogonal to all other parallelization techniques already described in Durdanovic et al. (2007) (see Section 7.4), and they can all be used together in this heterogeneous many-core setting.

We will mention only briefly one other parallelization possibility: multiple hardware accelerator cards in one machine. As we have already noted in Section 7.6.3, the PCI bus will eventually become a bottleneck, so this technique can be justified only for problems of a very large dimension. Our analysis shows that MNIST with $d = 784$ would saturate already for two cards, whereas NORB with $d = 5184$ would allow for four accelerator cards.

7.6.5 Beyond SVM

We have attempted to expand the hardware accelerator architecture presented here to encompass a wider variety of linear algebra operations and of variable precision (at the expense of available DSP units).

---

[17] DSP48e slice can perform $S[48]+ = A[25] * B[18] + C[48]$ multiply-accumulate operation (bit widths of operands are given in brackets).

The new version of massively parallel accelerator prototype is capable of accelerating many machine learning algorithms that use linear algebra routines as their core computation. We have successfully demonstrated acceleration of algorithms such as NN (neural networks), CNN (convolutional neural networks), GLVQ (generalized learning vector quantization), SSI (supervised semantic indexing), k-means, and SVM. For more details, we refer readers to our papers: Cadambi et al. (2009, 2010).

7.7 Results

The experimental system consisted of the AlphaData Virtex5 board and a variety of desktops and laptops that served as HOSTs. Here we report results for a dual Opteron (2.2GHZ, 12GB RAM) HOST.

To put results into perspective, the hardware accelerator prototype runs at only 125MHz (compared to a couple of gigahertz for the HOST) and consumes about 7 W (while the host consumes about 200 W). As a comparison, a GPU consumes about 130 W.

We used the MNIST dataset extended to 2M samples and the NORB dataset for comparing the performance of the accelerator prototype. The prototype is capable of sustained delivery of over 9G multiply-accumulate operations per second, which can be doubled and/or quadrupled by using the double clocking and double data computation (see Section 7.6.3) during mini-batch testing. The reported results in Table 7.3 are not the raw performance of the accelerator itself; rather, they reflect a more realistic overall speed of the HOST + accelerator system. The results are shown for four different implementations. For the FPU, all the computations were performed on the Opteron processor with two cores by the floating-point unit. For the MMX, the computation of the kernel values is done by the SIMD units of the Opteron processors. Table 7.3 presents the results obtained with the architecture described in Section 7.6. For a comparison, we also show the results obtained with a GPU (NVIDIA 8800). For training – where the core operation is vector-matrix multiplication – the maximum speed is lower than that obtained with the FPGA, despite the fact that the FPGA is running at 125MHz, while the GPU is clocked at 1.35GHz and also has 128 processing

Table 7.3. *Performance in G OP/s.*

MNIST	FPU	MMX	FPGA	GPGPU[a]
Training:	0.5	1.5	8.6	6.9
Testing:	0.67	1.67	14.5[b]	163[c]

[a] See Catanzaro, Sundaram, and Keutzer, (2008).

[b] This is with the double clocking; the raw performance is over 20G OP/s.

[c] The performance of NVIDIA 8800 is artificially high because all the test vectors were assumed to be known in advance and were pre-loaded into the GPGPU memory, allowing for the matrix-matrix (BLAS gemm) operation. The large increase in performance is a direct result of memory bandwidth not being the limiting factor: a matrix-matrix product requires $O(n^3)$ operations while using only $O(n^2)$ data.

units. For testing, all the test vectors were assumed to be known and were loaded onto the GPU board before starting the computation. More optimized matrix-matrix operations can then be used. Matrix-matrix products require $O(n^3)$ operations while using only $O(n^2)$ data, and therefore much higher speed can be achieved. Yet for real testing this is not realistic, because test vectors come in streaming mode and have to be transferred first to the GPU board. This emphasizes the significance of the data I/O for obtaining maximum performance. Ideally, for our architecture, the testing vectors would arrive in minibatches (of two or four) and could be computed in the same one-vector time.

7.8 Conclusion

We started with the SMO algorithm in its original form and have demonstrated how to scale it in various orthogonal ways: from massive macro to massive micro (custom processors) parallelization that scales to thousands of processing elements. Key for good performance is a balanced I/O speed versus compute speed. Distributed memory that is interleaved with the processing elements can reduce the required I/O bandwidth for many algorithms and is an effective way to increase performance.

What we demonstrate here is optimized for the SVM, but the same principles generalize to a wide range of algorithms. We developed a low-power massively parallel prototype hardware accelerator on an FPGA for linear algebra operations, and a great speedup for a variety of machine learning algorithms has been demonstrated (Cadambi et al. 2009). Given enough demand, a cheap, low-power processor can be produced from this prototype that would perform an order of magnitude better than the FPGA solution demonstrated here at a fraction of its cost.

References

Cadambi, S., Durdanovic, Igor, Jakkula, Venkata, Sankaradass, Murugan, Cosatto, Eric, Chakradhar, Srimat, and Graf, Hans Peter. 2009. A Massively Parallel FPGA-Based Coprocessor for Support Vector Machines. *Field-Programmable Custom Computing Machines, Annual IEEE Symposium on*, **0**, 115–122.

Cadambi, S., Majumdar, A., Becchi, M., Chakradhar, S. T., and Graf, H. P. 2010. A Programmable Parallel Accelerator for Learning and Classification.

Catanzaro, B., Sundaram, N., and Keutzer, K. 2008. Fast Support Vector Machine Training and Classification on Graphics Processors. Pages 104–111 of: *Proceedings of the 25th International Conference on Machine Learning (ICML 2008)*.

Chatterji, S., Narayanan, M., Duell, J., and Oliker, L. 2003. Performance Evaluation of Two Emerging Media Processors: VIRAM and Imagine. Page 229 of: *IPDPS*.

D'Apuzzo, M., and Marino, M. 2003. Parallel computational issues of an interior point method for solving large bound-constrained quadratic programming problems. *Parallel Computing*, **29**(4), 467–483.

Diamond, J. R., Robatmili, B., Keckler, S. W., van de Geijn, R. A., Goto, K., and Burger, D. 2008. High Performance Dense Linear Algebra on a Spatially Distributed Processor. Pages 63–72 of: *PPOPP*.

Durdanovic, I., Cosatto, E., and Graf, H. P. 2007. Large Scale Parallel SVM Implementation. In: Bottou, L., Chapelle, O., DeCoste, D., and Weston, J. (eds), *Large Scale Kernel Machines*. Cambridge, MA: MIT Press.

Fan, R.-E., Chen, P.-H., and Lin, C.-J. 2005. Working Set Selection Using Second Order Information for Training Support Vector Machines. *Journal of Machine Learning Research*, **6**, 1889–1918.

Graf, H. P., Cosatto, E., Bottou, L., Durdanovic, I., and Vapnik, V. 2005. Parallel Support Vector Machines: The Cascade SVM. Pages 521–528 of: Saul, L. K., Weiss, Y., and Bottou, L. (eds), *Advances in Neural Information Processing Systems 17*. Cambridge, MA: MIT Press.

Kapasi, U. J., Rixner, S., Dally, W. J., Khailany, B., Ahn, J. H., Mattson, P. R., and Owens, J. D. 2003. Programmable Stream Processors. *IEEE Computer*, **36**(8), 54–62.

Kelm, J. H., Johnson, D. R., Johnson, M. R., Crago, N. C., Tuohy, W., Mahesri, A., Lumetta, S. S., Frank, M. I., and Patel, S. J. 2009. Rigel: An Architecture and Scalable Programming Interface for a 1000-Core Accelerator. Pages 140–151 of: *ISCA*.

Owens, J. D., Luebke, D., Govindaraju, N., Harris, M., Krueger, J., Lefohn, A. E., and Purcell, T. J. 2007. A Survey of General-Purpose Computation on Graphics Hardware. *Computer Graphics Forum*, **26**(1), 80–113.

Platt, J. 1999. Fast Training of Support Vector Machines Using Sequential Minimal Optimization. Pages 185–208 of: Schölkopf, B., Burges, C. J. C., and Smola, A. J. (eds), *Advances in Kernel Methods – Support Vector Learning*. Cambridge, MA: MIT Press.

Rousseaux, S., Hubaux, D., Guisset, P., and Legat, J. 2007. A High Performance FPGA-Based Accelerator for BLAS Library Implementation. In: *Proceedings of the Third Annual Reconfigurable Systems Summer Institute (RSSI'07)*.

Seiler, L., Carmean, D., Sprangle, E., Forsyth, T., Abrash, M., Dubey, P., Junkins, S., Lake, A., Sugerman, J., Cavin, R., Espasa, R., Grochowski, E., Juan, T., and Hanrahan, P. 2008. Larrabee: A Many-Core x86 Architecture for Visual Computing. *ACM Transactions on Graphics*, **27**(3).

Taylor, M. B., Kim, J. S., Miller, J. E., Wentzlaff, D., Ghodrat, F., Greenwald, B., Hoffmann, H., Johnson, P., Lee, J.-W., Lee, W., Ma, A., Saraf, A., Seneski, M., Shnidman, N., Strumpen, V., Frank, M., Amarasinghe, S. P., and Agarwal, A. 2002. The Raw Microprocessor: A Computational Fabric for Software Circuits and General-Purpose Programs. *Institute of Electrical and Electronics Engineers Micro*, **22**(2), 25–35.

Zanghirati, G., and Zanni, L. 2003. A Parallel Solver for Large Quadratic Programs in Training Support Vector Machines. *Parallel Computing*, **29**(4), 535–551.

Zanni, L., Serafini, T., and Zanghirati, G. 2006. Parallel Software for Training Large Scale Support Vector Machines on Multiprocessor Systems. *Journal of Machine Learning Research*, 1467–1492.

Zhuo, L., and Prasanna, V. K. 2005. High Performance Linear Algebra Operations on Reconfigurable Systems. Page 2 of: *SC*.

CHAPTER 8

Large-Scale Learning to Rank Using Boosted Decision Trees

Krysta M. Svore and Christopher J. C. Burges

The web search ranking task has become increasingly important because of the rapid growth of the internet. With the growth of the web and the number of web search users, the amount of available training data for learning web ranking models has also increased. We investigate the problem of learning to rank on a cluster using web search data composed of 140,000 queries and approximately 14 million URLs. For datasets much larger than this, distributed computing will become essential, because of both speed and memory constraints. We compare a baseline algorithm that has been carefully engineered to allow training on the full dataset using a single machine, in order to evaluate the loss or gain incurred by the distributed algorithms we consider. The underlying algorithm we use is a boosted tree ranking algorithm called LambdaMART, where a split at a given vertex in each decision tree is determined by the split criterion for a particular feature. Our contributions are twofold. First, we implement a method for improving the speed of training when the training data fits in main memory on a single machine by distributing the vertex split computations of the decision trees. The model produced is equivalent to the model produced from centralized training, but achieves faster training times. Second, we develop a training method for the case where the training data size exceeds the main memory of a single machine. Our second approach easily scales to far larger datasets, that is, billions of examples, and is based on data distribution. Results of our methods on a real-world web dataset indicate significant improvements in training speed.

With the growth of the web, large datasets are becoming increasingly common – a typical commercial search engine may gather several terabytes per day of queries and web search interaction information. This opens a wide range of new opportunities, both because the best algorithm for a given problem may change dramatically as more data becomes available (Banko and Brill, 2001) and because such a wealth of data promises solutions to problems that could not be previously approached. In addition, powerful clusters of computers are becoming increasingly affordable. In light of these developments, the research area of understanding how to most effectively use both of these kinds of resources is rapidly developing. An example of a goal in this area might be to train a web search ranker on billions of documents, using user-clicks as labels, in a few minutes. Here, we concentrate on training a web search ranker on approximately 14 million labeled URLs, and our methods can scale to billions of URLs.

In this chapter, we investigate two synchronous approaches for learning to rank on a distributed computer that target different computational scenarios. In both cases, the base algorithm we use is LambdaMART (Wu et al., 2010; Burges, 2010), which we describe in more detail later. LambdaMART is a linear combination of regression trees and as such lends itself to parallelization in various ways. Our first method applies when the full training dataset fits in main memory on a single machine. In this case, our approach distributes the tree split computations, but not the data. Note that although this approach gives a speed-up due to parallelizing the computation, it is limited in the amount of data that can be used because all of the training data must be stored in main memory on every node.

This limitation is removed in our second approach, which applies when the full training dataset is too large to fit in main memory on a single machine. In this case, our approach distributes the training data samples and corresponding training computations and is scalable to very large amounts of training data. We develop two methods of choosing the next regression tree in the ensemble for our second approach and compare and contrast the resulting evaluation accuracy and training speed. In order to accurately investigate the benefits and challenges of our techniques, we compare to a stand-alone, centralized version that can train on the full training dataset on a single node. To this end, the stand-alone version has been carefully engineered (e.g., memory usage is aggressively trimmed by using different numbers of bits to encode different features).

Our primary contributions are:

- A boosted decision tree ranking algorithm with the computations for determining the best feature and value to split on at a given vertex in the tree distributed across cluster nodes, designed to increase the speed of training when the full training dataset fits in main memory. The model produced is equivalent to the centralized counterpart, but the speed is dramatically faster.
- A ranking algorithm with the training data and training computations distributed, designed to exploit the full training dataset, and to yield accuracy gains over training on the subset of training data that can be stored in main memory on a single machine. The model produced is not equivalent to the centralized counterpart. We assume in this case that a single machine can store only a small subset of the entire training dataset, and correspondingly assume that the centralized model cannot be trained on all of the training data.
- An investigation of two techniques for selecting the next regression tree in the ensemble.
- An investigation of using disjoint versus overlapping training datasets.
- A comprehensive study of the trade-offs in speed and accuracy of our distribution methods.

8.1 Related Work

There have been several approaches to distributed learning ranging from data sampling to software parallelization. A survey of approaches is given by Provost and Fayyad

(1999). Many distributed learning techniques have been motivated by the increasing size of datasets and their inability to fit into main memory on a single machine. A distributed learning algorithm produces a model that is either equivalent to the model produced by training on the complete dataset on a single node, or comparable but not equivalent.

We first review previous work on algorithms where the output model is equivalent. Caragea, Silvescu, and Honavar (2004) present a general strategy for transforming machine learning algorithms into distributed learning algorithms. They determine conditions for which a distributed approach is better than a centralized approach in training time and communication time. In van Uyen and Chung (2007), a synchronous, distributed version of AdaBoost is presented where subsets of the data are distributed to nodes. Exact equivalence is obtained by passing complete statistics about each sample to all other nodes. In Panda et al. (2009), a scalable approach to learning tree ensembles is presented. The approach uses the MapReduce model (Dean and Ghemawat, 2004) and can run on commodity hardware. The split computations are distributed, rather than the data samples, and are converted into Map and Reduce jobs. A challenge with the approach is that the communication cost is linear in the number of training samples, which may lead to prohibitively expensive communication costs for extremely large datasets.

The following distributed algorithms produce a model that is not equivalent to the model produced from training on a centralized dataset. In Domingos and Hulten (2000, 2001), learning algorithms, in particular k-means clustering, are scaled to arbitrarily large datasets by minimizing the number of data samples used at each step of the algorithm and by guaranteeing that the model is not significantly different from one obtained with infinite data. The training speed improvements come from sampling the training data; explicit distribution methods detailing communication costs are not presented. Fan, Stolfo, and Zhang (1999) present a distributed version of AdaBoost, where each node contains a subset of the training data. During each iteration, a classifier is built on a selected sample of training data. Two sampling methods are examined: r-sampling, where a set of samples are randomly chosen from the weighted training set, and d-sampling, where the weighted training set is partitioned into disjoint subsets, and a given subset is taken as a d-sample. After each round of boosting, the weights of all training samples are updated according to a global weight vector. The speed improvements are obtained through data sampling, whereas the communication cost scales with the number of training samples. The results indicate that their approach is comparable to boosting over the complete data set in only some cases. An extension of the work has been developed (Lazarevic, 2001; Lazarevic and Obradovic, 2002). Rather than add a classifier into the ensemble built from a single disjoint d-sample or r-sample, classifiers built from all distributed sites are combined into the ensemble. Several combination methods, including weighted voting and confidence-based weighting, are considered. Experimental results indicate that accuracy is the same or slightly better than boosting on centralized data. However, the large number of classifiers combined to form the ensemble and the communication of the global weight vector may be prohibitively expensive for practical use.

We present two methods of distributing LambdaMART. Our feature-distributed method is similar to the approach in Panda et al. (2009), except that our method has a communication cost that is constant in the number of training samples. Our data-distributed method differs from the previous methods in that (1) we aim to produce a comparable, but not equivalent, model; (2) we engineer our methods for a ranking task with billions of training samples; and (3) we use a minimal communication cost that is constant in the number of training samples. Previous methods have required communication of global statistics to achieve both exact and approximate models, and in each case the communication requirements scale with the number of training samples. Because our second approach distributes by data sample, the amount of training data (rather than the number of features) can scale with cluster size, which is usually more desirable than scaling with the number of features because the number of training samples tends to far exceed the number of features. Each tree in the ensemble is trained using a small subset of the data, and the best tree at a given iteration is chosen using the complement of its training data as a validation set, so the model is well regularized. In the remainder of this chapter, we describe our experiences with developing a distributed version of LambdaMART. We detail the benefits and challenges of our two approaches, including the communication costs, training times, and scalability to terabyte-size datasets.

8.2 LambdaMART

We use the LambdaMART algorithm for our boosted tree ranker (Wu et al., 2010; Burges, 2010). LambdaMART combines MART (Friedman, 2001) and LambdaRank (Burges et al., 2006; Burges, 2010). LambdaMART and LambdaRank were the primary components of the winning ranking system in the recent Yahoo! Learning to Rank Challenge for Web search (Yahoo! Learning to Rank Challenge, 2010; Burges et al., 2011). We briefly describe these algorithms here.

LambdaRank is a general method for learning to rank given an arbitrary cost function, and it circumvents the problem that most information retrieval measures have ill-posed gradients. It has been shown empirically that LambdaRank can optimize general Information Retrieval measures (Donmez, Svore, and Burges, 2009). A key idea in LambdaRank is to define the derivatives (of the cost with respect to the model scores) *after* the documents have been sorted by the current model scores, which circumvents the problem of defining a derivative of a measure whose value depends on the sorted order of a set of documents. These derivatives are called λ-*gradients*. A second key observation in LambdaRank is to note that many training algorithms (e.g., neural network training and MART) do not need to know the cost directly; they only need the derivatives of the cost with respect to the model scores.

For example, the λ-gradient for NDCG (Jarvelin and Kekalainen, 2000) for a pair of documents D_i and D_j, where D_i is more relevant to query q than D_j, can be defined as the product of the derivative of a convex cost C_{ij} and the NDCG gained by swapping the two documents:

$$\lambda_{ij} \equiv \left| \Delta\text{NDCG} \frac{\delta C_{ij}}{\delta o_{ij}} \right| \tag{8.1}$$

where o_{ij} is the difference in the model scores of the two documents. The λ-gradient for a single document is computed by marginalizing over the pairwise λ-gradients: $\lambda_i = \sum_{j \in P} \lambda_{ij}$, where the sum is over all pairs P for query q that contain document i.

MART is a class of boosting algorithms that may be viewed as performing gradient descent in function space, using regression trees. The final model maps an input feature vector $\mathbf{x} \in \mathbb{R}^d$ to a score $f(\mathbf{x}) \in \mathbb{R}$. MART is a class of algorithms, rather than a single algorithm, because it can be trained to minimize general costs (to solve, e.g., classification, regression, or ranking problems). The final score f can be written as

$$f(\mathbf{x}, N) = \sum_{n=1}^{N} \alpha_n f_n(\mathbf{x}) ,$$

where each $f_n(\mathbf{x}) \in \mathbb{R}$ is a function modeled by a single regression tree and the $\alpha_n \in \mathbb{R}$ are weights. Both the f_n and the α_n are learned during training. We refer to $\alpha_n f_n$ as the weak hypothesis h_n. A given f_n maps a given $\mathbf{x}$ to a real value by passing $\mathbf{x}$ down the tree, where the path (left or right) at a given node in the tree is determined by the value of a particular feature x_j, $j = 1, \ldots, d$, and where the output of the tree is taken to be a fixed value associated with each leaf, $v_{\ell n}$, $\ell = 1, \ldots, L$, $n = 1, \ldots, N$, where L is the number of leaves and N is the number of trees. For a given task (in our case, ranking), given training and validation sets, the user-chosen parameters of the training algorithm are the number of trees N, a fixed learning rate η (that multiplies every $v_{\ell n}$ for every tree), and the number of leaves[1] L. The binary decision functions at each node of each tree, and the $v_{\ell n}$ are learned during training; the decision functions are chosen to minimize a least-squares loss.

Clearly, since MART models derivatives and LambdaRank works by specifying the derivatives at any point during training, the two algorithms are well suited to each other. LambdaMART is the marriage of the two, and we refer the reader to Burges et al. (2006) and Burges (2010) for details. The set of M scores (one for each training sample) is computed, and the λ-gradient λ_m, $m = 1, \ldots, M$, of the cost function with respect to each model score is computed. Thus a single number is associated with each training sample, namely, the gradient of the cost with respect to the score that the model assigns to that sample. Tree f_n is then only a least-squares regression tree that models this set of gradients (so each leaf models a single value of the gradient). The overall cost is then reduced by taking a step along the gradient. This is often done by computing a Newton step $v_{\ell n}$ for each leaf, where the $v_{\ell n}$ can be computed exactly for some costs. Every leaf value is then multiplied by a learning rate η. Taking a step that is smaller than the optimal step size (i.e., the step size that is estimated to maximally reduce the cost) acts as a form of regularization for the model that can significantly improve test accuracy. The LambdaMART algorithm is outlined in Algorithm 18, where we have added the notion that the first model trained can be any previously trained model (step 3), which is useful for model adaptation tasks.

---

[1] One can also allow the number of leaves to vary at each iteration, but we do not consider such models here.

Algorithm 18: LambdaMART

1: **Input:** Training Data: $\{\mathbf{x}_m, y_m\}$, $m = 1, \ldots, M$;
   Number of Trees: N;
   Number of Leaves: L;
   Learning Rate: η;

2: **Output:** Model: $f(\mathbf{x}, N)$;

3: $f(\mathbf{x}, 0) = BaseModel(\mathbf{x})$ // *BaseModel may be empty*

4: **For** $n = 1$ to N **do**

5:    **For** $m = 1$ to M **do**

6:       $\lambda_m = G(q, \mathbf{x}, y, m)$ // *Calculate λ-gradient for sample m as a function of the query q and the documents and labels $\mathbf{x}$, y associated with q*

7:       $w_m = \frac{\partial \lambda_m}{\partial f(\mathbf{x}_m)}$ // *Calculate derivative of λ-gradient for sample m*

8:       $\{R_{\ell n}\}_{\ell=1}^{L}$ // *Create L-leaf regression tree on $\{\mathbf{x}_m, \lambda_m\}_{m=1}^{M}$*

9:       **For** $\ell = 1$ to L **do**

10:         $v_{\ell n} = \frac{\sum_{\mathbf{x}_m \in R_{\ell n}} \lambda_m}{\sum_{\mathbf{x}_m \in R_{\ell n}} w_m}$ // *Find the leaf values based on approximate Newton step*

11:    $f(\mathbf{x}_m, n) = f(\mathbf{x}_m, n - 1) + \eta \sum_{\ell} v_{\ell n} 1(\mathbf{x}_m \in R_{\ell n})$ // *Update model based on approximate Newton step and learning rate*

8.3 Approaches to Distributing LambdaMART

As previously noted, we focus on the task of ranking, in particular web search ranking, by learning boosted tree ensembles produced using LambdaMART. This means that the final model f is an ensemble defined as the sum $f(\mathbf{x}, N) = \sum_{n=1}^{N} h_n(\mathbf{x})$, where each h_n is a weak hypothesis. Moreover, f is constructed incrementally as weak hypotheses are added one by one. In this section, we present two approaches for distributed learning using LambdaMART:

1. Our first approach attempts to decrease training time by distributing the vertex split computations across the nodes and results in a solution that is equivalent to the solution resulting from training on all of the data on a single node (called the *centralized* model). We call this approach *feature-distributed* LambdaMART.

2. Our second approach distributes the training data across the nodes and does not produce a model equivalent to the centralized model. Rather, it attempts to dramatically reduce communication requirements without sacrificing accuracy and yields the possibility of training on billions of samples. We call this approach *data-distributed* LambdaMART. Within our second approach, we consider two weak hypothesis selection methods:
   - The master picks the weak hypothesis that maximizes the evaluation score (referred to as *full* selection)
   - The master picks a weak hypothesis at random, in order to decrease communication costs (referred to as *sample* selection)

Throughout the chapter, we assume that our distributed computer (cluster) has $K + 1$ nodes, one of which may be designated as *master*, while the others are *workers*. We denote the workers by $W_1, \ldots, W_K$ and use $[K]$ to denote the set $\{1, \ldots, K\}$.

8.3.1 A Synchronous Approach Based on Feature Distribution

In this section, we present feature-distributed LambdaMART, a synchronous distributed algorithm similar to the approach in Panda et al. (2009) that distributes the vertex split computations in the boosted decision trees. Our method differs from that in Panda et al. (2009) because the communication cost of our method is constant in the number of training samples (as opposed to linear). In addition, our method is based on MPI communication and does not use the MapReduce framework.

Recall that this approach targets the scenario where each node can store the full training dataset in main memory. Due to extensive engineering and optimization, we have been able to store a dataset with several thousand features and more than 14 million samples in main memory on a single machine. Our goal is to train on such a large dataset on a cluster more quickly than on a single machine, while outputting the same model as the centralized counterpart.

Our algorithm, detailed in Algorithm 19, proceeds as follows. Let there be K workers and no master. We are given a training set S of M instance-label pairs. Each node stores the full training set S in memory. Let A be the set of features. The features are partitioned into K subsets, $A_1, \ldots, A_K$, such that each subset is assigned to one of the K workers. Every worker maintains a copy of the ensemble $f(\mathbf{x}, n)$ and updates it after

---

Algorithm 19: Feature-Distributed LambdaMART

1: **Input:** Training Data: $\{x_m, y_m\}$, $m = 1, \ldots, M$;
    Number of Trees: N;
    Number of Leaves: L;
    Learning Rate: η;
    Number of Workers: K;
2: **Output:** Model: $f(\mathbf{x}, N)$;
3: **For** $k = 1$ to K **do**
4:    $f(\mathbf{x}, 0) = BaseModel(\mathbf{x})$ // *BaseModel may be empty*
5:    **For** $n = 1$ to N **do**
6:      **For** $m = 1$ to M **do**
7:        $\lambda_m = G(q, \mathbf{x}, y, m)$ // *Calculate λ-gradient for sample m as a function of the query q and the documents and labels $\mathbf{x}$, y associated with q*
8:        $w_m = \frac{\partial \lambda_m}{\partial f(\mathbf{x}_m)}$ // *Calculate derivative of λ-gradient for sample m*
9:      **For** $\ell = 1$ to $L - 1$ **do**
10:        φ_k // *Compute the optimal feature and split, φ_k, over features A_k on worker k*
11:        $Broadcast(\varphi_k)$ // *Broadcast φ_k to all other workers*
12:        $\varphi_* = \{\arg\max_k(\varphi_k)\}_{k=1}^K$ // *Find optimal φ_* across all φ_k's*
13:        $R_{\ell n}$ // *Create regression tree on φ_* and $\{\mathbf{x}_m, \lambda_m\}_{m=1}^M$*
14:      **For** $\ell = 1$ to L **do**
15:        $v_{\ell n} = \frac{\sum_{x_m \in R_{\ell n}} \lambda_m}{\sum_{x_m \in R_{\ell n}} w_\ell}$ // *Find the leaf values based on approximate Newton step*
16:      $f(\mathbf{x}_m, n) = f(\mathbf{x}_m, n - 1) + \eta \sum_\ell v_{\ell n} 1(\mathbf{x}_m \in R_{\ell n})$ // *Update model based on approximate Newton step and learning rate*

---

each boosting iteration n. During each boosting iteration, a regression tree $\{R_{\ell n}\}_{\ell=1}^{L}$ is constructed. Each vertex in the tree is described by an optimal feature, corresponding split threshold, and change in loss, collectively denoted by φ. Each worker k computes the optimal feature and corresponding split threshold among its set of features A_k and sends the optimal feature, threshold, and change in loss, denoted by φ_k, to all other workers.

Every worker, after it has received all of the φ_k's, determines the φ_k with the smallest loss, denoted by φ_*, creates the two new children for the model, and then computes which samples go left and which go right. Note that φ_* is the same for all workers, resulting in equivalent ensembles $f(\mathbf{x}, n)$ across all workers. The algorithm is synchronized as follows: each worker must wait until it receives all φ_k, $k = 1, \ldots, K$, before determining φ_*. Some workers will be idle while others are still computing their φ_k's.

The challenge of this approach is that it requires that every worker contain a copy of the full training dataset. A benefit is the corresponding reduction in communication: each worker sends only a limited amount of information about a single feature for each vertex split computation. The total communication cost depends on the number of leaves L in a tree and the number of workers K in the cluster, but does not depend on the number of training samples or on the number of features.

8.3.2 A Synchronous Approach Based on Data Distribution

Previous techniques of distributed boosted tree learning have focused on producing an ensemble that is equivalent to the ensemble produced by centralized training (Caragea et al., 2004; van Uyen and Chung, 2007; Panda et al., 2009). These approaches require that sufficient global statistics of the data be communicated among the master and the workers. Let there be a single master and K workers. The training set S is partitioned into K subsets, $S_1, \ldots, S_K$, and each subset resides on one of the workers of our distributed computer. For simplicity, assume that the subsets are equal in size, although this is not required in our derivation. However, we make no assumptions on how S is split, and specifically we do not require the subsets to be statistically equivalent.

Let data subset S_k reside on node k. To achieve a model equivalent to the centralized model, we could, for each vertex in the tree, send from each worker k to the master the split information for each feature, which includes which samples in S_k go left or right when split on that feature. The master then determines the best feature and split values based on S. In this case, the communication cost per regression tree is dependent on the number of vertices in the tree, the range of split values considered, the number of features, and the number of data samples. The communication resources per vertex have a linear dependence on the number of training samples, precluding the use of the approach when the number of samples is in the billions. We would like to devise an algorithm that achieves comparable accuracy but requires far less communication resources, namely, a communication cost that is independent of the number of training samples. We now describe our approach.

Assume that we have already performed $N - 1$ iterations of our algorithm and therefore the master already has an ensemble $f(\mathbf{x}, N - 1)$ composed of $N - 1$ weak hypotheses. The task is now to choose a new weak hypothesis to add to the ensemble. Each worker has a copy of $f(\mathbf{x}, N - 1)$ and uses its portion of the data to train a candidate weak hypothesis. Namely, worker k uses ensemble $f(\mathbf{x}, N - 1)$ and dataset S_k to generate the weak hypothesis $h_{N,k}(\mathbf{x})$ and sends it to all other workers.

Each worker now evaluates all of the candidates constructed by the other workers. Namely, worker k evaluates the set $\{h_{N,k}(\mathbf{x})\}_{[K]\setminus\{k\}}$, where $f_k(\mathbf{x}, N) = f(\mathbf{x}, N - 1) + h_{N,k}(\mathbf{x})$, and calculates the set of values $\{C_k(f_k(\mathbf{x}, N))\}_{[K]\setminus\{k\}}$ and returns these values to the master, where C is the evaluation measure.

The master then chooses the candidate with the largest evaluation score C on the entire training set S. This step of cross-validation adds a further regularization component to the training. We call this method the *full* selection method. Letting V denote the set of indices of candidates, the master calculates

$$C(f_k(\mathbf{x}, N)) = \sum_{i \in V} C_i(f_k(\mathbf{x}, N)) ,$$

for each candidate k. Finally, the master chooses the candidate with the largest average score, and sets

$$f(\mathbf{x}, N) = \arg\max f_k(\mathbf{x}, N) \, C(f_k(\mathbf{x}, N)) .$$

The master sends the index k of the selected weak hypothesis to all workers. Each worker then updates the model: $f(\mathbf{x}, N) = f(\mathbf{x}, N - 1) + h_{N,k}(\mathbf{x})$. On the next iteration, all of the workers attempt to add another weak learner to $f(\mathbf{x}, N)$. This procedure is shown in Algorithm 20.

The intuition behind our approach is that if the hypotheses are sufficiently diverse, then the hypotheses will exhibit dramatically different evaluation scores. The cross-validation ideally results in an ensemble of weak hypotheses that is highly regularized; we test this hypothesis through experiments in Section 8.4.

The communication cost of our approach is dependent on the size of the weak hypothesis and the number of workers, but is not dependent on the size of the training data. In addition, communication occurs only *once* per boosting iteration, removing the need to communicate once per vertex split computation. Each weak hypothesis must be communicated to all other workers, and the resulting evaluation scores must be communicated from each worker to the master. Essentially, the scores are an array of doubles, where the length of the array is the number of weak hypotheses evaluated. Once the master has determined the best weak hypothesis to add to the ensemble, the master need only communicate the index of the best model back to the workers. Each worker updates its model accordingly.

8.3.3 Adding Randomization

The straightforward data-distributed approach presented in Section 8.3.2 has the workers performing two different types of tasks: constructing candidate weak hypotheses and evaluating candidate ensembles that were constructed by others. If the training data size is fixed, and as the number of workers K increases, each worker trains on a smaller portion of the training data, namely $\frac{|S|}{K}$, then the task of constructing candidates can be completed faster. On the other hand, assuming that evaluation time is linear in the number of samples, the total time spent evaluating other candidates stays roughly constant. To see this, note that each worker has to evaluate $K - 1$ candidates on $\frac{|S|}{K}$ samples, for a total evaluation time on the order of $|S|\frac{K-1}{K}$. To resolve this problem, we need to reduce the number of evaluations; we accomplish this using the power of sampling. We call this method the *sample* selection method.

The algorithm proceeds as before: all of the workers are given the same ensemble $f(\mathbf{x}, N - 1)$ and use their datasets to construct candidates. Worker k constructs $f_k(\mathbf{x}, N)$. Rather than the master receiving K candidate weak hypotheses, it chooses a random worker k among the set and the chosen worker communicates $h_{N,k}(\mathbf{x})$ to all other workers (replacing steps 13–15 in Algorithm 20 with random selection of a hypothesis). The randomized selection of a candidate removes the need for extensive evaluation and requires only communicating the chosen candidate weak hypothesis from the master to the workers. This rough estimate may be enough to offer additional regularization over always choosing the same data sample to construct the weak hypothesis. It eliminates the expensive evaluation step previously required for each candidate at each boosting iteration in the full selection method and will work well if the hypotheses in fact exhibit very little diversity.

Algorithm 20: Data-Distributed LambdaMART

1: **Input:** Training Data: $\{x_m, y_m\}$, $m = 1, \ldots, M$;
    Number of Trees: N;
    Number of Leaves: L;
    Learning Rate: η;
    Number of Workers: K;

2: **Output:** Model: $f(\mathbf{x}, N)$;

3: **For** $k = 1$ to K **do**

4:    $f(\mathbf{x}, 0) = BaseModel(\mathbf{x})$ // *BaseModel may be empty*

5:    **For** $n = 1$ to N **do**

6:       **For each** $m \in S_k$ **do**

7:          $\lambda_m = G(q, \mathbf{x}, y, m)$ // *Calculate λ-gradient for sample m as a function of the query q and the documents and labels $\mathbf{x}$, y associated with q, where m is in the fraction of training data S_k on worker k*

8:          $w_m = \frac{\partial \lambda_m}{\partial f(\mathbf{x}_m)}$ // *Calculate derivative of λ-gradient for sample m*

9:          $\{R_{\ell n}\}_{\ell=1}^{L}$ // *Create L-leaf regression tree $\{R_{\ell n k}\}_{\ell=1}^{L}$ on $\{\mathbf{x}_m, \lambda_m\}$, $m \in S_k$*

10:         **For** $\ell = 1$ to L **do**

11:            $v_{\ell n} = \frac{\sum_{\mathbf{x}_m \in R_{\ell n}} \lambda_m}{\sum_{\mathbf{x}_m \in R_{\ell n}} w_m}$ // *Find the leaf values based on approximate Newton step*

12:         $f_k(\mathbf{x}_m, n) = f(\mathbf{x}_m, n - 1) + \eta \sum_\ell v_{\ell n} 1(\mathbf{x}_m \in R_{\ell n k})$ // *Update model based on approximate Newton step and learning rate*

13:         $\{C_k(f_k(\mathbf{x}, n))\}_{[K]\backslash\{k\}}$ // *Compute candidate weak hypotheses cost values*

14:         $C(f_k(\mathbf{x}, n)) = \sum_{i \in V} C_i(f_k(\mathbf{x}, n))$ // *Evaluate candidate weak hypotheses from all other workers*

15:         $f(\mathbf{x}, n) = \arg\max f_k(\mathbf{x}, n) C(f_k(\mathbf{x}, n))$ // *Choose best weak hypothesis and update model*

8.4 Experiments

In this section, we evaluate our proposed methods on a real-world web dataset. We ran all of our experiments on a 40-node MPI cluster, running Microsoft HPC Server 2008. One node serves as the cluster scheduler, and the remaining 39 are compute nodes. Each node has two 4-core Intel Xeon 5550 processors running at 2.67GHz and 48GB of RAM. Each node is connected to two 1Gb Ethernet networks: a private network dedicated to MPI traffic and a public network. Each network is provided by a Cisco 3750e Ethernet switch. The communication layer between nodes on our cluster was written using MPI.NET.

Total train time was measured as the time in seconds between the completion of the loading of the data on the cluster nodes and the completion of the final round of boosting. The time does not include loading data or testing the final model. To mitigate effects of varying cluster conditions, we ran each experimental setting three times and plot all three values.

We swept a range of parameter values for each experiment: we varied the learning rate η from 0.05 to 0.5 and the number of leaves L from 20 to 220, and trained for $N = 1000$ boosting iterations. We determined the best iteration and set of parameter values based on the evaluation accuracy of the model on a validation set.

8.4.1 Data

Our real-world web data collection contains queries sampled from query log files of a commercial search engine and corresponding URLs. All queries are English queries and contain up to 10 query terms. We perform some stemming on queries. Each query is associated with on average 150–200 documents (URLs), each with a vector of several thousand feature values extracted for the query–URL pair and a human-generated relevance label $l \in \{0, 1, 2, 3, 4\}$, with 0 meaning document d is not relevant to query q and 4 meaning d is highly relevant to q. The dataset contains 140,000 queries and corresponding URLs (14,533,212 query-URL pairs). We refer to the dataset size in terms of the number queries, where an n-query dataset means a dataset consisting of all query-URL pairs for those n queries.

We divide the dataset into train, valid, and test sets by selecting a random 80% of samples for training, a random 10% for validation, and a random 10% for test. We require that for a given query, all corresponding URLs (samples) reside in the same data split. In some experiments, we reduce the amount of training data by $\frac{1}{k}$, $k = \{2, 4, 8, 16, 32\}$. The resulting change in accuracy will indicate the sensitivity of the algorithms to the training data size.

8.4.2 Evaluation Measure

We evaluate using Normalized Discounted Cumulative Gain (NDCG) (Jarvelin and Kekalainen, 2000), a widely used measure for search metrics. It operates on multilevel relevance labels; in our work, relevance is measured on a five-level scale. NDCG for a given query q is defined as follows:

$$\text{NDCG@}T(q) = \frac{100}{Z} \sum_{r=1}^{T} \frac{2^{l(r)} - 1}{\log(1 + r)} \tag{8.2}$$

where $l(r) \in \{0, \ldots, 4\}$ is the relevance label of the document at rank position r and T is the truncation level to which NDCG is computed. Z is chosen such that the perfect ranking would result in $\text{NDCG@}T(q) = 100$. Mean NDCG@T is the normalized sum over all queries: $\frac{1}{Q} \sum_{q=1}^{Q} \text{NDCG@}T(q)$. NDCG is particularly well suited for web search applications because it accounts for multilevel relevance labels, and the truncation level can be set to model user behavior. In our studies, we evaluate our results using mean NDCG@1, 3, 10. For brevity, we write NDCG@1, 3, 10. We also perform a significance t-test with a significance level of 0.05. A significant difference should be read as significant at the 95% confidence level. All accuracy results are reported on the same 14K-query test set.

8.4.3 Time Complexity Comparison

We first examine the speed improvements and communication requirements of our distributed LambdaMART algorithms compared to the centralized LambdaMART algorithm. A major advantage of training a distributed learning algorithm over a centralized learning algorithm, in addition to being able to take advantage of more data, is the decrease in training time.

The total training time complexities of centralized LambdaMART, feature-distributed LambdaMART, and data-distributed LambdaMART are $O(|S||A|)$, $O(|S||A_k|)$, and $O(|S_k||A|)$, respectively, where $|S|$ is the size of the training data, $|A|$ is the number of features, and k indexes the node. Sample data-distributed LambdaMART requires only a constant additional communication cost and no evaluation cost. When the number of features is large, the feature-distributed algorithm is significantly more efficient than the centralized algorithm. When $|A| \ll |S|$, which is commonly the case, the sample data-distributed algorithm is significantly more efficient than both the centralized and feature-distributed algorithms.

Figures 8.1a–d show the difference in total training time between centralized LambdaMART and feature-distributed LambdaMART. We vary the number of workers K from 1 to 32, and the number of features $|A|$ from 500 to 4,000. For feature-distributed LambdaMART, $\frac{|A|}{K}$ features are assigned to each node. We employ the same set of parameters for each algorithm to provide fair training time comparisons; the parameters are set to $\eta = 0.1$, $N = 500$, and $L = 200$. We evaluated the total train time of feature-distributed LambdaMART on two types of clusters. The first cluster is as previously described, and we denote it as type I. Each node in the second cluster, denoted as type II, has 32.0 GB RAM and two quad-core Intel Xeon 5430 processors running at 2.67 GHz.

As shown in Figure 8.1, feature-distributed LambdaMART (solid lines) achieves significantly faster training times than centralized LambdaMART (dotted lines) on both clusters. When trained on type II with 500 features, feature-distributed LambdaMART with 8 workers achieves almost a two-fold speed-up over centralized LambdaMART

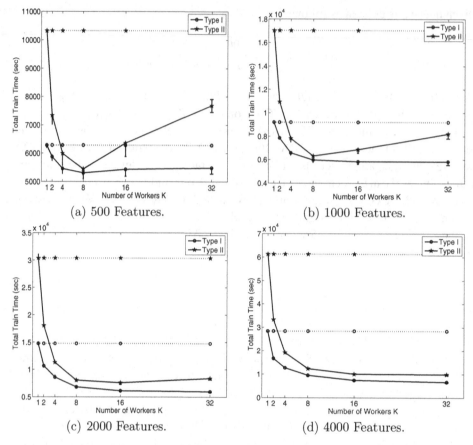

Figure 8.1 Number of workers K versus total training time in seconds for centralized (dotted) and feature-distributed (solid) LambdaMART, for 500–4,000 features and two cluster types. Centralized was trained on the full dataset for all K. Each experimental setting was run three times; times are shown by the bars around each point. Invisible bars indicate that times are roughly equivalent.

(Figure 8.1a). When the number of features is small, as the number of workers increases, the cost of communication among the workers outweighs the speed-ups due to feature distribution, as seen by the increase in time when $K \geq 8$ for type II (Figure 8.1a, b). However, as the number of features increases, communication occupies a smaller percentage of the training time, resulting in decreasing training times. For example, feature-distributed LambdaMART on type II with 4000 features (Figure 8.1d) exhibits decreasing training times as the number of workers increases and achieves a factor of 6 speed-up over centralized LambdaMART when trained on 32 workers. When trained on type I, feature-distributed LambdaMART exhibits decreasing training times as the number of workers grows; with 32 workers training on 4000 features, roughly a three-fold speed-up is obtained.

Our *full* data-distributed algorithm incurs an additional cost for the evaluation of weak hypotheses and the communication of the evaluation results and the chosen weak hypothesis. The evaluation cost is linear in the number of training samples $|S|$, but unlike previous methods, the communication cost is independent of the number of

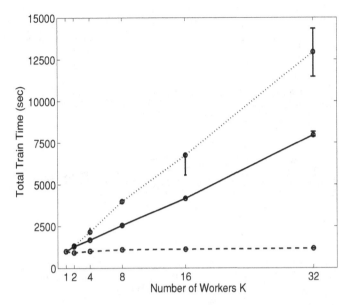

Figure 8.2 Number of workers K: total data used $= 3,500K$ queries versus training time in seconds for centralized (dotted), full data-distributed (solid), and sample data-distributed (dashed) LambdaMART with $L = 20$ leaves. Each experimental setting was run three times; times are shown by the bars around each point. Invisible bars indicate that times are roughly equivalent.

training samples; therefore, network communication is not a bottleneck as $|S|$ increases to billions of samples. The communication cost scales linearly with the number of nodes and is dependent on the size of the weak learner being broadcast, which is dependent on the number of leaves and the precision of the split thresholds (and is relatively small in practice). Previous approaches consider passing the weight vectors or passing data samples; these approaches are much more expensive in communication time.

The bottleneck of our full data-distributed approach is the cost of evaluation. Our *sample* data-distributed approach has only the additional cost of communicating the randomly chosen weak hypothesis to all nodes and does not require evaluation. Both data-distributed algorithms result in shorter training times than the centralized algorithm because the training data per worker k is smaller, $\frac{|S|}{k}$.

Figure 8.2 shows the number of workers versus the total training time in seconds, for weak hypotheses with varying numbers of leaves, for centralized and for full and sample data-distributed LambdaMART. The same parameter settings are used for the three approaches: $L = 20, N = 1,000$, and $\eta = 0.1$. The x-axis indicates the number of workers K, where each worker trains on $\frac{|S|}{32} \approx 3,500$ queries; with respect to centralized LambdaMART, the x-axis indicates the number of training queries residing on the single worker, $\frac{|S|}{32}K$. The point at $K = 1$ represents training centralized LambdaMART on $\frac{|S|}{32} \approx 3,500$ queries. As K increases, the total train time increases because the communication costs grow with the number of workers K. Because the evaluation and communication costs are almost negligible in sample data-distributed LambdaMART, the total train time is roughly equivalent to training on a single node, even though the amount of training data across the cluster increases with K.

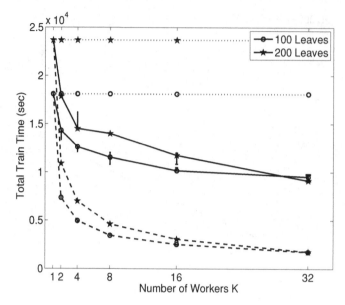

Figure 8.3 Number of workers K versus training time in seconds for centralized (dotted), full data-distributed (solid), and sample data-distributed (dashed) LambdaMART on 14 million samples (query–URL pairs). Each experimental setting was run three times; times are shown by the bars around each point.

We next evaluate the time required to train on $|S|$ queries, where the queries are split among K workers. For the centralized algorithm, a single worker trains on $|S|$ queries. We set $\eta = 0.1$, $L = \{100, 200\}$, and $N = 1000$. Figure 8.3 plots the number of workers K versus the total train time in seconds; every point represents a model trained on all $|S|$ queries. For the data-distributed algorithms, the training data S is split among K workers: as K increases, the number of queries on a single worker ($\frac{|S|}{K}$) decreases, but the total number of queries across all nodes remains constant ($|S|$). The two points at $K = 1$ represent the training times of centralized LambdaMART trained on fourteen million URLs. The central model at $K = 1$ is plotted at all K values for reference (shown by the dotted lines). When $K > 1$, the train times of full and sample data-distributed LambdaMART are significantly less than those of the centralized algorithm. Particularly notable is the reduction in train time obtained by the sample data-distributed LambdaMART algorithm.

8.4.4 Accuracy Comparison

In this section, we evaluate the prediction accuracy of our data-distributed algorithm using the full and sample selection strategies.[2] We consider the case where the training data S cannot fit in the main memory of a single machine. We compare the accuracy of our data-distributed algorithms and the accuracy of the centralized algorithm on a separate test set consisting of 14K queries, while varying the number of nodes K and

---

[2] Recall that the feature-distributed algorithm outputs the same model as the centralized algorithm and thus has the same prediction accuracy.

Table 8.1. *The learning rate η and the number of leaves L for centralized LambdaMART, and full and sample data-distributed LambdaMART, respectively. The first set of columns are the parameters when training on 3,500 queries per worker; in the central case, a single worker trains on 3,500K queries. The second set of columns are the parameters when training on 7,000 overlapping queries per worker; in the central case, a single worker trains on 7,000K queries. The final columns contain the parameters when training on $\frac{|S|}{K}$ queries per worker; in the central case, a single worker trains on $\frac{|S|}{K}$ queries.*

	3500		7000		All	
K	η	L	η	L	η	L
1	0.1, 0.1, 0.1	20, 20, 20	0.1, 0.1, 0.1	80, 80, 80	0.1, 0.1, 0.1	20, 20, 20
2	0.1, 0.05, 0.05	80, 80, 80	0.1, 0.1, 0.1	180, 180, 180	0.1, 0.1, 0.1	80, 190, 200
4	0.1, 0.1, 0.05	180, 80, 80	0.1, 0.05, 0.05	200, 200, 200	0.1, 0.05, 0.05	180, 170, 200
8	0.1, 0.05, 0.05	200, 120, 120	0.1, 0.05, 0.05	200, 200, 200	0.05, 0.05, 0.05	200, 180, 200
16	0.1, 0.05, 0.05	200, 140, 140	0.1, 0.05, 0.05	200, 200, 200	0.1, 0.05, 0.05	200, 170, 160
32	0.1, 0.05, 0.05	200, 140, 140	0.1, 0.05, 0.05	200, 140, 140	0.1, 0.05, 0.05	200, 100, 140

the amount of training data. Table 8.1 lists for each experimental setting the model parameters that produced the best validation accuracy.

The first experiment evaluates the change in accuracy of our data-distributed algorithms as the number of workers increases. We simulate memory constraints by assuming one worker can store at most 3,500 queries – in order to exploit more training data, the data must reside on separate workers. As the number of workers increases, it simulates the case where more and more training data is available, but the memory capacity of a single worker remains the same. The training set S is randomly partitioned into 32 disjoint subsets, and each subset resides on one of the 32 nodes in our cluster. Each partition contains roughly 3,500 queries and corresponding URLs. When $K = 1$, a single worker trains on 3,500 queries, when $K = 2$, two workers train on 3,500 queries each, and so on.

Figure 8.4 plots the number of workers K versus NDCG for full and sample data-distributed LambdaMART.[3] The training data distributed among the workers in the cluster acts as additional validation data because it is used for the evaluation and selection of the weak hypothesis. Full and sample selection strategies result, for each K, in similar NDCG scores, and exhibit NDCG accuracy increases as K increases. Having 3,500K queries in the cluster, for $K = \{8, 16, 32\}$, yields significant gains in NDCG@3 and 10 over training on 3,500 queries ($K = 1$). Thus, additional data, although mostly used for validation, significantly increases NDCG accuracy.

In Figure 8.4d, we analyze the effect of lifting the memory constraint and plot the centralized algorithm accuracy trained on 3,500K queries (dotted line) on a single worker, for increasing values of K. For $K = \{4, 8, 16, 32\}$, the resulting model is significantly better than the corresponding data-distributed models trained on 3,500K queries, indicating that when it is possible to use additional data directly for training, it is preferable to using it for cross-validation.

Somewhat surprisingly, as the amount of data increases, even though the data is highly distributed, the optimal values of the learning rate η and number of leaves L change dramatically for data-distributed LambdaMART (see Table 8.1). Even though

---

[3] The corresponding training time plots were given in Figure 8.2.

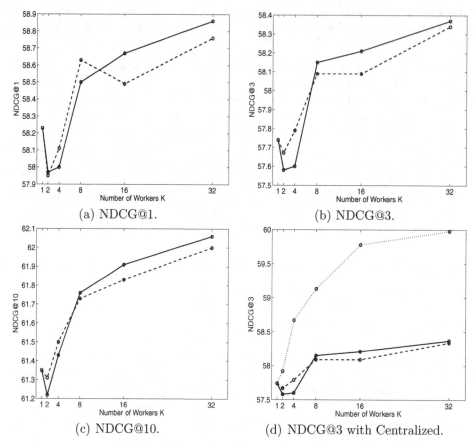

Figure 8.4 Number of workers K versus NDCG@1, 3, 10 for full (solid) and sample (dashed) data-distributed LambdaMART. Each worker trains on 3,500 queries. Figure (d) includes centralized LambdaMART (dotted) trained on $3,500K$ queries at each x-axis point. Signficant differences are stated in the text.

it is only the amount of validation data that increases as K increases, the parameters behave similarly to increasing the amount of centralized training data.

For our second experiment, we investigate how training on overlapping sets of data affects NDCG accuracy. Assume that a single worker can store at most 7,000 queries, and let the amount of training data available be $3,500K$ queries. We construct our overlapping sets as follows: The training data S is divided into K sets, $S_1, \ldots, S_K$. Worker k stores set S_k and set S_{k+1}, resulting in 7,000 queries. For example, when $K = 4$, $S_1 + S_2, S_2 + S_3, S_3 + S_4, S_4 + S_1$ reside on workers 1, 2, 3, 4, respectively. The total number of unique queries in the cluster remains $3,500K$. This approach can easily scale to larger datasets.

Figure 8.5 plots the number of workers K versus NDCG, where each worker contains an overlapping set of 7,000 queries, compared to 3,500 queries. The accuracy gains from training on 7,000 queries per worker instead of 3,500 are significant for all K at NDCG@3 and 10, further indicating that training on more data is better than validating over more data, and also indicating that the samples need not be unique across the workers. In particular, training $K = 8$ workers on overlapping 7,000-query sets results

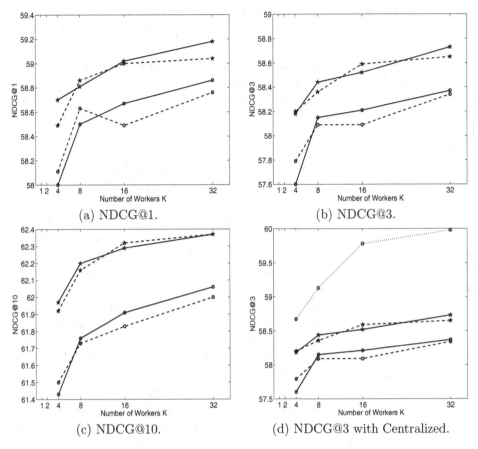

(a) NDCG@1. (b) NDCG@3.

(c) NDCG@10. (d) NDCG@3 with Centralized.

Figure 8.5 Number of workers K versus NDCG@1, 3, 10 for full (solid) and sample (dashed) data-distributed LambdaMART. Each worker trains on 7,000 overlapping queries (stars). Results from training on 3,500 queries per worker (circles) are plotted for comparison. Figure (d) includes centralized LambdaMART (dotted) trained on $3,500K$ queries at each x-axis point. Significant differences are stated in the text.

in similar accuracy to training $K = 32$ workers on 3,500-query sets. In all cases, full and sample selection strategies result in similar accuracies.

In Figure 8.5d, we again lift the memory constraint and plot the NDCG@3 accuracy of the central model on $3,500K$ queries (dotted line). The results highlight the benefit of increasing the amount of training data per worker over using additional validation data, as seen by the significant gap between the central and data-distributed models.

Even though the central model is superior in accuracy to our data-distributed models (assuming memory of a single worker is not constrained), our data-distributed algorithms exhibit significant gains when the memory of a single worker is exhausted. In this scenario, a benefit of our data-distributed algorithm is not only parallelized training, but also that the amount of information communicated between the master and the workers is independent of the amount of training data; it is dependent on the number of workers and the size of a weak hypothesis. Our full data-distributed algorithm relies on the diversity of each weak hypothesis, yet on examination of the NDCG scores of the weak hypotheses, we found that during early rounds of boosting, the weak hypotheses exhibited diversity, but after only a few rounds of boosting, the weak hypotheses achieved almost identical NDCG scores on the large validation data, indicating that we may be able to eliminate the evaluation step entirely and select a worker at random to produce the weak hypothesis at each iteration.

By eliminating the evaluation step at each iteration, the training time decreases dramatically, as previously shown in Figure 8.2, because the cost of evaluation is linear in the size of the largest split S_k, and the accuracies are equivalent to choosing the best weak hypothesis based on NDCG evaluation. Thus, our sample selection algorithm can be efficiently applied to billions of samples and achieve comparable accuracy to the full selection strategy. The sample selection algorithm also points to the advantages that an asynchronous distributed approach may have over a synchronous one. Because each worker k trains on a random subset S_k of the training data, then an asynchronous algorithm could assign idle workers different tasks, such as evaluating or training a regression tree for a future iteration. Such an approach could possibly yield improvements in speed or accuracy by taking advantage of the large number of workers available at any given time.

Our sample approach can also be applied to centralized training: at each round of boosting, sample the training data and train a weak hypothesis on that sample. If the complete training dataset fits in memory on a single machine, then the training time will decrease by training on a sample of the data during each boosting iteration. However, if the training data must reside on separate machines, then to train on a single machine, at each round of boosting, the sample must be sent to the machine and then loaded into memory on the machine. The sample must be sampled across all of the machines. The process of communicating the data samples from the many nodes that store the data will be costly and will prohibit the use of the algorithm on very large datasets.

8.4.5 Additional Remarks on Data-Distributed LambdaMART

We have shown that our data-distributed approach is a viable method for exploiting additional training data when the main memory of a single machine is exceeded. In this section, we consider the case where the main memory of the workers is not exhausted and we have a fixed amount of training data. One goal of a distributed learning algorithm is to achieve comparable or better accuracy compared to the centralized algorithm, but with much shorter training times. We conduct a series of experiments to determine if our data-distributed approach achieves comparable accuracy with shorter training times compared to the centralized algorithm.

We first determine the effect of decreasing the training data size on the centralized algorithm's accuracy. Let the size of the training set residing on the central machine decrease as $\frac{|S|}{K}$, with increasing values of K. Figure 8.6 plots the training set size versus NDCG for the centralized model (dotted line). When training on 50% of the training data, the NDCG@1, 3, 10 accuracy compared to training on 100% of the data is statistically similar. It is also noteworthy that as the training set size decreases, the optimal number of leaves decreases, whereas the optimal learning rate stays constant across the training data sizes (see Table 8.1).

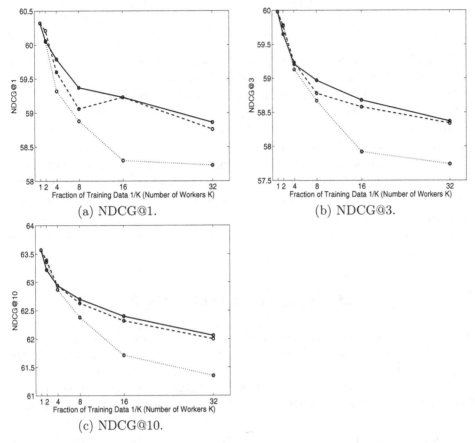

(a) NDCG@1.

(b) NDCG@3.

(c) NDCG@10.

Figure 8.6 Number of workers K versus NDCG@1, 3, 10 for centralized (dotted) and full (solid) and sample (dashed) data-distributed LambdaMART. Each worker trains on $\frac{|S|}{K}$ queries. The central model was trained on $\frac{|S|}{K}$ queries on a single worker. Significant differences are stated in the text.

We next determine the accuracy of full and sample data-distributed LambdaMART, where the training data S is split across K workers and each worker contains $\frac{|S|}{K}$ queries.[4] Figure 8.6 contains the centralized and full and sample data-distributed accuracy results. In the central case, the x-axis indicates the size of the training set on the single node. In the data-distributed cases, the x-axis indicates the number of workers K and correspondingly the amount of training data $\frac{|S|}{K}$ on a given worker. The results indicate that choosing a weak hypothesis among the K nodes, either by full or sample selection, is better than choosing the same weak hypothesis from the same node at each iteration. This is seen by looking at a given value of K: the data-distributed NDCG scores are consistently higher than the centralized NDCG scores and statistically significantly higher for $K \geq 16$. However, there is not a single point on the data-distributed curves that outperforms training on the full data set using the centralized algorithm (the point

---

[4] The corresponding training time plot was given in Figure 8.3.

at $K = 1$). Splitting the data across an increasing number of workers K causes a gradual and continual drop in accuracy, with significant losses compared to the point at $K = 1$ when $K \geq 4$.

The experiment additionally shows that choosing a single weak hypothesis from a worker at random (sample selection) performs similarly to choosing the best weak hypothesis among the K workers based on the evaluation step.

Finally, we determine if training on larger overlapping sets of data achieves comparable accuracy to the central model, but with less training time. We consider $K = 4$ workers and divide the training data S into four sets S_1, S_2, S_3, S_4. Each set contains 25% of the full training set. Worker k is assigned sets $S_k + S_{k+1} + S_{k+2}$ and thus produces a weak hypothesis based on 75% of the full training set. At each iteration, we use sample selection to produce the next weak hypothesis in the ensemble. We find that training on 75% of the training queries per node yields equivalent NDCG scores to the central model trained on 100% of the training data, but trains in less than half of the time.

8.5 Conclusions and Future Work

In summary, we have presented two approaches for distributing LambdaMART. The first distributes by feature by distributing the vertex split computations and requires that the full training set fit in main memory on each node in the cluster. Our feature-distributed approach achieves up to six-fold significant speed-ups over centralized LambdaMART while producing the same model and accuracy. Our second approach distributes the data across the nodes in the compute cluster and employs one of two strategies for selection of the next weak hypothesis: (1) select the next weak hypothesis based on evaluation scores on the training data residing on other nodes (full), or (2) select the next weak hypothesis at random (sample). We have shown that both selection strategies offer significant training-time speed-ups resulting in training up to 2–4 times faster than centralized LambdaMART. In particular, sample data-distributed LambdaMART demonstrates no significant accuracy loss compared to full data-distributed LambdaMART and achieves even more significant training time speed-ups. Unlike the feature-distributed approach, our data-distributed approaches can scale to billions of training samples.

Our data-distributed algorithms, however, do not match the centralized algorithm in accuracy. The accuracy results were disappointing and indicate that using data for massive cross-validation results in significant accuracy loss. In the future, it is worth determining a distributed method that can scale to billions of examples, but with accuracy that is equivalent or superior to training on centralized data, and with a communication cost that does not scale with the number of samples. Future work needs to be done to determine the bottlenecks of our data-distributed approaches and to determine how best to take advantage of distributed data without sacrificing the speed-ups obtained by our methods. We have developed a first step toward achieving this goal in that we have presented a method where the communication is independent of the number of samples.

8.6 Acknowledgments

We thank Ofer Dekel for his insightful ideas, his invaluable contributions to code and cluster development, and his assistance in running experiments.

References

Banko, M., and Brill, E. 2001. Scaling to Very Very Large Corpora for Natural Language Disambiguation. Pages 26–33 of: *Association for Computational Linguistics (ACL)*.

Burges, C. J., Svore, K. M., Benett, P. N., Pastusiak, A., and Wu, Q. 2011. Learning to Rank Using an Ensemble of Lambda-Gradient Models. *Special Edition of JMLR: Proceedings of the Yahoo! Learning to Rank Challenge*, **14**, 25–35.

Burges, C. J. C. 2010. *From RankNet to LambdaRank to LambdaMART: An Overview*. Technical Report MSR-TR-2010-82. Microsoft Research.

Burges, C. J. C., Ragno, R., and Le, Q. V. 2006. Learning to Rank with Non-Smooth Cost Functions. In: *Advances in Neural Information Processing Systems (NIPS)*.

Caragea, D., Silvescu, A., and Honavar, V. 2004. A Framework for Learning from Distributed Data using Sufficient Statistics and Its Application to Learning Decision Trees. *International Journal of Hybrid Intelligent Systems*, **1**(1–2), 80–89.

Dean, J., and Ghemawat, S. 2004. MapReduce: Simplified Data Processing on Large Clusters. In: *Symposium on Operating System Design and Implementation (OSDI)*.

Domingos, P., and Hulten, G. 2000. Mining High-Speed Data Streams. Pages 71–80 of: *SIGKDD Conference on Knowledge and Data Mining (KDD)*.

Domingos, P., and Hulten, G. 2001. A General Method for Scaling Up Machine Learning Algorithms and its Application to Clustering. In: *International Conference on Machine Learning (ICML)*.

Donmez, P., Svore, K., and Burges, C. J. C. 2009. On the Local Optimality of LambdaRank. In: *ACM SIGIR Conference on Research and Development in Information Retrieval (SIGIR)*.

Fan, W., Stolfo, S., and Zhang, J. 1999. The Application of AdaBoost for Distributed, Scalable and Online Learning. Pages 362–366 of: *SIGKDD Conference on Knowledge and Data Mining (KDD)*.

Friedman, J. 2001. Greedy Function Approximation: A Gradient Boosting Machine. *Annals of Statistics*, **25**(5), 1189–1232.

Jarvelin, K., and Kekalainen, J. 2000. IR Evaluation Methods for Retrieving Highly Relevant Documents. Pages 41–48 of: *ACM SIGIR Conference on Research and Development in Information Retrieval (SIGIR)*.

Lazarevic, A. 2001. The distributed boosting algorithm. Pages 311–316 of: *SIGKDD Conference on Knowledge Discovery and Data Mining (KDD)*.

Lazarevic, A., and Obradovic, Z. 2002. Boosting Algorithms for Parallel and Distributed Learning. *Distributed and Parallel Databases*, **11**, 203–229.

Panda, B., Herbach, J. S., Basu, S., and Bayardo, R. J. 2009. PLANET: Massively Parallel Learning of Tree Ensembles with MapReduce. In: *International Conference on Very Large Databases (VLDB)*.

Provost, F., and Fayyad, U. 1999. A Survey of Methods for Scaling Up Induction Algorithms. *Data Mining and Knowledge Discovery*, **3**, 131–169.

van Uyen, N. T., and Chung, T. 2007. A New Framework for Distributed Boosting Algorithm. Pages 420–423 of: *Future Generation Communication and Networking (FGCN)*.

Wu, Q., Burges, C. J. C., Svore, K. M., and Gao, J. 2010. Adapting Boosting for Information Retrieval Measures. *Journal of Information Retrieval*, **13**(3), 254–270.

Yahoo! Learning to Rank Challenge. 2010. http://learningtorankchallenge.yahoo.com/.

CHAPTER 9

The Transform Regression Algorithm

Ramesh Natarajan and Edwin Pednault

Massive training datasets, ranging in size from tens of gigabytes to several terabytes, arise in diverse machine learning applications in areas such as text mining of web corpora, multimedia analysis of image and video data, retail modeling of customer transaction data, bioinformatic analysis of genomic and microarray data, medical analysis of clinical diagnostic data such as functional magnetic resonance imaging (fMRI) images, and environmental modeling using sensor and streaming data. Provost and Kolluri (1999) in their overview of machine learning with massive datasets, emphasize the need for developing parallel algorithms and implementations for these applications.

In this chapter, we describe the Transform Regression (TReg) algorithm (Pednault, 2006), which is a general-purpose, non-parametric methodology suitable for a wide variety of regression applications. TReg was originally created for the data mining component of the IBM InfoSphere Warehouse product, guided by a challenging set of requirements:

1. The modeling time should be comparable to linear regression.
2. The resulting models should be compact and efficient to apply.
3. The model quality should be reliable without any further tuning.
4. The model training and scoring should be parallelized for large datasets stored as partitioned tables in IBM's DB2 database systems.

Requirements 1 and 2 were deemed necessary for a successful commercial algorithm, although this ruled out certain ensemble-based methods that produce high-quality models but have high computation and storage requirements. Requirement 3 ensured that the chosen algorithm did not unduly compromise the concomitant model quality in view of requirements 1 and 2. The TReg algorithm is able to achieve the balance between these conflicting requirements with a design and implementation that combines aspects of generalized additive models (Hastie and Tibshirani, 1990), gradient boosting (Friedman, 2001; Hastie, Tibshirani and Friedman, 2001), and linear regression trees (Natarajan and Pednault, 2002).

To satisfy requirement 4, a new, fully parallelized, database-embedded implementation was created based on our previous ProbE data mining engine (Apte et al., 2002;

Dorneich et al., 2006), which in turn provided the basis for the IBM Parallel Machine Learning (PML) toolbox described in a separate chapter in this book. The same TReg code, which runs in a database-embedded environment in the original ProbE, also runs on Linux clusters and the IBM Blue Gene line of supercomputers in the more recent database-independent PML environment. Given the relatively complex nature of the TReg algorithm, this provides a clear illustration of the ability of the ProbE/PML APIs to isolate algorithm-specific aspects of the implementation from the data access, inter-process communication, and control-specific aspects of the code on these diverse parallel-execution environments.

9.1 Classification, Regression, and Loss Functions

In classification, the goal is to predict a target value that represents a discrete outcome such as a class or category membership. In regression, on the other hand, the goal is to predict a target value that represents a continuous-valued outcome such as the conditional probability of a discrete outcome, a conditional mean, or a conditional quantile, and so forth depending on the context.

A wide range of regression applications can be accommodated by using a formulation based on the following optimization problem: Given a training dataset $\{x_i, y_i\}_{i=1}^{N}$, where the x is the vector of input features, y is the corresponding target feature, and N is the number of training data examples, along with a loss function $L(y, \hat{y})$ that measures the discrepancy between the target value y and a predicted value given by $\hat{y} = f(x)$, find the regression function $\hat{f}(x)$ that minimizes the average loss on the training data,

$$\hat{f}(x) = \arg\min_{f} \mathcal{L}(f), \tag{9.1}$$

where

$$\mathcal{L}(f) = \frac{1}{N} \sum_{i=1}^{N} L\big(y_i, f(x_i)\big). \tag{9.2}$$

Because the regression function $\hat{f}$ may overfit the training data, the optimization formulation Equation 9.1 can be regularized by controlling the class of functions for $f(x)$.

The distributional properties of the target feature y can be taken into account by choosing the loss function in Equation 9.2 appropriately. For example, assuming that y is Gaussian with mean $f(x)$ and constant variance (i.e., homoscedastic) leads to the familiar squared-error loss function

$$L\big(y, f(x)\big) = \tfrac{1}{2}\big(y - f(x)\big)^2. \tag{9.3}$$

Similarly, assuming that y takes discrete binary values 1 and -1, with the log-odds of obtaining the 1 versus -1 outcome being $f(x)$, leads to the logistic loss function

$$L\big(y, f(x)\big) = \log\big(1 + e^{-yf(x)}\big). \tag{9.4}$$

Other loss functions can have very different theoretical justifications; for instance, support vector machines consider a binary classification problem for a target feature y

with outcomes 1 and -1 and turn it into a regression problem by using the hinge loss function:

$$L(y, f(x)) = \max(0, yf(x)). \tag{9.5}$$

9.2 Background

We first consider the Gradient Boosting (GB) approach (Friedman, 2001; Hastie et al., 2001), which can incorporate all the various loss functions described in Section 9.1 for the optimization problem in Equation 9.1. In this approach, the regression function $\hat{f}(x)$ in Equation 9.1 is evaluated as a stagewise expansion of the form

$$f_T(x) = \sum_{t=1}^{T} \alpha_t g_t(x; \theta_t), \tag{9.6}$$

where the functions $g_t(x; \theta_t)$ are typically chosen from a low-order, adaptive basis-function family parameterized by θ_t. One example of a suitable basis-function family is regression trees of fixed depth (Friedman, 1999, 2001), where the parameter θ_t denotes the splitting conditions and leaf-node parameters.

As shown in Algorithm 21, each stage in Equation 9.6 is obtained by a two-step procedure. First, given the *pseudo-residuals* of the loss function with respect to the previous-stage model $f_{t-1}(x)$ evaluated in the form

$$r_{t,i} = -\left.\frac{\partial L(y_i, f)}{\partial f}\right|_{f=f_{t-1}(x_i)}, \tag{9.7}$$

as a target, the parameters θ_t are estimated from a least-squares regression fit in Equation 9.8. Second, the coefficient α_t is then obtained from a univariate line-search optimization in Equation 9.9. For the special case of the squared-error loss function shown in Equation 9.3, the pseudo-residuals $r_{t,i}$ are identical to the residuals $y_i - f_{t-1}(x_i)$, and the optimal coefficient α_t is always 1.

We consider the four aspects of the GB algorithm (Friedman, 2001) that are important for motivating the TReg algorithm.

First, the stage basis functions $g(x, \theta_t)$ in Equation 9.8 in Algorithm 21 are themselves regression models that are obtained using the squared-error loss function at each stage (irrespective of the overall loss function that is being minimized per Equation 9.1). This is computationally advantageous, because stage basis functions $g(x, \theta_t)$ can be computed in a rapid, modular fashion independent of the application (e.g., regression trees of small depth using the least-squares criterion, for which the parameters θ correspond to the split conditions and mean estimates in the leaf nodes of the regression trees). The use of the squared-error criterion in each stage implies that the selected basis function $g(x, \theta_t)$ is chosen to maximally correlate with pseudo-residual r_t. However, one disadvantage with using regression trees as stage basis functions is that even a simple regression function that is linear in the input features requires a large number of regression-tree basis functions in Equation 9.6 for a satisfactory fit.

Second, the univariate line-optimization step in Equation 9.9 need not be solved to optimality, because the same basis function can be reintroduced in subsequent stages in Equation 9.6 (in this sense, the GB algorithm is "self-correcting"). The use of

---

Algorithm 21: Overview of Gradient Boosting Algorithm

INITIALIZATION: Let $f_0(x) = 0, t = 0$

ITERATION: For $t = 1$ to T, compute the stage pseudo-residuals $r_t = -(\partial \mathcal{L}(f)/\partial f)_{f_{t-1}(x)}$

1. Compute the stage basis function $g_t(x; \theta_t)$ from the least-squares problem

$$\theta_t = \arg\min_{\theta} \sum_{i=1}^{N} (r_{t,i} - g_t(x_i; \theta))^2 \tag{9.8}$$

2. Compute α_t by solving the univariate optimization problem

$$\alpha_t = \arg\min_{\alpha} \sum_{i=1}^{N} L(y_i, f_{t-1}(x_i) + \alpha g_t(x_i; \theta_t)) \tag{9.9}$$

3. Set $f_t(x) = f_{t-1}(x_i) + \alpha_t g_t(x; \theta_t), t = t + 1$ and repeat

OUTPUT: Final model $f(x) = f_T(x)$

---

sub-optimal values for α_t may even be desirable in the initial few stages of the expansion in Equation 9.6 to avoid early-stage overfitting, which in this respect is akin to using explicit shrinkage factors in the stagewise expansions as mooted by Friedman (2001).

Third, in Algorithm 21, the coefficients α_1 through α_{t-1} in Equation 9.6 are not readjusted when the new basis function $g(x, \theta_t)$ is added to the model in stage t. This is in contrast with other stepwise regression procedures, where the coefficients of the existing regressors are always readjusted to reflect the addition or removal of features from the regression model.

Fourth, systematic errors in the model fit may arise from an inappropriate choice for the stage basis-function family. This is already a concern with the regression-tree basis function family, as mentioned previously when the target feature is known to have a linear dependence on certain input features, but more so when this dependence includes significant interaction effects among the input features. For example, regression trees of depth 1 can only model additive effects, and trees of depth 2 are required to model first-order interaction effects. Some experimentation is invariably required to find the "correct" stage basis-function family, because otherwise, particularly where interaction effects are concerned, the final GB model will have systematic errors that cannot be removed by simply adding more stages to the model expansion in Equation 9.6.

9.3 Motivation and Algorithm Description

There are many variations and subtleties in the implementation of the GB algorithm, such as the choice of expansion basis functions and learning-rate parameters, the use of data sub-sampling in the stage computations, and the tuning of the line-search optimization procedures (Friedman, 1999, 2001; Ridgeway, 2007). However, the overall GB procedure is fundamentally unsuitable for parallel computing with massive datasets, because of the fine-grained nature of the individual stage computations and the inherently sequential and I/O-inefficient nature of the stage expansion procedure.

The TReg algorithm may therefore be regarded as reformulation of the basic GB algorithm, which addresses the parallelization limitations mentioned previously in two ways: first, by increasing the computational requirement of each individual stage, and second, by reducing the number of sequential stages in the stagewise expansion.

Specifically, the TReg algorithm uses a broader class of multivariate basis functions for the expansion in Equation 9.6, when compared to the univariate "weak-learner" basis functions used in the GB algorithm. As a result, the overall number of stages required in Equation 9.6 for TReg is significantly reduced, and in principle, each stage in TReg is potentially comparable to several stages in the equivalent GB algorithm in terms of the resulting improvement in the stagewise model accuracy, as well as in terms of the computational work that is required. As described later, this makes it possible to obtain accurate regression models using TReg, with fewer overall training data scans, greater parallelism in the individual stage computations, and fewer sequential-execution constraints in the overall stagewise expansion than would be possible in the fine-grained and highly sequential GB algorithm.

The specific class of multivariate basis-function family that is used in the TReg algorithm relies crucially on the following two aspects of the PML toolbox.

The first is the ability in PML to provide the outputs of predictive models as "computed fields" in an "extended" input data record, so that these outputs can be used as dynamically generated "input" features for other predictive models in a feed-forward cascade. In fact, the GB algorithm is also an example of such a feed-forward cascade, albeit with a very simple structure, in which the output of the predictive model at the prior stage $t - 1$ (or more precisely, the pseudo-residual based on this output) is taken as the target feature for generating the basis functions at stage t. By contrast, in TReg, along with this prior-stage output, the entire sequence of all previous-stage model outputs is used in the stage t computations. As a result, the TReg algorithm has a more complex feed-forward cascade of composite model transformations when compared to the GB algorithm. Figure 9.1 schematically illustrates stage t of the TReg algorithm, showing the individual sub-steps and their inputs, outputs, and dependencies, which are described in further detail later.

The second is the integrated support provided in PML for model selection and model accuracy evaluation, without introducing additional parallelization or data I/O overheads. This is particularly crucial in the TReg algorithm because, as a result of the use of more complex stage basis functions, overfitting can occur within each individual stage computation itself. In PML, during each training data scan, the individual data records are systematically partitioned into cross-validation folds (used for model selection), a validation fold (used for iterative termination and model pruning), and a hold-out fold (used for obtaining an unbiased estimate of final model quality). Although the details are often omitted for brevity in the following discussion, these partitioned data folds are crucial for implementing the computation of the stage sub-basis shown later in Algorithm 23, the stage basis functions in Algorithm 24, and the iteration termination criterion in Algorithm 22.

The TReg stage basis functions can be explicitly written as

$$g_t(\boldsymbol{x}, \boldsymbol{\lambda}) = \sum_{j=1}^{M} \lambda_j h_{tj}(x_j; f_1, \ldots, f_{t-1}) + \sum_{j=1}^{t-1} \lambda_{M+j} \hat{h}_{tj}(f_j; f_1, \ldots, f_{j-1}), \quad (9.10)$$

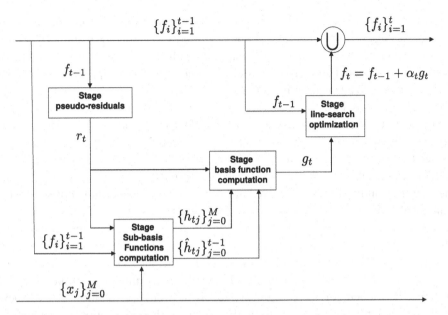

Figure 9.1 Schematic of stage t in the TReg algorithm.

which consists of a linear combination of certain $M + t - 1$ sub-basis functions with coefficients $\lambda = \{\lambda_j\}_{j=1}^{M+t-1}$, where M is the number of input features. Each sub-basis function is conceptually similar to a single stage basis function in the GB algorithm, but TReg uses piecewise-linear regression trees (Equation 9.10), which subsume the piecewise-constant regression trees used in the GB algorithm as a special case but are especially useful for succinctly modeling linear relationships that are common in regression problems, which would require an inordinate large number of piecewise-constant regression tree basis functions for comparable accuracy.

The notation $h_{tj}(x_j; f_1, \ldots, f_{t-1})$ in Equation 9.10 denotes the piecewise-linear regression tree, which is computed using the previous-stage pseudo-residual r_t as the target, with x_j being the only input feature used for splitting, while $\{x_j, f_1, \ldots, f_{t-1}\}$ are the only features used in the segment regression models. For simplicity in the implementation, and without any great loss of accuracy in practice, categorical input features x_j are used only as splitting features, while continuous input features x_j are used as splitting features and as segment regression model features (however, the restriction on categorical features can be easily removed by using dummy-coded representations of these features in the segment regression models).

Therefore, for continuous x_j, the relevant sub-basis function in Equation 9.10 can be written in the form

$$h_{tj}(x_j; f_1, \ldots, f_{t-1})$$
$$= \sum_{k=1}^{K_{tj}} (a_{k0j} + a_{k1j}f_1 + \cdots + a_{k(t-1)j}f_{t-1} + a_{ktj}x_j)I([x_j \in \Gamma_{t,jk}]), \quad (9.11)$$

where K_{tj} is the number of individual segments, $\Gamma_{t,jk}$ denotes the kth segment, and $I([x_j \in \Gamma_{t,jk}])$ denotes the indicator function for segment membership (the set of

segments $\{\Gamma_{t,jk}\}_{k=1}^{K_{tj}}$ is a mutually exclusive, collectively exhaustive univariate partition of x_j at stage t). For categorical x_j, these sub-basis functions (Equation 9.11) have
the same form but will exclude the linear term with coefficient a_{ktj}. The computations for the individual sub-basis functions (Equation 9.11) in Equation 9.10 can be
efficiently parallelized, as described in Section 9.4.1.

The choice of sub-basis functions (Equation 9.11) significantly reduces the number
of stages in Equation 9.6. First, using the outputs of the previous $(t-1)$ stages in Equation 9.6 as input features for the segment regression models $\{h_{tj}(x_j; f_1, \ldots, f_{t-1})\}_{j=1}^M$
in stage t, as shown in Equation 9.11, implicitly "orthogonalizes" the new stage sub-
basis function against all the previous-stage basis functions, and in this way, eliminates the possibility of introducing redundant terms in the expansion (Equation 9.6).
Orthogonalization occurs as a by-product of using least-squares fitting to construct
segment regression models – which, from a geometric standpoint, implicitly orthogonalizes x_j with respect to $f_1, \ldots, f_{t-1}$ when calculating the coefficient for x_j. Second,
because the previous-stage model outputs are also included as splitting features for
$\{\hat{h}_{tj}(f_j; f_1, \ldots, f_{j-1})\}_{j=1}^{t-1}$ in Equation 9.11, and because orthogonalization is implicitly being performed for these segment models as well, the addition of each new
sub-basis function $g_t(x)$ at stage t implicitly provides orthogonalization adjustments to
the previous-stage outputs. These two refinements in the TReg algorithm can be motivated by analogy with stepwise linear regression procedures, where new regressors
are implicitly or explicitly orthogonalized against existing model regressors in order
to avoid introducing redundant or collinear features in the model. Furthermore, in
these stepwise procedures, the coefficients of existing regressors in the model are also
readjusted to reflect the addition (or removal) of other regressors in the model. Thus,
Equation 9.10 may be regarded as a nonlinear generalization of these ideas, which
can lead to a substantial reduction in the overall number of stages in Equation 9.6,
with concomitant savings in the I/O and computational costs, particularly because the
required stage computations with these refinements can be implemented in parallel,
without no extra data I/O overhead.

Another important consequence of the choice of sub-basis functions arises in the
case when the regression function must incorporate complex, non-additive interaction
effects that cannot be captured by the set of untransformed piecewise-linear basis functions used in Equation 9.6. In TReg, these systematic errors can be reduced, and even
eliminated, by incorporating the entire set of previous-stage basis functions as splitting
features in the evaluation of the sub-basis functions $\{\hat{h}_{tj}(f_j; f_1, \ldots, f_{j-1})\}_{j=1}^{t-1}$ at stage t,
because this not only provides a mechanism for implicit readjustment of the coefficients
of the previous-stage basis function $\{f_1, \ldots, f_{j-1}\}$, but in addition, the piecewise-linear
regression tree transformations of the previous-stage basis functions also implicitly introduce cross-product terms into the regression function, arising from the nonlinear
transformation of the sums of previous-stage basis functions in Equation 9.6. The
resulting ability of Equation 9.6 to implicitly model non-additive and interaction effects has been illustrated by Pednault (2006) using a synthetic example, where it was
heuristically motivated by drawing an analogy between the expansion (Equation 9.6)
and the form of the universal approximating functions in Kolmogorov's Superposition Theorem (a similar analogy has also been used to motivate multi-layer neural
networks; Hecht-Nielsen, 1987). The use of input features that incorporate nonlinear

transformations of the previous-stage outputs in each stage in Equation 9.6, and the resulting ability of this expansion to model regression functions with complex feature interactions, is the rationale for the naming of the TReg algorithm.

9.3.1 Parallelization in ProbE/PML

Parallel algorithms are developed in ProbE/PML by implementing object classes that expose a set of interface methods that must be implemented by all algorithms. The chapter on PML describes these interface methods in detail, and the key steps are summarized here:

init: Initialize the algorithm object in preparation for training.
beginDataScan: Return true if an iteration over training data is needed.
serialize: Output an encoding of the algorithm object's internal state so the object can be reconstructed on other compute nodes.
processRecord: Update the algorithm object's internal state based on the data record that is provided as input.
mergeResults: Update the algorithm object's internal state by merging the results from the other algorithm object that is provided as input.
endDataScan: Perform post-data-scan processing and set up for the next data iteration.

The computationally intensive parts of the TReg algorithm (Algorithm 22) is implemented as component algorithms in terms of this interface, as described in greater detail later.

Following the description of the initialization and the termination steps, the component steps in the iteration in Algorithm 22, comprising the computation of the sub-basis functions (step 1), the stage basis function (step 2), and the line optimization (step 3), are individually described.

9.4 TReg Expansion: Initialization and Termination

The expansions in Algorithm 22 can be initialized in other ways besides taking $f_0(x) = 0$ as shown there. For example, in the least-squares regression application, $f_0(x)$ can be set to the unconditional mean of the target feature in the training data. However, the preferred alternative is to take $f_0(x)$ as the linear regression model based on the continuous input features, because this model can be computed as a "side effect" of the initial input data scan that is used to estimate the distributional properties of the individual input data fields (which are required in any case for discovering the values of categorical fields and for appropriately discretizing of the continuous fields, because these steps are needed for implementing the algorithms described in Section 9.4.1).

The expansions in Algorithm 22 can also be terminated in other ways besides the user-specified maximum number of stages shown there. However, the preferred termination criterion is to use the cross-validation estimate of the loss function (Equation 9.2), which can also be evaluated along with each stage of the corresponding stagewise expansion procedure, and statistical significance tests can be used to

---

Algorithm 22: Overview of Transform Regression Algorithm

INITIALIZATION: Let $f_0(\boldsymbol{x}) = 0, t = 0$

ITERATION: For $t = 1$ to T, let $r_t = -(\partial \mathcal{L}(f)/\partial f)_{f_{t-1}(\boldsymbol{x})}$ denote the stage pseudo-residuals

1. Compute the stage sub-basis functions $\{h_{tj}(x_j; x_j, f_1, \ldots, f_{t-1})\}_{j=1}^{M}$ and $\{\hat{h}_{tj}(f_j; f_1, \ldots, f_{j-1})\}_{j=1}^{t-1}$ in Equation 9.11, with r_t as target, as described in Section 9.4.1

2. Compute the stage basis function, $g_t(\boldsymbol{x}, \boldsymbol{\lambda}_t)$ in Equation 9.10 by solving the least-squares problem

$$\boldsymbol{\lambda}_t = \arg\min_{\boldsymbol{\lambda}} \sum_{i=1}^{N} (r_{t,i} - g_t(\boldsymbol{x}_i, \boldsymbol{\lambda}))^2, \tag{9.12}$$

   as described in Section 9.4.2

3. Compute α_t by solving the univariate optimization problem

$$\alpha_t = \arg\min_{\alpha} \sum_{i=1}^{N} L(y_i, f_{t-1}(\boldsymbol{x}_i) + \alpha g_t(\boldsymbol{x}, \boldsymbol{\lambda}_t)), \tag{9.13}$$

   as described in Section 9.4.3

4. Set $f_t(\boldsymbol{x}) = f_{t-1}(\boldsymbol{x}) + \alpha_t g_t(\boldsymbol{x}, \boldsymbol{\lambda}_t), t = t + 1$ and repeat

OUTPUT: Final model $f(\boldsymbol{x}) = f_T(\boldsymbol{x})$

---

determine whether the additional stages have not led to any decrease in this cross-validation loss estimate. The expansion can then be terminated and the expansion can be pruned back to the smallest number of stages in relation to the minimum cross-validation loss estimate.

9.4.1 Details of Sub-basis Function Computations

In PML, continuous-valued features x_j are pre-discretized into intervals based on certain "knot" points in the range of x_j (by default, these knot points are the deciles obtained from the empirical cumulative distribution of x_j), and the segments $\Gamma_{t,jk}$ that are used in Equation 9.11 correspond to a collection of contiguous intervals in this discretization. For categorical-valued features x_j, whose feature values are unordered, each segment $\Gamma_{t,k}$ can be an arbitrary collection of one or more category values in x_j.

The computation steps for obtaining one of the the stage sub-basis functions h_{tj} in Equation 9.11 is shown in Algorithm 23. The algorithm shown is essentially the Linear Regression Trees (LRT) algorithm of Natarajan and Pednault (2002), but specialized to split on a single feature x_j. The final segmentation $\Gamma_{t,jk}$, along with the corresponding segment linear models, can be generated in a single pass over the training data for all the sub-basis functions (Equation 9.10) required in each stage. The parallelization of this algorithm requires only two additional steps beyond those described by Natarajan and Pednault (2002): the `serialize` method to move objects between compute nodes

---

Algorithm 23: Parallel One-Pass Algorithm for the LRT Algorithm Used to Obtain One of the Sub-basis Functions (Equation 9.11) in TReg

---

init: On the Master node – For each initial segment $\{\Delta x_{jl}\}_{l=1}^{L_j}$, initialize the sufficient statistics $\{N_{tjl}, \boldsymbol{\mu}_{tjl}, S_{tjl}\}$ that will be used to obtain the LRT model for target r_t with he feature set $\boldsymbol{\xi}_{t,j}$

beginDataScan: Return true on first pass and false thereafter

serialize: Encode the segment sufficient statistics

processRecord: On Master and Worker nodes – Use the input data record to update the local copies of the sufficient statistics for all applicable segments

mergeResults: Incorporate the sufficient statistics from the input sub-basis function object

endDataScan: On the Master node – Starting with the initial segmentations $\{\Delta x_{jl}\}_{l=1}^{L_j}$, obtain the final segmentations by a sequence of bottom-up combine and top-down prune steps:

1. For each segment Δx_{jl}, estimate the optimal number of features in the segment regression model.
2. For each segment Δx_{jl}, estimate the regression coefficients and model variance with the optimal number of feature as above – mentioned.
3. For each segment Δx_{jl}, obtain an unbiased estimate $\mathcal{G}$ of the negative log-likelihood for the linear Gaussian model.
4. Combine the pair of admissible segments that lead to the maximum decrease in the negative log-likelihood for the linear Gaussian model in the combined segment.
5. Repeat the bottom-up combining steps (1)–(4) with the remaining pairs of admissible segments, to obtain a tree-like sequence.
6. Prune the resulting tree using the cross-validation estimate of the negative log-likelihood, to obtain the final segmentation $\{\Gamma_{t,jk}\}_{k=1}^{K_{tj}}$.

OUTPUT: For each feature x_j, the final segmentation given by $\{\Gamma_{t,jk}\}_{k=1}^{K_{tj}}$, and the corresponding sub-basis function given by h_{tj}

---

and the mergeResults method to combine sufficient statistics calculated on different worker nodes.

In Algorithm 23, the range of x_j is assumed to be pre-discretized into the intervals $\Delta x_{jl} = (x_{j(l)}, x_{j(l+1)})$. The data fields required for computing the LRT model for $h_{tj}(x_j; f_1, \ldots, f_{t-1})$ comprise an input data feature x_j and the computed features $f_1 \ldots f_{t-1}$, along with the target feature comprising the pseudo-residual from the previous stage r_t. This set of fields required for the segment models is denoted by $\boldsymbol{\xi}_{t,j} = \{x_j, f_1, \ldots, f_{t-1}, r_t\}$.

Starting with this initial segmentation, the LRT algorithm heuristically obtains a final segmentation $\Gamma_{t,jk}$ that minimizes the negative log-likelihood for the segmented linear Gaussian model, as follows. For a given interval Δx_{jl} in the pre-discretization of x_j, the sufficient statistics for the linear Gaussian model are the sample counts N_{tjl}, the multivariate sample means $\boldsymbol{\mu}_{tjl}$, and the sample covariance S_{tjl}, all computed over the relevant data fields $(\xi_{t,j})$ for the subset of data records with x_j in the interval Δx_{jl}. These sufficient statistics can be obtained for all the relevant segments using only a single data scan over the training data, and the only modifications required for parallelization are that each processor node updates a local copy of these sufficient statistics over its assigned parallel partition of the input data records. These partial local copies are then combined to obtain the global sufficient statistics for the entire dataset. The required updating and the merging formulas for this parallelization of the sufficient statistics computation are given by Natarajan and Pednault (2002).

The final step in the evaluation of the sub-basis functions is then performed on the master node (although this final step is not parallel, its computational and memory requirements are minuscule and no data I/O is required in this step). For each segment in the initial segmentation, comprising the intervals Δx_{jl} in the pre-discretization of x_j, the incremental Cholesky-based algorithm for solving the normal equations, described in detail in Natarajan and Pednault (2002) (and also used in Section 9.4.2), is used to obtain the linear models within each segment. Specifically, the optimal number of regression features (i.e., the model complexity) is first estimated for each of the segment linear regression models. The corresponding model coefficients $\{a_{lsj}\}_{s=0}^{t+1}$ and model variance σ_{jl} are then obtained for each segment Δx_{jl}. If $\tilde{\rho}_{jl}$ is an unbiased estimate for the squared residual error for this segment model, then excluding a constant term, the negative log-likelihood for the corresponding Gaussian error model is given by

$$\mathcal{G}_{tjl} = \frac{1}{2}\left[\log 2\pi\sigma_{jl}^2 + \frac{\tilde{\rho}_{jl}}{\sigma_{jl}}\right]. \qquad (9.14)$$

Thus, starting with the initial segmentation, a series of pairwise bottom-up combine steps are performed as follows. For continuous x_j, the sufficient statistics of adjacent segment pairs are combined whenever the resulting combined segment leads to a reduction in the negative log-likelihood for the respective segment linear Gaussian models. Specifically, if two adjacent segments are denoted by subscripts L and R, and their combined segment by $L + R$, respectively, and if the corresponding negative log-likelihoods for the linear Gaussian model are denoted by $\mathcal{G}_L$, $\mathcal{G}_L$, and $\mathcal{G}_{L+R}$, respectively, then

$$\Delta\mathcal{G} = N_{(L+R)}\mathcal{G}_{tj(L+R)} - (N_L\mathcal{G}_{tjL} - N_R\mathcal{G}_{tjR}) \qquad (9.15)$$

is evaluated, and the segment pairs for which $\Delta\mathcal{G}$ is maximally negative are combined. This bottom-up combine step typically does not increase the overall model complexity in the collection of segment models; for example, if n_L, n_R, and n_{L+R} denote the number of regression features in the linear models in the respective segments, then typically $n_{L+R} \leq n_L + n_R + 1$. However, occasionally the number of regression features increases with $n_{L+R} > n_L + n_R + 1$, in which case the segment pairs are not considered for combining. This bottom-up combine process is successively repeated until there is no further decrease in $\Delta\mathcal{G}$. The resulting tree, or collection of trees, is then pruned in a top-down manner using a cross-validation loss criterion to yield the required final segmentation $\{\Gamma_{t,jk}\}_{k=1}^{K_{tj}}$ for the feature x_j in Equation 9.11.

Figure 9.2 schematically illustrates the steps in the LRT algorithm for computing the sub-basis functions at stage t for a continuous feature x_j. A similar procedure is

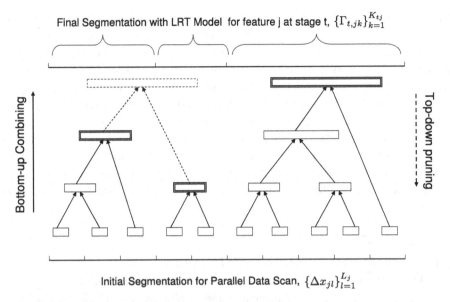

Figure 9.2 Schematic of the LRT algorithm for obtaining the sub-basis function at stage t for continuous feature x_j. The pruned sections are shown with dashed lines, and the final segments with double-lined boxes.

also used for a categorical feature x_j with the initial segmentation consisting of each category value. However, for categorical x_j, any two segments can be combined in the bottom-up procedure, unlike the case for continuous x_j, where only adjacent segments in the discretization could be combined.

Although the number of initial segment models in the LRT algorithm for obtaining the final sub-basis functions in Equation 9.11 can be very large, each of these segment models is typically of very low dimensionality. Specifically, the number of features used in a given stage t for each initial segment model is the dimension of $\boldsymbol{\xi}_{t,j}$, or equivalently $t+1$, which is always a small quantity, because the maximum number of stages in TReg almost never exceeds 5 to 10 in practice.

9.4.2 Details of Stage Basis Function Computations

From the sub-basis functions $\boldsymbol{\eta}_t = \{\{h_{t,j}\}_{j=1}^{M}, \{\hat{h}_{t,j}\}_{j=1}^{t-1}, r_t\}$ obtained as described in Section 9.4.1, the coefficients $\{\lambda_j\}_{j=1}^{M+t-1}$ in Equation 9.10 are estimated from the least-squares model (Equation 9.12).

The parallel LRT algorithm used for Equation 9.12 is essentially the same as that used for the independent segment models in the LRT algorithm (Algorithm 23); however, unlike the numerous but low-dimensional regression models in that case, here there is only a single high-dimensional linear regression model.

The incremental Cholesky factorization procedure described in Natarajan and Pednault (2002) is used for the solution of least-squares problem after the parallel step to obtain the required sufficient statistics. First, a cross-validation procedure is used to select the size of the linear regression model. For each cross-validation fold, starting with a null model, a sequence of nested linear regression models is obtained by a greedy forward-selection procedure. The cross-validation estimate of the loss is then computed and used to select the optimal number of regression features to be used in the linear regression model. This optimal number can correspond to the model size with the minimum cross-validation estimate of the loss, or to the size of the smallest model that is within one standard error of the best value (the so-called 1-SE rule). The latter criterion introduces shrinkage into the selection of the stage basis function and reduces the possibility of any overfitting within the computation of $g_t(x, \lambda)$ itself. Finally, the coefficients of the linear regression model with the selected optimal number of regression features are then estimated by pooling the data in the cross-validation folds. Algorithm 24 summarizes the overall basic function computation procedure.

Algorithm 24: Parallel One-Pass Linear Regression Algorithm Used for the Basis Function Computation (Equation 9.12) in TReg

---

init: On the Master node – For the linear regression model with r_t as target, and $\eta_t = \{\{h_{t,j}\}_{j=1}^{M}, \{\hat{h}_{t,j}\}_{j=1}^{t-1}\}$ as input features, initialize the sufficient statistics $\{N_t, \mu_t, S_t\}$

beginDataScan: Return true on first pass and false thereafter

serialize: Encode the sufficient statistics

processRecord: Master and Worker nodes – Use the input data record to update the local copy of the sufficient statistics

mergeResults: Incorporate the sufficient statistics from the input one-pass LRT object

endDataScan: *On the Master node –*

1. Compute a sequence of nested linear regression models and obtain the optimal number of regression features from a cross-validation estimate of the loss.
2. Compute the coefficients of the linear-regression model with the optimal number of regression features from (1) using a stepwise linear regression procedure.

OUTPUT: The final linear regression model for $g_t(x, \lambda)$

9.4.3 Line Search Optimization Details

For the squared-error loss, the line-search optimization step (Equation 9.13) is not required, because the optimum value of α_t is always 1. For the other loss functions, Equation 9.13 is equivalent to determining the coefficient in a regression fit for a linear model with offset $f_{t-1}(x)$ with input feature $g_t(x, \lambda_t)$ (for instance, with the logistic loss function, this is a single-feature Generalized Linear Model for estimating α_t). A more general approach that is applicable to all loss functions is univariate line-search optimization, which is also used with the GB algorithm (Friedman, 2001). However, all of these approaches require multiple training data scans for obtaining the optimal α_t and are therefore unsuitable for massive datasets.

In TReg, two approaches are used to obtain a good estimate for α_t using only a single data scan, although these estimates can be further improved using multiple data scans if required.

The first approach, termed the "one-step multi-α" method, is based on evaluating the objective function (Equation 9.13) on a grid of K values $\{\alpha_k\}_{k=1}^{K}$ (where typically $K \approx 100$), and α_t is the minimizer value from this set,

$$\alpha_t = \arg \min_{\alpha_k} \sum_{i=1}^{N} L(y_i, f_{t-1}(x_i) + \alpha_k g_t(x_i, \lambda_t)). \qquad (9.16)$$

The second approach, termed the "one-step Newton" method, is suitable for twice-differentiable loss functions (Equation 9.2) and uses the derivatives of $\mathcal{L}(f)$ evaluated at $\alpha = 0$,

$$\mathcal{L}_\alpha(f_{t-1}) = \sum_{i=1}^{N} \left(\frac{\partial L(y_i, f)}{\partial f} \right)_{f_{t-1}} g_t(x_i, \lambda_t),$$

$$\mathcal{L}_{\alpha\alpha}(f_{t-1}) = \sum_{i=1}^{N} \left(\frac{\partial^2 L(y_i, f)}{\partial f^2} \right)_{f_{t-1}} g_t(x_i, \lambda_t)^2, \qquad (9.17)$$

from which the one-step Newton estimate is given by

$$\alpha_t = -\frac{\mathcal{L}_\alpha(f_{t-1})}{\mathcal{L}_{\alpha\alpha}(f_{t-1})}. \qquad (9.18)$$

When applicable, the "one-step Newton" is generally preferable to the "one-step multi-α," because the choice of the initial set of grid values $\{\alpha_k\}_{k=1}^{K}$ for the function evaluation in Equation 9.16 can be quite arbitrary. Algorithm 25 summarizes the overall "one-step Newton" procedure.

Algorithm 25: Parallel One-Pass "One-Step Newton" Method Used for the Stage Coefficient Computation (Equation 9.18) in TReg

---

init: On the Master node – Provide the objects for calculating loss functions and their derivatives, and initialize the accumulators for summing the scores $\mathcal{L}_\alpha(f_{t-1})$ and $\mathcal{L}_{\alpha\alpha}(f_{t-1})$ in Equation 9.17

beginDataScan: Return true on first pass and false thereafter

serialize: Encode the accumulators and loss-function objects

processRecord: Master and Worker nodes – Pass the input record to the loss-function object to calculate and update the local accumulators for these scores for each parallel partition of the training dataset

mergeResults: Merge the local score accumulators to eventually obtain the the global scores based on the entire training dataset

endDataScan: On the Master node – Compute α_t from these global scores using Equation 9.18

OUTPUT: The coefficient α_t for stage t

9.5 Model Accuracy Results

The prediction accuracy of TReg is illustrated by comparison with MART (Friedman, 2001), as implemented in the gradient-boosting package gbm in R (Ridgeway, 2007). The default settings are used for the algorithms, except where noted; the MART results use 2-node trees for basis functions with 10-fold cross-validation, no learning-rate shrinkage, and no subsampling in the computations; the TReg results use 2-fold cross-validation, with stage expansions being terminated if four consecutive stages do not significantly reduce the cross-validation error.

Synthetic Data: We consider synthetic datasets generated from known regression functions in the form

$$y = f(x) + \epsilon \mathcal{N}(0, 1), \tag{9.19}$$

where x is a 20-dimensional vector of input features. The continuous features x_1 through x_{10} are obtained by uniform sampling the interval $(0, 1)$, and the 10 nominal features x_{11} through x_{20} by uniform sampling at four levels $\{1, 2, 3, 4\}$. The individual features are uncorrelated, but many of them are noise features in the following generated datasets.

Two specific regression functions are chosen for evaluation:

$$f_1(x) = 10(x_1 - 0.5)^2 - x_2 + \sin 2\pi x_2 - 3x_3 + 1.5I([x_{11} \in \{3, 4\}]), \tag{9.20}$$

which is an additive function of a subset of features, and

$$f_2(x) = \exp(-x_1 - x_2 + 2x_3) + 3(x_4 - x_5) + 2I([x_{11} \in \{3, 4\}] \cup [x_{12} \in \{1, 2\}]), \tag{9.21}$$

which is non-additive with high-order interaction effects among subsets of features (similar synthetic datasets are used by Li and Goel, 2007).

The training and test datasets consist of of 5,000 points each, and setting ϵ in Equation 9.19 to be 0.8 yields datasets with a roughly 2-to-1 signal-to-noise ratio.

The squared-error loss function was used for both MART and TReg. In the additive case, the holdout MSE for MART was 1.390 ± 0.027 and that for TReg was 0.777 ± 0.015. The holdout R^2 for MART was 0.61, and for TReg it was 0.77, respectively. The MART results required 247 stages, whereas the TReg results required only 8 stages. The MART results tend to be overfitted when more complex basis functions involving interaction effects are used; for instance, using 4-node trees instead of 2-node trees in MART, the holdout MSE was 1.468 ± 0.029 with an R^2 of 0.59.

In the non-additive case, the holdout MSE for MART was 1.676 ± 0.032 and for TReg was 0.845 ± 0.017. The holdout R^2 for MART was 0.564 and for TReg was 0.774. The MART results required 167 stages, and the TReg results required only 7 stages. However, using a 4-node tree instead of 2-node for MART, the holdout MSE was 1.673 ± 0.035 and the R^2 was 0.570, indicating that using basis functions that can incorporate non-additive effects is important for MART in this dataset; furthermore, TReg is able partially incorporate these non-additive effects, even though these effects are not explicitly modeled in the stage basis functions.

Table 9.1. *Model quality results for adult dataset.*

	Adult Census 36,632 (12,210) records			
	MART	TReg		
	Logistic	Logistic	Least-squares	Hinge-loss
Misclassification Error	0.153	0.141	0.140	0.147
Gini	0.804	0.819	0.823	0.785

In summary, compared to MART, TReg yields accurate results without overfitting, for both the additive and non-additive cases, and with no special algorithmic tuning being required.

California Housing Data: The California housing dataset (California, 2009) consists of eight continuous input features and a continuous target feature. The log of the target was modeled using the least-squares loss function, without trimming the input-feature outliers as in Li and Goel (2007). The original dataset with 20,640 records was randomly partitioned into training and holdout datasets with 13,960 and 6,680 records, respectively. The holdout MSE for MART was 0.0119 ± 0.0004 with 297 training stages, and for TReg was 0.01276 ± 0.0004 with 5 training stages. The holdout R^2 for MART was 0.798 and for TReg was 0.793.

Adult Data: The adult census dataset (Adult, 2009) consists of 15 input features (both continuous and categorical) and a binary target feature. The training and holdout datasets consist of 36,632 and 12,210 records, respectively. Table 9.1 shows the model quality in terms of the misclassification error, and the Gini coefficient obtained from the cumulative gains charts (Hand, 1997), and the results are quite comparable across the board. We note that the logistic models provide a direct estimate of the class probabilities, which is desirable in certain applications.

Spambase Data: The Spambase dataset (Spambase Data Set, 2009) consists of 57 continuous input features and a binary target feature. The original dataset with 4,603 records is randomly partitioned into a training set of 3,065 records and a holdout set of 1,536 records. The model quality results shown in Table 9.2 are quite comparable across the board. The MART solution required 114 stages, whereas the TReg solutions required 6 to 8 stages.

Table 9.2. *Model quality results for Spambase dataset.*

	Spambase 3,065 (1,536) records			
	MART	TReg		
	Logistic	Logistic	Least-squares	Hinge-loss
Misclassification Error	0.055	0.050	0.051	0.051
Gini	0.970	0.960	0.946	0.946

9.6 Parallel Performance Results

Parallel performance results were obtained on IBM Blue Gene/P (BG/P), which is a distributed memory supercomputer whose architecture and programming environment are described in IBM Blue Gene Team (2008).

9.6.1 Scalability Analysis

The parallel performance of PML applications can be characterized in terms of strong and weak scalability, as described next.

If T_p denotes the measured execution time for a parallel application on p nodes and T_b denotes the equivalent baseline time, then the parallel speedup is defined by $S_p = bT_p/T_b$ and the parallel efficiency by S_p/p. An objective measure for the baseline time T_b is the equivalent optimized serial program time on a single node ($b = 1$), but an equivalent serial program is often not available for performance benchmarking, and furthermore, the single-node execution time may be too long for the massive datasets of interest. For these reasons, in practice, the baseline performance is often obtained with the parallel program running on the smallest possible number of nodes that yields a reasonable execution time (on BG/P, for typical datasets, b ranged from 4 to 32 nodes).

For the strong scalability metric, the data size and various algorithm parameters are held fixed as p is increased, so that the memory requirement per node decreases. This metric is relevant when p is increased in order to reduce the execution time for a given problem of fixed size, and in the ideal case, the speedup S_p will be linearly proportional to p.

In contrast, for the weak scalability metric, the data size is also increased as p is increased, in such a way that the memory requirement per node remains fixed. This metric is relevant when p is increased so that problems of larger size require the same execution time, and in the ideal case, the speedup S_p stays close to 1 as p is increased.

9.6.2 PML Performance Optimizations

The `serialize` and `mergeResults` functions are customized for distributed-memory HPC platforms so that for p nodes, these operations are performed in $\log_2 p$ phases, with significant parallelism in each phase. This is similar to that used in the broadcast/reduce collective message primitives in MPI, but with PML-specific customization for matching and merging objects and for object serialization and materialization to ensure the best performance, particularly for large p.

9.6.3 Parallel Scalability Results

In machine learning applications, the strong-scalability analysis is relevant when the training dataset size is fixed in advance, whereas the weak-scalability analysis is

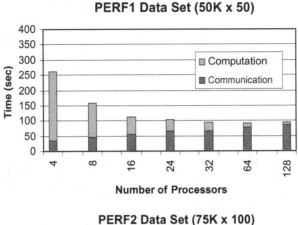

Figure 9.3 Performance results – communication and computation.

relevant for assessing model stability and accuracy with a sequence of larger training datasets.

To examine both these situations, two synthetic datasets from a known regression function were generated: PERF1, with 50,000 rows and 50 input features, and PERF2, with 75,000 rows and 100 input features (the parallel timing measurements in Algorithm 22 are for a single TReg iteration). Figure 9.3 shows the parallel timings for PERF1 and PERF2, also indicating the proportion of time spent in the communication and computation phases of the algorithm. As expected, with increasing P, the time for the highly parallel computational phase decreases, whereas the time for the communication phase increases. Because neither of these datasets could be run for the $P = 1$ case, the $P = 4$ case was used as the base to obtain the speedups for $P = 128$ processors, which was 2.79 for PERF1, and 3.46 for PERF2.

Figure 9.4 shows the same results, but indicating the proportion of time spent in the the three parts of the TReg iteration shown in Algorithm 22. The dominant fraction of the time is in the computation of the stage sub-basis functions; the computation of the stage basis functions and the line search optimization are a much smaller fraction of

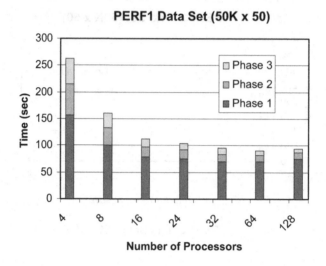

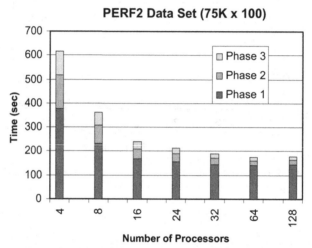

Figure 9.4 Performance results – time spent in each of the three phases of a TReg iteration.

the overall time. It is possible to further reduce the computation time by limiting the number of stage sub-basis functions, but the effect of these modifications on the PML model quality requires further study.

9.7 Summary

Transform regression (TReg) is a general-purpose regression algorithm whose implementation in the PML toolbox provides a unique parallel capability for massive datasets, with significant advantages over existing methods in terms of balancing the often-conflicting requirements of computational speed and efficiency, model accuracy and reliability, and parallel scalability.

References

Adult. 2009. Adult Census Data Set. http://archive.ics.uci.edu/ml/datasets/Adult.

Apte, C., Natarajan, R., Pednault, E. P. D., and Tipu, F. 2002. A Probabilistic Estimation Framework for Predictive Modeling Analytics. *IBM Systems Journal*, **41**(3), 438–448.

California. 2009. California Housing Data Set. http://lib.stat.cmu.edu/datasets/houses.zip.

Dorneich, A., Natarajan, R., Pednault, E., and Tipu, F. 2006. Embedded Predictive Modeling in a Parallel Relational Database. Pages 569–574 of: *SAC '06: Proceedings of the 2006 ACM Symposium on Applied Computing*. New York: ACM.

Friedman, J. H. 1999. Stochastic Gradient Boosting. *Computational Statistics and Data Analysis*, **38**, 367–378.

Friedman, J. H. 2001. Greedy Function Approximation: A Gradient Boosting Machine. *Annals of Statistics*, **29**, 1189–1232.

Hand, D. 1997. *Construction and Assessment of Classification Rules*. New York: Wiley.

Hastie, T., Tibshirani, R., and Friedman, J. H. 2001. *The Elements of Statistical Learning*. New York: Springer.

Hastie, T. J., and Tibshirani, R. J. 1990. *Generalized Additive Models*. London: Chapman & Hall.

Hecht-Nielsen, R. 1987. Kolmogorov Mapping Neural Network Existence Theorem. Pages 11–14 of: *Proceedings of IEEE International Conference on Neural Networks*, vol. 3.

IBM Blue Gene Team. 2008. Overview of the IBM Blue Gene/P project. *IBM Journal of Research and Development*, **52**, 199–220.

Li, B., and Goel, P. K. 2007. Additive regression trees and smoothing splines – predictive modeling and interpretation in data mining. *Contemporary Mathematics*, **443**, 83–101.

Natarajan, R., and Pednault, E. P. D. 2002. Segmented Regression Estimators for Massive Data Sets. In: *Proceedings of the Second SIAM International Conference on Data Mining*.

Pednault, E. P. D. 2006. Transform Regression and the Kolmogorov Superposition Theorem. In: *Proceedings of the Sixth SIAM International Conference on Data Mining*.

Provost, F. J., and Kolluri, V. 1999. A Survey of Methods for Scaling Up Inductive Learning Algorithms. *Data Mining and Knowledge Discovery*, **3**, 131–169.

Ridgeway, G. 2007. Generalized Boosted Models: A Guide to the GBM Package. http://cran.r-project.org/web/packages/gbm/vignettes/gbm.pdf.

Spambase Data Set. 2009. Spambase Data Set. http://archive.ics.uci.edu/ml/datasets/Spambase.

CHAPTER 10

Parallel Belief Propagation
in Factor Graphs

Joseph Gonzalez, Yucheng Low, and Carlos Guestrin

Probabilistic graphical models are used in a wide range of machine learning applications. From reasoning about protein interactions (Jaimovich et al., 2006) to stereo vision (Sun, Shum, and Zheng, 2002), graphical models have facilitated the application of probabilistic methods to challenging machine learning problems. A core operation in probabilistic graphical models is *inference* – the process of computing the probability of an event given particular observations. Although inference is NP-complete in general, there are several popular approximate inference algorithms that typically perform well in practice. Unfortunately, the approximate inference algorithms are still computationally intensive and therefore can benefit from parallelization. In this chapter, we parallelize *loopy belief propagation* (or loopy BP in short), which is used in a wide range of ML applications (Jaimovich et al., 2006; Sun et al., 2002; Lan et al., 2006; Baron, Sarvotham, and Baraniuk, 2010; Singla and Domingos, 2008).

We begin by briefly reviewing the sequential BP algorithm as well as the necessary background in probabilistic graphical models. We then present a collection of parallel shared memory BP algorithms that demonstrate the importance of *scheduling* in parallel BP. Next, we develop the Splash BP algorithm, which combines new scheduling ideas to address the limitations of existing *sequential* BP algorithms and achieve theoretically optimal *parallel* performance. Finally, we present how to efficiently implement loopy BP algorithms in the distributed parallel setting by addressing the challenges of distributed state and load balancing. Where possible, we provide both theoretical and real-world experimental analysis along with implementation-specific details addressing locking and efficient data structures. In addition, C++ code for the algorithms and experiments presented in this chapter can be obtained from our online repository at http://www.select.cs.cmu.edu/code.

10.1 Belief Propagation in Factor Graphs

Probabilistic graphical models provide a common language for studying, learning, and manipulating large *factorized distributions* of the form

$$\mathbf{P}\left(X_1 = x_1, \ldots, X_n = x_n \mid \theta\right) = \frac{1}{Z(\theta)} \prod_{\mathbf{A} \in \mathcal{C}} \psi_{\mathbf{A}}(\mathbf{x_A} \mid \theta), \qquad (10.1)$$

where $\mathbf{P}(x_1, \ldots, x_n)$ is the probability mass function for the set of variables $X = \{X_1, \ldots, X_n\}$. In this chapter we focus on distributions over discrete random variables $X_i \in \mathcal{X}_i = \{1, \ldots, |\mathcal{X}_i|\}$; however, many of the proposed methods may also be applied to settings with continuous variables.

Each $\mathbf{A} \in \mathcal{C}$ is a (typically small) subset $\mathbf{A} \subseteq \{1, \ldots, n\}$ of the indices of the random variables. The choice of subsets, $\mathcal{C}$, depends on the problem and encodes the conditional independence structure of the model. Each of the **factors** $\psi_{\mathbf{A}}$ is an un-normalized positive function, $\psi_{\mathbf{A}} : \mathcal{X}_{\mathbf{A}} \to \mathbb{R}^+$, over a subset $\mathbf{A} \in \mathcal{C}$ of the random variables. The factors are parametrized by the set of parameters θ. The **partition function** $Z(\theta)$ is the normalizing constant, which depends only on the parameters θ and has the value

$$Z(\theta) = \sum_{x_1 \in \mathcal{X}_1} \cdots \sum_{x_n \in \mathcal{X}_n} \prod_{\mathbf{A} \in \mathcal{C}} \psi_{\mathbf{A}}(\mathbf{x_A} \mid \theta) \ldots d\mathbf{x}, \qquad (10.2)$$

computed (in theory) by summing over the *exponentially* many joint assignments.

Because this chapter focuses on graphical model inference, we will assume that the model parameters (θ) and structure ($\mathcal{C}$) are fixed and known in advance and omit the parameters from the factors by writing $\psi_{\mathbf{A}}(\mathbf{x_A})$ instead of $\psi_{\mathbf{A}}(\mathbf{x_A} \mid \theta)$. Although in many applications the model parameters and structure are not known in advance and are instead learned from data, the algorithms for learning typically rely on inference as the core subroutine. Therefore, the parallel inference techniques presented in this chapter also can be used to accelerate learning.

Factorized distributions of the form Equation 10.1 may be naturally represented as an undirected bipartite graph $G = (V, E)$ called a *factor graph*. The vertices $V = \mathcal{X} \cup \mathcal{F}$ correspond to the variables ($\mathcal{X}$) on one side and the factors ($\mathcal{F}$) on the other, and the undirected edges $E = \{\{\psi_{\mathbf{A}}, X_i\} : i \in \mathbf{A}\}$ connect factors with the variables in their domain. To simplify notation, we use $\psi_{\mathbf{A}}, X_i \in V$ to refer to vertices when we wish to distinguish between factors and variables, and $i, j \in V$ otherwise. We define $\mathbf{N}[i]$ as the neighbors of i in the factor graph. In Figure 10.1 we illustrate a simple factor graph with four variables and two factors.

In Figure 10.2, we demonstrate how a factor graph can be used to reason about a noisy image. Suppose we are given a noisy image (Figure 10.2b) and our goal is to reconstruct the original image (Figure 10.2a). For each pixel measurement y_i, we introduce a latent random variable, X_i, which corresponds to the *true color* of the image at location i. We then introduce a "node" factor $\psi_{\{i\}}(X_i, y_i)$ that relates the true color of the image with the observed color y_i. For example, if we assume Gaussian noise, then a reasonable choice of node factor would be

$$\psi_{\{i\}}(X_i = x_i \mid Y_i = y_i) = \exp\left(-\frac{(x_i - y_i)^2}{2\sigma^2}\right). \qquad (10.3)$$

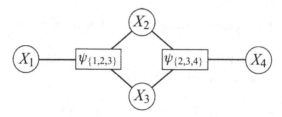

Figure 10.1 The factor graph corresponding to the factorized distribution $\mathbf{P}\left(x_1, x_2, x_3, x_4\right) \propto \psi_{\{1,2,3\}}(x_1, x_2, x_3)\psi_{\{2,3,4\}}(x_2, x_3, x_4)$. The circles represent variables, and the squares represent factors.

In "real-world" images, adjacent pixels typically have similar colors. We can encode this "smoothness" prior by constructing "edge" factors that connect adjacent pixels. These factors evaluate to large values when neighboring pixels are assigned similar colors and small values otherwise. A reasonable choice of similarity factor is the Laplace distribution:

$$\psi_{\{i,j\}}(X_i = x_i, X_j = x_j \mid \theta) = \exp\left(-\theta \left| x_i - x_j \right|\right). \tag{10.4}$$

Using the factors defined in Equations 10.3 and 10.4, we define the factor graph illustrated in Figure 10.2c. Graphical model inference is then used to recover the original image by solving for the expected color of each pixel ($\mathbf{E}[X_i]$) given the noisy pixel observations (y).

Factor graphs compactly represent a wide range of common graphical models, from Markov Logic Networks (MLNs) (Domingos et al., 2008) for natural language processing to pairwise Markov Random Fields (MRFs) for protein folding (Yanover and Weiss, 2002) and image processing (Saxena, Chung, and Ng, 2007).

10.1.1 Belief Propagation

Although graphical models provide a compact representation of factorized probability distributions, computing marginals and even the joint probability can often be intractable. In fact, computing exact marginals is NP-hard in general (Cooper, 1990) and even computing bounded approximations is NP-hard (Roth, 1993). Despite these discouraging results, there are several approximate inference algorithms that typically perform well in practice. In this chapter we focus on Loopy Belief Propagation

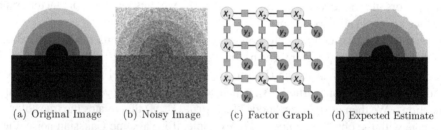

(a) Original Image   (b) Noisy Image   (c) Factor Graph   (d) Expected Estimate

Figure 10.2 Image denoising problem. (a) The synthetic noiseless original image. (b) The noisy pixel values observed by the camera. (c) A part of the factor graph used to denoise the image. Factors are included in this version of the drawing. (d) The expected assignment to each of the latent pixels as solved by BP.

(loopy BP), one of the more popular approximate inference algorithms, which is often considered to be an embarrassingly parallel algorithm (Mendiburu et al., 2007; Sun et al., 2002). In this chapter we explain why BP is not an embarrassingly parallel algorithm and provide a parallel variants that address the underlying sequential structure of graphical model inference.

Belief Propagation (BP), or the Sum-Product algorithm, was popularized by Pearl (1988) as an inference procedure for tree-structured models to estimate variable and clique marginals. The BP algorithm starts by placing a vector of parameters called a *message*[1] along each direction of every edge in the factor graph. The messages $m_{X_i \to \psi_A}$ and $m_{\psi_A \to X_i}$ along the edge connecting variable X_i to factor ψ_A are positive functions (tables) mapping assignments to X_i to the positive reals. In loopy graphs, it is difficult to provide a direct probabilistic interpretation of the messages. However, it may help to think of a message as encoding a distribution over the variable X_i.

The loopy BP algorithm begins by initializing all the messages to uniform distributions. Loopy BP then iteratively recomputes (updates) messages using the following update equations:

$$m_{X_i \to \psi_A}(x_i) \propto \prod_{\psi_B \in N[X_i] \setminus \psi_A} m_{\psi_B \to X_i}(x_i) \qquad (10.5)$$

$$m_{\psi_A \to X_i}(x_i) \propto \sum_{\mathbf{x}_A \setminus x_i} \psi_A(\mathbf{x}_A) \prod_{X_k \in N[\psi_A] \setminus X_i} m_{X_k \to \psi_A}(x_k) \qquad (10.6)$$

where Equation 10.5 is the message sent from variable X_i to factor ψ_A and Equation 10.6 is the message sent from factor ψ_A to variable X_i. The sum, $\sum_{\mathbf{x}_A \setminus x_i}$, is computed over all assignments to $\mathbf{x}_A$ excluding the variable x_i, and the product, $\prod_{X_k \in N[\psi_A] \setminus X_i}$, is computed over all neighbors of the vertex ψ_A excluding vertex X_i. The messages are normalized to ensure numerical stability. The procedure is then repeated until convergence.

At convergence, the local variable and factor marginals, also called the beliefs (b), are estimated using

$$\mathbf{P}(X_i = x_i) \approx b_{X_i}(x_i) \propto \prod_{\psi_A \in N[X_i]} m_{\psi_A \to X_i}(x_i) \qquad (10.7)$$

$$\mathbf{P}(\mathbf{X}_A = \mathbf{x}_A) \approx b_{\mathbf{X}_A}(\mathbf{x}_A) \propto \psi_A(\mathbf{x}_A) \prod_{X_j \in N[\psi_A]} m_{X_j \to \psi_A}(x_j).$$

In other words, the approximate marginal distribution of a variable is simply the (normalized) product of all of its incoming messages. Similarly, the approximate marginal of all variables within a factor can be estimated by multiplying the factor with all of its incoming messages.

The order in which messages are updated is called the *schedule* and plays an important role in efficient parallel loopy belief propagation. For instance, in tree graphical models, a simple procedure known as the forward-backward schedule was shown by Pearl (1988) to yield exact marginals using $O(2|E|)$ message calculations. First,

---

[1] Even though "message" is the traditional terminology and the words "send" and "receive" are frequently used, it should not be interpreted as a form of communication. The "message" is simply a numeric vector used in the derivation of the loopy BP algorithm in Pearl (1988).

messages are computed starting from the leaves and in the direction of an arbitrarily chosen root. The process is then reversed, computing all the messages in the opposite direction. The reader may observe from Equations 10.5 and 10.6 that this forward-backward (or perhaps upward-downward) schedule achieves exact convergence. That is, re-evaluation of any message using the message update equations will not change the message values.

Unfortunately, choosing the best schedule on loopy graphs is often difficult and can depend heavily on the factor graph structure and even the model parameters. For simplicity, many applications of loopy BP adopt a *synchronous* schedule in which all messages are *simultaneously* updated using messages from the previous iteration. Alternatively, some type of *asynchronous* schedule is employed, in which messages are updated *sequentially* using the most recent inbound messages. For example, the popular *round-robin* asynchronous schedule sequentially updates the messages in fixed order which is typically a random permutation over the vertices.

Advances by Elidan, McGraw, and Koller (2006) and Ranganathan, Kaess, and Dellaert (2007) have focused on *dynamic* asynchronous schedules, in which the message update order is determined as the algorithm proceeds. Other work by Wainwright, Jaakkola, and Willsky (2001) focuses on tree structured schedules, in which messages are updated along collections of spanning trees. By dynamically adjusting the schedule or by updating along spanning trees, these more recent techniques attempt to indirectly address the schedule dependence on the model parameters and structure. As we will see in this chapter, by varying the BP schedule we can affect the speed, convergence, and parallelism of BP.

Independent of the schedule, messages are computed until the change in message values between consecutive computations is bounded by small constant $\beta \geq 0$:

$$\max_{(i,j)\in E} \left\| m_{i \to j}^{(\text{new})} - m_{i \to j}^{(\text{old})} \right\|_1 \leq \beta. \tag{10.8}$$

Belief propagation is said to converge if at some point Equation 10.8 is achieved. Unfortunately, in cyclic graphical models there are few convergence guarantees (Tatikonda and Jordan, 2002; Ihler, Fischer, and Willsky, 2005; Mooij and Kappen, 2007). For a more complete introduction to loopy belief propagation as well as probabilistic graphical models, see Koller and Friedman (2009).

10.1.2 Opportunities for Parallelism in Belief Propagation

Belief propagation offers several opportunities for parallelism. At the graph level, multiple messages can be computed in parallel. At the factor level, individual message calculations (sums and products) can be expressed as matrix operations that can be parallelized relatively easily (Bertsekas and Tsitsiklis, 1989). For typical message sizes where the number of assignments is much less than the number of vertices ($\mathcal{X}_i << |V|$), graph-level parallelism provides more potential gains than factor-level parallelism. For instance, the message update equations do not offer much parallelism if all variables are binary. Therefore, we will ignore factor-level parallelism in this chapter and instead focus on graph-level parallelism. Running time will be measured in terms of the number of message computations, treating individual message updates as atomic unit time operations.

10.2 Shared Memory Parallel Belief Propagation

In this section we consider the shared memory setting and present the following parallel BP algorithms in order of increasing schedule complexity:

	Section	Asynch.	Dynamic	Difficulty
Synchronous	10.2.1			Simple
Round Robin	10.2.2	$\checkmark$		Moderate
Wildfire	10.2.3	$\checkmark$	$\checkmark$	Moderate
Residual	10.2.4	$\checkmark$	$\checkmark$	Challenging
Splash	10.2.5	$\checkmark$	$\checkmark$	Challenging

Although we ultimately advocate the use of the Splash BP algorithm, which typically outperforms the other algorithms, we believe that a better understanding of the parallel nature of BP can be obtained by examining each of the preceding algorithms. In addition, for some applications, simpler dynamic schedules, such as Wildfire, may perform adequately and may often be easier to implement.

10.2.1 Synchronous (MapReduce) BP

Synchronous BP is an inherently parallel algorithm. Given the messages from the previous iteration, all messages in the current iteration can be computed simultaneously and independently without inter-processor communication (Algorithm 26). The Synchronous BP algorithm requires two copies of each message to be maintained at all times. When the messages are updated, the values in $m^{(\text{old})}$ are used as input, while the resultant values are stored in $m^{(\text{new})}$. This form of completely independent computation is often deemed embarrassingly parallel. Because Synchronous BP is an embarrassingly parallel algorithm, it can naturally be expressed using the popular MapReduce framework.

Algorithm 26: Synchronous BP

   Input: Graph $G = (V, E)$ and all messages $\forall (i, j) \in E \, m_{i \to j}$

1 **while** *not converged* **do**

2   **forall** $j \in N[v]$ *in the neighbors of v* **do in parallel**

3   Compute Message $m_{v \to j}^{(\text{new})}$ using $\left\{ m_{i \to v}^{(\text{old})} \right\}_{i \in N[v]}$

4      $\text{Swap}(m^{(\text{old})}, m^{(\text{new})})$

The MapReduce framework, introduced by Dean and Ghemawat (2008), concisely and elegantly represents algorithms that consist of an embarrassingly parallel map phase followed by a reduction phase in which aggregate results are computed. It is important to note that the MapReduce abstraction was not originally designed for iterative algorithms, like belief propagation, and therefore standard implementations, like Hadoop, incur a costly communication and disk access penalty between iterations.

Algorithm 27: Map Function for Synchronous BP

Input: A vertex $v \in V$ and all inbound messages $\{m_{i \to v}\}_{i \in N[v]}$
Output: Set of outbound messages as key–value pairs $(j, m_{v \to j})$

1 **forall** $j \in N[v]$ *in the neighbors of v* **do in parallel**
2 $\quad\vert\quad$ Compute Message $m_{v \to j}$ using $\{m_{i \to v}\}_{i \in N[v]}$
3 $\quad\vert\quad$ Return key–value pair $(j, m_{v \to j})$

Nonetheless, Synchronous BP can naturally be expressed as an iterative MapReduce algorithm where the Map operation (defined in Algorithm 27) is applied to all vertices and emits destination-message key–value pairs and the Reduce operation (defined in Algorithm 28) joins messages at their destination vertex, updates the local belief, and prepares for the next iteration.

Algorithm 28: Reduce Function for Synchronous BP

Input: The key–value pairs $\{(v, m_{i \to v})\}_{i \in N[v]}$
Output: The belief b_v for vertex v as well as the $\{(v, m_{i \to v})\}_{i \in N[v]}$ pairs $(j, m_{v \to j})$

1 Compute the belief b_v for v using $\{(v, m_{i \to v})\}_{i \in N[v]}$
2 Return b_v and $\{(v, m_{i \to v})\}_{i \in N[v]}$

Although it is not possible to analyze the running time of Synchronous BP on a general cyclic graphical model, we can analyze the running time in the context of tree graphical models. In Theorem 10.1 we provide the running time of Synchronous BP when computing *exact* marginals without the *early-stopping* (see next subsection) typically used when running loopy BP.

Theorem 10.1 (Exact Synchronous BP Running Time) *Given an acyclic factor graph with $|V|$ vertices, longest path length l, and $p \leq 2(|V| - 1)$ processors, parallel synchronous belief propagation will compute exact marginals in time (as measured in number of vertex updates)*

$$\Theta \left(\frac{|V|l}{p} + l \right).$$

If we consider the running time given by Theorem 10.1, we see that the $|V|/p$ term corresponds to the parallelization of each synchronous update. The length l of the longest path corresponds to the limiting sequential component that cannot be eliminated by scaling the number of processors. As long as the number of vertices is much greater than the number of processors, the Synchronous BP algorithm achieves nearly linear parallel scaling and therefore appears to be an optimal parallel algorithm. However, an optimal parallel algorithm should also be *efficient*. That is, the total work done by all processors should be asymptotically equivalent to the work done by a single processor running the *optimal* sequential algorithm.

To illustrate the inefficiency of Synchronous BP, we analyze the running time on a chain graphical model with $|V|$ vertices. Chain graphical models act as a theoretical benchmark by directly capturing the limiting sequential structure of message passing

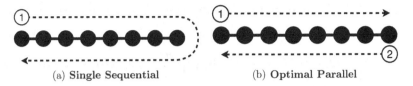

(a) **Single Sequential**   (b) **Optimal Parallel**

Figure 10.3 (a) The optimal forward-backwards message ordering for exact inference on a chain using a single processor. (b) The optimal message ordering for exact inference on a chain using two processors.

algorithms and can be seen as a sub-problem in both acyclic and cyclic graphical models.

It is well known that the forward-backward schedule (Figure 10.3a) for belief propagation on chain graphical models is optimal. The forward-backward schedule, as the name implies, sequentially computes messages from $m_{1\to2}$ to $m_{|V|-1\to|V|}$ in the forward direction and then sequentially computes messages from $m_{|V|\to|V|-1}$ to $m_{2\to1}$ in the backward direction. The running time of this simple schedule is therefore $\Theta(|V|)$ or exactly $2(|V|-1)$ message calculations.

If we run the Synchronous BP algorithm using $p = 2(|V|-1)$ processors on a chain graphical model of length $|V|$, we obtain a running time of exactly $|V|-1$. This means that parallel Synchronous BP algorithm obtains only a *factor of 2* speedup using two processors per edge, almost twice as many processors as the number of vertices. More surprisingly, if we use fewer than $|V|-1$ processors, the parallel synchronous algorithm will be *slower* than the simple sequential forward-backward algorithm running on a single processor. Finally, if we use any constant number of processors (e.g., $p = 2$), then the parallel Synchronous BP algorithm will run in *quadratic* time while the sequential single processor algorithm will run in *linear* time.

Although messages may be computed in any order, information is propagated *sequentially*. On every iteration of Synchronous BP, only a few message computations (in the case of chain graphical models, only two message computations) contribute to convergence while the rest are *wasted*. Unfortunately, there are no parallel schedules that achieve greater than a factor of 2 speedup for *exact* inference on arbitrary chain graphical models. Fortunately, there are parallel schedules that can achieve substantially better scaling by exploiting a frequently used *approximation* in loopy BP.

Stopping Early: The τ_ϵ Approximation

In almost all applications of loopy BP, the convergence threshold β in Equation 10.8 is set to a small value greater than zero, and the algorithm is terminated before reaching the true fixed point. Even when $\beta = 0$, the fixed floating-point precision of discrete processors result in early termination. Because the resulting approximation plays an important role in studying parallel belief propagation, we provide a brief theoretical characterization.

We can represent a single iteration of synchronous belief propagation by a function f_{BP} that maps all the messages $m^{(t)}$ on the tth iteration to all the messages $m^{(t+1)} = f_{\text{BP}}(m^{(t)})$ on the $(t+1)^{\text{th}}$ iteration. The fixed point is then the set of messages

$m^* = f_{BP}(m^*)$ that are invariant under f_{BP}. In addition, we define a max-norm for the message space

$$\left|\left|m^{(t)} - m^{(t+1)}\right|\right|_\infty = \max_{(i,j)\in E} \left|\left|m_{i\to j}^{(t)} - m_{i\to j}^{(t+1)}\right|\right|_1, \tag{10.9}$$

which matches the norm used in the standard termination condition, Equation 10.8. We define τ_ϵ as

$$\tau_\epsilon = \min_t t \quad \text{s.t.} \quad \left|\left|m^{(t)} - m^*\right|\right|_\infty \le \epsilon, \tag{10.10}$$

the number of synchronous iterations required to be within an ϵ ball of the BP fixed point. Therefore a τ_ϵ-approximation is the approximation obtained from running synchronous belief propagation for τ_ϵ iterations. In practice, it is typically impossible to determine τ_ϵ without first running the inference algorithm. Ultimately, we will rely on the idea of τ_ϵ-approximation and the τ_ϵ quantity as a theoretical tool for comparing inference algorithms and understanding parallel convergence behavior.

The definition of τ_ϵ directly leads to an *improved* parallel running time for Synchronous BP:

Theorem 10.2 (τ_ϵ-Approximate Synchronous BP Running Time) *Given an acyclic factor graph with $|V|$ vertices and $p \le 2(|V| - 1)$ processors, parallel synchronous belief propagation will compute τ_ϵ-approximate messages in time (as measured in number of vertex updates):*

$$\Theta\left(\frac{|V|\tau_\epsilon}{p} + \tau_\epsilon\right).$$

The important consequence of Theorem 10.2 is that the fundamental sequential component of Synchronous BP depends on the *effective* chain length determined by τ_ϵ. Models with weaker variable interactions will have a smaller τ_ϵ and will permit greater parallelism. We formalize this intuition through the following lower bound on τ_ϵ-approximations for chain graphical models.

Theorem 10.3 (τ_ϵ-Approximate BP Lower Bound) *For an arbitrary chain graph with $|V|$ vertices and p processors, a lower bound for the running time of a τ_ϵ-approximation is*

$$\Omega\left(\frac{|V|}{p} + \tau_\epsilon\right).$$

The bound provided in Theorem 10.3 is surprisingly revealing because it concisely isolates the fundamental parallel ($|V|/p$) and sequential (τ_ϵ) components of BP. Unfortunately, τ_ϵ could also grow with problem size, leading to an asymptotic inefficiency in Synchronous BP. As we present the remaining four parallel BP algorithms, we will see how the multiplicative dependence of $|V|\tau_\epsilon/p$ on τ_ϵ in Theorem 10.2 can be eliminated and the lower bound in Theorem 10.3 can be achieved. We also experimentally demonstrate how directly addressing this multiplicative τ_ϵ dependence can substantially improve performance in general factor graphs.

10.2.2 Round-Robin Belief Propagation

The Synchronous BP scheduling requires two copies of the graph, reading from the first copy, and writing to the second copy. However, if we perform the same schedule using only one copy of the graph by updating messages in-place, we obtain a form of asynchronous schedule known as Round-Robin BP. The round-robin schedule is defined over a fixed permutation σ of vertices V. The vertices in the graph are then updated in the order σ.

Because messages are updated in place, synchronization methods must be used to prevent processors from accessing the same message simultaneously. For instance, if one processor is writing a message while another processor is reading from it, the reader could end up with an inconsistent message. We demonstrate a simple synchronization strategy in Algorithm 29, which uses a *read-write lock* on each vertex. When SendMessages(v) is invoked on vertex v, we acquire a *write lock* on v and *read locks* on all adjacent vertices. To prevent deadlocks, all locks must be acquired in the same order on all processors. To achieve this, Algorithm 29 grabs vertex locks in the order of the vertex IDs. All locks are blocking, and so the processor does not proceed until the lock is acquired.

Algorithm 29: SendMessages(v)

    // Sort v and its neighbors (done in advance)
1 $o \leftarrow \text{Sort}(N[v] \cup \{v\})$ ordered by vertex ID
    // Lock v and its neighbors in order
2 **for** $i \in [1, \ldots, |o|]$ **do**
3   **if** $o_i = v$ **then** Acquire Write Lock on v
4   **else** Acquire Read Lock on neighbor o_i

    // Compute the new belief
5 $b_v \propto \prod_{u \in N[v]} m_{u \to v}$
6 **if** v *is a factor node* **then** $b_v \propto \psi_v \times b_v$
    // Compute outgoing messages
7 **for** $u \in \sigma(v)$ **do** $m_{v \to u} \propto \sum_{\mathbf{x}_v \setminus \mathbf{x}_u} b_v / m_{u \to v}$
    // Release all locks in the reverse order
8 **for** $i \in [|o|, \ldots, 1]$ **do**
9   **if** $o_i = v$ **then** Release Write Lock on o_i
10   **else** Release Read Lock on o_i

The parallel execution of the round-robin schedule may not always produce the same result as the sequential execution on that schedule. However, because of the locking mechanism used in SendMessages (Algorithm 29), it is possible to show *sequential consistency*: for every parallel execution, there is a corresponding sequential execution that produces the same result. Because the SendMessages routine ensures that the program state that is read or modified is locked throughout its execution, it is possible to arrange the simultaneous execution of SendMessages in a sequential order. A reader interested in learning more about memory consistency models is referred to

---

Algorithm 30: Atomic Parallel Round-Robin Algorithm

---

1   $\sigma \leftarrow$ Arbitrary permutation on $\{1, \ldots, |V|\}$
2   Atomic integer $i \leftarrow 1$
3   **do in parallel**
4   **while** *Not Converged* **do**
         // Reads the value of i and increments i atomically
5          $j = AtomicFetchAndIncrement(i)$
         // Get the vertex to update
6          $v = \sigma(j \bmod |V|)$
7   SendMessages(v)

Adve and Gharachorloo (1996). In practice we have found, surprisingly, that on some problems, disabling the locking mechanism seems to have little effect on the result with a minor improvement in parallel scaling. Indeed, work by Ihler et al. (2005) has shown that belief propagation is relatively robust to message errors.

Although there are several ways to implement a parallel round-robin algorithm, we present the simplest in Algorithm 30. The algorithm makes use of *atomic* operations, which are typically available on most modern processors. An atomic operation is an instruction that is guaranteed to complete without interrupt. For instance, the `AtomicFetchAndIncrement(i)`[2] operation increments i and returns its old value. Atomic operations cannot overlap: another `AtomicFetchAndIncrement(i)` issued by a different processor starts only after the current atomic operation completes.

In Algorithm 30, each processor runs independently, and the schedule is advanced by atomically reading and incrementing a shared counter, i. After a processor reads the shared counter, it executes `SendMessages`$(\sigma(i))$ on that vertex in the schedule σ and then checks for local convergence. The process is repeated until all vertices converge.

A slightly more efficient variation can be constructed by partitioning the vertices over the processors and executing a local round-robin schedule on each processor. However, because the processors run independently, the resulting schedule is not globally round-robin, and care must be taken to ensure that high-degree computationally expensive vertices do not cause individual processors to lag.

10.2.3 Wildfire Belief Propagation

In practice we find that the parallel Round-robin algorithm tends to converge faster than the parallel Synchronous algorithm. However, the Round-Robin algorithm still incurs a significant amount of unnecessary computation. For example, consider a graphical model that comprises two disconnected regions. The first region takes a iterations of Round-Robin scheduling to converge, while the second region takes b iterations, where $a \ll b$. Performing Round-Robin BP on the entire graph will therefore take b iterations to converge. The first region will run for $b - a$ more iterations than necessary, resulting in potentially substantial wasted computation.

---

[2] This function is provided in GCC (Gnu Compiler Collection) as _sync_fetch_and_add().

A simple solution to the problem of overscheduling an already converged region of the model is to simply skip vertices that have already converged. For both theoretical and practical reasons discussed in Gonzalez et al. (2009a), we introduced the *belief residual* defined as

$$r_v^{(t)} \leftarrow r_v^{(t-1)} + \left|\left| b_v^{(t)} - b_v^{(t-1)} \right|\right|_1. \qquad (10.11)$$

The belief residual accumulates the changes in belief between invocations of the SendMessages operation. After SendMessages is invoked on a vertex, its residual is set to zero, and the residuals of the neighboring vertices are increased by the corresponding change in belief. We also adopt the modified convergence criterion:

$$\max_{v \in V} r_v \leq \beta. \qquad (10.12)$$

Therefore, if $r_v \leq \beta$, then we no longer need to compute messages out of v.

The belief residual is an approximate measure of the amount of new information that has not yet been sent by vertex v. If we make a minor modification to the Round-Robin algorithm to skip vertices that have converged with respect to Equation 10.12, we obtain a parallel version of the Wildfire Algorithm (Ranganathan et al., 2007) shown in Algorithm 31. The Wildfire algorithm is almost identical to the Round-Robin Algorithm (Algorithm 30), except that vertices with insufficient residual are skipped.

Algorithm 31: Parallel Wildfire Algorithm Using Atomics

---

1   $\sigma \leftarrow$ Arbitrary permutation on $\{1, \ldots, |V|\}$
2   Atomic integer $i \leftarrow 1$
3   **do in parallel**
4   **while** *Not Converged* **do**
       // Reads the value of i and increments i atomically
5       $j = AtomicFetchAndIncrement(i)$
       // Get the vertex to update
6       $v = \sigma(j \mod |V|)$
7   **if** $r_v > \beta$ **then**
8   SendMessages(v)
9   Set $r_v = 0$ and update neighbors $r_{N[v]}$

10.2.4 Residual Belief Propagation

A natural extension to the Wildfire BP algorithm is to change the order in which vertices are updated by preferentially updating vertices that will exhibit the "largest change" (where change is defined by Equation 10.11). The resulting algorithm corresponds to a modified version of the residual belief propagation originally proposed by Elidan et al. (2006). The Residual BP algorithm in Algorithm 32 uses a priority queue to store the vertices in residual order. Each processor then picks the highest priority vertex from Q and executes SendMessages on it, updating all neighbor priorities along the way.

Algorithm 32: Residual Belief Propagation Algorithm

---

1 Priority Queue Q
2 Initialize Q with all vertices at ∞ priority
3 **do in parallel**
4   **while** `TopResid`$(Q) > \beta$ **do**
5          $v = $ `Top`(Q) `// Get vertex with highest residual`
6   `SendMessages`(v)
7   Set $r_v = 0$ and update neighbors $r_{N[v]}$

When the message computations are fairly simple, the priority queue becomes the central synchronizing bottleneck. An efficient implementation of a parallel priority queue is therefore the key to performance and scalability. There are numerous parallel priority queue algorithms in the literature (Driscoll et al., 1988; Crupi, Das, and Pinotti, 1996; Parberry, 1995; Sanders, 1998). Many require sophisticated fine-grained locking mechanisms while others employ binning strategies with constraints on the priority distribution. Because the residual priorities are a heuristic, we find that relaxing the strict ordering requirement can further improve performance by reducing priority queue contention. In our implementation we randomly assigned vertices to priority queues associated with each processor. Each processor then draws from its own queue but can update the priorities of vertices owned by other processors.

10.2.5 Splash Belief Propagation

Although often faster than Synchronous BP in practice, all the algorithms we have described so far share the same asymptotic $O\left(|V|\tau_\epsilon/p + \tau_\epsilon\right)$ performance on chain graphical models. The problem is, none of these algorithms directly address the forward-backward sequential element of inference. To address this problem, we introduced the Splash BP algorithm in Gonzalez, Low, and Guestrin (2009b), which combines the forward-backward element of tree-based schedules with the dynamic scheduling to achieve a provably optimal parallel BP algorithm. The Splash algorithm is composed of two core components, the Splash routine that generalizes the forward-backward scheduling to loopy BP, and a dynamic Splash scheduling (using belief residuals) that ultimately determines the shape, size, and location of Splashes.

The Splash operation (Algorithm 33 and Figure 10.4) generalizes the forward-backward scheduling illustrated in Figure 10.3a by constructing a small tree, which we call a Splash, and then executing a local forward-backward schedule on the tree.

By scheduling message calculations along a local tree, we directly address the sequential message dependencies and retain the optimal forward-backward schedule when applied to acyclic models. This also leads to substantial improvements in experimental performance.

The inputs to the Splash operation are the root vertex v and the maximum allowed size of the Splash, W. The maximum allowed size W is measured in terms of overall work, which is proportional to the number of floating-point operations associated with executing the Splash. We restrict our Splashes to be a fixed amount of work to ensure

---

Algorithm 33: Splash(v, W)

Input: Vertex v

Input: Maximum Splash size W

// Construct the breadth first search ordering with W
   message computations and rooted at v.

1 fifo $\leftarrow$ [] // FiFo Spanning Tree Queue

2 $\sigma \leftarrow (v)$ // Initial Splash ordering is the root v

3 AccumW $\leftarrow w_v$ // Accumulate the root vertex work

4 visited $\leftarrow \{v\}$ // Set of visited vertices

5 fifo.Enqueue($N[v]$)

6 **while** *fifo is not empty* **do**

7     $u \leftarrow$ fifo.Dequeue()

   // If adding u does not cause Splash to exceed limit

8   **if** $AccumW + w_u \leq W$ **then**

9   AccumW $\leftarrow$ AccumW $+ w_u$

10   Add u to the end of the ordering σ

11   **foreach** *neighbors* $v \in N[u]$ **do**

12   **if** *v is not in visited* **then**

13   fifo.Enqueue(v) // Add to boundary of spanning tree

14   visited $\leftarrow$ visited $\cup \{v\}$ // Mark Visited

// Forward Pass: sends messages from the leaves to root

16 **foreach** $u \in$ ReverseOrder(σ) **do**

17   SendMessages(u) // Update priorities if necessary.

// Backward Pass: sends messages from the root to leaves

19 **foreach** $u \in \sigma$ **do**

20   SendMessages(u) // Update priorities if necessary.

---

that each processor executes Splashes at similar rates. We define the work associated with each vertex u (which could be a variable or factor) as

$$w_u = |\mathbf{N}[u]| \times |\mathcal{X}_u| + \sum_{X_v \in \mathbf{N}[u]} |\mathcal{X}_v|, \qquad (10.13)$$

where $|\mathbf{N}[u]| \times |\mathcal{X}_u|$ represents the work required to recompute all outbound messages and $\sum_{X_v \in \mathbf{N}[u]} |\mathcal{X}_v|$ is the work required to update the beliefs of all the neighboring vertices. We account for updating the neighboring vertex beliefs because this is needed to maintain the belief residual defined in Equation 10.11. The work w_u defined in Equation 10.13 is therefore proportional to the running time of invoking SendMessages(u).

A Splash begins by constructing a local spanning tree rooted at v, adding vertices in breadth-first search order such that the total amount of work in the Splash does not exceed the limit set by W. Using the *reverse* of the breadth-first search ordering, the SendMessages operation is sequentially invoked on each vertex in the spanning tree starting at the leaves (line 16 of Algorithm 33), generalizing the forward sweep.

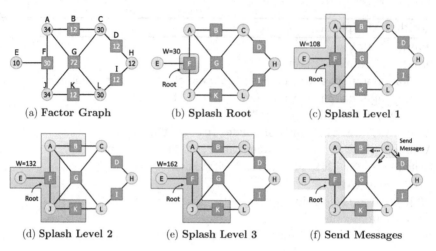

(a) **Factor Graph**   (b) **Splash Root**   (c) **Splash Level 1**

(d) **Splash Level 2**   (e) **Splash Level 3**   (f) **Send Messages**

Figure 10.4 A Splash of size $W = 170$ is grown starting at vertex F. The Splash spanning tree is represented by the shaded region. (a) The initial factor graph is labeled with the vertex work associated with each vertex. (b) The Splash begins rooted at vertex F. (c) The neighbors of F are added to the Splash, and the accumulated work increases to $w = 108$. (d) The Splash expands further to include vertex B and K but does not include vertex G, because doing so would exceed the maximum Splash size of $W = 170$. (e) The Splash expand, once more to include vertex C but can no longer expand without exceeding the maximum Splash size. The final Splash ordering is $\sigma = [F, E, A, J, B, K, C]$. (f) The SendMessages operation is invoked on vertex C, causing the messages $m_{C \to B}$, $m_{C \to G}$, and $m_{C \to D}$ to be recomputed.

Finally, messages are computed in the original σ ordering starting at the root (line 19 of Algorithm 33) and invoking SendMessages sequentially on each vertex, completing the backward sweep. Hence, with the exception of the root vertex v, all messages originating from each vertex in the Splash are computed twice, once in the forward sweep and once in the backward sweep.

By repeatedly executing p parallel Splashes of size $W = w|V|/p$ (where w is the work of updating a single vertex) placed evenly along the chain, we can achieve the *optimal* parallel BP running time:

Theorem 10.4 (Splash Optimality) *Given a chain graph with $|V|$ vertices and $p \leq |V|$ processors, then executing evenly spaced Splashes in parallel achieves a τ_ϵ level approximation for all vertices in time*

$$O\left(\frac{|V|}{p} + \tau_\epsilon\right).$$

We therefore achieve the runtime lower bound for τ_ϵ approximation described in Theorem 10.3 by using the Splash operation. The remaining challenge is determining how to place Splashes in arbitrary cyclic graphical models.

By combining the Splash operation with the belief residual scheduling to select Splash roots, we obtain the Splash BP algorithm given in Algorithm 34. The sequential Splash algorithm maintains a shared belief residual priority queue over vertices. The queue is initialized in a random order with the priorities of all vertices set to infinity. This ensures that every vertex is updated at least once. The Splash operation is applied

---

Algorithm 34: The Sequential Splash Algorithm

Input: Constants: maximum Splash size W, termination bound β

1 $Q \leftarrow$ InitializeQueue(Q)
2 Set All Residuals to ∞
3 **while** TopResid$(Q) > \beta$ **do**
4 $\quad\vert\quad v \leftarrow$ Top(Q)
5 $\quad\lfloor\quad$ Splash(Q, v, W) // Priorities updated after SendMessages

---

to the vertex at the top of the queue. During the Splash operation, the priorities of vertices in the Splash and along the boundary are updated.

To demonstrate the performance gains of the Sequential Splash algorithm on strongly sequential models, we constructed a set of synthetic chain graphical models and evaluated the running time on these models for a fixed convergence criterion while scaling the size of the Splash in Figure 10.5a and while scaling the size of the chain in Figure 10.5b. Each chain consists of binary random variables with weak random node potentials and strong attractive edge potentials. As the size of the Splash increases (Figure 10.5a), the total number of updates on the chain decreases, reflecting the optimality of the underlying forward-backward structure of the Splash.

In Figure 10.5b we compare the running time of Splash with Synchronous, Round-Robin, Residual, and Wildfire belief propagation as we increase the size of the model. The conventional Synchronous and Round-Robin algorithms are an order of magnitude slower than Wildfire, ResidualBP, and Splash and scale poorly, forcing separate comparisons for readability. Nonetheless, in all cases the Splash algorithm (with Splash size $W = 500$) is substantially faster and demonstrates better scaling with increasing model size.

The running time, computational efficiency, and accuracy of the sequential Splash algorithm were evaluated in the single-processor setting. In Figure 10.6a, b, and c, we plot the average belief accuracy, worst-case belief accuracy, and map prediction accuracy against the runtime on a subset of the UAI 2008 Probabilistic Inference Evaluation dataset (Darwiche et al. 2008). We ran each belief propagation algorithm to $\beta = 10^{-5}$ convergence and recorded the runtime in seconds and the marginal estimates for all variables. We compared against the exact marginals obtained using Ace 2.0 (Huang, Chavira, and Darwiche, 2006). In all cases the Splash algorithm obtained the most accurate belief estimates in the shortest time. The other baseline belief propagation algorithms follow a consistent pattern, with Wildfire and Residual belief propagation (dynamical scheduled algorithms) consistently outperforming round-robin and synchronous belief propagation (fixed schedules). We also assessed accuracy on a protein side-chain prediction task (Yanover, Schueler-Furman, and Weiss, 2007), where the goal is to estimate the orientations of each side chain in a protein structure. Here we find that all belief propagation algorithms achieve roughly the same prediction accuracy of 73% for χ_1 and χ_2 angles, which is consistent with the results of Yanover et al. (2007).

We assessed the convergence of the Splash belief propagation algorithm using several different metrics. In Figure 10.7a we plot the number of protein networks

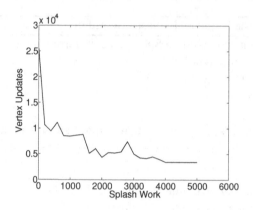

(a) **Runtime versus Splash Size**

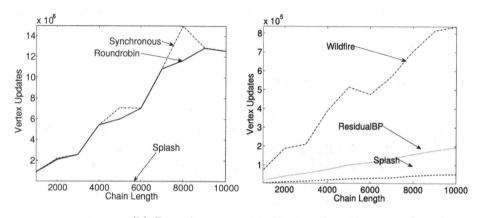

(b) **Runtime versus Chain Size**

Figure 10.5 In this figure, we plot the number of vertex updates on a randomly generated chain graphical model to convergence. Runtime to convergence is measured in vertex updates rather than wall clock time to ensure a fair *algorithmic* comparison and eliminate hardware and implementation effects that appear at the extremely short runtimes encountered on these simple models. (a) The number of vertex updates made by Sequential Splash BP, fixing the chain length to 1000 variables, and varying the Splash size. (b) The number of vertex updates made by various BP algorithms varying the length of the chain. Two plots are used to improve readability because the Splash algorithm is an order of magnitude faster than the Synchronous and Round-Robin algorithms; however, the Splash algorithm curve is the same for both plots.

that have converged ($\beta = 10^{-5}$) against the runtime. Here we find that not only does Splash belief propagation converge faster than other belief propagation algorithms, but it also converges more often. In Figure 10.7b we plot the number of protein networks that have converged against the number of message computations. Again, we see that Splash belief propagation converges sooner than other belief propagation algorithms.

The Parallel Splash Algorithm

We construct the Parallel Splash belief propagation algorithm from the Sequential Splash algorithm by executing multiple Splashes in parallel. The abstract Parallel

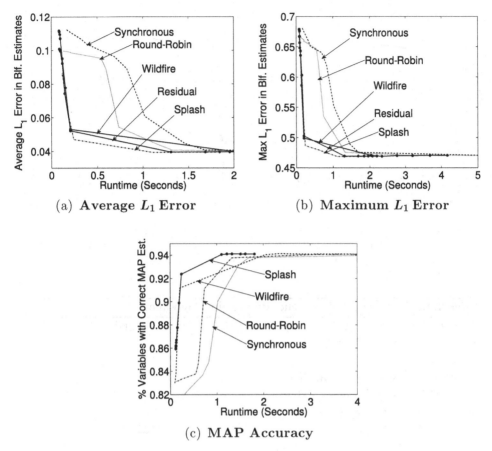

(a) **Average L_1 Error**   (b) **Maximum L_1 Error**

(c) **MAP Accuracy**

Figure 10.6 We assessed the accuracy of the Splash algorithm using the exact inference challenge networks from Darwiche et al. (2008) as well as the protein side chain prediction networks obtained from Yanover et al. (2007). In (a) and (b) we plot the average and max L_1 error in the belief estimates for all variables as a function of the running time. In (c) we plot the prediction accuracy of the MAP estimates as a function of the running time. In all cases we find that the Splash belief propagation achieves the greatest accuracy in the least time.

Splash algorithm is given in Algorithm 35. Notice that the Parallel Splash algorithm differs from the sequential Splash algorithm only in line 4, in which p processors are set to run the sequential Splash algorithm all drawing from the same shared queue.

Although we do not require that parallel Splashes contain disjoint sets of vertices, we do require that each Splash has a unique root which is achieved through the shared scheduling queue and atomic Push and Pop operations. To prevent redundant message update when Splashes overlap, if multiple processors simultaneously call SendMessages(i), all but one return immediately, ensuring a single update. To achieve maximum parallel performance, the parallel Splash BP algorithm (like the Residual BP algorithm) relies on an efficient parallel scheduling queue to minimize processor locking and sequentialization when Push, Pop, and UpdatePriority are invoked.

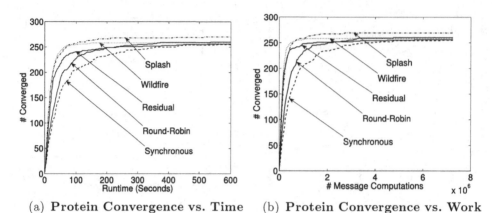

(a) **Protein Convergence vs. Time**   (b) **Protein Convergence vs. Work**

Figure 10.7 The Splash algorithm demonstrates faster and more consistent convergence than other baseline algorithms on a single processor. The number of converged ($\beta = 10^{-5}$) networks (out of 276) is plotted against the runtime (a) and number of message calculations (b).

Algorithm 35: Parallel Splash Belief Propagation Algorithm

Input: Constants: maximum Splash size W, termination bound β

1   $Q \leftarrow$ InitializeQueue(Q)

2   Set All Residuals to ∞

4   **forall** *processors* **do in parallel**

5   │   **while** *TopResidual(Q)* $> \beta$ **do**

6   │   │ $v \leftarrow$ Pop(Q) // Atomic

7   │   │   Splash(Q, v, W) // Updates vertex residuals

8   │   └ Q.Push((v, Residual(v))) // Atomic

Dynamic Splashes with Belief Residuals

A weakness of the Splash belief propagation algorithm is that it requires tuning of the Splash size (maximum work) parameter that affects the overall performance. If the Splash size is too large, then the algorithm will be forced to recompute messages that have already converged. Alternatively, if the Splash size is set too small, then we do not exploit the local sequential structure. To address this weakness in the Splash algorithm, we introduced Dynamic Splashes, which substantially improve performance in practice and eliminate the need to tune the Splash size parameter.

The key idea is that we can use belief residuals to automatically adapt the size and shape of the Splash procedure as the algorithm proceeds. In particular, we modify the initial breadth-first search phase of the Splash operation to exclude vertices with belief residuals below the termination condition. This ensures that we do not recompute messages that have already "converged," and more importantly allows the Splash operation to *adapt* to the local convergence patterns in the factor graph. As the algorithm approaches convergence, skipping low-belief residual vertices forces the breadth-first search to terminate early and causes the size of each Splash to shrink. As a consequence, the algorithm is less sensitive to the Splash size W. Instead we can fix Splash size

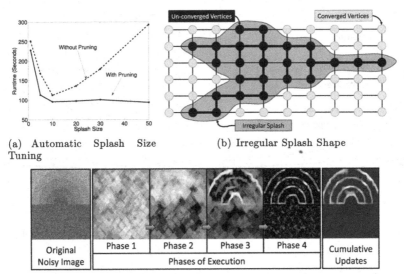

(a) Automatic Splash Size Tuning

(b) Irregular Splash Shape

(c) Execution of the Splash Algorithm on the Denoising Task

Figure 10.8 (a) The running time of the Splash algorithm using various different Splash sizes with and without pruning. (b) The vertices with high belief residual, shown in black, are included in the Splash, whereas vertices with belief residual below the termination threshold, shown in gray, are excluded. (c) To illustrate the execution of the Splash BP algorithm, we ran it on a simple image denoising task and took snapshots of the program state at four representative points (phases) during the execution. The cumulative vertex updates (number of times SendMessages was invoked since the last snapshot) are plotted, with brighter regions being updated more often than darker regions. Initially, large regular (rectangular) Splashes are evenly spread over the entire model. As the algorithm proceeds, the Splashes become smaller and more irregular, focusing on the *challenging* regions along the boundaries of the underlying image.

to a relatively large fraction of the graph (e.g., $|V|/p$) and let pruning automatically decrease the Splash size as needed.

In Figure 10.8a we plot the running time of the Parallel Splash algorithm with different Splash sizes W both with and without Splash pruning enabled. With Splash pruning disabled, there is a clear optimal Splash size. However, with Splash pruning enabled, increasing the size of the Splash beyond the optimal size does not reduce the performance. We have also plotted in Figure 10.8c examples of the Splashes at various phases of the algorithm on the classic image denoising task (see Figure 10.2). Initially the Splashes are relatively large and uniform, but as the algorithm converges, the Splashes shrink and adapt to the local shape of the remaining non-converged regions in the model.

10.3 Multicore Performance Comparison

We present runtime, speedup, work, and efficiency results as a function of the number of cores on protein-protein interaction networks obtained from Jaimovich et al. (2006) with over 14K binary variables, 20K factors, and 50K edges. The runtime, shown in Figure 10.9a, is measured in seconds of elapsed wall clock time before

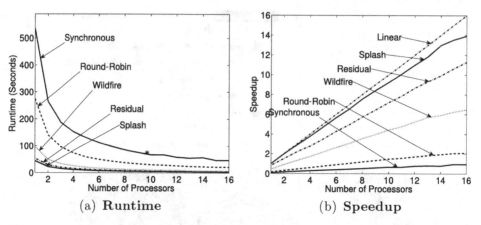

(a) **Runtime**   (b) **Speedup**

Figure 10.9 Multicore results for protein-protein interaction networks (Jaimovich et al., 2006).

convergence. An ideal runtime curve for p processors is proportional to $1/p$. On all of the models, we find that the Splash algorithm achieved a runtime that was strictly less than the standard belief propagation algorithms. We also find that the popular static scheduling algorithms, round-robin and synchronous belief propagation, are consistently slower than the dynamic scheduling algorithms, Residual, Wildfire, and Splash.

The speedup, shown in Figure 10.9b, is measured relative to the fastest single processor algorithm. As a consequence of the relative-to-best speedup definition, inefficient algorithms may exhibit a speedup less than 1. By measuring the speedup relative to the fastest single-processor algorithm, we ensure that wasted computation does not have an effect on the speedup curves.[3] Furthermore, we again see a consistent pattern in which the dynamic scheduling algorithms dramatically outperform the static scheduling algorithms. The inefficiency in the static scheduling algorithms (synchronous and round-robin) is so dramatic that the parallel variants seldom achieve more than a factor of 2 speedup using 16 processors.

10.4 Parallel Belief Propagation on Clusters

In this section we discuss some of the challenges and opportunities distributed memory architectures present in the context of parallel belief propagation and provide algorithmic solutions to several of the key challenges. Although the distributed setting often considers systems with network and processor failure, in this section we assume that all resources remain available throughout execution and that all messages eventually reach their destination.

In Algorithm 36 we present a generic distributed BP algorithm composed of a partitioning phase (line 2) after which each processor repeatedly executes BP updates

---

[3] An easy way to get "optimal" speedup is to have each thread perform additional unnecessary computation. This will produce strong speedup curves, but actual runtime will be suboptimal.

Algorithm 36: The Distributed BP Algorithm

---

2 $\mathcal{B} \leftarrow$ Partition(G, p) // Partition the graph over processors
3 DistributeGraph$(G, \mathcal{B})$
4 **forall** $b \in \mathcal{B}$ **do in parallel**
5   **repeat**
       // Perform BP Updates according to local schedule
7   BPUpdate(b)
8   RecvExternalMsgs() // Receive and integrate messages
9   SendExternalMsgs() // Transmit boundary messages
10   **until** *not Converged()* // Distributed convergence test
11

(line 7) using a local schedule, followed by inter-processor communication and a distributed convergence test. To achieve balanced computation and communication we employ weighted graph partitioning and overpartitioning, which we will now describe.

10.4.1 Partitioning the Factor Graph and Messages

To distribute the state of the program among p processors, we partition the factor graph and messages. We define a partitioning of the factor graph over p processors as a set $\mathcal{B} = \{B_1, \ldots, B_p\}$ of disjoint sets of vertices $B_k \subseteq V$ such that $\cup_{k=1}^p B_k = V$. Given a partitioning $\mathcal{B}$, we assign all the factor data associated with $\psi_i \in B_k$ to the kth processor. Similarly, for all (both factor and variable) vertices $i \in B_k$, we store the associated belief and all inbound messages on the processor k. Each vertex update is therefore a local procedure. For instance, if vertex i is updated, the processor owning vertex i can read factors and all incoming messages without communication. To maintain the locality invariant, after new outgoing messages are computed, they are transmitted to the processors owning the destination vertices.

Ultimately, we want to minimize communication and ensure balanced storage and computation; therefore, we can frame the minimum communication load balancing objective in terms of a graph partitioning. We formally define the graph partitioning problem as:

$$\min_{\mathcal{B}} \sum_{B \in \mathcal{B}} \sum_{(i \in B, j \notin B) \in E} (U_i + U_j) c_{ij} \tag{10.14}$$

$$\text{subj. to:} \quad \forall B \in \mathcal{B} \quad \sum_{i \in B} U_i w_i \leq \frac{\gamma}{p} \sum_{v \in v} U_v w_v \tag{10.15}$$

where U_i is the number of times SendMessages is invoked on vertex i, c_{ij} is the communication cost of the edge between vertex i and vertex j, w_i is the vertex work defined in Equation 10.13, and $\gamma \geq 1$ is the balance coefficient. The objective in Equation 10.14

(a) Denoise Uniformed Cut   (b) Denoise Overpartitioning

Figure 10.10 Overpartitioning can help improve work balance by more uniformly distributing the graph over the various processors. (a) A two-processor uninformed partitioning of the denoising factor graph can lead to one processor (CPU1) being assigned most of the work. (b) Overpartitioning by a factor of 6 can improve the overall work balance by assigning regions from the top and bottom of the denoising image to both processors.

minimizes communication while the constraint in Equation 10.15 ensures work balance for small γ and is commonly referred to as the k-way balanced cut objective, which is unfortunately NP-Hard in general. However, there are several popular graph partitioning libraries such as METIS (Karypis and Kumar, 1998) and Chaco (Hendrickson and Leland, 1994), which quickly produce reasonable approximation.

We define the communication cost as

$$c_{ij} = \mathcal{X}_i + C_{\text{comm}}, \tag{10.16}$$

the size of the message plus some additional constant network packet overhead C_{comm}.

In the case of static schedules, every vertex is updated the same number of times ($U_i = U_j : \forall i, j,$), and therefore U can be eliminated from both the objective and the constraints. Unfortunately, for dynamic schedules, the update counts U_i for each vertex are neither fixed or known. Furthermore, the update counts are difficult to estimate because they depend on the graph structure, factors, and progress toward convergence (Gonzalez et al., 2009a). Consequently, for dynamic BP algorithms, we advocate a randomized load balancing technique based on overpartitioning, which does not require knowledge of U_i.

Overpartitioning

If the graph is partitioned assuming constant update counts, there could be work imbalance due to dynamic update schedules. For instance, a frequently updated subgraph could be placed within a single partition as shown in Figure 10.10a. To decrease the chance of such an event, we can overpartition the graph, as shown in Figure 10.10b, into $k \times p$ balanced partitions and then randomly redistribute the partitions to the original p processors.

Choosing the optimal overpartitioning factor k is challenging and depends heavily on hardware, graph structure, and even factors. In situations where the algorithm may

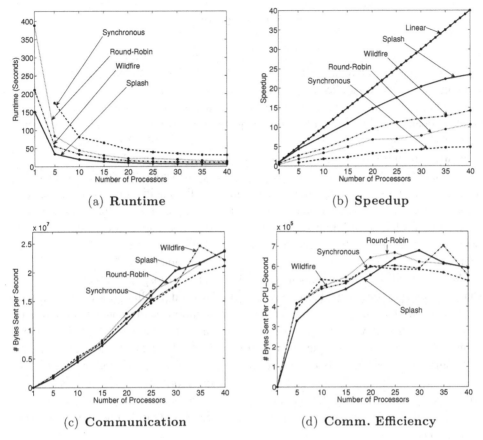

(a) **Runtime** (b) **Speedup**

(c) **Communication** (d) **Comm. Efficiency**

Figure 10.11 We assessed how each algorithm scales in the distributed setting on the protein-protein interaction network. Note that Synchronous BP failed to converge on a single processor. In (a) we plot the runtime in seconds as a function of the number of processors. In (b) we plot the speedup of each algorithm relative to the fastest single processor algorithm. The linear line represents the ideal linear speedup. Here we see that the Splash algorithm achieves the maximum speedup. Finally, in (c) and (d) we plot the bytes sent and bytes sent per CPU-second, respectively. Here we find that all algorithms share roughly the same communication requirements.

be run repeatedly, standard search techniques may be used. We find that in practice a small factor, such as $k = 5$, is typically sufficient.

10.4.2 Algorithm Comparison in the Distributed Setting

In Figure 10.11 we compare the different parallel BP algorithms in the distributed setting. In all cases we used the protein-protein interaction network from the multicore setting with the partitioning factor of $k = 5$. We implemented all the algorithms using MPICH2 (an open-source MPI implementation) on a commodity cluster consisting of five nodes, each with eight cores. We plot the runtime and speedup in Figure 10.11a and b, respectively. We plot speedup relative to the *fastest* single processor algorithm. In all cases, the Splash algorithm demonstrates the best performance.

10.5 Conclusion

In this chapter we first reviewed the natural parallelization of the belief propagation algorithm using the obvious synchronous schedule and demonstrated how this can lead to a highly inefficient parallel algorithm.

By explicitly considering the sequential structure of message-passing algorithms, we developed the Splash schedule, which sequentially moves messages along spanning trees. By running small tree schedules in parallel, we are able to construct a parallel schedule, which is more efficient than the popular synchronous schedule.

Often, in belief propagation, many of the messages will converge quickly while only a few small regions of the graph require substantial additional iteration. By updating the most divergent messages first and avoiding the re-computation of already converged messages, residual scheduling can dramatically improve the performance of belief propagation algorithms. To select to roots of the Splash operations and to prune the shape of the resulting Splashes, we introduced belief residual scheduling.

We discussed how to implement the Splash belief propagation algorithm in the shared memory setting using basic locking primitives and parallel priority queues. We identified load balancing and communication contention in the context of adaptive scheduling as they key challenges to a distributed implementation of the Splash algorithm and presented a the simple overpartitioning method to address these challenges.

Finally, we experimentally compared the Splash algorithm with the natural parallelization of several other adaptive belief propagation algorithms as well as the standard parallel synchronous belief propagation algorithm. We showed that in both the shared-memory and the distributed-memory setting, the Splash algorithm achieves the best performance.

The key concept in parallel machine learning addressed in this chapter is the importance of scheduling in the design of parallel algorithms. Although, synchronous algorithms often expose the most parallelism, by adopting dynamic asynchronous schedules with proper prioritization metrics it is often possible to produce parallel algorithms that both theoretically and experimentally outperform the simpler synchronous algorithms.

Acknowledgments

This work is supported by ONR Young Investigator Program grant N00014-08-1-0752, the ARO under MURI W911NF0810242, DARPA IPTO FA8750-09-1-0141, and the NSF under grants NeTS-NOSS, CNS-0625518, and IIS-0803333. Joseph Gonzalez is supported by the AT&T Labs Fellowship Program. We also thank Intel Research for cluster time and David O'Hallaron for his guidance in developing and implementing efficient multicore and distributed algorithms.

References

Adve, S. V., and Gharachorloo, K. 1996. Shared Memory Consistency Models: A Tutorial. *Computer*, **29**(12), 66–76.

Baron, D., Sarvotham, S., and Baraniuk, R. G. 2010. Bayesian compressive sensing via belief propagation. *IEEE Transactions on Signal Processing*, **58**(1), 269–280.

Bertsekas, D. P., and Tsitsiklis, J. N. 1989. *Parallel and Distributed Computation: Numerical Methods*. Englewood Cliffs, NJ: Prentice-Hall.

Cooper, G. F. 1990. The Computational Complexity of Probabilistic Inference using Bayesian Belief Networks. *Artificial Intelligence*, **42**, 393–405.

Crupi, V. A., Das, S. K., and Pinotti, M. C. 1996. Parallel and Distributed Meldable Priority Queues Based on Binomial Heaps. In: *International Conference on, Parallel Processing*, Vol. 1. IEEE Computer Society.

Darwiche, A., Dechter, R., Choi, A., Gogate, V., and Otten, L. 2008. *UAI' 08 Workshop: Evaluating and Disseminating Probabilistic Reasoning Systems*. http://graphmod.ics.uci.edu/uai08/.

Dean, J., and Ghemawat, S. 2008. MapReduce: Simplified Data Processing on Large Clusters. *Communications of the ACM*, **51**(1), 107–113.

Domingos, P., Kok, S., Lowd, D., Poon, H. F., Richardson, M., Singla, P., Sumner, M., and Wang, J. 2008. Markov Logic: A Unifying Language for Structural and Statistical Pattern Recognition. Page 3 of: *SSPR*.

Driscoll, J. R., Gabow, H. N., Shrairman, R., and Tarjan, R. E. 1988. Relaxed Heaps: An Alternative to Fibonacci Heaps with Applications to Parallel Computation. *Communications of the ACM*, **31**, 1343–1354.

Elidan, G., McGraw, I., and Koller, D. 2006. Residual Belief Propagation: Informed Scheduling for Asynchronous Message Passing. In: *UAI' 06*.

Gonzalez, J., Low, Y., Guestrin, C., and O'Hallaron, D. 2009a (July). Distributed Parallel Inference on Large Factor Graphs. In: *UAI' 09*.

Gonzalez, J., Low, Y., and Guestrin, C. 2009b. Residual Splash for Optimally Parallelizing Belief Propagation. In: *AISTATS' 09*.

Hendrickson, B., and Leland, R. 1994, Oct. *The Chaco User's Guide, Version 2.0*. Technical Report SAND94-2692. Sandia National Labs, Albuquerque, NM.

Huang, J., Chavira, M., and Darwiche, A. 2006. Solving MAP Exactly by Searching on Compiled Arithmetic Circuits. In: *AAAI' 06*.

Ihler, A. T. III, Fischer, J. W., and Willsky, A. S. 2005. Loopy Belief Propagation: Convergence and Effects of Message Errors. *Journal of Machine Learning Research*, **6**, 905–936.

Jaimovich, A., Elidan, G., Margalit, H., and Friedman, N. 2006. Towards an Integrated Protein-Protein Interaction Network: A Relational Markov Network Approach. *Journal of Computational Biology*, **13**(2), 145–164.

Karypis, G., and Kumar, V. 1998. Multilevel k-way Partitioning Scheme for Irregular Graphs. *Journal of Parallel Distributed Computing*, **48**(1).

Koller, D., and Friedman, N. 2009. *Probabilistic Graphical Models*. Cambridge, MA: MIT Press.

Lan, X. Y., Roth, S., Huttenlocher, D. P., and Black, M. J. 2006. Efficient Belief Propagation with Learned Higher-Order Markov Random Fields. In: *ECCV' 06*.

Mendiburu, A., Santana, R., Lozano, J. A., and Bengoetxea, E. 2007. A Parallel Framework for Loopy Belief Propagation. In: *GECCO' 07: Proceedings of the 2007 GECCO Conference Companion on Genetic and Evolutionary Computation*.

Mooij, J. M., and Kappen, H. J. 2007. Sufficient Conditions for Convergence of the Sum-Product Algorithm. *ITIT*, 4422–4437.

Parberry, I. 1995. Load Sharing with Parallel Priority Queues. *Journal of Computer and System Sciences*, **50**(1), 64–73.

Pearl, J. 1988. *Probabilistic Reasoning in Intelligent Systems: Networks of Plausible Inference*. San Francisco: Morgan Kaufmann.

Ranganathan, A., Kaess, M., and Dellaert, F. 2007. Loopy SAM. In: *IJCAI' 07*.

Roth, D. 1993. On the Hardness of Approximate Reasoning. Pages 613–618 of: *IJCAI' 93*.

Sanders, P. 1998. Randomized Priority Queues for Fast Parallel Access. *Journal of Parallel and Distributed Computing*, **49**(1), 86–97.

Saxena, A., Chung, S. H., and Ng, A. Y. 2007. 3-D Depth Reconstruction from a Single Still Image. *International Journal of Computer Vision*, **76**(1): 53–69.

Singla, P., and Domingos, P. 2008. Lifted First-Order Belief Propagation. In: *AAAI' 08*.

Sun, J., Shum, H. Y., and Zheng, N. N. 2002. Stereo Matching using Belief Propagation. In: *ECCV' 02*.

Tatikonda, S., and Jordan, M. I. 2002. Loopy Belief Propogation and Gibbs Measures. In: *UAI' 02*.

Wainwright, M., Jaakkola, T., and Willsky, A. S. 2001. Tree-Based Reparameterization for Approximate Estimation on Graphs with Cycles. In: *NIPS*.

Yanover, C., and Weiss, Y. 2002. Approximate Inference and Protein Folding. Pages 84–86 of: *NIPS*.

Yanover, C., Schueler-Furman, O., and Weiss, Y. 2007. Minimizing and Learning Energy Functions for Side-Chain Prediction. *Journal of Computational Biology*, 381–395.

CHAPTER 11

Distributed Gibbs Sampling for Latent Variable Models

Arthur Asuncion, Padhraic Smyth, Max Welling,
David Newman, Ian Porteous, and Scott Triglia

In this chapter, we address distributed learning algorithms for statistical latent variable models, with a focus on topic models. Many high-dimensional datasets, such as text corpora and image databases, are too large to allow one to learn topic models on a single computer. Moreover, a growing number of applications require that inference be fast or in real time, motivating the exploration of parallel and distributed learning algorithms.

We begin by reviewing topic models such as Latent Dirichlet Allocation and Hierarchical Dirichlet Processes. We discuss parallel and distributed algorithms for learning these models and show that these algorithms can achieve substantial speedups without sacrificing model quality. Next we discuss practical guidelines for running our algorithms within various parallel computing frameworks and highlight complementary speedup techniques. Finally, we generalize our distributed approach to handle Bayesian networks.

Several of the results in this chapter have appeared in previous papers in the specific context of topic modeling. The goal of this chapter is to present a comprehensive overview of distributed inference algorithms and to extend the general ideas to a broader class of Bayesian networks.

11.1 Latent Variable Models

Latent variable models are a class of statistical models that explain observed data with latent (or hidden) variables. Topic models and hidden Markov models are two examples of such models, where the latent variables are the topic assignment variables and the hidden states, respectively. Given observed data, the goal is to perform Bayesian inference over the latent variables and use the learned model to make inferences or predictions. In this section, we review two topic models, Latent Dirichlet Allocation and Hierarchical Dirichlet Processes.

11.1.1 Latent Dirichlet Allocation (LDA)

Latent Dirichlet Allocation (LDA) is a widely studied Bayesian latent variable model (Blei, Ng, and Jordan, 2003). LDA and its variants are referred to as "topic models" because these models represent each object in terms of a relatively small number of "topics" shared across the dataset. LDA has roots in dimensionality reduction techniques such as Principal Component Analysis (PCA) (Jolliffe, 2002), Latent Semantic Analysis (LSA) (Deerwester et al., 1990), and Probabilistic LSA (PLSA) (Hofmann, 2001). Buntine and Jakulin (2006) provide a comparative review of these related models. Topic models are also very similar to admixture models in genetics (Pritchard, Stephens, and Donnelly, 2000).

LDA is often used to model text corpora. Each document is represented as a vector of word counts over the vocabulary. The vocabulary is the entire set of words in the corpus, with stopwords (e.g., the, and) removed. To make this bag-of-words representation concrete, consider a toy example with four words in the vocabulary: cat, dog, fish, goat. A document containing fish once and cat twice is denoted by the vector [2 0 1 0]. Although word order is ignored, this is a powerful and efficient representation that allows meaningful topics to be learned. Variations of LDA have also been developed to leverage word order (see Griffiths et al., 2005; Wallach, 2006; Gruber, Rosen-Zvi, and Weiss, 2007).

Topic modeling has also been applied to non-text count data, such as image databases (Li and Perona, 2005) and collaborative filtering data (Porteous, Bart, and Welling, 2008b). For images, count data can be produced by running interest point detectors to identify informative locations in the image and representing each patch of pixels around every interest point through image descriptors (Lowe, 2004). These descriptors can be clustered into "visual words," which allows an image to be represented in bag-of-words form.

Formally, LDA is defined by the following generative process. Each of D documents in the corpus is modeled as a discrete distribution over K latent topics, and each topic is a discrete distribution over the vocabulary of W words. For document j, the distribution over topics, $\theta_{k|j}$, has a prior in the form of a Dirichlet distribution $\mathcal{D}[\alpha]$ with parameter α. Likewise, each topic, $\phi_{w|k}$, has a Dirichlet $\mathcal{D}[\beta]$ prior with parameter β. For the ith token in the document, a topic assignment z_{ij} is drawn from $\theta_{k|j}$ and then the word x_{ij} is drawn from the corresponding topic $\phi_{w|z_{ij}}$. LDA's graphical model is shown in Figure 11.1, and the generative process is summarized as

$$\theta_{k|j} \sim \mathcal{D}[\alpha] \qquad \phi_{w|k} \sim \mathcal{D}[\beta] \qquad z_{ij} \sim \theta_{k|j} \qquad x_{ij} \sim \phi_{w|z_{ij}}.$$

Given the observed data $\{x_{ij}\}$, the inference goal is to obtain the posterior distribution over the latent assignments $\{z_{ij}\}$, latent topics $\{\phi_{w|k}\}$, and latent document mixtures $\{\theta_{k|j}\}$. Although exact inference is intractable because of the coupling between the topics and mixtures induced by observing the data, a variety of approximate inference techniques for LDA have been developed, including variational techniques (Blei et al., 2003; Teh, Newman, and Welling, 2007; Asuncion et al., 2009b), MCMC sampling (Griffiths and Steyvers, 2004), hybrid variational/MCMC (Welling, Teh, and Kappen, 2008a), MAP estimation (Chien and Wu, 2008), and expectation propagation (Minka and Lafferty, 2002).

Table 11.1. *Example LDA topics learned on UCI/UCSD research papers.*

[mathematics]	[parallelization]	[politics]	[proteins]	[software]
theorem	processor	political	binding	software
lemma	parallel	social	protein	process
proof	data	policy	domain	tool
follow	performance	economic	site	project
constant	communication	china	receptor	development
bound	memory	law	interaction	design
exist	computation	government	complex	system

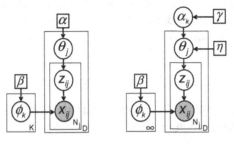

Figure 11.1 Graphical models for LDA (left) and HDP (right). Shaded/unshaded circles denote observed/latent variables, squares denote parameters, and plates denote replication across indices.

In this chapter, we focus on MCMC sampling techniques such as Gibbs sampling. Griffiths and Steyvers (2004) introduced the collapsed Gibbs sampler that is now commonly used for learning in LDA models. In this scheme, $\{\phi_{w|k}\}$ and $\{\theta_{k|j}\}$ are integrated out analytically and the algorithm samples topic assignments $\{z_{ij}\}$ according to the conditional distribution

$$p(z_{ij} = k | x_{ij} = w, z^{\neg ij}, x^{\neg ij}, \alpha, \beta) \propto \frac{N_{wk}^{\neg ij} + \beta}{\sum_w N_{wk}^{\neg ij} + W\beta} \left(N_{kj}^{\neg ij} + \alpha \right), \qquad (11.1)$$

where $N_{wjk} = \sum_i \mathbb{I}[x_{ij} = w, z_{ij} = k]$ is the number of times word w is assigned to topic k in document j, and W is the vocabulary size. In our notation, missing indices are summed out (e.g., $N_{wk} = \sum_j N_{wjk}$), and $\neg ij$ denotes that the current word is excluded from the counts or set of variables.

After obtaining samples from the posterior $p(z|x, \alpha, \beta)$ using collapsed Gibbs sampling, we can compute estimates for the topics $\{\phi_{w|k}\}$ and the topic mixtures $\{\theta_{k|j}\}$ (see Griffiths and Steyvers, 2004, for details). In Table 11.1, we show examples of topics learned on a corpus of research papers written by faculty at UC Irvine and UC San Diego, showing the seven most likely words in each topic, as well as a human-provided label in brackets.[1] Meanwhile, the learned topic mixtures $\theta_{k|j}$ can be used for document retrieval and clustering. Broadly speaking, LDA provides an automated unsupervised method for summarizing the semantic content of a corpus via learned topics and discovering the topics present in each document.

---

[1] Several topic browsers are available here: www.ics.uci.edu/~smyth/topics.html.

11.1.2 Hierarchical Dirichlet Processes

The Hierarchical Dirichlet Process (HDP) model consists of a hierarchical collection of Dirichlet processes and can be viewed as the nonparametric version of LDA (Teh et al., 2006). Whereas LDA requires a prespecified fixed number of topics K, the number of topics in HDP is unbounded. In practice, conditioned on the observed data, the number of instantiated HDP topics is finite and depends on the diversity of the dataset.

Although there are various ways to formulate the HDP, we define the HDP model by taking the following model in the limit as K goes to infinity. Let K be the number of topics and α_k be top-level Dirichlet variables sampled from a Dirichlet with parameter γ/K. For each document j, the mixture, $\theta_{k|j}$, is drawn from a Dirichlet with parameters $\eta\alpha_k$. Each topic, $\phi_{w|k}$, is similarly drawn from a base Dirichlet distribution with parameter β. As in LDA, z_{ij} is drawn from $\theta_{k|j}$ and x_{ij} is drawn from $\phi_{w|z_{ij}}$. The graphical model is as shown in Figure 11.1, and the generative process is summarized as

$$\alpha_k \sim \mathcal{D}[\gamma/K] \quad \theta_{k|j} \sim \mathcal{D}[\eta\alpha_k] \quad \phi_{w|k} \sim \mathcal{D}[\beta] \quad z_{ij} \sim \theta_{k|j} \quad x_{ij} \sim \phi_{w|z_{ij}}.$$

As in LDA, we integrate out $\{\phi_{w|k}\}$ and $\{\theta_{k|j}\}$ and Gibbs sample the topic assignments using the conditional distribution

$$p(z_{ij} = k | z^{\neg ij}, x, \alpha, \beta, \eta) \propto \begin{cases} \frac{N_{wk}^{\neg ij} + \beta}{\sum_w N_{wk}^{\neg ij} + W\beta} \left(N_{kj}^{\neg ij} + \eta\alpha_k \right), & \text{if } k \text{ prev. used} \\ \frac{\eta\alpha_{new}}{W}, & \text{if } k \text{ is new.} \end{cases} \tag{11.2}$$

Teh et al. (2006) provide the details for sampling α_k and the other hyper-parameters. A small amount of probability mass is reserved for instantiating a new topic, so the number of topics can grow during Gibbs sampling.

11.2 Distributed Inference Algorithms

We describe parallel and distributed inference algorithms for the LDA and HDP topic models. We assume the data, parameters, and computation are distributed over multiple processors. Our algorithms are amenable to any physical architecture of multiple processors. The processors can be physically distinct, such as in cloud computing or large-scale distributed processor environments, or of the shared-memory/multicore type. We also present asynchronous distributed schemes for learning these models.

11.2.1 Approximate Distributed LDA and HDP

We begin with the application of topic modeling to text data, where the input is the bag-of-words representation of the document set. The simplest partitioning of a document set is to arbitrarily distribute the D documents over P processors, with approximately $\frac{D}{P}$ documents on each processor. We partition the set $\{D\}$ of document IDs into P partitions, $\{D\} \rightarrow \{D_1\} \ldots \{D_P\}$, so that processor p performs computations over documents $j \in \{D_p\}$. Likewise, we partition words into $x = \{x_1, \ldots, x_p, \ldots, x_P\}$ and the corresponding topic assignments into $z = \{z_1, \ldots, z_p, \ldots, z_P\}$, where processor p stores x_p, the words from documents $j \in \{D_p\}$, and z_p, the topic assignments. Topic-document counts N_{kj}

are likewise distributed as N_{kjp}. Word-topic counts N_{wk} are also distributed, with each processor keeping a separate local copy N_{wkp} and N_{kp}.

Because Gibbs sampling for the collapsed LDA model is a strictly sequential process, it is difficult to recast the sampler as a parallel process without making approximations. To properly sample from the posterior distribution, the update of any topic assignment z_{ij} should not be performed concurrently with the update of any other $z_{i'j'}$. However, because there is typically a large number of word tokens compared to the number of processors, the dependence of the z_{ij}'s on each other is likely to be weak, and thus it is plausible that one can relax the requirement of sequential sampling of topic assignments and still learn a useful model. If two processors are concurrently sampling different words in different documents (i.e., $x_{ij} \neq x_{i'j'}$), concurrent sampling will be very similar to sequential sampling because the only term affecting the order of operations is the total topic count N_k in Equation 11.1.

Algorithm 37: AD-LDA: Collapsed Gibbs Sampling on a Distributed Set of Documents $D_1 \ldots D_P$ (Newman et al., 2008, 2009).

Partition documents $\{D\} \rightarrow \{D_1\} \ldots \{D_P\}$
Repeat
    For $p = 1 \ldots P$ *in parallel* **do**
        Copy global counts: $N_{wkp} = N_{wk}$
        Copy global counts: $N_{kp} = N_k$
        For each $j \in \{D_p\}, i \in \{1 \ldots N_j\}$ **do**
            Sample z_{ij} using LDA-Gibbs$(x_p, z_p, N_{kjp}, N_{wkp}, N_{kp}, \alpha, \beta)$
    Synchronize
    Update global counts: $N_{wk} = N_{wk} + \sum_p (N_{wkp} - N_{wk})$
    Update global counts: $N_k = N_k + \sum_p (N_{kp} - N_k)$
Until termination criterion satisfied

Pseudocode for our Approximate Distributed LDA (AD-LDA) algorithm is shown in Algorithm 37. After distributing data and parameters across processors, AD-LDA runs simultaneous Gibbs sampling sweeps on each of the P processors, using LDA's conditional distribution for z (Equation 11.1). After processor p sweeps through its local data and updates topic assignments z_p, the processor has modified count arrays N_{kjp}, N_{wkp}, and N_{kp}. The topic-document counts N_{kjp} are distinct across processors because of the document index, j, and will be consistent with the topic assignments z. However, the word-topic counts N_{wkp} and topic counts N_{kp} will be different on each processor and not globally consistent with z. To merge back to a single consistent set of word-topic and topic counts, we perform a reduce-sum operation on N_{wkp} and N_{kp} across all processors to update the global counts. After synchronization and update operations, each processor has the same values in the N_{wkp} and N_{kp} arrays, which are consistent with the global vector of assignments z. As in LDA, the algorithm can terminate either after a fixed number of iterations or based on a suitable Markov chain Monte Carlo (MCMC) convergence metric.

By using a different data distribution, it is possible to avoid the local copy of N_{wkp} on each processor and the global update for N_{wk} in shared-memory settings. If one partitions the data by both documents and words, then one only needs to synchronize topic counts, N_{kp} (see Yan, Xu, and Qi, 2009; Ihler, and Newman, 2009, for details). Ihler and Newman use this setup to bound the probability of making a sampling error at each AD-LDA step. In practice, we find that both versions of AD-LDA are able to learn very accurate models.

We also note that it is possible to slightly alter the LDA model by introducing a hierarchy over the topics ϕ in the graphical model. Having processor-specific ϕ_p variables allows each ϕ_p to be collapsed out of the model while facilitating exact concurrent Gibbs sampling of the z topic assignment variables. The details of this approach, known as Hierarchical Distributed LDA, are presented in Newman et al. (2009). Although this algorithm is performing exact Gibbs sampling on a slightly modified model, it is more complicated to implement than AD-LDA while producing very similar results, and so in practice we recommend the simpler AD-LDA method. In the same vein, we note that if θ and ϕ are not integrated out of the LDA model, one can perform exact parallel Gibbs sampling by concurrently sampling the z's conditional on θ and ϕ, and then in the global update step, sampling θ and ϕ given the z's. However, *collapsed* Gibbs sampling is widely preferred since it has reduced variance and is able to converge to accurate solutions more quickly (Newman et al., 2009). Another proper inference technique is to perform MCMC sampling with a Metropolis Hastings step, where one proposes a configuration achieved by approximate parallel sampling, and the algorithm either accepts or rejects this proposal. Doshi-Velez et al. (2009) use this technique to perform parallel inference for Indian Buffet Processes. For topic models, such a correction is not necessary, because the concurrent Gibbs sampling over the topic assignments produces very good results.

Analogous distributed algorithms exist for the HDP model. Our AD-HDP algorithm uses the same concurrent sampling technique as AD-LDA; however, because HDP is nonparametric, new local topics may be instantiated during the sampling sweep on each processor (see Equation 11.2). In AD-HDP, one needs to address the issue of combining newly instantiated local topics. Although naïve schemes, such as merging topics by topic ID, perform well, one can obtain improvements by merging topics based on similarity. The details of AD-HDP and topic merging heuristics are found in Newman et al. (2009).

11.2.2 Asynchronous Distributed Learning Techniques

The previous section described *synchronous* distributed algorithms. Next we discuss *asynchronous* distributed learning of topic models. We consider a "gossip-based" framework (Boyd et al., 2005) in which pairs of processors communicate to exchange topic statistics. Asynchronous algorithms have a number of potential benefits: no global synchronization across all processors is required; the system is fault-tolerant because of its decentralized nature; heterogeneous machines can be used; and processors with new data can be integrated into the system in an online fashion.

Because collapsed Gibbs sampling is performed on each processor based on its approximate view of the global set of topics, the algorithms are not sampling from the proper global posterior distribution. Yet, we find that these algorithms converge to high-quality solutions (Asuncion, Smyth, and Welling, 2009a).

Consider the problem of asynchronous learning of an LDA model where documents are distributed across P processors. Each processor p stores local variables: x_{ij}^p denotes the word type for each token i in document j on the processor p, and z_{ij}^p denotes the topic assignment for each token. $N_{wk}^{\neg p}$ is the global word-topic count matrix stored at the processor – this matrix stores counts of other processors gathered during the communication step and does not include the processor's local counts. N_{kj}^p is the local document-topic count matrix (derived from z^p), N_w^p is the word count on a processor (derived from x^p), and N_{wk}^p is the local word-topic count matrix (derived from z^p and x^p) containing only the counts of data on the processor.

During each iteration, processors concurrently perform a sweep of collapsed Gibbs sampling over their local topic assignment variables z^p according to the following conditional distribution (analogous to Equation 11.1):

$$P(z_{pij} = k | x_{pij} = w, z_p^{\neg ij}, x_p^{\neg ij}) \propto \frac{(N^{\neg p} + N^p)_{wk}^{\neg ij} + \beta}{\sum_w (N^{\neg p} + N^p)_{wk}^{\neg ij} + W\beta} \left(N_{pjk}^{\neg ij} + \alpha \right). \quad (11.3)$$

Once the sampling sweep over z^p is complete (and N_{wk}^p is updated), the processor finds another finished processor and initiates communication. Consider the case where two processors p and g have never met. In this case, processors simply exchange their local contributions to the global topic counts N_{wk}^p, and processor p adds N_{wk}^g to its $N_{wk}^{\neg p}$, and vice versa.

The case where two processors have met is more complex. Processors should not simply swap and add their local counts; rather, each processor should first remove from $N_{wk}^{\neg p}$ the previous influence of the other processor during their previous encounter, to prevent processors that frequently meet from overinfluencing each other. Because we are interested in situations where memory and communication bandwidth are both limited, we assume that processor p does not store in memory the previous counts of all the other processors that p has already met. Because the previous local counts of the other processor were already absorbed into $N_{wk}^{\neg p}$ and are thus not retrievable, we must infer a proxy set of counts. In Async-LDA, the processors exchange their N_{wk}^p, from which the count of words on each processor, N_w^g can be derived. Using processor g's N_w^g, processor p creates $\tilde{N}_{wk}^g$ by sampling N_w^g topic values randomly without replacement from collection $\{N_{wk}^{\neg p}\}$. This process is equivalent to sampling from a multivariate hypergeometric (MH) distribution. One can think of $\tilde{N}_{wk}^g$ as a "maximum entropy" proxy for the N_{wk}^g that processor p received during their previous encounter. We update $N_{wk}^{\neg p}$ by subtracting $\tilde{N}_{wk}^g$ and adding the current N_{wk}^g:

$$N_{wk}^{\neg p} \leftarrow N_{wk}^{\neg p} - \tilde{N}_{wk}^g + N_{wk}^g \quad \text{where} \quad \tilde{N}_{w,k}^g \sim \text{MH}\,[N_{w,k}^g; N_{w,1}^{\neg p}, .., N_{wk}^{\neg p}]. \quad (11.4)$$

Pseudocode for Async-LDA is shown in Algorithm 38. The asynchronous approach can be adapted to various computing settings with specific memory, bandwidth, and topology constraints and can also be applied to HDP (see Asuncion et al., 2009a, 2011, for an in-depth treatment).

Algorithm 38: Async-LDA: Collapsed Gibbs Sampling on a Distributed Document Set with Asynchronous Communications (Asuncion et al., 2009a; Asuncion, Smyth, and Welling, 2011).

Partition documents $\{D\} \rightarrow \{D_1\} \ldots \{D_P\}$
For $p = 1 \ldots P$ *in parallel* **do**
   Repeat
      Sample z^p locally (Equation 11.3)
      Receive N_{wk}^g from random processor g, and send N_{wk}^p to g
      If p has met g before **then**
         $N_{wk}^{\neg p} \leftarrow N_{wk}^{\neg p} - \tilde{N}_{wk}^g + N_{wk}^g$ (Equation 11.4)
      Else
         $N_{wk}^{\neg p} \leftarrow N_{wk}^{\neg p} + N_{wk}^g$
   Until termination criterion satisfied

11.3 Experimental Analysis of Distributed Topic Modeling

We analyze the behavior of our distributed algorithms, discussing accuracy and scalability results on real-world datasets. The distributed techniques produce substantial speedups while maintaining a high level of accuracy.

11.3.1 Accuracy of Distributed Algorithms

We begin with an empirical analysis for topic models. Of interest is comparing topic models learned using the distributed algorithms versus topic models learned using the standard sequential algorithm. Our evaluation is based on both the quality of the learned model and the rate of convergence when learning the model. The experiments in this section are based on simulations of parallel hardware that allow us to measure model quality as a function of the number of iterations. Experiments that assess parallel efficiency, using real parallel hardware, are discussed in Section 11.3.2.

Our datasets are shown in Table 11.2. For each corpus, D is the number of documents, W is the vocabulary size, and N is the total number of words. The NIPS and NEWSGROUPS data are used for accuracy experiments. Three larger datasets, NYT, WIKIPEDIA, and MEDLINE, are used for the speedup experiments in Section 11.3.2. These datasets can all be downloaded from the UCI Machine Learning Repository (Frank and Asuncion, 2007).

For AD-LDA and Async-LDA, we use symmetric Dirichlet parameters of $\alpha = 0.1$ and $\beta = 0.01$ per component. Although these hyperparameters were fixed in our experiments, they could also be learned. For AD-HDP, we set $\beta = 0.01$, $\eta \sim Gamma(2, 1)$,

Table 11.2. *Characteristics of datasets used in experiments.*

	NIPS	NEWSGROUPS	NYT	WIKIPEDIA	MEDLINE
D_{train}	1,500	19,500	300,000	2,051,929	8,200,000
W	12,419	27,059	102,660	120,927	141,043
N	2,166,058	2,057,207	99,542,125	344,941,756	737,869,083
D_{test}	184	498	–	–	–

and $\gamma \sim Gamma(10, 1)$, and we resample these hyperparameters to enable more robust topic growth (see Teh et al., 2006).

A standard evaluation measure for topic models is perplexity, which is based on the log-likelihood of test data and provides a characterization of the predictive quality of a model (lower is better). In speech recognition, perplexity has been found to be well-correlated with performance measures such as word-error rate (Jelinek et al., 1977). Perplexity is computed as $\mathrm{Perp}(x^{\mathrm{test}}) = \exp(-\frac{1}{N^{\mathrm{test}}} \log p(x^{\mathrm{test}}))$. For every test document, half the words at random are designated for "fold-in," and the remaining words are used for testing. The document mixture θ_j is learned using the fold-in part, and log probability of the test words is computed using this mixture, ensuring that the test words are not used in estimation of model parameters. For AD-LDA/AD-HDP, the perplexity computation exactly follows that of LDA/HDP, because a single set of topic counts N_{wk} are saved when a sample is taken. For Async-LDA, each processor has its own set of global topic counts, and thus we compute the perplexity on each processor and average across processors. Perplexities are computed for all algorithms using $S = 10$ samples from the posterior from 10 independent chains using the log-likelihood,

$$\log p(x^{\mathrm{test}}) = \sum_{j,w} N_{jw}^{\mathrm{test}} \log \frac{1}{S} \sum_{s} \sum_{k} \theta_{k|j}^s \phi_{w|k}^s \qquad (11.5)$$

$$\text{where} \quad \theta_{k|j}^s = \frac{\alpha + N_{kj}^s}{K\alpha + N_j^s}, \quad \phi_{w|k}^s = \frac{\beta + N_{wk}^s}{W\beta + N_k^s}.$$

This perplexity computation follows the standard practice of averaging over multiple samples when making predictions with LDA models trained via Gibbs sampling, as discussed in Griffiths and Steyvers (2004).

Using the NIPS data, we computed test set perplexities for different numbers of topics, K, and for numbers of processors, P, ranging from 1 to 1500. For each AD-LDA run, a sample was taken at 500 iterations of the Gibbs sampler, which is well after the typical burn-in period of the initial 200–300 iterations. For each run of HDP and AD-HDP, we allow the Gibbs sampler to run for 3,000 iterations, to allow the number of topics to equilibrate.

The perplexity results for NIPS in Figure 11.2 clearly show that the model perplexity is essentially the same for AD-LDA and AD-HDP at $P = 10$ and $P = 100$ as their single-processor versions at $P = 1$. The figure shows the test set perplexity, versus P, for different numbers of topics K for the LDA models, and also for the HDP models that learn the number of topics. The $P = 1$ perplexity is computed by LDA (circles) and HDP (triangles), and we use our distributed algorithms – AD-LDA (crosses), and AD-HDP (stars) – to compute the $P = 10$ and $P = 100$ perplexities. In this experiment, HDP instantiated 687 topics while AD-HDP instantiated 570 ($P = 10$) and 569 ($P = 100$) topics. AD-HDP instantiates fewer topics because of the merging across processors of newly created topics (see Newman et al., 2009); however, despite fewer topics, AD-HDP achieves essentially the same perplexity as HDP, because many topics have relatively small probability mass.

In the limit of a large number of processors, the perplexity for the distributed algorithms matches that for the sequential version. In fact, in the limiting case of only one document per processor, $P = 1500$ for NIPS, we see that the perplexities of AD-LDA are generally no different from those of LDA, as shown in the rightmost column

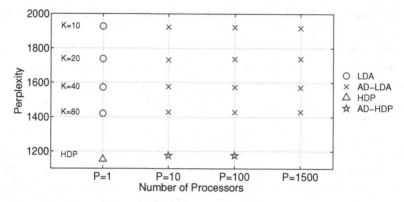

Figure 11.2 Test perplexity versus number of processors P, on NIPS data. $P = 1$ corresponds to LDA and HDP. At $P = 10$ and $P = 100$ we show AD-LDA and AD-HDP. We also show AD-LDA's limiting case of $P = 1500$. See Newman et al. (2009) for additional results.

of Figure 11.2. Despite no formal convergence guarantees for AD-LDA Algorithm 37, the approximate distributed algorithms, AD-LDA and AD-HDP, converged to good solutions in every experiment we conducted using multiple real-world datasets. The only case where AD-LDA fails is when synchronization between processors is not performed regularly after each local Gibbs sweep, and this case is apparent only when P is small (see Newman et al., 2009, for details). Newman et al. (2009) also found that AD-LDA and LDA had the same performance when evaluated using metrics such as mean precision on information retrieval tasks.

It is reasonable to believe that distributed algorithms might converge more slowly than single-processor algorithms. To see if this was the case, we performed experiments to see whether our distributed algorithms were converging at the same rate as their sequential counterparts. If the distributed algorithms were converging more slowly, the computational gains of parallelization would be reduced. Our experiments for AD-LDA consistently showed that the convergence rate for the distributed LDA algorithms was as fast as those for the single-processor case. As an example, Figure 11.3 shows test perplexity versus iteration of AD-LDA for the NIPS data at $K = 20$ topics. During

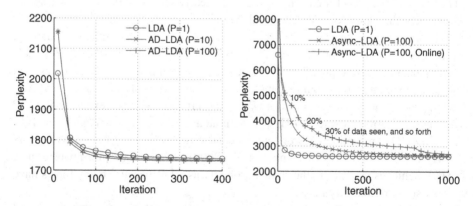

Figure 11.3 Convergence of test perplexity versus iteration: (left) AD-LDA using the NIPS data and $K = 20$ topics; (right) Async-LDA using NEWSGROUPS and $K = 40$ (see Newman et al., 2009, Asuncion et al., 2009a).

burn-in, up to iteration 200, the distributed algorithms are actually converging slightly faster than single-processor LDA. Note that one iteration of AD-LDA on a parallel multiprocessor computer takes only a fraction (at best $\frac{1}{P}$) of the wall-clock time of one iteration of LDA on a single-processor computer.

The asynchronous distributed algorithms (Async-LDA and Async-HDP) are also able to match the perplexities of the sequential samplers, producing results that are very similar to Figure 11.2 (Asuncion et al., 2009a). Figure 11.3 shows the convergence behavior of Async-LDA on NEWSGROUPS with $P = 100$ processors. Our simulation uses a gossip scheme over a fully connected network where each processor communicates topic counts with one other randomly selected processor at the end of every iteration (e.g., with $P = 100$, there are 50 pairs at each iteration). Although the final perplexity achieved is the same as standard LDA, Async-LDA converges more slowly, because the dissemination of information proceeds at a slower rate as a result of the restriction of asynchronous pairwise communication between processors. However, with count caching and forwarding, Async-LDA's rate of convergence can significantly improve (Asuncion et al., 2009b). Furthermore, Async-LDA provides other benefits such as online learning, as new processors with new data enter the system. We conducted an experiment where we introduced 10 new processors after every 100 iterations, with each processor containing 10% of the NEWSGROUPS data. Figure 11.3 shows the test perplexity achieved by this online scheme, suggesting that Async-LDA is also able to learn an accurate model in this setting.

11.3.2 Scalability on Real-World Datasets

The goal of distributed inference algorithms is to have highly scalable algorithms, in terms of memory and computation time. Memory and time complexity for LDA and AD-LDA are summarized in Table 11.3, where memory complexity is on a per-processor basis. For LDA, memory scales separately by the total number of words in the corpus, N, and the number of topics, K, while time scales as NK, the product of these two terms. The theoretical scalability of AD-LDA can be seen in the table by focusing on the terms that are multiplied by the factor of $\frac{1}{P}$. Because AD-LDA keeps a separate local copy of N_{wkp} on each processor, we see the additional KW term in memory. The CKW term is the communication cost, where C represents a combined bandwith/latency communication constant that converts from words transmitted per second to operations per second.

AD-HDP has time and memory complexity similar to that of AD-LDA; the difference is that the number of topics in AD-HDP is expected to grow as $\log(N)$. Async-LDA also has the same time complexity per iteration as AD-LDA, and the communication

Table 11.3. *Memory and time complexity of LDA and AD-LDA.*

	LDA	AD-LDA
Memory	$N + KD + KW$	$\frac{1}{P}(N + KD) + KW$
Time	NK	$\frac{1}{P}NK + CKW$

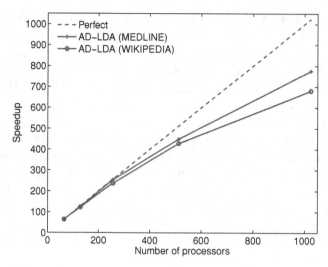

Figure 11.4 Parallel speedup results for AD-LDA using 64 to 1024 processors on multimillion-document datasets WIKIPEDIA and MEDLINE (Newman et al., 2009).

costs might be less because a global synchronization is not needed. If processors cache counts of other processors (to improve rate of convergence), Async-LDA would have a higher memory requirement than AD-LDA (by a constant factor).

We used two multimillion-document datasets, WIKIPEDIA and MEDLINE, for AD-LDA speedup experiments on a large-scale supercomputer. The supercomputer used was DataStar, a 15.6-TFlop terascale machine at San Diego Supercomputer Center built from 265 IBM P655 8-way compute nodes. We implemented a parallel version of AD-LDA using the Message Passing Interface protocol. We ran AD-LDA on WIKIPEDIA using $K = 1000$ topics and MEDLINE using $K = 2000$ topics distributed over $P = 64$, 128, 256, 512, and 1024 processors. The speedup results, shown in Figure 11.4, show relatively high parallel efficiency, with approximately 700 times speedup for WIKIPEDIA and 800 times speedup for MEDLINE when using $P = 1024$ processors, corresponding to parallel efficiencies of approximately 0.7 and 0.8, respectively. These speedups and parallel efficiencies are estimates, because actual speedup and parallel efficiency should be measured with respect to timings performed on a single processor. Because of our huge memory requirement (exceeding 100GB), it was impossible to run on a single processor. Therefore, we estimated speedup and parallel efficiency using a baseline computed using $P = 64$ processors. Specifically, our speedup was computed relative to the time per iteration when using $P = 64$ processors, that is, at $P = 64$, we assume perfect efficiency. Multiple runs were timed for both WIKIPEDIA and MEDLINE, and the resulting variation in timing was less than 1%, so error bars are not shown in the figure. We see slightly higher parallel efficiency for MEDLINE versus WIKIPEDIA because MEDLINE has a larger amount of computation per unit data communicated, $\frac{N}{PW}$.

This speedup dramatically reduces the learning time for large topic models. If we were to learn a $K = 2000$ topic model for MEDLINE using LDA on a single processor, it would require more than 300 days instead of the 10 hours required to learn the same model using AD-LDA on 1024 processors.

Async-LDA is also able to achieve substantial speedups. On a cluster with 32 processing cores, Async-LDA is able to achieve speedups of $15\times$ and $24\times$ on NYT and MEDLINE, respectively (Asuncion et al., 2009b).

11.4 Practical Guidelines for Implementation

We discuss a number of practical guidelines next for implementing our techniques, for a variety of distributed computing frameworks and for various inference techniques. We also show that it is possible to combine our distributed methods with other statistical acceleration methods.

11.4.1 Parallel and Distributed Hardware

The parallel and distributed inference algorithms discussed in this chapter can be realized in a variety of computing frameworks. For the results in this chapter, we have primarily utilized multicore and cluster computing frameworks, using standards such as OpenMP and the Message Passing Interface (MPI). However, the parallel Gibbs sampler for LDA has also been been implemented in other settings, including the Nvidia CUDA framework for graphics processing units (GPUs). For example, using an inexpensive off-the-shelf GPU card with 30 multiprocessors (with 8 thread processors each), Yan et al. (2009) have shown that parallel collapsed Gibbs sampling for LDA can obtain around $26\times$ speedup relative to a single-core processor. A related variational LDA algorithm for GPUs was investigated by Masada et al. (2009). One issue with GPUs is that the amount of memory on these cards is limited (e.g., 1 GB), and so very large datasets cannot fit in memory. However, this limitation can be overcome by (1) letting the processors share a single matrix of word-topic counts using the finer block-partitioning discussed in Section 11.2 and (2) streaming the data into the GPU as needed (Yan et al., 2009). Similar issues arise when using shared-memory systems via OpenMP.

These techniques have also been studied in large-scale computing settings. In particular, Wang et al. (2009) implemented the AD-LDA algorithm within Google's MapReduce framework and compared the MapReduce version of parallel LDA to the MPI version. They find that the MPI version actually produces greater speedups than MapReduce, because their MPI version uses efficient in-memory communication, while their MapReduce version uses disk I/O operations at each iteration. Of course there are other benefits to using the MapReduce framework, such as increased fault tolerance. In a similar vein, Wolfe, Haghighi, and Klein (2008) investigated large-scale EM techniques for models such as LDA. In comparing the MapReduce network topology to a junction tree topology, they found that using a junction tree topology can provide significant time and bandwidth savings. Recently, Smola and Narayanamurthy (2010) proposed a parallel blackboard architecture for LDA that uses a distributed caching system known as Memcached and performs both sampling and communication steps simultaneously. These studies suggest several guidelines: (1) avoid writing to disk as much as possible and (2) do not neglect communication and bandwidth costs.

Another choice to consider is whether one should perform synchronous or asynchronous distributed learning (Asuncion et al., 2009a). We generally recommend using synchronous inference techniques, because they are simpler to implement and converge more quickly as a result of the accessibility of the latest state information at each processor. Nonetheless, asynchronous techniques are useful in cases when global synchronization between processors is not feasible, or when decentralization is required for fault-tolerance.

11.4.2 Complementary Acceleration Techniques

Statistical acceleration techniques can be used in conjunction with parallel and distributed inference. One such method is Fast-LDA (Porteous et al., 2008a; see Yao, Mimno, and McCallum, 2009, for another efficient sampler). In this method, the core procedure of sampling from an unnormalized probability vector is accelerated by maintaining a bound on the partition function Z, which allows the sampler to avoid unnecessary calculations. This technique on its own can provide speedups of up to 5–8×. Fast-LDA can improve the performance of the parallel Gibbs sampler by replacing the core LDA procedure on each processor. However, Fast-LDA only replaces the core LDA procedure of parallel Gibbs sampling and does not mitigate the overhead required to synchronize the counts from multiple processors. As a consequence of Amdahl's law, the overall system speedup will be less than what one gets from Fast-LDA on a single CPU. We test the combined performance of AD-LDA and Fast-LDA ("Fast-AD-LDA") using MPI on 16 cores on the NYT data, and we find that we achieve over a 2× speedup relative to standard AD-LDA (Figure 11.5). Document length is not a factor in the complexity of combining statistics from multiple CPUs, and thus we expect that longer documents would result in an even larger speedup. It should also be possible to further reduce the communication overhead if one uses a shared-memory framework. Nonetheless, by combining a statistical acceleration technique with parallelization, we can achieve over 22× speedup on 16 cores.

Although we have focused on collapsed Gibbs sampling in this chapter, other inference techniques can also be used that can potentially accelerate learning. In previous work (Asuncion et al., 2009b), we compared methods for LDA such as ML/MAP estimation, variational inference, collapsed variational inference, and collapsed Gibbs

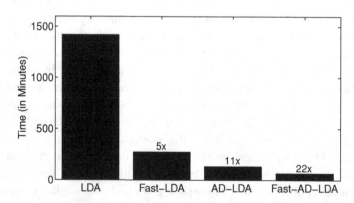

Figure 11.5 Time in minutes to perform 100 iterations for LDA, Fast-LDA, AD-LDA, and Fast-AD-LDA on NYT, with $K = 500$. AD-LDA and Fast-AD-LDA were run using $P = 16$.

sampling, and we found that all these techniques can learn LDA models at virtually the same accuracy, provided that the hyperparameters are also estimated in conjunction with each method. Computationally, there is a memory-time trade-off among these approaches. Variational methods are deterministic and allow for the entire uncertainty of the conditional distribution to be represented in the counts, which allows these methods to have a faster rate of convergence than collapsed Gibbs sampling; however, variational methods often require more memory to store these distributions. In settings where memory is not scarce, we recommend exploring fast variational methods to learn topic models, as these methods can be parallelized in the same fashion as collapsed Gibbs sampling (Nallapati, Cohen, and Lafferty, 2007; Asuncion et al., 2009b).

11.5 A Foray into Distributed Inference for Bayesian Networks

The distributed inference algorithms discussed so far are not limited to LDA and HDP. In the following sections, we argue that they naturally extend to Bayesian networks in general. Although the technical details are a little more involved, the line of reasoning remains very similar: conditional probability tables are integrated out and a Gibbs sampler is derived in the collapsed space. Because collapsing preserves the structure of the Bayesian network, forward-backward algorithms can be derived when the network structure has low tree-width. We illustrate this by working through the details of a particular hidden Markov model. Readers who are less familiar with the technical details of Bayesian network learning can safely skip this section.

11.5.1 Bayesian Networks

Topic models are members of a much broader class of directed models known as Bayesian networks (BN) (Pearl, 1988). To highlight this relationship, we reformulate LDA as a two-level BN in Figure 11.6. At the top level, there is a distribution τ over document ID labels. Given a document ID, d, we draw a topic assignment z from the distribution over topics, $\theta_{k|d}$. Given z, we draw x from the distribution over words, $\phi_{w|z}$. Both random variables $\{d\}$ and $\{x\}$ are observed; in fact, we observe N copies of pairs (d_i, x_i), $i = 1...N$, where i runs over all words across all documents. This view of LDA is a subcase of the standard BN formulation, where (1) N i.i.d. samples are drawn from a directed acyclic graphical model (DAG), (2) variable nodes can have an arbitrary number of parents and children, and (3) an arbitrary subset of those variables is observed. The general distribution for a BN is given by

$$P(\mathbf{z}|\boldsymbol{\pi}) = \prod_i \left[\prod_a p_a(z_{ai}|\mathrm{pa}(z_{ai})) \right], \tag{11.6}$$

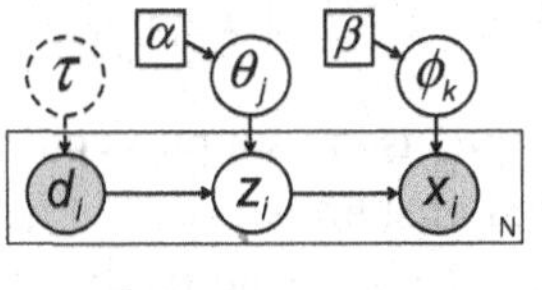

Figure 11.6 LDA depicted as a standard Bayesian network. Index i runs over all word tokens in the corpus. For each token, both the word-type x and the document label d are observed, while the topic variable z is hidden.

where $p_a(z_{ai}|\text{pa}(z_{ai}))$ is the conditional probability table (CPT), $\text{pa}(z_a)$ denotes the parents of z_a in the BN (where the parent set may be empty), the index a runs over variables in the BN, and the index i labels data cases (or data points). Note that the CPTs for LDA are τ, θ, and ϕ. For simplicity, we restrict ourselves to discrete random variables, but note that the derivations we present can be extended to any case where the observed variables follow a distribution in the exponential family. In particular, we use the notation

$$p_a(z_a = k|\text{pa}(z_a) = [j_1, .., j_J]) = \pi_{a,k,j_1,...,j_J}, \tag{11.7}$$

where $j_1, .., j_J$ is the joint state of the parent variables.

As in LDA, we introduce conjugate Dirichlet priors for the multinomial CPTs, $p(\boldsymbol{\alpha}_a) = \mathcal{D}(\alpha_{a1}, .., \alpha_{aK})$, with K being the domain size of z_a. We will also assume that this prior is the same (i.e., shared) for all possible parent states $\text{pa}(z_a)$. Inserting the multinomial distribution (11.7) into (11.6) and adding the Dirichlet priors, we arrive at the following joint distribution,

$$P(\mathbf{z}, \boldsymbol{\pi}|\boldsymbol{\alpha}) = \prod_a \prod_{j_1,...,j_J} \frac{\Gamma(\sum_k \alpha_{ak})}{\prod_k \Gamma(\alpha_{ak})} \prod_k \pi_{a,k,j_1,...,j_J}^{N_{k,j_1,...,j_J}^a + \alpha_{ak} - 1}, \tag{11.8}$$

where $N_{k,j_1,...,j_J}^a = \sum_i \mathbb{I}[z_{ai} = k, pa(z_{ai}) = [j_1, .., j_J]]$.

Because of the conjugacy between the CPT and the prior, we can analytically marginalize out all CPTs from the model. Doing so will induce dependencies between the data cases that were conditionally independent given the CPTs. The result of the marginalization is the collapsed joint distribution,

$$P(\mathbf{z}|\boldsymbol{\alpha}) = \prod_a \prod_{j_1,...,j_J} \frac{\prod_k \Gamma(N_{k,j_1,...,j_J}^a + \alpha_{ak})}{\Gamma(\sum_k (N_{k,j_1,...,j_J}^a + \alpha_{ak}))} \frac{\Gamma(\sum_k \alpha_{ak})}{\prod_k \Gamma(\alpha_{ak})}. \tag{11.9}$$

Although the original structure of the BN is preserved, we have introduced dependencies between the data cases. However, one can still derive a Gibbs sampler for this collapsed BN, where each variable z_{ai} for a single data point is sampled one at a time. The conditional probability is given by

$$p(z_{ai} = k|z^{\neg ai}) \propto p(z_{ai} = k|\text{pa}(z_{ai})) \prod_b p(\text{ch}_b(z_{ai})|\text{pa}(\text{ch}_b(z_{ai}))\backslash z_{ai}, z_{ai} = k), \tag{11.10}$$

where $\text{ch}_b(z_{ai})$ is the bth child variable of z_{ai}. The first factor corresponds to the CPT of z_{ai} given all its parent variables, whereas the second factor corresponds to all the children of z_{ai} given their parents (and note that one of these parents is z_{ai}). All these variables form the Markov blanket of z_{ai}. Inserting the explicit expression (11.9) into (11.10), we obtain the conditional,

$$p(z_{ai} = k|z^{\neg ai}) \propto (N_{k,j_1,...,j_J}^{a,\neg i} + \alpha_{ak}) \prod_b \frac{N_{m,l_1,..k,..l_L}^{b,\neg i} + \alpha_{bm}}{\sum_{m'} (N_{m',l_1,..k,..l_L}^{b,\neg i} + \alpha_{bm'})}. \tag{11.11}$$

This expression is somewhat imprecise to suppress clutter. The first term assumes that the parents of z_{ai} are instantiated at state $\text{pa}(z_{ai}) = [j_1, .., j_J]$. Moreover, the children of variable a are fixed in a state that we generically denote with "m", but every child can be in a different state "m_b". Similarly, the parents of the child nodes are assumed to be fixed in states that we denote with $l_1, .., l_L$, except for the parent node that actually corresponds to z_{ai}, which is of course assumed to be in state k. Once again, we suppress the dependence on b, although $l_{1b}, .., l_{Lb}$ is more precise. Gibbs sampling proceeds by cycling through all the variables $\{z_{ai}\}$ one by one, reading out the states of the variables in its Markov blanket, and computing the relevant counts associated with those states by counting how many *other* data cases are in the same states. Note that in computing these counts, one should not include the data case under consideration. Finally, we use Equation 11.11 to draw a new sample. We can estimate the value of the CPTs from the drawn samples by using the posterior mean estimate

$$\hat{\pi}_{k,j_1,...j_J} = \frac{N^a_{k,j_1,...,j_J} + \alpha_{ak}}{\sum_{k'} (N^a_{k',j_1,...,j_J} + \alpha_{ak'})}. \tag{11.12}$$

To reduce variance, one can average over multiple Gibbs samples.

Because the collapsed BN retains the structure of the original BN, we can adapt standard inference techniques used for BNs. For instance, if the BN is a tree, we can draw "perfect samples" from the full distribution by using "inward-filtering-outward-sampling" which is a generalization of forward-backward sampling (Scott, 2002). This technique computes probabilities $p(z_a, z_{\text{upstream}}|\text{downstream evidence})$, where z_{upstream} is the next variable toward the root. When we arrive at the root, we have access to the distribution $p(z_{\text{root}}|\text{all evidence})$ from which we draw a sample. We then traverse back to the leaf nodes by recursively sampling from $z_a \sim p(z_a, z_{\text{upstream}} = k|\text{downstream evidence})$. Because all upstream evidence is summarized in the sampled state $z_{\text{upstream}} = k$, the inward-outward pass samples from the full posterior $p(\mathbf{z}|\text{all evidence})$. When the BN has low tree-width, this technique can be extended to efficiently run on a junction tree. Other methods such as cutset sampling can also be employed (e.g., Bidyuk, and Dechter, 2003).

Nonparametric extensions of Bayesian networks have also been developed, where the number of hidden states is formally infinite (Welling, Porteous, and Bart, 2008b). The HDP can be understood as an instance of this class of models. We expect that the parallel inference techniques in Section 11.2 will be applicable to these infinite-state Bayesian networks as well.

11.5.2 Example: Hidden Markov Models

A popular example of a Bayesian network is the Hidden Markov Model (HMM) (Rabiner, 1990; Smyth, Heckerman, and Jordan, 1997), which has proven to be useful in many applications, such as speech recognition and machine translation. Consider an inhomogeneous HMM with time-varying transition parameters (Figure 11.7). In this

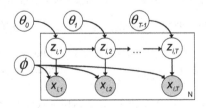

Figure 11.7 HMM with time-varying transition parameters.

model, the observed sequences, $\{x_i\}$, $1 \le i \le N$, are each of length T, where each x_{it} is discrete and can take one of M values. Each observed sequence has a corresponding hidden sequence z_i, and each z_{it} takes one of S state values. The transition matrices (of size $S \times S$) are denoted by θ_t (with the initial distribution being a vector θ_0), and the emission probability matrix (of size $S \times M$) is denoted by ϕ. The generative process is as follows:

$$\theta_0[\cdot] \sim \mathcal{D}[\alpha], \qquad \theta_t[\cdot|s] \sim \mathcal{D}[\alpha], \qquad \phi[\cdot|s] \sim \mathcal{D}[\beta]$$
$$z_{i,1} \sim \theta_0[\cdot], \qquad z_{i,t} \sim \theta_{t-1}[\cdot|z_{i,t-1}], \qquad x_{i,t} \sim \phi[\cdot|z_{i,t}].$$

We can integrate out θ from this HMM. Note that the Markov structure is retained because there is a different set of transition parameters per time step. Conditional on the data x_i and the emission probabilities ϕ, we can sample the entire hidden sequence z_i in block fashion, using the forward-backward (FB) sampler (Scott, 2002). Using the same type of derivation that we outlined for BNs, we can compute the probabilities needed by the FB sampler, using the counts $N_{t,r,s}^{-i} = \sum_{i' \ne i} \mathbb{I}[z_{i',t-1} = r, z_{i',t} = s]$:

$$p(z_{i,t} = s|z_{i,t-1} = r) \propto \frac{N_{t,r,s}^{-i} + \alpha}{\sum_{s'}^S N_{t,r,s'}^{-i} + S\alpha} \quad \text{and} \quad p(x_{i,t} = m|z_{i,t} = s) \propto \phi_{m|s}.$$

In the forward pass of the FB sampler, for each sequence i, we would need to build up probability matrices $\{P_2^i, P_3^i, .., P_T^i\}$, where $P_t^i = (p_{trs}^i)$ (see Scott, 2002, for details). We perform this computation recursively,[2]

$$p_{trs}^i \equiv p(z_{i,t-1} = r, z_{i,t} = s|x_{i,1:t})$$
$$\propto p(z_{i,t-1} = r, z_{i,t} = s, x_{i,t}|x_{i,1:(t-1)})$$
$$= p(x_{i,t}|z_{i,t} = s)p(z_{i,t} = s|z_{i,t-1} = r)p(z_{i,t-1} = r|x_{i,1:(t-1)})$$
$$= p(x_{i,t}|z_{i,t} = s)p(z_{i,t} = s|z_{i,t-1} = r) \sum_{r'} p_{t-1,r',r}^i.$$

After constructing these matrices up to $t = T$, we start the backward sampling pass. First, we sample the last state in the sequence, $z_{i,T} \sim \pi_T(\cdot)$, where $\pi_T(\cdot) \equiv \sum_r p_{Trs}^i$. Then, the state sequence is recursively sampled backward, using the appropriate column of each P matrix,

$$z_{i,t-1} \sim P_{t,\cdot,x_{i,t}}^i, \qquad \text{for } t = T, T-1, \dots, 2.$$

This forward-backward procedure is guaranteed to obtain an exact sample from the joint distribution $p(z_{i,1:T}|x_{i,1:T}, z^{-i}, x^{-i}, \phi, \alpha, \beta)$. Thus, we can perform Gibbs sampling by iteratively sampling each hidden sequence x_i conditional on the other hidden sequences and the data. After iterating through all the hidden sequences, the next step is to sample each $\phi_{\cdot|s}$ from $p(\phi_{\cdot|s}|x, z, \alpha, \beta)$, which is a posterior Dirichlet distribution,

$$\phi_{\cdot|s} \sim \mathcal{D}[N_{s,1} + \beta, N_{s,2} + \beta, \dots, N_{s,M} + \beta], \tag{11.13}$$

where $N_{s,m} = \sum_i \sum_t \mathbb{I}[z_{i,t} = s, x_{i,t} = m]$. This two-stage Gibbs sampler over z and ϕ is iteratively performed until convergence. This procedure yields samples for ϕ as well

---

[2] To avoid notational clutter, we do not include all the variables being conditioned on in the probabilities in this equation, but they can be inferred from context.

as a posterior mean estimate $\hat{\theta}$ that is computed in the same manner as Equation 11.12. Thus, given the observed data, we can learn in collapsed fashion the parameters of an inhomogeneous HMM.

11.5.3 Distributed Inference for Bayesian Networks

We can apply parallel sampling techniques to the more general case of Bayesian networks. We assume that the data cases are distributed across processors. In this approach, each processor runs its own inference procedure on local data. Then, each processor updates only a small fraction of the total counts, that is, $N = N^p + N^{\neg p}$, where N is processor p's estimate of the total count (for some family of variables $\{z_a, \mathrm{pa}(z_a)\}$), N^p are local counts based on the data updated by processor p, and $N^{\neg p}$ are the total counts received from the other processors. At specified times, the processors will exchange their counts and compute new (and up-to-date) total count arrays,

$$N^a_{k,j_1,...,j_J} = \sum_p N^{a,p}_{k,j_1,...,j_J} . \tag{11.14}$$

These global count arrays will then be communicated back to the processors, which proceed to update their own local count arrays N^p. This algorithm is not exact for Gibbs sampling, because a processor will not have the most recent update on the count arrays for the other processors. However, empirically this concurrent sampling procedure can produce accurate samples as long as the hidden variables are weakly coupled across processors. One can also develop asynchronous versions of this distributed algorithm.

In the specific case of the HMM discussed in Section 11.5.2, we can formulate an Approximate Distributed HMM (AD-HMM) algorithm as well. First, the observed sequences $\{x_i\}$ are distributed across processors. All the hidden sequences, $\{z_i\}$, are randomly initialized, and count matrices corresponding to θ are globally synchronized, as well as the instantiated ϕ variable. Each processor runs the forward-backward (FB) sampler described in Section 11.5.2 to sample its local hidden sequences; once the processors finish their local sweep, the counts are globally synchronized in the same fashion as Equation 11.14. At the global synchronization step, ϕ is sampled according to Equation 11.13. Then ϕ and the global counts for θ are sent back to the processors for another round of Gibbs sampling. As shown in the next section, this parallel sampling procedure for this class of HMMs can yield both significant computational speedups and accurate results.

Experimentally, we have found that our techniques are useful in this more general context of Bayesian networks. We performed an experiment comparing the single-processor collapsed Gibbs sampler for HMMs to AD-HMM. We used an HMM of length $T = 100$, with $S = 4$ hidden states and a domain size $M = 10$, for the observed variables. We simulated ground truth distributions ϕ_{true} and θ_{true} from a Dirichlet $\mathcal{D}[0.1]$. Given ϕ_{true} and θ_{true}, we simulated synthetic data consisting of a training set of $N = 1000$ observed sequences $\{x_{it}\}$, as well as a test set of 200 observed sequences. In this experiment, we distributed the sequences across processors and ran AD-HMM for 200 iterations with hyperparameter settings $\alpha = 0.1$ and $\beta = 0.1$. AD-HMM yields a sampled ϕ and a mean estimate, $\hat{\theta}$, and given ϕ and $\hat{\theta}$, it is easy to compute the log-likelihood of the test data using a standard HMM forward recursion. Figure 11.8

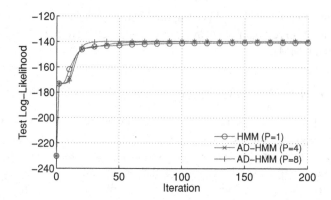

Figure 11.8 Test log-likelihood versus iteration, achieved by AD-HMM ($P = 4$ and $P = 8$) on synthetic sequence data.

shows the log-likelihood on test data achieved by both the single-processor sampler as well as AD-HMM for $P = 4$ and $P = 8$. These results suggest that AD-HMM can learn a model of the same quality as the sequential sampler. Furthermore, we ran the distributed algorithm for 200 iterations on a single multicore machine with eight cores, using MATLAB's parallel computing facilities (specifically the "parfor" construct), and AD-HMM with $P = 8$ was able to achieve a $6.8\times$ speedup over the single-processor sampler.

11.6 Conclusion

This chapter discussed a number of different parallel and distributed sampling algorithms for performing statistical inference on latent variable models such as topic models and hidden Markov models. Although some of these parallel MCMC sampling techniques use an approximation when performing concurrent sampling, our experimental analysis has shown that the models learned by these parallel samplers are as accurate as those learned by the standard sequential samplers. Furthermore, the distributed algorithms are able to achieve significant speedups and handle large amounts of data because of the increased amount of collective memory.

We also discussed the trade-offs of using various inference techniques and various computing infrastructures. As parallel and distributed computing frameworks mature and become more accessible to practitioners, we expect to see an increased use of hybrid techniques that take advantage of all the computational power available to the user, from the local processing cores available on the motherboard and graphics processing units, to large clusters of communicating machines, and eventually to cloud computing settings. Furthermore, as the statistical inference algorithms themselves continue to improve, the combination of statistical and computational acceleration techniques provides a promising opportunity to obtain compounded computational gains, opening the door to the learning of richer Bayesian models on even larger datasets.

Acknowledgments

This work is supported in part by NSF grants IIS-0083489 (PS, AA), IIS-0447903, and IIS-0535278 (MW), and an NSF graduate fellowship (AA), as well as ONR/MURI grants N00014-08-1-1015 (PS, AA) and 00014-06-1-073 (MW). PS is also supported by a Google research award. DN has been supported by NICTA. NICTA is funded by the Australian Government as represented by the Department of Broadband, Communications and the Digital Economy and the Australian Research Council through the ICT Centre of Excellence program.

References

Asuncion, A., Smyth, P., and Welling, M. 2009a. Asynchronous Distributed Learning of Topic Models. Pages 81–88 of: *Advances in Neural Information Processing Systems 21*.

Asuncion, A., Welling, M., Smyth, P., and Teh, Y. W. 2009b. On Smoothing and Inference for Topic Models. Pages 27–34 of: *Proceedings of the Twenty-Fifth Annual Conference on Uncertainty in Artificial Intelligence (UAI-09)*. Corvallis, OR: AUAI Press.

Asuncion, A., Smyth, P., and Welling, M. 2011. Asynchronous Distributed Estimation of Topic Models for Document Analysis. *Statistical Methodology*, **8**(1), 3–17.

Bidyuk, B., and Dechter, R. 2003. Cycle-Cutset Sampling for Bayesian Networks. Pages 297–312 of: *Advances in Artificial Intelligence, 16th Conference of the Canadian Society for Computational Studies of Intelligence*, Vol. 2671.

Blei, D. M., Ng, A. Y., and Jordan, M. I. 2003. Latent Dirichlet Allocation. *Journal of Machine Learning Research*, **3**, 993–1022.

Boyd, S. P., Ghosh, A., Prabhakar, B., and Shah, D. 2005. Gossip Algorithms: Design, Analysis and Applications. Pages 1653–1664 of: *Proceedings of INFOCOM: 24th Annual Joint Conference of the IEEE Computer and Communications Societies*, vol. 3. IEEE.

Buntine, W., and Jakulin, A. 2006. Discrete Component Analysis. *Lecture Notes in Computer Science*, **3940**, 1–33.

Chien, J. T., and Wu, M. S. 2008. Adaptive Bayesian Latent Semantic Analysis. *IEEE Transactions on Audio, Speech, and Language Processing*, **16**(1), 198–207.

Deerwester, S., Dumais, S. T., Furnas, G. W., Landauer, T. K., and Harshman, R. 1990. Indexing by Latent Semantic Analysis. *Journal of the American Society for Information Science*, **41**(6), 391–407.

Doshi-Velez, F., Knowles, D., Mohamed, S., and Ghahramani, Z. 2009. Large Scale Nonparametric Bayesian Inference: Data Parallelisation in the Indian Buffet Process. Pages 1294–1302 of: *Advances in Neural Information Processing Systems 22*.

Frank, A., and Asuncion, A. 2007. *UCI Machine Learning Repository*. www.ics.uci.edu/~mlearn/MLRepository.html.

Griffiths, T. L., and Steyvers, M. 2004. Finding Scientific Topics. *Proceedings of the National Academy of Sciences of the United States of America*, **101**(Suppl 1), 5228–5235.

Griffiths, T. L., Steyvers, M., Blei, D. M., and Tenenbaum, J. B. 2005. Integrating Topics and Syntax. Pages 537–544 of: *Advances in Neural Information Processing Systems 17*. Cambridge, MA: MIT Press.

Gruber, A., Rosen-Zvi, M., and Weiss, Y. 2007. Hidden Topic Markov Models. Pages 163–170 of: *AISTATS '07: Proceedings of 11th International Conference on Artificial Intelligence and Statistics*.

Hofmann, T. 2001. Unsupervised Learning by Probabilistic Latent Semantic Analysis. *Machine Learning*, **42**(1), 177–196.

Ihler, A., and Newman, D. 2009. *Bounding Sample Errors in Approximate Distributed Latent Dirichlet Allocation*. Large Scale Machine Learning Workshop, NIPS. UCI ICS Technical Report 09-06, www.ics.uci.edu/~ihler/papers/tr09-06.pdf.

Jelinek, F., Mercer, R. L., Bahl, L. R., and Baker, J. K. 1977. Perplexity – a Measure of the Difficulty of Speech Recognition Tasks. *Journal of the Acoustical Society of America*, **62**, S63.

Jolliffe, I. T. 2002. *Principal Component Analysis*, 2nd ed. New York: Springer.

Li, F. F., and Perona, P. 2005. A Bayesian Hierarchical Model for Learning Natural Scene Categories. Pages 524–531 of: *Proceedings of the 2005 IEEE Computer Society Conference on Computer Vision and Pattern Recognition (CVPR'05)*, vol. 2. IEEE Computer Society.

Lowe, D. G. 2004. Distinctive Image Features from Scale-Invariant Keypoints. *International Journal of Computer Vision*, **60**(2), 91–110.

Masada, T., Hamada, T., Shibata, Y., and Oguri, K. 2009. Accelerating Collapsed Variational Bayesian Inference for Latent Dirichlet Allocation with NVIDIA CUDA Compatible Devices. Pages 491–500 of: *Proceedings of the 22nd International Conference on Industrial, Engineering and Other Applications of Applied Intelligent Systems: Next-Generation Applied Intelligence*. New York: Springer.

Minka, T., and Lafferty, J. 2002. Expectation-Propagation for the Generative Aspect Model. Pages 352–359 of: *Proceedings of the Eighteenth Annual Conference on Uncertainty in Artificial Intelligence (UAI-02)*. San Francisco, CA: Morgan Kaufmann.

Nallapati, R., Cohen, W., and Lafferty, J. 2007. Parallelized Variational EM for Latent Dirichlet Allocation: An Experimental Evaluation of Speed and Scalability. Pages 349–354 of: *Proceedings of the Seventh IEEE International Conference on Data Mining Workshops*. Washington, DC: IEEE Computer Society.

Newman, D., Asuncion, A., Smyth, P., and Welling, M. 2008. Distributed Inference for Latent Dirichlet Allocation. Pages 1081–1088 of: *Advances in Neural Information Processing Systems 20*. Cambridge, MA: MIT Press.

Newman, D., Asuncion, A., Smyth, P., and Welling, M. 2009. Distributed Algorithms for Topic Models. *Journal of Machine Learning Research*, **10**, 1801–1828.

Pearl, J. 1988. *Probabilistic Reasoning in Intelligent Systems: Networks of Plausible Inference*. San Francisco, CA: Morgan Kaufmann.

Porteous, I., Newman, D., Ihler, A., Asuncion, A., Smyth, P., and Welling, M. 2008a. Fast Collapsed Gibbs Sampling for Latent Dirichlet Allocation. Pages 569–577 of: *KDD '08: Proceeding of the 14th ACM SIGKDD International Conference on Knowledge Discovery and Data Mining*. New York: ACM.

Porteous, I., Bart, E., and Welling, M. 2008b. Multi-HDP: A Non Parametric Bayesian Model for Tensor Factorization. Pages 1487–1490 of: *AAAI'08: Proceedings of the 23rd National Conference on Artificial Intelligence*. AAAI Press.

Pritchard, J. K., Stephens, M., and Donnelly, P. 2000. Inference of Population Structure using Multi-locus Genotype Data. *Genetics*, **155**, 945–959.

Rabiner, L. R. 1990. A Tutorial on Hidden Markov Models and Selected Applications in Speech Recognition. *Readings in Speech Recognition*, **53**(3), 267–296.

Scott, S. L. 2002. Bayesian Methods for Hidden Markov Models: Recursive Computing in the 21st Century. *Journal of the American Statistical Association*, **97**(457), 337–352.

Smola, A., and Narayanamurthy, S. 2010. An Architecture for Parallel Topic Models. Pages 703–710 at: Very Large Databases (VLDB).

Smyth, P., Heckerman, D., and Jordan, M. I. 1997. Probabilistic Independence Networks for Hidden Markov Probability Models. *Neural Computation*, **9**(2), 227–269.

Teh, Y. W., Jordan, M. I., Beal, M. J., and Blei, D. M. 2006. Hierarchical Dirichlet Processes. *Journal of the American Statistical Association*, **101**(476), 1566–1581.

Teh, Y. W., Newman, D., and Welling, M. 2007. A Collapsed Variational Bayesian Inference Algorithm for Latent DIrichlet Allocation. Pages 1353–1360 of: *Advances in Neural Information Processing Systems 19*. Cambridge, MA: MIT Press.

Wallach, H. M. 2006. Topic Modeling: Beyond Bag-of-Words. Pages 977–984 of: *ICML '06: Proceedings of the 23rd International Conference on Machine Learning*. New York: ACM.

Wang, Y., Bai, H., Stanton, M., Chen, W. Y., and Chang, E. Y. 2009. PLDA: Parallel Latent Dirichlet Allocation for Large-Scale Applications. Pages 301–314 of: *AAIM '09: Proceedings of the 5th International Conference on Algorithmic Aspects in Information and Management*. Berlin: Springer.

Welling, M., Teh, Y. W., and Kappen, H. 2008a. Hybrid Variational/Gibbs Collapsed Inference in Topic Models. Pages 587–594 of: *Proceedings of the Twenty-Fourth Annual Conference on Uncertainty in Artificial Intelligence (UAI-08)*. Corvallis, OR: AUAI Press.

Welling, M., Porteous, I., and Bart, E. 2008b. Infinite State Bayes-nets for Structured Domains. Pages 1601–1608 of: *Advances in Neural Information Processing Systems 20*. Cambridge, MA: MIT Press.

Wolfe, J., Haghighi, A., and Klein, D. 2008. Fully Distributed EM for Very Large Datasets. Pages 1184–1191 of: *ICML '08: Proceedings of the 25th International Conference on Machine Learning*. New York: ACM.

Yan, F., Xu, N., and Qi, Y. 2009. Parallel Inference for Latent Dirichlet Allocation on Graphics Processing Units. Pages 2134–2142 of: *Advances in Neural Information Processing Systems 22*.

Yao, L., Mimno, D., and McCallum, A. 2009. Efficient Methods for Topic Model Inference on Streaming Document Collections. Pages 937–946 of: *KDD '09: Proceedings of the 15th ACM SIGKDD International Conference on Knowledge Discovery and Data Mining*. New York: ACM.

CHAPTER 12

Large-Scale Spectral Clustering with MapReduce and MPI

Wen-Yen Chen, Yangqiu Song, Hongjie Bai, Chih-Jen Lin, and Edward Y. Chang

·

Spectral clustering is a technique for finding group structure in data. It makes use of the spectrum of the data similarity matrix to perform dimensionality reduction for clustering in fewer dimensions. Spectral clustering algorithms have been shown to be more effective in finding clusters than traditional algorithms such as k-means. However, spectral clustering suffers from a scalability problem in both memory use and computation time when the size of a dataset is large. To perform clustering on large datasets, in this work, we parallelize both memory use and computation using MapReduce and MPI. Through an empirical study on a document set of 534,135 instances and a photo set of 2,121,863 images, we show that our parallel algorithm can effectively handle large problems.

Clustering is one of the most important subfields of machine learning and data mining tasks. In the last decade, spectral clustering (e.g., Shi and Malik, 2000; Meila and Shi, 2000; Fowlkes et al., 2004), motivated by normalized graph cut, has attracted much attention. Unlike traditional partition-based clustering, spectral clustering exploits a pairwise data similarity matrix. It has been shown to be more effective than traditional methods such as k-means, which considers only the similarity between instances and k centroids (Ng, Jordan, and Weiss, 2001). Because of its effectiveness, spectral clustering has been widely used in several areas such as information retrieval and computer vision (e.g., Dhillon, 2001; Xu, Liu, and Gong, 2003; Shi and Malik, 2000; Yu and Shi, 2003). Unfortunately, when the number of data points (denoted as n) is large, spectral clustering can encounter a quadratic bottleneck (Fowlkes et al., 2004; Liu and Zhang, 2004) in computing pairwise similarities among n data points and in storing the large similarity matrix.

The most commonly used approach to address the computational and memory difficulties is to zero out some elements in the similarity matrix or to sparsify the matrix. From the obtained sparse similarity matrix, one then transforms it to a corresponding Laplacian matrix (defined in Section 12.1) and applies a sparse eigensolver. There are several methods available for sparsifying the similarity matrix (Luxburg, 2007). A sparse representation effectively handles the memory bottleneck, but some sparsification schemes still require calculating all elements of the similarity matrix. Another

Table 12.1. *Notation. The following notation is used in the chapter.*

n	number of data points
d	dimensionality of data points
k	number of desired clusters
p	number of nodes (number of computers in a distributed system)
t	number of nearest neighbors
m	Arnoldi length used in an eigensolver
$x_1, \ldots, x_n \in R^d$	data points
$S \in R^{n \times n}$	similarity matrix
$L \in R^{n \times n}$	Laplacian matrix
$v_1, \ldots, v_k \in R^n$	first k eigenvectors of L
$V \in R^{n \times k}$	eigenvector matrix
$E \in R^{n \times k}$	cluster indicator matrix
$c_1, \ldots, c_k \in R^d$	cluster centroids of k-means

popular approach to speedup spectral clustering is by using a dense sub-matrix of the similarity matrix (Fowlkes et al., 2004).

We consider the sparsification strategy of retaining nearest neighbors, and then investigate its parallel implementation. Our parallel implementation, which we call parallel spectral clustering (PSC), provides a systematic solution for handling challenges from calculating the similarity matrix to efficiently finding eigenvectors. PSC first distributes n data points onto p nodes. On each node, PSC computes the similarities between a subset of size n/p points and the whole dataset in a way that uses minimal disk I/O and distributedly stores the similarity matrix on nodes to reduce per-node memory use. Together with parallel eigensolver and k-means methods, PSC achieves good speedup on large datasets. In particular, we discuss the choice of MapReduce and MPI in implementing different steps. Part of this work has appeared in a paper (Chen et al., 2011).

12.1 Spectral Clustering

This section presents the spectral clustering algorithm and describes its resource bottlenecks. To assist readers, Table 12.1 defines terms and notation.

Given n data points $x_1, \ldots, x_n$, the spectral clustering algorithm constructs a similarity matrix $S \in R^{n \times n}$, where $S_{ij} \geq 0$ reflects the similarity relationship between x_i and x_j. It then uses the similarity information to group $x_1, \ldots, x_n$ into k clusters. There are several variants of spectral clustering. Here we consider the commonly used *normalized* spectral clustering (Ng et al., 2001).[1] An example similarity function is the Gaussian:

$$S_{ij} = \exp\left(-\frac{\|x_i - x_j\|^2}{2\sigma_i \sigma_j}\right), \tag{12.1}$$

where σ_i and σ_j are scaling parameters to control how rapidly the similarity S_{ij} reduces with the distance between x_i and x_j.

---

[1] For a survey of variants, refer to Luxburg (2007).

Spectral clustering finds the eigenvectors of a specific graph Laplacian matrix (Luxburg, 2007). Consider the normalized Laplacian matrix (Chung, 1997):

$$L = I - D^{-1/2}SD^{-1/2}. \tag{12.2}$$

The matrix D, used for normalizing S, is a diagonal matrix with

$$D_{ii} = \sum_{j=1}^{n} S_{ij}, \quad \text{for } i = 1, \ldots, n.$$

It has been shown that for any S with $S_{ij} \geq 0$, the Laplacian matrix is symmetric positive semi-definite (Luxburg, 2007). In the ideal case, data in one cluster are not related to those in others, so $S_{ij} = 0$ if x_i and x_j are in different clusters. Then nonzero elements of S (and hence L) occur in a block diagonal form:

$$L = \begin{bmatrix} L_1 & & \\ & \ddots & \\ & & L_k \end{bmatrix}.$$

In practice, we do not know cluster assignment beforehand, so choosing an appropriate similarity function is hard. The choice in Equation (12.1) is reasonable because S_{ij} is larger if x_i is closer to x_j. Luxburg (2007, Proposition 4) shows that the block diagonal matrix L has k zero-eigenvalues, which are also the k smallest ones. Their corresponding eigenvectors $v_i \in R^n, \forall i$ are

$$V = [v_1, v_2, \ldots, v_k] = D^{1/2}E, \quad \text{and} \quad E = \begin{bmatrix} e_1 & 0 & \cdots & 0 \\ 0 & e_2 & & \vdots \\ \vdots & & \ddots & 0 \\ 0 & \cdots & 0 & e_k \end{bmatrix}, \tag{12.3}$$

where $e_i, i = 1, \ldots, k$ are vectors of all 1s (vectors may be of different lengths). Because $D^{1/2}E$ has the same nonzero pattern as E, simple clustering algorithms such as k-means can easily cluster the n rows of V into k groups. Thus, what one needs to do is to find the first k eigenvectors of L (i.e., the eigenvectors corresponding to the k smallest eigenvalues). Practically the obtained eigenvectors are in the form of

$$V = D^{1/2}EQ,$$

where Q is an orthogonal matrix. Ng et al. (2001) propose normalizing V so that

$$U_{ij} = \frac{V_{ij}}{\sqrt{\sum_{r=1}^{k} V_{ir}^2}}, i = 1, \ldots, n, j = 1, \ldots, k. \tag{12.4}$$

Each row of U has a unit length. Because Q is orthogonal, Equation 12.4 is equivalent to

$$U = EQ = \begin{bmatrix} Q_{1,1:k} \\ \vdots \\ Q_{1,1:k} \\ Q_{2,1:k} \\ \vdots \end{bmatrix}, \tag{12.5}$$

where $Q_{i,1:k}$ indicates the ith row of Q. Then U's n rows correspond to k orthogonal points on the unit sphere. The n rows of U can thus be easily clustered by k-means (Ng et al., 2001) or other simple techniques.

In summary, spectral clustering assumes $S_{ij} = 0$ if x_i and x_j are in different classes, obtains a block diagonal similarity matrix S, constructs the Laplacian matrix, conducts eigendecomposition, and obtains a matrix V, whose rows can be easily clustered. For the practical use of spectral clustering, we choose suitable similarity functions to construct a matrix S (and L) close to be block diagonal.

12.2 Spectral Clustering Using a Sparse Similarity Matrix

A serious bottleneck for spectral clustering is the memory use for storing S, whose number of elements is the square of the number of data points. For instance, storing $n = 10^6$ data points (assuming double-precision storage) requires 8TB of memory, which is not available on a general-purpose machine. Approximation techniques have been proposed to avoid storing the dense matrix, such as zeroing out random entries in the similarity matrix (Achlioptas, McSherry, and Schölkopf, 2002), using the t-nearest-neighbor approach or the ϵ-neighborhood approach (Luxburg, 2007), or using the Nyström approximation to store only several columns (or rows) of the similarity matrix S (Fowlkes et al., 2004). Existing comparisons of approximation methods for constructing the similarity matrix include, for example, Fowlkes et al. (2004); Chen et al. (2011). A taxonomy of different approximation approaches is given in Chen et al. (2011, Figure 1). In this chapter, we focus on studying the method of using t nearest neighbors.

Algorithm 39: Spectral Clustering Using a Sparse Similarity Matrix

---

Input: Data points $x_1, \ldots, x_n$;
    k: number of desired clusters.
    Construct similarity matrix $S \in R^{n \times n}$
    Modify S to be a sparse matrix
    Compute the Laplacian matrix L by Equation 12.2
    Compute the first k eigenvectors of L; and collect these eigenvectors as a matrix $V \in R^{n \times k}$
    Compute the normalized matrix U of V by Equation 12.4
    Use k-means algorithm to cluster n rows of U into k groups

---

Algorithm 39 presents spectral clustering using the t-nearest-neighbor method for sparsification. We follow exactly the same procedure in Section 12.1, although S is modified to be a sparse matrix. In the rest of this section we examine Algorithm 39's computational cost and memory use. We omit discussing some inexpensive steps.

Construct a Sparse Similarity Matrix: To generate a sparse similarity matrix, we retain only S_{ij} where the ith point (or the jth point) is among the t nearest neighbors of the jth point (or the ith point). A typical implementation is as follows. By keeping a max heap of size t, we sequentially insert the distance that is smaller than the maximal value of the heap and then restructure the heap. Because restructuring a max heap is on the order of $\log t$, the complexity of generating a sparse matrix S is

$$O(n^2 d) + O(n^2 \log t) \text{ time and } O(nt) \text{ memory.} \qquad (12.6)$$

The $O(n^2 d)$ cost may be slightly reduced using some advanced techniques; see the discussion in Section 12.5. Studying these techniques is beyond the scope of this chapter because in particular their parallelization may be difficult. We thus focus only on a precise method to find t nearest neighbors.

The foregoing construction may lead to a non-symmetric matrix. We can easily make it symmetric. If either the (i, j) or the (j, i) element is nonzero, we set both positions to have the same value S_{ij}. Making the matrix symmetric leads to at most $2t$ nonzero elements per row. As $2t \ll n$, the symmetric matrix is still sparse.

Compute the First k Eigenvectors by Lanczos/Arnoldi Factorization: Once we have obtained a sparse similarity matrix S and its Laplacian matrix L by Equation (12.2), we can use sparse eigensolvers. In particular, we desire a solver that can quickly obtain the first k eigenvectors of L. Some example solvers include ARPACK (Lehoucg, Sorensen, and Yang, 1998) and SLEPc (Hernandez, Roman, and Vidal, 2005b); see (Hernandez et al., 2005a) for a comprehensive survey. Most existing approaches are variants of the Lanczos/Arnoldi factorization (explained later). These variants have similar time complexity, so the discussion here is quite general. We employ a popular one called ARPACK and briefly describe its basic concepts hereafter; more details can be found in the user's guide for ARPACK. The main computation involved in ARPACK is the implicitly restarted Arnoldi factorization. The m-step Arnoldi factorization finds two matrices $\bar{V}$ and H such that

$$L\bar{V} = \bar{V}H + \text{(a matrix of small values)}, \qquad (12.7)$$

where $\bar{V} \in R^{n \times m}$ has orthonormal columns and $H \in R^{m \times m}$ is an upper Hessenberg matrix with zero entries below the first subdiagonal (Lehoucg et al., 1998). If the "matrix of small values" in Equation 12.7 is indeed zero, then $\bar{V}$'s m columns are L's first m eigenvectors (details not derived here). Therefore, Equation 12.7 provides a way to check how well we approximate eigenvectors of L. To know how good the approximation is, one needs all eigenvalues of the dense matrix H, a procedure taking $O(m^3)$ operations. ARPACK employs an iterative procedure called "implicitly restarted" Arnoldi. Users specify an Arnoldi length m with $m > k$ and $m \ll n$. Then at each iteration (restarted Arnoldi) one uses $\bar{V}$ and H from the previous iteration to conduct the eigendecomposition of H and find a new Arnoldi factorization. An Arnoldi factorization at each iteration involves at most $(m - k)$ steps, where each step's main computational complexity is $O(nm)$ for a few dense matrix-vector products and $O(nt)$ for a sparse matrix-vector product. In particular, $O(nt)$ is for

$$Lv, \qquad (12.8)$$

where v is a vector of length n. Because each row of L has no more than $2t$ nonzero elements, the cost of this sparse matrix-vector product is $O(nt)$.

After finishing the implicitly restarted Arnoldi procedure, we can obtain the required matrix V by collecting the first k columns of final $\bar{V}$. Based on the preceding analysis, the overall cost of ARPACK is upper-bounded by

$$\left(O(m^3) + (O(nm) + O(nt)) \times (m - k)\right) \times \text{(restarted Arnoldi iterations)}. \quad (12.9)$$

Note that the number of inner steps at each restarted Arnoldi iteration is no more than $m - k$. Obviously, the selected value m affects the computation time. One often sets m to be several times larger than k. As $m \ll n$, $O(m^3)$ is not the dominant term in each restarted Arnoldi iteration. For the number of restarted Arnoldi iterations, ARPACK may take a few dozen in a typical run. The memory use of ARPACK is $O(nt) + O(nm)$.

Use k-means to Cluster the Normalized Matrix U: Let $\boldsymbol{u}_j$, $j = 1, \ldots, n$, be vectors corresponding to U's n rows. The k-means algorithm aims at minimizing the total intra-cluster variance:

$$\sum_{i=1}^{k} \sum_{\boldsymbol{u}_j \in C_i} ||\boldsymbol{u}_j - \boldsymbol{c}_i||^2. \quad (12.10)$$

We assume that data are in k clusters C_i, $i = 1, 2, \ldots, k$, and $\boldsymbol{c}_i \in R^k$ is the centroid of the cluster C_i.

The k-means algorithm employs an iterative procedure. At each iteration, one finds each data point's nearest centroid and assigns it to the corresponding cluster. Cluster centroids are then recalculated. Because the algorithm evaluates the distances between any data point and the current k cluster centroids, the time complexity of k-means is

$$O(nk^2) \times \text{(k-means iterations)}. \quad (12.11)$$

Note that each data point or centroid here is a vector of length k. In this work, we terminate k-means execution if the relative difference between the two values of the objective function 12.10 in consecutive iterations is less than 0.001.

Overall Analysis: From Equations 12.6, 12.9, and 12.11, the $O(n^2 d) + O(n^2 \log t)$ computation time in constructing sparse similarity matrix is the main bottleneck for spectral clustering. This bottleneck has been well discussed in previous works (e.g., Fowlkes et al., 2004; Liu and Zhang, 2004).

12.3 Parallel Spectral Clustering (PSC) Using a Sparse Similarity Matrix

We now present PSC using t-nearest-neighbor sparse similarity matrices. We have both Message Passing Interface (MPI) (Snir and Otto, 1998) and MapReduce (Dean and Ghemawat, 2008) systems on our distributed environments. We illustrate their differences and present our implementation of the parallel spectral clustering algorithm.

12.3.1 MPI and MapReduce

MPI (Snir and Otto, 1998) is a message-passing library specification for parallel programming. An MPI program is loaded into the local memory of each machine, where

Table 12.2. *Sample MPI functions (Snir and Otto, 1998).*

MPI_Bcast:	Broadcasts information to all processes.
MPI_AllGather:	Gathers the data contributed by each process on all processes.
MPI_AllReduce:	Performs a global reduction and returns the result on all processes.

every processor/process (each processor will be assigned only one process for maximum performance) has a unique ID. When needed, the processes can communicate and synchronize with others by calling MPI library routines. Examples of MPI functions are shown in Table 12.2.

MapReduce is a Google parallel computing framework (Dean and Ghemawat, 2008). As an abstract programming model, different implementations of MapReduce are available depending on the architecture (shared or distributed environments). The one considered here is the implementation used in Google distributed clusters. For both map and reduce phases, the program reads and writes results to disks. With the disk I/O, MapReduce provides a fault-tolerant mechanism. That is, if one node fails, MapReduce restarts the task on another node. In contrast, MPI lacks this feature because its functions send and receive data to and from a node's memory. MPI users need to employ check points in their programs to achieve fault tolerance. In general, MapReduce is suitable for non-iterative algorithms where nodes require little data exchange to proceed (*non-iterative* and *independent*); MPI is appropriate for iterative algorithms where nodes require data exchange to proceed (*iterative* and *dependent*).

In Algorithm 39, constructing the sparse similarity matrix is a non-iterative and independent procedure; thus, we use MapReduce. Besides, as this construction is the most time consuming step, having a fault tolerant mechanism is essential. For finding the first k eigenvectors, we use MPI as eigensolvers are iterative and dependent procedures. For k-means, we use MPI as well.

We conclude the section by providing some implementation details. To ensure fast file I/O, we use the Google file system (GFS) (Ghemawat, Gobioff, and Leung, 2003) and store data in the SSTable file format (Chang et al., 2006). In contrast to traditional file I/O, where we sequentially read data from the beginning of the file, using SSTable allows us to easily access any data point. This property is useful in calculating the similarity matrix; see the discussion in Section 12.3.2. Regarding MPI implementations, we modify the underlying communication layer of MPICH2[2] (Gropp, Lusk, and Skjellum, 1999) to work in Google's system.

12.3.2 Similarity Matrix and Nearest Neighbors

To construct the sparse similarity matrix using t nearest neighbors, we perform three steps. First, for each data point, we compute its distance to all data points, and find its t nearest neighbors. Second, we modify the sparse matrix obtained from the first step to be symmetric. Finally, we compute the similarities using distances; see Equation 12.1. These three steps are implemented using MapReduce, as described later.

---

[2] MPICH2 is a popular MPI implementation. www.mcs.anl.gov/research/projects/mpich2.

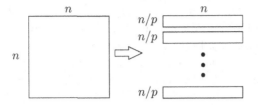

Figure 12.1 The distance matrix is distributedly computed and stored on multiple machines. The matrix is then modified to be the similarity matrix by Equation 12.1.

Compute Distances and Find Nearest Neighbors: In this step, for each data point, we compute its distance (e.g., Euclidean or cosine distance) to all data points and find the t nearest neighbors. Suppose p nodes are allocated in a distributed environment. Figure 12.1 shows that we construct n/p rows of the distance matrix at each node. To handle very large datasets, we need to carefully consider the memory usage in calculating the distances. In our implementation, we do not assume that all data points can be loaded into the memory of each single node in the distributed environment. However, we require that each node can keep n/p data points in memory. This can be achieved by increasing p, the number of nodes.

The map phase creates intermediate keys/values so that we make every n/p data points have the same key. In the reduce phase, these n/p data points are loaded to the memory of a node. We refer to them as the local data. We then scan the whole dataset: given an x_i, we calculate $\|x_i - x_j\|$ for all x_j of the n/p local data points. We use n/p max heaps so each maintains a local data point's t nearest neighbors so far. If the Euclidean distance is used, then

$$\|x_i - x_j\|^2 = \|x_i\|^2 + \|x_j\|^2 - 2x_i^T x_j.$$

We precompute all $\|x_j\|^2$ of local data to conserve time. The use of SSTable allows us to easily access arbitrary data points in the file. Thus, reading the n/p local points does not require scanning the whole input file. On each node, we store the resulting n/p sparse rows in the compressed row format.

Modify the Distance Matrix to Be Symmetric: The sparse distance matrix computed previously is not symmetric. In this step, if either (i, j) or (j, i) element of the t-nearest-neighbor distance matrix contains the distance between x_i and x_j, we set both positions to have the same value.

In the map phase, for each nonzero element in the sparse distance matrix, we generate two key–value pairs. The first key is the row ID of the element, and the corresponding value is the column ID and the distance. The second key is the column ID, and the corresponding value is the row ID and the distance. When the reduce function is called, elements with the same key correspond to values in the same row of the desired symmetric matrix. These elements are then collected. However, duplicate elements may occur, so we keep a hash map to do an efficient search and deletion. Each row contains no greater than $2t$ nonzero elements after symmetrization.

Compute Similarities: We could easily compute the similarities in the previous step, if σ_i and σ_j in Equation 12.1 are set to constants. However, for better performance, we selftune σ_i and σ_j by defining σ_i as the average of t distance values to x_i's t nearest neighbors (Zelnik-Manor and Perona, 2005). Therefore, we have a separate MapReduce step to compute similarities. In the map phase, we calculate the average distance of each row of the distance matrix. Each reduce function obtains a row of the distance matrix and all parameters, and then computes the similarity values by Equation 12.1.

12.3.3 Parallel Eigensolver

After we have obtained the sparse similarity matrix, it is important to use a parallel eigensolver. Several works have studied parallel eigendecomposition (Hernandez et al., 2005b; Marques, 1995; Maschhoff and Sorensen, 1996; Wu and Simon, 1999). We use PARPACK (Maschhoff and Sorensen, 1996), a parallel ARPACK implementation based on MPI. Assume p is the number of nodes in the distributed system. We let each MPI node store n/p rows of the matrix L as depicted in Figure 12.1. For the eigenvector matrix $\bar{V}$ (see Equation 12.7) generated during the call to ARPACK, we also split it into p partitions, each of which possesses n/p rows. Note that if k (and m) is larger than the average number of nonzero elements in each row of the sparse similarity matrix, then $\bar{V}$, an $R^{n \times m}$ dense matrix, will consume more memory. Hence, $\bar{V}$ should be distributedly stored on different nodes. As mentioned in Section 12.2, major operations at each step of the Arnoldi factorization include a sparse and a few dense matrix-vector products, which cost $O(nt)$ and $O(nm)$, respectively. We parallelize these computations so that the complexity of finding eigenvectors becomes

$$\left(O(m^3) + (O(\frac{nm}{p}) + O(\frac{nt}{p})) \times (m - k) \right) \times \text{(restarted Arnoldi iterations)}. \quad (12.12)$$

The communication between nodes occurs in the following three situations:

1. Calculate the 2-norm of a distributed vector, which is used for calculating the "matrix of small values" in Equation 12.7. Thus, we need to sum p values and broadcast the result to p nodes.
2. Parallel sparse matrix-vector product: Equation 12.8.
3. Parallel dense matrix-vector product: Sum p vectors of length m and broadcast the resulting vector to all p nodes.

The first and the third cases transfer only short vectors, but the second case may move a larger vector $v \in R^n$ to several nodes. Because of this high communication cost, we next discuss the parallel sparse matrix-vector product in detail.

Figure 12.2 shows matrix L and vector v. Suppose $p = 5$. The figure indicates that both L and v are horizontally split into five parts and each part is stored on one computer node. Take node 1 as an example. It is responsible for performing

$$L_{1:n/p, 1:n} \times v, \quad (12.13)$$

where $v = [v_1, \ldots, v_n]^T$. $L_{1:n/p, 1:n}$, the first n/p rows of L, is stored on node 1, but only $v_1, \ldots, v_{n/p}$ are available there. Hence other nodes must send to node 1 the elements $v_{n/p+1}, \ldots, v_n$. Similarly, node 1 should dispatch its $v_1, \ldots, v_{n/p}$ to other nodes. This task is a gather operation (*MPI_AllGather*, see Table 12.2): data on each node are

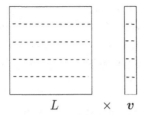

$$L \quad \times \quad v$$

Figure 12.2 Sparse matrix-vector product. We assume $p = 5$ here. L and v are respectively separated to five block partitions.

gathered on all nodes. Note that one often assumes the following cost model for transferring data between two nodes (Barnett et al., 1994):

$$\alpha + \beta \cdot (\text{length of data transferred}),$$

where α, the startup time of a transfer, is a constant independent of the message size. The value β is the transfer time per unit of data. Depending on α, β of the distributed environment and the size of data, one can select a suitable algorithm for implementing the *MPI_AllGather* function. After some experiments, we use the *recursive doubling* algorithm (Thakur, Rabenseinfer, and Gropp, 2005). In the recursive doubling algorithm, nodes that are distance 1, 2, 4, and so on, apart sequentially exchange their data. Thus, the amount of data accumulated at a node doubles at each step. If p is a power-of-2 number, all the nodes can receive all the data in $\log(p)$ steps. The total communication cost to gather v on all nodes is

$$O\left(\alpha \cdot \log(p) + \beta \cdot \frac{p-1}{p}n\right), \tag{12.14}$$

where n is the length of the vector v. For this implementation, the number of machines must be a power of two. On our distributed environment (cheap PCs in a data center), the initial cost α of any point-to-point communication is expensive. Thus, the recursive doubling is very suitable because among various approaches discussed in Thakur et al. (2005) for the gather operation, Equation 12.14 has the smallest coefficient related to α.

12.3.4 Parallel k-Means

Once the eigensolver computes the first k eigenvectors of the Laplacian matrix, the matrix V is distributedly stored. Thus, the normalized matrix U can be computed in parallel and stored on p machines. Each row of the matrix U is regarded as one data point in the k-means algorithm. We implement the k-means algorithm using MPI. Several prior works have studied parallel k-means (e.g., Chu et al., 2007; Dhillon and Modha, 1999; Gürsoy, 2003; Xu and Zhang, 2004).

To start the k-means procedure, the master machine chooses a set of initial cluster centroids and broadcasts them to all machines. In the ideal case, the cluster centroids calculated from the matrix U are orthogonal to each other. Thus, an intuitive initialization of centroids can be done by selecting a subset of U's n rows whose elements are almost orthogonal (Yu and Shi, 2003). To begin, we use the master machine to randomly choose a point as the first cluster centroid. Then it broadcasts the centroid to all machines. Each machine identifies the most orthogonal point to this centroid by finding the minimal cosine similarity (inner product) between its points and the centroid. By collecting the p minimal cosine similarities, we choose the most orthogonal point to the first centroid as the second centroid. This procedure is repeated to obtain k centroids.

Once the initial centroids are broadcasted, each data point on each machine is assigned to the closest cluster and the local sums of clusters are calculated without any inter-machine communication. The master machine then obtains the sum of all data points in each cluster to calculate new centroids and broadcasts them to all machines. Most of the communication occurs here, and this requires a reduction operation in MPI (*MPI_AllReduce*, see Table 12.2). The loss function, Equation 12.10, can also be computed in parallel in a similar way. Therefore, the computation time for parallel k-means is reduced to $1/p$ of that in Equation 12.11. Regarding the communication, as local sums on each machine are k vectors of length k, the communication cost per k-means iteration is on the order of k^2. Note that the *MPI_AllReduce* function used here has a similar cost to the *MPI_AllGather* function discussed previously. We here explain that the communication overhead of the k-means algorithm is less than that in Equation 12.8 for the sparse matrix-vector product of eigendecomposition. For each sparse matrix-vector product, we gather $O(n)$ values. From Table 12.3, there are $(m - k) \times$ (restarted Arnoldi iterations) sparse matrix-vector products. For k-means, in each iteration we transfer $O(k^2)$ values after calculating the distance between n/p points and k cluster centroids. In a typical run, (restarted Arnoldi iterations) is of the same scale as (k-means iterations), so the total number of sparse matrix-vector products is larger than the number of k-means iterations. If $n \geq k^2$, then the communication overhead in eigendecomposition is more serious than in k-means. We will clearly observe this result in Section 12.4.2.

We summarize the computation time complexity of each step of the spectral clustering algorithm before and after parallelization in Table 12.3.

Table 12.3. *Time complexity of each step of the spectral clustering algorithm before and after parallelization. Communication time is excluded.*

	Before parallelization
Getting a sparse similarity matrix	$O(n^2d + n^2 \log t)$
Finding the first k eigenvectors	$(O(m^3) + (O(nm) + O(nt)) \times (m - k))$ $\times$(restarted Arnoldi iterations)
Performing k-means	$O(nk^2) \times$ (k-means iterations)

	After parallelization
Getting a sparse similarity matrix	$O(\frac{n^2d}{p} + \frac{n^2 \log t}{p})$
Finding the first k eigenvectors	$(O(m^3) + (O(\frac{nm}{p}) + O(\frac{nt}{p})) \times (m - k))$ $\times$(restarted Arnoldi iterations)
Performing k-means	$O(\frac{nk^2}{p}) \times$ (k-means iterations)

12.4 Experiments

We designed experiments to evaluate spectral clustering algorithms and investigate the performance of our parallel implementation. Our experiments used three datasets: (1) 20 Newsgroups, a collection of 19,928 newsgroup documents; (2) RCV1 (Reuters Corpus Volume I), a filtered collection of 534,135 documents; and (3) 2,121,863 photos collected from PicasaWeb.

20 Newsgroups: This is a collection of 19,974 non-empty newsgroup documents (Lang, 1995). We consider the dataset processed and partitioned (nearly) evenly across 20 categories by Rennie (2001).[3] We then obtained 19,928 documents in 20 categories. The vocabulary size is 62,061. Each document is represented by a cosine normalization of a log-transformed TF-IDF feature vector. We grouped the data into 20 clusters and set the Arnoldi length m to 40 (we often set $m = 2k$ for the Arnoldi length).

RCV1: This is an archive of 804,414 labeled newswire stories from Reuters Ltd (Lewis et al., 2004). The news documents are categorized into hierarchies with respect to three controlled vocabularies: *industries*, *topics*, and *regions*. Data instances were split into 23,149 training documents and 781,256 test documents. We used the relabeled categorization (Bekkerman and Scholz, 2008). It maps the entire dataset to the second level of RCV1 *topic* hierarchy. Documents that have only third- or fourth-level labels are mapped to the parent category of their second-level label. Documents that have only first-level labels are not mapped to any category. In this clustering experiment, documents with multiple labels were not used. We then obtained 534,135 documents in 53 categories. Each document is represented by a cosine normalization of a log transformed TF-IDF feature vector. The Arnoldi length m is set to be 106.

PicasaWeb: Picasa is an online platform for users to upload, share, and manage images. The PicasaWeb dataset we collected consists of 2,121,863 images. For each image, we extracted 144 features including color, texture, and shape as the image's representation (Li, Chang, and Wu, 2003). We performed feature scaling so features were on the same scale. We grouped the data into 1,000 clusters and set the Arnoldi length m to 2,000.

12.4.1 Clustering Quality of Using a Sparse Similarity Matrix

To justify our decision to use a sparse similarity matrix, we compare the results with those obtained by using a full similarity matrix. The 20 Newsgroups dataset is considered because the full similarity matrix can be stored in the memory of one computer. As a side comparison, we also report the performance of traditional k-means. We used *document categories* in the 20 Newsgroups dataset as the ground truth for evaluating cluster quality. We measured the quality via the Normalized Mutual

---

[3] Data available at www.csie.ntu.edu.tw/~cjlin/libsvmtools/datasets.

Information (NMI) between the produced clusters and the ground-truth categories. The NMI between two random variables CAT (category label) and CLS (cluster label) is defined as

$$\text{NMI}(\text{CAT}; \text{CLS}) = \frac{\text{I}(\text{CAT}; \text{CLS})}{\sqrt{\text{H}(\text{CAT})\text{H}(\text{CLS})}}, \tag{12.15}$$

where I(CAT; CLS) is the mutual information between CAT and CLS. The entropies H(CAT) and H(CLS) are used for normalizing the mutual information to be in the range of [0, 1]. More formally, we made use of the following formulation to estimate the NMI score (Strehl and Ghosh, 2002):

$$\text{NMI} = \frac{\sum_{i=1}^{k} \sum_{j=1}^{k} n_{i,j} \log\left(\frac{n \cdot n_{i,j}}{n_i \cdot n_j}\right)}{\sqrt{\left(\sum_i n_i \log \frac{n_i}{n}\right)\left(\sum_j n_j \log \frac{n_j}{n}\right)}}, \tag{12.16}$$

where n is the number of documents, n_i and n_j denote the number of documents in category i and cluster j, respectively, and $n_{i,j}$ denotes the number of documents in category i as well as in cluster j. The NMI score is 1 if the clustering results perfectly match the category labels, and the score is close to 0 if data are randomly partitioned (Zhong and Ghosh, 2003). The higher the NMI score, the better the clustering quality.

We compared three different clustering algorithms, including

- k-means algorithm based on Euclidean distance (k-means)
- spectral clustering using a full similarity matrix (SC-full)
- spectral clustering using a t-nearest-neighbor sparse similarity matrix (SC-sparse)

We checked the performance of SC-sparse by searching a set of numbers of nearest neighbors ($t = 20, 50, 100, \dots, 17500$).

Table 12.4 presents the comparison results. Each result is an average over 10 runs. The results show that spectral clustering algorithm using a sparse similarity matrix (SC-sparse) outperforms k-means and SC-full. However, selecting the number of nearest neighbors for SC-sparse may be hard because the true cluster assignment is not known in practice. Therefore, we change the number of nearest neighbors for SC-sparse and examine the performance. Figure 12.3 shows the NMI score for SC-sparse. SC-sparse performs the best when using 100 nearest neighbors. However, the clustering quality deteriorates when using more than 2,000 nearest neighbors. Nevertheless, because a small t is chosen in practice, in general SC-sparse is competitive. The poor result of $t = 17,500$ is surprising because it should be close to that of using the full similarity matrix (i.e., $t = 19,928$). We investigated this issue further by examining their similarity matrices and eigenvalues. Section 12.1 indicated that spectral clustering requires a positive semi-definite (PSD) L, which is guaranteed if $S_{ij} \geq 0$. Although S does not

Table 12.4. *20 Newsgroups. NMI comparisons for k-means, spectral clustering using a full similarity matrix (SC-full), and spectral clustering using a spare similarity matrix (SC-sparse). The SC-sparse result is obtained by using 100 nearest neighbors.*

Algorithms	k-means	SC-full	SC-sparse
NMI	0.4369(±0.0110)	0.4826(±0.0029)	0.5210(±0.0036)

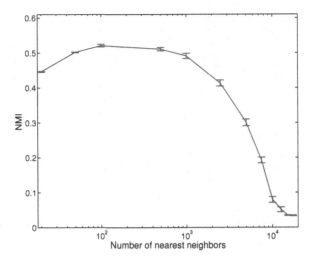

Figure 12.3 A clustering quality comparison of SC-sparse using the 20 Newsgroups data. We use $t = 20, 50, 100, 500, 1000, 2500, 5000, 7500, 10000, 12500, 15000$, and 17500 as the number of nearest neighbors.

need to be PSD, we found that this property might be important for this data. It is known that S by Equation 12.1 is PSD, but after some elements being removed, S might not be PSD any more (Micchelli, 1986). We found that the S's eigenvalues of using $t = 17,500$ and $t = 19,928$ (i.e., full S) are very different.

12.4.2 Speedup and Scalability in Distributed Environments

We used the two large datasets (RCV1 and a PicasaWeb) to conduct speedup and scalability experiments. We ran experiments on up to 256 machines at a data center. Although not all machines are identical, each machine is configured with a CPU faster than 2GHz and memory larger than 4GB. Our experiments begin with detailed runtime and speedup analysis by varying the number of machines. We discuss individual steps of Algorithm 39 as well as the whole procedure. Next, we fix the number of machines and report the speedup results by varying the problem size. Finally, the scalability of our implementation is investigated.

Getting a Sparse Similarity Matrix: Tables 12.5 and 12.6 report the runtime and speedup for getting a sparse similarity matrix on RCV1 and PicasaWeb datasets, respectively. For the PicasaWeb dataset, storing the similarity matrix and the matrix $\bar{V} \in R^{n \times m}$ with $m = 2,000$ requires more than 32GB of memory.[4] This memory configuration is not available on off-the-shelf machines. We had to use at least 16 machines to perform spectral clustering. Therefore, we used 16 machines as the baseline and assumed a speedup of 16. We separate the running time into three parts according to the discussion in Section 12.3.2: computing distances and finding nearest neighbors, modifying the distance matrix to be symmetric, and computing similarities. Because the similarity matrix calculation involves little communication between nodes, the

---

[4] If we assume the double precision storage, we need $2 \times 10^6 \times 2000 \times 8 = 32$ GB.

Table 12.5. *RCV1 dataset. Runtime and speedup for getting the sparse similarity matrix on different number of machines.* $n = 534,135, k = 53, m = 106, t = 100.$

Machines	CompDistance	Symmetric	CompSimilarity	Total	Speedup
1	494312s	837s	335s	495484s	1.00
2	242324s	452s	142s	242918s	2.04
4	117907s	273s	83s	118263s	4.19
8	59602s	238s	65s	59905s	8.27
16	29923s	115s	35s	30073s	16.48
32	15725s	122s	31s	15878s	31.21
64	7840s	82s	30s	7952s	62.31
128	4001s	89s	31s	4121s	120.23

speedup is almost linear if machines have similar configurations and loads (when we ran experiments). To obtain the sparse similarity matrix with $t = 100$, the RCV1 dataset takes 1.1 hours using 128 machines and the PicasaWeb dataset takes 15.2 hours using 256 machines.

Finding the First k Eigenvectors and Performing k-means: Here k-means refers to Step 6 in Algorithm 39. In Tables 12.7 and 12.8, we report the runtime and speedup on the RCV1 dataset for finding the first k eigenvectors and performing k-means, respectively. We separate running time for finding the first k eigenvectors into two parts: all dense operations and sparse matrix-vector products. Each part is further separated into computation, communication (message passing between nodes), and synchronization time (waiting for the slowest machine). As shown in Table 12.7, these two types of operations have different runtime behaviors. Tables 12.7 and 12.8 indicate that neither finding the first k eigenvectors nor performing k-means can achieve linear speedup when the number of machines is beyond a threshold. This result is expected because of communication and synchronization overheads. Note that other jobs may be run simultaneously with ours on each machine, though we chose a data center with a light load.

As shown in Table 12.7 for the RCV1 dataset, when the number of machines increases, the computation time decreases almost linearly. However, the communication cost of conducting sparse matrix-vector products becomes the bottleneck in finding the first k eigenvectors because a vector $v \in R^n$ is gathered to all nodes. For dense matrix-vector products, the communication cost is less for vectors of size m, but it also takes up a considerable ratio of the total time. For the total time, we can see that when 64 machines were used, the parallel eigensolver achieved 9.54 times speedup. When

Table 12.6. *PicasaWeb dataset. Runtime and speedup for getting the sparse similarity matrix on different number of machines.* $n = 2,121,863, k = 1,000, m = 2,000, t = 100.$

Machines	CompDistance	Symmetric	CompSimilarity	Total	Speedup
16	751912s	348s	282s	752542s	16.00
32	376591s	205s	205s	377001s	31.94
64	191691s	128s	210s	192029s	62.70
128	100918s	131s	211s	101260s	118.91
256	54480s	45s	201s	54726s	220.02

Table 12.7. *RCV1 dataset. Runtime and speedup for finding the first k eigenvectors on different numbers of machines. n = 534,135, k = 53, m = 106, t = 100.*

Machines	Dense Matrix Operations within ARPACK			Sparse Matrix Vector Product			Total	Speedup
	Comp	Comm	Sync	Comp	Comm	Sync		
1	3012s	0s	0s	4066s	0s	0s	7078s	1.00
2	1430s	3s	19s	1981s	134s	49s	3616s	1.96
4	605s	9s	40s	889s	213s	35s	1791s	3.95
8	258s	20s	44s	493s	280s	40s	1135s	6.24
16	123s	44s	43s	271s	384s	53s	918s	7.71
32	63s	52s	40s	145s	411s	58s	769s	9.20
64	30s	85s	51s	73s	458s	45s	742s	9.54
128	14s	133s	66s	41s	604s	51s	909s	7.79

more machines were used, the speedup decreased. Regarding the computation time for performing k-means, as shown in Table 12.8, it is less than finding eigenvectors. When using more nodes, the communication time for performing k-means did not increase as much as it did for finding eigenvectors. This observation is consistent with the explanation in Section 12.3.4.

Next, we looked into the speedup on the PicasaWeb dataset. Tables 12.9 and 12.10 report the runtime and speedup for finding the first k eigenvectors and performing k-means, respectively. Compared to the results with the RCV1 dataset, here computation time takes a much larger ratio of the total time in obtaining eigenvectors. As a result, we could achieve nearly linear speedups for 32 machines. Even when using 256 machines, a speedup of 69.14 is obtained. As in Table 12.7, the communication cost for sparse matrix-vector products dominates the total time when p is large. This is due to the large $\alpha \log p$ term explained in Equation 12.14. If one has a dedicated cluster with a better connection between nodes, then α is smaller and a higher speedup can be achieved. For k-means, we achieve an excellent speedup. It is nearly linear up to $p = 64$.

End-to-End Runtime and Speedup: Tables 12.11 and 12.12 show the end-to-end runtime and speedup on RCV1 and PicasaWeb datasets, respectively. We achieve near-linear speedup when using 32 machines on RCV1 and 128 machines on PicasaWeb.

Table 12.8. *RCV1 dataset. Runtime and speedup for performing k-means on different number of machines. n = 534,135, k = 53, m = 106, t = 100.*

Machines	Comp	Comm	Sync	Total	Speedup
1	70.53s	0.00s	0.00s	70.53s	1.00
2	35.41s	0.12s	0.56s	36.09s	1.95
4	17.11s	0.27s	1.79s	19.17s	3.68
8	8.49s	0.52s	1.70s	10.71s	6.59
16	4.28s	0.92s	1.02s	6.22s	11.34
32	2.15s	1.41s	1.23s	4.79s	14.72
64	1.08s	2.02s	1.42s	4.52s	15.60
128	0.57s	2.38s	1.44s	4.39s	16.07

Table 12.9. *PicasaWeb dataset. Runtime and speedup for finding the first k eigenvectors on different numbers of machines. $n = 2,121,863$, $k = 1,000$, $m = 2,000$, $t = 100$.*

Machines	Dense Matrix Operations within ARPACK			Sparse Matrix Vector Product			Total	Speedup
	Comp	Comm	Sync	Comp	Comm	Sync		
16	18196s	118s	430s	3351s	2287s	667s	25049s	16.00
32	7757s	153s	345s	1643s	2389s	485s	12772s	31.38
64	4067s	227s	495s	913s	2645s	404s	8751s	45.80
128	1985s	347s	423s	496s	2962s	428s	6641s	60.35
256	977s	407s	372s	298s	3381s	362s	5797s	69.14

Table 12.10. *PicasaWeb dataset. Runtime and speedup for performing k-means on different number of machines. $n = 2,121,863$, $k = 1,000$, $m = 2,000$, $t = 100$.*

Machines	Comp	Comm	Sync	Total	Speedup
16	18053s	29s	142s	18223s	16.00
32	9038s	36s	263s	9337s	31.23
64	4372s	46s	174s	4591s	63.51
128	2757s	79s	108s	2944s	99.04
256	1421s	91s	228s	1740s	167.57

Table 12.11. *RCV1 dataset. End-to-end runtime and speedup for parallel spectral clustering on different number of machines. $n = 534,135$, $k = 53$, $m = 106$, $t = 100$.*

Machines	SimilarityMatrix	Eigendecomp	k-Means	Total	Speedup
1	495484s	7078s	70.53s	502632.53s	1.00
2	242918s	3616s	36.09s	246570.09s	2.04
4	118263s	1791s	19.17s	120073.17s	4.19
8	59905s	1135s	10.71s	61050.71s	8.23
16	30073s	918s	6.22s	30997.22s	16.22
32	15878s	769s	4.79s	16651.79s	30.18
64	7952s	742s	4.52s	8698.52s	57.78
128	4121s	909s	4.39s	5034.39s	99.84

Table 12.12. *PicasaWeb dataset. End-to-end runtime and speedup for parallel spectral clustering on different number of machines. $n = 2,121,863$, $k = 1,000$, $m = 2,000$, $t = 100$.*

Machines	SimilarityMatrix	Eigendecomp	k-Means	Total	Speedup
16	752542s	25049s	18223s	795814s	16.00
32	377001s	12772s	9337s	399110s	31.90
64	192029s	8751s	4591s	205371s	62.00
128	101260s	6641s	2944s	110845s	114.87
256	54726s	5797s	1740s	62263s	204.50

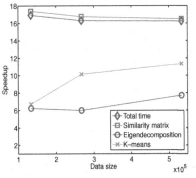
(a) RCV1: speedup versus data sizes.

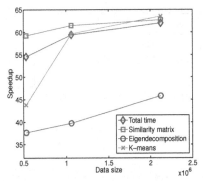
(b) PicasaWeb: speedup versus data sizes.

Figure 12.4 Speedup versus data sizes. For RCV1, we use 16 machines and three different data sizes: 133,534; 267,068; and 534,135. For PicasaWeb, we use 64 machines and three different data sizes: 530,474; 1,060,938; and 2,121,863.

Speedup versus Data Sizes: Figure 12.4a shows the speedup for varying data sizes on the RCV1 dataset using 16 machines. We use three different data sizes: 133,534; 267,068; and 534,135. We observe that the larger the dataset, the more speedup we can gain for finding the first k eigenvectors and performing k-means. Because several computationally intensive steps grow faster than the communication cost, the larger the dataset, the greater the opportunity for parallelization to gain speedup. In addition, the speedup for the eigendecomposition step is lower than for other steps. This is because, when compared to other steps, the communication cost of eigendecomposition step takes a higher ratio of the runtime. Figure 12.4b shows the speedup for varying data sizes on the PicasaWeb dataset using 64 machines. We use three different data sizes: 530,474; 1,060,938; and 2,121,863. Results are similar to those for the RCV1 dataset. However, in Figure 12.4b the line of speedup for the "total time" is not as close to the line of speedup for the "similarity matrix" as in Figure 12.4a. This is because eigendecomposition and k-means steps take a relatively larger portion of the total time on the PicasaWeb data.

Scalability: Because of the communication overhead, we have observed that with a given data size, speedup goes down as the number of machines increases. In the parallel computation community, researchers thus define the scalability by taking the problem size into consideration. As defined in recent publications (Grama et al., 2003; Llorente et al., 1996), a parallel system is scalable if the speedup can be kept constant as the number of machines and the data sizes are both increased. Figure 12.5a presents the scalability of the RCV1 dataset. The y-axis presents the speedup, and in the x-axis, we check three different pairs of number of machines and data size: (16, 133534), (32, 267068), and (64, 534135). Except for eigendecomposition, the speedup for the whole procedure as well as for each step is almost doubled when doubling both number of machines and data size. That is, the curve has a constant slope of 2. Figure 12.5b presents the scalability on the PicasaWeb dataset. We use three different pairs of number of machines and data size: (64, 530474), (128, 1060938), and (256, 2121863). Similarly, the speedup is doubled except for eigendcomposition. Overall, our parallel

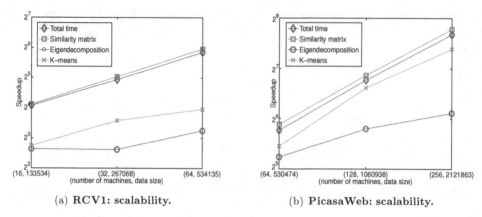

(a) RCV1: scalability.   (b) PicasaWeb: scalability.

Figure 12.5 Scalability: speedup versus number of machines and data sizes. For RCV1, we use (16, 133534), (32, 267068), and (64, 534135) as pairs of number of machines and data size. For PicasaWeb, we use (64, 530474), (128, 1060938), and (256, 2121863) as pairs of number of machines and data size.

implementation scales reasonably well as the number of machines and the data size both increase.

Benchmarking Parallel Programs in a Data Center Environment: To evaluate a parallel program, we often prefer a dedicated data center for accurate timing. However, few data centers are constructed for such a purpose. Though we ran jobs in a lightly loaded center, we find that the variance of running time can sometimes be high. We share our experiences and observations here. First, among the three major steps of PSC (see Table 12.3), k-means has the smallest variance of running time, whereas calculating the similarity matrix has the largest. This result indicates that a job with longer running time may be more affected by other jobs that compete for resources. Second, the running time of a MapReduce program fluctuates more than that of an MPI program. Take the RCV1 data as an example: one run to get the similarity matrix may need 50% more time than another. To obtain Tables 12.5 and 12.6, we averaged the numbers of three runs with the smallest running time. It is not yet clear to us why MapReduce and MPI behave differently on the stability of running time. This issue needs further investigation.

12.5 Conclusions

In this chapter, we have investigated an approximation approach for large-scale spectral clustering by t-nearest-neighbor sparsification. We propose a parallel implementation and evaluate its scalability. A slightly modified version of our code is available at http://code.google.com/p/pspectralclustering/, in which the construction of the similarity matrix is implemented based on MPI instead of MapReduce. We plan to study the following research issues.

Very Large Number of Clusters: A large k implies a large m in the process of Arnoldi factorization. Then $O(m^3)$ for finding the eigenvalues of the dense matrix H becomes the dominant term in Equation 12.9. How to handle the case of large k and parallelize the $O(m^3)$ operation are thus interesting issues.

Reducing the Cost for Obtaining the Sparse Similarity Matrix: The expensive $O(n^2 d)$ cost shown in Equation 12.6 may be reduced by KD-trees (Bentley, 1975), LSH (Gionis, Indyk, and Motwani, 1999), Spill-tree (Liu et al., 2004), or others. These methods may be effective only under certain circumstances or only for approximations in getting t nearest neighbors. Because they are more complicated than a precise method of getting t nearest neighbors, the parallelization may be difficult and deserves further investigation.

Reducing the Communication Cost of Sparse Matrix-Vector Products: Taking the sparsity of L into consideration may further reduce the communication cost of sparse matrix-vector products Lv. The reduction depends on the sparsity and the structure of the matrix.

Parallelization of other Approximation Methods for Spectral Clustering: Besides methods mentioned in Section 12.2, recently some new and effective approximation methods have been proposed (e.g., Yan, Huang, and Jordan, 2009). Their parallelization, though beyond the scope of this chapter, is worth future investigation.

In summary, this chapter gives a general and systematic study of parallel spectral clustering methods and techniques and demonstrates that despite communication and synchronization overheads, it is possible to build a system to effectively cluster large-scale data in a distributed environment.

References

Achlioptas, D., McSherry, F., and Schölkopf, B. 2002. Sampling Techniques for Kernel Methods. Pages 335–342 of: *Proceedings of NIPS*.

Barnett, M., Gupta, S., Payne, D. G., Shuler, L., Geijn, R., and Watts, J. 1994. Interprocessor Collective Communication Library (InterCom). Pages 357–364 of: *Proceedings of the Scalable High Performance Computing Conference*.

Bekkerman, R., and Scholz, M. 2008. Data Weaving: Scaling Up the State-of-the-Art in Data Clustering. Pages 1083–1092 of: *Proceedings of CIKM*.

Bentley, J. L. 1975. Multidimensional Binary Search Trees Used for Associative Searching. *Communications of the ACM*, **18**(9), 509–517.

Chang, F., Dean, J., Ghemawat, S., Hsieh, W. C., Wallach, D. A., Burrows, M., Chandra, T., Fikes, A., and Gruber, R. E. 2006. Bigtable: A Distributed Storage System for Structured Data. Pages 205–218 of: *Proceedings of OSDI*.

Chen, W.-Y., Song, Y., Bai, H., Lin, C.-J., and Chang, E. Y. 2011. Parallel Spectral Clustering in Distributed Systems. *IEEE Transactions on Pattern Analysis and Machine Intelligence*, **33**(3), 568–586.

Chu, C.-T., Kim, S. K., Lin, Y.-A., Yu, Y., Bradski, G., Ng, A. Y., and Olukotun, K. 2007. Map-Reduce for Machine Learning on Multicore. Pages 281–288 of: *Proceedings of NIPS*.

Chung, F. 1997. *Spectral Graph Theory*. Number 92 in CBMS Regional Conference Series in Mathematics. American Mathematical Society.

Dean, J., and Ghemawat, S. 2008. MapReduce: Simplified Data Processing on Large Clusters. *Communications of the ACM*, **51**(1), 107–113.

Dhillon, I. S. 2001. Co-clustering Documents and Words Using Bipartite Spectral Graph Partitioning. Pages 269–274 of: *Proceedings of SIGKDD*.

Dhillon, I. S., and Modha, D. S. 1999. A Data-Clustering Algorithm on Distributed Memory Multi-processors. Pages 245–260 of: *Large-Scale Parallel Data Mining*.

Fowlkes, C., Belongie, S., Chung, F., and Malik, J. 2004. Spectral Grouping Using the Nyström Method. *IEEE Transactions on Pattern Analysis and Machine Intelligence*, **26**(2), 214–225.

Ghemawat, S., Gobioff, H., and Leung, S.-T. 2003. The Google File System. Pages 29–43 of: *Proceedings of SOSP*. New York: ACM.

Gionis, A., Indyk, P., and Motwani, R. 1999. Similarity Search in High Dimensions via Hashing. Pages 518–529 of: *Proceedings of VLDB*.

Grama, A., Karypis, G., Kumar, V., and Gupta, A. 2003. *Introduction to Parallel Computing*, 2nd ed. Reading, MA: Addison-Wesley.

Gropp, W., Lusk, E., and Skjellum, A. 1999. *Using MPI-2: Advanced Features of the Message-Passing Interface*. Cambridge, MA: MIT Press.

Gürsoy, A. 2003. Data Decomposition for Parallel *k*-Means Clustering. Pages 241–248 of: *PPAM*.

Hernandez, V., Roman, J. E., Tomas, A., and Vidal, V. 2005a. *A Survey of Software for Sparse Eigenvalue Problems*. Technical Report. Universidad Politecnica de Valencia.

Hernandez, V., Roman, J. E., and Vidal, V. 2005b. SLEPc: A Scalable and Flexible Toolkit for the Solution of Eigenvalue Problems. *ACM Transactions on Mathematical Software*, **31**, 351–362.

Lang, Ken. 1995. NewsWeeder: Learning to Filter Netnews. Pages 331–339 of: *Proceedings of ICML*.

Lehoucg, R. B., Sorensen, D. C., and Yang, C. 1998. *ARPACK User's Guide*. SIAM.

Lewis, D. D., Yang, Y., Rose, T. G., and Li, F. 2004. RCV1: A New Benchmark Collection for Text Categorization Research. *Journal of Machine Learning Research*, **5**, 361–397.

Li, B., Chang, E. Y., and Wu, Y.-L. 2003. Discovery of a Perceptual Distance Function for Measuring Image Similarity. *Multimedia Systems*, **8**(6), 512–522.

Liu, R., and Zhang, H. 2004. Segmentation of 3D meshes through spectral clustering. In: *Proceedings of Pacific Graphics*.

Liu, T., Moore, A., Gray, A., and Yang, K. 2004. An Investigation of Practical Approximate Nearest Neighbor Algorithms. In: *Proceedings of NIPS*.

Llorente, I. M., Tirado, F., and Vázquez, L. 1996. Some Aspects about the Scalability of Scientific Applications on Parallel Architectures. *Parallel Computing*, **22**(9), 1169–1195.

Luxburg, U. 2007. A Tutorial on Spectral Clustering. *Statistics and Computing*, **17**(4), 395–416.

Marques, O. A. 1995. *BLZPACK: Description and User's Guide*. Technical Report TR/PA/95/30. CERFACS, Toulouse, France.

Maschhoff, K., and Sorensen, D. 1996. A Portable Implementation of ARPACK for Distributed Memory Parallel Architectures. In: *Proceedings of CMCIM*.

Meila, M., and Shi, J. 2000. Learning Segmentation by Random Walks. Pages 873–879 of: *Proceedings of NIPS*.

Micchelli, Charles A. 1986. Interpolation of Scattered Data: Distance Matrices and Conditionally Positive Definite Functions. *Constructive Approximation*, **2**, 11–22.

Ng, A. Y., Jordan, M. I., and Weiss, Y. 2001. On Spectral Clustering: Analysis and an Algorithm. Pages 849–856 of: *Proceedings of NIPS*.

Rennie, J. D. M. 2001. *Improving Multi-class Text Classification with Naive Bayes*. M.Phil. thesis, Massachusetts Institute of Technology.

Shi, J., and Malik, J. 2000. Normalized Cuts and Image Segmentation. *IEEE Transactions on Pattern Analysis and Machine Intelligence*, **22**(8), 888–905.

Snir, M., and Otto, S. 1998. *MPI – The Complete Reference: The MPI Core*. Cambridge, MA: MIT Press.

Strehl, A., and Ghosh, J. 2002. Cluster Ensembles – A Knowledge Reuse Framework for Combining Multiple Partitions. *Journal of Machine Learning Research*, **3**, 583–617.

Thakur, R., Rabenseinfer, R., and Gropp, W. 2005. Optimization of Collective Communication Operations in MPICH. *International Journal of High Performance Computing Applications*, **19**(1), 49–66.

Wu, K., and Simon, H. 1999. *TRLAN User Guide*. Technical report. LBNL-41284. Lawrence Berkeley National Laboratory.

Xu, S. T., and Zhang, J. 2004. A Hybrid Parallel Web Document Clustering Algorithm and Its Performance Study. *Journal of Supercomputing*, **30**(2), 117–131.

Xu, W., Liu, X., and Gong, Y. 2003. Document Clustering Based on Non-negative Matrix Factorization. Pages 267–273 of: *Proceedings of SIGIR*.

Yan, D., Huang, L., and Jordan, M. I. 2009. Fast Approximate Spectral Clustering. Pages 907–916 of: *Proceedings of the 15th ACM SIGKDD International Conference on Knowledge Discovery and Data Mining*.

Yu, S. X., and Shi, J. 2003. Multiclass Spectral Clustering. Page 313 of: *Proceedings of ICCV*.

Zelnik-Manor, L., and Perona, P. 2005. Self-Tuning Spectral Clustering. Pages 1601–1608 of: *Proceedings of NIPS*.

Zhong, S., and Ghosh, J. 2003. A Unified Framework for Model-Based Clustering. *Journal of Machine Learning Research*, **4**, 1001–1037.

CHAPTER 13

Parallelizing Information-Theoretic Clustering Methods

Ron Bekkerman and Martin Scholz

Facing a problem of clustering a multimillion-data-point collection, a machine learning practitioner may choose to apply the simplest clustering method possible, because it is hard to believe that fancier methods can be applicable to datasets of such scale. Whoever is about to adopt this approach should first weigh the following considerations:

- **Simple clustering methods are rarely effective.** Indeed, four decades of research would not have been spent on data clustering if a simple method could solve the problem. Moreover, even the simplest methods may run for long hours on a modern PC, given a large-scale dataset. For example, consider a simple online clustering algorithm (which, we believe, is machine learning folklore): first initialize k clusters with one data point per cluster, then iteratively assign the rest of data points into their closest clusters (in the Euclidean space). If k is small enough, we *can* run this algorithm on one machine, because it is unnecessary to keep the entire data in RAM. However, besides being slow, it will produce low-quality results, especially when the data is highly multi-dimensional.
- **State-of-the-art clustering methods *can* scale well**, which we aim to justify in this chapter.

With the deployment of large computational facilities (such as Amazon.com's EC2, IBM's BlueGene, and HP's XC), the *Parallel Computing* paradigm is probably the only currently available option for tackling gigantic data processing tasks. Parallel methods are becoming an integral part of any data processing system, and thus getting special attention (e.g., universities introduce parallel methods to their core curricula; see Johnson et al., 2008).

Although parallel data clustering methods have been developed for more than 25 years (see, e.g., Tilton and Strong, 1984), most efforts have focused on parallelizing k-means-like methods (see Section 13.2 for a short survey). Despite its popularity, the k-means algorithm (in its traditional formulation, i.e., minimization of mean squared error in the Euclidean space) shows rather poor results on real-world datasets (see Section 13.5). In the text domain, for example, traditional k-means usually produces a highly unbalanced clustering (i.e., one huge cluster and a few tiny ones).[1] In this chapter, we go beyond parallelizing k-means. We focus on two families of data clustering methods:

- **Multi-modal (or multivariate) clustering** is a framework for simultaneously clustering a few interacting types (or *modalities*) of the data. Example: construct a clustering of web pages, while constructing a clustering of words from those pages, as well as a clustering of URLs hyperlinked from those pages. It is commonly believed that multi-modal clustering is able to achieve better performance than traditional, unimodal methods. The two-modal case (often called *co-clustering*, *bi-clustering*, or *double clustering*) has been widely explored in the literature (see, e.g., El-Yaniv and Souroujon, 2001; Dhillon, Mallela, and Modha, 2003), whereas a more general m-modal case has recently attracted close attention of the research community (Gao et al., 2005; Bekkerman, El-Yaniv, and McCallum, 2005, and others).
- **Information-theoretic clustering (ITC)** (see, e.g., Slonim, Friedman, and Tishby, 2002) is an adequate solution to the problem of clustering highly multi-dimensional data, such as documents or genes. ITC methods optimize an information-theoretic objective function. One of the strict advantages of ITC methods is that they are not limited to take a *data affinity matrix* as their input. Affinity matrices are quadratic in the number of data instances (and therefore prohibitively large for the tasks we are concerned with). ITC methods operate in a sub-quadratic space, which makes them attractive for large-scale tasks. For the definition and discussion of ITC, see Section 13.1.

We distinguish between *stepwise* and *sequential* clustering methods. Stepwise methods, such as k-means, first accumulate all data points that are candidates for reassignment from clusters to clusters, and then actually reassign all the candidates at once. In contrast, sequential methods reassign a data point as soon as a better assignment has been found for it. Stepwise methods suffer from a tribe effect: a group of data points can be candidates for moving into a cluster $\tilde{x}$ because they are similar to a group of $\tilde{x}$'s members that are candidates for moving out of $\tilde{x}$. Once the reassignment is done, the two similar groups are still not in the same cluster. This would not happen in sequential clustering, where data points are reassigned one after another. Although stepwise methods are intuitively less accurate than sequential methods, they are often easier to parallelize.

One of the most popular ITC methods, *information-theoretic co-clustering (IT-CC)* proposed by Dhillon et al. (2003), belongs to the family of stepwise clustering methods. In Section 13.2.1, we show a fairly straightforward method for its parallelization. The IT-CC algorithm turns out to be conservative in optimizing the clustering objective, that is, it often gets stuck in local optima. In Section 13.3, we discuss the *sequential*

---

[1] The traditional k-means assigns instances to clusters based on the Euclidean distances between data points and centroids. Because text is usually sparse and high-dimensional, documents typically have only few terms in common. As a consequence, the l^2 norms of terms and centroids often dominate in the calculation of their Euclidean distances. Because the l^2 norms of centroids naturally decrease with increasing the cluster size, instances tend to be reassigned to clusters that are already large, and smaller clusters disappear over time.

co-clustering (SCC) method and show analytically that it is more aggressive in optimizing the objective.

In Section 13.4, we present a scheme for parallelizing sequential clustering methods, called *data weaving* (Bekkerman and Scholz, 2008). It works like a loom: it propagates data clusters through a rack of processors, at each of which two clusters meet and make a "knot". This way, $\frac{k}{2}$ cluster knots are made in parallel (where k is the number of clusters). At the next step, $\frac{k}{2}$ other cluster knots are made, and so on. We apply this mechanism to parallelizing the SCC method, which leads to constructing a highly scalable, information-theoretic, multi-modal clustering algorithm, called *DataLoom*.

In the experimentation part of this chapter (Section 13.5) we first compare DataLoom with its original, non-parallel version (SCC), as well as with IT-CC and two more baseline methods on four small datasets (including the benchmark 20 Newsgroups). We show that the use of parallelization does not compromise the clustering quality. Finally, we apply DataLoom to two large datasets: RCV1 (Lewis et al., 2004), where we cluster documents and words, and Netflix KDD'07 Cup data,[2] where we cluster customers and movies. If represented as contingency tables, both datasets contain billions of entries. On both of them, DataLoom significantly outperforms parallelized IT-CC.

13.1 Information-Theoretic Clustering

Over the past decade, information-theoretic clustering methods have proven themselves to be the state-of-the-art in clustering highly multi-dimensional data. In this chapter, we focus on *hard* clustering (a many-to-one mapping of data points to cluster identities), as opposed to *soft* clustering (a many-to-many mapping, where each data point is assigned a probability distribution over cluster identities). Hard clustering can be viewed as a lossy compression scheme – this observation opens a path to applying various information-theoretic methods to clustering. Examples include the application of the minimum description length principle (Böhm et al., 2006), compression distances (Cilibrasi and Vitányi, 2005), and rate-distortion theory (Tishby, Pereira, and Bialek, 1999; Crammer, Talukdar, and Pereira, 2008).

The pioneering work on information-theoretic clustering was done by Tishby et al. (1999), who proposed the powerful *Information Bottleneck (IB)* principle, which then led to dozens of extensions. In Information Bottleneck, the data is modeled as a random variable X, which is clustered with respect to an interacting variable Y: the clustering $\tilde{X}$ is represented as a low-bandwidth channel (a *bottleneck*) $X \leftrightarrow \tilde{X} \leftrightarrow Y$ between the input signal X and the output signal Y. This channel is constructed to minimize communication error while maximizing compression:

$$\max_{\tilde{X}} \left[I(\tilde{X}; Y) - \beta I(\tilde{X}; X) \right], \tag{13.1}$$

---

[2] http://cs.uic.edu/~liub/Netflix-KDD-Cup-2007.html.

where I is *Mutual Information (MI)*,[3] and β is a Lagrange multiplier. A variety of optimization procedures have been derived for the Information Bottleneck principle, including agglomerative (Slonim and Tishby, 2000), divisive (Bekkerman et al., 2001), and sequential (Slonim et al., 2002).

To illustrate the intuition behind Information Bottleneck, let us consider the following example. We are given a set of documents $\mathcal{X}$, over which a multinomial (empirical) random variable X is defined. We define a multinomial Y over the set of words that occur in those documents. The clustering objective is to construct a random variable $\tilde{X}$ (defined over disjoint subsets of $\mathcal{X}$, such that $p(\tilde{x}) = \sum_{x \in \tilde{x}} p(x)$) by maximizing mutual information $I(\tilde{X}; Y)$, while keeping mutual information $I(\tilde{X}; X)$ as low as possible. Maximizing $I(\tilde{X}; Y)$ will guarantee that the constructed clustering $\tilde{X}$ contains topically coherent clusters (as words bear documents' topicality); minimizing $I(\tilde{X}; X)$ leads to maximizing compression (i.e., to constructing a small number of large clusters).[4]

Friedman et al. (2001) generalize the IB principle to the multivariate case. In its simplest form of clustering two variables X and Y, the generalization is relatively straightforward: a channel $X \leftrightarrow \tilde{X} \leftrightarrow \tilde{Y} \leftrightarrow Y$ is constructed to optimize the objective

$$\max_{\tilde{X}, \tilde{Y}} \left[I(\tilde{X}; \tilde{Y}) - \beta_1 I(\tilde{X}; X) - \beta_2 I(\tilde{Y}; Y) \right]. \tag{13.2}$$

Following our previous example, this optimization performs *co-clustering* of documents and their words. When more than two variables are clustered (e.g., documents, words, and authors of the documents), the mutual information $I(\tilde{X}; \tilde{Y})$ is generalized into its multivariate version, called *multi-information*. The complexity of computing multi-information grows exponentially while adding more variables, and is therefore restrictive in practice.

Information-theoretic co-clustering (IT-CC) was proposed by Dhillon et al. (2003) as an alternative to multivariate IB, for the two-variate case when the numbers of clusters $|\tilde{X}|$ and $|\tilde{Y}|$ are fixed. In this case, it is quite natural to drop the compression constraints $I(\tilde{X}; X)$ and $I(\tilde{Y}; Y)$ in Equation 13.2, and directly minimize the *information loss*:

$$\min_{\tilde{X}, \tilde{Y}} \left[I(X; Y) - I(\tilde{X}; \tilde{Y}) \right] = \max_{\tilde{X}, \tilde{Y}} I(\tilde{X}; \tilde{Y}), \tag{13.3}$$

as $I(X; Y)$ is a constant for a given dataset. To optimize this objective, Dhillon et al. proposed an elegant optimization method that resembles the traditional k-means.

---

[3] Mutual Information between two random variables Z_1 and Z_2 is the amount of information each variable provides on the other:

$$I(Z_1; Z_2) = \sum_{z_1, z_2} p(z_1, z_2) \log \frac{p(z_1, z_2)}{p(z_1)p(z_2)}.$$

---

[4] Note that without the compression constraint, this optimization would lead to a trivial solution of one document per cluster.

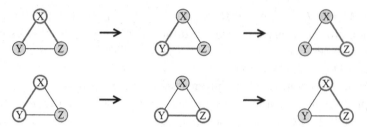

Figure 13.1 Difference between ICM (upper) and CWO (lower) optimization methods (nodes that are being optimized are unshaded bold). ICM iterates over G's nodes (in round-robin) and optimize each of them based on its Markov blanket. CWO iterates over cliques in G (edges, in the simplest case) and locally optimizes the corresponding model while ignoring the rest of the interaction graph.

Bekkerman et al. (2005) generalize IT-CC to the multivariate case, while avoiding the trap of multi-information, which is replaced with a (weighted) sum of pairwise MI terms:

$$\max_{\tilde{X}_1,\ldots,\tilde{X}_m} \left[\sum_{e_{ij}\in E} w_{ij} I(\tilde{X}_i; \tilde{X}_j) \right],$$

where data variables $\mathbf{X} = \{X_1, \ldots, X_m\}$ are organized in an *interaction graph* $G = (\mathbf{X}, \mathbf{E})$,[5] with edges e_{ij} corresponding to pairs of interacting variables (X_i, X_j). Weights w_{ij} are chosen to bring MI terms to the same scale. Bekkerman et al. propose a complex optimization method that utilizes *Iterative Conditional Modes* (ICM; see Besag, 1986) for traversing the graph G, and then performs a hybrid hierarchical/sequential clustering step for each of G's nodes. An illustration of ICM is given in Figure 13.1 (upper).

Bekkerman and Scholz (2008) propose an alternative to the ICM optimization that avoids extra parametrization (through weights w_{ij}): instead of iterating over nodes (as in ICM), one can iterate over edges e_{ij} and maximize only one MI term $I(\tilde{X}_i; \tilde{X}_j)$ at a time (see the lower part of Figure 13.1). This method is called *Clique-Wise Optimization (CWO)* in analogy to *pairwise training* (Sutton and McCallum, 2005), a similar optimization scheme within the supervised learning framework.

13.2 Parallel Clustering

This chapter discusses scaling up information-theoretic clustering algorithms to the very large amounts of data, by parallelizing them over a "shared nothing" cluster of computers connected via a high-bandwidth local area network. Note that the clustering problem can be large-scale along several dimensions: not only can the number of data instances be very large, but data can also be very highly dimensional. For example, 10,000 features is common even for small text corpora, easily reaching millions in larger collections. Whenever the task of clustering data collections requires capturing the underlying structure of a dataset at a fine level, using a very large number of clusters is also common. Our goal is to reduce the total computational costs to a tractable level in order to obtain the best possible clustering results on very large data collections.

---

[5] Lauritzen (1996) defines an interaction graph as a generalization of a graphical model.

One of the early approaches explicitly addressing the clustering scalability problem along those three dimensions is Canopy (McCallum et al., 2000), a non-distributed clustering algorithm that avoids many expensive distance computations by aggregating objects at a coarse level; only objects in a common "canopy" are assumed to be close enough to potentially be in the same cluster. In Canopy, scaling up drastically may compromise the clustering quality. Also (unlike ITC), Canopy operates on the data affinity matrix, which imposes limitations on its applicability to large data (see discussion in the chapter's introduction).

Several authors addressed the scalability issue of clustering by parallelizing specific algorithms, most prominently k-means (Judd, McKinley, and Jain, 1998; Dhillon and Modha, 2000) and its generalizations (Forman and Zhang, 2000) that cover, for example, the EM algorithm. The parallelization strategies exploit the stepwise nature and mathematical properties of k-means that allow computing a global solution from a set of local solutions, in the following manner. Each node is responsible for a subset of the data. It determines the closest cluster for each of its instances, computes the new local cluster means (or parameters for EM, respectively), communicates these means to a master node that aggregates them, and distributes the aggregated centroids (or parameters) for the next iteration. This parallelization procedure yields algorithms that obtain results identical to those of their non-parallel counterparts.

On the technical side, the literature usually shows that these algorithms can be realized on top of a specific low-level communication framework (Forman and Zhang, 2000; Dhillon and Modha, 2000; Hadjidoukas and Amsaleg, 2006) when running on a "shared nothing" cluster, but they are clearly not limited to this kind of architecture. It has recently been discussed that the same kind of parallelization works very well in combination with the popular MapReduce paradigm (Dean and Ghemawat, 2004). Parallelizing the clustering algorithms k-means and EM (mixture of Gaussians) via MapReduce is covered in Chu et al. (2006).

So far, not much progress has been made on parallelizing clustering algorithms of a non-k-means nature. In this section, we show why parallelizing those algorithms is an important task. After a detailed discussion on IT-CC (Dhillon et al., 2003), which is an effective k-means-like algorithm, we prove that a *sequential* information-theoretic clustering algorithm outperforms IT-CC in optimizing the clustering objective and therefore is capable of obtaining better empirical results.

13.2.1 Parallel IT-CC

The information-theoretic co-clustering of Dhillon et al. is a k-means-style algorithm that *locally* optimizes the global information-theoretic objective function (13.3). We first briefly sketch the formal background of IT-CC, before proposing its parallelization.

The goal of IT-CC is to approximate a given joint probability distribution p over two modalities X and Y with a "simpler" distribution q, where the statistical dependencies are captured in a lower-dimensional *cluster space*:

$$q(x, y) := p(x) \cdot p(y) \cdot \frac{p(\tilde{x}, \tilde{y})}{p(\tilde{x}) \cdot p(\tilde{y})}, \qquad (13.4)$$

where $x \in X$, $y \in Y$, $p(x)$ and $p(y)$ denote marginals; $\tilde{x}$ and $\tilde{y}$ are the corresponding clusters of x and y, respectively; and $p(\tilde{x})$ and $p(\tilde{y})$ are marginal probabilities of these clusters. Dhillon et al. show that optimization of the objective function 13.3 is equivalent to minimization of the KL divergence $D_{KL}(p(X, Y)||q(X, Y))$ of the joint distribution p and its approximation q.

Like many other co-clustering algorithms, IT-CC alternates iterations that update the clustering assignments $\tilde{X}$ and $\tilde{Y}$. The IT-CC algorithm is a k-means-style algorithm in a sense that it first assigns all data points to their closest clusters, and then it recomputes cluster representatives based on the data points that now belong to each cluster.

Let us focus on a IT-CC iteration where the clustering $\tilde{X}$ is updated given the clustering $\tilde{Y}$ (the opposite case is symmetric). Unlike the traditional k-means that uses the Euclidean distance metric, IT-CC defines the proximity of a data point x to a cluster $\tilde{x}$ in terms of the KL divergence between $p(Y|x)$ and $q(Y|\tilde{x})$, where the latter is computed using

$$q(y|\tilde{x}) = q(y|\tilde{y}) \cdot q(\tilde{y}|\tilde{x}). \tag{13.5}$$

During the data point assignment process, the conditionals $q(Y|\tilde{x})$ do not change, thus playing the role of the centroids. That is, when x is reassigned from one cluster to another, this does not automatically cause $q(Y|\tilde{x})$ to change. Only once the reassignment process is over is $q(Y|\tilde{x})$ recomputed.

Dhillon et al. prove that the co-clustering strategy of assigning data points x to clusters $\tilde{x}$ by minimizing the local objective $D_{KL}(p(Y|x)||q(Y|\tilde{x}))$, monotonically decreases the global objective function, which guarantees the algorithm's convergence. The following transformations illustrate how to simplify computations without changing the optimization problem, that is, without changing the total order of its solutions. We remove terms that are constants in the context of optimizing cluster assignment $\tilde{X}$ and rewrite

$$\arg\min_{\tilde{x}} D_{KL}(p(Y|x)||q(Y|\tilde{x})) = \arg\min_{\tilde{x}} \sum_y p(y|x) \log \frac{p(y|x)}{q(y|\tilde{x})}$$

(applying Equation (13.5) for $q(y|\tilde{x})$:)

$$= \arg\max_{\tilde{x}} \sum_y p(y|x) \log(q(y|\tilde{y})q(\tilde{y}|\tilde{x})) = \arg\max_{\tilde{x}} \sum_{\tilde{y}} p(\tilde{y}|x) \log q(\tilde{y}|\tilde{x})$$

(using the fact that $q \equiv p$ in the space of clusters:)

$$= \arg\max_{\tilde{x}} \sum_{\tilde{y}} p(\tilde{y}|x) \log p(\tilde{y}|\tilde{x}). \tag{13.6}$$

The preceding transformation shows that rather than computing the centroids $q(Y|\tilde{x})$, the algorithm only needs to compute $q(\tilde{x}, \tilde{y}) = p(\tilde{x}, \tilde{y})$ for each cluster pair $(\tilde{x}, \tilde{y})$ at each iteration.

We argue that the same simplification allows selection of an optimal clustering $\tilde{X}^{opt}$ from a set of candidate clusterings by *only* referring to cluster joints $p(\tilde{x}, \tilde{y})$.

Let $q_{(\tilde{X},\tilde{Y})}$ be the distribution q induced by a specific pair of clusterings $\tilde{X}$ and $\tilde{Y}$. We have

$$\tilde{X}^{opt} = \arg\min_{\tilde{X}} D_{KL}(p(X,Y)\|q_{(\tilde{X},\tilde{Y})}(X,Y)) = \arg\min_{\tilde{X}} \sum_{x,y} p(x,y) \log \frac{p(x,y)}{q_{(\tilde{X},\tilde{Y})}(x,y)}$$

$$= \arg\max_{\tilde{X}} \sum_{\tilde{x}} p(\tilde{x}) \sum_{\tilde{y}} p(\tilde{y}|\tilde{x}) \log q(\tilde{y}|\tilde{x}) = \arg\max_{\tilde{X}} \sum_{\tilde{x}} p(\tilde{x}) \sum_{\tilde{y}} p(\tilde{y}|\tilde{x}) \log p(\tilde{y}|\tilde{x})$$

as our new, equivalent formulation of the IT-CC optimization problem.

Following the outline of parallel k-means and the preceding description, we can adapt IT-CC to the parallel case as follows. We alternate the optimization of $\tilde{X}$ and $\tilde{Y}$. During each of these optimizations, parallel processes hold disjoint subsets of the data. We will describe the case of computing a new clustering of X; clustering Y works analogously. Process i will be responsible for data instances $\mathcal{X}^{(i)} \subset \mathcal{X}$. All cluster "centroids" $p(\tilde{x}, \tilde{y})$ are distributed to all nodes, where the new cluster assignments are computed based on the KL divergence 13.6. Given the new assignments, each process i computes the local joints $q^{(i)}(\tilde{x}, \tilde{y}) = \sum_{x \in \tilde{x} \cap \mathcal{X}^{(i)}} p(x, \tilde{y})$ for each (new) cluster $\tilde{x}$ and transmits them to a master node. The master computes the new global "centroids" $q(\tilde{x}, \tilde{y}) = \sum_i q^{(i)}(\tilde{x}, \tilde{y})$. They can then be broadcasted back to the slave nodes to start the next round of refining $\tilde{X}$, or the algorithm can switch to clustering Y instead. Note that this process yields exactly the same results as in the non-parallelized case.

We consider the parallel IT-CC algorithm as a strong baseline for the DataLoom algorithm proposed in Section 13.4. Before moving on, let us discuss the potential of DataLoom by taking a closer look at the difference between IT-CC and the (non-parallelized) sequential information bottleneck.

13.3 Sequential Co-clustering

DataLoom originates from a multi-modal version of the *sequential Information Bottleneck (sIB)* algorithm (Slonim et al., 2002). In sIB, at its initialization step, all data points are uniformly at random assigned into k clusters. The algorithm iterates over the data points chosen in a random order. Each data point is pulled out of its current cluster and probed into every cluster. It is finally assigned to the cluster such that the objective function 13.1 is maximized. The algorithm is executed until its full convergence.

We focus on the multi-modal variation of sIB – we call it *sequential co-clustering* (SCC). The SCC algorithm iterates over the data modalities organized in an interaction graph (see Section 13.1). At each iteration, it applies the sIB's optimization procedure to maximize the co-clustering objective (13.3). It improves clusterings by continuously updating cluster memberships of individual data points. To decide whether to change a cluster membership, it directly evaluates the objective (in its primal form).

Theorem 13.1 *The set of clustering pairs $(\tilde{X}, \tilde{Y})$ that are local optima of SCC are a subset of the clustering pairs that are local optima of IT-CC.*

It is sufficient to show that whenever IT-CC reads a pair of clusterings $(\tilde{X}, \tilde{Y})$ and outputs a pair of clusterings $(\tilde{X}', \tilde{Y}')$ with a higher score of the objective function,

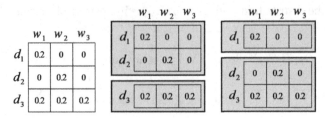

Figure 13.2 An illustration to the difference between IT-CC and SCC optimization procedures, used in Theorem 13.2.

SCC will improve the objective function on $(\tilde{X}, \tilde{Y})$ as well. See Bekkerman and Scholz (2008) for the proof.

Theorem 13.2 *The subset relationship proved in Theorem 13.1 is strict.*

PROOF We prove this by presenting an example where IT-CC gets stuck in a local optimum while SCC is able to overcome it. We look at three documents with the following sets of words: $d_1 = \{w_1\}$, $d_2 = \{w_2\}$, and $d_3 = \{w_1, w_2, w_3\}$. Initially, the first two documents belong to cluster $\tilde{d}_1$, while the third document belongs to cluster $\tilde{d}_2$. For simplicity, we assume that each word sits in a separate cluster over the words' modality W. Figure 13.2 shows the joint probability matrix p (left) and the initial aggregation to clusters (middle). The conditional distributions are hence $p(\tilde{W}|\tilde{d}_1) = (\frac{1}{2}, \frac{1}{2}, 0)$ (upper cluster) and $p(\tilde{W}|\tilde{d}_2) = (\frac{1}{3}, \frac{1}{3}, \frac{1}{3})$ (lower cluster). It can be easily verified by applying Equation 13.6 that IT-CC will not modify any cluster. However, SCC will move either d_1 or d_2 into the second cluster (Figure 13.2 right). By applying this modification, SCC will almost double the mutual information (13.3) from 0.171 (middle) to 0.322 (right). □

Theorems 13.1 and 13.2 reveal that IT-CC gets stuck in local minima more often than SCC. At the level of updating individual cluster memberships, IT-CC is more conservative. More specifically, this suggests that the sequential strategy might both converge faster (because at every iteration it will perform a few updates that IT-CC will miss) and to a better local optimum. We leave verification of this conjecture to the empirical part of this chapter.

13.4 The DataLoom Algorithm

Intuitively, sequential co-clustering can be parallelized by simply moving multiple data points in parallel, while each move maximizes the SCC objective function $I(\tilde{X}; \tilde{Y})$ independently of the others. However, we can easily come up with examples where two advantageous moves will hurt the objective when done in parallel. In a sequential process, one of the two moves would make another one disadvantageous and thus would prevent it. Therefore, this naive parallelization scheme is not applicable to SCC.

Our parallelization of SCC is based on the following fairly straightforward consideration: mutual information $I(\tilde{X}; \tilde{Y})$ is *additive* over either of its arguments. That is, when SCC optimizes $\tilde{X}$ with respect to $\tilde{Y}$ and a data point $x' \in \tilde{x}'$ asks to move to cluster

$\tilde{x}^*$, only the portion of the mutual information that corresponds to clusters $\tilde{x}'$ and $\tilde{x}^*$ is affected. Indeed, by definition,

$$I(\tilde{X}; \tilde{Y}) = \sum_{\tilde{x}} \sum_{\tilde{y}} p(\tilde{x}, \tilde{y}) \log \frac{p(\tilde{x}, \tilde{y})}{p(\tilde{x})p(\tilde{y})} = \sum_{\tilde{x} \neq \tilde{x}' \wedge \tilde{x} \neq \tilde{x}^*} \sum_{\tilde{y}} p(\tilde{x}, \tilde{y}) \log \frac{p(\tilde{x}, \tilde{y})}{p(\tilde{x})p(\tilde{y})}$$
$$+ \sum_{\tilde{y}} \left[p(\tilde{x}', \tilde{y}) \log \frac{p(\tilde{x}', \tilde{y})}{p(\tilde{x}')p(\tilde{y})} + p(\tilde{x}^*, \tilde{y}) \log \frac{p(\tilde{x}^*, \tilde{y})}{p(\tilde{x}^*)p(\tilde{y})} \right].$$

To check whether or not moving x' into $\tilde{x}^*$ increases our objective function, it is sufficient to compute the delta between its value before the move and after the move. Again, only terms that correspond to $\tilde{x}'$ and $\tilde{x}^*$ are involved in the delta computation. Also, the marginals $p(\tilde{y})$ cancel out:

$$\Delta I(\tilde{X}; \tilde{Y}) = I_{\text{after}}(\tilde{X}; \tilde{Y}) - I_{\text{before}}(\tilde{X}; \tilde{Y})$$
$$= \sum_{\tilde{y}} \left[p\left(\tilde{x}' \setminus \{x'\}, \tilde{y}\right) \log \frac{p\left(\tilde{x}' \setminus \{x'\}, \tilde{y}\right)}{p\left(\tilde{x}' \setminus \{x'\}\right)} + p\left(\tilde{x}^* \cup \{x'\}, \tilde{y}\right) \log \frac{p\left(\tilde{x}^* \cup \{x'\}, \tilde{y}\right)}{p\left(\tilde{x}^* \cup \{x'\}\right)} \right.$$
$$\left. - p(\tilde{x}', \tilde{y}) \log \frac{p(\tilde{x}', \tilde{y})}{p(\tilde{x}')} - p(\tilde{x}^*, \tilde{y}) \log \frac{p(\tilde{x}^*, \tilde{y})}{p(\tilde{x}^*)} \right]. \tag{13.7}$$

This observation leads us to the idea that probing the moves $x' \rightarrow \tilde{x}^*$ can be performed in parallel if all the clusters in $\tilde{X}$ are split into disjoint pairs.[6] Each such probing can then be executed as a separate process. Because the communication is generally expensive, it is beneficial to sequentially probe *all* data points in both $\tilde{x}'$ and $\tilde{x}^*$. If the probe shows that the objective can be increased, the data point is immediately moved from its cluster into the other. Once all the data points are probed (and some get moved), each process will be ready to "shuffle" another pair of clusters. Using this approach, we lose one ingredient of SCC: data points do not necessarily move into the cluster such that the objective function is *maximized*, but only *increased*. Despite the fact that intuitively such a loss might be crucial, Bekkerman, Sahami, and Learned-Miller, (2006) empirically show that both approaches perform comparably, as soon as the number of optimization steps is about the same. The latter can be achieved by iterating over *all* cluster pairs.

The DataLoom system consists of a master process and $\lceil \frac{k}{2} \rceil$ slave processes (where k is the number of clusters). The master's algorithm is shown in Algorithm 40, the slave's in Algorithm 41. After constructing the initial set of cluster pairs and sending them to the slave processes, the master node switches to the sleep state, while the slave processes work autonomously, communicating with each other. Each slave process receives two clusters and shuffles them while optimizing the objective. After the shuffling task is completed, each slave is ready to send and receive clusters to another slave process. It is enough to send (and receive) only *one* cluster of each pair – by which means the communication cost is kept at its minimum.

In order to make each pair of clusters meet and get shuffled, we use a communication protocol that is a variation of the *round-robin tournament* (see, e.g., Brent and Luk, 1985), optimized to minimize the communication cost. Round-robin tournament

---

[6] For example, a set of six clusters $\{\tilde{x}_1, \tilde{x}_2, \tilde{x}_3, \tilde{x}_4, \tilde{x}_5, \tilde{x}_6\}$ can be divided into three pairs $\{\{\tilde{x}_1, \tilde{x}_3\}, \{\tilde{x}_2, \tilde{x}_6\}, \{\tilde{x}_4, \tilde{x}_5\}\}$.

Algorithm 40: Master Process

Input: G – interaction graph of nodes $\{X_1, \ldots, X_m\}$ and edges $\mathbf{E}$
$p(X_i, X_j)$ – pairwise joint distributions, for each edge e_{ij}
l – number of optimization iterations
Output: Clusterings $\{\tilde{X}_1^{(l)}, \ldots, \tilde{X}_m^{(l)}\}$
  Initialization:

For each node X **do**
  Assign values x to clusters $\tilde{x}$ uniformly at random
  Main loop:

For each iteration $t = (1, \ldots, l)$ **do**
  For each edge $e_{ij} = (X_i, X_j)$ **do**
    For each ordering $(X, Y) \in \{(X_i, X_j), (X_j, X_i)\}$ **do**
      For each random restart **do**
        Randomly split the set of clusters to pairs $(\tilde{x}, \tilde{x}')$
        Assign each pair $(\tilde{x}, \tilde{x}')$ to a slave process
        Prepare input $\{p(x, \tilde{Y}) | x \in (\tilde{x}, \tilde{x}')\}$ for each slave
        Repeat
          Run slave processes
          Wait and monitor
          If system failure **then** kill all slave processes
        Until all slave processes successfully completed
        Compute $I(\tilde{X}; \tilde{Y})$
      Choose clustering $\tilde{X}^{(t)} = \arg\max_{\tilde{X}} I(\tilde{X}; \tilde{Y})$ among all random restarts

---

Algorithm 41: Slave Process

Input: $(\tilde{x}, \tilde{x}')$ – two clusters from $\tilde{X}$
$p(x, \tilde{Y})$ – rows of probability table $p(X, \tilde{Y})$ for $\forall x \in (\tilde{x}, \tilde{x}')$
l – overall number of slave processes
$r \in [0..(l-1)]$ – my process ID
Output: New clusters $(\tilde{x}, \tilde{x}')$
  Main loop:

For each iteration $t = (1, \ldots, l - 1)$ **do**
  Build a random permutation Ψ of all values $x \in (\tilde{x}, \tilde{x}')$
  For each $x \in \Psi$ **do**
    Move x from its cluster into another if this leads to $\Delta I(\tilde{X}; \tilde{Y}) > 0$ (from Equation (13.7))
  If iteration number t is odd **then**
    If $r == 0$ **then** swap clusters $\tilde{x}$ and $\tilde{x}'$
    Send cluster $\tilde{x}$ to process with ID $(r + 1)\%l$
    Receive cluster $\tilde{x}$ from process with ID $(l + r - 1)\%l$
  Else
    Send cluster $\tilde{x}'$ to process with ID $(l + r - 1)\%l$
    Receive cluster $\tilde{x}'$ from process with ID $(r + 1)\%l$
  Synchronize with all the other slave processes

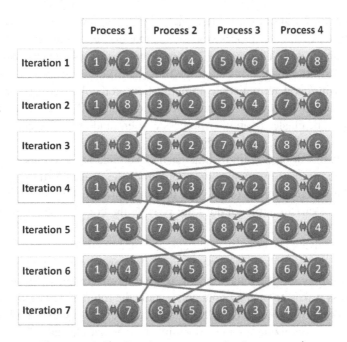

Figure 13.3 The DataLoom communication protocol.

algorithms are based on the analogy with chess tournaments in which each player has to meet each other player once. Most round-robin tournament algorithms are not designed to minimize the communication cost (in a chess tournament, for example, it is not a problem if both players leave the table when the game is over). In our case, however, we make sure that only one player will leave the table. For now, let us assume that k is even, and then the parallel computation is performed over $\frac{k}{2}$ slave processes that are organized in a list sorted by their IDs. After each process shuffles its pair of clusters $(\tilde{x}, \tilde{x}')$, it sends $\tilde{x}$ to the next process in the list, shuffles the new pair, and sends $\tilde{x}'$ to the previous process in the list. An exception is one cluster that never leaves its process – this cluster breaks the symmetric order in which clusters are sent and received and therefore enables the process to cover all the pairs.

Figure 13.3 illustrates our communication protocol on eight clusters (handled by four slave processes). To cover all the pairs, seven parallel computing iterations should be performed. After one shuffling iteration, each process sends one cluster to the right. After another iteration, each process sends the "older" cluster to the left. Cluster 1 always stays at process 1. Note that if the number of clusters k is odd, the only change that should be done to our communication protocol is to leave the "seat" of cluster 1 unoccupied.

Theorem 13.3 *The DataLoom communication protocol guarantees that every pair of clusters meets exactly once.*

See Bekkerman and Scholz (2008) for the proof.

Theorem 13.4 *The DataLoom communication protocol minimizes the communication cost.*[7]

---

[7] We assume that transmitting any cluster takes a unit of time.

The proof is straightforward: after each shuffle, a slave process has to send at least one cluster to another process (otherwise two clusters would meet twice, which contradicts the result of Theorem 13.3). Our protocol ensures that each process sends *exactly* one cluster.

Together with the deterministic communication protocol described previously, we propose a stochastic protocol, in which, after the cluster shuffling is completed, a slave process sends one cluster to another process chosen randomly. The exact protocol is precomputed by the master and then distributed to the slaves. It keeps track of the cluster transfers such that at each point of time each slave node has two clusters to process. The stochastic protocol overcomes the problem of the deterministic protocol, which preserves the initial ordering of clusters that may presumably be disadvantageous. However, the stochastic protocol does not provide the completeness guarantee given in Theorem 13.3.

The collection of slave processes operates as a loom, which uses the communication protocol as a shuttle. If a slave process fails, the communication protocol gets out of synchronization and the data weaving routine never completes. In that case, the master process wakes up on a timeout and restarts the routine. After the data weaving routine is successfully completed, the master process collects all the resulting clusters and switches to optimizing another modality (e.g., when clusters of documents are constructed, the algorithm switches to constructing clusters of words, and so forth). Our method can be generalized to handle any number of modalities organized in an interaction graph to be traversed by the master. The method's complexity increases only linearly with increasing the number of edges in the interaction graph.

The computational complexity of one DataLoom iteration is $O(nk^2m)$, where n is the size of the largest modality ($n = \max_i |\mathcal{X}_i|$); k is the maximum number of clusters (among clusterings of all modalities); and m is the number of modalities (which is typically a small number, such as 2 or 3). In the worst case (when a clustering is *unbalanced*, resulting in a few large clusters and many small ones), a slave process iterates over $O(n)$ data points, while it takes $O(km)$ time units to probe one data point. Each slave process runs $O(k)$ times to finish one DataLoom iteration. Note that our objective function is designed to produce *balanced* clusterings, which in the best case makes the slave process iterate over $O(\frac{n}{k})$ data points only, and the overall complexity is then $O(nkm)$.

As far as only the computational complexity is concerned (without communication), the DataLoom algorithm is no more expensive than parallel k-means. At each iteration, each slave process probes each data point it holds – exactly once. Throughout the course of the algorithm, we probe each data point $k - 1$ times; therefore we perform no more point-cluster probes than parallel k-means and parallel IT-CC do.

13.5 Implementation and Experimentation

In our implementation of the DataLoom algorithm, the communication is based on the Message Passing Interface (MPI) (Snir et al., 1998). We decided to apply MPI instead of the popular MapReduce scheme because an iterative application of MapReduce requires a disk access to back-propagate the data from a reducer to the next mapper, which can be expensive in our setup. The DataLoom algorithm was deployed on a Hewlett-Packard XC Linux cluster system consisting of 62 eight-core machines with 16GB RAM each.

As a baseline for our large-scale experiments, together with the parallelized IT-CC algorithm, we used a parallelized version of the double k-means algorithm (see, e.g., Rocci and Vichi, 2008). Double k-means is basically the IT-CC optimization procedure that minimizes the traditional k-means objective (the sum of Euclidean distances of data points to their centroids). We parallelized it analogously to the IT-CC parallelization (see Section 13.2.1).

13.5.1 Comparison with Sequential Co-clustering

Our first objective is to show that the performance of the DataLoom algorithm is comparable to the performance of its sequential ancestor. To meet this objective, we replicate the experimental setup of Bekkerman et al. (2005), where ITC algorithms are tested on six relatively small textual datasets. Our evaluation measure is *micro-averaged accuracy*[8] of document clustering, which is the portion of data points that belong to dominant categories. Formally, let $\mathcal{C}$ be the set of ground truth categories. For each cluster $\tilde{x}$, let $\mu_{\mathcal{C}}(\tilde{x})$ be the maximal number of elements of $\tilde{x}$ that belong to one category, and let $|\tilde{x}|$ be the size of cluster $\tilde{x}$. We define the precision of $\tilde{x}$ with respect to $\mathcal{C}$ as $Prec(\tilde{x}, \mathcal{C}) = \mu_{\mathcal{C}}(\tilde{x})/|\tilde{x}|$. The micro-averaged precision of the entire clustering $\tilde{X}$ is

$$Prec(\tilde{X}, \mathcal{C}) = \frac{\sum_{\tilde{x}} \mu_{\mathcal{C}}(\tilde{x})}{\sum_{\tilde{x}} |\tilde{x}|} = \frac{\sum_{\tilde{x}} \mu_{\mathcal{C}}(\tilde{x})}{|\mathcal{X}|}, \tag{13.8}$$

where $|X|$ is the size of the dataset. If the number of clusters k is equal to the number of categories $|\mathcal{C}|$, then $Prec(\tilde{X}, \mathcal{C})$ equals micro-averaged recall and thus equals clustering *accuracy*.

For simplicity, we choose four of the six datasets used by Bekkerman et al. (2005) – those that have an even number of categories. Three of the datasets (*acheyer*, *mgondek*, and *sanders-r*) are small collections of 664, 297, and 1188 email messages, grouped into 38, 14, and 30 folders, respectively. The fourth dataset is the widely used benchmark 20 Newsgroups (20NG) dataset, which consists of 19,997 postings submitted to 20 newsgroups. About 4.5% of the 20NG documents are duplications – we do not remove them, for better replicability. For all the four datasets, we simultaneously cluster documents and their words. For email datasets, we also cluster the third modality, which is the names of email correspondents. For the three-way clustering, we use our CWO optimization scheme (see Section 13.1).

The summary of our results is given in Table 13.1. Besides comparing to SCC and IT-CC, we compared DataLoom against the standard unimodal k-means, as well as against *Latent Dirichlet Allocation (LDA)* (Blei, Ng, and Jordan, 2003) – a popular generative model for representing document collections. In LDA, each document is represented as a distribution of topics, and parameters of those distributions are learned from the data. Documents are then clustered based on their posterior distributions (given the topics).

---

[8] As used by Slonim et al. (2002), Dhillon et al. (2003), Bekkerman et al. (2005), and others.

Table 13.1. *Clustering accuracy on small datasets. Standard error of the mean is shown after the ± sign.*

Algorithm	acheyer	mgondek	sanders-r	20NG
k-means	24.7	37.0	45.5	16.1
LDA	44.3 ± 0.4	68.0 ± 0.8	63.8 ± 0.4	56.7 ± 0.6
IT-CC	39.0 ± 0.6	61.3 ± 1.5	56.1 ± 0.7	54.2 ± 0.7
SCC	46.1 ± 0.3	63.4 ± 1.1	60.2 ± 0.4	57.7 ± 0.2
2way DataLoom (deterministic)	43.7 ± 0.5	63.3 ± 1.8	59.8 ± 0.9	55.1 ± 0.7
2way DataLoom (stochastic)	42.4 ± 0.5	64.6 ± 1.2	61.3 ± 0.8	55.6 ± 0.7
3way DataLoom (stochastic)	46.7 ± 0.3	73.8 ± 1.7	66.5 ± 0.2	N/A

We used Xuerui Wang's LDA implementation (McCallum, Corrada-Emmanuel, and Wang, 2005) that applies Gibbs sampling with 10,000 sampling iterations.

As we can see in the table, the empirical results approve our theoretical argumentation from Section 13.3 – sequential co-clustering significantly outperforms the IT-CC algorithm. Our two-way parallelized algorithm demonstrates very reasonable performance: only in two of the four cases is it inferior to the SCC. It is highly notable that our three-way DataLoom algorithm achieves the best results, outperforming by more than 5% (on the absolute scale) all its competitors on *mgondek*. When comparing the deterministic and stochastic communication protocols, we notice that they perform comparably. For the rest of our experiments, we use the stochastic version.

13.5.2 The RCV1 Dataset

The RCV1 (Lewis et al., 2004) dataset is one of the largest fully labeled benchmark text categorization datasets. It consists of 806,791 documents, each of which belongs to a hierarchy of categories. The top level of the hierarchy contains only 4 categories, while the second level contains 55 categories. In our experiment, we ignored the top level and mapped categories from all the lower levels onto their parents from the second level (using this scheme, 27,076 documents were not assigned into any category and therefore were always considered as wrongly categorized). We removed stopwords and low-frequency words (leaving 150,032 distinct words overall). Represented as a contingency table, the resulting data contains more than 120 billion entries. We built 800 document clusters and 800 word clusters. We plotted the clustering precision (Equation 13.8) over the clustering iterations and compared DataLoom with the parallelized IT-CC, as well as with parallelized double *k*-means. The results are presented in Figure 13.4 (left), where DataLoom has a clear advantage over the other methods. We also plot the mutual information $I(\tilde{X}; \tilde{Y})$ after each iteration and show that DataLoom is able to construct clusterings with 20% higher mutual information.

13.5.3 The Netflix Dataset

Another dataset we used in our experiments was taken from the Netflix challenge. It contains ratings of 17,770 movies given by 480,189 users. We did not consider the actual values of ratings, but wanted to predict for a number of given user–movie pairs whether or not this user rated this movie. This resembles one of the tasks of KDD'07 Cup, and we used its evaluation set. We built 800 user clusters and 800 movie clusters.

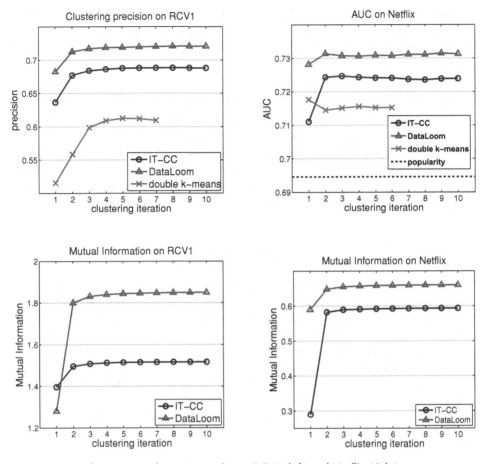

Figure 13.4 Clustering results on RCV1 (left) and Netflix (right).

Our prediction method is directly based on the the natural approximation q (defined in Equation 13.4) of our (normalized) Boolean movie–user rating matrix p. The quality of this approximation is prescribed by the quality of the co-clustering. The intuition behind our experiment is that capturing more of the structure underlying this data helps in better approximating the original matrix. We ranked all the movie–user pairs in the hold-out set with respect to the predicted probability of q. Then we computed the Area Under the ROC Curves (AUC) for the three co-clustering algorithms. To establish a lower bound, we also ranked the movie–user pairs based on the pure popularity score $p(x)p(y)$. The results are shown in Figure 13.4 (right). In addition to that, as in the RCV1 case, we directly compared the objective function values of the co-clusterings produced by DataLoom and IT-CC. Here again, DataLoom shows an impressive advantage over the other methods.

13.6 Conclusion

This chapter describes an attempt to dramatically scale up a strong data clustering method while applying parallelization. The resulting algorithm is applied to two large labeled data corpora, RCV1 and Netflix, of hundreds of thousands of data instances each. The algorithm is by all means applicable to datasets orders of magnitude larger than that, but we decided on these two publicly available datasets for the sake of replicability only.

As far as the speedup is concerned, on small datasets (see Section 13.5.1) the DataLoom method is not gaining a particularly impressive advantage over non-parallelized methods. Naturally, small datasets can be clustered using sequential clustering as is. On large datasets, however, the parallelization is vital. Basically, SCC is not applicable to large datasets: on RCV1, for example, it would have run for months (assuming that it can fit the RAM), whereas it completes within a few hours on a 400-core cluster.[9] Thus, applying the data weaving parallelization makes real what would have been infeasible otherwise.

References

Bekkerman, R., and Scholz, M. 2008. Data Weaving: Scaling Up the State-of-the-Art in Data Clustering. Pages 1083–1092 of: *Proceedings of CIKM-17*.

Bekkerman, R., El-Yaniv, R., Tishby, N., and Winter, Y. 2001. On Feature Distributional Clustering for Text Categorization. Pages 146–153 of: *Proceedings of SIGIR*.

Bekkerman, R., El-Yaniv, R., and McCallum, A. 2005. Multi-Way Distributional Clustering via Pairwise Interactions. Pages 41–48 of: *Proceedings of ICML-22*.

Bekkerman, R., Sahami, M., and Learned-Miller, E. 2006. Combinatorial Markov Random Fields. In: *Proceedings of ECML-17*.

Besag, J. 1986. On the Statistical Analysis of Dirty Pictures. *Journal of the Royal Statistical Society*, **48**(3).

Blei, D. M., Ng, A. Y., and Jordan, M. I. 2003. Latent Dirichlet Allocation. *Journal of Machine Learning Research*, **3**, 993–1022.

Böhm, C., Faloutsos, C., Pan, J.-Y., and Plant, C. 2006. Robust Information-Theoretic Clustering. Pages 65–75 of: *Proceedings of ACM SIGKDD*.

Brent, R. P., and Luk, F. T. 1985. The Solution of Singular-Value and Symmetric Eigenvalue Problems on Multiprocessor Arrays. *SIAM Journal on Scientific and Statistical Computing*, **6**, 69–84.

Chu, C.-T., Kim, S. K., Lin, Y.-A., Yu, Y. Y., Bradski, G. R., Ng, A. Y., and Olukotun, K. 2006. MapReduce for Machine Learning on Multicore. In: *Advances in Neural Information Processing Systems (NIPS)*.

Cilibrasi, R., and Vitányi, P. 2005. Clustering by Compression. *IEEE Transactions on Information Theory*, **51**(4), 1523–1545.

Crammer, K., Talukdar, P., and Pereira, F. 2008. A Rate-Distortion One-Class Model and Its Applications to Clustering. In: *Proceedings of the 25st International Conference on Machine Learning*.

Dean, J., and Ghemawat, S. 2004. MapReduce: Simplified Data Processing on Large Clusters. *Symposium on Operating System Design and Implementation (OSDI)*, 137–150.

Dhillon, I. S., and Modha, D. S. 2000. A Data Clustering Algorithm on Distributed Memory Multiprocessors. In: *Large-Scale Parallel Data Mining*. Lecture Notes in Artificial Intelligence, vol. 1759.

---

[9] One co-clustering iteration of DataLoom completes in about 50 minutes on the Netflix dataset and in about 75 minutes on RCV1. As we can see from the bottom graphs in Figure 13.4, no more than three or four DataLoom iterations are necessary.

Dhillon, I. S., Mallela, S., and Modha, D. S. 2003. Information-Theoretic Co-clustering. Pages 89–98 of: *Proceedings of SIGKDD-9*.

El-Yaniv, R., and Souroujon, O. 2001. Iterative Double Clustering for Unsupervised and Semi-supervised Learning. In: *Advances in Neural Information Processing Systems (NIPS-14)*.

Forman, G., and Zhang, B. 2000. Distributed Data Clustering Can Be Efficient and Exact. *SIGKDD Exploration Newsletter*, **2**(2), 34–38.

Friedman, N., Mosenzon, O, Slonim, N., and Tishby, N. 2001. Multivariate Information Bottleneck. In: *Proceedings of UAI-17*.

Gao, B., Liu, T.-Y., Zheng, X., Cheng, Q.-S., and Ma, W.-Y. 2005. Consistent Bipartite Graph Co-partitioning for Star-Structured High-Order Heterogeneous Data Co-clustering. In: *Proceedings of ACM SIGKDD*.

Hadjidoukas, P. E., and Amsaleg, L. 2006. Parallelization of a Hierarchical Data Clustering Algorithm Using OpenMP. In: *Proceedings of the International Workshop on OpenMP (IWOMP)*.

Johnson, M., Liao, R. H., Rasmussen, A., Sridharan, R., Garcia, D., and Harvey, B. 2008. Infusing Parallelism into Introductory Computer Science using MapReduce. In: *Proceedings of SIGCSE: Symposium on Computer Science Education*.

Judd, D., McKinley, P. K., and Jain, A. K. 1998. Large-Scale Parallel Data Clustering. *IEEE Transactions on Pattern Analysis and Machine Intelligence*, **20**(8), 871–876.

Lauritzen, S. L. 1996. *Graphical Models*. Oxford: Clarendon Press.

Lewis, D. D., Yang, Y., Rose, T. G., and Li, F. 2004. RCV1: A New Benchmark Collection for Text Categorization Research. *JMLR*, **5**, 361–397.

McCallum, A., Nigam, K., and Ungar, L. H. 2000. Efficient Clustering of High-dimensional Data Sets with Application to Reference Matching. Pages 169–178 of: *Proceedings of ACM SIGKDD*.

McCallum, A., Corrada-Emmanuel, A., and Wang, X. 2005. Topic and Role Discovery in Social Networks. Pages 786–791 of: *Proceedings of IJCAI-19*.

Rocci, R., and Vichi, M. 2008. Two-Mode Multi-partitioning. *Computational Statistics and Data Analysis*, **52**(4).

Slonim, N., and Tishby, N. 2000. Agglomerative Information Bottleneck. Pages 617–623 of: *Advances in Neural Information Processing Systems 12 (NIPS)*.

Slonim, N., Friedman, N., and Tishby, N. 2002. Unsupervised Document Classification Using Sequential Information Maximization. In: *Proceedings of SIGIR-25*.

Snir, M., Otto, S. W., Huss-Lederman, S., Walker, D. W., and Dongarra, J. 1998. *MPI – The Complete Reference: Volume 1, The MPI Core*, 2nd ed. Cambridge, MA: MIT Press.

Sutton, C., and McCallum, A. 2005. Piecewise Training of Undirected Models. In: *Proceedings of UAI-21*.

Tilton, J. C., and Strong, J. P. 1984. Analyzing Remotely Sensed Data on the Massively Parallel Processor. Pages 398–400 of: *Proceedings of 7th International Confecrence on Pattern Recognition*.

Tishby, N., Pereira, F., and Bialek, W. 1999. The Information Bottleneck Method. Invited paper to the *37th Annual Allerton Conference on Communication, Control, and Computing*.

PART THREE
Alternative Learning Settings

CHAPTER 14

Parallel Online Learning

Daniel Hsu, Nikos Karampatziakis, John Langford,
and Alex J. Smola

One well-known general approach to machine learning is to repeatedly greedily update a partially learned system using a single labeled data instance. A canonical example of this is provided by the perceptron algorithm (Rosenblatt, 1958), which modifies a weight vector by adding or subtracting the features of a misclassified instance. More generally, typical methods compute the gradient of the prediction's loss with respect to the weight vector's parameters and then update the system according to the negative gradient. This basic approach has many variations and extensions, as well as at least two names. In the neural network literature, this approach is often called "stochastic gradient descent," whereas in the learning theory literature it is typically called "online gradient descent". For the training of complex nonlinear prediction systems, the stochastic gradient descent approach was described long ago and has been standard practice for at least two decades (Bryson and Ho, 1969; Rumelhart, Hinton, and Williams, 1986; Amari, 1967).

Algorithm 42 describes the basic gradient descent algorithm we consider here. The core algorithm uses a differentiable loss function $\ell = \ell(\cdot, y)$ to measure the quality of a prediction $\hat{y}$ with respect to a correct prediction y, and a sequence of learning rates (η_t). Qualitatively, a "learning rate" is the degree to which the weight parameters are adjusted to predict in accordance with a data instance. For example, a common choice is squared loss where $\ell(\hat{y}, y) = (y - \hat{y})^2$ and a common learning rate sequence is $\eta_t = 1/\sqrt{t}$.

There are several basic observations regarding efficiency of online learning approaches.

- At a high level, many learning system make a sequence of greedy improvements. For such systems, it is difficult to reduce these improvements to one or only a few steps of greedy improvement, simply because the gradient provides local information relevant only to closely similar parameterizations, whereas successful prediction is a global property. This observation applies to higher order gradient information such as second derivatives as well. An implication of this observation is that multiple steps must be

---

Algorithm 42: Gradient Descent

---

input loss function l, learning rate schedule η_t
initialize for all $i \in \{1, \ldots, n\}$, weight $w_i := 0$
For $t = 1$ to T **do**

    Get next feature vector $x \in \mathbb{R}^n$
    Compute prediction $\hat{y} := \langle w, x \rangle$
    Get corresponding label y
    For $i \in \{1, \ldots, n\}$ compute gradient $g_i := \frac{\partial \ell(\hat{y}, y)}{\partial w_i} \left(= \frac{\partial \ell(\langle w, x \rangle, y)}{\partial w_i} \right)$
    For $i \in \{1, \ldots, n\}$ update $w_i := w_i - \eta_t g_i$

---

taken, and the most efficient way to make multiple steps is to take a step after each instance is observed.

- If the same instance occurs twice in the data, it is useful to take advantage of data as it arrives. Take the extreme case where every instance is replicated n times. Here an optimization algorithm using fractions of $1/n$ of the data at a time would enjoy an n-fold speedup relative to an algorithm using full views of the data for optimization. Although in practice it is difficult to ascertain these properties beforehand, it is highly desirable to have algorithms that can take advantage of redundancy and similarity as data arrives.

- The process of taking a gradient step is generally amortized by prediction itself. For instance, with the square loss $\ell(\hat{y}, y) = \frac{1}{2}(\hat{y} - y)^2$, the gradient is given by $(\hat{y} - y)x_i$ for $i \in \{1, \ldots, n\}$, so the additional cost of the gradient step over the prediction is roughly a single multiply-and-store per feature. Similar amortization can also be achieved with complex nonlinear circuit-based functions, for instance, when they are compositions of linear predictors.

- The process of prediction can often be represented in vectorial form such that highly optimized linear algebra routines can be applied to yield an additional performance improvement.

Both the practice of machine learning and the basic preceding observations suggest that gradient descent learning techniques are well suited to address large-scale machine learning problems. Indeed, the techniques are so effective, and modern computers are so fast, that we might imagine no challenge remains. After all, a modern computer might have eight cores operating at 3GHz, each core capable of four floating-point operations per clock cycle, providing a peak performance of 96GFlops. A large dataset by today's standards is about webscale, perhaps 10^{10} instances, each 10^4 features in size. Taking the ratio, this suggests that a well-implemented learning algorithm might be able to process such a dataset in less than 20 minutes. Taking into account that GPUs are capable of delivering at least one order of magnitude more computation and that FPGAs might provide another order of magnitude, this suggests no serious effort should be required to scale up learning algorithms, at least for simple linear predictors.

However, considering only floating-point performance is insufficient to capture the constraints imposed by real systems: the limiting factor is not computation, but rather network limits on bandwidth and latency. This chapter is about dealing with these limits in the context of gradient descent learning algorithms. We take as our baseline gradient descent learning algorithm a simple linear predictor, which we typically train to minimize squared loss. Nevertheless, we believe our findings with respect to these limitations qualitatively apply to many other learning algorithms operating according to gradient descent on large datasets.

Another substantial limit is imposed by label information – it is difficult in general to cover the cost of labeling 10^9 instances. For large datasets relevant to this work, it is typically the case that label information is derived in some automated fashion – for example, a canonical case is web advertisement, where we might have 10^{10} advertisements displayed per day, of which some are clicked on and some are not.

14.1 Limits Due to Bandwidth and Latency

The bandwidth limit is well illustrated by the Stochastic Gradient Descent (SGD) implementation (Bottou, 2008). Léon Bottou released it as a reference implementation along with a classification problem with 781K instances and 60M total (non-unique) features derived from RCV1 (Lewis et al., 2004). On this dataset, the SGD implementation might take 20 seconds to load the dataset into memory and then learn a strong predictor in 0.4 seconds. This illustrates that the process of loading the data from disk at 15MB/s is clearly the core bottleneck.

But even if that bottleneck were removed, we would still be far from peak performance: 0.4 seconds is about 100 times longer than expected given the peak computational limits of a modern CPU. A substantial part of this slowdown is due to the nature of the data, which is sparse. With sparse features, each feature might incur the latency to access either cache or RAM (typically a $10\times$ penalty), imposing many-cycle slowdowns on the computation. Thus, performance is sharply limited by bandwidth and latency constraints that in combination slow down learning substantially.

Luckily, gradient-descent style algorithms do not require loading all data into memory. Instead, one data instance can be loaded, a model updated, and then the instance discarded. A basic question is: can this be done rapidly enough to be an effective strategy? For example, a very reasonable fear is that the process of loading and processing instances one at a time induces too much latency, slowing the overall approach unacceptably.

The Vowpal Wabbit (VW) software (Langford, Li, and Strehl, 2007) provides an existence proof that it is possible to have a fast fully online implementation that loads data as it learns. On the preceding dataset, VW can load and learn on the data simultaneously in about 3 seconds, an order of magnitude faster than SGD. A number of tricks are required to achieve this, including a good choice of cache format, asynchronous parsing, and pipelining of the computation. A very substantial side benefit of this style of learning is that we are no longer limited to datasets that fit into memory. A dataset can be streamed either from disk or over the network, implying that the primary bottleneck is bandwidth, and the learning algorithm can handle datasets with perhaps 10^{12} non-unique features in a few hours.

The large discrepancy between bandwidth and available computation suggests that it should be possible to go beyond simple linear models without a significant computational penalty: we can compute nonlinear features of the data and build an extended linear model based on those features. For instance, we may use the random kitchen sink features (Rahimi and Recht, 2008) to obtain prediction performance comparable with Gaussian RBF kernel classes. Furthermore, although general polynomial features are computationally infeasible, it is possible to obtain features based on the outer product of two sets of features efficiently by explicitly expanding such features on the fly. These outer product features can model interaction between two sources of information; for example, the interaction of (query,result) feature pairs is often relevant in internet search settings.

VW allows the implicit specification of these outer product features via specification of the elements of the pairs. The outer product features thus need not be read from disk, implying that the disk bandwidth limit is not imposed. Instead, a new limit arises based on random memory access latency and to a lesser extent on bandwidth constraints. This allows us to perform computation in a space of up to 10^{13} features with a throughput on the order of 10^8 features/second. Note that VW can additionally reduce the dimensionality of each instance using feature hashing (Shi et al., 2009; Weinberger et al., 2009) , which is essential when the (expanded) feature space is large, perhaps even exceeding memory size. The core idea here is to use a hash function, which sometimes collides features. The learning algorithm learns to deal with these collisions, and the overall learning and evaluation process happens much more efficiently because of substantial space savings.

This quantity remains up to two orders of magnitude below the processing limit imposed by a modern CPU (we have up to 100 Flops available per random memory access). This means that there is plenty of room to use more sophisticated learning algorithms without substantially slowing the learning process. Nevertheless, it also remains well below the size of the largest datasets, implying that our pursuit of a very fast, efficient algorithm is not yet complete.

To make matters more concrete assume we have datasets of 10TB size (which is not uncommon for web applications). If we were to stream this data from disk, we cannot expect a data stream of more than 100MB/s per disk (high performance arrays might achieve up to $5\times$ this throughput, albeit often at a significant CPU utilization). This implies that we need to wait at least 10^5 seconds, that is, 30 hours, to process this data on a single computer. This is assuming an optimal learning algorithm that needs to see each instance only once and a storage subsystem that is capable of delivering sustained peak performance for over a day. Even with these unrealistic assumptions, this is often too slow.

14.2 Parallelization Strategies

Creating an online algorithm to process large amounts of data directly limits the designs possible. In particular, it suggests decomposition of the data either in terms of instances or in terms of features as depicted in Figure 14.1. Decomposition in terms of instances automatically reduces the load per computer because we need to process and store only a fraction of the data on each computer. We refer to this partitioning as "instance sharding".[1]

---

[1] In the context of data, "shard" is typically used to define a partition without any particular structure other than size.

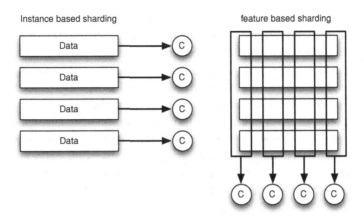

Figure 14.1 Two approaches to data splitting. Left: instance shards. Right: feature shards.

An alternative is to decompose data in terms of its features. Although it does *not* reduce the number of *instances* per computer, it reduces the data per computer by reducing the number of features associated with an instance for each computer, thus increasing the potential throughput per computer.

A typical instance shard scheme runs the learning algorithm on each shard, combines the results in some manner, and then runs a learning algorithm again (perhaps with a different initialization) on each piece of the data. An extreme case of the instance shard approach is given by parallelizing statistical query algorithms (Chu et al., 2007), which compute statistics for various queries over the entire dataset and then update the learned model based on these queries, but there are many other variants as well (Mann et al., 2009; McDonald, Hall, and Mann, 2010). The instance shard approach has a great virtue – it is straightforward and easy to program.

A basic limitation of the instance shard approach is the "combination" operation, which does not scale well with model complexity. When a predictor is iteratively built based on statistics, it is easy enough to derive an aggregate statistic. When we use an online linear predictor for each instance shard, some averaging or weighted averaging style of operation is provably sensible. However, when a nonlinear predictor is learned, it is unclear how to combine the results. Indeed, when a nonlinear predictor has symmetries, and the symmetries are broken differently on different instance shards, a simple averaging approach might cancel the learning away. An example of a symmetry is provided by a two-layer neural network with two hidden nodes. By swapping the weights in the first hidden node with the weights of the second hidden node and similarly swapping the weights in the output node, we can build a representationally different predictor with identical predictions. If these two neural networks then have their weights averaged, the resulting predictor can perform very poorly.

We have found a feature shard approach more effective after the (admittedly substantial) complexity of programming has been addressed. The essential idea in a feature shard approach is that a learning algorithm runs on a subset of the features of each instance, then the predictions on each shard are combined to make an overall prediction for each instance. In effect, the parameters of the global model are partitioned over different machines. One simple reason why the feature shard approach works well is due to caching effects – any learned model is distributed across multiple nodes and hence better fits into the cache of each node. This combination process can be a simple addition, or the predictions from each shard can be used as features for a final prediction process, or the combination could even be carried out in a hierarchical fashion. After a prediction is made, a gradient-based update can be made to weights at each node in the process. Because we are concerned with datasets less than 10^{12} in size, the bandwidth required to pass a few bytes per instance around is not prohibitive.

One inevitable side effect of either the instance shard or the feature shard approach is a delayed update, as explained later. Let m be the number of instances and n be the number of computation nodes. In the instance shard approach, the delay factor is equal to m/n, because m/n updates can occur before information from a previously seen instance is incorporated into the model. With the feature shard approach, the latency is generally smaller, but more dependent on the network architecture. In the asymptotic limit when keeping the bandwidth requirements of all nodes constant, the latency grows as $O(\log(n))$ when the nodes are arranged in a binary tree hierarchy; in this case, the prediction and gradient computations are distributed in a divide-and-conquer fashion and are completed in time proportional to the depth of the recursion, which is $O(\log(n))$. In the current implementation of VW, a maximum latency of 2048 instances is allowed. It turns out that any delay can degrade performance substantially, at least when instances arrive adversarially, as we outline next.

14.3 Delayed Update Analysis

We have argued that both instance sharding and feature sharding approaches require delayed updates in a parallel environment. Here we state some analysis of the impact of delay, as given by the delayed gradient descent algorithm in Algorithm 43. We assume that at time t we observe some instance x with associated label y. Given the instance x, we generate some prediction $\langle w, x \rangle$. Based on this, we incur a loss $\ell(\langle w, x \rangle, y)$, such as $\frac{1}{2}(y - \langle w, x \rangle)^2$.

Algorithm 43: Delayed Gradient Descent

Input: Loss function l, learning rate η_t and delay $\tau \in \mathbb{N}$
initialize for all $i \in \{1, \dots, n\}$, weight $w_i := 0$
Set $x_1 \dots, x_\tau := 0$ and compute corresponding g_t for $\ell(0, 0)$
For $t = \tau + 1$ **to** $T + \tau$ **do**
　Get next feature vector $x \in \mathbb{R}^n$
　Compute prediction $\hat{y} := \langle w, x \rangle$
　Get corresponding label y
　For $i \in \{1, \dots, n\}$ compute gradient $g_{t,i} := \frac{\partial \ell(\hat{y}, y)}{\partial w_i}$
　For $i \in \{1, \dots, n\}$ update $w_i := w_i - \eta_t g_{t-\tau, i}$

Given this unified representation we consider the following optimization algorithm template. It differs from Algorithm 42 because the update is delayed by τ rounds. This aspect models the delay due to the parallelization strategy for implementing the gradient descent computation.

14.3.1 Guarantees

We focus on the impact of delay on the convergence rate of the weight vector learned by the algorithm. Convergence rate is a natural performance criterion for online learning algorithms, as it characterizes the trade-off between running time and learning accuracy (measured specifically in number of instances versus error rate).

Introducing delay between data presentation and updates can lead to a substantial increase in error rate. Consider the case where we have a delay of τ between the time we see an instance and when we are able to update w based on the instance. If we are shown τ duplicates of the same data, that is, $x_t, \ldots, x_{t+\tau-1} = \bar{x}$ in sequence, we have no chance of responding to $\bar{x}$ in time and the algorithm cannot converge to the best weight vector any faster than $\frac{1}{\tau}$ times the rate of an algorithm that is able to respond instantly. Note that this holds even if we are told beforehand that we will see the same instance τ times.

This simple reasoning shows that for an adversarially chosen sequence of instances the regret (defined later) induced by a delay of τ can never be better than that of the equivalent no-delay algorithm whose convergence speed is reduced by a factor of $\frac{1}{\tau}$. It turns out that these are the very rates we are able to obtain in the adversarial setting. On the other hand, in the non-adversarial setting, we are able to obtain rates that match those of no-delay algorithms, albeit with a sizable additive constant that depends on the delay.

The guarantees we provide are formulated in terms of a *regret*, that is, as a discrepancy relative to the best possible solution w^* defined with knowledge of all events. Formally, we measure the performance of the algorithm in terms of

$$\text{Reg}[\underbrace{w_1, \ldots, w_T}_{=:W}] := \sum_{t=1}^{T} \left[\ell(\hat{y}_t, y_t) - \ell(\hat{y}_t^*, y_t) \right] \tag{14.1}$$

$$\text{where } y_t^* = \left\langle x_t, \arg\min_w \sum_{t'=1}^{T} \ell(\hat{y}, y_{t'}) \right\rangle$$

Theorem 14.1 (Worst Case Guarantees for Delayed Updates; Langford, Smola, and Zinkevich, 2009) *If* $\|w^*\| \leq R^2$ *and the norms of the gradients* $\nabla_w \ell(\langle w, x \rangle, y)$ *are bounded by* L, *then*

$$Reg[W] \leq 4RL\sqrt{\tau T} \tag{14.2}$$

when we choose the learning rate $\eta_t = \frac{R}{L\sqrt{2\tau t}}$. *If, in addition,* $\ell(\langle w, x \rangle, y)$ *is strongly convex with modulus of convexity* c, *we obtain the guarantee*

$$Reg[W] \leq \frac{L^2}{c} [\tau + 0.5] \log T + C(\tau, L, c)$$

with learning rate $\eta_t = \frac{1}{c(t-\tau)}$, *where* C *is a function independent of* T.

In other words, the average error of the algorithm (as normalized by the number of seen instances) converges at rate $O(\sqrt{\tau/T})$ whenever the loss gradients are bounded and at rate $O(\tau \log T / T)$ whenever the loss function is strongly convex. This is exactly what we would expect in the worst case: an adversary may reorder instances so as to maximally slow down progress. In this case a parallel algorithm is no faster than a sequential code. Although such extreme cases hardly occur in practice, we have observed experimentally that for sequentially correlated instances, delays can rapidly degrade learning.

If subsequent instances are only weakly correlated or IID, it is possible to prove tighter bounds where the delay does not directly harm the update (Langford et al., 2009). The basic structure of these bounds is that they have a large delay-dependent initial regret after which the optimization essentially degenerates into an averaging process for which delay is immaterial. These bounds have many details, but a very crude alternate form of analysis can be done using sample complexity bounds. In particular, if we have a set H of predictors and at each timestep t choose the best predictor on the first $t - \tau$ timesteps, we can bound the regret to the best predictor h according to the following:

Theorem 14.2 (IID Case for delayed updates) *If all losses are in $\{0, 1\}$, for all IID data distributions D over features and labels, for any δ in $(0, 1)$, with probability $1 - \delta$*

$$\min_{h \in H} \sum_{t=1}^{T} [\ell(h(x_t), y_t) - \ell(h_t(x_t), y_t)] \leq \tau + \sqrt{T \ln \frac{3|H|T}{\delta}} + \sqrt{\frac{T \ln \frac{3}{\delta}}{2}}. \quad (14.3)$$

PROOF   The proof is a straightforward application of the Hoeffding bound. At every timestep t, we have $t - \tau$ labeled data instances. Applying the Hoeffding bound for every hypothesis h, we have that with probability $2\delta/3|H|T$, $\left| \frac{1}{t-\tau} \sum_{i=1}^{t-\tau} \ell(h(x_t), y_t) - E_{(x,y) \sim D} \ell(h(x), y) \right| \leq \sqrt{\frac{\ln 3|H|T/\delta}{2(t-\tau)}}$. Applying a union bound over all hypotheses and timesteps implies the same holds with probability at least $2\delta/3$. The algorithm that chooses the best predictor in hindsight therefore chooses a predictor with expected loss at most $\sqrt{\frac{2 \ln 3|H|T/\delta}{t-\tau}}$ worse than the best. Summing over T timesteps, we get: $\tau + \sqrt{2 \ln 3|H|T/\delta} \sum_{t=1}^{T-\tau} \frac{1}{\sqrt{t}} \leq \tau + \sqrt{2T \ln 3|H|T/\delta}$. This is a bound on an expected regret. To get a bound on the actual regret, we can simply apply a Hoeffding bound again yielding the theorem result.   □

14.4 Parallel Learning Algorithms

We have argued that delay is generally bad when doing online learning (at least in an adversarial setting), and that it is also unavoidable when parallelizing. This places us in a bind: How can we create an effective parallel online learning algorithm? We discuss two approaches based on multicore and multinode parallelism.

14.4.1 Multicore Feature Sharding

A multicore processor consists of multiple CPUs that operate asynchronously in a shared memory space. It should be understood that because multicore parallelization does not address the primary bandwidth bottleneck, its usefulness is effectively limited to those datasets and learning algorithms that require substantial computation per raw instance used. In the current implementation, this implies the use of feature pairing, but there are many learning algorithms more complex than linear prediction where this trait may also hold.

The first version of Vowpal Wabbit used an instance sharding approach for multi-core learning, where the set of weights and the instance source were shared among multiple identical threads that each parsed the instance, made a prediction, and then did an update to the weights. This approach was effective for two threads, yielding a near factor-of-2 speedup because parsing of instances required substantial work. However, experiments with more threads on more cores yielded no further speedups because of lock contention. Before moving on to a feature sharding approach, we also experimented with a dangerous parallel programming technique: running with multiple threads that *do not* lock the weight vector. This did yield improved speed, but at a cost in reduced learning rate and nondeterminism that was unacceptable.

The current implementation of Vowpal Wabbit uses an asynchronous parsing thread that prepares instances into the right format for learning threads, each of which computes a sparse-dense vector product on a disjoint subset of the features. The last thread completing this sparse-dense vector product adds together the results and computes an update, which is then sent to all learning threads to update their weights, and then the process repeats. Aside from index definition related to the core hashing representation (Shi et al., 2009; Weinberger et al., 2009) Vowpal Wabbit employs, the resulting algorithm is identical to the single thread implementation. It should be noted that although processing of instances is fully synchronous, there is a small amount of non-determinism between runs due to order-of-addition ambiguities between threads. In all our tests, this method of multicore parallelization yielded virtually identical prediction performance with negligible overhead compared to non-threaded code and sometimes substantial speedups. For example, with four learning threads, about a factor of 3 speedup is observed.

We anticipate that this approach to multicore parallelization will not scale to large numbers of cores, because the very tight coupling of parallelization requires low latency between the different cores. Instead, we believe that multinode parallelization techniques will ultimately need to be used for multicore parallelization, motivating the next section.

14.4.2 Multinode Feature Sharding

The primary distinction between multicore and multinode parallelization is latency, with the latency between nodes many orders of magnitude larger than for cores. In particular, the latency between nodes is commonly much larger than the time to process an individual instance, implying that any per-instance blocking operation, as was used for multicore parallelization, is unacceptable.

This latency also implies a many-instance delayed update that, as we have argued, incurs a risk of substantially degrading performance. In an experiment to avoid this risk, we investigated the use of updates based on information available to only one node in the computation, where there is *no* delay. Somewhat surprisingly, this worked better than our original predictor.

Tree Architectures

Our strategy is to employ feature sharding across several nodes, each of which updates its parameters online as a single-node learning algorithm would. So, ignoring the overhead due to creating and distributing the feature shards (which can be minimized by reorganizing the dataset), we have so far fully decoupled the computation. The issue now is that we have n independent predictors, each using a subset of the features (where n is the number of feature shards), rather than a single predictor utilizing all of the features. We reconcile this in the following manner: (1) we require that each of these nodes compute and transmit a prediction to a master node after receiving each new instance (but before updating its parameters); and (2) we use the master node to treat these n predictions as features, from which the master node learns to predict the label in an otherwise symmetric manner. Note that the master node must also receive the label corresponding to each instance, but this can be handled in various ways with minimal overhead (e.g., it can be piggybacked with one of the subordinate node's predictions). The end result, illustrated in Figure 14.2, is a two-layer architecture for online learning with reduced latency at each node and no delay in parameter updates.

Naturally, the strategy described previously can be iterated to create multi-layered architectures that further reduce the latency at each node. At the extreme, the architecture becomes a (complete) binary tree: each leaf node (at the bottom layer) predicts using a single feature, and each internal node predicts using the predictions of two subordinate nodes in the next lower layer as features (Figure 14.3). Note that each internal node may incur delay proportional to its fan-in (in-degree), so reducing fan-in is desirable; however, this comes at the cost of increased depth and thus prediction latency. Therefore, in practice the actual architecture that is deployed may be somewhere in between the binary tree and the two-layer scheme. Nevertheless, we will study the binary tree structure further because it illustrates the distinctions relative to a simple linear prediction architecture.

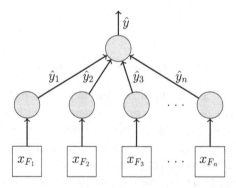

Figure 14.2 Architecture for no-delay multinode feature sharding.

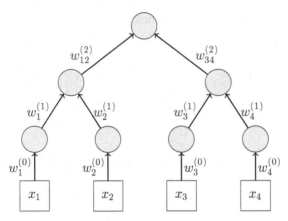

Figure 14.3 Hierarchical architecture for no-delay multinode feature sharding. Each edge is associated with a weight learned by the node at the arrowhead.

Convergence Time versus Representation Power

The price of the speedup that comes with the no-delay approach (even with the two-layer architecture) is paid in representation power. That is, the no-delay approach learns restricted forms of linear predictors relative to what can be learned by ordinary (delayed) gradient descent. To illustrate this, we compare the resulting predictors from the no-delay approach with the binary tree architecture and the single-node linear architecture. Let $x = (x_1, \ldots, x_n) \in \mathbb{R}^n$ be a random vector (note that the subscripts now index the features) and $y \in \mathbb{R}$ be a random variable. Gradient descent using a linear architecture converges toward the least-squares linear predictor of y from x, that is,

$$w^* := \arg \min_{w \in \mathbb{R}^n} \mathbf{E}\left[\frac{1}{2}(\langle x, w \rangle - y)^2\right] = \Sigma^{-1}b \in \mathbb{R}^n$$

where

$$\Sigma := \mathbf{E}[xx^\top] \in \mathbb{R}^{n \times n} \quad \text{and} \quad b := \mathbf{E}[xy] \in \mathbb{R}^n,$$

in time roughly linear in the number of features n (Haussler, Kivinen, and Warmuth, 1995).

The gradient descent strategy with the binary tree architecture, on the other hand, learns weights locally at each node; the weights at each node therefore converge to weights that are locally optimal for the input features supplied to the node. The final predictor is linear in the input features but can differ from the least-squares solution. To see this, note first that the leaf nodes learn weights $w_1^{(0)}, \ldots, w_n^{(0)}$, where

$$w_i^{(0)} := \frac{b_i}{\Sigma_{i,i}} \in \mathbb{R}.$$

Then, the $(k+1)$th layer of nodes learns weights from the predictions of the kth layer; recursively, a node whose input features are the predictions of the ith and jth nodes from layer k learns the weights $(w_i^{(k+1)}, w_j^{(k+1)}) \in \mathbb{R}^2$. By induction, the prediction of the ith node in layer k is linear in the subset S_i of variables that are descendants of this node in the binary tree. Let $w_{S_i}^{(k)} \in \mathbb{R}^{|S_i|}$ denote these weights and $x_{S_i} \in \mathbb{R}^{|S_i|}$ denote the corresponding feature vector. Then $(w_i^{(k+1)}, w_j^{(k+1)}) \in \mathbb{R}^2$ can be expressed as

$$
\begin{bmatrix} w_i^{(k+1)} \\ w_j^{(k+1)} \end{bmatrix} = \begin{bmatrix} \left\langle w_{S_i}^{(k)}, \Sigma_{S_i,S_i} w_{S_i}^{(k)} \right\rangle & \left\langle w_{S_i}^{(k)}, \Sigma_{S_i,S_j} w_{S_j}^{(k)} \right\rangle \\ \left\langle w_{S_j}^{(k)}, \Sigma_{S_j,S_i} w_{S_i}^{(k)} \right\rangle & \left\langle w_{S_j}^{(k)}, \Sigma_{S_j,S_j} w_{S_j}^{(k)} \right\rangle \end{bmatrix}^{-1} \begin{bmatrix} \left\langle w_{S_i}^{(k)}, b_{S_i} \right\rangle \\ \left\langle w_{S_j}^{(k)}, b_{S_j} \right\rangle \end{bmatrix}
$$

where $\Sigma_{S_i,S_j} = \mathbf{E}[x_{S_i} x_{S_j}^\top]$ and $b_{S_i} = \mathbf{E}[x_{S_i} y]$. Then, the prediction at this particular node in layer $k + 1$ is

$$
w_i^{(k+1)} \left\langle w_{S_i}^{(k)}, x_{S_i} \right\rangle + w_j^{(k+1)} \left\langle w_{S_j}^{(k)}, x_{S_j} \right\rangle,
$$

which is linear in (x_{S_i}, x_{S_j}). Therefore, the overall prediction is linear in x, with the weight attached to x_i being a product of weights at the different levels. However, these weights can differ significantly from w^* when the features are highly correlated, as the tree architecture only ever considers correlations between (say) x_{S_i} and x_{S_j} through the scalar summary $\left\langle w_{S_i}^{(k)}, \Sigma_{S_i,S_j} w_{S_j}^{(k)} \right\rangle$. Thus, the representational expressiveness of the binary tree architecture is constrained by the local training strategy.

The tree predictor can represent solutions with complexities between Naïve Bayes and a linear predictor. Naïve Bayes learns weights identical to the bottom layer of the binary tree, but stops there and combines the n individual predictions with a trivial sum: $w_1^{(0)} x_1 + \cdots + w_n^{(0)} x_n$. The advantage of Naïve Bayes is its convergence time: because the weights are learned independently, a union bound argument implies convergence in $O(\log n)$ time, which is exponentially faster than the $O(n)$ convergence time using the linear architecture!

The convergence time of gradient descent with the binary tree architecture is roughly $O(\log^2 n)$. To see this, note that the kth layer converges in roughly $O(\log(n/2^k))$ time because there are $n/2^k$ parameters that need to converge, plus the time for the $(k-1)$th layer to converge. Inductively, this is $O(\log n + \log(n/2) + \cdots + \log(n/2^k)) = O(k \log n)$. Thus, all of the weights have converged by the time the final layer ($k = \log_2 n$) converges; this gives an overall convergence time of $O(\log^2 n)$. This is slightly slower than Naïve Bayes, but still significantly faster than the single-node linear architecture.

The advantage of the binary tree architecture over Naïve Bayes is that it can account for variability in the prediction power of various feature shards, as the following result demonstrates.

Proposition 14.3 There exists a data distribution for which the binary tree architecture can represent the least-squares linear predictor but Naïve Bayes cannot.

PROOF Suppose the data comes from a uniform distribution over the following four points:

	x_1	x_2	x_3	y
Point 1	+1	+1	−1/2	+1
Point 2	+1	−1	−1	−1
Point 3	−1	−1	−1/2	+1
Point 4	−1	+1	+1	+1

Naïve Bayes yields the weights $w = (−1/2, 1/2, 2/5)$, which incurs mean squared-error 0.8. On the other hand, gradient descent with the binary tree architecture learns additional weights:

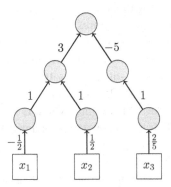

which ultimately yields an overall weight vector of

$$(−1/2 \cdot 1 \cdot 3, \ 1/2 \cdot 1 \cdot 3, \ 2/5 \cdot 1 \cdot −5) = (−3/2, \ 3/2, \ −2)$$

which has zero mean-squared error.   □

In the proof example, the features are, individually, equally correlated with the label y. However, the feature x_3 is correlated with the two individually uncorrelated features x_1 and x_2, but Naïve Bayes is unable to discover this, whereas the binary tree architecture can compensate for it.

Of course, as mentioned before, the binary tree architecture (and Naïve Bayes) is weaker than the single-node linear architecture in expressive power because of its limited accounting of feature correlation.

Proposition 14.4 There exists a data distribution for which neither the binary tree architecture nor Naïve Bayes can represent the least-squares linear predictor.

PROOF Suppose the data comes from a uniform distribution over the following four points:

	x_1	x_2	x_3	y
Point 1	+1	−1	−1	−1
Point 2	−1	+1	−1	−1
Point 3	+1	+1	−1	+1
Point 4	+1	+1	−1	+1

The optimal least-squares linear predictor is the all-ones vector $w^* = (1, 1, 1)$ and incurs zero squared-error (because $1 \cdot x_1 + 1 \cdot x_2 + 1 \cdot x_3 = y$ for every point). However, both Naïve Bayes and the binary tree architecture yield weight vectors in which zero weight is assigned to x_3, because x_3 is uncorrelated with y; any linear predictor that assigns zero weight to x_3 has expected squared error at least $1/2$. □

14.4.3 Experiments

Here, we detail experimental results conducted on a medium-sized proprietary ad display dataset. The task associated with the dataset is to derive a good policy for choosing an ad given user, ad, and page display features. This is accomplished via pairwise training concerning which of two ads was clicked on and element-wise evaluation with an offline policy evaluator (Langford, Strehl, and Wortman, 2008). There are several ways to measure the size of this dataset – it is about 100GB when gzip compressed, has around 10M instances, and has about 125G non-unique nonzero features. In the experiments, VW was run with $2^{24} \simeq 16M$ weights, which is substantially smaller than the number of unique features. This discrepancy is accounted for by the use of a hashing function, with 2^{24} being chosen because it is large enough such that a larger number of weights does not substantially improve results.

In the experimental results, we report the ratio of progressive validation squared losses (Blum, Kalai, and Langford, 1999) and wall clock times to a multicore parallelized version of Vowpal Wabbit running on the same data and the same machines. Here, the progressive validation squared loss is the average over t of $(y_t - \hat{y}_t)^2$ where critically, $\hat{y}_t$ is the prediction prior to an update. When data is independent, this metric has deviations similar to the average loss computed on held-out evaluation data.

Every node has eight CPU cores and is connected via gigabit Ethernet. All learning results are obtained with single-pass learning on the dataset using learning parameters optimized to control progressive validation loss. The precise variant of the multinode architecture we experimented with is detailed in Figure 14.4. In particular, note that we worked with a flat hierarchy using 1–8 feature shards (internal nodes). All code is available in the current Vowpal Wabbit open source code release.

Results are reported in Figure 14.5. The first thing to note in Figure 14.5a is that there is essentially no loss in time and precisely no loss in solution quality for using two machines (shard count = 1): one for a no-op shard (used only for sending data to the other nodes) and the other for learning. We also note that the running time does not decrease linearly in the number of shards, which is easily explained by saturation of the network by the no-op sharding node. Luckily, this is not a real bottleneck, because the process of sharding instances is stateless and (hence) completely parallelizable. As expected, the average solution quality across feature shards also clearly degrades with the shard count. This is because the increase in shard count implies a decrease in the number of features per nodes, which means each node is able to use less information on which to base its predictions.

On examination of Figure 14.5b, we encounter a major surprise – the quality of the final solution substantially improves over the single node solution because the relative squared loss is less than 1. We have carefully verified this. It is most stark when there

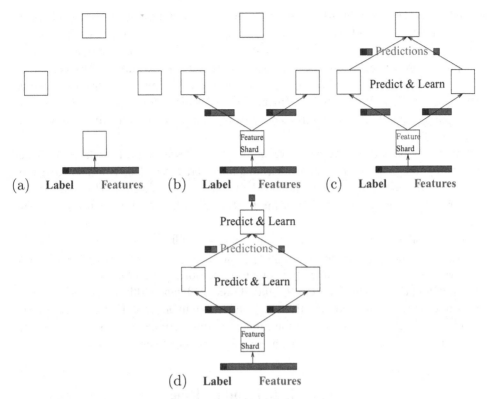

Figure 14.4 Diagram of the parallel algorithm used in the experiments. Step (a) starts with a full data instance. Step (b) splits the instance's features across each shard while replicating the label to each shard. In our experiments, the number of feature shards varies between 1 and 8. Step (c) does prediction and learning at each feature shard using only local information. Step (d) combines these local predictions, treating them as features for a final output prediction.

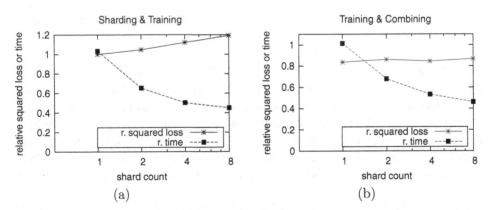

Figure 14.5 Plots of running time and loss versus shard count. (a) Ratio of time and progressive squared loss of the shard and local train steps to a multicore single-machine instance of VW. Here the squared loss reported is the average of the squared losses at each feature shard, without any aggregation at the final output node. (b) Ratio of time and squared loss for learning at the local nodes and passing information to the final output node where a final prediction is done.

is only one feature shard, where we know that the solution on that shard is identical to the single node solution. This output prediction is then thresholded to the interval [0, 1] (as the labels are either 0 or 1) and passed to a final prediction node that uses the prediction as a feature and one (default) constant feature to make a final prediction. This very simple final prediction step is where the large improvement in prediction quality occurs. Essentially, because there are only two features (one is constant!), the final output node performs a very careful calibration that substantially improves the squared loss.

Note that one may have the false intuition that because each node does linear prediction, the final output is equivalent to a linear predictor. This is in fact what was suggested in the previous description of the binary tree architecture. However, this is incorrect because of thresholding of the final prediction of each node to the interval [0,1].

Figure 14.5b shows that the improved solution quality degrades mildly with the number of feature shards and the running time is again not decreasing linearly. We believe this failure to scale linearly is due to limitations of Ethernet where the use of many small packets can result in substantially reduced bandwidth.

A basic question is: how effective is this algorithm in general? Further experiments on other datasets (later) show that the limited representational capacity does degrade performance on many other datasets, motivating us to consider global update rules.

14.5 Global Update Rules

So far we have outlined an architecture that lies in between Naïve Bayes and a linear model. In this section, we investigate various trade-offs between the efficiency of local training procedure of the previous section and the richer representation power of a linear model trained on a single machine. Before we describe these trade-offs, let us revisit the proof of Proposition 14.4. In that example, the node that gets the feature that is uncorrelated with the label learns a zero weight because its objective is to minimize its own loss, not the loss incurred by the final prediction at the root of the tree. This can be easily fixed if we are willing to communicate more information on each link. In particular, when the root of the tree has received all the information from its children, it can send back to them some information about its final prediction. Once a node receives some information from its master, it can send a similar message to its children. In what follows we show several different ways in which information can be propagated and dealt with on each node. We call these updates global because, in contrast to the local training of the previous section, they use information about the *final prediction of the system* to mitigate the problems that may arise from pure local training.

14.5.1 Delayed Global Update

An extreme example of global training is to avoid local training altogether and simply rely on the update from the master. At time t the subordinate node sends to its master a prediction p_t using its current weights and does not use the label until time $t + \tau$, when the master replies with the final prediction $\hat{y}_t$ of the system. At this point the subordinate node computes the gradient of the loss as if it had made the final prediction itself (i.e., it computes $g_{dg} = \frac{\partial \ell}{\partial \langle w,x \rangle}\big|_{\langle w,x \rangle = \hat{y}_t} x$, where x are the node's features) and updates its weights using this gradient.

14.5.2 Corrective Update

Another approach to global training is to allow local training when an instance is received but use the global training rule *and undo the local training* as soon as the final prediction is received. More formally, at time t the subordinate node sends a prediction p_t to its master and then updates its weights using the gradient $g = \frac{\partial \ell}{\partial \langle w,x \rangle}\big|_{\langle w,x \rangle = p_t} x$. At time $t + \tau$ it receives the final prediction $\hat{y}_t$ and updates its weights using $g_{cor} = \frac{\partial \ell}{\partial \langle w,x \rangle}\big|_{\langle w,x \rangle = \hat{y}_t} x - \frac{\partial \ell}{\partial \langle w,x \rangle}\big|_{\langle w,x \rangle = p_t} x$. The rationale for using local training is that it might be better than doing nothing while waiting for the master, as in the case of the delayed global update. However, once the final prediction is available, there is little reason to retain the effect of local training, and the update makes sure it is forgotten.

14.5.3 Delayed Back-Propagation

Our last update rule treats the whole tree as a composition of linear functions and uses the chain rule of calculus to compute the gradients in each layer of the architecture. For example, the tree of Figure 14.3 computes the function

$$f(x) = w_{12}^{(2)} f_{12}(x_1, x_2) + w_{34}^{(2)} f_{34}(x_3, x_4)$$
$$f_{12}(x_1, x_2) = w_1^{(1)} f_1(x_1) + w_2^{(1)} f_2(x_2)$$
$$f_{34}(x_3, x_4) = w_3^{(1)} f_3(x_3) + w_4^{(1)} f_4(x_4)$$
$$f_j(x_j) = w_j^{(0)} x_j \quad j = 1, 2, 3, 4.$$

As before let $\hat{y} = f(x)$ and $\ell(\hat{y}, y)$ be our loss. Then partial derivatives of ℓ with respect to any parameter $w_i^{(j)}$ can be obtained by the chain rule as shown in the following examples:

$$\frac{\partial \ell}{\partial w_3^{(1)}} = \frac{\partial \ell}{\partial f} \frac{\partial f}{\partial f_{34}} \frac{\partial f_{34}}{\partial w_3^{(1)}} = \frac{\partial \ell(\hat{y}, y)}{\partial \hat{y}} w_{34}^{(2)} f_3$$

$$\frac{\partial \ell}{\partial w_3^{(0)}} = \frac{\partial \ell}{\partial f} \frac{\partial f}{\partial f_{34}} \frac{\partial f_{34}}{\partial f_3} \frac{\partial f_3}{\partial w_3^{(0)}} = \frac{\partial \ell(\hat{y}, y)}{\partial \hat{y}} w_{34}^{(2)} w_3^{(1)} x_3$$

Notice here the modularity implied by the chain rule: once the node that outputs f_{34} has computed $\frac{\partial \ell}{\partial w_3^{(1)}}$, it can send to its subordinate nodes the product $\frac{\partial \ell(\hat{y}, y)}{\partial \hat{y}} w_{34}^{(2)}$ as well as the weight it uses to weigh their predictions (i.e., $w_3^{(1)}$ in the case of the node that outputs f_3). The subordinate nodes then have all the necessary information to compute partial derivatives with respect to their own weights. The chain rule suggests that nodes whose predictions are important for the next level are going to be updated more aggressively than nodes whose predictions are effectively ignored in the next level.

The preceding procedure is essentially the same as the back-propagation procedure, the standard way of training with many layers of learned transformations as in multi-layer neural networks. In that case the composition of simple nonlinear functions yields improved representational power. Here the gain from using a composition of linear functions is not in representational power, because $f(x)$ remains linear in x, but in the improved scalability of the system.

Another difference from the back-propagation procedure is the inevitable delay between the time of the prediction and the time of the update. In particular, at time t the subordinate node performs local training and then sends a prediction $\bar{p}_t$ using the updated weights. At time $t + \tau$ it receives from the master the gradient of the loss with respect to $\bar{p}_t$: $g = \frac{\partial \ell}{\partial \bar{p}_t}\Big|_{\langle w,x \rangle = \hat{y}_t}$. It then computes the gradient of the loss with respect to its weights using the chain rule: $g_{bp} = g \cdot \frac{\partial \bar{p}_t}{\partial w}$. Finally, the weights are updated using this gradient.

14.5.4 Minibatch Gradient Descent

Another class of delay-tolerant algorithms is "minibatch" approaches that aggregate predictions from several (but not all) examples before making an aggregated update. Minibatch has even been advocated over gradient descent itself (see Shalev-Shwartz, Singer, and Srebro, 2007), with the basic principle being that a less noisy update is possible after some amount of averaging.

A minibatch algorithm could be implemented either on an example shard organized data (as per Dekel et al., 2010) or on feature shard organized data. On an example shard-based system, minibatch requires transmitting and aggregating the gradients of all features for an example. In terms of bandwidth requirements, this is potentially much more expensive than a minibatch approach on a feature shard system, regardless of whether the features are sparse or dense. On the latter only a few bytes/examples are required to transmit individual and joint predictions at each node. Specifically, the minibatch algorithms use global training without any delay: once the master has sent all the gradients in the minibatch to its subordinate nodes, they perform an update and the next minibatch is processed.

Processing the examples in minibatches reduces the variance of the used gradient by a factor of b (the minibatch size) compared to computing the gradient based on one example. However, the model is updated only once every b examples, slowing convergence.

Online gradient descent has two properties that might make it insensitive to the advantage provided by the minibatch gradient:

- Gradient descent is a somewhat crude method: it immediately forgets the gradient after it uses it. Contrast this with, say, bundle methods (Teo et al., 2009), which use the gradients to construct a global approximation of the loss.
- Gradient descent is very robust. In other words, gradient descent converges even if provided with gradient estimates of bounded variance.

Our experiments in the next section confirm our suspicions and show that, for simple gradient descent, the optimal minibatch size is $b = 1$.

14.5.5 Minibatch Conjugate Gradient

The drawbacks of simple gradient descent suggest that a gradient computed on a minibatch might be more beneficial to a more refined learning algorithm. An algorithm that is slightly more sophisticated than gradient descent is the nonlinear conjugate gradient (CG) method. Nonlinear CG can be thought as gradient descent with momentum where principled ways for setting the momentum and the step sizes are used. Empirically, CG can converge much faster than gradient descent when noise does not drive it too far astray.

Apart from the weight vector w_t, nonlinear CG maintains a direction vector d_t, and updates are performed in the following way:

$$d_t = -g_t + \beta_t d_{t-1}$$
$$w_{t+1} = w_t + \alpha_t d_t$$

where $g_t = \sum_{\tau \in m(t)} \nabla_w \ell(\langle w, x_\tau \rangle, y_\tau)\big|_{w=w_t}$ is the gradient computed on the tth minibatch of examples, denoted by $m(t)$. We set β_t according to a widely used formula (Gilbert and Nocedal, 1992):

$$\beta_t = \max \left\{ 0, \frac{\langle g_t, g_t - g_{t-1} \rangle}{||g_{t-1}||^2} \right\},$$

which most of the time is maximized by the second term, known as the Polak-Ribière update. Occasionally $\beta_t = 0$ effectively reverts back to gradient descent. Finally, α_t is set by minimizing a quadratic approximation of the loss, given by its Taylor expansion at the current point:

$$\alpha_t = -\frac{\langle g_t, d_t \rangle}{\langle d_t, H_t d_t \rangle}$$

where H_t is the Hessian of the loss at w_t on the tth minibatch. This procedure avoids an expensive line search and takes advantage of the simple form of the Hessian of a decomposable loss, which allows fast computation of the denominator. In general, $H_t = \sum_{\tau \in m(t)} \ell''_\tau x_\tau x_\tau^\top$ where $\ell''_\tau = \frac{\partial^2 \ell(\hat{y}, y_\tau)}{\partial \hat{y}^2}\big|_{\hat{y}=\langle w_t, x_\tau \rangle}$ is the second derivative of the loss with respect to the prediction for the τth example in the minibatch $m(t)$. Hence the denominator is simply $\langle d_t, H_t d_t \rangle = \sum_{\tau \in m(t)} \ell''_\tau \langle d_t, x_\tau \rangle^2$.

At first glance it seems that updating w_t will be an operation involving two dense vectors. However, we have worked out a way to perform these operations in a lazy fashion so that all updates are sparse. To see how this could work, assume for now that $\beta_t = \beta$ is fixed throughout the algorithm and that the ith element of the gradient is nonzero at times t_0 and $t_1 > t_0$ and zero for all times τ in between. We immediately see that

$$d_{i,\tau} = \prod_{s=t_0}^{\tau} \beta_s d_{i,t_0} = d_{i,t_0} \beta^{\tau-t_0}.$$

Hence, we can compute the direction at any time by storing a timestamp for each weight recording its last modification time. To handle the case of varying β, we first conceptually split the algorithm's run in phases. A new phase starts whenever

$\beta_t = 0$, which effectively restarts the CG method. Hence, within each phase $\beta_t \neq 0$. To compute the direction, we need to keep track of B_t, the cumulative product of the β's from the beginning of the phase up to time t, and use $\prod_{s=t_0}^{\tau} \beta_s = \frac{B_\tau}{B_{t_0}}$. Next, because each direction d_t changes w by a different amount α_t in each iteration, we must keep track of $A_t = \sum_{s=1}^{t} \alpha_s B_s$. Finally, at time t the update for a weight whose feature i was last seen at time τ is

$$w_{t,i} = w_{\tau,i} + \frac{A_t - A_{\tau-1}}{B_\tau} d_{\tau,i}.$$

14.5.6 Determinizing the Updates

In all of the preceding updates, delay plays an important role. Because of the physical constraints of the communication, the delay τ can be different for each instance and for each node. This can have an adverse effect on the reproducibility of our results. To see this, it suffices to think about the first time a leaf node receives a response. If that varies, then the number of instances for which this node will send a prediction of zero to its master varies, too. Hence, the weights that will be learned are going to be different. To alleviate this problem and ensure reproducible results, our implementation takes special care to impose a deterministic schedule of updates. This has also helped in the development and debugging of our implementation. Currently, the subordinate node switches between local training on new instances and global training on old instances in a round-robin fashion, after an initial period of local training only, that maintains $\tau = 1024$ (which is half the size of the node's buffer). In other words, the subordinate node will wait for a response from its master if doing otherwise would cause $\tau > 1024$. It would also wait for instances to become available if doing otherwise would cause $\tau < 1024$, unless the node is processing the last 1024 instances in the training set.

14.6 Experiments

Here we experimentally compare the predictive performance of the local, the global, and the centralized update rules. We derived classification tasks from the two datasets described in Table 14.1, trained predictors using each training algorithm, and then measured performance on separate test sets. For each algorithm, we perform a separate search for the best learning rate schedule of the form $\eta_t = \frac{\lambda}{\sqrt{t+t_0}}$ with $\lambda \in \{2^i\}_{i=0}^{9}$, $t_0 \in \{10^i\}_{i=0}^{6}$. We report results with the best learning rate we found for each algorithm and task. For the minibatch case we report a minibatch size of 1024, but we also tried smaller sizes, even though there is little evidence that they can be parallelized efficiently.

Table 14.1. *Description of datasets in global experiments.*

Name	# Training Data	# Testing Data
RCV1	780K	23K
Webspam	300K	50K

Finally, we report the performance of a centralized stochastic gradient descent (SGD) that corresponds to minibatch gradient descent with a batch size of 1.

We omit results for the Delayed Global and Corrective update rules because they have serious issues with delayed feedback. Imagine trying to control a system (say, driving a car) that responds to actions after much delay. Every time an action is taken (such as steering in one direction) it is not clear how much it has affected the response of the system. If our strategy is to continue performing the same action until its effect is noticeable, it is likely that by the time we receive all the delayed feedback, we will have produced an effect much larger than we desired. To reduce the effect, we can try to undo our action, which of course can produce an effect much smaller than what was desirable. The system then oscillates around the desired state and never converges there. This is exactly what happens with the delayed global and corrective update rules. Delayed back-propagation is less susceptible to this problem because the update is based on both the global and the local gradient. Minibatch approaches completely sidestep this problem because the information they use is always a gradient at the current weight vector.

In Figure 14.6 we report our results on each dataset. We plot the test accuracy of each algorithm under different settings. "Backprop $\times 8$" is the same as backprop where the gradient from the master is multiplied by 8 (we also tried 2, 4, and 16 and obtained qualitatively similar results) – we tried this variant as a heuristic way to balance the relative importance of the backprop update and that of the local update. In the first row of Figure 14.6, we show that the performance of both local and global learning rules degrades as the degree of parallelization (number of workers) increases. However, this effect is somewhat lessened with multiple passes through the training data and is milder for the delayed backprop variants, as shown in in the second row for the case of 16 passes. In the third and fourth rows, we show how performance improves with the number of passes through the training data, using 1 worker and 16 workers. Notice that SGD, Minibatch, and CG are not affected by the number of workers because they are global-only methods. Among these methods, SGD dominates CG, which in turn dominates minibatch. However, SGD is not parallelizable, whereas minibatch CG is.

14.7 Conclusion

Our core approach to scaling up and parallelizing learning is to first take a very fast learning algorithm and then speed it up even more. We found that a core difficulty with this is dealing with the problem of delay in online learning. In adversarial situations, delay can reduce convergence speed by the delay factor, with no improvement over the original serial learning algorithm.

We addressed these issues with parallel algorithms based on feature sharding. The first is simply a very fast multicore algorithm that manages to avoid any delay in weight updates by virtue of the low latency between cores. The second approach, designed for multinode settings, addresses the latency issue by trading some loss of representational power for local-only updates, with the big surprise that this second algorithm actually

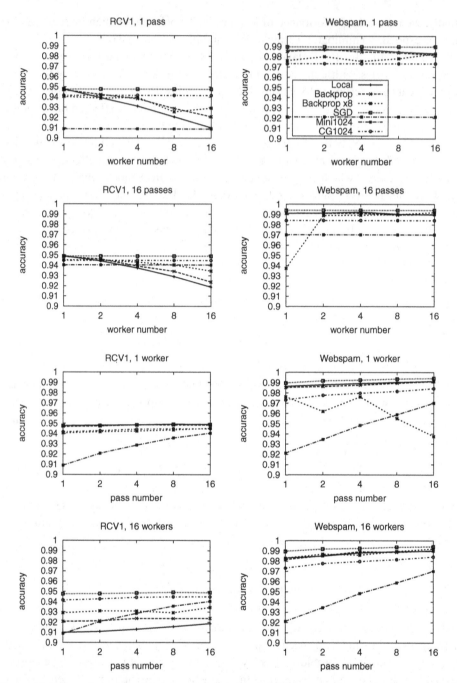

Figure 14.6 Experimental results compare global to local learning rules. In the first two rows, we see how performance degrades for various rules as the number of workers increases. In the last two rows, we show how performance changes with multiple passes. All plots share the same legend, shown in the top right plot.

improved performance in some cases. The loss of representational power can be addressed by incorporating global updates either based on back-propagation on top of the local updates or using a minibatch conjugate gradient method; experimentally, we observed that the combination of local and global updates can improve performance significantly over the local-only updates.

The speedups we have found so far are relatively mild because of working with a relatively small number of cores and a relatively small number of nodes. Given that we are starting with an extraordinarily fast baseline algorithm, these results are unsurprising. A possibility does exist that great speedups can be achieved on a large cluster of machines, but this requires further investigation.

References

Amari, S. 1967. A Theory of Adaptive Pattern Classifiers. *IEEE Transactions on Electronic Computers*, **16**, 299–307.

Blum, A., Kalai, A., and Langford, J. 1999. Beating the Hold-out: Bounds for *k*-Fold and Progressive Cross-Validation. Pages 203–208 of: *Proceedings of 12th Annual Conference on Computational Learning Theory*. New York: ACM.

Bottou, Léon. 2008. *Stochastic Gradient SVMs*. http://leon.bottou.org/projects/sgd.

Bryson, A. E., and Ho, Y.-C. 1969. *Applied Optimal Control: Optimization, Estimation, and Control*. Blairsdell.

Chu, C., Kim, S. K., Lin, Y., Yu, Y., Bradski, G., Ng, A. Y., and Olukotun, K. 2007. Map-Reduce for Machine Learning on Multicore. In: *Neural Information Processing Systems (NIPS) 19*.

Dekel, O., Gilad-Bachrach, R., Shamir, O., and Xiao, L. 2010. Optimal Distributed Online Prediction using Mini-Batches. In: *Learning on Cores, Clusters, and Clouds Workshop*.

Gilbert, J. C., and Nocedal, J. 1992. Global Convergence Properties of Conjugate Gradient Methods for Optimization. *SIAM Journal on Optimization*, **2**(1), 21–42.

Haussler, D., Kivinen, J., and Warmuth, M. K. 1995. Tight Worst-Case Loss Bounds for Predicting with Expert Advice. Pages 69–83 of: *Computational Learning Theory: EuroColt '95*. New York: Springer.

Langford, J., Li, L., and Strehl, A. 2007. *Vowpal Wabbit Online Learning Project*. http://hunch.net/?p=309.

Langford, J., Strehl, A., and Wortman, J. 2008. Exploration Scavenging. In: *Proceedings of International Conference on Machine Learning (ICML)*.

Langford, J., Smola, A.J., and Zinkevich, M. 2009. *Slow Learners Fast*. arXiv:0911.0491.

Lewis, D. D., Yang, Y., Rose, T. G., and Li, F. 2004. RCV1: A New Benchmark Collection for Text Categorization Research. *Journal of Machine Learning Research*, **5**, 361–397.

Mann, G., McDonald, R., Mohri, M., Silberman, N., and Walker, D. 2009. Efficient Large-Scale Distributed Training of Conditional Maximum Entropy Models. In: *Neural Information Processing Systems (NIPS)*.

McDonald, R., Hall, K., and Mann, G. 2010. Distributed Training Strategies for the Structured Perceptron. In: *North American Association for Computational Linguistics (NAACL)*.

Rahimi, A., and Recht, B. 2008. Random Features for Large-Scale Kernel Machines. In: Platt, J. C., Koller, D., Singer, Y., and Roweis, S. (eds), *Advances in Neural Information Processing Systems 20*. Cambridge, MA: MIT Press.

Rosenblatt, F. 1958. The Perceptron: A Probabilistic Model for Information Storage and Organization in the Brain. *Psychological Review*, **65**(6), 386–408.

Rumelhart, D. E., Hinton, G. E., and Williams, R. J. 1986. Learning Internal Representations by Error Propagation. Pages 318–362 of: *Parallel Distributed Processing*. Cambridge, MA: MIT Press.

Shalev-Shwartz, S., Singer, Y., and Srebro, N. 2007. Pegasos: Primal Estimated sub-GrAdient Solver for SVM. In: *Proceedings of International Conference on Machine Learning*.

Shi, Q., Petterson, J., Dror, G., Langford, J., Smola, A., Strehl, A., and Vishwanathan, S. V. N. 2009. *Hash Kernels*. Society for Artificial Intelligence and Statistics.

Teo, C. H., Vishwanthan, S. V. N., Smola, A. J., and Le, Q. V. 2009. Bundle Methods for Regularized Risk Minimization. *Journal of Machine Learning Research*, **11**, 311–365.

Weinberger, K., Dasgupta, A., Attenberg, J., Langford, J., and Smola, A. J. 2009. Feature Hashing for Large Scale Multitask Learning. In: Bottou, L., and Littman, M. (eds), *International Conference on Machine Learning*.

CHAPTER 15

Parallel Graph-Based
Semi-Supervised Learning

Jeff Bilmes and Amarnag Subramanya

Semi-supervised learning (SSL) is the process of training decision functions using small amounts of labeled and relatively large amounts of unlabeled data. In many applications, annotating training data is time consuming and error prone. Speech recognition is the typical example, which requires large amounts of meticulously annotated speech data (Evermann et al., 2005) to produce an accurate system. In the case of document classification for internet search, it is not even feasible to accurately annotate a relatively large number of web pages for all categories of potential interest. SSL lends itself as a useful technique in many machine learning applications because one need annotate only relatively small amounts of the available data. SSL is related to the problem of *transductive learning* (Vapnik, 1998). In general, a learner is transductive if it is designed for prediction on only a closed dataset, where the test set is revealed at training time. In practice, however, transductive learners can be modified to handle unseen data (Sindhwani, Niyogi, and Belkin, 2005; Zhu, 2005a). Chapter 25 in Chapelle, Scholkopf, and Zien (2007) gives a full discussion on the relationship between SSL and transductive learning. In this chapter, SSL refers to the semi-supervised transductive classification problem.

Let $\mathbf{x} \in \mathbf{X}$ denote the input to the decision function (classifier), f, and $y \in Y$ denote its output label, that is, $f : \mathbf{X} \to Y$. In most cases $f(\mathbf{x}) = \text{argmax}_{y \in Y}\, p(y|\mathbf{x})$. In SSL, certain reasonable assumptions are made so that properties of the distribution $p(\mathbf{x})$ (which is available from the unlabeled data sampled from $p(\mathbf{x})$) can influence $p(y|\mathbf{x})$. These assumptions are as follows:

1. *Manifold Assumption* – The data items $\mathbf{x} \in \mathbf{X}$ lie on a low-dimensional manifold embedded within a high-dimensional space. There are two ways to interpret this. First, the data may lie, irrespective of class, on one global low-dimensional manifold embedded within a high-dimensional space. Second, the data for each class might lie on its own specific manifold, and the manifolds for different classes might or might not intersect. Although the first case is more commonly discussed, in either case the decision boundary between classes can be more accurately determined using not only the labeled but also the unlabeled data.

2. *Smoothness Assumption* – If two points x_1 and x_2 in a high-density region are close based on a given distance measure on X (which might depend on the manifold), then their corresponding output labels are also likely to be close or identical. Stated differently, a decision boundary between classes will lie in a low-density region. A third way to state this is, if between two points there exists a trajectory that always lies within the same connected high-density region, then the two points will likely have the same label. Here, a high-density region is a subset of X that has high probability according to $p(x)$. This is sometimes also called the *cluster assumption*.

These assumptions often being essentially true for real-world data is the reason why a large set of semi-supervised learning algorithms work quite well for many applications.

SSL has a long history of previous research. Early work includes methods such as *self-training* (Scudder, 1965), which involves training the decision function using data annotated during a previous classification run over the unlabeled data. This so-called labeled data needs to be carefully chosen and/or filtered, or else it would amount to adding noise (i.e., incorrectly labeled samples) to the training set. In general, self-training offers no guarantees except under certain conditions (Haffari and Sarkar, 2007). *Co-training* is a related algorithm where one uses two sets of decision functions with one learning from the output of the other and vice versa. The co-training algorithm is one of the more well-studied SSL algorithms (Goldman and Zhou, 2000; Balcan and Blum, 2005). *Expectation-maximization* (EM) (Dempster et al., 1977; Bilmes, 1998) can also be seen as an SSL algorithm. EM is a general procedure to maximize the likelihood of data given a model with hidden variables and is guaranteed to converge to a local optimum. EM lends itself naturally to SSL because the labels of the unlabeled samples can be treated as missing (or hidden). Examples of algorithms that use EM within a SSL setting include Hosmer (1973), Nigam (2001), and McLachlan, and Ganesalingam (1982). Self-training, co-training, and EM all make use of the smoothness assumption in one way or another.

Transductive support vector machines (TSVM) (Vapnik, 1998) are based on the premise that the decision boundary must avoid high-density regions in the input space (i.e., the low-density separation assumption). They are related to support vector machines (SVM) used for supervised learning. Computing the exact TSVM solution is in general NP hard and a number of approximation algorithms have been proposed (Zhu, 2005a). Gaussian processes with a "null category noise model" are yet another technique for SSL (Lawrence and Jordan, 2005) and are related to TSVMs.

Graph-based SSL algorithms are an important sub-class of SSL techniques that have received much attention in the recent past (Blum and Chawla, 2001; Zhu, Ghahramani, and Lafferty, 2003; Joachims, 2003; Belkin, Niyogi, and Sindhwani, 2005; Corduneanu and Jaakkola, 2003; Tsuda, 2005; Szummer and Jaakkola, 2001; Zhu and Ghahramani, 2002a; Zhu, 2005a; Chapelle, Scholkopf, and Zien, 2007; Subramanya and Bilmes, 2008, 2009b,a, in press). Here one assumes that the data (both labeled and unlabeled) lies on a low-dimensional manifold that may be reasonably approximated by a graph (this constitutes the manifold assumption). Each data sample is represented by a vertex in an edge-weighted graph with the weights providing a measure of similarity between vertices. We discuss graph-based SSL in Section 15.2. We refer the reader to Seeger

(2000), Zhu (2005a), Chapelle et al. (2007), Blitzer and Zhu (2008), and Zhu and Goldberg (2009) for additional discussion regarding SSL in general.

In the present chapter, we discuss the scalability to very large problems sizes (>100 million nodes) of graph-based SSL algorithms on different types of parallel machines, either shared-memory symmetric multi-processors (SMPs) or distributed computers. A common feature of most graph-based algorithms that we exploit is that their optimization can be expressed as simple and efficient messages passed along edges of the graph (see Figure 15.1). This is also true of a recent graph-based SSL algorithm proposed by the authors that seems to perform better than most other graph-based SSL algorithms (Subramanya and Bilmes, 2009a, in press). For shared-memory SMPs, we propose a simple generic linear-time (in the number of graph nodes) cache-cognizant node ordering heuristic to improve the efficiency of message passing. On distributed computers, we propose a modification of this heuristic that is still linear time and generic, but that is more intelligent regarding the nonuniform memory access on such machines. We test these heuristics on a large semi-supervised learning task consisting of a graph with 120 million nodes and show that for both a 16-node SMP and a 1000-node distributed computer, significant improvements in machine efficiency can be obtained.

15.1 Scaling SSL to Large Datasets

Because SSL is based on the premise that unlabeled data is easily obtained and adding large quantities of unlabeled data leads to improved performance,[1] it is important that SSL algorithms scale easily to large amounts of (unlabeled) data. In recent times, the degree to which an algorithm scales has become practically synonymous with the ease and efficiency at which it can be parallelized.

In general, previous work has focused more on improving SSL algorithms and less on parallelization. For example, in the case of TSVMs, which as stated previously are NP hard, early work could handle only a few thousand samples (Bie and Cristianini, 2003). Therefore, Collobert et al. (2006) proposed a method based on the convex-concave procedure (CCCP) to scale TSVMs to larger dataset sizes. More recently, Sindhwani and Selvaraj (2006) proposed an efficient implementation of TSVMs with linear kernels suitable for text applications. Current state-of-the-art TSVMs can handle only tens of thousands of samples when using an arbitrary kernel. For example, Karlen et al. (2008) report that for a problem with about 70,000 samples (both labeled and unlabeled included), a CCCP-TSVM took about 42 hours to train.

In the case of graph-based approaches, Delalleau, Bengio, and Roux (2005) proposed to create a small graph with a subset of the unlabeled data, thereby enabling fast computation. We are not aware, however, of a published principled algorithm to choose such a subset. Garcke and Griebel (2005) proposed the use of sparse grid for semi-supervised learning. The idea was to approximate the function space with a finite basis with sparse grids. Although their approach scales linearly in the number of

---

[1] Note that there are recent exceptions (Nadler, Srebro, and Zhou, 2010) where more data can in fact hurt certain algorithms.

samples, in practice it works only for relatively low-dimensional (< 20) data. Karlen et al. (2008) solved a graph transduction problem with 650,000 samples using a neural network. They made use of standard stochastic gradient techniques to scale the approach. However, the lack of convexity of the neural network training objective means that there are no convergence guarantees. Gradient-based approaches, moreover, pose other challenges such as the setting of learning rates and convergence criteria. Note that we are not arguing against the general use of stochastic gradient techniques to find optima of nonconvex objectives (e.g., the discriminative training of hidden Markov models [HMMs], or our own previous work on the semi-supervised training of parametric discriminative classifiers [Malkin, Subramanya, and Bilmes, 2009]); however, when other convex alternatives are available (such as the ones described later) and are suitable for a given application, and when they work well in practice, it may be more prudent to use the convex formulations. To the best of our knowledge, the largest graph-based SSL problem solved to date had about 900,000 samples (including both labeled and unlabeled data) (Tsang and Kwok, 2006). Clearly, this is a fraction of the amount of unlabeled data at our disposal. For example, on the internet, society creates more than 1.6 billion blog posts, 60 billion emails, 2 million photos, and 200,000 videos every day (Tomkins, 2008). SSL holds promise to produce a proper and practical taxonomy of this enormous wealth of information.

15.2 Graph-Based SSL

In general, graph-based SSL algorithms often have a global objective (see, e.g., Section 15.2.2). This objective might even be convex and have an analytic solution that uses matrix inversion (Zhu et al., 2003; Belkin et al., 2005) or eigen-based matrix decomposition (Joachims, 2003), but because of the inherent $O(m^3)$ computation associated with these approaches (where m is the dataset size), they are difficult to scale to large problems.

We are interested in graph-based SSL algorithms, however, for the following important reasons:

1. Time and again, and for many applications, they have performed better than most other SSL algorithms in comparative evaluations (see chapter 21 in Chapelle et al., 2007).
2. Most graph-based methods have a convex objective, thereby providing convergence guarantees, making them attractive for solving large-scale problems.
3. For most graph-based SSL approaches, optimizing the objective can be achieved via message passing on graphs. Each iteration of the algorithm consists of a set of updates to each graph node. An updated node value is computed based on the node's current value as well as the neighbors' current set of values (see Figure 15.1). Unlike other algorithms such as Transductive SVMs that require a specialized design and implementation, a majority of the graph-based SSL algorithms may be represented within this common framework of message passing with respect to a given graph (further discussion of this framework is given in Section).
4. The message-passing approach to optimizing a graph-based SSL objective will often have its own convergence guarantees. For example, it can sometimes be shown that the

simple message-passing algorithm linearly converges to the true global optimum of the convex objective (Subramanya and Bilmes, in press).

5. It is possible (as we show in the present chapter) to derive simple fast heuristics that enable such algorithms to scale to large parallel machines with good machine efficiency.

Graph-based SSL algorithms broadly fall under two categories – those that use the graph structure to spread labels from labeled to unlabeled samples (Szummer and Jaakkola, 2001; Zhu and Ghahramani, 2002a; Baluja et al., 2008) and those that optimize a loss function based on smoothness constraints derived from the graph (Blum and Chawla, 2001; Zhu, Ghahramani, and Lafferty, 2003; Joachims, 2003; Belkin et al., 2005; Corduneanu and Jaakkola, 2003; Tsuda, 2005). These categories, however, are often different only in form rather than in their underlying goal. For example, label propagation (Zhu and Ghahramani, 2002a) and the harmonic functions algorithm (Zhu, Ghahramani, and Lafferty, 2003; Bengio, Delalleau, and Roux, 2007) optimize a similar loss function (Zhu, 2005b; Bengio et al., 2007). Next, we describe some of the previous work in graph-based SSL in more detail.

Spectral graph transduction (SGT) (Joachims, 2003) is an approximate solution to the NP-hard normalized cut problem. The use of norm-cut instead of a min-cut (as in Blum and Chawla, 2001) ensures that the number of unlabeled samples in each side of the cut is more balanced. SGT requires that one compute the eigen-decomposition of an $m \times m$ matrix, which can be challenging for very large datasets (where m is the total number of samples in the dataset). *Manifold regularization* (Belkin et al., 2005) proposes a general framework where a parametric loss function is defined over the labeled samples and is regularized by a graph smoothness term defined over both the labeled and unlabeled samples. When the loss function satisfies certain conditions, it can be shown that the representer theorem applies and so the solution is a weighted sum over kernel computations. The goal of the learning process is thus to discover these weights. When the parametric loss function is based on least squares, the approach is referred to as *Laplacian Regularized Least Squares* (LapRLS) (Belkin et al., 2005) and when the loss function is based on hinge loss, the approach is called *Laplacian Support Vector Machines* (LapSVM) (Belkin et al., 2005). In the case of LapRLS, the weights have a closed-form solution that involves inverting an $m \times m$ matrix, whereas in the case of LapSVM, optimization techniques used for SVM training may be used to solve for the weights. In general, it has been observed that LapRLS and LapSVM give similar performance (see chapter 21 in Chapelle et al., 2007). Note that although LapSVM minimizes hinge loss (over the labeled samples), which is considered more optimal than squared loss for classification, the graph regularizer is still based on squared error.

A majority of the graph-based SSL algorithms discussed previously attempt to minimize squared loss. Although squared loss is optimal under a Gaussian noise model, it is not optimal in the case of classification problems. We discuss more about the relative merits of using a squared-loss based objective in Section 15.2.2. Another potential drawback in the case of some graph-based SSL algorithms (Blum and Chawla, 2001; Joachims, 2003; Belkin et al., 2005) is that they assume binary classification tasks and thus require the use of suboptimal (and often computationally expensive) approaches such as one versus rest to solve multi-class problems. Yet another issue relates to the use of priors – most graph-based SSL algorithms are not capable of tightly integrating

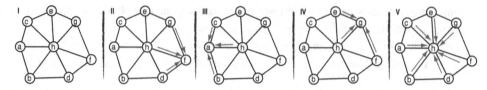

Figure 15.1 I: A graph $G = (V, E)$ with $V = \{a, b, c, d, e, f, g, h\}$ and edges as indicated. II–V: Various messages on the graphs are given. For example, in II, node f is being processed, which requires reading information not only from f but also from all of f's neighbors $\mathbf{N}(f) = \{d, g, h\}$ – this essentially constitutes a "message" being sent to node f from its neighbors.

priors into their training objective. To address the preceding issues, in Subramanya and Bilmes (2008, 2009a, in press), we have proposed a graph-based SSL algorithm based on minimizing *Kullback-Leibler divergence* (KLD) between probability distributions that we call *Measure Propagation*. We discuss this in more detail in Section 15.2.2. Next, we describe the two stages of solving a semi-supervised learning problem using graph-based methods–(I) graph construction and (II) the use of the graph as a regularizer to solve the graph-based SSL problem.

15.2.1 Graph Construction

Let $\mathcal{D}_l = \{(\mathbf{x}_i, r_i)\}_{i=1}^{l}$ be the set of labeled samples, $\mathcal{D}_u = \{\mathbf{x}_i\}_{i=l+1}^{l+u}$ the set of unlabeled samples and tr $\overset{\triangle}{=} \{\mathcal{D}_l, \mathcal{D}_u\}$. Here r_i is an encoding of the labeled data and will be explained shortly. We are interested in solving the transductive learning problem, that is, given tr, the task is to predict the labels of the samples in $\mathcal{D}_u$ (for inductive extensions, see Subramanya and Bilmes, 2009a, in press). We are given an undirected weighted graph $\mathbf{G} = (V, E)$, where the vertices (equivalently nodes) $V = \{1, \ldots, m\}$ (with $m = l + u$) represent the data points in tr and the edges $E \subseteq V \times V$ connect related nodes. Let $V_l \cup V_u = V$ be a partition of V where V_l is the set of labeled vertices and V_u the set of unlabeled vertices. $\mathbf{G}$ may be represented via a matrix $\mathbf{W} = \{w_{ij}\}_{i,j}$ with nonnegative values referred to as the weight or affinity matrix. If $w_{ij} > 0$, we say that vertices i and j are adjacent or are neighbors in G. Given a vertex $v \in V$, let $\mathbf{N}(v) \subseteq V$ denote the set of neighbors of the vertex v, and given a set $S \subset V$, let $\mathbf{N}(S) \subseteq V$ be the set of neighbors of nodes in S. Thus, by definition, $\mathbf{N}(v) = \mathbf{N}(\{v\})$ for a single vertex v. For example, in Figure 15.1-I, $\mathbf{N}(a) = \{c, h, b\}$ and $\mathbf{N}(\{a, f\}) = \{c, h, b, d, g\}$. Also, $\mathbf{N}(S)$ might include some or all of S when $|S| > 1$–in the figure, $\mathbf{N}(\{a, b\}) = \{c, h, d, a, b\}$, so $\mathbf{N}(S) \setminus S$ is the set of neighbors of S not including S. In this work, no two vertices have more than one edge between them, and thus $|\mathbf{N}(i)|$ represents vertex i's degree.

There are many ways of constructing a graph for a given dataset. In some applications, it might be a natural result of a relationship between the samples in tr. For example, consider the case where each vertex represents a web page and the edges represent the links between web pages. In other cases, such as the work of Wang and Zhang (2006), the graph is generated by performing an operation similar to local linear embedding (LLE) with the constraint that the LLE weights are nonnegative. In the majority of applications, including those considered in this chapter, we use *k*-nearest neighbor (k-NN) graphs. In fact, we make use of symmetric k-NN graphs with edge weights $w_{ij} = [\mathbf{W}]_{ij}$ given by

$$w_{ij} = \begin{cases} \text{sim}(\mathbf{x}_i, \mathbf{x}_j) & \text{if } j \in \mathbf{K}(i) \text{ or } i \in \mathbf{K}(j) \\ 0 & \text{otherwise} \end{cases}$$

where $\mathbf{K}(i)$ is the set of k-NNs of $\mathbf{x}_i$ ($|\mathbf{K}(i)| = k, \forall i$) according to sim, and $\text{sim}(\mathbf{x}_i, \mathbf{x}_j)$ is a measure of similarity between $\mathbf{x}_i$ and $\mathbf{x}_j$ (which are represented by nodes i and j). We note that sim is implicit in $\mathbf{K}(i)$, in that $\mathbf{K}(i)$ contains the k data points nearest to i based on sim. The neighbors function, $\mathbf{N}(i)$, on the other hand, is based on a graph once it has already been constructed.

It is assumed that the similarity measure is symmetric, that is, $\text{sim}(x, y) = \text{sim}(y, x)$. Further, $\text{sim}(x, y) \geq 0$. Choosing the correct similarity measure and k are crucial steps in the success of any graph-based SSL algorithm as it determines the graph. Some popular similarity measures include

$$\text{sim}(\mathbf{x}_i, \mathbf{x}_j) = e^{-\frac{\|\mathbf{x}_i - \mathbf{x}_j\|_2^2}{2\sigma}} \quad \text{or} \quad \text{sim}(\mathbf{x}_i, \mathbf{x}_j) = \cos(\mathbf{x}_i, \mathbf{x}_j) = \frac{\langle \mathbf{x}_i, \mathbf{x}_j \rangle}{\| \mathbf{x}_i \|_2 \| \mathbf{x}_j \|_2}$$

where $\| \mathbf{x}_i \|_2$ is the L_2 norm and $\langle \mathbf{x}_i, \mathbf{x}_j \rangle$ is the inner product of $\mathbf{x}_i$ and $\mathbf{x}_j$. The first similarity measure is a radial-basis-function (RBF) kernel of width σ applied to the squared Euclidean distance, whereas the second is cosine similarity. The choice of $\mathbf{W}$ depends on a number of factors such as whether $\mathbf{x}_i$ is continuous or discrete and characteristics of the problem at hand.

15.2.2 Graph Regularization

For each $i \in V$ and $j \in V_l$, we define multinomial distributions p_i and r_j, respectively, over the set of classifier outputs Y. That is, for each vertex in the graph, we define a measure p_i, and for each labeled vertex we also define r_i (we explain the reason for including r_i shortly). Here $|Y| = 2$ yields binary classification while $|Y| > 2$ yields multi-class classification. Note that $p_i(y)$ represents the probability that the sample represented by vertex i belongs to class y. We assume that there is at least one labeled sample for every class.

We have that $\sum_y p_i(y) = 1$, $p_i(y) \geq 0$, $\sum_y r_i(y) = 1$, and $r_i(y) \geq 0$. Thus, p_i and r_i lie within a $|Y|$-dimensional probability simplex that we depict using $\triangle_{|Y|}$ and so $p_i, r_i \in \triangle_{|Y|}$ (henceforth, we abbreviate $\triangle_{|Y|}$ as $\triangle$). Also, let $p \stackrel{\triangle}{=} (p_1, \ldots, p_m) \in \triangle^m$ denote the set of distributions to be learned, and $r \stackrel{\triangle}{=} (r_1, \ldots, r_l) \in \triangle^l$ be the set of measures (representing labels; more on this later) that are given. Here, $\triangle^m \stackrel{\triangle}{=} \triangle \times \ldots \times \triangle$ (the Cartesian product of $\triangle$ repeated m times). Finally, let u be the uniform probability measure defined over Y, that is, $u(y) = \frac{1}{|Y|} \forall y \in Y$.

The $\{r_i\}_i$'s represent the labels of the supervised portion of the training data and are derived in one of the following ways: (1) if $\hat{y}_i$ is the single supervised label for input $\mathbf{x}_i$ then $r_i(y) = \delta(y = \hat{y}_i)$, which means that r_i gives unity probability for y equaling the label $\hat{y}_i$; (2) if $\hat{y}_i = \{\hat{y}_i^{(1)}, \ldots, \hat{y}_i^{(t)}\}$, $t \leq |Y|$ is a *set* of possible outputs for input $\mathbf{x}_i$, meaning an object validly falls into all of the corresponding categories, we set $r_i(y) = (1/t)\delta(y \in \hat{y}_i)$ meaning that r_i is uniform over only the possible categories and zero otherwise; (3) if the labels are given in the form of a set of nonnegative scores, or even a probability distribution itself, we set r_i to be equal to those scores (possibly) normalized to become a valid probability distribution. Thus, the r_i's can represent various degrees of *label uncertainty*, ranging from completely certain (the label is a single integer) to fairly uncertain (r_i has relatively high entropy), and there can be differing degrees of uncertainty associated with different labels. It is important to distinguish between the classical multi-label problem and the use of uncertainty in r_j. In our case, if there are two nonzero outputs during training as in $r_j(\bar{y}_1), r_j(\bar{y}_2) > 0$, $\bar{y}_1, \bar{y}_2 \in Y$, it does not imply that the input $\mathbf{x}_j$ is necessarily a member of both of the two corresponding classes. Rather, there is *uncertainty* regarding truth, and we utilize a discrete probability measure over the labels to represent this uncertainty. This can be useful in the document classification task where in the case of a majority of documents, there is an uncertainty associated with the appropriate topic (label) for the document (Subramanya and Bilmes 2008). To express the alternate case, where an $\mathbf{x}_j$ can be a member of more than one class, we would need multiple binary distributions for each data point – we do not consider this case further in the present chapter.

We define two graph-based SSL objectives. The first uses a squared-error objective, whereas the second makes use of KLD to measure distance between probability distributions at the vertices.

Algorithm Based on Squared Error: Consider the optimization problem $\mathcal{P}_1$: $\min_{\mathrm{p} \in \Delta^m} C_1(\mathrm{p})$ where

$$C_1(\mathrm{p}) = \sum_{i=1}^{l} \| r_i - p_i \|^2 + \mu \sum_{i=1}^{m} \sum_{j \in \mathbf{N}(i)} w_{ij} \| p_i - p_j \|^2 + \nu \sum_{i=1}^{m} \| p_i - u \|^2$$

where $\| p \|^2 = \sum_y p^2(y)$. $\mathcal{P}_1$ can also be seen as a multi-class extension of the *quadratic cost criterion* (Bengio et al., 2007) or as a variant of one of the objectives in Zhu and Ghahramani (2002b) or Talukdar and Crammer (2009).

The goal of the preceding objective is to find the best set of measures p_i that attempt to: (1) agree with the labeled data r_j wherever it is available (the first term in C_1); (2) agree with each other when they are close according to a graph (the second graph-regularizer term in C_1); and (3) not be overconfident (the last term in C_1). In essence, SSL on a graph consists of finding a labeling for $\mathcal{D}_u$ that is consistent with both the labels provided in $\mathcal{D}_l$ and the geometry of the data induced by the graph. In this case, the error is measured using squared loss.

$\mathcal{P}_1$ can be reformulated as the following equivalent optimization problem $\mathcal{P}_1$: $\min_{\mathrm{p} \in \Delta^m} C_1(\mathrm{p})$ where

$$C_1(\mathrm{p}) = \mathrm{Tr}\left((S\mathrm{p} - \mathrm{r}')(S\mathrm{p} - \mathrm{r}')^T\right) + 2\mu\mathrm{Tr}(\mathcal{L}\mathrm{pp}^T) + \nu\mathrm{Tr}((\mathrm{p} - \mathrm{u})(\mathrm{p} - \mathrm{u})^T),$$

$$S \stackrel{\triangle}{=} \begin{pmatrix} \mathbf{I}_l & 0 \\ 0 & 0 \end{pmatrix}, \quad \mathrm{r}' \stackrel{\triangle}{=} \begin{pmatrix} \mathrm{r} & 0 \\ 0 & 0 \end{pmatrix}, \quad \mathrm{u} \stackrel{\triangle}{=} (u, \ldots, u) \in \Delta^m,$$

$\mathbf{1}_m \in \mathbb{R}^m$ is a column vector of 1's, and $\mathbf{I}_l$ is the $l \times l$ identity matrix. Here $\mathcal{L} \stackrel{\triangle}{=} \Delta - \mathbf{W}$ is the unnormalized graph Laplacian and Δ is a diagonal matrix given by

$d_i = [\mathbf{\Delta}]_{ii} = \sum_j w_{ij}$. C_1 is convex if $\mu, \nu \geq 0$ and, as the constraints that ensure $p \in \Delta$ are linear, we can make use of the KKT conditions (Bertsekas, 1999) to show that the solution to $\mathcal{P}_1$ is given by

$$\hat{p} = (S + 2\mu\mathcal{L} + \nu\mathbf{I}_m)^{-1}\left[Sr + \nu u + \frac{2\mu}{|Y|}\mathcal{L}\mathbf{1}_m\mathbf{1}_{|Y|}^T \right].$$

Henceforth we refer to the preceding approach to solving $\mathcal{P}_1$ as *SQ-Loss-C*. The preceding closed-form solution involves inverting a matrix of size $m \times m$. As a result, it may not be amenable to very large problems. In such cases, one may solve $\mathcal{P}_1$ in an iterative fashion. It can be shown that the iterative update for each p_i is given by

$$p_i^{(n)}(y) = \frac{r_i(y)\delta(i \leq l) + \nu u(y) + \mu\sum_j w_{ij}p_j^{(n-1)}(y)}{\delta(i \leq l) + \nu + \mu\sum_j w_{ij}}.$$

Here n is the iteration index. More interestingly, it can be shown that $p^{(n)} \to \hat{p}$ (Bengio et al., 2007). We refer to the iterative approach to solving $\mathcal{P}_1$ as *SQ-Loss-I*.

Measure Propagation: Next we consider a graph regularization framework based on KLD (Subramanya and Bilmes 2009a, in press). Consider the optimization problem $\mathcal{P}_2 : \min_{p \in \Delta^m} C_2(p)$ where

$$C_2(p) = \sum_{i=1}^{l} D_{KL}(r_i\|p_i) + \mu\sum_{i=1}^{m}\sum_{j \in N(i)} w_{ij}D_{KL}(p_i\|p_j) - \nu\sum_{i=1}^{n} H(p_i).$$

Here $H(p) = -\sum_y p(y)\log p(y)$ is the Shannon entropy of p and $D_{KL}(p_i\|q_j)$ is the KLD between measures p_i and q_j and is given by $D_{KL}(p\|q) = \sum_y p(y)\log\frac{p(y)}{q(y)}$. (μ, ν) are hyper-parameters that can be set via cross-validation. The three terms in $C_2(p)$ have the same purpose as the three terms in $C_1(p)$, but in this case, loss is measured in the KLD sense. We note that C_2 is still convex in p. We solve $C_2(p)$ using alternating minimization (AM), and the updates are given by

$$p_i^{(n)}(y) = \frac{\exp\{\frac{\mu}{\gamma_i}\sum_j w'_{ij}\log q_j^{(n-1)}(y)\}}{\sum_y \exp\{\frac{\mu}{\gamma_i}\sum_j w'_{ij}\log q_j^{(n-1)}(y)\}} \quad \text{and}$$

$$q_i^{(n)}(y) = \frac{r_i(y)\delta(i \leq l) + \mu\sum_j w'_{ji}p_j^{(n)}(y)}{\delta(i \leq l) + \mu\sum_j w'_{ji}}$$

where $\gamma_i = \nu + \mu\sum_j w'_{ij}$, and where $q^{(n)} \triangleq (q_1^{(n)}, \ldots, q_m^{(n)}) \in \Delta^m$ is another set of m distributions that are learned simultaneously with p. In Subramanya and Bilmes (2009a, in press) we show that $\lim_{n\to\infty} D_{KL}(q_i^{(n)}\|p_i^{(n)}) = 0$ for each i and moreover that they both converge to the minimum of C_1. We call this iterative procedure *measure propagation* (MP).

There are number of reasons to prefer the KLD-based objective to the one defined in terms of squared error. First, as shown in Subramanya and Bilmes, (2008, 2009b,a), the KLD-based objective outperforms other squared-loss based approaches on a wide variety of datasets. Second, although squared-error has worked well in the

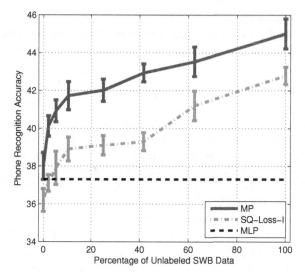

Figure 15.2 Phone accuracy versus percentage of switchboard (SWB) I training data. The STP portion of SWB is fully described in Section 15.3. Phone accuracy was measured on the STP data. Note that when all the switchboard I data was added, the resulting graph had 120 million vertices! The dashed black line shows the performance of a multi-layered perceptron (MLP) in the no-unlabeled-data case, measured using the same training, development, and test sets as MP and LP. That is, the MLP here is trained fully supervised, unlike in our other work (Malkin et al., 2009). More details may be found in Subramanya and Bilmes (in press).

case of regression problems (Bishop, 1995),[2] for classification, it is often argued that squared-loss is not the optimal criterion and alternative loss functions such as the cross-entropy (Bishop, 1995), logistic (Ng and Jordan, 2002), and hinge-loss (Vapnik, 1998) have been proposed. Third, for measuring the dissimilarity between measures, KLD is said to be asymptotically consistent w.r.t. the underlying probability distributions (Bishop, 1995). Finally, KLD-based loss is based on relative error rather than absolute error as in the case of squared error. Indeed, the results given in Figure 15.2 show that the KLD-based SSL objective significantly outperforms algorithms based on the squared-error objective, and also based on a multi-layered perceptron (MLP) trained using only on the labeled data.

Table 15.1 gives a summary of the update equations for different graph-based algorithms. Note that SQ-Loss-C and SQ-Loss-I are in fact reformulations of the popular squared-loss based objectives in terms of multinomial distributions. MP, SQ-Loss-I, and LP, however, are iterative and in fact correspond precisely to message passing on graphs as depicted in Table 15.1. SQ-Loss-C has a closed-form solution that involves inverting an $m \times m$ matrix. In practice, such a matrix will be sparse, but implementing SQ-Loss-C is arguably not as straightforward as the iterative message-passing cases. Moreover, in the message-passing cases, the updates at every vertex are a function of the values of its neighbors and so are quite easy to parallelize. We thus turn our attention to how best to parallelize such message-passing algorithms.

---

[2] Assuming a Gaussian noise model in a regression problem leads to an objective based on squared loss.

Table 15.1. *A summary of update equations for various graph-based SSL algorithms. μ and ν are hyper-parameters.*

Algorithm	Update Equation(s)
MP (Subramanya and Bilmes 2009a)	$p_i^{(n)}(y) = \frac{\exp\{\frac{\mu}{\gamma_i}\sum_j w'_{ij}\log q_j^{(n-1)}(y)\}}{\sum_y \exp\{\frac{\mu}{\gamma_i}\sum_j w'_{ij}\log q_j^{(n-1)}(y)\}}$ $q_i^{(n)}(y) = \frac{r_i(y)\delta(i\le l)+\mu\sum_j w'_{ji}p_i^{(n)}(y)}{\delta(i\le l)+\mu\sum_j w'_{ji}}$ $\gamma_i = \nu + \mu\sum_j w'_{ij}$
SQ-Loss-C	$\hat{p} = (S + 2\mu\mathcal{L} + \nu I_m)^{-1}\left[Sr + \nu u + \frac{2\mu}{|Y|}\mathcal{L}\mathbf{1}_m\mathbf{1}_c^T\right]$ $\mathcal{L} \stackrel{\triangle}{=} \Delta - W, [\Delta]_{ii} = \sum_j w_{ij}$
SQ-Loss-I	$p_i^{(n)}(y) = \frac{r_i(y)\delta(i\le l)+\nu u(y)+\mu\sum_j w_{ij}p_j^{(n-1)}(y)}{\delta(i\le l)+\nu+\mu\sum_j w_{ij}}$
LP (Zhu and Ghahramani, 2002a)	$p_i^{(n)}(y) = \frac{r_i(y)\delta(i\le l)+\delta(i>l)\sum_j w_{ij}p_j^{(n-1)}(y)}{\delta(i\le l)+\delta(i>l)\sum_j w_{ij}}$

15.3 Dataset: A 120-Million-Node Graph

Our interest in this chapter is on fast parallel implementations of message-passing-based semi-supervised learning algorithms, and we therefore need a large real-world dataset that is deserving of our efforts.

We therefore utilized the popular speech dataset Switchboard I (SWB) which is a collection of about 2,400 two-sided telephone conversations among 543 speakers (302 male, 241 female) from all areas of the United States (Godfrey, Holliman, and McDaniel, 1992). A computer-driven system handled the calls, giving the caller appropriate recorded prompts, selecting and dialing another person (the callee) to take part in a conversation, introducing a topic for discussion, and recording the speech from the two subjects into separate channels until the conversation was finished. SWB consists of about 300 hours of speech data and is very popular in the speech recognition community for the training of large-vocabulary conversational speech recognition systems (Evermann et al., 2005; Subramanya et al., 2007).

SWB has been annotated in multiple ways. There are manually produced word-level transcriptions. In addition, one also has access to less reliable phone-level annotations generated in an automatic manner by a speech recognizer with a nonzero error rate (Deshmukh et al., 1998).

Most interesting from the perspective of SSL, the *Switchboard Transcription Project* (STP) (Greenberg, 1995; Greenberg, Hollenback, and Ellis, 1996) was undertaken to accurately annotate SWB at the phonetic and syllabic levels. Within the annotated portion of the STP data, every phone (or syllabic) segment is marked with a temporally high-resolution start and end time and a phone (or syllable) identity, and this is done painstakingly by a human annotator. These segments can be used to make a decision regarding the phone identity of every 25 ms (millisecond) window of speech, a process known as *frame* annotation. One of the hopes for the STP data was that it could be used to improve the performance of conversational speech recognition systems – each frame label could be used to train an HMM by having a phonetic label determine each state variable at each time frame during training. As the transcription task was time consuming, costly, and error prone, only 75 minutes of speech selected from different SWB conversations was annotated at the phone level. Completing this annotation task is thus the perfect job for transductive SSL: produce labels for the unlabeled data. Having access to such annotations for all of SWB could potentially be useful for large-vocabulary speech recognition and speech research in general, and this, in fact, was the process we undertook (Subramanya and Bilmes, 2009b). This data is also an ideal real-world task for SSL, and accuracy results showed that measure propagation was significantly more accurate than alternatives on this data (Subramanya and Bilmes, 2009a, in press). The STP data is useful for a third purpose, because it corresponds to a very large real-world graph (approximately 120 million nodes, corresponding to 120 million speech frames), suitable for developing scalable SSL algorithms, the topic of this chapter (also see Figure 15.2).

The following process was used to construct this graph from the STP data. The speech wave files were first segmented and then windowed using a Hamming window of size 25 ms at 100 Hz (15-ms window overlap). We then extracted 13 Perceptual Linear Prediction (PLP) (Huang, Acero, and Hon, 2001) coefficients from these windowed features and appended both deltas and double deltas resulting in a 39-dimensional feature vector. To increase context information, we used a 7-Frame context window (3 frames in the past and 3 in the future) yielding a 273-dimensional sample $\mathbf{x}_i$. We used

$$\text{sim}(\mathbf{x}_i, \mathbf{x}_j) = \exp\{-(\mathbf{x}_i - \mathbf{x}_j)^T \Sigma^{-1} (\mathbf{x}_i - \mathbf{x}_j)\}$$

as the similarity measure to generate the weights w_{ij}, where Σ is the "grand" covariance matrix computed using all the data. Our task is the phone classification problem, and so Y is the set of phones (an approximately 40-class multi-class classification problem). We constructed a symmetrized k-NN graph using the preceding data with each vertex having at least $k = 10$ neighbors, using the procedure described in Section 15.3.1. The graph, hereinafter referred to as the *SWB graph*, had about 120 million vertices. More details are given in Subramanya and Bilmes (2009a; in press).

15.3.1 Graph Construction in Large Problems

Graph construction is an important step in the use of a graph-based algorithm for solving a SSL problem. At a very high level, the graph determines how information flows from one sample to another, and thus an incorrect choice of a neighborhood can lead to poor results. Improper choice of a graph can also lead to degenerate solutions (where either all samples belong to a single class or all samples have a uniform distributions) (Blum and Chawla, 2001; Joachims, 2003). In general, graph construction "is more of an art, than science" (Zhu, 2005b) and is an active research area (Alexandrescu and Kirchhoff, 2007).

Constructing a graph over a large number of samples (>1 million) itself poses an interesting computational challenge – conventional brute-force construction of k-NN graphs does not scale to large datasets as it is $O(m^2)$. Nearest-neighbor search is a well-researched problem, however, with many approximate solutions. A large number of solutions to this problem are based on variations of the classic *kd-tree* data structure (Friedman, Bentley, and Finkel, 1977). However, kd-trees or their derivatives are not ideally suited to the case of high-dimensional data, as we have shown.

Because we have continuous data in this work, we make use of the Approximate Nearest Neighbor (ANN) library (see www.cs.umd.edu/~mount/ANN/) (Arya and Mount, 1993; Arya et al., 1998). It constructs a modified version of the kd-tree data structure that is then used to query the NNs. The query process requires that one specify an error term, ϵ, and guarantees that $\text{sim}(\mathbf{x}_i, \text{N}(\mathbf{x}_i))/\text{sim}(\mathbf{x}_i, \text{N}_\epsilon(\mathbf{x}_i)) \leq 1 + \epsilon$ where $\text{N}(\mathbf{x}_i)$ is a function that returns the exact nearest neighbor of $\mathbf{x}_i$ while $\text{N}_\epsilon(\mathbf{x}_i)$ returns the approximate NN. Larger values of ϵ improve the speed of the nearest neighbor search at the cost of accuracy. For more details, see Arya and Mount (1993) and Arya et al. (1998). We note that one could also use b-matching (Jebara, Wang, and Chang, 2009) to obtain a symmetrized k-NN graph, but it is quadratic in the graph size and so does not scale well to problem at hand.

15.4 Large-Scale Parallel Processing

In the next few sections, we discuss the scaling up of graph-based message passing algorithms for SSL learning on both a shared-memory computer (the next section) and a distributed memory computer (see Section 15.4.3).

15.4.1 Inference on a Shared-Memory Symmetric Multiprocessor

In an SMP, all processing units share the same address space and are often cache coherent. Such computing environments are important, because individual modern microprocessors are becoming ever more like SMPs, with multicore (and soon "many core") units being available in a single package.

Recall from Table 15.1 that in the case of most graph-based algorithms, the update at each node is a function of the current value of its neighbors. In the case of Measure Propagation (MP), for example, we see that one set of measures is held fixed while the other set is updated without any required communication among set members, so there is no write contention. In the case of SQ-Loss-I, the same holds if one considers $p^{(n-1)}$ as the set of measures that are held fixed while a new separate $p^{(n)}$ may change. This immediately yields a T-threaded implementation where the graph is evenly but otherwise arbitrarily T-partitioned and each thread operates over only a size $m/T = (l + u)/T$ subset of the graph nodes, the intent being of course that each of the T threads runs in parallel.

We implemented such a multi-threaded application and ran timing tests on the aforementioned graph with about 120 million nodes. We ran a timing test on a 16-core SMP with 128GB of RAM, each core operating at 1.6GHz. We varied the number T of threads from 1 (single threaded) up to 16, in each case running three iterations of MP (i.e., three each of p and q updates). Each experiment was repeated 10 times, and we measured the minimum CPU time over these 10 runs. CPU time does not include the time taken to load data structures from disk. The speedup for T threads is typically defined as the ratio of time taken for single thread to time taken for T threads. The solid line on the left side of Figure 15.4 (later) represents the ideal case (a linear speedup), that is, when using T threads results in a speedup of T. The pointed shows the actual speedup of the preceding procedure, typically less than ideal because of interprocess communication and poor shared L1 and/or L2 microprocessor cache interaction. When $T \leq 4$, the speedup (green) is close to ideal, but for increasing T the algorithm increasingly falls away from the ideal case.

15.4.2 Graph Reordering Algorithm for SMP

We assert that the sub-linear speedup is due to the poor cache cognizance of the algorithm. At a given point in time, suppose thread $t \in \{1, \ldots, T\}$ is operating on node i_t. The collective set of neighbors that are being used by these T threads are $\{\cup_{t=1}^{T} \mathbf{N}(i_t)\}$, and this, along with nodes $\cup_{t=1}^{T} \{i_t\}$ (and all memory for the associated measures), constitutes the current *working set*. The working set should be made as small as possible to increase the chance that it will fit in any shared machine caches, but this becomes decreasingly likely as T increases because the working set is monotonically increasing with T. Our goal, therefore, is for the nodes that are being simultaneously operated on to have a large amount of neighbor overlap, thus minimizing the working set size.

Recall that $\mathbf{N}(v)$ is the set of v's neighbors. Also, $\mathbf{N}(\mathbf{N}(v))$ is the set of v's neighbors' neighbors or equivalently, the neighbors of v's neighbors. For example, in Figure 15.1-I, $\mathbf{N}(a) = \{c, h, b\}$ and $\mathbf{N}(\mathbf{N}(a)) = V$. Note that $v \in \mathbf{N}(\mathbf{N}(v))$, but this will not affect any decisions made by our procedure. For notational simplicity, for a given set $S \subseteq V$, we define $\mathbf{N}^2(S) \stackrel{\triangle}{=} \mathbf{N}(\mathbf{N}(S))$.

Viewed as the optimization problem, our goal is to find a partition of V into a set of clusters $(V_1, V_2, \ldots, V_{m/T})$ that minimizes $\max_{j \in \{1, \ldots, m/T\}} |\cup_{v \in V_j} \mathbf{N}(v)|$, where $|V_i| = T$ and the nodes in V_i are run in parallel. With such a partition, we may also produce an order $\pi = (\pi_1, \ldots, \pi_{m/T})$ of the clusters so that the neighbors of V_{π_i} would have maximal overlap with the neighbors of $V_{\pi_{i+1}}$. We then schedule the clusters according to this order, so that the nodes in V_{π_i} run simultaneously, which would also act to prefetch many of the neighbors of the nodes in $V_{\pi_{i+1}}$.

The time to produce such a partition, of course, must not dominate the time to run the algorithm itself. Therefore, we propose a simple linear-time (i.e., $O(m)$) *node* ordering procedure (Algorithm 44) that can be run once before the parallelization begins. The algorithm produces a node ordering $\sigma = (\sigma_1, \sigma_2, \ldots, \sigma_m)$ such that successive nodes are likely to have a high amount of neighbor overlap with each other and, by transitivity, with nearby nodes in the ordering. It does this by, given a current node v, choosing as the next node v' in the order (from among v's neighbors' neighbors) the one that has the largest number of shared neighbors. We need not search all m nodes for this, because anything other than v's neighbors' neighbors has no overlap with the neighbors of v.

Algorithm 44: Graph Node Ordering Algorithm Pseudocode, SMP Case

---

Input: A Graph $G = (V, E)$

Result: A node ordering, by when they are marked

1 Select an arbitrary node v ;

2 **while** *There are unselected nodes remaining* **do**

3 $\quad$ Select an unselected $v' \in \mathbf{N}^2(v)$ that maximizes $|\mathbf{N}(v) \cap \mathbf{N}(v')|$. If the intersection is empty, select an arbitrary unselected v'. ;

4 $\quad$ Mark v' as selected.; $\qquad\qquad$ // v' is next node in the order

5 $\quad$ $v \leftarrow v'$. ;

Assuming that the nodes are ordered according to σ (something that in practice is done only implicitly), the tth thread operates on nodes $\{t, t + m/T, t + 2m/T, \dots\}$. If the threads proceed synchronously at the graph node level (which we do not enforce in our implementation), the set of nodes being processed by multiple processors at time instant j are $V_j = \{1 + jm/T, 2 + jm/T, \dots, T + jm/T\}$. This assignment is beneficial not only for maximizing the set of neighbors being simultaneously used, but also for successive chunks of T nodes, because once a chunk of T nodes have been processed, it is likely that many of the neighbors of the next chunk of T nodes will already have been prefetched into the caches. With the graph represented as an adjacency list and sets of neighbor indices sorted, our algorithm is $O(mk^3)$ in time and linear in memory because the intersection between two sorted lists may be computed in $O(k)$ time. Here k is the number of neighbors of a given vertex in the graph. This can be better than $O(m \log m)$ because $k^3 < \log m$ for very large m.

The utility of this heuristic is depicted in Figure 15.3. On the left, we see a partition that might at first look reasonable, because each cluster consists of neighboring nodes (e.g., V1 consists of nodes $\{c, e\}$), but this clustering is poor because each pair of nodes, in all clusters but one, shares only one neighbor (e.g., c and e in V1 have only one neighbor in common, namely h). On the right, we see a much better clustering, where each pair of nodes in all clusters shares two neighbors (e.g., e and a in V1 share neighbors c and h). In fact, this clustering can result from running Algorithm 44.

We ordered the SWB graph nodes and ran timing tests using MP as explained previously. To be fair, the CPU time required for ordering the nodes by the heuristic is included in every run along with the time for running MP. The results are shown in Figure 15.4(left) (pointed line) where the results are much closer to ideal, and there are no obvious diminishing returns like in the unordered case. Running times are given in Figure 15.4(right). Moreover, the ordered case showed better performance even for a single thread $T = 1$ (the CPU time is about 790 minutes for the ordered case, versus about 815 minutes for the unordered case, on two iterations of MP). The reason for this difference is that the ordering heuristic exhibits better cache behavior even on a single node, because nearby nodes in the order tend to share neighbors (see Figure 15.5).

Finally, we note that because we made use of speech data to generate the graph, it is already naturally well ordered by time. This is because human speech is a slowly changing signal, so the nodes corresponding to consecutive frames are similar, and

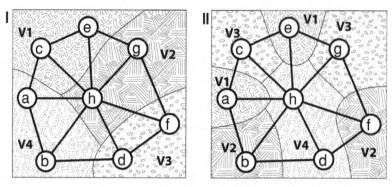

Figure 15.3 I, left: The graph from Figure 15.1 that has been partitioned into four subsets of nodes (marked as regions V1, V2, V3, and V4), where each subset is to be processed on a separate processor (on a four-processor parallel machine). Within V1, V3, and V4, each node has only one common neighbor with the other node, whereas in region V2, the two nodes (g and h) have two neighbors in common (e and f). In regions V1, V3, and V4, therefore, reading one node's neighbors will not prefetch as much useful information as in region V2, thereby slowing down the entire parallel computation. II, Right: Here, every node in each region has a neighbor overlap of 2 with the other node in its region. For example, in region V1, nodes e and a both have as neighbors nodes {c, h}. Therefore, processing the neighbors of one node in each region will prefetch more of what the other node in a region needs. This region allocation is what Algorithm 44 can produce, when starting at node a – the ordering is (a, e, f, b, c, g, d, h).

can be expected to have similar neighbors. This is confirmed by Figure 15.5, which shows the average neighbor overlap as a function of distance, for a random order, the speech order, and for an ordering produced by our heuristic. Therefore, we expect our "baseline" speech graph to be better than an arbitrary order, one that might be encountered in a different application domain. In order to measure performance for such arbitrarily ordered graphs, we took the original graph and reordered uniformly at random (a uniform node shuffle). As seen in Figure 15.5, the random order had the least degree of neighbor overlap at nearby distances. We ran timing experiments on the

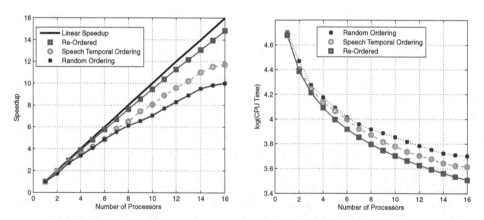

Figure 15.4 (Left) Speedup versus number of threads for the SWB graph. The process was run on a 128GB, 16-core machine with each core at 1.6GHz. (Right) The actual CPU times in seconds on a *log scale* versus number of threads for with and without ordering cases. "Random" corresponds to the case where we choose a random unselected node rather than the one with maximum overlap (see Algorithm 44).

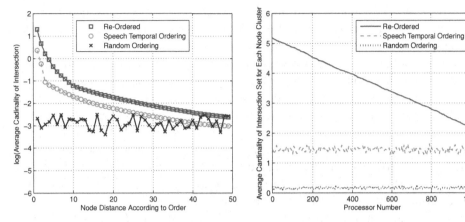

Figure 15.5 Left: Average cardinality of the intersection between neighbors of node i and node $i+k$ where k was varied between 1 and 50 (all using natural logarithm). "Speech Temporal Ordering" is the graph generated from the data, "Re-ordered" is the preceding graph ordered using Algorithm 44, and "Random Ordering" is a random shuffle of the nodes. Right: With the nodes ordered according to Algorithm 45, and with the clustering as specified in Section 15.4.3, this plot shows the average cardinality of neighbor intersection for successive nodes as a function of the cluster index (equivalent to processor number). Note that the overall average in this figure is approximately equal to the distance-1 average on the left figure ($\ln(3.5) \approx 1.25$). Note also that, because of the greedy nature of Algorithm 45, the average intersection decreases as the heuristic proceeds.

resulting graph, and the results are shown in Figure 15.4 as "Random". As can be seen, there is indeed a benefit from the speech order, and relative to this random baseline, our node ordering heuristic improves machine efficiency quite significantly.

We conclude this section by noting that: (1) reordering may be considered a pre-processing (offline) step; (2) the SQ-Loss algorithm may also be implemented in a multi-threaded manner, and this is supported by our implementation; and (3) our reordering algorithm is general and fast and can be used for any graph-based algorithm where the iterative updates for a given node are a function of its neighbors (i.e., the updates are *harmonic* w.r.t. the graph; Zhu et al., 2003).

15.4.3 Inference in a Distributed Computing Environment

Our results in the previous section for the SMP show that it is possible to get good efficiency on an SMP using only a simple node-ordering heuristic. Unfortunately, an SMP does not scale to tens of thousands (or even thousands) of processing units, as is typical in large distributed computing environments. Distributed computers do not have shared memory, and any communication between them is typically done via a form of messaging library. Such environments, moreover, are likely to be more realistic for the case when one wishes to utilize inexpensive massive parallelism. In this section, we see how it is possible to modify our SMP reordering algorithm for the distributed computer case, while retaining its linear time.

On a distributed computer, things are quite different than on an SMP. On each individual distributed computer node, there is still a benefit for successive nodes to have a large amount of neighbor overlap. The reason is that if node i is adjacent to a set of neighbors common with node $i + 1$, node i will essentially prefetch, into microprocessor caches, data useful for node $i + 1$. This is the reason for the single-thread speedup exhibited in Section 15.4.2.

Assume we have a T processor distributed computer. We then we want to partition the graph $G = (V, E)$ into T clusters $(V_1 \cup V_2 \cup \cdots \cup V_T)$, where the nodes in V_i are to be run by processor t. Each of the nodes in V_i can thus be ordered locally on each processor using Algorithm 44 to maximize within-processor neighbor overlap to take advantage of the node's local caches. On the other hand, there should be as little communication cross processing elements as possible, to reduce potential waiting time for necessary data. This means that the neighbors of nodes assigned to different processors $|\Gamma(V_i) \cap \Gamma(V_j)|$, for $i \neq j$ should be as small as possible, reducing the chance that any processing element will need to wait for data.

One possible solution to this problem is to perform a minimum T-cut (or T-partition) of the graph, which is a known NP-complete optimization problem (Vazirani, 2001). This, if solved optimally, would produce a graph clustering that minimizes the total number of edges that cross between any two clusters. The good news is that this can be constant-factor $(2 - 2/T)$ approximated. The bad news, however, is that even this approximation algorithm is too expensive for the large graphs we wish to use (the approximation algorithm requires a Gomory-Hu tree (Vazirani, 2001), which requires computing $|V| - 1$ (s, t)-cuts). Perhaps even more problematic, we have another constraint, which is that each cluster should have about the same number of nodes to achieve a good load balance (and thereby, high computer efficiency). The approximation algorithm for T-cut is quite outlier sensitive, and some processors could easily end up with very little work to do. Therefore, we desire a procedure for normalized T-partition, and it needs to run very fast. Performing even normalized 2-partition is NP-complete (Shi and Malik, 2000), however, so we must resort to a heuristic.

Fortunately, our SMP heuristic (Algorithm 44) can be modified to suit the distributed case, and the clues on how to do so lie within Figure 15.5. We see that in the re-ordered case, successive nodes have many neighbors in common. Because of transitivity, nearby nodes also have neighbors in common. As we move away in distance, the number of neighbors in common decreases. Moreover, the degree of neighbor overlap is much higher than the speech ordering, and also much higher than the random order, which, as expected, has very little neighbor overlap. Although such a random order might seem to be pointless, we can exploit this property of random orders to ensure that V_i and V_j, for $i \neq j$, have a small neighbor intersection.

Thus, a very simple heuristic is to do the following: Produce a hybrid node ordering heuristic that switches between: (1) choosing the next node from the set of neighbors' neighbors, based on maximizing the neighbor overlap, and (2) choosing the next node uniformly at random. Under the assumption of uniform load balance (i.e., every processor gets m/T nodes allocated to it, but see later where this assumption no longer holds), the transitions in the order between processors are at locations $\ell m/T$ for $\ell = 0 \ldots T$. Let $R = \{\ell m/T : \ell = 0 \ldots T\}$ be the set of transitions. Let i refer to the current position in the ordering. When i is nowhere near any of the transitions, nearby nodes should have a large degree of neighbor overlap, but as i approaches one of the transitions (i.e., i is on the "boundary" regions), the amount of neighbor overlap should decrease. We can choose a threshold τ such that if i is within τ nodes of a transition, it is a boundary node, and it should be chosen at random. This is described in Algorithm 45, lines 3 through 10.

Algorithm 45: Graph Node Ordering Algorithm for a Distributed Computer

---

Input: A Graph $G = (V, E)$ with $m = |V|$ nodes. Parameter T indicating the number of compute nodes. A positive integer threshold τ

Result: A node ordering, by when they are marked

1   Select an arbitrary node v ;

2   $i \leftarrow 0$;

3   **while** *There are unselected nodes remaining* **do**

4   **if** $\min_\ell |i - \ell m/T| < \tau$ **then**   // near a transition

5 | Select uniformly at random any unselected node v' ;

6   **else**   // not near a transition

7 | Select an unselected $v' \in \mathbf{N}^2(v)$ that maximizes $|\mathbf{N}(v) \cap \mathbf{N}(v')|$. If the intersection is empty, select an arbitrary unselected v'. ;

8   Mark v' as selected.;   // v' is next node in the order

9     $v \leftarrow v'$;

10    $i \leftarrow i + 1$;

11 **foreach** ℓ **do**   // randomly scatter boundary nodes to internal locations

12   Define segment ℓ boundary node indices as
$B_\ell = \{i : 0 \le i - \ell m/T < \tau \text{ or } 0 \le (\ell + 1)m/T - i < \tau\}$;

13   **foreach** $i \in B_\ell$ **do**

14 | Insert node i uniformly at random between nodes $\ell m/T + \tau$ and $(\ell + 1)m/T - \tau$;

We implemented this heuristic on a 1,000-node distributed computer. We did not have available detailed information about this computer such as speed and/or topology of the communications network. Therefore, the heuristics we describe in this section are generic, rather than being specific to this (or any) distributed computer. As a result, given more information about the machine, we believe it would be possible to further improve machine efficiency over what our current results for these heuristics show.

Figure 15.6 shows the results. The first thing to note is that a purely random order (marked as "Random") does poorly, as it did for an SMP in Figure 15.4. The random order is what we might expect using an arbitrary order for a given application. When we use the speech temporal order, the situation improves. Further improvement can be acquired by running the SMP heuristic (Algorithm 44) on the distributed computer, marked as "SMP Heuristic" in the figure. As mentioned previously, this heuristic makes no attempt to ensure that $|\Gamma(V_i) \cap \Gamma(V_j)|$ is small for $i \ne j$. When we use a heuristic consisting of *only* lines 3 through 10 in Algorithm 45, we see a significant efficiency improvement over the SMP heuristic – this is marked as "Dist. Heuristic" in the figure. The results correspond to a $\tau = 25$, which was obtained empirically, but other values might be better still.

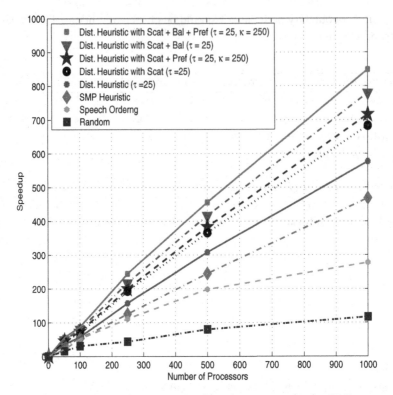

Figure 15.6 Speedup versus number of processors for the SWB.

On the other hand, there is still a problem in that all communication on the machine is happening simultaneously. That is, when only lines 3 through 10 are executed, the message-passing algorithm has two phases with very different communications network behavior. Phase 1 is when all processors are operating on non-boundary nodes (and there is very little network communication). Phase 2 is when all processors are operating on boundary nodes and the communications network is being flooded with requests for data. To mitigate this problem, we can randomly scatter the boundary nodes onto points internal to a segment, as done in lines 11–14 of Algorithm 45. Performing this scatter results in improved efficiency, as shown in Figure 15.6 as "Dist. Heuristic with Scat".

A further improvement can be obtained by taking advantage of the fact that once the scatter has been performed, we still know exactly which nodes are likely to have most or all off their neighbors on processor (i.e., those that have not been scattered) and which are likely to have most or all of their neighbors off processor (i.e., those that have been scattered). This information can be exploited by prefetching the cross-processor neighbors of the scattered nodes early. This is controlled by parameter κ, which states that scattered node i's off-processor neighbors should be asynchronously prefetched at the time that we are processing node $i - \kappa$. With $\kappa = 250$, this results in further improvements, as shown in Figure 15.6, "Dist. Heuristic with Scat + Pref".

Both Algorithm 44 and Algorithm 45 are "greedy" in the sense that they select and then commit to the next node that looks best at the time, without regard to how this decision might adversely affect decisions made later. There are some cases where greedy algorithms are indeed optimal (White, 1986), but we do not expect this to be one of them. Indeed, Figure 15.5 (right) shows that as the distributed heuristic proceeds, the average cardinality of neighbor intersection (over adjacent nodes in the order, and within each cluster) decreases from about 5.2 at the beginning of the heuristic to about 2.3 at the end. Therefore, processor 0 has a set of nodes with significantly more neighbor overlap on average than processor 1,000. Although this was not a significant issue on the SMP (with only 16 processors), on a large distributed computer this decreases efficiency significantly. We note that any imbalance between processors is, in this case, due only to the fact that previous processors will have better locality properties in their local caches. One solution to this problem is for multiple orderings to be deduced simultaneously (and in parallel) along with a collision avoidance scheme and a restart mechanism on reaching a dead end. On the other hand, a simpler solution is to simply give previous processors more nodes than later processors, thus recovering balance. We have done this and show the results in Figure 15.6, "Dist. Heuristic with Scat + Bal". To achieve balance, we derived a simple re-balance mechanism based on a fraction of the slope of the plot in Figure 15.5 (right). This fraction corresponds to how important local cache misses on each processor are relative to their computational workloads and network communication costs. As can be seen, further significant improvements are obtained.

Last, prefetching and load balancing can be utilized simultaneously to achieve further gains as shown in Figure 15.6, "Dist. Heuristic with Scat + Bal + Pref". As mentioned previously, these heuristics are fairly generic and could be easily exploited on any distributed computer. With more knowledge about the latency and bandwidth of the underlying communications network, we expect that we could improve machine efficiency even further.

15.5 Discussion

In this chapter we have proposed graph node reordering heuristics that make it possible to scale graph-based SSL algorithms to large datasets. We have shown that it is possible to recover a near-linear speedup relative to standard order on an SMP and have achieved an 85% efficiency on a 1,000-node distributed computer. In Subramanya and Bilmes, (2009b,a, in press), we use the preceding SMP implementation of measure propagation on STP data and show that it significantly outperforms the only other SSL algorithms that can scale to such large datasets (label propagation). More importantly, we found that the performance on the STP data improves with the addition of increasing amounts of unlabeled data, and MP seems to get a better benefit with this additional unlabeled data, although even SQ-Loss-I has not reached the point where unlabeled data starts becoming harmful (Nadler et al., 2010). This portends well for large-scale semi-supervised learning approaches.

We also wish to point out that since the graph-based SSL algorithms listed in Table 15.1 are all instances of the more general procedure of message passing on graphs, which includes random walks (Woess, 2000), (loopy) belief propagation (Pearl, 1988), affinity propagation (Frey and Dueck, 2007), and others Baluja et al., 2008).

All of these algorithms could stand to benefit from the simple node-ordering algorithms presented in this work.

References

Alexandrescu, A., and Kirchhoff, K. 2007. Graph-Based Learning for Statistical Machine Translation. In: *Proceeding of the Human Language Technologies Conference (HLT-NAACL)*.

Arya, S., and Mount, D. M. 1993. Approximate Nearest Neighbor Queries in Fixed Dimensions. In: *ACM-SIAM Symposium on Discrete Algorithms (SODA)*.

Arya, S., Mount, D. M., Netanyahu, N. S., Silverman, R., and Wu, A. 1998. An Optimal Algorithm for Approximate Nearest Neighbor Searching. *Journal of the ACM*.

Balcan, M.-F., and Blum, A. 2005. A PAC-Style Model for Learning from Labeled and Unlabeled Data. Pages 111–126 of: *COLT*.

Baluja, S., Seth, R., Sivakumar, D., Jing, Y., Yagnik, J., Kumar, S., Ravichandran, D., and Aly, M. 2008. Video Suggestion and Discovery for YouTube: Taking Random Walks through the View Graph. Pages 895–904 of: *Proceeding of the 17th International conference on World Wide Web*. ACM.

Belkin, M., Niyogi, P., and Sindhwani, V. 2005. On Manifold Regularization. In: *Proceedings of the Conference on Artificial Intelligence and Statistics (AISTATS)*.

Bengio, Y., Delalleau, O., and Roux, N. L. 2007. Label Propagation and Quadratic Criterion. In: *Semi-Supervised Learning*. Cambridge, MA: MIT Press.

Bertsekas, D. 1999. *Nonlinear Programming*. Athena Scientific.

Bie, T. D., and Cristianini, N. 2003. Convex Methods for Transduction. Pages 73–80 of: *Advances in Neural Information Processing Systems 16*. Cambridge, MA: MIT Press.

Bilmes, J. A. 1998. *A Gentle Tutorial on the EM Algorithm and Its Application to Parameter Estimation for Gaussian Mixture and Hidden Markov Models*. Technical Report ICSI-TR-97-021. University of Berkeley.

Bishop, C. (ed). 1995. *Neural Networks for Pattern Recognition*. New York: Oxford University Press.

Blitzer, J., and Zhu, J. 2008. *ACL 2008 Tutorial on Semi-supervised Learning*. http://ssl-acl08.wikidot .com/.

Blum, A., and Chawla, S. 2001. Learning from Labeled and Unlabeled Data Using Graph Mincuts. Pages 19–26 of: *Proceedings of the 18th International Conference on Machine Learning*. San Francisco, CA: Morgan Kaufmann.

Chapelle, O., Scholkopf, B., and Zien, A. 2007. *Semi-Supervised Learning*. Cambridge, MA: MIT Press.

Collobert, R., Sinz, F., Weston, J., Bottou, L., and Joachims, T. 2006. Large Scale Transductive SVMs. *Journal of Machine Learning Research*.

Corduneanu, A., and Jaakkola, T. 2003. On Information Regularization. In: *Uncertainty in Artificial Intelligence*.

Delalleau, O., Bengio, Y., and Roux, N. L. 2005. Efficient Non-parametric Function Induction in Semi-Supervised Learning. In: *Proceedings of the Conference on Artificial Intelligence and Statistics (AISTATS)*.

Dempster, A. P., Laird, N. M., Rubin, D. B., et al. 1977. Maximum Likelihood from Incomplete Data via the EM Algorithm. *Journal of the Royal Statistical Society, Series B (Methodological)*, **39**(1), 1–38.

Deshmukh, N., Ganapathiraju, A., Gleeson, A., Hamaker, J., and Picone, J. 1998 (November). Resegmentation of Switchboard. Pages 1543–1546 of: *Proceedings of the International Conference on Spoken Language Processing*.

Evermann, G., Chan, H. Y., Gales, M. J. F., Jia, B., Mrva, D., Woodland, P. C., and Yu, K. 2005. Training LVCSR Systems on Thousands of Hours of Data. In: *Proceedings of ICASSP*.

Frey, B. J., and Dueck, D. 2007. Clustering by Passing Messages between Data Points. *Science*, **315**(5814), 972.

Friedman, J. H., Bentley, J. L., and Finkel, R. A. 1977. An Algorithm for Finding Best Matches in Logarithmic Expected Time. *ACM Transaction on Mathematical Software*, **3**.

Garcke, J., and Griebel, M. 2005. Semi-supervised Learning with Sparse Grids. In: *Proceedings of the 22nd ICML Workshop on Learning with Partially Classified Training Data*.

Godfrey, J., Holliman, E., and McDaniel, J. 1992 (March). SWITCHBOARD: Telephone Speech Corpus for Research and Development. Pages 517–520 of: *Proceedings of the IEEE International Conference on Acoustics, Speech, and Signal Processing*, vol. 1.

Goldman, S., and Zhou, Y. 2000. Enhancing Supervised Learning with Unlabeled Data. Pages 327–334 of: *Proceedings of the 17th International Conference on Machine Learning*. San Francisco, CA: Morgan Kaufmann.

Greenberg, S. 1995. *The Switchboard Transcription Project*. Technical Report, The Johns Hopkins University (CLSP) Summer Research Workshop.

Greenberg, S., Hollenback, J., and Ellis, D. 1996. Insights into Spoken Language Gleaned from Phonetic Transcription of the Switchboard Corpus. Pages 24–27 of: *ICSLP*.

Haffari, G.R., and Sarkar, A. 2007. Analysis of Semi-supervised Learning with the Yarowsky Algorithm. In: *UAI*.

Hosmer, D. W. 1973. A Comparison of Iterative Maximum Likelihood Estimates of the Parameters of a Mixture of Two Normal Distributions under Three Different Types of Sample. *Biometrics*.

Huang, X., Acero, A., and Hon, H. 2001. *Spoken Language Processing*. Englewood Cliffs, NJ: Prentice-Hall.

Jebara, T., Wang, J., and Chang, S.F. 2009. Graph Construction and b-Matching for Semi-supervised Learning. In: *International Conference on Machine Learning*.

Joachims, T. 2003. Transductive Learning via Spectral Graph Partitioning. In: *Proceedings of the International Conference on Machine Learning (ICML)*.

Karlen, M., Weston, J., Erkan, A., and Collobert, R. 2008. Large Scale Manifold Transduction. In: *International Conference on Machine Learning, ICML*.

Lawrence, N. D., and Jordan, M. I. 2005. Semi-supervised Learning via Gaussian Processes. In: *Neural Information Processing Systems*.

Malkin, J., Subramanya, A., and Bilmes, J.A. 2009 (September). On the Semi-Supervised Learning of Multi-Layered Perceptrons. In: *Proceedings of the Annual Conference of the International Speech Communication Association (INTERSPEECH)*.

McLachlan, G. J., and Ganesalingam, S. 1982. Updating a Discriminant Function on the Basis of Unclassified Data. *Communication in Statistics: Simulation and Computation*.

Nadler, B., Srebro, N., and Zhou, X. 2010. Statistical Analysis of Semi-supervised Learning: The Limit of Infinite Unlabelled Data. In: *Advances in Neural Information Processing Systems (NIPS)*.

Ng, A., and Jordan, M. 2002. On Discriminative vs. Generative Classifiers: A Comparison of Logistic Regression and Naive Bayes. In: *Advances in Neural Information Processing Systems (NIPS)*.

Nigam, G. 2001. *Using Unlabeled Data to Improve Text Classification*. Ph.D. thesis, CMU.

Pearl, J. 1988. *Probabilistic Reasoning in Intelligent Systems: Networks of Plausible Inference*. San Francisco, CA: Morgan Kaufmann.

Scudder, H. J. 1965. Probability of Error of Some Adaptive Pattern-Recognition Machines. *IEEE Transactions on Information Theory*, **11**.

Seeger, M. 2000. *Learning with Labeled and Unlabeled Data*. Technical Report, University of Edinburgh, UK.

Shi, J., and Malik, J. 2000. Normalized Cuts and Image Segmentation. *IEEE Transactions on Pattern Analysis and Machine Intelligence.*

Sindhwani, V., and Selvaraj, S.K. 2006. Large Scale Semi-Supervised Linear SVMs. In: *SIGIR '06: Proceedings of the 29th Annual International ACM SIGIR.*

Sindhwani, V., Niyogi, P., and Belkin, M. 2005. Beyond the Point Cloud: From Transductive to Semi-supervised learning. In: *Proceedings of the International Conference on Machine Learning (ICML).*

Subramanya, A., and Bilmes, J. 2008. Soft-Supervised Text Classification. In: *EMNLP.*

Subramanya, A., and Bilmes, J. 2009a. Entropic Regularization in Non-parametric Graph-Based Learning. In: *NIPS.*

Subramanya, A., and Bilmes, J. 2009b. The Semi-supervised Switchboard Transcription Project. In: *Interspeech.*

Subramanya, A., and Bilmes, J. 2011. Semi-Supervised Learning with Measure Propagation. *Journal of Machine Learning Research.*

Subramanya, A., Bartels, C., Bilmes, J., and Nguyen, P. 2007. Uncertainty in Training Large Vocabulary Speech Recognizers. In: *Proceedings of the IEEE Workshop on Speech Recognition and Understanding.*

Szummer, M., and Jaakkola, T. 2001. Partially Labeled Classification with Markov Random Walks. In: *Advances in Neural Information Processing Systems,* vol. 14.

Talukdar, P. P., and Crammer, K. 2009. New Regularized Algorithms for Transductive Learning. In: *European Conference on Machine Learning (ECML-PKDD).*

Tomkins, A. 2008. *Keynote Speech.* CIKM Workshop on Search and Social Media.

Tsang, I. W., and Kwok, J. T. 2006. Large-Scale Sparsified Manifold Regularization. In: *Advances in Neural Information Processing Systems (NIPS) 19.*

Tsuda, K. 2005. Propagating Distributions on a Hypergraph by Dual Information Regularization. In: *Proceedings of the 22nd International Conference on Machine Learning.*

Vapnik, V. 1998. *Statistical Learning Theory.* New York: Wiley.

Vazirani, V. V. 2001. *Approximation Algorithms.* New York: Springer.

Wang, F., and Zhang, C. 2006. Label Propagation through Linear Neighborhoods. Pages 985–992 of: *Proceedings of the 23rd International Conference on Machine Learning.* New York: ACM.

White, N. 1986. *Theory of Matroids.* Cambridge University Press.

Woess, W. 2000. Random Walks on Infinite Graphs and Groups. *Cambridge Tracts in Mathematics 138.* New York: Cambridge University Press.

Zhu, X. 2005a. *Semi-Supervised Learning Literature Survey.* Technical Report 1530. Computer Sciences, University of Wisconsin–Madison.

Zhu, X. 2005b. *Semi-Supervised Learning with Graphs.* Ph.D. thesis, Carnegie Mellon University.

Zhu, X., and Ghahramani, Z. 2002a. *Learning from Labeled and Unlabeled Data with Label Propagation.* Technical Report, Carnegie Mellon University.

Zhu, X., and Ghahramani, Z. 2002b. *Towards Semi-supervised Classification with Markov Random Fields.* Technical Report CMU-CALD-02-106. Carnegie Mellon University.

Zhu, X., and Goldberg, A.B. 2009. *Introduction to Semi-supervised Learning.* Morgan & Claypool.

Zhu, X., Ghahramani, Z., and Lafferty, J. 2003. Semi-supervised Learning using Gaussian Fields and Harmonic Functions. In: *Proceedings of the International Conference on Machine Learning (ICML).*

CHAPTER 16

Distributed Transfer Learning via Cooperative Matrix Factorization

Evan Xiang, Nathan Liu, and Qiang Yang

Machine learning and data-mining technologies have already achieved significant success in many knowledge engineering areas including web search, computational advertising, recommender systems, etc. A major challenge in machine learning is the data sparsity problem. For example, in the domain of online recommender systems, we attempt to recommend information items (e.g., movies, TV, books, news, images, web pages, etc.) that are likely to be of interest to the user. However, the item space is usually very large and the amount of user preference values is small. When the user data are too sparse, it is difficult to obtain a reliable and useful model for recommendation. Whereas large online sites like Amazon and Google can easily access huge volumes of user data, the enormous number of smaller online business sites, which collectively constitute the long tail of the web, are much more likely to have very sparse user data and have difficulty in generating accurate recommendations. One potential solution to the data sparsity problem is to transfer knowledge from other information sources (e.g., Mehta and Hofmann, 2007; Li, Yang, and Xue, 2009). Such techniques for knowledge transfer are called *transfer learning* (see, e.g., Pan and Yang, 2010). An additional issue is that, in reality, many small websites often attract similar users and/or provide similar items, if not the identical ones, which implies that data about such users/items could potentially be distributed across different systems. For example, Delicious and Digg are both popular online social bookmarking tools. However, users often choose Delicious to maintain their favorite websites, and Digg is more often used to discover popular online news stories. Similarly, aided by product search engines, a user may easily purchase from many different online vendors, and thus, each vendor may record only a subset of the user's transactions. In all these scenarios, we can find that the user datasets held by different systems are complementary and can potentially be combined to model users more accurately.

In this chapter, we consider the case when different systems may form a *coalition*, in which the participating systems can cooperate and share information. A naive approach to enabling different systems to cooperate is to simply aggregate the data from individual systems, build a model using the aggregated data for the union of all the entities, and then pass the relevant part of the model back to the individual systems. However, such a centralized approach is often unfavorable and impractical for several reasons:

- *Communication and storage cost*: Transferring each task's data to a common central system would incur high communication and storage cost.
- *Computational cost*: The scale of the aggregated data from a large number of systems could be enormous. Processing such data on a centralized server can require highly scalable software and hardware infrastructure.

In recent years, scaling up data-mining algorithms to massive datasets using distributed computing techniques has become an increasingly popular research topic. In Das et al. (2007), a MapReduce (Dean and Ghemawat, 2008) implementation of the popular probabilistic latent semantic analysis model is described for collaborative filtering in online news personalization. More recently, Chen et al. (2009) designed a parallel Gibbs sampling algorithm for the latent Dirichlet allocation model (Blei, Ng, and Jordan, 2003). The general idea behind these algorithms is to divide the data into small sections that can be handled at an individual computing node and coordinate a large number of computing nodes to achieve scalability.

Our goal is slightly different from these works. In order to solve the data sparsity problem, we aim to transfer more knowledge from some other systems, without aggregating their raw data. Thus, we introduce a novel framework called *distributed coalitional learning* (DisCo), which enables multiple systems to form a coalition (Figure 16.1) and cooperate in order to build more accurate learning models. To address the aforementioned problems of a centralized approach, the DisCo framework is particularly designed to enable multiple systems to cooperate in a decentralized fashion so that their respective models can be jointly learnt without the need for data aggregation. There are two advantages of the DisCo framework. First, DisCo is based on the cooperative matrix factorization (CoMF) model, which extends the popular matrix factorization model by allowing multiple matrices with shared entities to be jointly factorized, so that datasets within different systems may complement and enhance each other. Second, it is easy to design distributed learning algorithms for the CoMF model,

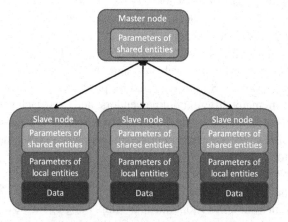

Figure 16.1 The coalitional learning framework for distributed transfer learning. Different tasks form a coalition, and knowledge transfer is achieved on the master node by exchanging the information carried by the parameters of shared entities.

while allowing each system to hold its own database and be responsible for updating its own model parameters. This avoids data aggregation/integration while achieving scalability by letting multiple systems divide and counterpoise the computing workload. Once the distributed learning finishes, each system would obtain a complete model for its own set of data and be able to draw inference independently in the prediction phase.

In recent years, an emerging technology trend for web applications is to embrace principles such as collective intelligence, openness, interoperability, and decentralized control/power structure.[1] These emerging patterns have enabled novel applications, such as mashups (e.g., fickrvision.com) and meta-social networks (e.g., friendfeed.com), that allow data and functionalities from multiple web sources to be easily reused and combined to create new services. This motivated the design of DisCo framework, which can be viewed as an extension of such a paradigm to the application domain of recommender systems. In the following sections, we first illustrate the basic framework for the distributed coalitional learning based on the cross system collaborative filtering tasks and show empirically the efficiency gain for transfer learning. Then, we discuss variations of the framework for its extension to other types of tasks. We provide some experimental results on real-world datasets, which successfully demonstrate that individual systems can improve their prediction accuracy using DisCo.

16.1 Distributed Coalitional Learning

Since our goal is to transfer knowledge from other parallel tasks to assist our target task, our first objective is to form a compact coalitional model that aggregates information from each individual task. Then, a second objective is to make each parallel system be able to exchange some useful information with such coalitional model to improve the performance of their respective tasks. Our distributed coalitional learning framework (DisCo) consists of two core components. The first is the cooperative matrix factorization (CoMF) model, which provides the basis for aggregating and transferring knowledge across different related tasks. The second is a distributed learning algorithm for solving the CoMF model, which allows coalitional learning to be implemented in a scalable manner.

16.1.1 Cooperative Matrix Factorization

For simplicity, we assume that the data for each task involve only the relationship between two types of entities, such as document-words or user-items, and thus can be represented by a matrix $\mathbf{X} \in \mathbb{R}^{m \times n}$. The DisCo framework is mainly based on the CoMF model, which allows multiple matrices with some shared entities to be jointly factorized. In this framework, datasets within different systems may complement and enhance each other.

Suppose that there are S recommender systems in a coalition. The sth system is associated with m_s users and n_s items denoted by $\mathcal{U}_s$ and $\mathcal{V}_s$, respectively. For

---

[1] http://en.wikipedia.org/wiki/Web_2.0.

each system s, we observe a sparse rating matrix $\mathbf{X}_s \in \mathbb{R}^{m_s \times n_s}$ with entries $X_{s,ij}$. Let $\mathcal{R}_s = \{(i, j, r) : r = X_{s,ij}, \text{where } X_{s,ij} \neq 0\}$ denote the set of observed ratings in each system. A basic assumption of the coalitional learning framework is that some users and items may be shared and serve as an "information bridge" to connect different individual systems. More formally, this implies that $\exists i, j : \mathcal{U}_i \cap \mathcal{U}_j \neq \emptyset$ or $\mathcal{V}_i \cap \mathcal{V}_j \neq \emptyset$. We refer the set of such users and items as *shared users* and *shared items*, denoted by $\widetilde{\mathcal{U}}$ and $\widetilde{\mathcal{V}}$. Let $\mathcal{U}^* = \mathcal{U}_1 \bigcup \mathcal{U}_2 \bigcup \cdots \bigcup \mathcal{U}_S$ and $\mathcal{V}^* = \mathcal{V}_1 \bigcup \mathcal{V}_2 \bigcup \cdots \bigcup \mathcal{V}_S$ denote the union of the collections of users and items in this coalition of S recommender systems, where $m^* = |\mathcal{U}^*|$ and $n^* = |\mathcal{V}^*|$ denote the total number of unique users and items in the coalition.

In order to derive a coalitional model for the collaborative filtering tasks, we introduce here CoMF. In CoMF, we model the users $\mathcal{U}^*$ and the items $\mathcal{V}^*$ in the coalition by a user factor matrix $\mathbf{U} \in \mathbb{R}^{k \times m^*}$ and an item factor matrix $\mathbf{V} \in \mathbb{R}^{k \times n^*}$, where the ith user and jth item are represented by $\mathbf{u}_i$ and $\mathbf{v}_j$, corresponding to the ith and jth column of $\mathbf{U}$ and $\mathbf{V}$, respectively. Let $\mathbf{U}_s \in \mathbb{R}^{k \times m_s}$ denote the matrix formed by the rows in $\mathbf{U}$ that correspond to $\mathcal{U}_s$. Similarly, let $\mathbf{V}_s \in \mathbb{R}^{k \times n_s}$ denote the matrix formed by the rows in $\mathbf{V}$ that correspond to $\mathcal{V}_s$. The goal is to approximate each rating matrix $\mathbf{X}_s$ by multiplying the factor matrices $\mathbf{U}_s$ and $\mathbf{V}_s$, i.e., $\mathbf{X}_s \approx \mathbf{U}_s^T \mathbf{V}_s$. In the CoMF model, the factor matrices $\mathbf{U}$ and $\mathbf{V}$ can be learned by minimizing the following loss function:

$$\mathcal{L} = \sum_{s=1}^{S} (\sum_{(i,j) \in \mathcal{R}_s} \left(\mathbf{u}_i^T \mathbf{v}_j - X_{s,ij} \right)^2 + \lambda (\parallel \mathbf{U} \parallel_F^2 + \parallel \mathbf{V} \parallel_F^2)), \qquad (16.1)$$

where λ controls the trade-off between the rating matrix approximation errors and model complexity reflected by the Frobenius norm of the factor matrices.

In the CoMF model, the multiple rating matrices $\mathbf{X}_s$ are jointly factorized and the set of factor matrices $\mathbf{U}_1, \ldots, \mathbf{U}_S$ and $\mathbf{V}_1, \ldots, \mathbf{V}_S$ for different systems becomes interdependent because the features of a shared user or a shared item are required to be the same when factorizing different rating matrices. This is in contrast to a non-cooperative approach, which would treat $\mathbf{U}_s$ and $\mathbf{V}_s$ for each of the S systems independently by minimizing the loss function:

$$\mathcal{L}_s = \sum_{(i,j) \in \mathcal{R}_s} \left(\mathbf{u}_i^T \mathbf{v}_j - X_{s,ij} \right)^2 + \lambda (\parallel \mathbf{U}_s \parallel_F^2 + \parallel \mathbf{V}_s \parallel_F^2) \qquad (16.2)$$

In order to find the optimal solution for the CoMF model, we can use the *alternating least squares* (ALS) algorithm (Zhou et al., 2008) (Algorithm 46) to minimize the loss function in Equation 16.1 with respect to $\mathbf{U}$ and $\mathbf{V}$.

When one of the factor matrices is fixed, minimizing $\mathcal{L}$ with respect to the other factor matrix is equivalent to solving a least squares problem. We can easily compute the gradient of the loss function $\mathcal{L}$ with respect to the user features $\mathbf{u}_i$:

$$\nabla_{\mathbf{u}_i} \mathcal{L} = \sum_{s=1}^{S} \sum_{j \in \mathcal{V}_{s,i}} (\mathbf{u}_i^T \mathbf{v}_j - X_{s,ij}) \mathbf{v}_j + \lambda \mathbf{u}_i$$

$$= (\sum_{s=1}^{S} \sum_{j \in \mathcal{V}_{s,i}} \mathbf{v}_j \mathbf{v}_j^T + \lambda E_k) \mathbf{u}_i - \sum_{s=1}^{S} \sum_{j \in \mathcal{V}_{s,i}} X_{s,ij} \mathbf{v}_j,$$

where E_k denotes a $k \times k$ identity matrix and $\mathcal{V}_{s,i}$ denotes the set of items rated by user i in system s. By setting the gradient $\nabla_{\mathbf{u}_i} \mathcal{L}$ to zero, we obtain the following closed-form expression for updating $\mathbf{u}_i$:

$$\mathbf{u}_i = \mathbf{A}_i^{-1} \mathbf{b}_i, \tag{16.3}$$

where

$$\mathbf{A}_i = \sum_{s=1}^{S} \sum_{j \in \mathcal{V}_{s,i}} \mathbf{v}_j \mathbf{v}_j^T + \lambda E_k \tag{16.4}$$

is a $k \times k$ matrix and

$$\mathbf{b}_i = \sum_{s=1}^{S} \sum_{j \in \mathcal{V}_{s,i}} X_{s,ij} \mathbf{v}_j \tag{16.5}$$

is a k-dimensional vector.

Similarly, to update the item features $\mathbf{v}_j$, we fix $\mathbf{U}$ and minimize $\mathcal{L}$ with respect to $\mathbf{v}_j$, which yields the following updating formulas:

$$\mathbf{v}_j = \mathbf{A}_j^{-1} \mathbf{b}_j, \tag{16.6}$$

where

$$\mathbf{A}_j = \sum_{s=1}^{S} \sum_{i \in \mathcal{U}_{s,j}} \mathbf{u}_i \mathbf{u}_i^T + \lambda E_k \tag{16.7}$$

is a $k \times k$ matrix and

$$\mathbf{b}_j = \sum_{s=1}^{S} \sum_{i \in \mathcal{U}_{s,j}} \mathbf{X}_{s,ij} \mathbf{u}_i \tag{16.8}$$

is a k-dimensional vector.

16.1.2 Distributed Learning for CoMF

Here, we introduce a distributed learning algorithm in such a way that different systems can cooperatively build their respective models by exchanging only a minimal amount of information of the compact model parameters of each participating system. In particular, our design adopts a master/slave communication model, which is based on the message passing interface (MPI) platform (Snir et al., 1998). Each system in the coalition acts as a slave node on which all the system-dependent data reside. In the case of the CoMF model, the local data include a system's rating matrix $\mathbf{X}_s$ and its factor matrices $\mathbf{U}_s$ and $\mathbf{V}_s$. A problem with this distributed scheme is that now the parameters of the shared users and shared items would be replicated across multiple systems that involve those shared entities. Here, we consider the simplest knowledge-sharing strategy; i.e., under the CoMF model, the features of shared users and shared items in different systems are required to be the same. Therefore, it is necessary to ensure that relevant portions of the factor matrices $\mathbf{U}_s$ and $\mathbf{V}_s$, which correspond to the shared entities in different systems, conform to one another. Therefore, we designate a master node that maintains a shared user factor matrix $\widetilde{\mathbf{U}} \in \mathbb{R}^{k \times |\widetilde{\mathcal{U}}|}$ and a shared item factor matrix $\widetilde{\mathbf{V}} \in \mathbb{R}^{k \times |\widetilde{\mathcal{V}}|}$. For each shared user i or shared item j, the master node maintains a list of slave nodes $\mathcal{S}_i = \{s | i \in \mathcal{V}_s\}$ that involve that user or item. As a result, whenever a shared entity's parameter $\widetilde{\mathbf{u}}_i$ (or $\widetilde{\mathbf{v}}_j$) is updated, the master will send a message to all slave nodes $\mathcal{S}_i$ to ensure that features for the shared entities remain consistent across different slave nodes. The design of our algorithm is based on the following two observations about the ALS algorithm (Algorithm 46). First, in each iteration of the ALS algorithm, the computation required for updating non-shared users and items in each system can be performed locally at each system using Equations 16.3 and 16.6. In particular, for a non-shared user $i \in \mathcal{U}_s \setminus \widetilde{\mathcal{U}}$, $\mathbf{A}_i$ and $\mathbf{b}_i$ depend only on ratings in $\mathbf{X}_s$ and parameters in $\mathbf{V}_s$. Analogously, for a non-shared item $j \in \mathcal{V}_s \setminus \widetilde{\mathcal{V}}$, expressions $\mathbf{A}_j$ and $\mathbf{b}_j$ required for updating $\mathbf{v}_j$ also depend only on ratings $\mathbf{X}_s$ and parameters in $\mathbf{U}_s$. Thus, as long as the user factor matrix (or the item factor matrix) conforms with the location of a non-shared user, the update of the parameters of the non-shared entities can be carried out at the slave node locally.

Algorithm 46: Alternating Least Squares

---

1. Initialize $\mathbf{U}$ and $\mathbf{V}$ with small random numbers
2. **while** $\mathcal{L}$ has not converged **do**
3.   Update $\mathbf{V}$ using Equation 16.6
4.   Update $\mathbf{U}$ using Equation 16.3

Second, the update of the parameters of shared entities would require information at multiple slave nodes. In particular, at slave node s, for each shared user $i \in \mathcal{U}_s \cap \widetilde{\mathcal{U}}$, we produce the following two messages to pass to the master node in order to compute expressions $\mathbf{A}_i$ and $\mathbf{b}_i$ needed for updating $\widetilde{\mathbf{u}}_i$ using Equation 16.3:

$$\mathcal{M}^A_{s,i} = \sum_{j \in \mathcal{U}_{s,i}} \mathbf{v}_j \mathbf{v}_j^T \qquad (16.9)$$

$$\mathcal{M}^b_{s,i} = \sum_{j \in \mathcal{U}_{s,i}} X_{s,ij} \mathbf{v}_j \qquad (16.10)$$

At the master node, once it receives all the messages for updating shared users, expressions $\mathbf{A}_i$ and $\mathbf{b}_i$ can be easily computed:

$$\mathbf{A}_i = \sum_{s \in \mathcal{S}_i} \mathcal{M}^A_{s,i} + \lambda E_k \qquad (16.11)$$

$$\mathbf{b}_i = \sum_{s \in \mathcal{S}_i} \mathcal{M}^b_{s,i} \qquad (16.12)$$

Then, using Equation 16.3, the shared user factor matrix $\widetilde{\mathbf{U}}$ can be easily updated. Next, the master node sends the rows of $\widetilde{\mathbf{U}}$ corresponding to $\mathcal{U}_s \cap \widetilde{\mathcal{U}}$ to each slave node so that slave nodes' user factor matrices $\mathbf{U}_s$ are updated. This completes the process of updating user parameters. The item factor matrices $\mathbf{V}_1, \ldots, \mathbf{V}_S$ and $\widetilde{\mathbf{V}}$ could then

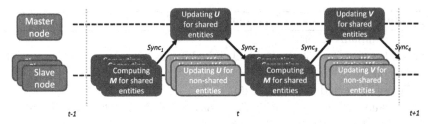

Figure 16.2 The distributed coalitional learning procedure for CoMF.

be updated following a similar procedure. It is evident that the distributed algorithm updates the user and item parameters in exactly the same way as the ALS algorithm does. The only difference from the centralized ALS lies in the fact that the computation for learning the non-shared entities is distributed to the slave nodes.

The detailed procedure at the master node and slave node is shown in Algorithms 47 and 48, respectively. On the one hand, using the distributed algorithm, parameters of non-shared entities are updated at each slave node completely locally, and the different slave processes are executed in parallel at their respective computing nodes (Figure 16.2). On the other hand, parameters of shared entities are updated at the master node on the basis of the messages passed from each slave node, and broadcast between the master and the slave nodes after each update. To maximally parallelize computation both at the master node and the slave nodes, special care is taken while ordering the operations at the slave nodes. In particular, when updating either the user or the item parameters, we first compute messages $\mathcal{M}_{s,i}^A$ and $\mathcal{M}_{s,i}^b$ and send them to the master node. This is immediately followed by updating the non-shared entities' parameters, whereas receiving results from the master node is the final step. This ensures that, while the master node is updating the parameters of shared entities, the slave nodes can carry out the computation that does not depend on the results from the master node.

Algorithm 47: Master Node Procedure for CoMF

---

1. Initialize $\widetilde{\mathbf{U}}$ and $\widetilde{\mathbf{V}}$ with small random numbers
2. **Sync$_0$**: Send each slave node the columns in $\widetilde{\mathbf{U}}$ and $\widetilde{\mathbf{V}}$ that correspond to $\mathcal{U}_s \cap \widetilde{\mathcal{U}}$ and $\mathcal{V}_s \cap \widetilde{\mathcal{V}}$
3. **while** convergence not reached **do**
4.   **Sync$_1$**: Receive and aggregate messages $\mathcal{M}_{s,i}^A$ and $\mathcal{M}_{s,i}^b$ from each slave node using Equations 16.11 and 16.12
5.   Update user parameters $\widetilde{\mathbf{U}}$ using Equation 16.3
6.   **Sync$_2$**: Send each slave node s the updated columns of $\widetilde{\mathbf{U}}$ that correspond to $\mathcal{U}_s \cap \widetilde{\mathcal{U}}$
7.   **Sync$_3$**: Receive and aggregate messages $\mathcal{M}_{s,j}^A$ and $\mathcal{M}_{s,j}^b$ from each slave node s
8.   Update item parameters $\widetilde{\mathbf{V}}$ using Equation 16.6
9.   **Sync$_4$**: Send each slave node s the updated columns of $\widetilde{\mathbf{V}}$ that correspond to $\mathcal{V}_s \cap \widetilde{\mathcal{V}}$

Algorithm 48: Slave Node s Procedure for CoMF

---

1. Random initialize $\mathbf{U}_s$ and $\mathbf{V}_s$
2. **Sync$_0$**: Receive from the master node initial values for columns of $\mathbf{U}_s$ and $\mathbf{V}_s$ that correspond to $\mathcal{U}_s \cap \widetilde{\mathcal{U}}$ and $\mathcal{V}_s \cap \widetilde{\mathcal{V}}$
3. **while** not instructed to terminate **do**
4.   Compute $\mathcal{M}_{s,i}^A$ and $\mathcal{M}_{s,i}^b$ using Equations 16.9 and 16.10 for each shared user i in $\mathcal{U}_s \cap \widetilde{\mathcal{U}}$
5.   **Sync$_1$**: Send $\mathcal{M}_{s,i}^A$ and $\mathcal{M}_{s,i}^b$ to the master node
6.   Update $\mathbf{u}_i$ using Equation 16.3 for each non-shared user i in $\mathcal{U}_s \setminus \widetilde{\mathcal{U}}$
7.   **Sync$_2$**: Receive updated columns of $\mathbf{U}_s$ that correspond to $\mathcal{U}_s \cap \widetilde{\mathcal{U}}$ from the master node
8.   Compute $\mathcal{M}_{s,j}^A$ and $\mathcal{M}_{s,j}^b$ for each item j in $\mathcal{V}_s \cap \widetilde{\mathcal{V}}$
9.   **Sync$_3$**: Send $\mathcal{M}_{s,j}^A$ and $\mathcal{M}_{s,j}^b$ to the master node
10.   Update $\mathbf{v}_j$ using Equation 16.6 for each non-shared item j in $\mathcal{V}_s \setminus \widetilde{\mathcal{V}}$
11.   **Sync$_4$**: Receive updated columns of $\mathbf{V}_s$ that correspond to $\mathcal{V}_s \cap \widetilde{\mathcal{V}}$ from the master node

---

Complexity Analysis

At each slave node, computing all $\mathbf{A}_i$ and $\mathbf{b}_i$ in each iteration would take a total running time of $O(N_s k^2)$, where $N_s = |\mathcal{R}_s|$ is the number of nonzero entries in X_s. Assuming $O(k^3)$ as the cost for inverting $\mathbf{A}_i$, the total running time for computing new parameter values for the non-shared entities using Equations 16.3 and 16.6 is $O((m'_s + n'_s)k^3)$, where $m'_s = |\mathcal{U}_s \setminus \widetilde{\mathcal{U}}|$ and $n'_s = |\mathcal{V}_s \setminus \widetilde{\mathcal{V}}|$. Therefore, the total running time for each iteration at the slave node is $O(N_s k^2 + (m'_s + n'_s)k^3)$.

At the master node, the running time for aggregating all the messages using Equations 16.11 and 16.12 is $O((m^* + n^*)k^2)$, where $m^* = |\widetilde{\mathcal{U}}|$ and $n^* = |\widetilde{\mathcal{V}}|$. Computing new values for all the parameters takes $O((m^* + n^*)k^3)$, which leads to a total running time of $O((m^* + n^*)k^3)$.

Since k is significantly smaller than m and n (e.g., 20), the running time of each slave node mainly depends on m'_s and n'_s, and the running time of the master node mainly depends on m^* and n^*.

Next, we analyze the communication cost. Since each shared entity can appear in at most S systems, the total cost of transferring all $\mathcal{M}_{s,i}^A$ and $\mathcal{M}_{s,i}^b$ is $O(S(m^* + n^*)k^2)$. Sending the updated parameters to all slave nodes would cost $O(S(m^* + n^*)k)$. Hence, the total communication cost for each iteration is bounded by $O(S(m^* + n^*)k^2)$.

Efficiency Test

To evaluate efficiency, we compare the run time of the distributed implementation of DisCo executed on a cluster of machines with that of a non-distributed version executed on a single machine, which implements the standard ALS algorithm for the CoMF model. We conducted different sets of experiments to answer the following questions: (1) How does the number of systems in a coalition affect the efficiency of DisCo? (2) How does the proportion of shared entities affect the efficiency of DisCo?

Table 16.1. *Running time of CoMF with varying number of systems (shared entities = 40%).*

ALS (centralized)		DisCo	
Number of systems	Time (s)	Time (s)	Speedup (×)
2	320	162	2.0
4	640	164	3.9
10	1,600	180	8.9
20	3,230	281	11.4
30	4,860	385	12.6
40	6,500	460	14.1

In this section, we compare the running time of DisCo with that of an undistributed implementation of the standard ALS algorithm that runs on a single machine with all the rating data from all systems. To test DisCo, we used a LAN-based cluster of 40 PCs each with an AMD Opteron 2.6GHz CPU and 2GB memory. The master and slave processes were executed on separate machines.

Dataset Description As it is difficult to obtain rating data from many real-world recommender systems, in order to evaluate the effectiveness of DisCo systematically, we use the large Netflix dataset[2] to synthesize a number of rating datasets to simulate multiple related recommender systems. We randomly sample 40 sub-matrices from the complete rating matrix, each comprising 5,000 items and 20,000 users. The average sparsity of these sub-matrices is about 0.7%. During the sampling process, if a particular entry in the original rating matrix is sampled multiple times, it is randomly assigned to only one of the samples to ensure that the different sub-matrices remain disjoint. For the shared entities, we also sample a proportion of users and items from each dataset that have also appeared in at least two datasets. For all of the following experiments, the latent factor k for matrix factorization is set to 10.

In the first set of experiments, we compare the running time for 20 iterations of DisCo and centralized ALS as the number of systems increases, while keeping the proportion of shared entities in each system fixed at 40% (Table 16.1). The speedup achieved by DisCo along with the ideal case of linear speedup is shown in Figure 16.3. We can observe that near linear speedup can be achieved when the number of systems is small. In addition, we note that, as the number of systems increases, the speedup increases slower comparatively as communication overhead becomes dominant.

In the second set of experiments, we compare the running time of DisCo and centralized ALS when the number of systems is fixed at 20, and the proportion of shared entities in each system increases from 0% to 100% (Table 16.2). The speedup achieved by DisCo is shown in Figure 16.4. We can observe that initially the speedup is significant because the number of shared entities is small. Thereafter, the running time of DisCo increases quickly with the proportion of shared entities. This is because the communication cost in the distributed learning algorithm is dominated by sending and receiving messages and parameters for updating parameters of the shared entities; hence, the communication cost would increase with the number of entities shared by

[2] http://www.netflixprize.com/

Table 16.2. *Running time of CoMF with varying proportion of shared entities (number of systems = 20).*

ALS (centralized)		DisCo	
Shared entities	Time (s)	Time (s)	Speedup ($\times$)
20%	3,230	215	15.0
40%	3,230	281	11.4
60%	3,230	400	8.1
80%	3,230	520	6.2
100%	3,230	800	4.0

the different systems. An extreme case occurs when the shared proportion of entities reaches 100%, we can observe that DisCo can still achieve a speedup of 4$\times$. The reason for such a speedup is that, although the parameter updating process for the shared entities is centralized on the master node, the computation of Equations 16.9 and 16.10 can still be distributed to the individual slave nodes.

16.1.3 CoMF for Knowledge Transfer

So far, we have shown that DisCo is able to scale up with a large number of cooperative learning tasks. Here, we illustrate the effectiveness of DisCo in knowledge transfer. In particular, we compare DisCo with traditional collaborative filtering methods that do not consider cooperation between multiple systems. Our first baseline method is the matrix factorization model (Koren, Bell, and Volinsky, 2009) built on an individual system's rating matrix independently to obtain each system's baseline, which we refer to as the independent matrix factorization (IMF) approach. The second baseline is the average filling (AF) method, which makes predictions using a linear combination of the target user's and item's mean ratings. We conducted experiments in order to answer the following questions: (1) Can we transfer knowledge among multiple related recommender systems to improve their performance by establishing cooperation among them using DisCo? (2) How does the number of tasks in a coalition affect the knowledge

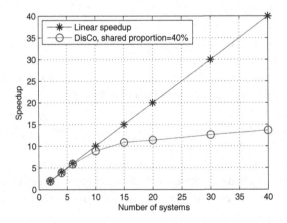

Figure 16.3 DisCo speedups for CoMF with varying different numbers of systems.

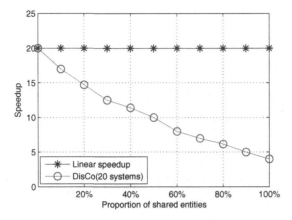

Figure 16.4 DisCo speedups for CoMF with varying proportions of shared entities.

transfer effectiveness of DisCo? (3) How does the proportion of shared entities affect the effectiveness of DisCo?

Dataset Description In order to evaluate the effectiveness of DisCo systematically, we use the Netflix dataset to synthesize a number of rating datasets to simulate multiple related recommender systems. We randomly sample 40 sub-matrices from the complete rating matrix in the way mentioned previously, each comprising 5,000 items and 20,000 users with sparsity around 0.7%. For each dataset, we randomly select 20% of the ratings as the test set.

We use root mean square error (RMSE) to evaluate the prediction quality of different models. The metric RMSE is defined as

$$\text{RMSE} = \sqrt{\frac{\sum_{i,j}(X_{i,j} - \widehat{X}_{i,j})^2}{N}}, \tag{16.13}$$

where $X_{i,j}$ and $\widehat{X}_{i,j}$ are the observed rating and predicted rating, respectively, and N is the total number of ratings used in the test set. As coalitional collaborative filtering involves multiple systems, we evaluate the overall performance using the average of the RMSEs computed on each system's test set.

Varying Proportion of Shared Entities

The entities shared by different systems are critical for bridging different recommender systems in the DisCo framework. Intuitively, the more entities the different systems have in common, the more they are expected to benefit from cooperating. To examine this effect, we vary the proportion of shared entities exposed by each system to the server from 0% to 100% while running DisCo. As this proportion increases, an increasing number of shared entities in the systems would conform to those in other systems rather than being independently updated by each system itself. In addition, we also compare the following three possible settings for DisCo: (1) DisCo(U) – where there exist only shared users in different systems, which is the case when different systems provide different but complementary items; (2) DisCo(I) – where there exist only shared items

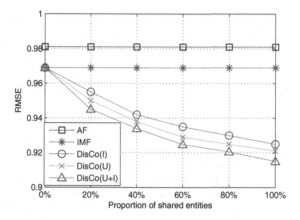

Figure 16.5 Effect on RMSE with the different proportions of shared entities for CoMF.

in different systems, which can be the case when user identities are anonymized; (3) DisCo(U+I) – where there exist both shared users and items in different systems. We measure the performance as the average of RMSEs on the 20 test sets for all systems. The results for all three settings are plotted in Figure 16.5. In this figure, the horizontal line on the top corresponds to the performance of the baseline model IMF, which is consistently outperformed by DisCo in all settings. This clearly indicates that different systems can indeed benefit from the coalition. Moreover, the performance consistently improves as more and more entities are shared among different systems. Among the three settings, having shared items appears to be more helpful than having shared users, whereas the most effective setting appears to be when different systems have both shared users and shared items. An extreme case occurs when the shared proportion reaches 100%, the effect of DisCo is equivalent to directly factorizing a huge rating matrix that is aggregated from all the systems.

Effect of the Additiveness of Coalitional Systems

Another important factor in DisCo is the number of different systems in a coalition. To evaluate this effect, we randomly associate each system with a varying number of other systems and examine how its performance changes within coalitions of increasing sizes. Again, we test the same three settings for DisCo introduced in the previous section. The proportion of shared entities is set to 40%. The results are plotted in Figure 16.6. We can observe that, as the number of systems increases, the average performance of the participating systems consistently improves. This is because, as more systems join a coalition, it is more likely for each system to be able to transfer knowledge from other systems via shared entities. This indicates that the DisCo framework exhibits the *network effect*, i.e., the more systems in the coalition, the more each participating system may benefit from DisCo.

16.1.4 Summary

In this section, we use the collaborative filtering tasks as an example to illustrate how a collection of related learning tasks can be jointly modeled as a coalition. The

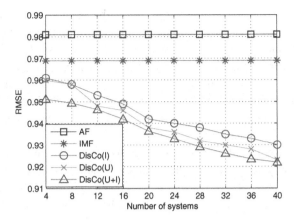

Figure 16.6 Effect on EMSE while varying the number of systems for CoMF.

key to integrate the related learning tasks together is to seek some shared entities to serve as an information bridge among different tasks. We also demonstrate that such coalitional model can be solved in a distributed manner. We can also observe that there is a trade-off between the effectiveness and efficiency of such distributed coalitional models. In order to guarantee the knowledge-sharing ratio, we hope to involve more and more shared entities. However, doing this will sacrifice the learning efficiency of the distributed model.

16.2 Extension of DisCo to Classification Tasks

In the previous section, we have illustrated a basic distributed coalitional learning framework using collaborative filtering tasks. In this section, we introduce an extension of DisCo to the coalition of classification tasks, which can help readers establish a connection between DisCo and traditional transfer learning problems.

16.2.1 Supervised Cooperative Matrix Factorization

Consider a classification task. Coalitional classification is different from collaborative filtering in that the goal of the latter tasks is to predict the ratings in a matrix. In contrast, classification tasks infer the labels of entire rows in a data matrix. In order to generalize the CoMF model to cope with classification tasks, we need to seek a way for knowledge sharing among different classification tasks.

A common approach in traditional transfer learning is to discover feature clusters that are shared among different tasks (Dai et al., 2007; Xue et al., 2008). In this vein, we select features as shared entities for knowledge sharing and adopt the supervised matrix factorization model (Zhu et al., 2007) for the local learning process of each task; i.e., two entities, instances, and class labels are used only in the local learning, whereas features are used in both local and global learning.

Supervised matrix factorization is a supervised learning model that can be easily extended for solving semi-supervised learning problems. Let C be the set of classes. For simplicity, we first consider binary classification problems, i.e., $C = \{-1, +1\}$.

Here, we still adopt similar terminologies as for the collaborative filtering problem. Suppose that there are S classification tasks in a coalition. The sth task is associated with m_s instances and n_s features, denoted by $\mathcal{U}_s$ and $\mathcal{V}_s$, respectively. For each task s, we observe a sparse feature matrix $\mathbf{X}_s \in \mathbb{R}^{m_s \times n_s}$ with entries $X_{s,ij}$, together with a partial label matrix $\mathbf{Y}_s$ with entries $Y_{s,ic} \in \{-1, +1, \emptyset\}$ ($\emptyset$ means that some instances are not labeled in the training set; the supervised matrix factorization model can also work in a semi-supervised learning mode). Similar to the coalitional collaborative filtering framework, we assume that some features serve as bridges to transfer the label information among different tasks. More formally, we have $\exists i, j : \mathcal{V}_i \cap \mathcal{V}_j \neq \emptyset$. Adopting a similar symbol, we refer the set of such features as *shared features* denoted by $\widetilde{\mathcal{V}}$. Let $\mathcal{U}^* = \mathcal{U}_1 \bigcup \mathcal{U}_2 \bigcup \cdots \bigcup \mathcal{U}_S$ and $\mathcal{V}^* = \mathcal{V}_1 \bigcup \mathcal{V}_2 \bigcup \cdots \bigcup \mathcal{V}_S$ denote the union of instances and features in this coalition of the S classification tasks, where $m^* = |\mathcal{U}^*|$ and $n^* = |\mathcal{V}^*|$ denote the total number of unique instances and features in the coalition.

In DisCo, we adopt the CoMF model, which extends traditional matrix factorization with the capability to jointly factorize multiple feature matrices from different tasks. In the CoMF model, we represent instances $\mathcal{U}^*$ and features $\mathcal{V}^*$ in the coalition by an instance factor matrix $\mathbf{U} \in \mathbb{R}^{k \times m^*}$ and a feature factor matrix $\mathbf{V} \in \mathbb{R}^{k \times n^*}$, where the ith instance and jth feature are represented by $\mathbf{u}_i$ and $\mathbf{v}_j$ that correspond to the ith and jth column of $\mathbf{U}$ and $\mathbf{V}$, respectively. Let $\mathbf{U}_s \in \mathbb{R}^{k \times m_s}$ denote the matrix formed by the rows in $\mathbf{U}$ that correspond to $\mathcal{U}_s$. Similarly, let $\mathbf{V}_s \in \mathbb{R}^{k \times n_s}$ denote the matrix formed by the rows in $\mathbf{V}$ that correspond to $\mathcal{V}_s$. For the collaborative filtering problem, the goal is to approximate each rating matrix $\mathbf{X}_s$ by multiplying the factor matrices $\mathbf{U}_s$ and $\mathbf{V}_s$, i.e., $\mathbf{X}_s \approx \mathbf{U}_s^T \mathbf{V}_s$. However, in order to solve the classification problem, we need to introduce another set of parameters for capturing the label information carried by $\mathbf{Y}_s$.

Assume that we know the labels $\{y_i\}$ for instances in $\mathcal{U}_s$. We aim to find a hypothesis $h_s : \mathcal{U}_s \to \mathbb{R}$, such that we set y_i to 1 when $h_s(\mathbf{u}_i) \geq 0$, and -1 otherwise. We assume that a transform from the latent space to $\mathbb{R}$ is linear, i.e.,

$$h_s(\mathbf{u}_i) = \mathbf{W}_s^T \mathbf{u}_i + w_0, \tag{16.14}$$

where $\mathbf{W}_s$ and w_0 are the parameters to be estimated. We can rewrite Equation 16.14 in a matrix form as

$$\mathbf{H}_s = \mathbf{U}_s \mathbf{W}_s^T \tag{16.15}$$

Unlike the loss on $\mathbf{X}_s$ (shown in Equation 16.2) in the collaborative filtering tasks, there is a second objective for the classification tasks, that is, to minimize the loss on $\mathbf{Y}_s$:

$$\mathcal{L}_{s,Y}(\mathbf{Y}_s, \mathbf{U}_s, \mathbf{W}_s) = \sum_C \sum_{m_s} g(\mathbf{Y}_s \cdot \mathbf{H}_s), \tag{16.16}$$

where $\mathbf{Y}_s$ is the class label, $\mathbf{W}_s$ is the parameter matrix for task s, and $\cdot$ is the elementwise product. We introduce another loss term $\mathcal{L}_{s,Y}(\mathbf{Y}_s, \mathbf{U}_s, \mathbf{W}_s)$ to capture the supervision information in each task, where the loss function $\mathcal{L}_{s,Y}$ can be instantiated with the needs of different tasks, such as smoothed hinge loss (Zhu et al., 2007) for classification or square loss for regression problems. Here, we adopt the smoothed hinge loss:

$$
g(x) = \begin{cases} 0, & \text{when} & x \geq 2 \\ 1 - x, & \text{when} & x \leq 0 \\ \dfrac{1}{4}(x-2)^2, & \text{when} & 0 \geq x \leq 2 \end{cases}
\tag{16.17}
$$

The object of supervised CoMF is to minimize the loss function:

$$
\mathcal{L} = \sum_{s=1}^{S} \Big(\sum_{(i,j)\in\mathcal{R}_s} \big(\alpha(\mathbf{u}_i^T \mathbf{v}_j - X_{s,ij}) \big)^2 + \beta \mathcal{L}_{s,Y}(\mathbf{Y}_s, \mathbf{U}_s, \mathbf{W}_s)
$$
$$
+ \frac{\lambda}{2}(\| \mathbf{U}_s \|_F^2 + \| \mathbf{V}_s \|_F^2 + \| \mathbf{W}_s \|_F^2))
\tag{16.18}
$$

16.2.2 Distributed Learning for Supervised CoMF

In order to find the optimal parameters for the supervised CoMF model, we use a gradient descent algorithm to minimize the loss function in Equation 16.18. We can alternatively seek the optimal factor matrix by minimizing $\mathcal{L}$ with respect to the other factor matrices. We can easily compute the gradient of the loss function $\mathcal{L}$ with respect to different factors:

$$
\nabla_{\mathbf{v}_j} \mathcal{L} = \left(\sum_{s=1}^{S} \sum_{i\in\mathcal{U}_{s,j}} \mathbf{u}_i \mathbf{u}_i^T + \lambda E_k \right) \mathbf{v}_j
$$
$$
- \sum_{s=1}^{S} \sum_{i\in\mathcal{U}_{s,j}} \mathbf{X}_{s,ij} \mathbf{u}_i
\tag{16.19}
$$

$$
\nabla_{\mathbf{u}_{s,i}} \mathcal{L} = \left(\sum_{j\in\mathcal{V}_{s,i}} \mathbf{v}_j \mathbf{v}_j^T + \lambda E_k \right) \mathbf{u}_i
$$
$$
- \sum_{j\in\mathcal{V}_{s,i}} \mathbf{X}_{s,ij} \mathbf{v}_j + \beta G_{s,i*} \mathbf{W}_s
\tag{16.20}
$$

$$
\nabla_{\mathbf{W}_s} \mathcal{L} = \beta G_s^T \mathbf{U}_s + \lambda \mathbf{U}_s,
\tag{16.21}
$$

where E_k denotes a $k \times k$ identity matrix and $\mathcal{V}_{s,i}$ denotes the set of features contained in instance i in task s. G_s is an $m_s \times |C|$ matrix, whose icth element is $Y_{s,ic} g'(Y_{s,ic} H_{s,ic})$, and g' is the derivative of g. Adopting the gradient-based method, we can iteratively update $\mathbf{u}_i$ and $\mathbf{W}$:

$$
\mathbf{u}_i = \mathbf{u}_i - \epsilon (\mathbf{A}_i \mathbf{u}_i - \mathbf{b}_i)
\tag{16.22}
$$
$$
\mathbf{W}_s = \mathbf{W}_s - \epsilon \left(\beta G_s^T \mathbf{U}_s + \lambda \mathbf{U}_s \right),
\tag{16.23}
$$

where

$$
\mathbf{A}_i = \sum_{j\in\mathcal{V}_{s,i}} \mathbf{v}_j \mathbf{v}_j^T + \lambda E_k
\tag{16.24}
$$

is a $k \times k$ matrix and

$$\mathbf{b}_i = \sum_{j \in \mathcal{V}_{s,i}} X_{s,ij} \mathbf{v}_j \tag{16.25}$$

is a k-dimensional vector.

Similarly, to update the feature factor $\mathbf{v}_j$, we fix $\mathbf{U}$ and minimize $\mathcal{L}$ with respect to $\mathbf{v}_j$, which yields the following updating formulas:

$$\mathbf{v}_j = \mathbf{v}_j - \epsilon (\mathbf{A}_j \mathbf{v}_j - \mathbf{b}_j), \tag{16.26}$$

where

$$\mathbf{A}_j = \sum_{s=1}^{S} \sum_{j \in \mathcal{V}_{s,i}} \mathbf{u}_i \mathbf{u}_i^T + \lambda E_k \tag{16.27}$$

is a $k \times k$ matrix and

$$\mathbf{b}_j = \sum_{s=1}^{S} \sum_{i \in \mathcal{U}_{s,j}} X_{s,ij} \mathbf{u}_i \tag{16.28}$$

is a k-dimensional vector.

Some parameters of shared features serve as an information bridge for knowledge transfer among different tasks, which would require information at multiple slave nodes. In particular, at slave node s, for each shared feature $j \in \mathcal{V}_s \cap \widetilde{\mathcal{V}}$, we produce the following two messages to pass to the master node in order to compute expressions $\mathbf{A}_j$ and $\mathbf{b}_j$ needed for updating $\widetilde{\mathbf{v}}_j$ using Equation 16.26:

$$\mathcal{M}_{s,j}^A = \sum_{i \in \mathcal{V}_{s,j}} \mathbf{u}_i \mathbf{u}_i^T \tag{16.29}$$

$$\mathcal{M}_{s,j}^b = \sum_{i \in \mathcal{V}_{s,j}} X_{s,ij} \mathbf{u}_i \tag{16.30}$$

On the master side, once the node has received all the messages for updating shared features, expressions $\mathbf{A}_j$ and $\mathbf{b}_j$ can be easily computed and sent back to each slave node:

$$\mathbf{A}_j^* = \sum_{s \in \mathcal{S}_j} \mathcal{M}_{s,j}^A + \lambda E_k \tag{16.31}$$

$$\mathbf{b}_j^* = \sum_{s \in \mathcal{S}_j} \mathcal{M}_{s,j}^b \tag{16.32}$$

Then using Equation 16.26, the shared feature factor matrix $\widetilde{\mathbf{V}}$ can be easily updated.

The detailed procedures at the master node and slave node are shown in Algorithms 49 and 50, respectively. Using the distributed algorithm, parameters of non-shared features and instances are updated at each slave completely locally, and the different slave processes are executed in parallel at their respective computing node (Figure 16.7). Likewise, parameters of shared features are aggregated at the master

---

Algorithm 49: Master Node Procedure for Supervised CoMF

---

1. Initialize $\widetilde{\mathbf{V}}$ with small random numbers
2. **Sync$_0$**: Send each slave node s the columns in $\widetilde{\mathbf{V}}$ that correspond to $\mathcal{V}_s \cap \widetilde{\mathcal{V}}$
3. **while** convergence not reached **do**
4.   **Sync$_1$**: Receive and aggregate messages $\mathcal{M}_{s,j}^A$ and $\mathcal{M}_{s,j}^b$ from each slave node using Equations 16.31 and 16.32
5.   **Sync$_2$**: Send each slave node s the aggregated messages $\mathcal{M}_{s,j}^{A*}$ and $\mathcal{M}_{s,j}^{b*}$

Algorithm 50: Slave Node s Procedure for Supervised CoMF

---

1. Random initialize $\mathbf{W}_s$, $\mathbf{U}_s$, and $\mathbf{V}_s$
2. **Sync$_0$**: Receive from the master node initial values for columns of $\mathbf{V}_s$ that correspond to $\mathcal{V}_s \cap \widetilde{\mathcal{V}}$
3. **while** not instructed to terminate **do**
4.   Compute $\mathcal{M}_{s,j}^A$ and $\mathcal{M}_{s,j}^b$ using Equations 16.29 and 16.30 for each feature j in $\mathcal{V}_s \cap \widetilde{\mathcal{V}}$
5.   **Sync$_1$**: Send $\mathcal{M}_{s,j}^A$ and $\mathcal{M}_{s,j}^b$ to the master node
6.   Update $\mathbf{v}_j$ using Equation 16.26 for each non-shared feature j in $\mathcal{V}_s \setminus \widetilde{\mathcal{V}}$
7.   **Sync$_2$**: Receive aggregated messages $\mathcal{M}_{s,j}^{A*}$ and $\mathcal{M}_{s,j}^{b*}$ from the master node
8.   Update $\mathbf{v}_j$ using Equation 16.26 for each shared feature j in $\mathcal{V}_s \cap \widetilde{\mathcal{V}}$
9.   Update $\mathbf{u}_i$ using Equation 16.22 for each instance i in $\mathcal{U}_s$
10.   Update $\mathbf{W}_s$ using Equation 16.23

---

node on the basis of the messages from each slave node and broadcast between the master and the slaves after each update. To maximally parallelize computation both at the master and the slave nodes, similarly to DisCo for CoMF, care was taken in re-ordering the operations at the slave node. In particular, when updating the feature parameters, we first compute messages $\mathcal{M}_{s,j}^A$ and $\mathcal{M}_{s,j}^b$ and send them to the master node. This is immediately followed by updating the non-shared feature parameters, whereas receiving results from the master node is the final step. This ensures that, while the master node is updating the shared features' parameters, the slave nodes can carry out the computation that does not depend on the results from the master node.

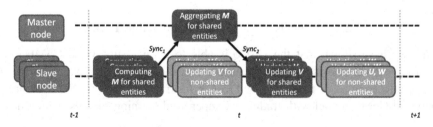

Figure 16.7 The distributed coalitional learning procedure for supervised CoMF.

Efficiency Test

In order to validate the efficiency of the distributed learning algorithm for the supervised CoMF model, we compare the running time of the distributed implementation of DisCo executed on a cluster of machines with that of a non-distributed version executed on a single machine. For testing DisCo, we used a LAN-based cluster of 50 PCs each with an AMD Opteron 2.6GHz CPU and 2GB memory. The master and slave processes were executed on separate machines.

Dataset Description We generate a number of classification tasks to simulate multiple related systems. We form 50 binary text classification tasks by randomly sampling and pairing subsets of documents from the tier 2 sub-categories in 20 Newsgroups[3] and tier 3 sub-categories in ODP[4]. Totally, we sampled more than 500,000 documents with 100,000 features. Each task consists of 2,000–3,000 items and 20,000 features on average, while no instance is shared among any pair of tasks. There are about 5,000 features shared by more than 80% of classification tasks, and we use them as shared features for information sharing across different tasks. This means that the proportion of shared features for each task is 25% on average.

In the first set of experiments, we compare the running time for 30 iterations of the centralized version (i.e., SMF) and the distributed version (i.e., DisCo) of supervised CoMF and obtain the speedup ratio as

$$\text{Speedup} = \frac{\text{time(SMF)}}{\text{time(DisCo)}} \tag{16.33}$$

When the number of systems is 10, it takes 380 seconds for SMF and 60 seconds for DisCo to finish 30 iterations of training. When the number of systems becomes 50, the running time of SMF is 1,600 seconds, whereas the running time of DisCo is only 130 seconds. The speedup achieved by DisCo along with the ideal case of linear speedup is shown in Figure 16.8. We can observe that a near linear speedup can be achieved when the number of tasks is small. However, when the number of systems increases, the speedup becomes less and less optimal. This effect may be due to the fact that the master node is burdened by aggregating the gradients from a large number of slaves. For simplicity, we only introduce the basic master/slave mode algorithm for DisCo in this chapter. One possible solution to this problem is to change the master/slave architecture to the peer-to-peer mode, which can distribute the computation of gradient aggregation to the other slaves.

16.2.3 Supervised CoMF for Knowledge Transfer

So far, we have shown that the DisCo is able to learn a supervised CoMF model with a large number of cooperative learning classification tasks. Next, we will validate the effectiveness of the supervised CoMF for transfer learning. We compare the supervised CoMF model with traditional supervised learning models, which do not

---

[3] http://people.csail.mit.edu/jrennie/20Newsgroups/.
[4] http://www.dmoz.org/

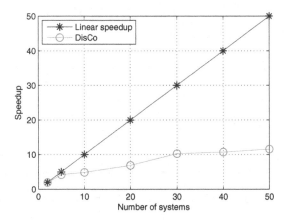

Figure 16.8 DisCo speedups for supervised CoMF with different numbers of systems.

consider cooperation between multiple classification tasks. We set the baseline method as building supervised matrix factorization models (Zhu et al., 2007) on each task's data independently to obtain each system's baseline, which we refer to as the independent supervised matrix factorization (ISMF) approach.

Dataset Description We conducted our experiments on the datasets used in the efficiency test. For each task, 150 instances are labeled, i.e., 5–8%, and the remaining instances also participate in the training process as unlabeled data. We use the true labels of the remaining 92–95% instances to evaluate the learned coalitional classification model.

Each task is a binary classification problem. We can use the standard accuracy to evaluate the prediction quality of different models. The accuracy for binary classification is defined as

$$\text{Accuracy} = \frac{TP + TN}{N}, \tag{16.34}$$

where TP and TN stand for correctly classified positive and negative instances, respectively, and N is the total number of instances used in the test set.

Effect of Additiveness of Coalitional Systems

In this experiment, we start with a coalition of five tasks. We continue to evaluate the averaged accuracy on these five initial tasks while adding more and more classification tasks into the coalition. The averaged accuracy values, compared with those for the ISMF model, are plotted in Figure 16.9. We can observe that as the number of systems increases, the average performance of the initial tasks consistently improves. Such results are quite impressive, because no matter the initial five or the further added tasks contain only 150 labeled instances each, which is insufficient to training an accurate classification model. From the results of ISMF, we find that we could achieve an accuracy of only around 80% for each individual task. In addition, such results demonstrate that, given a large number of weakly labeled datasets, we still can form a powerful coalition for knowledge transfer among different tasks.

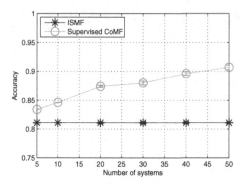

Figure 16.9 Effect of accuracy while varying the numbers of systems for supervised CoMF.

16.2.4 Summary

In this section, we use the classification tasks as an example to illustrate how the distributed coalitional model is flexible to be extended to solve other types of learning tasks. The key to switching between different types of learning tasks is to quickly find out what entities can be used as shared entities to serve as an information bridge for knowledge transfer. In other words, we need to think about what is invariant or stable among our target tasks. Then, we need to seek a trade-off between the effectiveness and efficiency for such distributed coalitional model.

16.3 Conclusion

In this chapter, we introduced a novel distributed coalitional collaborative filtering (DisCo) framework for enabling multiple related recommender systems to cooperate in order to build more accurate prediction models. In DisCo, knowledge transfer across different recommender systems or classification tasks is achieved using the CoMF model, which is solved using distributed learning algorithms that are scalable and efficient. Extensive experiments on real-world movie ratings and text classification datasets have demonstrated DisCo's effectiveness and efficiency.

Furthermore, the DisCo framework is flexible to be extended in several directions. First, rather than requiring different systems to adopt matrix factorization as their homogeneous models, heterogeneous models can be allowed in different individual systems. Second, the current distributed algorithms are based on the master/slave communication model. One may be interested in alternative architectures such as peer-to-peer based models that may require no additional master component and lower communication costs.

References

Blei, D. M., Ng, A. Y., and Jordan, M. I. 2003. Latent Dirichlet Allocation. *Journal of Machine Learning Research*, **3**, 993–1022.

Chen, W.-Y., Chu, J.-C., Luan, J., Bai, H., Wang, Y., and Chang, E. Y. 2009. Collaborative Filtering for Orkut Communities: Discovery of User Latent Behavior. Pages 681–690 of: *WWW '09: Proceedings of the 18th International Conference on World Wide Web.*

Dai, W., Xue, G.-R., Yang, Q., and Yu, Y. 2007. Co-clustering Based Classification for Out-of-Domain Documents. Pages 210–219 of: *Proceedings of the 13th ACM SIGKDD International Conference on Knowledge Discovery and Data Mining, KDD 2007*, San Jose, California, USA.

Das, A. S., Datar, M., Garg, A., and Rajaram, S. 2007. Google News Personalization: Scalable Online Collaborative Filtering. Pages 271–280 of: *WWW '07: Proceedings of the 16th International Conference on World Wide Web.*

Dean, J., and Ghemawat, S. 2008. MapReduce: Simplified Data Processing on Large Clusters. *Communications of the ACM*, **51**(1), 107–113.

Koren, Y., Bell, R., and Volinsky, C. 2009. Matrix Factorization Techniques for Recommender Systems. *IEEE Computer*, **42**(8), 30–37.

Li, B., Yang, Q., and Xue, X. 2009. Can Movies and Books Collaborate? Cross-domain Collaborative Filtering for Sparsity Reduction. Pages 2052–2057 of: *International Joint Conference on Artificial Intelligence (IJCAI).*

Mehta, B., and Hofmann, T. 2007. Cross System Personalization and Collaborative Filtering by Learning Manifold Alignments. Pages 244–259 of: *KI 2006: Advances in Artificial Intelligence.*

Pan, S. J., and Yang, Q. 2010. A Survey on Transfer Learning. *IEEE Transactions on Knowledge and Data Engineering*, **22**(10), 1345–1359.

Snir, M., Otto, S., Huss-Lederman, S., Walker, D., and Dongarra, J. 1998. *MPI-The Complete Reference, Vol. 1: The MPI Core.*

Xue, G.-R., Dai, W., Yang, Q., and Yu, Y. 2008. Topic-bridged PLSA for Cross-domain Text Classification. Pages 627–634 of: *Proceedings of the 31st Annual International ACM SIGIR Conference on Research and Development in Information Retrieval, SIGIR 2008*, Singapore, July 20–24.

Zhou, Y., Wilkinson, D., Schreiber, R., and Pan, R. 2008. Large-scale Parallel Collaborative Filtering for the Netflix Prize. Pages 337–348 of: *AAIM '08: Proceedings of the 4th International Conference on Algorithmic Aspects in Information and Management.*

Zhu, S., Yu, K., Chi, Y., and Gong, Y. 2007. Combining Content and Link for Classification Using Matrix Factorization. Pages 487–494 of: *SIGIR '07: Proceedings of the 30th Annual International ACM SIGIR Conference on Research and Development in Information Retrieval.*

CHAPTER 17

Parallel Large-Scale Feature Selection

Jeremy Kubica, Sameer Singh, and Daria Sorokina

The set of features used by a learning algorithm can have a dramatic impact on the performance of the algorithm. Including extraneous features can make the learning problem more difficult by adding useless, noisy dimensions that lead to *over-fitting* and increased computational complexity. Conversely, excluding useful features can deprive the model of important signals. The problem of feature selection is to find a subset of features that allows the learning algorithm to learn the "best" model in terms of measures such as accuracy or model simplicity.

The problem of feature selection continues to grow in both importance and difficulty as extremely high-dimensional datasets become the standard in real-world machine learning tasks. Scalability can become a problem for even simple approaches. For example, common feature selection approaches that evaluate each new feature by training a new model containing that feature require learning a linear number of models each time they add a new feature. This computational cost can add up quickly when we iteratively add many new features. Even those techniques that use relatively computationally inexpensive tests of a feature's value, such as mutual information, require at least linear time in the number of features being evaluated.

As a simple illustrative example, consider the task of classifying websites. In this case, the dataset could easily contain many millions of examples. Including very basic features such as text unigrams on the page or HTML tags could easily provide many thousands of potential features for the model. Considering more complex attributes such as bigrams of words or co-occurrences of particular HTML tags can dramatically drive up the complexity of the problem.

Similar large-scale, high-dimensional problems are now common in other applications such as internet algorithms, computational biology, or social link analysis. Thus, as we consider feature selection on modern datasets, traditional single machine algorithms may no longer be feasible to produce models in reasonable time.

In this chapter, we examine parallelizing feature selection algorithms for logistic regression using the MapReduce framework. In particular, we examine the setting of *forward* feature selection in which at every step new features are added to an existing model. We describe and compare three different techniques for evaluating new features: full forward feature selection (Whitney 1971), single feature optimization (SFO; Singh et al., 2009), and grafting (Perkins, Lacker, and Theiler, 2003). Although all these techniques provide fast greedy approaches to the full feature selection problem, they still scale poorly with the number of features. We show how each of these techniques can naturally be parallelized to gracefully scale to much larger feature sets.

Our discussion focuses on the logistic regression learning algorithm. Recent comparison studies of machine learning algorithms in high-dimensional data have shown that logistic regression, along with Random Forests and SVMs, is a top performing algorithm for high-dimensional data (Caruana, Karampatziakis, and Yessenalina, 2008). Given the fact that logistic regression is often faster to train than more complex models like Random Forests and SVMs (Komarek and Moore, 2005), in many situations it can be a preferred method for dealing with large-scale high-dimensional datasets.

17.1 Logistic Regression

Logistic regression is a simple model for predicting the probability of an event and is often used for binary classification. Assume that we have a dataset containing N data points $\{(\vec{x}_i, y_i)\}$, $1 \leq i \leq N$, where $\vec{x}_i$ are the vectors of input feature values and $y_i \in \{0, 1\}$ are binary response values. Logistic regression represents log odds of the event as a linear model:

$$\log\left(\frac{p}{1-p}\right) = \vec{\beta} \cdot \vec{x} \tag{17.1}$$

Here $p = P(y = 1)$ is the predicted probability of a positive outcome and $\vec{\beta}$ is the vector of model parameters. Equation 17.1 is equivalent to the following representation of p:

$$p = f_{\vec{\beta}}(\vec{x}) = \frac{e^{\vec{\beta} \cdot \vec{x}}}{1 + e^{\vec{\beta} \cdot \vec{x}}} \tag{17.2}$$

Therefore, the logistic regression model is completely defined by the vector of coefficients $\vec{\beta}$. The *link function* $f_{\vec{\beta}}(\vec{x})$ defines a sigmoid that translates the linear function of $\vec{\beta} \cdot \vec{x}$ onto the range [0, 1]. It is useful to note that this model can be extended to categorical prediction using the multinomial logit and that many of the techniques described later can similarly be adapted.

Logistic regression models are most often learned by *maximum likelihood estimation*, which finds the $\vec{\beta}$ that maximizes the probability of the data given the model

$$\vec{\beta}_{learned} = \arg\max_{\vec{\beta}} P(\mathbf{Y}|\vec{\beta}, \mathbf{X})$$

$$= \arg\max_{\vec{\beta}} \left(\prod_{i=1}^{N} f_{\vec{\beta}}(\vec{x}_i)^{y_i} (1 - f_{\vec{\beta}}(\vec{x}_i))^{(1-y_i)}\right), \tag{17.3}$$

where $\mathbf{X} = \{\vec{x}_1, \vec{x}_2, \cdots, \vec{x}_N\}$ is the full $N \times D$ dataset. Equivalently, we can maximize the model's log-likelihood:

$$\vec{\beta}_{learned} = \arg\max_{\vec{\beta}} \sum_{i=1}^{N} \left(y_i \ln f_{\vec{\beta}}(\vec{x}_i) + (1 - y_i) \ln(1 - f_{\vec{\beta}}(\vec{x}_i)) \right),$$

(17.4)

which simplifies the mathematics. Since there is no closed-form solution to this maximization, the standard approach to solving it is to use an iterative algorithm such as Newton Raphson (Hastie, Tibshirani, and Friedman, 2001), Fisher's scoring (Komarek and Moore, 2005), or coordinate descent (Friedman, Hastie, and Tibshirani, 2008). These approaches can still be computationally intensive, especially for high-dimensional problems.

For the rest of the discussion, we assume that the values of $\vec{x}$ are binary or continuous. For general categorical attributes, we use the standard technique of unrolling categorical attributes into disjoint binary attributes. For example, we can represent a single categorical attribute COLOR $\in$ { RED, BLUE, GREEN } as three Boolean attributes: COLOR_IS_RED, COLOR_IS_BLUE, and COLOR_IS_GREEN. Thus, a k-valued feature becomes k disjoint binary features that form a logical group, called a *feature class*. Features in a feature class are by definition constrained to be completely disjoint.

17.2 Feature Selection

The goal of feature selection is to find a subset of features that produces the "best" model $f_{\vec{\beta}}(\vec{x})$ for the dataset $\{(\vec{x}, y)\}$. Often, this means finding a small model that performs well on a given loss metric. In this chapter, we focus primarily on cases where "best" is defined as the model's (unpenalized) likelihood on the training or test set. However, the techniques described can easily be adapted to other scoring measures.

An exhaustive approach for feature selection on a set of D possible features would simply learn models for all 2^D possible combinations of features and directly evaluate their performance. However, the cost of this approach grows exponentially with the number of features, and this method becomes completely unfeasible for even small feature sets.

A range of feature selection techniques have been developed to avoid this combinatorial explosion while still accurately finding good sets of features. These techniques vary widely in how they measure quality of the features and their knowledge of the underlying algorithm. One common split is between *wrapper* algorithms, techniques that utilize knowledge of the underlying model, and *filter* algorithms that are independent of the underlying learning algorithm.

In this chapter, we focus on the *forward selection* wrapper framework introduced by Whitney (1971). Forward selection algorithms incrementally build feature sets by adding new features to the current model. Such methods are expected to perform well, but often at the cost of high computational complexity (John, Kohavi, and Pfleger, 1994). In the following, we describe three different techniques for evaluating new features in this framework: full forward feature selection (Whitney 1971), SFO

(Singh et al., 2009), and grafting (Perkins et al., 2003). For a good discussion of other feature selection techniques, see also Guyon and Elisseeff (2003).

17.2.1 Forward Feature Selection

Forward feature selection is a heuristic that significantly reduces the number of feature sets that are evaluated (Whitney, 1971). We begin with an empty model. Then, on each iteration of the algorithm, we choose a feature that gives the best performance when added to the current set of features. Each feature is evaluated by adding it to the current set of features, relearning the whole model, and evaluating the model under the desired score metric. This means that on dth iteration we build $D - (d - 1)$ models, where D is the original number of candidate features. Thus, the overall number of models to build and evaluate becomes quadratic in the number of features. It is better than exponential, but the complexity is still very high when all $\vec{\beta}$ in every model are learned by a complex iterative method.

Throughout the rest of the chapter, we use the notation x_{id} and β_d to denote features and coefficients in the current model, respectively, and we use the notation x'_{id} and β'_d to denote features that are being evaluated for addition to the model. In this notation, forward feature selection starts with an empty set of features, $\vec{x} = \{\}$, and repeatedly adds the best feature from $\vec{x}''$ to $\vec{x}$.

17.2.2 Single Feature Optimization

Ideally, we would evaluate each new feature in the context of a fully learned model containing both that feature and the current set of features. However, as described previously, this presents a computational challenge. For even moderate dataset sizes and numbers of features, this may not be feasible.

The SFO heuristic speeds up this evaluation by retaining coefficients from the current best model and optimizing only the coefficient β'_d of the new feature (Singh et al., 2009). The result is an approximate model that can be evaluated. In this way, we create $D - (d - 1)$ *approximate* models on each iteration of forward selection. After evaluating them and choosing the best feature, we rerun the full logistic regression to produce a fully learned model that includes the newly selected feature(s). We begin with this model for the next iteration of feature selection, so the approximation errors do not compound. As we rerun the full logistic regression solver only once on each iteration, we need to learn D models – linear in the number of features as opposed to quadratic.

We can quickly learn an approximate model by limiting the optimization only to the coefficient of the new feature. We hold the previous model parameters constant and perform one-dimensional optimization over the new coefficient. For each new feature x'_d, we compute an estimated coefficient β'_d by maximizing the log-likelihood L with the new feature:

$$\arg\max_{\beta'_d} \sum_{i=1}^{N} \left(y_i \ln f_{\vec{\beta}^{(d)}}(\vec{x}_i^{(d)}) + (1 - y_i) \ln(1 - f_{\vec{\beta}^{(d)}}(\vec{x}_i^{(d)})) \right), \qquad (17.5)$$

where $\vec{x}_i^{(d)} = \vec{x}_i \cup \{x'_{id}\}$ is the set of features in the model and the candidate feature. Similarly, $\vec{\beta}^{(d)}$ includes the candidate coefficient β'_d. Thus,

$$f_{\vec{\beta}^{(d)}}(\vec{x}_i^{(d)}) = \frac{e^{\vec{\beta} \cdot \vec{x}_i + x'_{id}\beta'_d}}{1 + e^{\vec{\beta} \cdot \vec{x}_i + x'_{id}\beta'_d}} \qquad (17.6)$$

There are a variety of optimization approaches that we could use to solve Equation 17.5. We use Newton's method to maximize the log-likelihood L:

$$\frac{\partial L}{\partial \beta'_d} = 0 \qquad (17.7)$$

We start at $\beta'_d = 0$ and iteratively update β'_d using the standard update,

$$\beta'_d = \beta'_d - \frac{\frac{\partial L}{\partial \beta'_d}}{\frac{\partial^2 L}{\partial \beta_d'^2}}, \qquad (17.8)$$

until convergence. In the case where L is the log-likelihood in Equation 17.5, the derivatives simplify to

$$\frac{\partial L}{\partial \beta'_d} = \sum_{i=1}^{N} x'_{id}(y_i - f_{\vec{\beta}^{(d)}}(\vec{x}_i^{(d)})) \qquad (17.9)$$

$$\frac{\partial^2 L}{\partial \beta_d'^2} = -\sum_{i=1}^{N} x_{id}'^2 f_{\vec{\beta}^{(d)}}(\vec{x}_i^{(d)})(1 - f_{\vec{\beta}^{(d)}}(\vec{x}_i^{(d)})) \qquad (17.10)$$

This optimization needs only to iterate over those records that contain the new feature, $x'_{id} = 1$, and thus can be very efficient for sparse data.

Once we have the approximate model containing the new feature(s), it is trivial to use it to compute standard performance metrics such as log-likelihood, AUC, or prediction error. Thus, we can score the new feature class by directly evaluating the approximate model.

An obvious drawback of such SFO is that we do not relearn the remaining coefficients. Therefore, we can get only an approximate estimate of the effect of adding the new feature. For example, we will *underestimate* the performance of the new model on training set metrics. Despite this potential drawback, this limited optimization can still provide a strong signal.

Feature Class Optimization

Many real-world problems contain categorical attributes that can be exploded into a series of binary features. As noted previously, the resulting features from a single feature class are by definition disjoint. Since we hold all other coefficients fixed, we can optimize each feature *independently* of others and later combine the resulting coefficients to form a complete model. Further, each of these optimizations needs to run only over those records that contain the relevant feature. For a k-valued categorical attribute that has been unrolled into $\{x'_1, \ldots, x'_k\}$, we estimate $\{\beta'_1, \ldots, \beta'_k\}$ by solving Equation 17.5 independently for each of the resulting binary feature. Thus, we can trivially break the problem of evaluating categorical attributes into a series of smaller independent optimizations. Such unrolling is particularly well suited for the SFO described previously.

17.2.3 Grafting

Perkins et al. (2003) propose using the loss function's gradient with respect to the new feature to decide whether to add this feature. The gradient of the loss function with respect to the new feature is used as an indication of how much the new feature would help the model. As with SFO, this gradient is computed independently for each feature using the current coefficients in the model.

More formally, grafting uses the magnitude of gradient with respect to that feature's coefficient:

$$\left|\frac{\partial L}{\partial \beta_d'}\right| = \left|\sum_i x_{id}'(y_i - p_i)\right|, \tag{17.11}$$

where p_i is the model's prediction for the feature vector $\vec{x}_i$.

At each step, the feature with the largest magnitude of gradient is added to the model:

$$\arg\max_{\beta_d'} \left|\frac{\partial L}{\partial \beta_d'}\right| \tag{17.12}$$

In a gradient-descent algorithm, this is equivalent to initially fixing coefficients at zero and at each step allowing the parameter with the greatest effect on the objective function to move away from zero. As with full forward feature selection and SFO, the non-zero coefficients are added one at a time and the model is fully relearned after each feature is added.

17.2.4 Multi-Class Prediction Problems

The forward feature selection techniques can also be easily applied to multi-class prediction problems. One standard approach is to learn a separate model for each class, by treating the problem as a series of binary classification problems. Each model is queried at prediction time and the class label with the highest predicted value is chosen. Thus, if we have C different class labels, we need to train and query C models.

In the case of feature evaluation, we aim to find the best feature to add for each of these models. We can do this in several different ways. The easiest approach is to create a separate training dataset for each classification label and run feature evaluation for each of these datasets. This approach is also equivalent to creating a single dataset that creates C modified copies of each record by appending the corresponding class label to each feature in that record, including the bias key. The result is a dataset with $N \cdot C$ records that effectively represents C different datasets.

For concreteness, consider a classification problem with three labels: a, b, and c. In this case, a single input record with features and label a, $\{1, 2, 3\} = a$, would be transformed into three records: $\{a : 1, a : 2, a : 3\} = 1$, $\{b : 1, b : 2, b : 3\} = 0$, and

$\{c : 1, c : 2, c : 3\} = 0$. Since the modified copies of the features are completely disjoint for each model, the overall model acts as C independent models.

17.3 Parallelizing Feature Selection Algorithms

All three of the forward feature evaluation methods described previously can become computationally expensive as the size of the data grows. Even the SFO and gradient evaluations require at least a single pass through the dataset for each iteration of the feature evaluation algorithm. One approach for scaling up these algorithms to even larger datasets is to parallelize the evaluation and distribute the cost over many machines.

17.3.1 Parallel Full Forward Feature Selection

The basic forward feature selection approach is trivial to parallelize by only partitioning evaluation of features. At each iteration of forward feature selection, we aim to determine the "best" feature to add. We can do this in parallel by partitioning the D features to be evaluated into K subsets and evaluate each subset of features independently on K machines. Each machine then needs to learn and evaluate only $\frac{D}{K}$ full models per iteration. This can lead to significant savings over a single-machine implementation for large D.

The disadvantage of this approach is that, although the work is distributed over K machines, we still have to relearn a full model for each feature – which can be costly. Thus, this approach does not help us scale to large datasets in terms of the number of records.

17.3.2 Parallel SFO

The SFO heuristic is especially well suited for parallelization. In particular, we can effectively partition the computation first over the records and then over the candidate features. This allows SFO to scale to both high dimensionality and a large number of records. We developed the SFO evaluation algorithm in the context of the MapReduce framework (Dean and Ghemawat, 2004).

At a high level, the MapReduce framework consists of two distinct phases, mapping and reducing, which parallelize the computation over the training records and potential features, respectively. During the mapping phase, the algorithm iterates over the input records and collects the statistics needed to estimate the candidate coefficients for each feature. During the reduce phase, the algorithm operates on these per-feature sets of data to compute the estimated coefficients; see Figure 17.1 for an illustration of the process.

More formally, the SFO MapReduce algorithm consists of three steps:

1. **Mapping Phase** (*parallel over records, Algorithm 51*): Iterate over the training records, computing the raw information needed to later estimate the coefficients. For each training record, $(\vec{x}_i, y_i, \vec{x}_i')$, compute the predicted probability of the current model

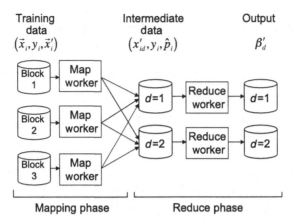

Figure 17.1 Conceptual data flow of the feature evaluation MapReduce with three input data blocks and two features. In the mapping stage, separate processors operate on blocks of training data $(\vec{x}_i, y_i, \vec{x}_i')$ to produce datasets of statistics $(\vec{x}_i', y_i, p_i)$ for each new feature in the record $\vec{x}_i'$. In the reduce phase, separate processors operate on each of these datasets, computing estimated coefficients for the new features β_d'.

Algorithm 51: The SFO Map Function (Takes a data block $\{\mathbf{X}, \vec{y}\}$ and a vector of coefficients $\vec{\beta}$. Produces a dataset $T_d = \bigcup_{\{i:x_{id}'=1\}} (\vec{x}_i', y_i, p_i)$ of statistics for each candidate feature.)

> **For each** record $\{\vec{x}_i, y_i, \vec{x}_i'\}$ in the data $\{\mathbf{X}, \vec{y}\}$ **do**
> Compute the predicted probability: $p_i = f_{\vec{\beta}}(\vec{x}_i)$
> **For each** active candidate feature $x_{id}' \in \vec{x}_i'$ **do**
> > Output $(\vec{x}_i', y_i, p_i)$

$p_i = f_{\vec{\beta}}(\vec{x}_i)$. Then, for each of the candidate features that is active in this record, output the necessary statistics, $(\vec{x}_i', y_i, p_i)$, to the reduce phase. We can collect the lists of predicted probabilities and true outcomes in a separate, intermediate dataset for each of the candidate features: $T_d = \bigcup_{\{i:x_{id}'=1\}} (\vec{x}_i', y_i, p_i)$. The reduce phase will then be able to use each of these lists to independently compute the coefficients. Note that, since the input features are binary, we need to collect statistics for a candidate feature only in those records where that feature is active.

2. **Reduce Phase** (*parallel over features, Algorithm 52*): For each feature being evaluated, use the corresponding outputs of the mapping phase, $T_d = \bigcup_{\{i:x_{id}'=1\}} (\vec{x}_i', y_i, p_i)$, to compute an estimated coefficient β_d' as in Section 17.2.2. Here, we compute an approximate coefficient by learning a correction to the predicted probabilities for the records in which this feature occurs. We can also aggregate estimated changes in training set log-likelihood by using the estimated coefficients.

3. **Post-Processing**: Aggregate the coefficients for all features in the same feature class.

Since the features are always treated independently up to the post-processing phase, we can also use this algorithm to evaluate different non-disjoint feature classes in a single run. This allows us to trivially explore *all* potential feature classes in parallel.

Algorithm 52: The SFO Reduce Function (Takes a dataset $T_d = \bigcup_{\{i:x'_{id}=1\}}$ $(\vec{x_i}', y_i, p_i)$ for a candidate feature. Produces an estimated coefficient β'_d for that feature.)

$\beta'_d = 0$

while β'_d has not converged **do**

Initialize the first and second derivatives: $\frac{\partial L}{\partial \beta'_d} = \frac{\partial^2 L}{\partial \beta'^2_d} = 0$

For each record $(\vec{x_i}, y_i, p_i) \in T_d$ **do**

$a_i = \log\left(\frac{p_i}{1-p_i}\right)$

Compute the new prediction under β'_d: $p'_i = \frac{e^{a_i+\beta'_d}}{1+e^{a_i+\beta'_d}}$

Update the first derivative sum: $\frac{\partial L}{\partial \beta'_d} = \frac{\partial L}{\partial \beta'_d} + (y_i - p'_i)x'_{id}$

Update the second derivative sum: $\frac{\partial^2 L}{\partial \beta'^2_d} = \frac{\partial^2 L}{\partial \beta'^2_d} - p'_i(1 - p'_i)x'^2_{id}$

Update the estimate of β'_d using a Newton's step: $\beta'_d = \beta'_d - \frac{\partial L}{\partial \beta'_d} / \frac{\partial^2 L}{\partial \beta'^2_d}$

In the ideal case, parallelizing this computation over K machine reduces the runtime by a factor of K. We can know this by looking at the running time of the component phases. The running time of the mapping phase is approximately $O(\frac{N \cdot D_{max}}{K})$, where N is the number of records and D_{max} is the maximum number of features active in any record. This running time follows directly from the $O(D_{max})$ cost of computing a predicted probability using the current feature set and storing it for each active candidate feature that is required for each of the N records. Similarly, the running time of the reduce phase is $O(\frac{N_{max} \cdot D}{K})$, where N_{max} is the maximum number of records containing a single new feature. This follows from the cost of computing the estimated coefficient for each candidate feature. Note that the N_{max} cost can be significant for common features, such as the bias term. Singh et al. (2009) describe a method for further reducing this running time by using histograms.

However, it is important to note that we do not expect to see this ideal speedup often in practice. In real-world systems, there is also a (nontrivial) per-machine start-up cost that limits the benefit of adding more machines.

We can also use the same framework to compute test set metrics with a second MapReduce-based algorithm. We can then use these test set metrics to rank the candidate features and select the best one. In this case, the algorithm knows the estimated coefficients $\vec{\beta}'$ of all the candidate features and the phases become:

1. **Map Phase** (*parallel over records*): Iterate over the test records $(\vec{x_i}, y_i, \vec{x_i}')$, and for each new feature $\vec{x}'_{id}$, compute the predicted probabilities under the old model $p_i = f_{\vec{\beta}}(\vec{x_i})$ and the new model $p'_{id} = f_{\vec{\beta}'(d)}(\vec{x_i})$.
2. **Reduce Phase** (*parallel over features*): For each evaluated feature β'_d use the predictions from the old model p_i and new model p'_{id} to compute the model scores and difference in scores.
3. **Post-Processing**: Aggregate the score changes for all features in the same feature class.

17.3.3 Parallel Grafting

We can also apply a similar MapReduce framework to other feature evaluation methodologies, such as grafting (Perkins et al., 2003). The grafting approach to feature evaluation chooses the feature that has the largest magnitude gradient. Formally, we choose the next feature using

$$\arg\max_{\beta'_d} \left| \frac{\partial L}{\partial \beta'_d} \right| = \arg\max_{\beta'_d} \left| \sum_i x'_{id}(y_i - p_i) \right| \tag{17.13}$$

Here, we note that we can compute the gradient independently for each record and aggregate the sum of the gradients independently for each feature.

The grafting MapReduce algorithm (Algorithms 53 and 54) consists of three steps:

1. **Map Phase** (*parallel over records*): Iterate over the training records $(\vec{x}_i, y_i, \vec{x}_i')$, computing which new features are active in $\vec{x}_i'$, the predicted probability of the current model $p_i = f_{\vec{\beta}}(\vec{x}_i)$, and the gradient:

$$\frac{\partial L_i}{\partial \beta'_d} = y_i - p_i \quad \forall x'_{id} \in \vec{x}_i' \tag{17.14}$$

2. **Reduce Phase** (*parallel over features*): For each evaluated feature β'_d, compute the absolute value of the sum of the per-record gradients.
3. **Post-Processing**: Aggregate the gradients for all features in the same feature class.

Since the features are always treated independently up to the post-processing phase, we can trivially explore all potential feature classes in parallel.

Algorithm 53: The Grafting Map Function (Takes a data block $\{\mathbf{X}, \vec{y}\}$ and a vector of coefficients $\vec{\beta}$. Produces a dataset T_d for each candidate feature.)

For each record $\{\vec{x}_i, y_i, \vec{x}_i'\}$ in the data $\{\mathbf{X}, \vec{y}\}$ **do**
    Compute the gradient for that record: $g_i = y_i - f_{\vec{\beta}}(\vec{x}_i)$
    For each active candidate feature $x'_{id} \in \vec{x}_i'$ **do**
    Output g_i: $T_d = T_d \cup \{g_i\}$

Algorithm 54: The Grafting reduce() Function (Takes a dataset T_d for a candidate feature. Produces an absolute sum of gradient G_d.)

$G_d = 0$
For each record $g_i \in T_d$ **do**
    $G_d = G_d + g_i$

17.3.4 Other Related Algorithms

There exist a wide range of other feature selection algorithms and methodologies that can also be parallelized to improve scalability. Although a full discussion of approaches is beyond the scope of this chapter, we provide here a brief high-level discussion of some other types of feature selection methodologies. Many of these techniques can easily be adapted to use the parallelization techniques described in this chapter.

In this chapter, we focus on the category of wrapper methods. One easy approach to scaling techniques of this type is to parallelize the evaluation of features as described in Section 17.3.1. For example, Garcia et al. (2006) describe an approach that evaluates many random subsets of features in parallel and then merges the best performing subsets. López et al. (2006) describe an evolutionary algorithm that parallelizes the evaluation, combination, and improvement of the solution population by distributing the work for different subsets of the population. This general approach could also be applied to many other recent forward-wrapper techniques, such as the algorithm of Della Pietra, Della Pietra, and Lafferty (1997) and that of McCallum (2003), by evaluating new features in parallel. Della Pietra et al. (1997) describe a feature selection method for random fields that holds the features in the current model fixed and selects the new feature by minimizing the KL-divergence between the model and the empirical distribution. McCallum (2003) introduces a similar method for conditional random fields, but like SFO his algorithm chooses the feature that maximizes the new model's log-likelihood. The same approach could apply to *backward elimination* techniques, which start with a full feature set and iteratively remove the least helpful feature. As noted by Abe (2005), backward feature selection also suffers from potentially high computational costs when the models are fully relearned.

In contrast to wrapper methods, filter methods attempt to select features using signals independent of the underlying model. Again, some of these techniques could naturally be parallelized by distributing the computation by records or features. Some techniques such as mutual information feature selection, which uses the mutual information between a feature and the class label (Lewis, 1992; Battiti, 1994), could even be implemented within the MapReduce framework. In this case, the map phase would consist of counting feature occurrences and the reduction phase would consist of summing these counts and computing the mutual information. Similarly, Fleuret (2004) proposes a filter method based on conditional mutual information that chooses the feature that maximizes the minimum mutual information with the response variable conditioned on each of the features already in the model. This technique could also be implemented similarly to the SFO algorithm with the current feature set used during mapping to compute counts of joint occurrences between the response variable, candidate features, and the current features.

Another general approach to feature selection is to automatically select features during the model training process. For example, LASSO (Tibshirani, 1996) is a well-known algorithm of this type. It uses regularization with an L_1 penalty to force the coefficients of non-useful attributes toward zero, encouraging sparsity in the model. Genkin, Lewis, and Madigan (2005) provide a good discussion on using regularization for sparsity in high-dimensional problems. More recently Krishnapuram, Carin, and Hartemink (2004) proposed Bayesian methods for joint learning and feature selection. Since these algorithms rely on the learning algorithm itself for feature selection, both the parallelization and scalability are determined by the algorithms.

17.4 Experimental Results

We conduct a series of experiments to test the algorithms' effectiveness in determining the "next" feature to add to a model. Since our intention is to provide an accurate approximation of a full forward selection step, we empirically evaluate the performance of the approximate algorithms by using full forward feature selection as the ground truth. Note that it is not our intention to compare greedy forward selection against the full space of feature selection approaches.

In the following experiments, we consider feature selection starting with differently sized base models. We randomly choose a set F_B of *base* features from a pool of frequently occurring features and train a full model. By varying the size of the base feature set, we can examine the algorithms' performance as the incremental benefit of adding features decreases. We also choose a set F_E of candidate *evaluation* features from the remaining features to be evaluated for inclusion in the model. We then evaluate each of the candidate features with each algorithm and compare the results to full forward feature selection.

We also ran the same experimental setup to examine the accuracy of the resulting learning models. In these runs, we held out a 10% test set and computed the AUC and log-likelihood on these data. Each evaluation model was trained on all of the training data using the full set of base features and the feature selected by the feature selection algorithm. Results are reported for average improvement in AUC and average percent improvement in log-likelihood. This test gives an indication of how much the selected feature helps on the actual prediction task.

In addition to SFO and grafting, we also consider two baseline feature evaluation approaches: random selection (rand) and mutual information (MI). Random selection provides a baseline by choosing the best feature to add at random without using the current model or data. Mutual information, a common filter algorithm, provides a more principled baseline by choosing the feature with the highest mutual information between that feature and the label:

$$MI_d = \sum_{y\in\{0,1\}} \sum_{x'_d\in\{0,1\}} P(x'_d, y) \log \left(\frac{P(x'_d, y)}{P(x'_d)P(y)} \right), \qquad (17.15)$$

where $P(x'_d, y)$, $P(x'_d)$, and $P(y)$ are the probabilities empirically computed from the data. It is important to note that, when we evaluate the performance of the algorithms in choosing the same features as forward feature selection, we do *not* try to compare the overall accuracy of mutual information versus the other techniques. Instead, we use mutual information as a baseline to help compare how well the approximate forward feature selection algorithms perform relative to each other.

We use a publicly available IRLS logistic regression package[1] to learn the logistic regression models (Komarek and Moore, 2005). In particular, this solver is used to learn the base models, fully retrained models, and full-forward feature selection models.

---

[1] Available at http://www.autonlab.org/.

Table 17.1. *Empirical results on the UCI Internet Ads data. The fraction of runs where SFO, grafting, mutual information, and random selection selected the same feature as full forward feature selection.*

$|F_B|$	SFO	Grafting	MI	Rand
0	0.96	0.96	0.84	0.00
50	1.00	0.88	0.68	0.00
100	0.84	0.84	0.64	0.00
150	0.96	0.64	0.52	0.00
200	0.88	0.84	0.72	0.04
250	0.88	0.80	0.72	0.00

17.4.1 UCI Internet Ads Dataset

First, we examine the performance of the algorithms on a small-scale simple dataset from the UCI repository (Asuncion and Newman, 2007), the Internet Ads dataset. The Internet Ads dataset includes 3,279 image instances that are labeled as "Ad" or "Non-Ad" and contains 1,558 features. We use the 1,555 binary features for our candidate feature set. As described previously, we examine the performance of the algorithms as the size of the base features is increased. Experiments are run 25 times in each setting with randomly chosen base features and 100 candidate features.

The results of the empirical evaluation, given in Table 17.1, show a strong performance for the parallel algorithms in approximating full forward feature evaluation. Both SFO and grafting perform well above random selection ($\sim 1\%$ accuracy). As expected, the results also show that the features selected by mutual information often differ from those by forward feature selection.

Table 17.2 presents the average improvement in accuracy as a result of adding the feature selected by each method. Here, we see a strong and often comparable performance on all four feature selection approaches. All four approaches perform better than random selection.

Table 17.2. *Empirical accuracy results on the UCI Internet Ads data using a 10% holdout test set. Average improvement of AUC (top) and percent improvement on log-likelihood (bottom) for a full trained model containing the feature selected by each technique.*

$|F_B|$	Full	SFO	Grafting	MI	Rand
0	0.064	0.065	0.068	0.065	0.005
50	0.058	0.057	0.055	0.056	0.004
100	0.012	0.014	0.007	0.011	0.002
200	0.010	0.009	0.008	0.008	0.001
0	3.28	3.33	3.36	3.27	0.04
50	4.21	4.09	4.12	4.10	0.10
100	2.29	2.33	2.15	2.26	0.05
200	2.06	1.91	1.80	1.60	0.15

17.4.2 RCV1 Dataset

To demonstrate a more realistic data size for the distributed algorithms, we apply the algorithms to the RCV1 data (Lewis et al., 2004). These data consist of stemmed tokens from text articles on a range of topics. We examine accuracy for the binary prediction problem for each of the five largest subcategories (C15, C18, GPOL, M13, and M14) as the size of the base model is increased. For our purposes, we combine the original training set and four test datasets into a single dataset with $N = 804,679$ records. Furthermore, in order to bias the set of evaluation features to potentially beneficial features, we filter the feature set to include only those features that appear at least 5,000 times in the data. This results in $D = 1,992$ possible features. Experiments were run 25 times in each setting with randomly chosen base features and 25 candidate features.

On the task of selecting the same features as full forward feature selection, the results in Table 17.3 show that the parallel algorithms perform well. Both SFO and grafting perform well above random selection ($\sim 4\%$ accuracy), but below the performance of the full forward evaluation. Of the two approximate parallel algorithms, SFO often outperforms grafting.

It is also interesting to note that the mutual information selects many of the same features as full forward feature selection when the number of base features is small. In fact, for empty models, $|F_B| = 0$, mutual information is often one of the top performing algorithms on this metric. However, as the size of the base model increases, the selections of mutual information begin to differ. This is expected, because, unlike both SFO and grafting, mutual information does not use information about the features currently in the model. Thus, it can select features that look good on their own, but correlate with features already in the model.

Table 17.4 shows the average percent improvement in test set log-likelihood as a result of adding the feature selected by each method. Both full forward feature selection

Table 17.3. *Empirical results on the RCV1 data. The fraction of runs where SFO, grafting, mutual information, and random selection selected the same feature as full forward feature selection.*

Label	$|F_B|$	SFO	Grafting	MI	Rand
C15	0	0.96	0.68	0.96	0.08
C15	100	0.76	0.72	0.60	0.04
C15	500	0.60	0.44	0.36	0.00
C18	0	0.88	0.88	0.96	0.00
C18	100	0.72	0.72	0.68	0.04
C18	500	0.68	0.72	0.52	0.08
GPOL	0	1.00	0.80	1.00	0.00
GPOL	100	0.80	0.44	0.52	0.04
GPOL	500	0.76	0.80	0.60	0.00
M13	0	0.96	0.72	0.96	0.00
M13	100	0.76	0.56	0.56	0.04
M13	500	0.84	0.72	0.64	0.00
M14	0	0.88	0.64	0.96	0.00
M14	100	0.96	0.72	0.80	0.04
M14	500	0.88	0.64	0.52	0.00

Table 17.4. *Empirical accuracy results on the RCV1 data using a 10% holdout test set. Average percent improvement of log-likelihood on a full trained model containing the feature selected by each technique.*

Label	$|F_B|$	Full	SFO	Grafting	MI	Rand
C15	0	530.8	530.8	500.2	530.8	85.0
C15	100	318.9	314.6	291.4	270.0	76.0
C15	200	203.2	201.0	186.4	188.4	5.5
C18	0	86.6	86.3	80.5	86.3	8.0
C18	100	110.5	98.0	101.3	103.8	25.5
C18	200	82.9	81.9	78.4	80.7	1.5
GPOL	0	385.8	385.1	375.7	385.8	38.0
GPOL	100	123.7	123.1	118.3	117.2	21.9
GPOL	200	90.4	89.4	87.8	85.5	6.6
M13	0	165.9	165.7	154.4	166.2	12.9
M13	100	236.6	236.0	227.2	228.8	6.6
M13	200	129.8	122.9	120.1	123.6	2.8
M14	0	334.8	332.6	257.4	334.8	58.0
M14	100	183.3	196.9	167.1	190.2	27.3
M14	200	162.1	161.1	152.9	136.9	25.1

and SFO perform well, often selecting the features that provide good improvement in test set log-likelihoods. Mutual information is often also a strong contender, especially for smaller base models. As in the Internet Ads experiments, the test set AUC results, which are not shown here to save space, show little difference among the feature selection approaches.

17.4.3 Timing Results

To examine the effectiveness of using the MapReduce framework, we can examine the wall clock running time of the algorithm as we vary the number of machines K. In the following, we look at the *speedup* over the single machine:

$$\text{Speedup}(K) = \frac{\text{Running time with 1 machine}}{\text{Running time with } K \text{ machines}} \tag{17.16}$$

An ideal speedup is linear in K indicating perfect parallelization.

Simulated Data

We initially look at SFO's speedup over two simulated datasets: one with 1,000,000 records and 50,000 features, and the other with 10,000,000 records and 100,000 features. The data were generated from random models with coefficients in the range $[-0.5, 0.5]$. Each record contains exactly 20 active features selected randomly without replacement. The base model has a uniform prior probability of 0.5 of generating a true label.

Figure 17.2 shows a clear benefit as we increase the number of machines. The deviation from ideal when using a higher number of machines in the speedup plots (Figures 17.2a and b) occurs since the benefit of adding machines decreases as the per-machine startup costs begin to become an increasing factor. These overheads can

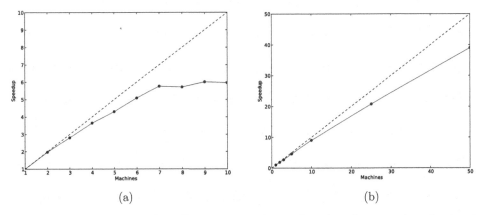

(a)   (b)

Figure 17.2 Speedup plots of parallel SFO versus the number of machines used on simulated data for (a) 1,000,000 records/50,000 features and (b) 10,000,000 records/100,000 features. The dashed lines represent ideal behavior.

include such factors as launching the relevant programs and copying the data to the machine. For example, in Figure 17.2a, we do not see a benefit past seven machines, because at that point we are dealing with a small problem of less than 150,000 records per machine.

Despite the decreasing returns with the number of machines, we expect this parallelization to provide significant wall clock savings for large datasets or feature sets. As observed, this happens because the deviation from ideal is less for the larger dataset (for the same number of machines). Further, we expect the marginal benefit of adding machines to *increase* with the computational cost of computing the features. This type of parallelization becomes more important when considering nontrivial features, such as those requiring string parsing, because we distribute the expensive computation over more machines.

RCV1 Data

In looking at the RCV1 data, we can further scale up the size of the problem by using the fact that the RCV1 is actually a multi-class problem. We can choose C labels and learn binary models to predict the outcome for each label. As discussed in Section 17.2.4, we can learn independent models for each class label by effectively replicating the dataset C times. For each class label L we create a new copy of the dataset such that:

1. A record is positive if and only if its class label is L in the original data.
2. We create new copies of each attribute that include the label.

For example, in the RCV1 data, we could modify the record { world, qualify, ⋯ } to be { C15:world, C15:qualify, ⋯ } in the dataset for the C15 label. Once we have the C datasets, we can merge them into a single large dataset and train a single model over them. In doing so, we effectively learn a separate binary model for each label. Further, we can use a single iteration of the feature selection algorithms to choose the best feature for *each* model by selecting the best feature for each label.

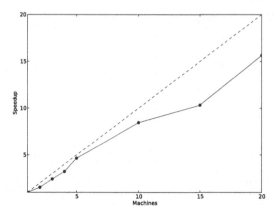

Figure 17.3 Speedup plot of parallel SFO versus the number of machines on the RCV1 data. The dashed line represents ideal behavior.

We used the previous multi-class approach to test the scalability of the SFO algorithm. In our tests, we looked at feature evaluation for the $C = 9$ subcategories that have $\geq 40{,}000$ positive records: C15, C17, C18, C31, E21, GPOL, M11, M13, M14. This provides a total data size of approximately 7.2 million records and 2.6 million features.

Figure 17.3 shows a clear benefit as we increase the number of machines. Although we have increased both the number of records and the dimensionality by a factor of 9, we have also increased the sparsity of dataset. In particular, in the reduce phase the workers only need to process the data from the records that contain a given feature in the context of a given class label. This means that they have $C * D$ smaller chunks of work instead of D larger ones.

17.5 Conclusions

In this chapter, we have described three parallel algorithms for forward feature selection in logistic regression: full forward feature selection, SFO, and grafting. Both SFO and grafting provide computationally efficient approximations of the full evaluation of which features provide the most signal to the model. Both of these approximations are easily parallelizable within the MapReduce framework.

Empirically, we show that the SFO heuristic results in a good performance and is comparable to techniques that relearn the whole model. In addition, the approximate model can also be used to evaluate the feature's impact on a range of other metrics and on validation set performance. Further, the coefficients estimated by the SFO heuristic can provide useful starting points to relearn the model and can provide insights into the structure of the problem.

References

Abe, S. 2005. Modified backward feature selection by cross validation. In: *13th European Symposium on Artificial Neural Networks*.

Asuncion, A., and Newman, D. 2007. *UCI Machine Learning Repository*.

Battiti, R. 1994. Using Mutual Information for Selecting Features in Supervised Neural Net Learning. *IEEE Transactions on Neural Networks*, **5**, 537–550.

Caruana, R., Karampatziakis, N., and Yessenalina, A. 2008. An Empirical Evaluation of Supervised Learning in High Dimensions. In: *Proceedings of the 25th International Conference on Machine Learning (ICML 2008)*.

Dean, J., and Ghemawat, S. 2004. MapReduce: Simplified Data Processing on Large Clusters. In: *OSDI'04: Sixth Symposium on Operating System Design and Implementation*.

Della Pietra, S., Della Pietra, V., and Lafferty, J. 1997. Inducing Features of Random Fields. *IEEE Transactions on Pattern Analysis and Machine Intelligence*, **19**(4), 380–393.

Fleuret, F. 2004. Fast Binary Feature Selection with Conditional Mutual Information. *Journal of Machine Learning Research*, **5**, 1531–1555.

Friedman, J., Hastie, T., and Tibshirani, R. 2008. *Regularized Paths for Generalized Linear Models via Coordinate Descent*. http://www.stat.stanford.edu/~hasti/Papers/glmnet.pdf.

Garcia, D., Hall, L., Goldgof, D., and Kramer, K. 2006. A parallel feature selection algorithm from random subsets. In: *Proceedings of the 17th European Conference on Machine Learning and the 10th European Conference on Principles and Practice of Knowledge Discovery in Databases*.

Genkin, A., Lewis, D., and Madigan, D. 2005. *Sparse Logistic Regression for Text Categorization*.

Guyon, I., and Elisseeff, A. 2003. An Introduction to Variable and Feature Selection. *Journal of Machine Learning Research*, **3**(March), 1157–1182.

Hastie, T., Tibshirani, R., and Friedman, J. 2001. *The Elements of Statistical Learning*. New York: Springer.

John, G., Kohavi, R., and Pfleger, K. 1994. Irrelevant Features and the Subset Selection Problem. Pages 121–129 of: *Proceedings of the Eleventh International Conference on Machine Learning (ICML 1994)*. San Francisco, CA: Morgan Kauffmann.

Komarek, P., and Moore, A. 2005. Making Logistic Regression a Core Data Mining Tool with TR-IRLS. In: *Proceedings of the 5th International Conference on Data Mining Machine Learning*.

Krishnapuram, B., Carin, L., and Hartemink, A. 2004. Joint Classifier and Feature Optimization for Comprehensive Cancer Diagnosis Using Gene Expression Data. *Journal of Computational Biology*, **11**(2–3), 227–242.

Lewis, D. 1992. Feature Selection and Feature Extraction for Text Categorization. Pages 212–217 of: *Proceedings of the Workshop on Speech and Natural Language*.

Lewis, D., Yang, Y., Rose, T., and Li, F. 2004. RCV1: A New Benchmark Collection for Text Categorization Research. *Journal of Machine Learning Research*, **5**, 361–397.

López, F., Torres, M., Batista, B., Pérez, J., and Moreno-Vega, M. 2006. Solving Feature Subset Selection Problem by a Parallel Scatter Search. *European Journal of Operational Research*, **169**(2), 477–489.

McCallum, A. 2003. Efficiently Inducing Features of Conditional Random Fields. In: *Conference on Uncertainty in Artificial Intelligence (UAI)*.

Perkins, S., Lacker, K., and Theiler, J. 2003. Grafting: Fast, Incremental Feature Selection by Gradient Descent in Function Space. *Journal of Machine Learning Research*, **3**, 1333–1356.

Singh, S., Kubica, J., Larsen, S., and Sorokina, D. 2009. Parallel Large Scale Feature Selection for Logistic Regression. In: *SIAM International Conference on Data Mining (SDM)*.

Tibshirani, R. 1996. Regression Shrinkage and Selection via the Lasso. *Journal of the Royal Statistical Society*, **58**(1), 267–288.

Whitney, A. 1971. A Direct Method of Nonparametric Measurement Selection. *IEEE Transactions on Computers*, **20**(9), 1100–1103.

PART FOUR

Applications

CHAPTER 18

Large-Scale Learning for Vision with GPUs

Adam Coates, Rajat Raina, and Andrew Y. Ng

Computer vision is a challenging application area for learning algorithms. For instance, the task of object detection is a critical problem for many systems, like mobile robots, that remains largely unsolved. In order to interact with the world, robots must be able to locate and recognize large numbers of objects accurately and at reasonable speeds. Unfortunately, off-the-shelf computer vision algorithms do not yet achieve sufficiently high detection performance for these applications. A key difficulty with many existing algorithms is that they are unable to take advantage of large numbers of examples. As a result, they must rely heavily on prior knowledge and hand-engineered features that account for the many kinds of errors that can occur. In this chapter, we present two methods for improving performance by scaling up learning algorithms to large datasets: (1) using graphics processing units (GPUs) and distributed systems to scale up the standard components of computer vision algorithms and (2) using GPUs to automatically learn high-quality feature representations using deep belief networks (DBNs). These methods are capable of not only achieving high performance but also removing much of the need for hand-engineering common in computer vision algorithms.

The fragility of many vision algorithms comes from their lack of knowledge about the multitude of visual phenomena that occur in the real world. Whereas humans can intuit information about depth, occlusion, lighting, and even motion from still images, computer vision algorithms generally lack the ability to deal with these phenomena without being engineered to account for them in advance. Despite these considerable disadvantages, vision algorithms have nevertheless been able to perform reasonably well on a variety of detection tasks, such as finding faces (Viola and Jones, 2001; Rowley, Baluja, and Kanade, 1995; Schneiderman and Kanade, 2000) or people (Dalal and Triggs, 2005; Felzenszwalb, Mcallester, and Ramanan, 2008) in images – well enough, in fact, to become deployable in consumer devices such as digital cameras. Other objects can also be detected with varying degrees of accuracy (Felzenszwalb et al., 2008; Opelt, Pinz, and Zisserman, 2006; Schneiderman and Kanade, 2004; Winn, Criminisi, and Minka, 2005; Torralba, Murphy, and Freeman, 2007b. Unfortunately, the general task of object detection (even for rigid objects) remains extremely difficult:

competitors in the PASCAL Challenge frequently score below 50% (Everingham et al., 2009). These numbers are no surprise considering the difficulties described earlier: there are simply too many things that can go wrong. For example, cluttered background imagery and lighting effects provide endless varieties of shapes and shades that can easily be mistaken for a target object if that particular background pattern has never been seen before, and it is unlikely that we can avoid all of these mistakes by clever engineering. Although the assumptions on which many successful algorithms are built work well most of the time, it is not clear how they can be tweaked to work well in the remaining "hard" or "unusual" cases that inevitably show up.

Recent research suggests that there may be another way to improve performance: rather than focusing on creating more clever methods for handling the complexities of real images, we could instead focus on creating simple algorithms that are both general and highly scalable. By "general" we mean that the algorithms include few hardwired assumptions that might be violated by real data, and by "scalable" we mean that these algorithms should be able to handle large numbers of examples gracefully and, even better, should become faster and more capable as computing resources grow more plentiful. An algorithm that has these characteristics could, by virtue of learning from millions upon millions of training examples, learn all of the structure necessary to perform difficult vision tasks on its own – mitigating the need for complex, hand-tuned systems. It has already been shown in several settings that even very simple, general-purpose learning algorithms can perform well when trained from large amounts of data (Banko and Brill, 2001; Torralba, Fergus, and Freeman, 2007a; Torralba, Fergus, and Weiss, 2008; Nister and Stewenius, 2006). Our goal in this chapter is to apply this approach to difficult tasks in computer vision.

We start with a brief introduction to what we regard as a "standard" pipeline for a broad class of computer vision algorithms and explain the difficulties encountered when we attempt to apply this pipeline to complex problems and large datasets. This will motivate our introduction of two different approaches to "scaling up" the pipeline to tackle problems in computer vision.

18.1 A Standard Pipeline

Computer vision algorithms for detection and recognition tasks come in many forms, but a large number of them follow a standard learning pipeline. For concreteness, we describe an instantiation of this pipeline for a specific scenario related to the applications we explore later. In particular, we assume that each input image contains either an entire object or random imagery, and thus, we can label each input image as either a "positive" example (meaning that it contains a nicely framed instance of the target object) or a "negative" example.[1] We ultimately seek to train a classifier that makes binary decisions about such an input image, labeling it as a positive image (of the target object) or as a negative image. This pipeline is shown in Figure 18.1.

---

[1] For multi-class problems we can, of course, use multiple labels. To simplify discussion, we refer only to the binary case.

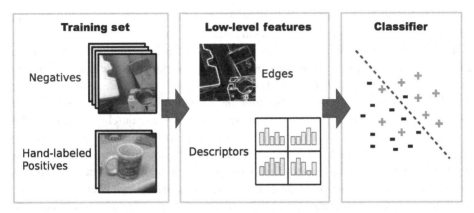

Figure 18.1 A standard learning pipeline used in computer vision. A training set is collected and labeled by hand. Hand-engineered, low-level image features are computed for each example, and then a classifier is trained to distinguish positive example images from negative example images based on these features.

The first step is to collect and label a corpus of training data. We must first collect a set of images and, for each image, label it as a positive or negative example. Second, given a new input image, the next step is to compute a vector of low-level features to convert the raw pixel intensities into a form useful for learning. Finally, all of the labeled examples are given to an appropriate machine learning algorithm that trains a classifier to recognize the positive instances. If all goes well, this classifier will output decisions for new test images, labeling each as either a positive instance of an object from the training set or as a negative image containing nothing of interest.

Although there is nothing wrong with this recipe in general, its actual implementation is fraught with bottlenecks. For instance, the first step requires us to collect and label data by hand. This process limits the number of examples we can reasonably expect to obtain for a new learning task. For some widely studied classes of objects, such as people, relatively large labeled datasets do exist: the LabelMe dataset (Russell et al., 2005) presently contains approximately 27,000 labeled persons. However, if we aim to identify a less common object, such as a claw hammer, we will not likely be able (or willing) to collect hundreds or thousands of unique training images. If a large number of examples are really necessary for algorithms to achieve good generalization, this limitation will translate directly into decreased performance.

For the second stage of the pipeline, we usually choose some hand-engineered feature representation. These features aim to simplify the image structure to make the learning problem easier. For instance, a common choice is edge responses that can be computed easily using the gradient of pixel intensities at different locations. Although the gradients (finite differences) are linear functions of the input pixels, it is common practice to normalize the responses to adjust for intensity and contrast variation and to combine the gradients from multiple locations. The Sobel operator, for instance, yields responses that roughly approximate the outlines of objects by computing the norm of a smoothed gradient at each location (as in the top center of Figure 18.1). As another example, Lowe's scale invariant feature transform (SIFT) (Lowe, 1999) computes histograms of local intensity gradients for small regions of the image; normalizes for intensity, contrast, orientation, and scale; and then outputs a high-dimensional "descriptor" vector that describes the local image content.

In selecting our features, we are forced to consider a computational trade-off: we can choose fast, simple features or slower but highly expressive features. Since the features must be computed at hundreds or even thousands of locations for each image, our choice can have a significant impact on the amount of data we can reasonably use for training. Very simple features, such as edge responses, are quickly computable but are usually too simple to convey all of the information our learning algorithm may need. Meanwhile, detailed features such as SIFT descriptors are somewhat slower and produce a large number of output values (a high-dimensional vector) that we will have to sort out during the learning stage. If we are intent on using large numbers of images to boost performance, it makes sense to try to use expressive features where possible, but we would certainly aim to compute these features in a reasonable amount of time.

Another caveat is that the choice of features often depends on the application, and very few features work well for all situations. If we choose poor features, our learning algorithm, no matter how intelligent, may not be able to create a classifier that generalizes well. Hand-engineered features are often brittle since they incorporate many assumptions that are, as rules of thumb, quite reasonable but can fail in general. For instance, SIFT normalizes for rotations and scale, yet there is no way to know when this is a good thing or a bad thing to do. Although such normalizations work well for many applications, our goal in learning from large training sets is to perform well even when faced with cases that otherwise beguile existing algorithms. These are the "hard" cases where it is unclear, even to an expert, what types of features will be important. One can imagine that we might improve the performance of our systems by eliminating these hardwired assumptions and instead trying to learn a feature representation that will allow us to achieve high performance. In Section 18.4, we describe such an algorithm and its application to large datasets.

Finally, in the last stage of the pipeline, all of our labeled feature vectors are passed to a machine learning algorithm. Common choices of learning algorithm include Support Vector Machines (Felzenszwalb et al., 2008; Grauman and Darrell, 2005; Osuna, Freund, and Girosi, 1997) and boosted decision trees (Viola and Jones, 2001, 2004; Torralba et al., 2007b). Depending on the implementation of these algorithms, one is usually forced to load all of the training data into the main memory on a single machine (thus limiting our training set sizes), or else use incremental or online algorithms that can stream data from disk. Again, we are faced with a trade-off imposed by computing power: training on data stored entirely in main memory is fast, but training on data from disk allows us to use more data even though it can be orders of magnitude slower.

In order to tackle large datasets, we need to make improvements on each of these three pipeline stages. We must acquire larger training sets, develop features that are not only expressive and general but also quickly computable, and we must choose a training algorithm that can handle large numbers of training examples without extremely long training times. In the remainder of this chapter, we describe two different approaches to solving the issues outlined earlier. The first combines several standard components, but retools them to capitalize on hardware trends so that they can scale up to huge datasets. The second approach exploits large unlabeled datasets using Deep Belief Networks (DBNs). Both approaches harness the rising power of GPUs (which have previously been applied to accelerate various machine learning and vision tasks) (Catanzaro, Sundaram, and Keutzer, 2008; Heymann et al., 2007). To this end, we thus briefly describe how GPUs work and their relationship to traditional parallel processing before continuing.

18.2 Introduction to GPUs

GPUs have been steadily growing in computational capabilities since their introduction into the computer graphics and games market over a decade ago. Although initially designed solely for graphics operations, with specialized processors to perform basic operations such as geometry and lighting transforms, these units have evolved into self-contained, general-purpose computing platforms living on expansion cards. The advantage of GPUs lies in their choice of design trade-offs. Central processing units (CPUs) are designed to perform well on heterogeneous workloads and thus devote a great deal of their hardware budget to complex execution logic, such as instruction reordering, cache management, and branch prediction. They are optimized for traditional jobs that are typically serial. GPUs, on the other hand, have been optimized for tasks that are all naturally parallel, for example applying a common calculation on every pixel of an image. Thus, GPUs devote virtually all of their transistors to computational units and improving throughput (nVidia, 2009). In this section, we briefly describe the programming model for GPUs and how this differs from traditional parallel programming on CPUs (e.g., threaded applications). We also describe the caveats associated with GPU programming, which will inform our choice of algorithms later.

18.2.1 Data-Parallel Programming

Typical multi-CPU computer systems rely on the application programmer to design their program for parallel execution. This is usually done through a software threading library: each "thread" is a single path of execution through a piece of code. Each thread is free to execute a completely different code path without any relationship to the operation of other threads. GPUs can have hundreds of cores on a single chip, but unlike CPUs, the threads running on these cores are not programmed independently: each thread executes essentially the same piece of code but on a different piece of data. This is referred to as "data-parallel computation" and is similar to the "vector processing" capabilities of CPUs where a single arithmetic unit performs the same operation on multiple pieces of data at once. Figure 18.2 illustrates the data-parallel threading model.

18.2.2 CUDA Programming Model

For concreteness we describe the basic concepts from nVidia's CUDA programming model (nVidia, 2009), but the basic concepts map closely to the hardware architecture of current GPUs and are thus widely applicable.

Figure 18.3 shows a simplified schematic of a typical nVidia GPU. The GPU hardware provides two levels of parallelism: there are several multiprocessors (MPs), and

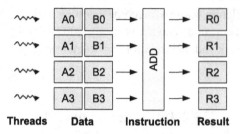

Figure 18.2 Data-parallel programs execute the same instruction sequence in parallel on multiple pieces of data. For instance, if four threads all execute an "add" instruction at the same time on different pieces of data, this operation can be parallelized.

each multiprocessor contains several stream processors (SPs) that perform actual computation. These two levels of parallelism are exposed to the programmer: each program is broken into "threads" that execute on the SPs, and these threads are grouped together into "thread blocks" that are scheduled to run together on each multiprocessor. All threads within a block execute together on the same multiprocessor and are able to cooperate with each other (synchronizing with each other as necessary during execution). In addition, each block of threads has access to a small (e.g., 16KB) but extremely fast shared cache memory as well as the larger global main memory (up to 6GB). In contrast, since each block of threads is scheduled separately on a different processor, potentially at different times, threads in one block cannot communicate with threads in another block.

Conceptually, this implies that any job that runs on the GPU must first be broken into "blocks" of computation that can be run independently without communicating or sharing their results. Within these blocks, the work must be divided up into smaller tasks that will be performed by individual threads of execution (which may cooperate with other threads working on the same block of the computation). Typically, a block will consist of between 32 and 512 threads, with each thread running a common piece of code on a different piece of data (as in Figure 18.2).

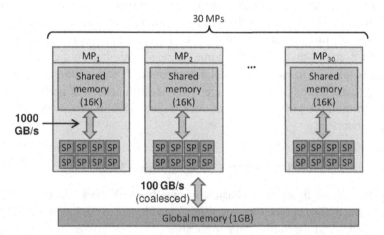

Figure 18.3 A simplified schematic for the nVidia GeForce GTX 280 graphics card, with 240 total cores (30 multiprocessors with 8 stream processors each).

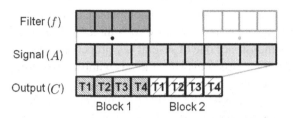

Filter (f)

Signal (A)

Output (C)

Block 1 Block 2

Figure 18.4 Given a filter of length 4 and a signal of length 11, we must compute 8 outputs. We can map this to blocks and threads in the following way: each thread within a block (labeled T1 through T4 above) computes a single output value as a dot product between the filter and a segment of the input signal. We then create enough blocks to compute all of the outputs. In the given example, exactly 2 blocks are needed to compute all 8 outputs (using 4 threads in each block).

18.2.3 Example: Convolutions on GPUs

To illustrate this framework, we briefly explain a common operation for which GPUs are well-suited: performing cross-correlation (convolution) between images and linear filters. For simplicity, we use 1D inputs in this example, as the generalization to 2D inputs as used in vision applications is straightforward. We will also use this example to explain a few issues that are encountered when implementing algorithms on GPUs: global memory access and using the shared memory cache.

Suppose we are given a linear filter, $f \in \Re^m$, and an input signal[2] $A \in \Re^n$. We compute the cross-correlation between these two arrays using the formula

$$C[i] = \sum_{j=0}^{m-1} A[i+j] \cdot f[j], \ 0 \leq i < n - m + 1$$

Since each $C[i]$ depends only on the inputs, each can be computed independently. Thus, we can divide this problem into "blocks" where each block is responsible for, say, 32 of the outputs in C. Each of the 32 threads within a block will then use this formula to compute a single $C[i]$ as a function of the inputs. Figure 18.4 illustrates this division of labor for a small signal and filter.

Algorithmically, there is nothing more to do. This algorithm can be implemented straightforwardly using the CUDA framework. In order to fully take advantage of the GPU's capabilities, however, optimization is necessary. For instance, implementing cross-correlation directly as described earlier will mean making many accesses to the A and f arrays in the GPU's global memory. It turns out that this is quite slow: global memory accesses involve latencies of hundreds of cycles. The CUDA architecture provides two (hardware supported) avenues for avoiding this penalty: (1) coalesced memory accesses, where many values can be accessed from global memory at once, and (2) the shared memory cache.

Memory access requests from threads in a block are said to be coalesced if the threads access memory in sequence (i.e., the ith thread accesses the ith consecutive location in

---

[2] In vision applications, the input "signal" is a 2D image, and the filter is a 2D array of real numbers.

memory).[3] It is easy to see that if thread i computes $C[i]$ in the formula given earlier, then accesses to A will be coalesced, since each thread will access adjacent entries of A. This example demonstrates one of several key properties we seek in algorithms that run on GPUs: memory accesses made by threads within a block should be adjacent (or nearly so) in main memory.

The second way to avoid the overhead of main memory access is to use the user-controlled[4] shared cache memory. By first loading data into the cache (ideally, using coalesced memory accesses), we can subsequently access these cached values at much higher speeds. Under some conditions, these accesses can be as fast as register access, and thus we should use the cache whenever possible instead of accessing main memory. The advantages of the cache are even greater when many threads share the same data, since this data can be loaded once into the cache and then accessed repeatedly by all of the threads. This is true for cross-correlation, for instance, where each thread reuses many of the same input values while computing its output $C[i]$. Since the cache is small, however, this places a constraint on the amount of work we can expect to do at once without touching main memory. Thus, this points to a second characteristic of GPU-friendly algorithms: each block is able to fit most (if not all) of the data it needs for computation into the shared cache and should exhibit a high degree of data reuse across threads.

18.2.4 GPU Conclusions

The previous example demonstrates that although GPUs have great computational power, not all algorithms are easily implemented in a way that achieves good performance. Specifically, algorithms that make poor use of cache memory or make incoherent accesses to global memory will run slowly. The example of convolution shown earlier is one situation where it is easy to satisfy these constraints and achieve very high throughput. Though we will not discuss the many other issues in detail, it should be noted that other common operations such as branching can also carry a speed penalty and should be avoided where feasible. Hence, in order to leverage the full capabilities of GPUs in our applications, we must choose algorithms that work well with the memory and execution patterns for which the hardware is optimized.

18.3 A Standard Approach Scaled Up

Our goal is to modify the standard learning approach described in Section 18.1 so that it can gracefully scale to extremely large datasets. In the introduction, we characterized our ideal system as one that is both general and scalable. More specifically, we would like our system to be general purpose, with few built-in assumptions that might prevent us from maximizing performance as datasets grow. This suggests, for instance, that

---

[3] Recent GPUs relax this constraint, allowing for more general access patterns; however, the threads must still access memory locations in a small contiguous region.

[4] Newer GPUs also have options for automated cache management.

learning parametric models will not be sufficient since the modeling assumptions that we choose will undoubtedly affect our results.

In terms of scalability, we must also consider how our choice of algorithms fits with current trends in computing hardware. In light of our discussion of the benefits of GPUs, we should consider algorithms whose characteristics make them GPU-friendly and aim to use algorithms that can benefit from the strengths of current and future hardware. This will allow our system to train on more data in the future and potentially achieve higher accuracy as hardware improves.

In this section, we present a different instantiation of each component in the standard learning pipeline designed to make it scale to very large datasets. In particular, for training data, we use synthetic examples derived from a small number of hand-collected images. As low-level features, we select a representation that is both well suited to GPU implementation as well as reasonably general. Finally, we present a training method for boosted decision trees that scales easily up to 100 million training examples.

18.3.1 Synthetic Training Data

A major bottleneck in the standard pipeline described previously is data collection and labeling. One way that we might avoid this burden is by using synthetic data. This approach has been used before in computer vision (e.g., LeCun, Huang, and Bottou, 2004). Although synthetic data is generally not as good as real data, it has the advantage of allowing us to generate unlimited numbers of training examples from a small pool of real examples, cutting our data collection time drastically. The synthetic examples are artificially distorted to simulate geometric and photometric changes that often occur in real images. Through this process, we can try to teach a learning algorithm to be invariant to processes in the real world that we would otherwise have to explicitly engineer our way around.

We briefly describe one way to perform this data synthesis, though there are many different methods and variations that could be used. We use a "green screen" approach similar to those used by LeCun et al. (2004) and Sapp, Saxena, and Ng (2008). A typical image and mask captured from our system is shown in the left two images of Figure 18.5.

By using the (known) background color, a mask is computed that covers the object in the image frame. Using the captured image and mask, we then apply a series of distortions to generate new positive examples. These distorted examples attempt to capture variations that frequently appear in real data. These include (1) random backgrounds, (2) random perspective distortions, (3) nonlinear lighting changes, and

Figure 18.5 From left to right: an image captured from our green screen system, the object mask, and three synthesized positive training examples.

(4) blurring. In addition, we also overlay a texture on top of the object to add additional variation. Several synthetic examples from this procedure are shown in Figure 18.5.

By using synthetic data, we now only need to locate instances of the object class that we would like to detect and photograph them each from various orientations. The rest of the training data can then be generated using the techniques described earlier. In the experiments presented later in this section, we use up to 9 million such synthetic examples.

18.3.2 GPU-Friendly Features

Our classification algorithm will operate on a set of features computed from each example image. As explained previously, we would like to use features that are amenable to implementation on GPUs. Thus, their computation should be simple and not require complex logic that breaks data parallelism, and they should be able to take advantage of the caching system of the GPU. We have chosen to use the 2D patch features described by Torralba et al. (2007b).

We begin by constructing a dictionary from small image fragments (typically around a thousand). Each fragment f is randomly extracted from positive examples of an object. Each patch is also annotated with a rectangle $\mathcal{R}$ specifying its approximate location relative to the object center (Figure 18.6). Specifically, a dictionary patch will be defined as a pair $\langle f, \mathcal{R} \rangle$.

Given an input example image, a feature value is computed by first computing the (normalized) cross-correlation of the dictionary patch over the input image region $\mathcal{R}$. We then take the max value achieved over this region. Loosely speaking, this can be thought of as a simple "template matcher": we find the location in $\mathcal{R}$ that looks most like the filter patch f, and then use a (normalized) dot product (which measures how similar f is to the input) as the feature value. The maximization step here is often referred to as "max pooling" and provides some translation and noise invariance. We have chosen these features because they are general purpose yet sufficiently specialized that we expect them to work well with a wide range of objects. Since the feature definitions are acquired from data, we can create new features from new data whenever the necessity arises.

The output of cross-correlation over the region $\mathcal{R}$ is an image in which each pixel measures the similarity (response) of the dictionary patch (filter) f with the input image

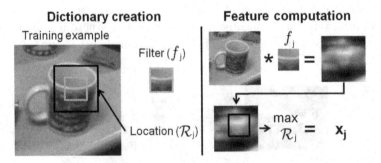

Figure 18.6 We extract linear filters from positive examples of a target object. The response of this feature is max-pooled over a rectangle around the location from which it was extracted.

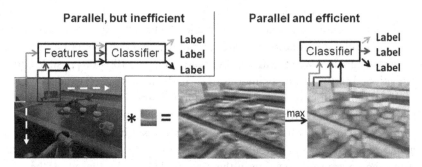

Figure 18.7 Illustration of the "sliding window" approach to object detection. Note that computing features separately for each window is naturally parallelizable but inefficient (left side). Instead, we perform the filter cross-correlation and max pooling on the GPU in two highly efficient passes before running the sliding window. Then, we can simply extract features from each location in the response image and feed them directly to the classifier (right side).

at one location. We now need to compute the maximum response over each of these pixels. The "max pooling" operation can similarly be thought of as running a nonlinear "filter" in a convolutional manner over the resulting response image obtained from the cross-correlation step. However, instead of performing a dot product (as in cross-correlation) between windows of the input and the filter f, we simply compute the max over each sub-window. The result is an output image that, at each pixel, contains the max-pooled response for a dictionary patch.

Importantly, these two passes can be performed efficiently for large images using GPUs and the approach described in Section 18.2.3. Notice, however, that each feature involves a convolution over only a small region $\mathcal{R}$ for each example image. GPUs excel at handling large, pipelined workloads, and computing convolutions over small regions separately takes away many of the performance benefits. We will see in Section 18.3.3, though, that these features mesh naturally with the "sliding window approach" to object detection, allowing us to computing all of the features for an entire scene in parallel.

18.3.3 Sliding Window Object Detection and Convolutions

The sliding window is a common way to turn a classifier trained to make binary decisions about the presence of an object in an image (as described in Section 18.1) into a detector that locates all instances of the object within a larger image (see, e.g., Dalal and Triggs, 2005; Rowley et al., 1995; Ferrari et al., 2008). This is done by running the classifier independently on a large number of sub-windows at different locations and scales within the larger image (Figure 18.7). Sub-windows where the classifier outputs a "positive" decision are bounded with a rectangle and reported as a detected object instance.[5]

---

[5] In practice, classifiers tend to report many positive detections in the close vicinity of an object. For this reason, a suppression step is usually applied that removes any weak detections, returning only the strongest detection in a region.

The sliding window procedure is (evidently) quite parallelizable, since each window of the image can be classified separately in parallel. Unfortunately, we must compute the features (and the classifier output) for an extremely large number of possible locations. For standard image sizes we may need to evaluate more than 100,000 possible windows, and as mentioned earlier, the convolutions over small pieces of each window will not be efficient if done individually. Instead, we can compute the features at every location of the entire scene first: we perform the convolution over the entire image using each filter, then perform the "max pooling" operation over the resulting filter response images. To evaluate our classifier in a given window, we now only need to extract the feature value from the appropriate location in the max-pooled results (based on the window location, and the position of the pooling region $\mathcal{R}$ associated with each patch).

Not only is this property useful for speeding the runtime execution of the classifier, but it can also be used to generate features for large numbers of negative examples very quickly. Given a large image that does not contain any instances of the target object, we can gather a large number of negative examples by taking many overlapping sub-windows of the image. For reasonable amounts of overlap, these examples are not too correlated, and we can use the sliding window machinery to compute feature vectors for these sub-windows much more quickly than can be done for independent windows. Hence, we can leverage the GPU's performance to compute features for large numbers of negative images very quickly, allowing us to build up a huge corpus of negative examples for training.

18.3.4 Classification

The last stage of the pipeline is classification. Here, we must build a classifier that takes in a feature vector describing an image (which is usually a sub-window of a larger image) and decides whether the image contains an instance of the target object. Our choice of learning algorithm is again influenced by the same considerations as the other parts of the pipeline: we want an algorithm that scales gracefully when presented with increasing quantities of data and makes as few assumptions about the data as possible.

In our work, we have used the Gentle Boost (Friedman, Hastie, and Tibshirani, 1998) algorithm with decision trees. Previous work has demonstrated the effectiveness of this particular combination of algorithms in practice (Viola and Jones, 2001; Quigley et al., 2009; Torralba et al., 2007b), but our choice is also motivated by the ability to scale this particular combination of algorithms to large amounts of data. For instance, if we know how to train a simple "weak" classifier efficiently from a large dataset (e.g., by distributing the data across a large cluster of machines), boosting algorithms give us a way to build a stronger classifier by adding these "weak" functions together. Ensembles of weak classifiers generated in this way are capable of representing extremely complex decision functions, which are likely to be necessary for difficult classification tasks such as those in computer vision.

Our system uses decision trees as weak learners. This is motivated partly by their compact structure and their (very) sparse dependence on the elements of the feature vector, which has the benefit of reducing the number of features used to be proportional to the number of boosting rounds. However, it is also easy to train these simple classifiers quickly on a large cluster of machines, as we show later.

We can gain two main benefits from distributed training: (1) the use of multicore systems to process the training data repeatedly in parallel, reducing training time, and (2) the ability to leverage the abundance of RAM on multiple machines to hold massive training sets in main memory, thus avoiding expensive disk and network transfers. These features are in line with our desire to build a system that scales well with hardware: as we buy more machines with more memory and more CPU cores, the algorithm's capacity and speed (or both) can expand without requiring any changes. To create a distributed version of Gentle Boost, we only need to train the weak learners (decision trees, in our case) in a distributed fashion; the remaining steps are easy to run on a single desktop PC for enormous datasets.

Our decision trees are trained similarly to the well-known CART algorithm (Breiman et al., 1984) to minimize the squared error in label predictions using the Gini coefficient as split criterion:

$$g(\theta, j) = \frac{1}{N} \left(N_L^+ (1 - \frac{N_L^+}{N_L}) + N_R^+ (1 - \frac{N_R^+}{N_R}) \right),$$

where N is the total number of examples, N_L is the number of examples with $x_j < \theta$, and N_L^+ is the number of these with positive label. N_R and N_R^+ are defined analogously. This is the (average) squared prediction error if the left and right nodes output constant-valued predictions.[6]

To make our training algorithm distributed, however, we cannot simply compute the decision tree splits for the entire dataset on a single machine (at least not without streaming data from disk). Instead, we use an approximation that has seen success in the data-mining community: we distribute the data to a set of worker machines and have each worker accumulate the feature values for each training example into a histogram, which serves as a sufficient statistic for that feature (Alsabti, Ranka, and Singh, 1998). Each histogram has 256 buckets (we use fixed bounds, since our features are all normalized to the range $[-1,+1]$) and thus they are easy to store or transmit, and we only need two histograms per feature[7] for each machine participating in the training. Once the sufficient statistics (histograms) have been accumulated over the entire training set by all of the workers, the histograms are sent to a master machine and summed together. The resulting histogram for each dimension allows us to compute the decision tree splits using the Gini coefficient as defined earlier, and also to compute the appropriate prediction values for each leaf (Figure 18.8). It is not difficult to generalize this procedure to training full trees.

We have available to us a 40 processor-core cluster (10 machines), with 3GB of RAM available per core (12GB per machine). Each training example is stored on our distributed file system with the feature values quantized to 8-bit integers.[8] Thus,

---

[6] The Gentle Boost algorithm assumes that the weak learner approximates $\mathbb{E}[y|x]$. It is possible to use other split criteria though greedily minimizing the squared error in this way is a natural choice.

[7] We typically keep one histogram for positive examples and one histogram for negative examples, as in Figure 18.8.

[8] The loss of precision in storing our features this way is irrelevant since the histograms used during training have only 256 bins.

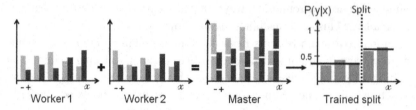

Figure 18.8 A decision tree node can be trained by accumulating a histogram of the feature values for the positive and negative examples reaching a node. This can be done in a distributed fashion by accumulating histograms for subsets of the data on separate worker machines, then summing the histograms together on a master machine. The histograms can be used to compute the conditional probability of the label for each bin of feature values, which in turn allows us to find the best split point (vertical dashed line) and output values for the leaves (horizontal lines).

using the previous procedure, we can accommodate more than 100GB of training data or, assuming a 1,000-dimensional feature vector, more than 100 million training examples.

18.3.5 Experimental Results

We have applied this approach to the problem of object detection for an office assistance robot. A common task that we might like such a robot to perform is that of inventorying a handful of different types of objects. In this task, the robot enters an office and takes several pictures of the room. It must then detect instances of the objects it is trained to seek and report the locations of any objects that it finds. Being able to recognize a wide variety of objects reliably in uncontrolled environments such as homes and offices is a critical capability for robots if they are expected to behave well in realistic scenarios, like putting away items left out on tables.

In Coates et al. (2009), the features and the classifier training algorithm described earlier were used along with (typically about 700) hand-labeled positive examples and a large corpus of negative examples (up to 1 million). We extract a dictionary of 1,200 image patches randomly from positive examples of each class, thus giving 1,200 features for each example. Training on our 10-machine (40-core) cluster takes about a half hour for 200 rounds of boosting using trees of depth 3. Classifiers were trained to find coffee mugs, coffee cups, office staplers, and bananas in images.[9] The first two of these objects have many similar features, making them easy to confuse with one another, while the other two objects are elongated and appear different from various orientations.

These classifiers were tested on 20 images using the sliding window algorithm described in Section 18.3.2. The results of these experiments are summarized in Table 18.1, with some representative examples of the object detections shown in Figure 18.9. Note that for mugs and cups, whose appearance does not change too drastically with viewpoint, extremely high performance can be achieved using a

---

[9] The robot also collects range data that can be included easily with the usual 2D image data: our choice of patch features works well for both visual and range data.

Table 18.1. *Object detection accuracy.*

Object	Count	True Positive	False Positive	Precision	Recall
Mug	67	63	1	0.984	0.940
Cup	43	41	0	1	0.953
Stapler	55	30	0	1	0.54
Banana	21	5	0	1	0.23

 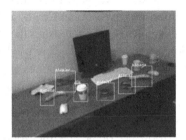

Figure 18.9 Resulting object detections from Coates et al. (2009).

single classifier. Staplers and bananas, which exhibit a great deal of intra-class variation and appear different from differing viewing angles, are much more difficult.[10] To put these numbers in perspective, it helps to consider the number of examples the classifier has actually been tested on: because of the sliding window algorithm, each classifier has actually classified almost 2 million windows (100,000 windows in each of 20 images) during this task, finding 95% of mugs and cups and more than half of the staplers with virtually no false positives.[11] The fact that such low false-positive rates are necessary to achieve reasonable performance is one of the challenges inherent in this type of vision task. Nevertheless, since the classifier is trained on large numbers of examples, the probability that our detector makes such mistakes is kept quite low.

In addition to the accuracy of the classifiers, we are also concerned about the running time. The running times for the learned detectors are shown in Table 18.2 for a GTX9800 GPU running our GPU-based features and a 2.66GHz Xeon CPU running an optimized implementation of the same algorithms (based on OpenCV's highly tuned cross-correlation code). We can see that the GPU implementation is up to 100 times faster than the CPU version. A quad-core CPU (which costs roughly the same amount as a mid-range GPU, as of 2010) would thus remain 25 times slower at best. Although the quick running times are a major benefit during testing, they are also helpful during training: the fast feature computations are what allow us to use large numbers of negative examples.

One can ask how much of a difference large datasets can make. If 1 million negative examples and a few hundred hand-labeled positive examples yield results as shown,

---

[10] These issues can be helped by using a separate classifier with separate feature dictionaries for each view of an object; see Coates and Ng (2010) for discussion.

[11] The test examples seen by the classifier correlate because they are extracted from overlapping windows – we might expect a higher error rate on truly independent data.

Table 18.2. *Detector running times for several objects.*

Object	Dictionary size	GPU time (s)	CPU time (s)	Factor speedup ($\times$)
Mug	590	2.96	286	96
Cup	540	3.13	320	102
Stapler	472	3.90	372	95
Banana	827	4.16	302	72

what happens when we move to synthetic positive examples and even more negatives? This question was explored in Coates and Ng (2010), where up to 9 million synthetic positive examples (generated using the green screen approach described earlier) and 90 million negative examples were used to train a detector to find claw hammers. The detector used the same patch features and the classifier training algorithm described in this chapter, as well as histogram of oriented gradient (HoG) features. Unfortunately, the HoG features are much slower than the patch features, and thus we use them more sparingly.

The performance of the classifier for different training set sizes (with a 10-to-1 ratio of negative to positive examples), expressed as area under the precision-recall curve of the classifier, is plotted in Figure 18.10. On our cluster of 10 machines, the full training procedure for the largest dataset (100 million examples) takes about 15 hours (400 patch features, 200 HoG features, 400 rounds of boosting, depth 3 trees).

While the performance asymptotes above roughly 5 million examples, the performance of the classifier does continue to improve slowly and, indeed, happens to peak at 100 million examples. These results suggest that we should aim to use up to 10 million examples (1 million positives) for a high-quality classifier – a number far beyond the dataset sizes presently used in most computer vision applications (Table 18.3).

The reason for the performance ceiling reached in Figure 18.10 is not entirely clear. Other experiments have shown that only slightly higher performance can be obtained by using deeper trees or more rounds of boosting. This suggests that the system may be hamstrung by either our use of synthetic data or the choice of features.

Our second approach to scalability, presented in Section 18.4, takes a different tack that may ultimately allow us to solve these problems. In particular, we look at a way to *learn* good features while also allowing us to leverage large amounts of unlabeled data (rather than relying on synthetic data).

18.4 Feature Learning with Deep Belief Networks

In the previous section we described a reworking of the learning pipeline for computer vision that combined standard algorithms but scaled them up to extremely large datasets.

Table 18.3. *Dataset sizes.*

Dataset	Positive examples per class
Caltech 256 (Griffin, Holub, and Perona, 2007)	≤ 827
LabelMe (Person) (Russell et al., 2008)	27,719
NORB (LeCun et al. 2004)	38,880
Coates and Ng (2010)	10^7

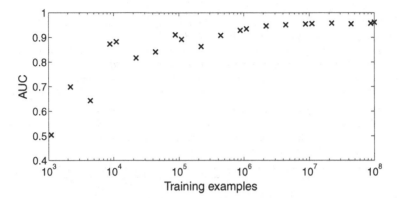

Figure 18.10 The performance (area under precision-recall curve) of a detector for claw hammers trained on up to 100 million examples 10 to 1 negatives-to-positives ratio.

We saw that we could achieve high performance on a difficult vision task as a result of using these algorithms with large datasets and that our performance improves greatly as the training set size grows. We also noted, though, that our choice of features and reliance on synthetic data may be blocking us from achieving even higher performance. Our chosen features, like most in vision, were hand-engineered. Likewise, our synthetic data, although reasonable looking, is generated using hand-picked heuristics. To make our vision algorithms even better, we could try to design better features, and develop improved data synthesizers. However, this is a somewhat unsatisfactory way to make progress on hard computer vision problems – this approach does not scale very well to future problems because of the requirement for human expertise and ingenuity in designing features and heuristics.

A promising alternative approach to scale up the standard vision pipeline is to use the input data itself to automatically compute good features to use. For example, we might be able to examine a large number of images on the internet, even without knowing what objects occur in them and find that most images consist of certain types of edges, and that these edges combine to make certain types of shapes and objects. We could then use those common building blocks as features for new images, so that supervised learning algorithms can then reason about edges and shapes (or whatever other features are found to be "optimal" for the input data), instead of about raw pixels. Further, the examples used to learn features can be *unlabeled*, thus solving the "data-collection" problem in many vision applications.

18.4.1 Deep Belief Networks

We consider the "deep belief network (DBN)" model for learning such features. A DBN is a multi-layer neural network that learns a hierarchical representation for its input data, such that the input layer contains the raw inputs (e.g., raw pixel intensities for images), the subsequent lower layers are computed from the input layer and capture low-level correlations between inputs (e.g., edges and contours for images), and the higher layers computed from the lower-layer representations attempt to capture larger

Table 18.4. *A rough estimate of the number of free parameters (in millions) in some recent deep belief network applications reported in the literature, compared to our desired model. To pick the applications, we looked through several research papers and picked the ones for which we could reliably tell the number of parameters in the model.*

Published source	Application	Params (in million)
Hinton and Salakhutdinov (2006)	Digit images	1.6
Hinton et al. (2006)	Face images	3.8
Salakhutdinov and Hinton (2007)	Semantic hashing	2.6
Ranzato and Szummer (2008)	Text	3
Our model		100 million

and more robust correlations (e.g., various types of shapes or objects in images). For computer vision, a DBN can compute the higher-layer representation for a given image, and thus represent the input in terms of those robust, object-level features, instead of in terms of the original raw pixel-level features. Also, current algorithms for learning DBNs can work with unlabeled input data, which is very readily available. DBNs promise to significantly enhance the standard vision pipeline by providing an automated, optimized way of generating features.

DBNs have been successfully applied to a variety of machine learning applications (Hinton and Salakhutdinov, 2006; Salakhutdinov and Hinton, 2007; Ranzato and Szummer, 2008). Due to their recent importance, there is interest in scaling up DBN algorithms, and several ingenious methods have been devised specifically for efficient DBN learning (Hinton, Osindero, and Teh, 2006; Bengio et al., 2006). However, conventional single-core learning algorithms do not scale very well to using millions of input examples or high-dimensional input data. Table 18.4 lists some recent applications of DBNs and contrasts them with the typical scale for our computer vision application. All the applications do not implement exactly the same algorithm, and the applications cited may not have used the largest-scale models possible, so this is not an exact comparison – but the order of magnitude difference between our desired model and recent work is striking, and suggests that significant benefits can be achieved by using GPUs for large-scale DBN learning.

We follow the unsupervised learning algorithm proposed by Hinton et al. (2006), in which the DBN is greedily built up layer by layer, starting from the input data. Each layer is learned using a probabilistic model called a restricted Boltzmann machine (RBM). Briefly, an RBM contains a set of stochastic hidden units h that are fully connected in an undirected probabilistic model to a set of stochastic visible (input) units x; the visible units could represent the raw input vector, and the hidden unit could represent the feature representation computed by a single RBM layer. Assuming binary-valued units, the RBM defines the following joint distribution over x and h:

$$P(x, h) \propto \exp \left(\sum_{i,j} x_i w_{ij} h_j + \sum_i c_i x_i + \sum_j b_j h_j \right),$$

where the weights w and biases b and c are parameters to be learned. The learning algorithms typically rely on the observation that the conditional distributions can be analytically computed:

$$P(h_j|x) = \text{sigmoid}(b_j + \sum_i w_{ij}x_i) \tag{18.1}$$

$$P(x_i|h) = \text{sigmoid}(c_i + \sum_j w_{ij}h_j) \tag{18.2}$$

where $\text{sigmoid}(a) = 1/(1 + e^{-a})$. Maximum likelihood parameter learning for an RBM can be efficiently approximated by contrastive divergence updates (Hinton, 2002): given an unlabeled example, start by initializing the visible units x to the unlabeled example, alternately sample the hidden units h and visible units x using Gibbs sampling (Equations 18.1 and 18.2), and update the parameters as:

$$w_{ij} := w_{ij} + \eta \left(\langle x_i h_j \rangle_{\text{data}} - \langle x_i h_j \rangle_{\text{sample}} \right) \tag{18.3}$$

$$c_i := c_i + \eta \left(\langle x_i \rangle_{\text{data}} - \langle x_i \rangle_{\text{sample}} \right) \tag{18.4}$$

$$b_j := b_j + \eta \left(\langle h_j \rangle_{\text{data}} - \langle h_j \rangle_{\text{sample}} \right) \tag{18.5}$$

where η is the learning rate, $\langle \cdot \rangle_{\text{data}}$ represents expectations with the visible units tied to the input examples, and $\langle \cdot \rangle_{\text{sample}}$ represents expectations after $T \geq 1$ iterations of Gibbs sampling. Since each update requires a Gibbs sampling operation – which scales as the product of the input dimension and the number of hidden units – and the updates have to be applied over millions of unlabeled examples to reach convergence, unsupervised learning of the parameters can take *several days* to complete on a modern CPU.

Recent work has shown that several popular learning algorithms such as logistic regression, linear SVMs, and others can be easily implemented in parallel on multicore architectures, by having each core perform the required computations for a subset of input examples, and then combining the results centrally (Dean and Ghemawat, 2004; Chu et al., 2006). However, standard algorithms for DBNs are difficult to parallelize with such "data-parallel" schemes, because they involve iterative, stochastic parameter updates, such that any update depends on the previous updates. This makes the updates hard to massively parallelize at a coarse, data-parallel level (e.g., by computing the updates in parallel and summing them together centrally) without losing the critical stochastic nature of the updates. Instead, the DBN learning algorithms can be successfully parallelized using the fine-grained parallelism offered by GPUs.

18.4.2 GPUs for DBN Learning

The contrastive divergence algorithm follows a standard template for machine learning algorithms: pick a small number of input examples, compute an update (using the contrastive divergence equation), and apply it to the parameters. To successfully apply GPUs to accelerate such an algorithm, we need to satisfy two major requirements. First, memory transfers between RAM and the GPU's global memory need to be minimized or grouped into large chunks. For machine learning applications, we can achieve this by storing all parameters permanently in GPU global memory during learning. Input examples usually cannot all be stored in global memory, but they should be transferred only occasionally into global memory in as large chunks as possible. With both parameters and input examples in GPU global memory, the updates can be computed without any memory transfer operations, with any intermediate computations also stored in global memory.

A second requirement is that the learning updates should be implemented to fit the two-level GPU hierarchy of blocks and threads, in such a way that shared memory can be used where possible and global memory accesses can be coalesced. Often, blocks can exploit data parallelism (e.g., each block can work on a separate input example), while threads can exploit more fine-grained parallelism because they have access to very fast shared memory and can be synchronized (e.g., each thread can work on a single feature of the input example assigned to the block). Further, the graphics hardware can hide memory latencies for blocks waiting on global memory accesses by scheduling a ready-to-run block in that time. To fully use such latency hiding, it is beneficial to use a large number of independently executing blocks.

Both principles are easy to apply to the contrastive divergence updates in Equations 18.3–18.5. The parameters w, c, and b for all the DBN layers are maintained permanently in global memory during training. The updates require repeated Gibbs sampling using the distributions in Equations 18.1 and 18.2. These distributions can be rewritten using matrix notation:

$$P(h|x) = \text{vectorSigmoid}(b + w^T x)$$
$$P(x|h) = \text{vectorSigmoid}(c + wh)$$

where $\text{vectorSigmoid}(\cdot)$ represents the elementwise sigmoid function and x, h are vectors containing a feature corresponding to each visible and hidden unit, respectively. The foregoing computations can be batched together for several examples for efficiency. The matrix operations can be performed in parallel using optimized linear algebra packages for the GPU; other operations are simply elementwise operations (e.g., the sigmoid computation and sampling) and can be done by a simple parallelization scheme where each block works on a single example and each thread in the block works on a single feature of the example. Finally, once the samples have been generated, the updates can again be applied in parallel using linear algebra packages: for example, $w := w + \eta \left(\langle x^T h \rangle_{\text{data}} - \langle x^T h \rangle_{\text{sample}} \right)$. As we will see later, this simple GPU-based scheme turns out to work remarkably well.

We extend our method to learning DBNs with "overlapping patches" as shown in Figure 18.11. This model is most easily understood with hidden and visible units arranged in a 2D array (e.g., when the input is an image and each visible unit is a pixel). The input image is fully tiled by equally spaced, equal-sized patches (or receptive fields), and each patch is fully connected to a unique group of hidden units. This is very similar to the convolutional DBN model of Lee et al. (2009), except that there is no forced sharing of weights in this model, and each connection is parametrized by a free parameter. Because of the overlapping patches, all the parameters in the model depend on each other, making learning hard. However, Gibbs sampling can still be performed in parallel for this model: each visible unit depends on hidden units at many different locations, but the sampling operation $x|h$ can be implemented using only coalesced

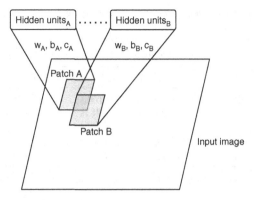

Figure 18.11 A schematic diagram of the overlapping patches model for deep belief networks. Two patches A and B in the input image are shown, with each patch connected to a different set of hidden units. The connections are parameterized by their own sets of parameters w_A, b_A, c_A and w_B, b_B, c_B.

global memory accesses (implementation details omitted; see the previous example of implementation of convolutions on GPUs).

These overlapping patch RBMs can be stacked on top of each other, such that the second-layer RBM contains hidden units connected locally to first-layer hidden units, and so on. The resulting deep networks have a very large number of units but only sparse, local connections, which make learning tractable even for models with more than 100 million parameters.

18.4.3 Experimental Results

In Raina, Madhavan, and Ng (2009), we compare this GPU-based algorithm against CPU-based methods using the following multicore hardware:

- **GPU:** Nvidia GeForce GTX 280 graphics card with 1GB memory. The machine had a dual-core CPU @ 3.16GHz. The reported running time results show the total running time (including all computation, memory transfer, and soforth).
- **Single CPU:** Single core @ 3.16GHz.
- **Dual-core CPU:** Two cores, each @ 3.16GHz. (Identical machine as for the GPU result.)
- **Quad-core* CPU:** Four cores, each @ 2.40GHz.[12]

The CPU-based method was implemented using two highly optimized multi-threaded linear algebra packages: ATLAS BLAS (Whaley, Petitet, and Dongarra, 2001) and Goto BLAS (Goto and Van De Geijn, 2008). Consistent with previous results, we found that Goto BLAS was faster (Bengio, 2007), so we report CPU results using it. As input, we used a large dataset of natural images (van Hateren and van der Schaaf, 1998) and obtained input examples by randomly extracting square image patches of

---

[12] Note that each core in our quad-core machine is somewhat slower than the single CPU core, so that the peak processing power of the quad-core is a little more than three times that of the single CPU. For this reason, the quad-core machine does not always perform better than the single- dual-core machine. We put an asterisk on quad-core* everywhere to remind the reader of this distinction.

Table 18.5. *Average running time in seconds for processing 1 million input examples for learning an RBM, with contrastive divergence updates applied in batches of 192 examples each. The size of the RBM in each column is denoted by the number of visible units × number of hidden units. The GPU speedup is computed w.r.t. the fastest CPU-based result.*

Package	Architecture	576 × 1024	1024 × 4096	2304 × 16000	4096 × 11008
Goto BLAS	Single CPU	563s	3638s	172803s	223741s
Goto BLAS	Dual-core CPU	497s	2987s	93586s	125381s
Goto BLAS	Quad-core* CPU	777s	3785s	70175s	95537s
	GPU	38.6s	184s	1376s	1726s
	GPU Speedup	**12.9×**	**16.2×**	**51.0×**	**55.4×**

Table 18.6. *Average time in seconds for processing 1 million examples for the overlapping patch model, with contrastive divergence updates applied in batches of 192 examples each. The model size in each column is denoted by the number of visible units × number of hidden units (but note that the units are not fully connected). Overall, the models have 28 million and 54 million free parameters, respectively.*

Package	Arch.	20,736 × 49,152	36,864 × 92,928
Goto	Single CPU	38455s	77246s
Goto	Dual-core	32236s	65235s
	GPU	3415s	6435s
	GPU Speedup	**9.4×**	**10.1×**

the required size. Following previous work, we used Gaussian visible units and binary hidden units and trained a sparse RBM by adding an additional penalty term to the objective (Lee, Chaitanya, and Ng, 2007) – these modifications do not affect the running time results significantly. For learning, we performed one-step contrastive divergence updates using a mini-batch of 192 examples.

Table 18.5 shows the running time for processing 1 million examples for RBMs of varying size (denoted by number of visible units × number of hidden units). The GPU method is between 12 and 55 times faster than the fastest CPU-based configuration. The speedup obtained is highest for large RBMs, where the computations involve large matrices and can be more efficiently parallelized by using a large number of concurrent blocks (which allows the graphics hardware to better hide memory latencies). The largest model in Table 18.5 has 45 million parameters, and our GPU method can update these parameters using 1 million examples in about 29 minutes. In comparison, our multicore CPU configuration takes more than a day per million examples. Since we would ideally want to use tens of millions of training examples for learning such a large model, the CPU method is impractical for such tasks.

Table 18.6 shows a similar running time comparison for two "overlapping patch" models (see table caption for details).[13] The GPU method is about 10 times faster than

---

[13] Other details: the two models were created by taking 144 × 144 pixel and 192 × 192 pixel inputs respectively; the size of each patch is 24 × 24 pixels, there are 192 hidden units connected to each patch, and neighboring patches are 8 pixels apart.

the dual-core CPU. This speedup is somewhat lower than the speedup observed for a fully connected RBM (see Table 18.5), because Gibbs sampling in the overlapping patch model requires many operations involving small matrices (one weight matrix per patch), instead of only a few operations involving large matrices. By using the overlapping patch model, we can learn a four-layer DBN with 96 million parameters and 25,600, 82,944, 8,192, 4,608, and 1,024 units, respectively, in the input layer and the four successive hidden layers. Such models are at least an order of magnitude larger than previously published work on DBNs and can potentially provide fully automated feature learning for computer vision with large input images.

18.5 Conclusion

In this chapter, we have described two different approaches to improving performance in difficult vision tasks using large datasets. The first approach uses (carefully chosen) traditional algorithms that have been enhanced to take advantage of GPUs and distributed systems. Specifically, we have shown that synthetic data, GPU-friendly image features, and a distributed decision tree training system can allow us to use extremely large training sets of up to 10^8 examples – orders of magnitude more than standard vision systems. This new "scaled up" pipeline allows us to achieve high performance on a realistic application: detecting objects in images captured by a mobile robot. The results suggest that, in fact, learning from large training sets can free us from many of the difficult engineering tasks involved in computer vision.

However, we have also noted that despite the flexibility of our learning algorithm, synthetic data and hand-engineered features may still be barriers to maximum performance. We thus explore an alternative approach to scaling up the learning pipeline: using DBNs to leverage large unlabeled datasets to learn higher level feature representations. These representations allow us not only to achieve higher performance but also to avoid the costly task of collecting and labeling data. Despite the computational requirements of the DBN learning algorithms, we have shown that, again, GPUs can be used to accelerate learning in order to scale the algorithm to large datasets.

Both of these approaches have key strengths. The first, using distributed training algorithms, although more traditional, can train on extremely large amounts of data, limited only by the number of machines we devote to the task. The second, using unsupervised DBN training, promises to yield highly general feature representations that perform better and require less human engineering. Meanwhile, these algorithms also free us from the difficult task of collecting and labeling training data. In either case it is clear that scalability, in one direction or another, is a major benefit and can provide significant performance gains for many difficult vision applications.

References

Alsabti, K., Ranka, S., and Singh, V. 1998. CLOUDS: A decision tree classifier for large datasets. In: *4th International Conference on Knowledge Discovery and Data Mining*.

Banko, M., and Brill, E. 2001. Scaling to Very Very Large Corpora for Natural Language Disambiguation. In: *39th Annual Meeting on Association for Computational Linguistics*.

Bengio, Y. 2007. Speeding Up Stochastic Gradient Descent. In: *Advances in Neural Information Processing Systems: Workshop on Efficient Machine Learning*.

Bengio, Y., Lamblin, P., Popovici, D., and Larochelle, H. 2006. Greedy Layer-wise Training of Deep Networks. Pages 153–160 of: *Advances in Neural Information Processing Systems*.

Breiman, L., Friedman, J., Olshen, R., and Stone, C. 1984. *Classification and Regression Trees*. Monterey, CA: Wadsworth and Brooks.

Catanzaro, B., Sundaram, N., and Keutzer, K. 2008. Fast support vector machine training and classification on graphics processors. In: *Proceedings of the 25th International Conference on Machine Learning*.

Chu, C. T., Kim, S. K., Lin, Y. A., Yu, Y., Bradski, G. R., Ng, A. Y., and Olukotun, K. 2006. Map-Reduce for Machine Learning on Multicore. Pages 281–288 of: *Neural Information Processing Systems*.

Coates, A., and Ng, A. Y. 2010. Multi-camera Objection Detection for Robotics. In: *IEEE International Conference on Robotics and Automation*.

Coates, A., Baumstarck, P., Le, Q., and Ng, A. Y. 2009. Scalable Learning for Object Detection with GPU Hardware. In: *IEEE/RSJ International Conference on Intelligent Robots and Systems*.

Dalal, N., and Triggs, B. 2005. Histograms of Oriented Gradients for Human Detection. In: *IEEE Conference on Computer Vision and Pattern Recognition*.

Dean, J., and Ghemawat, S. 2004. MapReduce: Simplified Data Processing on Large Clusters. In: *Sixth Symposium on Operating System Design and Implementation*.

Everingham, M., Van Gool, L., Williams, C. K. I., Winn, J., and Zisserman, A. 2009. *The PASCAL Visual Object Classes Challenge 2009 (VOC2009) Results*. http://www.pascalnetwork.org/challenges/VOC/voc2009/workshop/index.html.

Felzenszwalb, P., Mcallester, D., and Ramanan, D. 2008. A Discriminatively Trained, Multiscale, Deformable Part Model. In: *IEEE International Conference on Computer Vision and Pattern Recognition*.

Ferrari, V., Fevrier, L., Jurie, F., and Schmid, C. 2008. Groups of Adjacent Contour Segments for Object Detection. *IEEE Transactions on Pattern Analysis and Machine Intelligence*.

Friedman, J., Hastie, T., and Tibshirani, R. 1998. *Additive Logistic Regression: A Statistical View of Boosting*. Technical Report, Department of Statistics, Stanford University.

Goto, K., and Van De Geijn, R. 2008. High-performance Implementation of the Level-3 BLAS. *ACM Transactions on Mathematical Software*, **35**(1), 1–14.

Grauman, K., and Darrell, T. 2005. The Pyramid Match Kernel: Discriminative Classification with Sets of Image Features. In: *Tenth IEEE International Conference on Computer Vision*.

Griffin, G., Holub, A., and Perona, P. 2007. *Caltech-256 Object Category Dataset*. Technical Report, California Institute of Technology.

Heymann, S., Miller, K., Smolic, A., Frhlich, B., and Wiegand, T. 2007. SIFT implementation and optimization for general-purpose GPU. In: *15th International Conference in Central Europe on Computer Graphics, Visualization and Computer Vision*.

Hinton, G. E. 2002. Training Products of Experts by Minimizing Contrastive Divergence. *Neural Computation*, **14**, 1771–1800.

Hinton, G. E., and Salakhutdinov, R. R. 2006. Reducing the Dimensionality of Data with Neural Networks. *Science*, **313**(5786), 504–507.

Hinton, G. E., Osindero, S., and Teh, Y.-W. 2006. A Fast Learning Algorithm for Deep Belief Nets. *Neural Computation*, **18**(7), 1527–1554.

LeCun, Y., Huang, F. J., and Bottou, L. 2004. Learning Methods for Generic Object Recognition with Invariance to Pose and Lighting. In: *IEEE Conference on Computer Vision and Pattern Recognition*.

Lee, H., Chaitanya, E., and Ng, A. Y. 2007. Sparse deep belief net model for visual area V2. Pages 873–880 of: *Advances in Neural Information Processing Systems.*

Lee, H., Grosse, R., Ranganath, R., and Ng, A. Y. 2009. Convolutional Deep Belief Networks for Scalable Unsupervised Learning of Hierarchical Representations. In: *Proceedings of the 26th International Conference on Machine Learning.*

Lowe, D. G. 1999. Object Recognition from Local Scale-invariant Features. Pages 1150–1157 of: *Seventh IEEE International Conference on Computer Vision,* vol. 2.

Nister, D., and Stewenius, H. 2006. Scalable Recognition with a Vocabulary Tree. Pages 2161–2168 of: *IEEE Conference on Computer Vision and Pattern Recognition.*

nVidia. 2009. *nVidia CUDA Programming Guide.* NVIDIA Corporation, 2701 San Tomas Expressway, Santa Clara, CA.

Opelt, A., Pinz, A., and Zisserman, A. 2006. Incremental Learning of Object Detectors Using a Visual Shape Alphabet. In: *IEEE Conference on Computer Vision and Pattern Recognition.*

Osuna, E., Freund, R., and Girosi, F. 1997. Training Support Vector Machines: An Application to Face Detection. In: *Computer Vision and Pattern Recognition, IEEE Computer Society Conference on.*

Quigley, M., Batra, S., Gould, S., Klingbeil, E., Le, Q. V., Wellman, A., and Ng, A. Y. 2009. High-accuracy 3D Sensing for Mobile Manipulation: Improving Object Detection and Door Opening. In: *IEEE International Conference on Robotics and Automation.*

Raina, R., Madhavan, A., and Ng, A. 2009. Large-Scale Deep Unsupervised Learning Using Graphics Processors. Pages 873–880 of: Bottou, L., and Littman, M. (eds), *Proceedings of the 26th International Conference on Machine Learning.* Montreal: Omnipress.

Ranzato, M. A., and Szummer, M. 2008. Semi-supervised Learning of Compact Document Representations with Deep Networks. Pages 792–799 of: *Proceedings of the 25th International Conference on Machine Learning.*

Rowley, H. A., Baluja, S., and Kanade, T. 1995. Human Face Detection in Visual Scenes. In: *Advances in Neural Information Processing Systems.*

Russell, B. C., Torralba, A., Murphy, K. P., and Freeman, W. T. 2005. *Labelme: A Database and Web-based Tool for Image Annotation.* Technical Report MIT-CSAIL-TR-2005-056, Massachusetts Institute of Technology.

Russell, B. C., Torralba, A., Murphy, K. P., and Freeman, W. T. 2008. LabelMe: A Database and Web-based Tool for Image Annotation. *International Journal of Computer Vision,* **77**(May), 157–173.

Salakhutdinov, R., and Hinton, G. 2007. Semantic Hashing. In: *SIGIR Workshop on Information Retrieval and Applications of Graphical Models.*

Sapp, B., Saxena, A., and Ng, A. Y. 2008. A Fast Data Collection and Augmentation Procedure for Object Recognition. In: *AAAI'08: Proceedings of the 23rd National Conference on Artificial Intelligence.*

Schneiderman, H., and Kanade, T. 2000. A Statistical Method for 3D Object Detection Applied to Faces and Cars. In: *IEEE Conference on Computer Vision and Pattern Recognition.*

Schneiderman, H., and Kanade, T. 2004. Object Detection Using the Statistics of Parts. *International Journal of Computer Vision.*

Torralba, A., Fergus, R., and Freeman, W. T. 2007a. 80 Million Tiny Images: A Large Dataset for Non-parametric Object and Scene Recognition. *IEEE Transactions on Pattern Analysis and Machine Intelligence.*

Torralba, A., Murphy, K. P., and Freeman, W. T. 2007b. Sharing Visual Features for Multiclass and Multiview Object Detection. *IEEE Transactions on Pattern Analysis and Machine Intelligence.*

Torralba, A., Fergus, R., and Weiss, Y. 2008. Small Codes and Large Image Databases for Recognition. In: *IEEE Conference on Computer Vision and Pattern Recognition.*

van Hateren, J. H., and van der Schaaf, A. 1998. Independent Component Filters of Natural Images Compared with Simple Cells in Primary Visual Cortex. *Proceedings of the Royal Society of London B*, **265**, 359–366.

Viola, P., and Jones, M. J. 2001. Robust Real-time Object Detection. *International Journal of Computer Vision*.

Viola, P., and Jones, M. J. 2004. Robust Real-Time Face Detection. *International Journal of Computer Vision*.

Whaley, R. C., Petitet, A., and Dongarra, J. J. 2001. Automated Empirical Optimization of Software and the ATLAS Project. *Parallel Computing*, **27**(1–2), 3–35.

Winn, J., Criminisi, A., and Minka, T. 2005. Object Categorization by Learned Universal Visual Dictionary. In: *Tenth IEEE International Conference on Computer Vision*.

CHAPTER 19

Large-Scale FPGA-Based Convolutional Networks

Clément Farabet, Yann LeCun, Koray Kavukcuoglu,
Berin Martini, Polina Akselrod, Selcuk Talay,
and Eugenio Culurciello

Micro-robots, unmanned aerial vehicles, imaging sensor networks, wireless phones, and other embedded vision systems all require low cost and high-speed implementations of synthetic vision systems capable of recognizing and categorizing objects in a scene.

Many successful object recognition systems use dense features extracted on regularly spaced patches over the input image. The majority of the feature extraction systems have a common structure composed of a filter bank (generally based on oriented edge detectors or 2D Gabor functions), a nonlinear operation (quantization, winner-take-all, sparsification, normalization, and/or pointwise saturation), and finally a pooling operation (max, average, or histogramming). For example, the scale-invariant feature transform (SIFT) (Lowe, 2004) operator applies oriented edge filters to a small patch and determines the dominant orientation through a winner-take-all operation. Finally, the resulting sparse vectors are added (pooled) over a larger patch to form a local orientation histogram. Some recognition systems use a single stage of feature extractors (Lazebnik, Schmid, and Ponce, 2006; Dalal and Triggs, 2005; Berg, Berg, and Malik, 2005; Pinto, Cox, and DiCarlo, 2008).

Other models such as HMAX-type models (Serre, Wolf, and Poggio, 2005; Mutch, and Lowe, 2006) and convolutional networks use two more layers of successive feature extractors. Different training algorithms have been used for learning the parameters of convolutional networks. In LeCun et al. (1998b) and Huang and LeCun (2006), pure supervised learning is used to update the parameters. However, recent works have focused on training with an auxiliary task (Ahmed et al., 2008) or using unsupervised objectives (Ranzato et al., 2007b; Kavukcuoglu et al., 2009; Jarrett et al., 2009; Lee et al., 2009).

This chapter presents a scalable hardware architecture for large-scale multi-layered synthetic vision systems based on large parallel filter banks, such as convolutional networks. This hardware can also be used to accelerate the execution (and partial learning) of recent vision algorithms such as SIFT and HMAX (Lazebnik et al., 2006; Serre et al., 2005). This system is a dataflow vision engine that can perform real-time detection, recognition, and localization in megapixel images processed as pipelined streams. The system was designed with the goal of providing categorization of an arbitrary number of objects while consuming very little power.

Graphics processing units (GPUs) are becoming a common alternative to custom hardware in vision applications, as demonstrated in Coates et al. (2009). Their advantages over custom hardware are numerous: they are inexpensive, available in most recent computers, and easily programmable with standard development kits, such as nVidia CUDA SDK. The main reasons for continuing developing custom hardware are twofold: performance and power consumption. By developing a custom architecture that is fully adapted to a certain range of tasks (as is shown in this chapter), the product of power consumption by performance can be improved by a factor of 100.

19.1 Learning Internal Representations

One of the key questions of vision science (natural and artificial) is how to produce good internal representations of the visual world. What sort of internal representation would allow an artificial vision system to detect and classify objects into categories, independently of pose, scale, illumination, conformation, and clutter? More interestingly, how could an artificial vision system *learn* appropriate internal representations automatically, the way animals and humans seem to learn by simply looking at the world? In the time-honored approach to computer vision (and to pattern recognition in general), the question is avoided: internal representations are produced by a handcrafted feature extractor, whose output is fed to a trainable classifier. While the issue of learning features has been a topic of interest for many years, considerable progress has been achieved in the past few years with the development of so-called *deep learning* methods.

Good internal representations are hierarchical. In vision, pixels are assembled into edglets, edglets into motifs, motifs into parts, parts into objects, and objects into scenes. This suggests that recognition architectures for vision (and for other modalities such as audio and natural language) should have multiple trainable stages stacked on top of each other, one for each level in the feature hierarchy. This raises two new questions: what to put in each stage? and how to train such *deep, multi-stage architectures*? Convolutional Networks (ConvNets) are an answer to the first question. Until recently, the answer to the second question was to use gradient-based supervised learning, but recent research in *deep learning* has produced a number of unsupervised methods that greatly reduce the need for labeled samples.

19.1.1 Convolutional Networks

Convolutional Networks (LeCun et al., 1990, 1998b) are trainable architectures composed of multiple stages. The input and output of each stage are sets of arrays called *feature maps*. For example, if the input is a color image, each feature map would be a 2D array containing a color channel of the input image (for an audio input each feature map would be a 1D array, and for a video or volumetric image, it would be a 3D array). At the output, each feature map represents a particular feature extracted at all locations on the input. Each stage is composed of three layers: a *filter bank layer*, a *nonlinearity layer*, and a *feature pooling layer*. A typical ConvNet is composed of one, two, or three such three-layer stages, followed by a classification module.

Each layer type is now described for the case of image recognition. We introduce the following convention: banks of images will be seen as 3D arrays in which the first dimension is the number of independent maps/images, the second is the height of the maps, and the third is the width. The input bank of a module is denoted as x, the output bank as y, an image in the input bank as x_i, and a pixel in the input bank as x_{ijk}.

- **Filter Bank Layer – F:** The input is a 3D array with n_1 2D *feature maps* of size $n_2 \times n_3$. Each component is denoted as x_{ijk}, and each feature map is denoted as x_i. The output is also a 3D array y composed of m_1 feature maps of size $m_2 \times m_3$. A trainable filter (kernel) k_{ij} in the filter bank has size $l_1 \times l_2$ and connects input feature map x_i to output feature map y_j. The module computes

$$y_j = b_j + \sum_i k_{ij} * x_i \tag{19.1}$$

where b_j is a trainable bias parameter and $*$ is the 2D discrete convolution operator:

$$(k_{ij} * x_i)_{pq} = \sum_{m=-l_1/2}^{l_1/2-1} \sum_{n=-l_2/2}^{l_2/2-1} k_{ij,m,n} x_{i,p+m,q+n} \tag{19.2}$$

Each filter detects a particular feature at every location on the input. Hence, spatially translating the input of a feature detection layer will translate the output but leave it otherwise unchanged.

- **Nonlinearity Layer – R, N:** In traditional ConvNets, this simply consists in a pointwise tanh function applied to each site (ijk). However, recent implementations have used more sophisticated nonlinearities. A useful one for natural image recognition is the rectified tanh: $R_{abs}(x) = abs(g_i \cdot \tanh(x))$ where g_i is a trainable gain parameter per each input feature map i. The rectified tanh is sometimes followed by a subtractive and divisive local normalization N, which enforces local competition between adjacent features in a feature map and between features at the nearby spatial locations. Local competition usually results in features that are decorrelated, thereby maximizing their individual role. The subtractive normalization operation for a given site x_{ijk} computes

$$v_{ijk} = x_{ijk} - \sum_{ipq} w_{pq} \cdot x_{i,j+p,k+q}, \tag{19.3}$$

where w_{pq} is a normalized truncated Gaussian weighting window (typically of size 9×9). The divisive normalization computes

$$y_{ijk} = \frac{v_{ijk}}{\max(mean(\sigma_{jk}), \sigma_{jk})}, \tag{19.4}$$

where $\sigma_{jk} = (\sum_{ipq} w_{pq} \cdot v_{i,j+p,k+q}^2)^{1/2}$. The local contrast normalization layer is inspired by visual neuroscience models (Lyu and Simoncelli, 2008; Pinto et al., 2008).

- **Feature Pooling Layer – P:** This layer treats each feature map separately. In its simplest instance, called P_A, it computes the average values over a neighborhood in each feature map. The neighborhoods are stepped by a stride larger than 1 (but smaller than or equal to the pooling neighborhood). This results in a reduced-resolution output feature map that is robust to small variations in the location of features in the previous layer. The average operation is sometimes replaced by a max operation, P_M. Traditional ConvNets use a pointwise tanh() after the pooling layer, but more recent models do not. Some ConvNets dispense with the separate pooling layer entirely, but use strides larger than one in the filter bank layer to reduce the resolution (LeCun et al., 1989; Simard, Steinkraus, and Platt, 2003). In some recent versions of ConvNets, the pooling also pools similar features at the same location, in addition to the same feature at nearby locations (Kavukcuoglu et al., 2009).

Supervised training is performed using online stochastic gradient descent to mini-mize the discrepancy between the desired output and the actual output of the network. All the coefficients in all the layers are updated simultaneously by the learning proce-dure for each sample. The gradients are computed with the back-propagation method. Details of the procedure are given in LeCun et al. (1998b), and methods for efficient training are detailed in LeCun et al. (1998a).

19.1.2 History and Applications

ConvNets can be seen as a representatives of a wide class of models that we will call *multi-stage Hubel-Wiesel architectures*. The idea is rooted in Hubel and Wiesel's classic 1962 work on the cat's primary visual cortex. It identified orientation-selective *simple cells* with local receptive fields, whose role is similar to that of the ConvNets filter bank layers, and *complex cells*, whose role is similar to that of the pooling layers. The first such model to be simulated on a computer was Fukushima's Neocognitron (Fukushima and Miyake, 1982), which used a layerwise, unsupervised competitive learning algo-rithm for the filter banks, and a separately trained supervised linear classifier for the output layer. The innovation in LeCun et al. (1989, 1990) was to simplify the architec-ture and to use the back-propagation algorithm to train the entire system in a supervised fashion.

The approach was very successful, and led to several implementations, ranging from optical character recognition (OCR) to object detection, scene segmentation, and robot navigation:

- Check reading (handwriting recognition) at AT&T (LeCun et al., 1998b) and Mi-crosoft (Simard et al., 2003; Chellapilla, Shilman, and Simard, 2006).
- Detection in images, including faces with record accuracy and real-time perfor-mance (Vaillant, Monrocq, and LeCun, 1994; Garcia and Delakis, 2004; Osadchy, LeCun, and Miller, 2007; Nasse, Thurau, and Fink, 2009), license plates and faces in Google's StreetView (Frome et al., 2009), or customers' gender and age at NEC.
- More experimental detection of hands/gestures (Nowlan and Platt, 1995), logos and text (Delakis and Garcia, 2008).
- Vision-based navigation for off-road robots: In the DARPA-sponsored LAGR program, ConvNets were used for long-range obstacle detection (Hadsell et al., 2009). In Hadsell et al. (2009), the system is pre-trained offline using a combination of unsupervised learning (as described in Section 19.1.3) and supervised learning. It is then adapted online, as the robot runs, using labels provided by a short-range stereovision system (see videos at http://www.cs.nyu.edu/~yann/research/lagr).
- Interesting new applications include image restoration (Jain and Seung, 2008) and image segmentation, particularly for biological images (Ning et al., 2005).

Over the years, other instances of the multi-stage Hubel-Wiesel architecture have appeared that are in the tradition of the Neocognitron: unlike supervised ConvNets, they use a combination of hand-crafting and simple unsupervised methods to design the filter banks. Notable examples include Mozer's visual models (Mozer, 1991) and the so-called HMAX family of models from T. Poggio's lab at MIT (Serre et al., 2005; Mutch and Lowe, 2006), which uses hardwired Gabor filters in the first stage and a simple unsupervised random template selection algorithm for the second stage. All stages use pointwise nonlinearities and max pooling. From the same institute, Pinto et al. (2008) have identified the most appropriate nonlinearities and normalizations by running systematic experiments with a single-stage architecture using GPU-based parallel hardware.

19.1.3 Unsupervised Learning of ConvNets

Training deep, multi-stage architectures using supervised gradient back-propagation requires many labeled samples. However, in many problems labeled data is scarce, whereas unlabeled data is abundant. Recent research in deep learning (Hinton and Salakhutdinov, 2006; Bengio et al., 2007; Ranzato, Boureau, and LeCun, 2007a) has shown that *unsupervised learning* can be used to train each stage one after the other using only unlabeled data, reducing the requirement for labeled samples significantly. In Jarrett et al. (2009), using abs and normalization nonlinearities, unsupervised pre-training, and supervised global refinement has been shown to yield excellent performance on the Caltech-101 dataset with only 30 training samples per category (more on this later). In Lee et al. (2009), good accuracy was obtained on the same set using a very different unsupervised method based on sparse restricted Boltzmann machines. Several works at NEC have also shown that using *auxiliary tasks* (Ahmed et al., 2008; Weston, Rattle, and Collobert, 2008) helps regularizing the system and produces excellent performance.

Unsupervised Training with Predictive Sparse Decomposition

The unsupervised method we propose, to learn the filter coefficients in the filter bank layers, is called predictive sparse decomposition (PSD) (Kavukcuoglu, Ranzato, and LeCun, 2008). Similar to the well-known sparse coding algorithms (Olshausen and Field, 1997), inputs are approximated as a sparse linear combination of dictionary elements:

$$Z^* = \min_Z \|X - WZ\|_2^2 + \lambda |Z|_1 \qquad (19.5)$$

In conventional sparse coding (19.5), for any given input X, an expensive optimization algorithm is run to find the optimal sparse representation Z^* (the "basis pursuit" problem). PSD trains a nonlinear feed-forward regressor (or *encoder*) $C(X, K) = g.(\tanh(X * k + b))$ to approximate the sparse solution Z^*. During training, the feature vector Z^* is obtained by minimizing the following compound energy:

$$E(Z, W, K) = \|X - WZ\|_2^2 + \lambda \|Z\|_1 + \|Z - C(X, K)\|_2^2, \qquad (19.6)$$

where W is the matrix whose columns are the dictionary elements and $K = k, g, b$ are the encoder filter, bias, and gain parameters. For each training sample X, one first finds Z^* that minimizes E, then W and K are adjusted by one step of stochastic gradient descent to lower E. Once training is complete, the feature vector for a given input is simply approximated with $Z^* = C(X, K)$; hence, the process is extremely fast (feed-forward).

Results on Object Recognition

In this section, various architectures and training procedures are compared to determine which nonlinearities are preferable, and which training protocol makes a difference.

Generic Object Recognition Using Caltech 101 Dataset: Caltech 101 is a standard dataset of labeled images, containing 101 categories of objects in the wild.

We use a two-stage system, the first stage of which is composed of an F layer with 64 filters of size 9×9, followed by different combinations of nonlinearities and pooling. The second-stage feature extractor is fed with the output of the first stage and extracts 256 output feature maps, each of which combines a random subset of 16 feature maps from the previous stage using 9×9 kernels. Hence, the total number of convolution kernels is $256 \times 16 = 4,096$.

Table 19.1 summarizes the results for the experiments, where U and X denote unsupervised pre-training and random initialization, respectively and "+" denotes supervised fine-tuning of the whole system:

1. Excellent accuracy of 65.5% is obtained using unsupervised pre-training and supervised refinement with abs and normalization nonlinearities. The result is on par with the popular model based on SIFT and pyramid match kernel SVM (Lazebnik et al., 2006). It is clear that abs and normalization are crucial for achieving good performance. This

Table 19.1. *Average recognition rates on Caltech-101 with 30 training samples per class. Each row contains results for one of the training protocols (U = unsupervised, X = random, $+$ = supervised fine-tuning), and each column for one type of architecture (F = filter bank, P_A = average pooling, P_M = max pooling, R = rectification, N = normalization).*

	Single stage [$64.F^{9\times9} - R/N/P^{5\times5}$ − logreg]			
	$F - R_{\mathrm{abs}} - N - P_A$ (%)	$F - R_{\mathrm{abs}} - P_A$ (%)	$F - N - P_M$ (%)	$F - P_A$ (%)
U^+	54.2	50.0	44.3	14.5
X^+	54.8	47.0	38.0	14.3
U	52.2	43.3	44.0	13.4
X	53.3	31.7	32.1	12.1

	Two stages [$256.F^{9\times9} - R/N/P^{4\times4}$ − logreg]			
	$F - R_{\mathrm{abs}} - N - P_A$ (%)	$F - R_{\mathrm{abs}} - P_A$ (%)	$F - N - P_M$ (%)	$F - P_A$ (%)
U^+	65.5	60.5	61.0	32.0
X^+	64.7	59.5	60.0	29.7
U	63.7	46.7	56.0	9.1
X	62.9	33.7	37.6	8.8

is an extremely important fact for users of convolutional networks, which traditionally use only tanh().

2. Astonishingly, *random filters without any filter learning whatsoever achieve decent performance* (62.9% for X), as long as abs and normalization are present ($R_{abs} - N - P_A$). A more detailed study on this particular case can be found in Jarrett et al. (2009).

3. Comparing experiments from rows X versus X^+, U versus U^+, we see that supervised fine-tuning consistently improves the performance, particularly with weak nonlinearities.

4. It seems that unsupervised pre-training (U, U^+) is crucial when newly proposed nonlinearities are not in place.

Handwritten Digit Classification Using MNIST Dataset: MNIST is a dataset of handwritten digits (LeCun and Cortes, 1998): it contains 60,000 28×28 image patches of digits on uniform backgrounds, and a standard testing set of 10,000 different samples, widely used by the vision community as a benchmark for algorithms. Each patch is labeled with a number ranging from 0 to 9.

By using the evidence gathered in previous experiments, we used a two-stage system with a two-layer fully connected classifier to learn the mapping between the samples' pixels and the labels. The two convolutional stages were pre-trained unsupervised (without the labels), and refined supervised (with the labels). An error rate of 0.53% was achieved on the test set. To our knowledge, *this is the lowest error rate ever reported on the original MNIST dataset, without distortions or preprocessing.* The best previously reported error rate was 0.60% (Ranzato et al., 2007a).

Connection with Other Approaches in Object Recognition

Many recent successful object recognition systems can also be seen as single or multi-layer feature extraction systems followed by a classifier. Most common feature extraction systems such as SIFT (Lowe, 2004) and HoG (Dalal and Triggs, 2005) are composed of filter banks (oriented edge detectors at multiple scales) followed by nonlinearities (winner-take-all) and pooling (histogramming). A pyramid match kernel (PMK) SVM (Lazebnik et al., 2006) classifier can also be seen as another layer of feature extraction since it performs a K-means based feature extraction followed by local histogramming.

19.2 A Dedicated Digital Hardware Architecture

Biologically inspired vision models and more generally image processing algorithms are usually expressed as sequences of operations or transformations. They can be well described by a modular approach in which each module processes an input image bank and produces a new bank. Figure 19.1 is a graphical illustration of this approach. Each module requires the previous bank to be fully (or at least partially) available before computing its output. This causality prevents simple parallelism from being implemented across modules. However, parallelism can easily be introduced within a module and at several levels, depending on the kind of underlying operations.

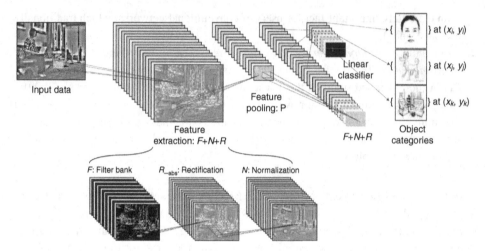

Figure 19.1 Architecture of a typical convolutional network for object recognition. This implements a convolutional feature extractor and a linear classifier for generic N-class object recognition. Once trained, the network can be computed on arbitrary large input images, producing a classification map as output.

In the following discussion, banks of images will be seen as 3D arrays in which the first dimension is the number of independent maps/images, the second is the height of the maps, and the third is the width. As in Section 19.1.1, the input bank of a module is denoted as x, the output bank y, an image in the input bank x_i, and a pixel in the input bank x_{ijk}. Input banks' dimensions will be noted $n_1 \times n_2 \times n_3$, output banks $m_1 \times m_2 \times m_3$. Each module implements a type of operation that requires K operations per input pixel x_{ijk}. The starting point of the discussion is a general-purpose processor composed of an arithmetic unit, a fast internal cache of size S_{INT}, and an external memory of size $S_{EXT} \gg S_{INT}$. The bandwidth between the internal logic and the external memory array will be noted B_{EXT}.

The coarsest level of parallelism can be obtained at the image bank level. A module that applies a unary transformation to produce one output image for each input image ($n_1 = m_1$) can be broken up in n_1 independent threads. This is the most basic form of parallelism, and it finds its limits when $n_2 \times n_3$ becomes larger than a threshold, closely related to S_{INT}. In fact, past a certain size, the number of pixels that can be processed in a given time equals $B_{EXT}/(2 \times K)$ (bandwidth is shared between writes and reads). In other terms, the amount of parallelism that can be introduced at this level is limited by B_{EXT}/K.

A finer level of parallelism can be introduced at the operation level. The cost of fetching pixels from the external memory being very high, the most efficient form of parallelism can occur when pixels are reused in multiple operations ($K > 1$). It can be shown that optimal performances are reached if K operations can be produced in parallel in the arithmetic unit. In other terms, the amount of parallelism that can be introduced at this level is limited by B_{EXT}.

If the internal cache size S_{INT} is large enough to hold all the images of the entire set of modules to compute, then the overall performance of the system is defined by B_{INT}, the bandwidth between the arithmetic unit and the internal cache. The size of internal memory caches growing according to Moore's law, more data can fit internally, which naturally pulls performances of computations from $K \times B_{EXT}$ to $K \times B_{INT}$.

For a given technology though, S_{INT} has an upper bound, and the only part of the system we can act upon is the internal architecture. On the basis of these observations, our approach is to tackle the problem of producing the K parallel operations by rethinking the architecture of the arithmetic units, while conserving the traditional external memory storage. Our problem can be stated simply:

Problem 19.1 K being the number of operations performed per input pixel and B_{EXT} being the bandwidth available between the arithmetic units and the external memory array, we want to establish an architecture that produces K operations in parallel, so that B_{EXT} is fully utilized.

19.2.1 A Dataflow Approach

The dataflow hardware architecture was initiated by Adams (1969) and quickly became an active field of research (Dennis and Misunas, 1974; Hicks et al., 1993; Gaudiot et al., 1994). Cho et al. (2008) presents one of the latest dataflow architectures that has several similarities to the approach presented here.

Figure 19.2 shows a dataflow architecture whose goal is to process homogeneous streams of data in parallel (Farabet et al., 2010). It is defined around several key ideas:

- A 2D grid of N_{PT} Processing Tiles (PTs) that contain the following:
  - A bank of processing operators. An operator can be anything from a FIFO to an arithmetic operator, or even a combination of arithmetic operators. The operators are connected to local data lines.
  - A routing multiplexer (MUX). The MUX connects the local data lines to global data lines or to neighboring tiles.
- A Smart direct memory access module (Smart DMA) that interfaces off-chip memory and provides asynchronous data transfers, with priority management.
- A set of N_{global} global data lines used to connect PTs to the Smart DMA, $N_{global} \ll N_{PT}$.
- A set of local data lines used to connect PTs with their four neighbors,
- A runtime configuration bus, used to reconfigure many aspects of the grid at runtime – connections, operators, Smart DMA modes, and so on (the configurable elements are depicted as squares in Figure 19.2).
- A controller that can reconfigure most of the computing grid and the Smart DMA at runtime.

On Runtime Reconfiguration

One of the most interesting aspects of this grid is its configuration capabilities. Many systems have been proposed that are based on 2D arrays of processing elements interconnected by a routing fabric that is reconfigurable. Field programmable gate arrays (FPGAs), for instance, offer one of the most versatile grid of processing elements.

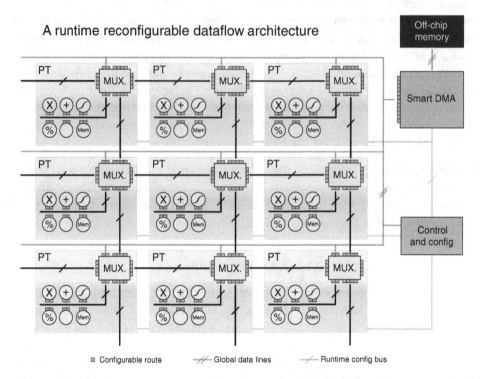

Figure 19.2 A dataflow computer. A set of runtime configurable processing tiles are connected on a 2D grid. They can exchange data with their four neighbors and with an off-chip memory via global lines.

Each of these processing elements – usually a simple look-up table – can be connected to any of the other elements of the grid, which provides with the most generic routing fabric one can think of. Thanks to the simplicity of the processing elements, the number that can be packed in a single package is in the order of 10^4 to 10^5. The drawback is the reconfiguration time, which takes in the order of milliseconds, and the synthesis time, which takes in the order of minutes to hours depending on the complexity of the circuit.

At the other end of the spectrum, recent multicore processors implement only a few powerful processing elements (in the order of 10s to 100s). For these architectures, no synthesis is involved, instead, extensions to existing programming languages are used to explicitly describe parallelism. The advantage of these architectures is their relative simplicity of use: the implementation of an algorithm rarely takes more than a few days, whereas months are required for a typical circuit synthesis for FPGAs.

The architecture presented here is at the middle of this spectrum. Building a fully generic dataflow computer is a tedious task. Reducing the spectrum of applications to the image processing problem – as stated in Problem 19.1 – allows us to define the following constraints:

- High throughput is a top priority; low latency is not. Indeed, most of the operations performed on images are replicated over both dimensions of these images, usually bringing the amount of similar computations to a number that is much larger than the typical latencies of a pipelined processing unit.

- Therefore, each operator has to provide with a maximum throughput (e.g., one operation per clock cycle) to the detriment of any initial latency and has to be stallable (e.g., must handle discontinuities in data streams).
- Configuration time has to be low, or more precisely in the order of the system's latency. This constraint simply states that the system should be able to reconfigure itself between two kinds of operations in a time that is negligible compared to the image sizes. That is a crucial point to allow runtime reconfiguration.
- The processing elements in the grid should be as coarse grained as permitted, to maximize the ratio between *computing logic* and *routing logic*. Creating a grid for a particular application (e.g., ConvNets) allows the use of very coarse operators. On the other hand, a general-purpose grid has to cover the space of standard numeric operators.
- The processing elements, which also might be complex, should not have any internal state but should passively process any incoming data. The task of sequencing operations is done by a global control unit that simply configures the entire grid for a given operation, lets the data flow in, and prepares the following operation.

The first two points of this list are crucial to create a flexible dataflow system. Several types of grids have been proposed in the past (Dennis and Misunas, 1974; Hicks et al., 1993; Kung, 1986), often trying to solve the dual latency/throughput problem and often providing a computing fabric that is too rigid.

The grid proposed here provides a flexible processing framework, which is due to the stallable nature of the operators. Indeed, any paths can be configured on the grid, even paths that require more bandwidth that is actually feasible. Instead of breaking, each operator will stall its pipeline when required. This is achieved by the use of FIFOs at the input and output of each operators, which compensate for bubbles in the data streams and force the operators to stall when they are full. Any sequence of operators can then be easily created, without concern for bandwidth issues.

The third point is achieved by the use of a runtime configuration bus, common to all units. Each module in the design has a set of configurable parameters, routes, or settings (depicted as squares on Figure 19.2) and possesses a unique address on the network. Groups of similar modules also share a broadcast address, which dramatically speeds up reconfiguration of elements that need to perform similar tasks.

The last point depicts the dataflow idea of having (at least theoretically) no state or instruction pointer. In the case of the system presented here, the grid has no state, but a state does exit in a centralized control unit. For each configuration of the grid, no state is used, and the presence of data drives the computations. Although this leads to an optimal throughput, the system presented here strives to be as general as possible, and having the possibility of configuring the grid quickly to perform a new type of operation is crucial to run algorithms that require different types of computations.

A typical execution of an operation on this system is as follows: (1) the control unit configures each tile to be used for the computation and each connection between the tiles and their neighbors and/or the global lines, by sending a configuration command to each of them; (2) it configures the Smart DMA to prefetch the data to be processed, and to be ready to write results back to off-chip memory; (3) when the DMA is ready,

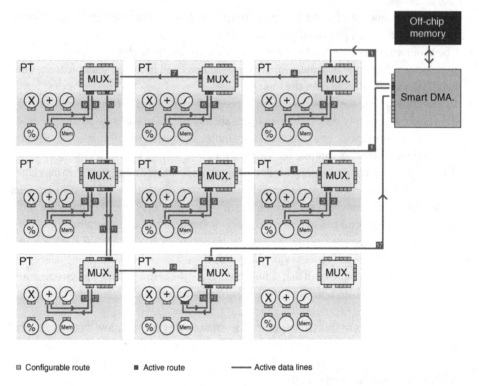

■ Configurable route   ■ Active route   ——— Active data lines

Figure 19.3 The grid is configured for a complex computation that involves several tiles: the three top tiles perform a 3×3 convolution, the three intermediate tiles another 3×3 convolution, the bottom left tile sums these two convolutions, and the bottom center tile applies a function to the result.

it triggers the streaming out; (4) each tile processes its respective incoming streaming data, and passes the results to another tile, or back to the Smart DMA; and (5) the control unit is notified of the end of operations when the Smart DMA has completed.

Example 19.2 Such a grid can be used to perform arbitrary computations on streams of data, from plain unary operations to complex nested operations. As stated previously, operators can be easily cascaded and connected across tiles, independently managing their flow by the use of input/output FIFOs.

Figure 19.3 shows an example of configuration, where the grid is configured to compute a sum of two convolutions followed by a nonlinear activation function:

$$y_{1,i,j} = Tanh(\sum_{m=0}^{K-1}\sum_{n=0}^{K-1} x_{1,i+m,j+n}w_{1,m,n} + \sum_{m=0}^{K-1}\sum_{n=0}^{K-1} x_{2,i+m,j+n}w_{2,m,n}) \qquad (19.7)$$

The operator $\sum \prod$ performs a sum of products, or a dot-product between an incoming stream and a local set of weights (preloaded as a stream as well). Therefore, each tile performs a 1D convolution, and three tiles are used to compute a 2D convolution with a 3×3 kernel. All the paths are simplified, of course, and in some cases one line represents multiple parallel streams.

It can be noted that this last example provides a nice solution to Problem 19.1. Indeed, the input data being two images x_1 and x_2, and the output data one image

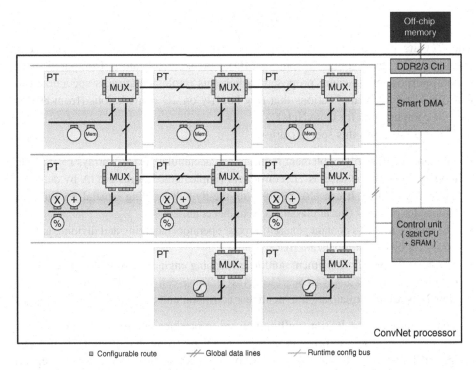

Figure 19.4 Overview of the ConvNet Processor system. A grid of multiple full-custom processing tiles tailored to ConvNet operations, and a fast streaming memory interface (Smart DMA).

y_1, the K operations are performed in parallel, and the entire operation is achieved at a bandwidth of $B_{EXT}/3$.

19.2.2 An FPGA-Based ConvNet Processor

Recent DSP-oriented FPGAs include a large number of hardwired MAC units and several thousands of programmable cells (look-up tables), which allows fast prototyping and real-time simulation of circuits, but also actual implementations to be used in final products.

In this section we present a concrete implementation of the ideas presented in Section 19.2.1, specially tailored for ConvNets. We refer to this implementation as the *Convnet Processor*. The architecture presented here has been fully coded in hardware description languages (HDLs) that target both ASIC synthesis and programmable hardware such as FPGAs.

A schematic summary of the *ConvNet Processor* system is presented in Figure 19.4. The main components of our system are: (1) a *Control Unit* (implemented on a general-purpose CPU), (2) a grid of *Processing Tiles (PTs)*, and (3) a *Smart DMA* interfacing external memory via a standard controller.

In this implementation, the Control Unit is implemented by a *general-purpose CPU*. This is more convenient than a custom state machine as it allows the use of standard C compilers. Moreover, the CPU has full access to the external memory (via global data lines), and it can use this large storage to store its program instructions.

Specialized Processing Tiles

The *PTs* are independent processing tiles laid out on a 2D grid. As presented in Section 19.2.1, they contain a routing MUX and local operators. Compared to the general-purpose architecture proposed earlier, this implementation is specialized for ConvNets and other applications that rely heavily on 2D convolutions (from 80% to 90% of computations for ConvNets).

Figure 19.4 shows this specialization:

- The top-row PTs only implement multiply and accumulate (MAC) arrays ($\sum \prod$ operators), which can be used as 2D convolvers (implemented in the FPGA by dedicated hardwired MACs). It can also perform on-the-fly subsampling (spatial pooling) and simple dot-products (linear classifiers) (Farabet et al., 2009).
- The middle-row PTs contain general-purpose operators (squaring and dividing are necessary for divisive normalization).
- The bottom-row PTs implement nonlinear mapping engines, used to compute all sorts of functions from $Tanh()$ to $Sqrt()$ or $Abs()$. Those can be used at all stages of the ConvNets, from normalization to nonlinear activation units.

The operators in the PTs are fully pipelined to produce one result per clock cycle. Image pixels are stored in off-chip memory as Q8.8 (16-bit, fixed-point), transported on global lines as Q8.8 but scaled to 32-bit integers within operators, to keep full precision between successive operations. The numeric precision, and hence the size of a pixel, will be noted P_{bits}.

The 2D convolver can be viewed as a dataflow grid itself, with the only difference that the connections between the operators (the MACs) are fixed. The reason for having a full-blown 2D convolver within a tile (instead of a 1D convolver per tile, or even simply one MAC per tile) is that it maximizes the ratio between actual computing logic and routing logic, as stated previously. Of course it is not as flexible, and the choice of the array size is a hardwired parameter, but it is a reasonable choice for an FPGA implementation and for image processing in general. For an ASIC implementation, having a 1D dot-product operator per tile is probably the best compromise.

The pipelined implementation of this 2D convolver (as described in Farabet et al., 2009), computes Equation 19.8 at every clock cycle:

$$y_{1,i,j} = x_{2,i,j} + \sum_{m=0}^{K-1} \sum_{n=0}^{K-1} x_{1,i+m,j+n} w_{1,m,n} \qquad (19.8)$$

In Equation 19.8, $x_{1,i,j}$ is a value in the input plane, $w_{1,m,n}$ is a value in a $K \times K$ convolution kernel, $x_{2,i,j}$ is a value in a plane to be combined with the result, and y_1 is the output plane.

Both the kernel and the image are streams loaded from the memory, and the filter kernels can be pre-loaded in local caches concurrently to another operation: each new pixel thus triggers $K \times K$ parallel operations.

All the nonlinearities in neural networks can be computed with the use of look-up tables or piecewise linear decompositions.

A look-up table associates one output value for each input value and, therefore, requires as much memory as the range of possible inputs. It is the fastest method to compute a nonlinear mapping, but the time required to reload a new table is prohibitive if different mappings are to be computed with the same hardware.

A piecewise linear decomposition is not as accurate (f is approximated by g, as in Equation 19.9), but only requires a couple of coefficients a_i to represent a simple mapping such as a hyperbolic tangent or a square root. It can be reprogrammed very quickly at runtime, allowing multiple mappings to reuse the same hardware. Moreover, if the coefficients a_i follow the constraint given by Equation 19.10, the hardware can be reduced to shifters and adders only:

$$g(x) = a_i x + b_i \quad for \quad x \in [l_i, l_{i+1}] \tag{19.9}$$

$$a_i = \frac{1}{2^m} + \frac{1}{2^n} \quad m, n \in [0, 5] \tag{19.10}$$

Smart DMA Implementation

A critical part of this architecture is the direct memory access (DMA) module. Our *Smart DMA* module is a full-custom engine that has been designed to allow N_{DMA} ports to access the external memory totally asynchronously.

A dedicated arbiter is used as hardware *Memory Interface* to multiplex and demultiplex access to the external memory with high bandwidth. Subsequent buffers on each port ensure continuity of service on a port while the others are utilized.

The DMA is *smart*, because it complements the Control Unit. Each port of the DMA can be configured to read or write a particular chunk of data, with an optional stride (for 2D streams), and communicate its status to the Control Unit. Although this might seem trivial, it respects one of the foundations of dataflow computing: while the Control Unit configures the grid and the DMA ports for each operation, an operation is driven exclusively by the data, from its fetching to its writing back to off-chip memory.

If the PTs are synchronous to the memory bus clock, the following relationship can be established between the memory bandwidth B_{EXT}, the number of possible parallel data transfers $MAX(N_{DMA})$, and the bits per pixel P_{bits}:

$$MAX(N_{DMA}) = \frac{B_{EXT}}{P_{bits}} \tag{19.11}$$

For example, $P_{bits} = 16$ and $B_{EXT} = 128$-bit/cyc allows $MAX(N_{DMA}) = 7$ simultaneous transfers.

19.2.3 Compiling ConvNets for the ConvNet Processor

Before being run on the ConvNet Processor, a ConvNet has to be trained offline, on a regular computer, and then converted to a compact representation that can be interpreted by the Control Unit to generate controls/configurations for the system.

Offline, the training is performed with existing software such as Lush (LeCun and Bottou, 2002) or Torch-5 (Collobert, 2008). Both libraries use the modular approach described in the introduction of Section 19.2.

On board, the Control Unit of the ConvNet Processor decodes the representation, which results in several grid reconfigurations, interspersed with data streams. This representation will be denoted as *bytecode* from now on. Compiling a ConvNet for the ConvNet Processor can be summarized as the task of mapping the offline training results to this bytecode.

Extensive research has been done on the question of how to schedule dataflow computations (Lee and David, 1987) and how to represent streams and computations on streams (Gaudiot et al., 1994). In this section, we only care about how to schedule computations for a ConvNet (and similar architectures) on our ConvNet Processor engine.

It is a more restricted problem, and can be stated simply:

Problem 19.3   Given a particular ConvNet architecture, and trained parameters, and given a particular implementation of the dataflow grid, what is the sequence of grid configurations that yields the shortest computation time? Or in other terms, for a given ConvNet architecture, and a given dataflow architecture, how do we produce the bytecode that yields the shortest computing time?

As described in the introduction of Section 19.2, there are three levels at which computations can be parallelized:

1. Across modules: Operators can be cascaded, and multiple modules can be computed on the fly (average speedup).
2. Across images, within a module: Can be done if multiple instances of the required operator exist (poor speedup, as each independent operation requires its own input/output streams, which are limited by B_{EXT}).
3. Within an image: Some operators naturally implement that (the 2D convolver, which performs all the MACs in parallel); in some cases, multiple tiles can be used to parallelize computations.

Parallelizing computations across modules can be done in special cases. Example 19.2 illustrates this case: two operators (each belonging to a separate module) are cascaded, which speeds up this computation by a factor of 2.

Parallelizing computations across images is straightforward but very limited. The following example illustrates this point.

Example 19.4   The dataflow system built has 3 PTs with 2D convolvers, 3 PTs with standard operators, and 2 PTs with nonlinear mappers (as depicted in Figure 19.4), and the exercise is to map a fully connected filter bank with 3 inputs and 8 outputs, for example, a filter bank where each of the 8 outputs is a sum of 3 inputs convolved with a different kernel:

$$y_j = \sum_{i=0}^{2} k_{ij} * x_i \quad \text{for} \quad j \in [0, 7] \tag{19.12}$$

For the given hardware, the optimal mapping is as follows: each of the three 2D convolvers is configured to convolve one of the three inputs x_i with a kernel k_{ij}, and a standard PT is configured to accumulate those three streams in one and produce y_j.

Although optimal (three images are processed in parallel), four simultaneous streams are created at the Smart DMA level, which imposes a maximum bandwidth of $B_{EXT}/4$ per stream.

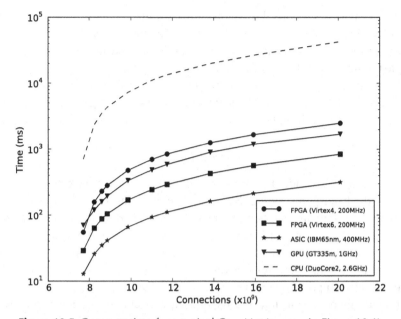

Figure 19.5 Compute time for a typical ConvNet (as seen in Figure 19.1).

Parallelizing computations within images is what this grid is best at. Example 19.2 is a perfect example of how an operation (in that case a sequence of operations) can be done in a single pass on the grid.

19.2.4 Performance

Figure 19.5 reports a performance comparison for the computation of a typical ConvNet on multiple platforms:

- The CPU data was measured from compiled C code (GNU C compiler and Blas libraries) on a Core 2 Duo 2.66GHz Apple Macbook PRO laptop operating at 90 W (30 to 40 W for the CPU).
- The FPGA data was measured on both a Xilinx Virtex-4 SX35 operating at 200MHz and 7 W and a Xilinx Virtex-6 VLX240T operating at 200MHz and 10 W.
- The GPU data was obtained from a CUDA-based implementation running on a laptop-range nVidia GT335m operating at 1GHz and 40 W.
- The ASIC data is simulation data gathered from an IBM 65 nm CMOS process. For an ASIC-based design with a speed of 400MHz (speeds of >1GHz are possible), the projected power consumption is simulated at 3 W.

The test ConvNet is composed of a nonlinear normalization layer, three convolutional layers, two pooling layers, and a linear classifier. The convolutional layers and pooling layers are followed by nonlinear activation units (hyperbolic tangent). Overall, it possesses N_{KER} $K \times K$ learned kernels, N_{POOL} $P \times P$ learned pooling kernels, and N 200 dimension classification vectors.

Figure 19.5 was produced by increasing the parameters N_{KER}, N_{POOL}, K, and P simultaneously and estimating the time to compute the ConvNet for each set of parameters. The x-axis reports the overall number of linear connections in the ConvNet (e.g., the number of multiply and accumulate operations to perform).

Note: On the spectrum of parallel computers described in Section 19.2.1, GPUs belong to the small grids (hundreds of elements) of large and complex processing units (full-blown streaming processors). Although they offer one of the most interesting ratios of computing power to price, their drawback is their high power consumption (from 40 W to 200 W per unit).

Precision

Recognition rates for standard datasets were obtained to benchmark the precision loss induced by the fixed-point coding. By using floating-point representation for training and testing, the following results were obtained: for *NORB*, 85% recognition rate was achieved on the test dataset; for *MNIST*, 95%; and for *UMASS* (faces dataset), 98%. The same tests were conducted on the ConvNet Processor with fixed-point representation (Q8.8), and the results were, respectively, 85%, 95%, and 98%, which confirms the assumptions made a priori on the influence of quantization noise.

To provide more insight into the fixed-point conversion, the number of weights being zeroed with quantization was measured, in the case of the NORB object detector. Figure 19.6 shows the results: at 8-bits, the quantization impact is already significant (10% of weights become useless), although it has no effect on the detection accuracy.

19.3 Summary

The convolutional network architecture is a remarkably versatile, yet conceptually simple, paradigm that can be applied to a wide spectrum of perceptual tasks. Although

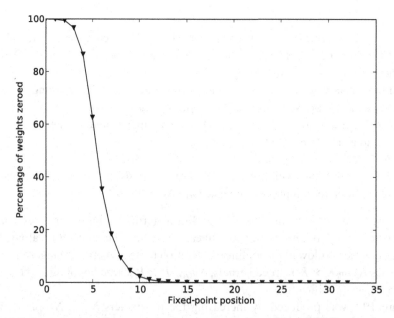

Figure 19.6 Quantization effect on trained networks: the x-axis shows the fixed-point position, the y-axis shows the percentage of weights being zeroed after quantization.

traditional ConvNets trained with supervised learning are very effective, training them requires a large number of labeled training samples. We have shown that using simple architectural tricks such as rectification and contrast normalization, and using unsupervised pre-training of each filter bank, the need for labeled samples is considerably reduced.

We presented a dataflow computer that could be optimized to compute convolutional networks. Different use cases were studied, and it was seen that mapping/unrolling a convolutional network was straightforward on such an architecture, thanks to their relatively uniform design.

Because of their applicability to a wide range of tasks, ConvNets are perfect candidates for hardware implementations and embedded applications, as demonstrated by the increasing amount of work in this area. We expect to see many new embedded vision systems based on ConvNets in the next few years.

Future work on our dataflow architecture will aim at making it more general, to open the doors to more complex and generic recognition tasks. Multiple object detection (LeCun, Huang, and Bottou, 2004) or online learning for adaptive robot guidance (Hadsell et al., 2009) are tasks that will be largely improved by this system.

References

Adams, D. A. 1969. *A Computation Model with Data Flow Sequencing*. Ph.D. thesis, Stanford University.

Ahmed, A., Yu, K., Xu, W., Gong, Y., and Xing, E. 2008. Training Hierarchical Feed-Forward Visual Recognition Models Using Transfer Learning from Pseudo-Tasks. In: *ECCV*. New York: Springer.

Bengio, Y., Lamblin, P., Popovici, D., and Larochelle, H. 2007. Greedy Layer-Wise Training of Deep Networks. In: *NIPS*.

Berg, A. C., Berg, T. L., and Malik, J. 2005. Shape Matching and Object Recognition Using Low Distortion Correspondences. In: *CVPR*.

Chellapilla, K., Shilman, M., and Simard, P. 2006. Optimally Combining a Cascade of Classifiers. In: *Proceedings of Document Recognition and Retrieval 13, Electronic Imaging, 6067*.

Cho, M. H., Cheng, C,-C., Kinsy, M., Suh, G. E., and Devadas, S. 2008. *Diastolic Arrays: Throughput-Driven Reconfigurable Computing*.

Coates, A., Baumstarck, P., Le, Q., and Ng, A.Y. 2009. Scalable Learning for Object Detection with GPU Hardware. Pages 4287–4293 of: *Proceedings of the 2009 IEEE/RSJ International Conference on Intelligent Robots and Systems*. Citeseer.

Collobert, R. 2008. *Torch*. Presented at the *Workshop on Machine Learning Open Source Software, NIPS*.

Dalal, N., and Triggs, B. 2005. Histograms of Oriented Gradients for Human Detection. In: *CVPR*.

Delakis, M., and Garcia, C. 2008. Text Detection with Convolutional Neural Networks. In: *International Conference on Computer Vision Theory and Applications (VISAPP 2008)*.

Dennis, J. B., and Misunas, D. P. 1974. A Preliminary Architecture for a Basic Data-Flow Processor. *SIGARCH Computer Architecture News*, **3**(4), 126–132.

Farabet, C., Poulet, C., Han, J. Y., and LeCun, Y. 2009. CNP: An FPGA-Based Processor for Convolutional Networks. In: *International Conference on Field Programmable Logic and Applications (FPL'09)*. Prague: IEEE. .

Farabet, C., Martini, B., Akselrod, P., Talay, S., LeCun, Y., and Culurciello, E. 2010. Hardware Accelerated Convolutional Neural Networks for Synthetic Vision Systems. In: *International Symposium on Circuits and Systems (ISCAS'10)*. Paris: IEEE.

Frome, A., Cheung, G., Abdulkader, A., Zennaro, M., Wu, B., Bissacco, A., Adam, H., Neven, H., and Vincent, L. 2009. Large-Scale Privacy Protection in Street-Level Imagery. In: *ICCV'09*.

Fukushima, K., and Miyake, S. 1982. Neocognitron: A New Algorithm for Pattern Recognition Tolerant of Deformations and Shifts in Position. *Pattern Recognition*, **15**(6), 455–469.

Garcia, C., and Delakis, M. 2004. Convolutional Face Finder: A Neural Architecture for Fast and Robust Face Detection. *IEEE Transactions on Pattern Analysis and Machine Intelligence*.

Hadsell, R., Sermanet, P., Scoffier, M., Erkan, A., Kavackuoglu, K., Muller, U., and LeCun, Y. 2009. Learning Long-Range Vision for Autonomous Off-Road Driving. *Journal of Field Robotics*, **26**(2), 120–144.

Hicks, J., Chiou, D., Ang, B. S., and Arvind. 1993. *Performance Studies of Id on the Monsoon Dataflow System*.

Hinton, G. E., and Salakhutdinov, R. R. 2006. Reducing the Dimensionality of Data with Neural Networks. *Science*.

Huang, F.-J., and LeCun, Y. 2006. Large-Scale Learning with SVM and Convolutional Nets for Generic Object Categorization. In: *Proceedings of Computer Vision and Pattern Recognition Conference (CVPR'06)*. IEEE.

Jain, V., and Seung, H. S. 2008. Natural Image Denoising with Convolutional Networks. In: *Advances in Neural Information Processing Systems 21 (NIPS 2008)*. Cambridge, MA: MIT Press.

Jarrett, K., Kavukcuoglu, K., Ranzato, M. A., and LeCun, Y. 2009. What Is the Best Multi-Stage Architecture for Object Recognition? In: *Proceedings of International Conference on Computer Vision (ICCV'09)*. IEEE.

Kavukcuoglu, K., Ranzato, M. A., and LeCun, Y. 2008. *Fast Inference in Sparse Coding Algorithms with Applications to Object Recognition*. Technical Report CBLL-TR-2008-12-01.

Kavukcuoglu, K., Ranzato, M. A., Fergus, R., and LeCun, Y. 2009. Learning Invariant Features through Topographic Filter Maps. In: *Proceedings of International Conference on Computer Vision and Pattern Recognition (CVPR'09)*. IEEE.

Kung, H. T. 1986. Why Systolic Architectures? 300–309.

Gaudiot, J. L., Bic, L., Dennis, J., and Dennis, J. B. 1994. Stream Data Types for Signal Processing. In: *In Advances in Dataflow Architecture and Multithreading*. IEEE.

Lazebnik, S., Schmid, C., and Ponce, J. 2006. Beyond Bags of Features: Spatial Pyramid Matching for Recognizing Natural Scene Categories. Pages 2169–2178 of: *Proceedings of Computer Vision and Pattern Recognition*. IEEE.

LeCun, Y., and Bottou, L. 2002. *Lush Reference Manual*. Technical Report Code available at http://lush.sourceforge.net.

LeCun, Y., and Cortes, C. 1998. *MNIST Dataset*. http://yann.lecun.com/exdb/mnist/.

LeCun, Y., Boser, B., Denker, J. S., Henderson, D., Howard, R. E., Hubbard, W., and Jackel, L. D. 1989. Backpropagation Applied to Handwritten Zip Code Recognition. *Neural Computation*.

LeCun, Y., Boser, B., Denker, J. S., Henderson, D., Howard, R. E., Hubbard, W., and Jackel, L. D. 1990. Handwritten Digit Recognition with a Back-Propagation Network. In: *NIPS'89*.

LeCun, Y., Bottou, L., Orr, G., and Muller, K. 1998a. Efficient BackProp. In: Orr, G., and Muller, K., (eds), *Neural Networks: Tricks of the Trade*. New York: Springer.

LeCun, Y., Bottou, L., Bengio, Y., and Haffner, P. 1998b. Gradient-Based Learning Applied to Document Recognition. *Proceedings of the IEEE*, **86**(11), 2278–2324.

LeCun, Y., Huang, F.-J., and Bottou, L. 2004. Learning Methods for Generic Object Recognition with Invariance to Pose and Lighting. In: *Proceedings of CVPR'04*. IEEE.

Lee, E. A., and David. 1987. Static Scheduling of Synchronous Data Flow Programs for Digital Signal Processing. *IEEE Transactions on Computers*, **36**, 24–35.

Lee, H., Grosse, R., Ranganath, R., and Ng, A., Y. 2009. Convolutional Deep Belief Networks for Scalable Unsupervised Learning of Hierarchical Representations. In: *Proceedings of the 26th International Conference on Machine Learning (ICML'09)*.

Lowe, D. G. 2004. Distinctive Image Features from Scale-Invariant Keypoints. *International Journal of Computer Vision.*

Lyu, S., and Simoncelli, E. P. 2008. Nonlinear Image Representation Using Divisive Normalization. In: *CVPR.*

Mozer, M. C. 1991. *The Perception of Multiple Objects: A Connectionist Approach.* Cambridge, MA: MIT Press.

Mutch, J., and Lowe, D. G. 2006. Multiclass Object Recognition with Sparse, Localized Features. In: *CVPR.*

Nasse, F., Thurau, C., and Fink, G. A. 2009. *Face Detection Using GPU-Based Convolutional Neural Networks.*

Ning, F., Delhomme, D., LeCun, Y., Piano, F., Bottou, L., and Barbano, P. 2005. Toward Automatic Phenotyping of Developing Embryos from Videos. *IEEE Transactions on Image Processing.* Special issue on Molecular and Cellular Bioimaging.

Nowlan, S., and Platt, J. 1995. A Convolutional Neural Network Hand Tracker. Pages 901–908 of: *Neural Information Processing Systems.* San Mateo, CA: Morgan Kaufmann.

Olshausen, B. A., and Field, D. J. 1997. Sparse Coding with an Overcomplete Basis Set: A Strategy Employed by V1? *Vision Research.*

Osadchy, M., LeCun, Y., and Miller, M. 2007. Synergistic Face Detection and Pose Estimation with Energy-Based Models. *Journal of Machine Learning Research*, **8**(May), 1197–1215.

Pinto, N., Cox, D. D., and DiCarlo, J. J. 2008. Why Is Real-World Visual Object Recognition Hard? *PLoS Computer Biology*, **4**(1), e27.

Ranzato, M. A., Boureau, Y.-L., and LeCun, Y. 2007a. Sparse Feature Learning for Deep Belief Networks. In: *NIPS'07.*

Ranzato, M. A., Huang, F.-J., Boureau, Y.-L., and LeCun, Y. 2007b. Unsupervised Learning of Invariant Feature Hierarchies with Applications to Object Recognition. In: *Proceedings of Computer Vision and Pattern Recognition Conference (CVPR'07).* IEEE.

Serre, T., Wolf, L., and Poggio, T. 2005. Object Recognition with Features Inspired by Visual Cortex. In: *CVPR.*

Simard, P. Y., Steinkraus, D., and Platt, J. C. 2003. Best Practices for Convolutional Neural Networks Applied to Visual Document Analysis. In: *ICDAR.*

Vaillant, R., Monrocq, C., and LeCun, Y. 1994. Original Approach for the Localisation of Objects in Images. *IEEE Proceedings on Vision, Image, and Signal Processing*, **141**(4), 245–250.

Weston, J., Rattle, F., and Collobert, R. 2008. Deep Learning via Semi-Supervised Embedding. In: *ICML.*

CHAPTER 20

Mining Tree-Structured Data on Multicore Systems

Shirish Tatikonda* and Srinivasan Parthasarathy

Mining frequent subtrees in a database of rooted and labeled trees is an important problem in many domains, ranging from phylogenetic analysis to biochemistry and from linguistic parsing to XML data analysis. In this work, we revisit this problem and develop an architecture-conscious solution targeting emerging multicore systems. Specifically, we identify a sequence of memory-related optimizations that significantly improve the spatial and temporal locality of a state-of-the-art sequential algorithm – alleviating the effects of memory latency. Additionally, these optimizations are shown to reduce the pressure on the front-side bus, an important consideration in the context of large-scale multicore architectures. We then demonstrate that these optimizations, although necessary, are not sufficient for efficient parallelization on multicores, primarily because of parametric and data-driven factors that make load balancing a significant challenge. To address this challenge, we present a methodology that adaptively and automatically modulates the type and granularity of the work being shared among different cores. The resulting algorithm achieves near perfect parallel efficiency on up to 16 processors on challenging real-world applications. The optimizations we present have general-purpose utility, and a key outcome is the development of a general-purpose scheduling service for moldable task scheduling on emerging multicore systems.

The field of knowledge discovery is concerned with extracting actionable knowledge from data efficiently. Although most of the early work in this field focused on mining simple transactional datasets, recently there has been a significant shift toward analyzing data with complex structure such as trees and graphs. A number of applications ranging from bioinformatics to XML databases, from the World Wide Web to computational linguistics, are now generating and processing large amounts of semi-structured data. This chapter focuses on analyzing datasets with hierarchical data records that are represented using tree structures.

---

* This work was done while Shirish Tatikonda was a student at the Ohio State University.

Frequent pattern mining is a fundamental task in knowledge discovery process that deals with mining useful and common patterns from massive datasets. In the context of transactional datasets, this problem is popularly referred to as *frequent itemset mining*. An equivalent problem for tree-structured data is often cited as *frequent subtree mining*. Recently this problem has gained a lot of interest in a number of application domains. For example, in bioinformatics, the secondary structure of an RNA molecule is represented as a rooted ordered tree (Zhang, 1998). Common substructures discovered from a database of such trees help in discovering new functional relationships among corresponding RNAs (Gan, Pasquali, and Schlick, 2003). These substructures are known to be useful in predicting RNA folding (Le et al., 1989) and in functional studies of RNA processing mechanisms (Shapiro and Zhang, 1990). Similar techniques can be extended to other biological entities such as *glycans* and *phylogenetic trees* (Shasha and Zhang, 2004; Zaki, 2005).

Techniques to mine frequent substructures are also useful in a number of other application domains – in web log mining (Zaki, 2005), in analyzing XML repositories (Zaki and Aggarwal, 2003), in designing caching policies for XML indices (Yang, Lee, and Hsu, 2004), in designing automatic language parsers (Charniak, 1996), in examining parse trees (Baxter et al., 1998), in automatically building mediated schema (Termier, Rousset, and Sebag, 2002), to name a few. The essential problem in these instances can be abstracted to that of *discovering frequent subtrees from a set of rooted ordered trees* (Asai et al., 2002; Chi et al., 2004; Nijssen and Kok, 2003; Tan et al., 2006; Tatikonda, Parthasarathy, and Kurc, 2006; Wang et al., 2004; Zaki, 2005) – the focus of this chapter.

Recent research in *architecture-conscious data analysis and management* has shown that careful algorithmic restructuring coupled with methods that effectively leverage the underlying hardware are essential for handling massive datasets (Buehrer, Parthasarathy, and Chen, 2006; Ghoting et al., 2005; Parthasarathy et al., 2008). In this chapter, we put forth several such techniques that scale up frequent subtree mining on multicore systems. In multicore or chip-multiprocessing (CMP) systems, multiple processors operating at low frequencies are packed on a single chip to deliver better performance at smaller power envelopes. For such systems, there is a need to alleviate the problem of memory access latency as well as to reduce the bandwidth pressure since technology constraints are likely to limit off-chip bandwidth to memory as one scales up the number of cores per chip (Kumar et al., 2003). Equally important is the design of scalable parallel algorithms to deliver efficient performance on multicore chips. As most data mining workloads possess highly irregular and complex access patterns with many control and data dependencies, it is difficult to achieve good load balance among different processing elements.

The rest of this chapter is organized as follows. We discuss the challenges posed by multicores in Section 20.1. We then define the problem and discuss the limitations of existing works in Section 20.2. We present our memory-related optimizations in Section 20.3 and our parallelization strategies in Section 20.4. Empirical results are shown in Section 20.5. We finally conclude the chapter in Section 20.6 with a discussion on broader applicability of our contributions.

20.1 The Multicore Challenge

Multicore processor designs range from the general-purpose (AMD, Intel) to the specialized (Cell, Sun) to the niche markets (GPUs). Although current commodity chips have up to eight cores per CPU, chip makers promise systems with hundreds of cores in near future. We now discuss the challenges in deploying large-scale data mining and data management algorithms on these modern architectures.

Memory Bandwidth: The classic memory-wall problem that refers to the disparity between speeds of CPU and RAM is aggravated in multicore systems. While the *latency to main memory* continues to be an important factor for efficient performance, applications on CMPs must also focus on *memory bandwidth*. Since all cores share the same front-side bus, bandwidth to main memory is likely to be a precious shared commodity. In this context, *controlling the memory footprint* becomes very important as excessive memory usage forces OS to rely on virtual memory and increases the memory bus contention, thereby slowing down the application performance. Large memory footprints also hinder the development of effective parallelization methods. Therefore, restricting the memory usage is very critical to achieve good performance on CMPs.

Locality of Reference: Multicores typically have shared caches, although other variants are possible (Kumar et al., 2003). Since a sizable portion of the chip's real estate is occupied by the cores themselves, the available cache for each core decreases as the number of cores increases. Thus, algorithms that exhibit good data locality are critical. Poor data locality along with excessive memory usage amplifies the pressure on the (shared) front-side bus, potentially resulting in *thrashing*. Guaranteeing good data locality on large-scale data mining problems is nontrivial because of highly irregular access patterns – while the spatial locality is deterred by pointer-based data structures, the temporal locality is hindered by huge search space.

Working Set Size: The size of a working set is defined as the amount of data that is actively used by the program during a particular phase of computation. If the working set of an algorithm is not held in the cache, then the off-chip traffic increases because of constant data swapping between cache and memory. Since the amount of cache available per core is small in CMP systems, algorithms that maintain small working sets must be developed for efficient performance. Since each core used in the computation maintains its own separate working set, the sum of all per-core working sets must be smaller than the available cache.

Load Balance: Load balancing is critical to achieve efficiency. Paramount to leveraging the additional compute capability in CMPs are the effective work partitioning strategies that distribute the work among different cores. The data, control, and parameter dependencies in data mining workloads make it difficult to estimate the lifetime of a task, and hence static work scheduling methods are ineffective. Parallel efficiency on irregular mining algorithms can only be achieved by (1) *adaptively modulating* the type and granularity of the work being shared; and (2) efficiently handling the skew present in the data. Furthermore, algorithms must also expose and subsequently exploit *fine-grained parallelism* (Saha, 2007).

Dynamic Data Structures: Since the algorithms developed for multicore systems operate in shared-memory environments, the use of dynamic data structures must be limited. The system calls to dynamic memory allocation and de-allocation on the heap are serialized. Excessive use of dynamic data structures thus hinders the parallel performance.

20.2 Background

In graph theoretic terms, a *rooted tree* $T = (V, E, r)$ is a connected acyclic graph where V and E are the sets of vertices and edges, respectively. The node $r \in V$ is called the root node of T. A tree $S_i = (V_i, E_i)$ is said to be an *induced* subtree of T if S_i is connected, $V_i \subseteq V$, and $E_i \subseteq E$. In other words, $\forall e = (v_p, v_c) \in E_i$, v_p is the parent of v_c in T. Any induced subtree of T can be obtained simply by deleting vertices and adjacent edges from T. Similarly, a tree $S_e = (V_e, E_e)$ is said to be an *embedded* subtree of T if S_e is connected, $V_e \subseteq V$, and $\forall e = (v_a, v_d) \in E_e$, v_a is the ancestor of v_d in T. Whereas an induced subtree preserves parent–child relationships from T, an embedded subtree respects the ancestor–descendant relationships. Each occurrence of a subtree S in a tree T is called an *embedding* of S in T. An embedding refers to the set of vertices in T that are matched with vertices in S.

20.2.1 Problem Definition

Let T be a tree and S be a small subtree. Let $\delta_T(S)$ be the number of embedded or induced occurrences of S in T. Define an indicator variable d_T such that $d_T(S) = 1$ if $\delta_T(S) > 0$ and $d_T(S) = 0$ if $\delta_T(S) = 0$. The *support* of a subtree S can be defined in two ways – *transaction-based* and *occurrence-based*. The former counts the number of trees in which S occurs and the latter counts the total number of *embeddings* (or matches) in the database. Consider a database $D = \{T_1, T_2, \ldots, T_n\}$.

$$\text{Transaction Support}: \ sup^t(S, D) = \sum_{i=1}^{n} d_{T_i}(S)$$
$$\text{Occurrence Support}: \ sup^o(S, D) = \sum_{i=1}^{n} \delta_{T_i}(S)$$

In this chapter, we consider the transaction-based definition even though our techniques are not limited by the support definition.

Definition 20.1 *Frequent Subtree Mining*: Given a database of rooted ordered trees, enumerate the set of all frequent embedded subtrees (FS), that is, the subtrees whose support is greater than a user-defined minimum support threshold *minsup*.

A variant of this problem mines for *induced* subtrees that preserve parent–child relationships, as opposed to *embedded* subtrees that preserve ancestor–descendant relationships. Example database trees and patterns are shown in Figure 20.1a.

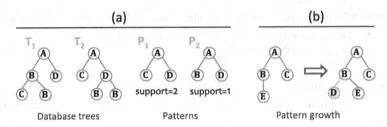

Figure 20.1 (a) Example database and patterns. (b) Illustration of *edge extension* or *point growth*.

The mining process is divided into two logical phases – *candidate generation* and *support counting*. The first phase generates all candidate subtrees, which are then evaluated for their frequency in the second phase. The challenge in the first phase is to efficiently *traverse the search space* to generate candidates so that no candidate is generated more than once. The second phase requires efficient isomorphism checks to determine the frequency of each candidate – nontrivial for tree-structured data (especially with embedded subtrees) and graph-structured data.

Pattern mining algorithms can be classified into two categories. The first class of methods, known as a priori-style methods, process *all* patterns of size k *before* generating any pattern of size larger than k. The other class of techniques are known as *pattern-growth approaches*, in which a frequent subtree S is repeatedly *grown* with new edges (equivalently, new nodes) to yield larger candidate subtrees. The newly added edge is called an *extension*, and the process of edge addition is referred to as *point growth* (see Figure 20.1b). The set of all subtrees generated from a single pattern S via one or more pattern growths is called its *equivalence class*, which is denoted by $[S]$. If S is a single node v, then the set $[S]$ contains all subtrees whose root node is v. Pattern-growth approaches typically exhibit better data locality and maintain smaller memory footprints when compared to a priori-style methods.

20.2.2 State of the Art

A majority of existing algorithms reduce the time spent in expensive (embedded) subtree isomorphism checks by employing special data structures called *embedding lists* (ELs). These lists store the matches of smaller patterns, so that the matches for bigger patterns can be found without an explicit subtree isomorphism check. For example, all matches of a path A–B–C can be enumerated quickly if the locations at which the edge A–B occurs in the database are stored. This strategy essentially trades memory for improved execution time. However, in practice, these lists can grow exponentially in size and affect both the memory and runtime performance. As discussed in Section 20.1, algorithms with larger memory footprints are not suitable for CMPs. We first briefly review the existing methods for frequent tree pattern mining and then point out their limitations.

Seminal work on tree pattern mining was done by Zaki in which he proposed an algorithm known as *TreeMiner* (Zaki, 2005). TreeMiner represents the dataset in vertical format as opposed to the traditional transactional format. The set of all matches for a given pattern P are summarized and stored in a data structure known as a scope-list. Each entry in the scope-list corresponds to a single occurrence of P, which is uniquely denoted as a 3-tuple (*tid, prefix, scope*) – *tid* is a tree in which P occurs as a subtree; *prefix* is the embedding (i.e., list of matching nodes) of P's parent pattern; and *scope* denotes a range of candidate nodes in *tid* with which P can be grown to create bigger patterns. Larger patterns are generated by intersecting the scope-lists of smaller patterns. Note that the size of scope-lists governs both the memory usage and the runtime performance of TreeMiner.

Tan et al. have proposed iMB3, which uses *occurrence lists* to store the embeddings (Tan et al., 2006). Their approach also maintains two more data structures that are *persistent* across the entire execution – *dictionary* for representing the data and *descendant lists* to track *all* descendants of a frequent node.Although the original iMB3 uses the occurrence-based support, it can be tuned to use the transaction-based definition – which we refer to as *iMB3-T*. The performance of both TreeMiner and iMB3-T suffer because of large memory footprints and poor data locality. Wang et al. (2004) proposed two algorithms, *Chopper* and *XSpanner*. Chopper recasts the subtree mining problem into a sequence mining problem. XSpanner, in contrast, employs a recursive projection strategy that is inspired by the popular itemset mining algorithm FPGrowth (Han, Pei, and Yin, 2000). This method, however, is too complex and results in pointer-chasing and thus in poor performance. There exist several other algorithms that primarily differ in the type of subtrees that they mine (Asai et al., 2002; Chi et al., 2004; Nijssen and Kok, 2003; Ruckert and Kramer, 2004; Shasha and Zhang, 2004; Termier, Rousset, and Sebag, 2004). Further details on these methods can be found in the survey article (Chi et al., 2005).

We present several memory optimizations and parallelization strategies in the context of an existing algorithm known as Trips (Tatikonda, Parthasarathy, and Kurc, 2006). This algorithm transforms all database trees into sequences and subsequently operates completely on sequences. Such sequence-based processing enables better spatial data locality. Although our algorithms are presented in the context of Trips, they are generic in nature and can be adopted for many other tree mining and graph mining techniques. We next briefly review the details of Trips algorithm.

20.2.3 Trips Algorithm

Trips relies on an injective transformation between trees and sequences. Each database tree T is encoded as two sequences: Numbered Prüfer Sequence NPS_T and Label Sequence LS_T. They are constructed iteratively on the basis of post-order traversal numbers (PON) of tree nodes. In every iteration, a node (say, v) with the smallest PON is removed. The label of v is appended to LS_T, and the PON of v's parent is added to NPS_T. An example tree and its associated Prüfer sequence is shown in Figure 20.2. Note that each edge corresponds to an entry in the sequence pair.

The given database D of trees is first transformed into equivalent Prüfer sequences (D') and all frequent nodes (F_1) are found (see Algorithm 20.3). For each $f \in F_1$, the function *mineTrees* is called to mine subtrees whose root is f, that is, those subtrees that belong to the equivalence class $[f]$. Each invocation of the recursive *mineTrees* procedure mines for extensions (bigger patterns) resulting from *newpat* (*pat + extension*) by scanning the projected database *tidlist*, the list of trees in which *pat* is present.

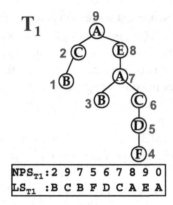

Figure 20.2 Prüfer sequence.

Here, the extension refers to point growths, that is, the addition of a new edge or a node. More specifically, an extension (*label*, *pos*) of *pat* defines a new subtree *newpat* (in line 1) that is obtained by attaching a node with label *label* to a node in *pat* whose PON is equal to *pos*. Note that each extension uniquely identifies a subtree grown from a given pattern.

Lines 3–5 of the algorithm in Figure 20.3 modify the embedding lists with the matches for *pat* into those with the occurrences of *newpat* by scanning each tree in *tidlist* for (*label*, *pos*). Lines 8–10 scan all nodes from all trees in *newtidlist* to produce extensions of *newpat*, whose counts are collected by a hash-table *H*. Those extensions whose frequency is greater than *minsup*, that is, the *frequent* subtrees grown from *newpat*, are processed further in lines 13–15.

Limitations of Existing Tree Mining Algorithms: The embedding lists (ELs), which affect both the memory and runtime performance of an algorithm, can grow arbitrarily large in size. Consider the worst-case scenario of a *chain tree* (a path) *T* of size *n*, where every node has the same label (say, *A*). Let the number of entries in EL be

---

Input: $D = \{T_1, T_2, \ldots, T_N\}, minsup$
$(D', F_1) = \text{Transform}(T_i): 1 \le i \le N$
For each f in F_1 **do**
  mineTrees ($NULL, (f, -1), D'$)
mineTrees (*pat*, extension (*label*,*pos*), *tidlist*)
1: $newpat \leftarrow pat + (label, pos)$ // pattern extension
2: output *newpat*
3: **For each** T in *tidlist* **do**
4:     **If** (*label*, *pos*) is an extension point for *pat* in T **then**
5:       update the embedding list of T i.e., $EL(T)$
6:       add T to *newtidlist* // indicates *newpat* occurs in T
7: $H = NULL$
8: **For each** T in *newtidlist* **do**
9:     **For each** node v in T **do**
10:       **For each** match m in $EL(T)$ **do**
11:          **If** v is a valid extension to m **then**
12:             add the extension point to H
13: **For each** *ext* in H **do**
14:    **If** *ext* is frequent **then**
15:       mineTrees (*newpat*, *ext*, *newtidlist*)

Figure 20.3 Trips algorithm.

Table 20.1. *Characterization of existing tree mining algorithms.*

	TreeMiner	iMBT	Trips
Working set (KB)	256	128	64
Memory usage (GB)	7	32	4

denoted as $|EL|$. When a single-node pattern $S = A$ is being processed, $|EL| = \binom{n}{1} = n$ entries, where each entry corresponds to a match of S in T. As S is extended to an edge pattern $A\text{–}A$, the list is extended to record all $\binom{n}{2}$ matches of the edge; hence, $|EL| = \binom{n}{1} + \binom{n}{2} = \frac{n(n+1)}{2}$ entries. Similarly, when S is grown into a pattern of size n (i.e., the complete path), $|EL| = \sum_{i=1}^{n} \binom{n}{i} = 2^n - 1$. It can be seen that the worst-case size of an embedding list is exponential in tree size. Such worst-case scenarios often occur in real-world datasets. For example, in the Cslogs dataset (see Section 20.5), as a 3-node pattern is grown into a 6-node pattern, the number of matches sharply increases from 141,574 to 474 million. All existing algorithms diligently store the location of each of those 474 million matches, thereby resulting in very large memory footprints.

Table 20.1 presents a detailed characterization of memory performance of existing algorithms on Treebank dataset ($minsup = 85\%$). Large embedding lists maintained in these algorithms lead to several limitations: (1) they increase the memory footprints, making it difficult to realize efficient performance when the algorithms are executed on multicore chips; (2) since embedding lists are dynamic data structures, they complicate the memory management, especially when implemented in shared-memory environments; and (3) they severely limit the parallelization of algorithms as they introduce dependencies among different tasks.

Parallel Data Mining Algorithms: There has been some research on parallel data mining algorithms for shared-memory multiprocessor (SMP) systems. Parthasarathy et al. (2001) have studied the impact of several issues like synchronization overhead, degree of parallelism, and data locality on workload parallelization. Zaki (1999a) has proposed methods for mining sequence databases on SMP systems. There also exists work focusing on parallelizing other data mining tasks such as classification and clustering (Olson, 1995). These studies focus on much simpler problems than semi-structured data mining. Furthermore, they are not readily applicable for multicores.

Buehrer et al. (2006) have developed techniques for *adaptive state management* and *adaptive parallelization* for graph mining workloads on CMP systems. Since the subgraph isomorphism problem is hard, adaptation of the trade-off between space and runtime is the key for efficient performance. Liu et al. have proposed lock-free data structures for itemset mining that exploit the fine-grained parallelism on multicores. A list of such architecture-conscious techniques was recently compiled by Parthasarathy et al. (2008).

20.3 Memory Optimizations

The architecture of our enhanced version of Trips, which is called *Memory Conscious Trips* (MCT), is shown in Figure 20.4. All trees in a given database D are first transformed into sequences ($T(D)$) (see Section 20.2.3). Subsequently, the sequences

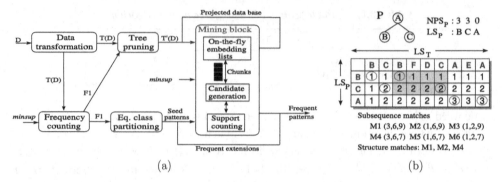

(a)   (b)

Figure 20.4 (a) Framework of our MCT algorithm. (b) Example pattern and its R-matrix with respect to the database tree from Figure 20.2.

are trimmed by removing all infrequent nodes whose support is less than *minsup* to form $T'(D)$. Both $T'(D)$ and the set of frequent nodes F_1 are fed to the mining block that has three different phases: on-the-fly embedding lists *OEL* (see Section 20.3.1), candidate generation *CG*, and support counting *SC*. The *CG* phase invokes *OEL* to produce pattern matches ondemand. They are subsequently processed by *SC* to generate frequent extensions, which are fed back into the mining block to yield larger patterns.

20.3.1 On-the-Fly Embedding List Creation (NOEM)

Unlike existing algorithms that store embedding lists (ELs) explicitly, we adopt a strategy that dynamically *constructs* the list, *uses* it, and then *de-allocates* it. In graph-theoretic terms, constructing a dynamic EL is equivalent to finding the set of all (embedded) subtree isomorphisms of a given pattern in the database. We construct these lists by employing a dynamic programming-based approach that is inspired by recent research in XML indexing (Tatikonda et al., 2007; Zezula et al., 2003). However, as shown in Section 20.5, a direct application of these techniques results in poor runtime performance. We therefore propose methods that reorganize the computation to improve the data locality and execution time (see Section 20.3.3). Note that dynamic list construction affects only lines 3–6 of the algorithm in Figure 20.3 – the correctness of the overall algorithm is *still intact*.

Say we need to find matchings of subtree $S = (LS_S, NPS_S)$ in a tree $T = (LS_T, NPS_T)$. Let $|S| = m$ and $|T| = n$. Prüfer sequences, because of the way they are constructed, possess an important property that if S is an embedded subtree of T, then the label sequence LS_S is a subsequence of LS_T, that is, being a subsequence is a *necessary but not sufficient* condition for subtree isomorphism. On the basis of this observation, we design a three-step process to enumerate all matches of S in T.

First, we check whether LS_S is a subsequence of LS_T or not by computing the length of their longest common subsequence (LCS) using a traditional dynamic programming approach (Wagner and Fischer, 1974) (see Algorithm 55). This approach constructs a matrix R using Equation 20.1, so that the length of LCS is given by the matrix entry

---

Algorithm 55: On-the-Fly Embedding List Construction

Input: $P = (LS_P, NPS_P), T = (LS_T, NPS_T)$
    $R \leftarrow$ computeLcsMatrix(LS_P, LS_T);
    say $m \leftarrow |LS_P|, n \leftarrow |LS_T|$
    if $R[m][n] \mathrel{!=} m$ **then return**
    else processR $(m, n, 0)$

processR (p_i, t_j, L)

1: **If** $p_i = 0$ or $t_j = 0$ **then return**
2: **If** $L = m$ **then**
3:     **If** $SM[..]$ corresponds to a subtree **then**
4:         update $EMList[T]$ with SM
5:     **return**
6: **If** $LS_P[p_i] = LS_T[t_j]$ **then**
7:     $SM[m - L] \leftarrow t_j$
8:     processR $(p_i - 1, t_j - 1, L + 1)$
9:     processR $(p_i, t_j - 1, L)$
10: **Else If** $R[p_i, t_j - 1] < R[p_i - 1, t_j]$ **then**
11:     processR $(p_i, t_j - 1, L)$

$R[m, n]$. If $R[m, n] \neq m$ then we conclude that S is *not* a subtree of T (see Figure 20.4b).

$$R[i, j] = \begin{cases} 0, & \text{if } i = 0, j = 0 \\ R[i - 1, j - 1] + 1, & \text{if } LS_S[i] = LS_T[j] \\ max(R[i - 1, j], R[i, j - 1]), & \text{if } LS_S[i] \neq LS_T[j] \end{cases} \tag{20.1}$$

Second, if LS_S is a subsequence of LS_T, then we enumerate all subsequence matches of LS_S in LS_T by backtracking from $R[m, n]$ to $R[1, 1]$ (lines 6–11 in Algorithm 55). A subsequence match (SM) is denoted by $(i_1, \ldots, i_m)$, where i_k's are the locations in T at which the match occurs, that is, $LS_P[k] = LS_T[i_k]$ for $1 \leq k \leq m$ (see Figure 20.4b). It is worth noting that, unlike in a classical sequence-matching problem, here we are interested in obtaining all matches. Since backtracking is performed in backward, the matches are generated from *right to left*.

Third, we filter the false-positive subsequences by matching the structure (given by NPS) of $SM = (i_1, \ldots, i_m)$ with that of S (line 3 in Algorithm 55). Such a structural match (*map*) maps every parent–child relation in S into an ancestor–descendant relation in SM, that is, in T. We first set $map[m] = i_m$ (root node). For $k = m-1\ldots1$, we check if $map[NPS_S[k]]$ either is equal to $NPS_T[i_k]$ or is a nearest mapped ancestor of $NPS_T[i_k]$ – that is, the parent of the kth node in S is mapped to an ancestor of the i_k^{th} node in T. Since nodes are considered in reverse post order, structure match is also established from right to left (i.e., root to leaf). The resulting match is finally added to the dynamically constructed embedding list (line 4 in Algorithm 55).

Example: Figure 20.4b shows an example three-node pattern P and the R-matrix that is obtained with respect to the database tree from Figure 20.2. The length of LCS between two label sequences LS_P and LS_T is given by the bottom rightx corner entry, whose value is 3. Since this value is equal to the $|LS_P|$, we enumerate all six subsequence matches of

LS_P in LS_T. Out of these six matches, only M_1, M_2, and M_4 are actual subtree matches. For M_3: at $k = 3$, the root node is mapped to node $i_3 = 9$ in T, that is, $map[3] = 9$. At $k = 2$ ($NPS_S[k] = 3$), we set $map[2] = i_k = 2$ because $map[3] = NPS_T[i_k]$. However, at $k = 1$ ($i_k = 1$), $map[3] \neq NPS_T[i_k]$ and $map[3]$ is not the nearest mapped ancestor of i_1 in T. Since the check fails, M_3 is declared as a false-positive. For M_5 and M_6, the check fails at $k = 1$ and $k = 2$, respectively.

20.3.2 Optimizations for Tree Matching

The following three optimizations reduce the number of redundant computations in Algorithm 55. The first two reduce the recursion overhead incurred while backtracking; the third reduces the overhead due to false positives.

1. *Label Filtering (LF)*: Before constructing the R-matrix, we remove those nodes in T that do not appear in S. In Figure 20.4b, the columns corresponding to nodes D, E, and F can be safely deleted as they do not help in establishing the subsequence match.
2. *Dominant Match Processing (DOM)*: Observe that a subsequence match is established only at the entries (called as *dominant matches*) where both LS_S and LS_T match (condition 2 in Equation 20.1). Backtracking on the rest of the entries is redundant and must be avoided. In Figure 20.4b, dominant matches are circled. For example, $R[2, 6]$ and $R[1, 3]$ are dominant and all the other shaded cells simply carry LCS value from one to the other. Recursion from $R[2, 6]$ can directly jump to $R[1, 3]$, avoiding all the other shaded cells.
3. *Simultaneous Matching (SIMUL)*: Here, observe that both subsequence and structure matching phases operate from right to left in reverse post order. Therefore, instead of performing the structure matching after generating all subsequence matches, both the matchings can be done simultaneously. As soon as a subsequence match is established at position k, we perform the structure match at that position. Such an *embedding of structural constraints* into subsequence matching detects the false positives as early as possible and never generates them completely.

20.3.3 Computation Chunking (CHUNK)

Since the size of EL is proportional to the number of matches, our dynamic embedding lists can also grow exponentially, in the worst case. CHUNK optimization completely eliminates the lists by *coalescing both tree matching and tree mining* algorithms. It operates in three steps: *loop inversion, quick checking,* and *chunking*. The computation in algorithm in Figure 20.3 is reorganized by inverting the loops in lines 9 and 10, that is, T is scanned for each match m instead of processing m for each node in T. The second step, *quick checking*, notes that the extensions associated with two different matches m_i and m_j ($i < j$) are independent of each other. Thus, m_i need not wait until m_j is generated, and thus it need not be stored explicitly in EL. Finally, *chunking* improves the locality by grouping a fixed number of matches into chunks. T is then scanned for each chunk instead of for each match m. Once the extensions against all the matches in one chunk are found, we proceed to the next chunk.

Algorithm 56: Memory Conscious Trips (MCT)

---

mineTrees (*pat*, extension *e*, tidlist)

  A: **for each** T in tidlist **do**

    B: construct R-Matrix for T and *newpat*

    C: processR (m, n, m)

  D: **for each** *ext* in H **do**

    E: mineTrees (*newpat*, *ext*) recursively

processR (p_i, t_j, L)

  1: **If** $p_i = 0$ or $t_j = 0$ **then return**

  2: **If** $L = 0$ **then**

  3:    add *SM* to *EMList* and add T to *newtidlist*

  4:    **If** $|EMList| \% 10 = 0$ **then**

  5:      **For each** match m in *EMList* **do**

  6:        **For each** node v in T **do**

  7:          **If** v is a valid extension with m **then**

  8:            add the resulting extension to H

  9:    *EMList* $\leftarrow$ *null*

10:    **return**

11: **for** $k = t_j$ to 1 **do**

12:    **If** $R[p_i][k]$ is dominant & $R[p_i][k] = L$ **then**

13:      $SM[k] \leftarrow (LS_T[t_j], NPS_T[t_j])$

14:      **If** agreeOnStructure (P, SM, k) **then**

15:        processR ($p_i - 1$, $t_j - 1$, $L - 1$)

The complete MCT is shown as Algorithm 56. Since it always keeps a fixed number of matches in memory, MCT maintains a *constant-sized* memory footprint throughout the execution. Further, chunking *localizes* the computation to higher-level caches, improving both locality and working sets.

20.4 Adaptive Parallelization

We now consider the parallelization of MCT for multicore systems. Direct parallelization of the Trips algorithm resulted in inefficient performance as embedding lists led to a large memory footprint and high pressure on the memory bus. The inherent dependency structure of lists poses difficulties in sharing them, leading to coarse-grained work partitioning and poor load balance (see Section 20.5.3). Essentially, *parallelization without identifying the memory optimizations*, presented in the previous section, is extremely inefficient.

Our parallel framework employs a *multi-level work sharing* approach that adaptively modulates the type and granularity of the work that is being shared among threads. Each core C_i in the CMP system runs a single instantiation (i.e., a thread) of our parallel algorithm. Henceforth, the terms *core*, *thread*, and *process* are used interchangeably and are referred by C_i. A *job* refers to a piece of work that is executed by any thread.

The set of all threads consume jobs from a *job pool* (JP) and possibly produce new jobs into it. The jobs from a job pool are dequeued and executed by threads on a "first come, first serve" basis.

Control Flow: Our work-sharing parallelization technique is a simple *lock-based* algorithm that is driven by the amount of remaining work in the system. Whenever a thread C_i finds the job pool to be empty, it votes for termination by joining the *thread pool* (TP) and detaches itself (i.e., blocks itself) from execution. Each thread monitors TP at pre-set points during its runtime, and if it is not empty, then it may choose to fork off new jobs onto JP, and notify the threads waiting in TP. The mining process terminates when *all* threads vote for termination.

In our multi-level approach, all threads operate in three different levels. Each level corresponds to a different execution mode, which dictates the type and granularity of the jobs in that mode. The three execution modes are *task-parallel*, *data-parallel*, and *chunk-parallel*. The first one exploits the parallelism across different portions of the search space. The data-parallel mode parallelizes the work required to mine a single pattern. Finally, at the finest level of granularity, the chunk-parallel mode obtains the matches of a pattern within a single tree in parallel. For a simpler design, we used different job pools for different modes: *task pool* (JP_T), *tree pool* (JP_D), and *column pool* (JP_C), respectively. Alternatively, one can implement it as a single job pool with prioritized jobs. Shared access to these pools is protected using simple locks. Jobs in these job pools are uniquely identified by *job descriptors*. Each job descriptor J is a 6-tuple as shown here:

$$J = (J.t, J.i, J.f, J.c, J.o, J.r), \quad J.t = \begin{cases} task, & if \ J \in JP_T \\ data, & if \ J \in JP_D \\ chunk, & if \ J \in JP_C \end{cases}$$

Job type $J.t$ corresponds to the execution mode, and it defines the remaining entries. Given a job J, a thread starts with the inputs $J.i$, and applies the function $J.f$ to produce an output $J.o$. The control is then returned to the job that created J if return flag $J.r$ is set to *true*. A condition $J.c$ is evaluated at pre-set points to determine whether or not to spawn new jobs from J.

$J.t$ also determines the type of new jobs that J can spawn. A task-level job can create either new tasks or a single job of type *data*. A chunk-level job in JP_C can be created only by a data-parallel job in JP_D. And, jobs in JP_C cannot create new jobs, that is, $\forall J \in JP_C, J.c = false$. The granularity of jobs in JP_T is more than that in JP_D, which in turn is greater than the granularity of jobs in JP_C. Such a design *adaptively adjusts the granularity* by switching between the execution modes. The high-level control flow of our parallel strategy is shown as the algorithm in Figure 20.5.

20.4.1 Task-Parallel Mode

In this mode, each thread processes jobs from the task pool JP_T where each *task* corresponds to the process of mining either the complete or a portion of an equivalence class $[S]$. Therefore, every job $J \in JP_T$ is associated with a subtree $J.i = S$. The output

```
 1: initialize( ) // I1
 2: identifyGranularities( ) // I3, I4, I5
 3: while true do
 4:    If  JP_T is empty then
 5:       If  JP_D is empty then
 6:          If  JP_C is empty then
 7:             vote for termination
 8:             block itself from execution
 9:             if { all threads voted } break
10:          Else
11:             process  JP_C  //  chunk-parallel
                 (I8, sync)
12:       Else
13:          process  JP_D  //  data-parallel (I8,
              sync, I9)
14:    Else
15:       mine a task from  JP_T  // task-parallel
           (I8, I9)
16: finishUp( ) // I2
```

Figure 20.5 Parallel tree mining.

$J.o$ is the set of subtrees produced from S by invoking $J.f$ (*mineTrees* in Algorithm 56). Further, $J.r$ is always set to *false* in this mode.

In this mode, one can devise different strategies based on the way the search space is *partitioned* into tasks. A naive strategy is to partition the space by equivalence classes – EQ in Figure 20.6 – and schedule different classes (F_1 in Figure 20.3) on different cores. This coarse-grained strategy is called equivalence class task partitioning (EqP) (Zaki, 1999b). Another strategy is to partition the search space such that each pattern is treated as a different job – P in Figure 20.6. Each extension that is produced is enqueued into the job pool as new tasks (i.e., $J.c$ is a tautology). Such a technique is referred to as pattern-level task partitioning (PaP) (Zaki, 1999b). Although EqP delivers poor performance because of inherent skew in the size of different equivalence classes, the aggressive job sharing in PaP suffers from high computation overhead. PaP also suffers from locality issues since the subtrees may not be mined at the places where they were created.

Instead of these two extremes, we design an adaptive task partitioning (AdP) strategy where the search space is partitioned *on demand*. New tasks are created only when

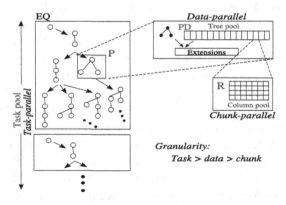

Figure 20.6 Schematic of different job granularities.

there are idle threads waiting (for work) in the thread pool TP. Unlike EqP and PaP, this method *adaptively modulates* the task granularity at runtime. It can be described as

$$JP_T = \{ J \mid J.i = \text{a frequent subtree} \wedge J.c = (TP \neq \Phi \wedge |Ext| \geq 1) \}$$

|Ext| is the number of extensions that are *yet to be* processed. Note that $TP \neq \Phi$ implies that the job pool is empty, that is, new jobs are created only if the job pool is empty and some threads are in wait state. The pre-set points to evaluate $J.c$ are between lines D and E in Algorithm 56, that is, $J.c$ is evaluated before processing each extension point. Since AdP dynamically modulates the task granularity, it not only *achieves good load balance* but also exhibits *good locality* since extensions are mined, whenever possible, on the processor that created them.

20.4.2 Data-Parallel Mode

The task partitioning strategies primarily process the search space in parallel. They inherently assume that all patterns are of similar complexity. They do not take the underlying *data distribution* into account. Efficiency can be improved by dividing the work associated with more expensive patterns. We parallelize the job of mining a single subtree S by looking at its projected database PD_S, 8–12 in the algorithm in Figure 20.3 (PD in Figure 20.6). We put all trees from PD_S into the job pool JP_D and treat each tree as a different job that is scheduled on to a processing core. We devise an adaptive strategy, called hybrid work partitioning (HyP), by combining this basic data partitioning method with the task partitioning strategy AdP. Here, a core C_i that is currently mining a task-level job $J \in JP_T$ with $J.i = S$ forks off new jobs on to JP_D only when it finds any idle threads while finding extensions from S. Once all trees in JP_D are processed, the core C_i performs a reduction operation to combine the partial sets of extensions obtained from each tree in PD_S. If needed, J may now proceed to create new tasks according to *AdP*. Therefore, a task-level job may either create new tasks or new jobs of type *data* – the spawning condition thus needs to be augmented as follows:

$$\forall J \in JP_T, J.c = \begin{cases} \text{add tasks to } JP_T, & \text{if } TP \neq \Phi \wedge |Ext| \geq 1 \\ \text{add jobs to } JP_D, & \text{if } TP \neq \Phi \wedge \frac{c(J.i)}{s(J.i)} < \theta \end{cases}$$

Although the first condition is evaluated between lines D and E of Algorithm 56 (same as AdP), the second one is checked between lines A and B. The second condition governs the creation of data-parallel jobs, and it depends on the amount of work that is remaining to complete the task $J.i$. A rough estimate for the amount of remaining work is given by $\frac{c(J.i)}{s(J.i)}$, where $c(J.i)$ is the number of matches found so far and $s(J.i)$ is the support of $J.i$ (known from line 14 in the algorithm in Figure 20.3). If this ratio is smaller than a threshold θ (we use $\theta = 20\%$ in our evaluation), then it means that there is a lot of work to be done and it can be shared with others. Such a method essentially decides whether it is worth dividing the work into jobs of finer granularity.

Once the tree pool is created, we sort the trees in decreasing order of their size. This is similar to classical job scheduling where the jobs are sorted in decreasing order of their processing time. We sort based on tree size because the mining time that depends on the number of matches in a given tree is *likely* to be proportional to the tree size.

20.4.3 Chunk-Parallel Mode

A much more fine-grained parallelism can be realized by exploiting the skew among trees, that is, processing of one tree may be more expensive than that of the other tree. For example in bioinformatics, one glycan or RNA structure may be very large when compared to the other. Such large trees, as well as trees with large numbers of matches, will introduce load imbalance while using HyP. To deal with such a skew, the job of mining a single tree, that is, the process of finding matches and corresponding extensions from a given tree should be parallelized. This fine-grained parallelism is obtained by parallelizing at the level of *chunks*, which are generated in lines 3 and 4 of Algorithm 56. Since chunks are created from individual columns of the R-matrix, we treat each column as a separate job and schedule them on to different cores.

This mode is entered only when all the available parallelism in the data-parallel mode is fully exploited. A job of type *data* in JP_D switches to this mode based on the following condition:

$$\forall J \in JP_D, J.c = \{\text{spawn jobs onto } JP_C, \text{ if } TP \neq \Phi\}.$$

One can also design $J.c$ based on pattern size, the number of matches found so far, and the portion of R-matrix that is yet to be explored. This condition is evaluated between lines 13 and 14 of Algorithm 56.

For each job J in column pool JP_C, the input is a column from the R-matrix and the partial match that is constructed so far (by J's parent job in JP_D). $J.f$ backtracks from the input column to discover the remaining part of the match and extensions from that match ($J.o$). $J.r$ in this mode is always set to *true* so that extensions generated from different column jobs can be combined at the parent job. Also, $J.c$ is always set to *false*.

20.4.4 Cost Analysis

The performance of our parallel framework depends on the overhead incurred in creating, sharing, and managing jobs and job pools. This overhead is minimal for the following reasons: (1) we avoid the use of meta data structures, making it easier to fork off new jobs from the current computation; (2) all jobs have very small-sized inputs (a small pattern, a tree id, or a column id), and so it is easy to share the jobs; (3) all jobs are shared using simple queueing and locking mechanisms; and (4) all job spawning conditions can be evaluated in constant time.

We now develop theoretical bounds on an another type of overhead, the number of context switches between different execution modes. Let $N(t, S)$ be the number of times the spawning condition *that results in* jobs of type t is evaluated to *true*, while processing S. Let $N(S)$ be the number context switches (of any type) while mining S, and N be the total number of context switches during the entire execution, that is, $N = \sum_S N(S)$, where $N(S) = N(task, S) + N(data, S) + N(chunk, S)$. We now construct the worst-case bounds for $N(t, S)$ for each t.

New tasks from S are created only through AdP, whose spawning conditions are evaluated after all extensions are produced from S. Therefore, any subtree can produce new tasks at most once, that is, $\forall S, N(task, S) \leq 1$. Thus, we have $\sum_S N(task, S) \leq |FS|$, where FS is the set of all frequent subtrees.

Similarly, when a task J spawns jobs onto the tree pool, each unexplored tree in $J.i$'s projected database is created as a new job. For any subtree, the switch from task-parallel mode to data-parallel mode can happen at most once, that is, $\forall S, N(data, S) \leq 1$. We thus have $\sum_S N(data, S) \leq |FS|$.

Finally, $N(chunk, S)$ is equal to the number of trees in S's projected database that spawn the chunk-level jobs. From Section 20.4.3, jobs of type *chunk* are created only when TP is empty. We can thus infer that $N(chunk, S)$ is always less than the number of cores. If $N(chunk, S) \geq |C|$ then TP cannot be empty. We then have $\sum_S N(chunk, S) \leq |FS| * (|C| - 1)$. The upper bound on N can then be derived as follows:

$$N = \sum_S N(S) = \sum_S N(task, S) + \sum_S N(data, S) + \sum_S N(chunk, S)$$
$$\leq |FS| + |FS| + |FS| * (|C| - 1)$$
$$\leq |FS| * (|C| + 1)$$

We can conclude that the number of context switches per pattern is bounded by a constant, and the total number N is in the order of $|FS|$. However, in practice, these numbers are very, very small since the algorithm moves to a lower granularity only when the parallelism at current granularity is *completely* exploited. For example, many subtrees would have already been enumerated by the time the first data-parallel job is created, that is, $\sum_S N(data, S) \ll |FS|$.

20.4.5 Scheduling Service

A key outcome of our efforts in adaptive parallelization is a task scheduling service that has been ported to two multicore chips and one SMP system. We believe that such services will be ubiquitous as systems grow more complex and are essential to realize performance commensurate with technology advances. For simplicity, we limit our discussion to the basic interface shown in Algorithm 57. Functions *startService()* and *stopService()* are basic startup and cleanup routines. The *register()* method specifies the list and the order (specified via *gOrder*) in which different granularities are to be exploited. It also creates different job pools and other data structures used for scheduling. For each granularity, *bind()* defines an application handle that is invoked to execute the jobs of that granularity. The optional *finalize()* routine registers a synchronization callback handle (for cases where $J.c$ is *true*). *schedule()* is responsible for scheduling

---

Algorithm 57: Prototype Interface for Scheduling Service

I_1	void startService ()
I_2	void stopService ()
I_3	int register (int *granularities, int size, int *gOrder)
I_4	int bind (int gran, void (*callback) (void *))
I_5	int finalize (int gran, void (*sync) (void *))
I_6	void schedule ()
I_7	int createJob (int gran, void *inputs)
I_8	int executeJob (job *j);
I_9	bool evaluateForSpawning (job *j)

and completing all jobs by performing context switches, if needed. *createJob()* and *executeJob()* are invoked for the creation and execution of jobs. *evaluateForSpawning()* is a check-point function used to evaluate whether or not to switch between different granularities. A sample use case scenario for these interface routines is shown in the algorithm in Figure 20.5.

Such a job scheduling service can be used for a range of pattern mining tasks (from itemsets to graphs) as well as other data mining tasks. This service is also capable of producing several useful performance statistics, which we use in designing a performance monitoring tool that provides *real-time* feedback to applications.

20.5 Empirical Evaluation

We evaluate our algorithms using two commonly used real-world datasets (Tatikonda and Parthasarathy, 2009), Treebank (TB) and Cslogs (CS) (Zaki, 2005) – derived from computation linguistics and web usage mining, respectively. The number of trees and the average tree size (in number of nodes) in CS and TB are (59,691, 12.94) and (52,581, 68.03), respectively. While the trees in TB possess a very deep recursive structure with high associativity, the tree nodes in CS exhibit a high variance in their label frequencies. Such a high variance in CS significantly increases the average number of matches per frequent pattern. We use a 900-MHz Intel Itanium 2 dual-processor system with 4GB RAM, and if more memory is required (typically by extant algorithms), we use a system with 32GB RAM (same processor) instead of relying on virtual memory. Hereafter, *DS-minsup* denotes an experiment where *DS* is a dataset and *minsup* is the support.

20.5.1 Sequential Performance

Effect of Optimizations: We highlight the benefits from our optimizations in Figure 20.7 by considering the runtime and memory usage of Trips as the baseline. Note that the *y*-axis in Figures 20.7b and d is shown in *reverse* direction to indicate the reduction in memory usage. The memory footprint of algorithms is approximated as its resident set size (RSS) obtained from the "top" command. The results shown for each optimization include the benefits from all the other optimizations presented before that. So, *CHUNK* refers to the fully optimized Algorithm 56 (MCT).

Although NOEM reduces the memory consumption of Trips, computational overhead due to recursions in Algorithm 55 affects the execution time. In case of TB-40K alone, NOEM slowed down Trips by 3.6 times – because of 10 billion recursions to find just 413 million subsequences, in which 289 million are false positives (about 7 out of 10). Although LF and DOM reduce the number of recursions to a mere 554 million, SIMUL eliminates all 289 million false positives – giving a 23% runtime improvement over Trips. More importantly, these optimizations improve the runtime *without affecting* the memory benefits from NOEM. Subsequently, the computation reorganization from CHUNK (or MCT) improves the locality and reduces the working sets, resulting in a very good runtime and memory performance. When compared to Trips, on TB-30K, MCT performs 24% faster and uses 45 times less memory.

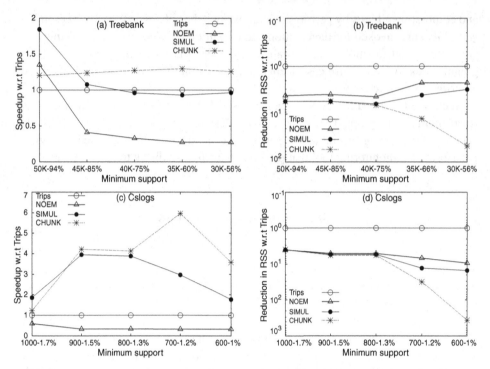

Figure 20.7 Runtime comparison with Trips as the baseline. (a,b) Treebank; (c,d) Cslogs.

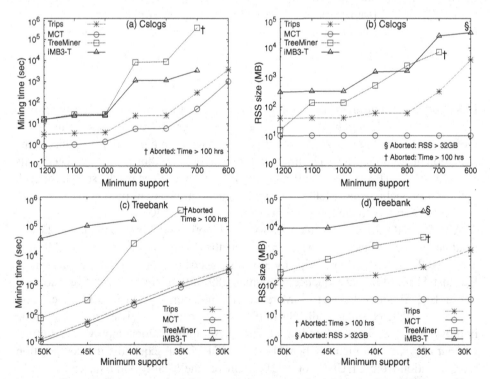

Figure 20.8 Memory performance comparison. (a,b) Cslogs; (c,d) Treebank.

Similarly, on CS-600, our optimizations improve the memory usage 366-fold and runtime 3.7 times.

Comparison with TreeMiner and iMB3-T: The performance of TreeMiner is primarily limited by the number and the size of scope-lists. For example in Cslogs, as a frequent edge is grown into a 6-node pattern, the number of matches increased sharply from 11,339 to 141,574 to 2,337,127 to 35,884,361 to 474,716,009 – resulting in large scope-lists that are later used in expensive joins. Similarly, multiple persistent data structures employed in iMB3-T severely affect the memory performance, which indirectly hinders the execution time. Although the memory usage of these algorithms grows exponentially with decreasing *minsup*, MCT always maintains a *constant-sized* footprint – 10.72MB on Cslogs and 34MB on Treebank – irrespective of *minsup*. Since chunking keeps a fixed number of matches in memory at any given point in time, MCT is able to regulate the memory usage – a significant result for CMPs where the bandwidth to memory is precious. Overall, we observed that the memory and runtime performance of MCT is orders of magnitude better than existing algorithms. For example, on CS-700, MCT exhibits a 7,200-fold speedup along with a 660-fold reduction in memory usage when compared to TreeMiner. Similarly, MCT is better than iMB3-T by 66 times and 2,300 times, respectively.

20.5.2 Characterization Study for CMP Architectures

We now present a detailed performance study of our optimizations to show that they are suitable for multicore systems. We measure several metrics such as cache miss rates and branch mispredictions via hardware performance counters using the *PAPI* toolkit.[1] All results in this section are obtained by running a TB-45K experiment on a system with a 1.4GHz Itanium 2 processor and 32GB memory – on-chip caches: 16KB L1-data; 16KB L1-instruction; 256KB L2; and 3MB L3.

Analysis of Cache Performance: The impact of our optimizations on the cache hit ratio is demonstrated in Figure 20.9a, by taking NOEM in Algorithm 55 as the baseline. Although the tree matching optimizations improve the cache performance by more than 19 times because of reducing the number of accesses to the R-matrix, CHUNK *localizes* the computation to higher-level caches to improve the L1 misses of NOEM by a factor of 1,442.

Analysis of Bandwidth Pressure: Since all the cores of a CMP system share a single memory bus, memory bandwidth becomes a key factor to application performance. We devise a novel and simple method to approximate the memory bandwidth by observing the amount of traffic on the front-side bus (i.e., off-chip). We first divide the execution time (x-axis in Figure 20.9b–d) into small 1-ms slices – a coarse-grained analysis. Then the amount of off-chip traffic during each slice (y-axis) is approximated to be the product of L3 line size and the number of L3 misses in that slice (recorded by PAPI).

---

[1] http://icl.cs.utk.edu/papi/index.html.

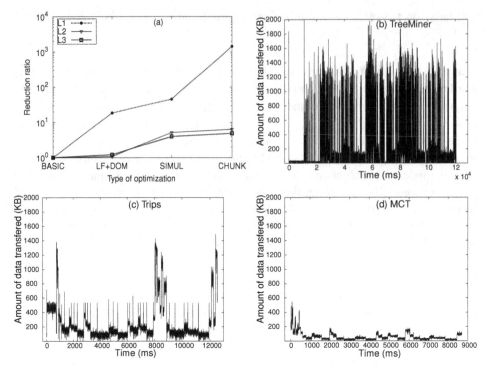

Figure 20.9 Characterization of memory optimizations.

Figures 20.9b–d show the variations in off-chip traffic for TreeMiner, Trips, and MCT, respectively. iMB3-T is not considered here because of its poor runtime and memory performance. Initial spikes in these figures denote cold L3 misses incurred while bootstrapping (e.g., reading the dataset). Frequent accesses to large memory-bound scope-lists result in very high off-chip traffic for TreeMiner. In contrast, well-structured computation in MCT results in more uniform and small-sized memory requests. On average, accesses made by MCT are well below 200KB per millisecond whereas the accesses made by TreeMiner and Trips are greater than 1100KB and 600KB per millisecond, respectively. From this coarse-grained study, it appears that each core in TreeMiner, and to a lesser extent in Trips, aggressively attempts to access main memory (because of embedding lists). For instance, on a dual quad-core system from Section 20.5.3, we observed a sustained *cumulative* bandwidth of 1.5GB per second. With 1,100KB per millisecond accesses (i.e., 1GB per second per core) by TreeMiner, the bandwidth is likely to saturate when it is executed on multiple cores. Overall, our optimizations reduce the off-chip traffic and its variability, making them viable for CMPs.

Analysis of Working Set Size: We empirically examined the working sets maintained by different algorithms using the tool *Cachegrind*. We monitored the change in L1 miss rate by varying the L1 size from 2KB to 256KB (L2 size and its associativity is fixed). We found that the L1 miss rate of MCT reduced sharply between 8KB and 16KB and stayed constant for L1 size > 16KB, indicating that the working set size is between 8KB and 16KB. As shown in Table 20.1, other algorithms maintain relatively large

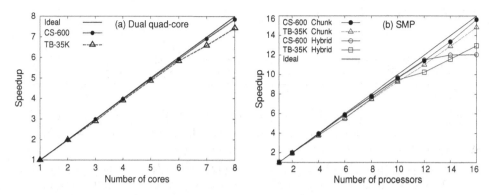

Figure 20.10 Parallel performance.

working sets. This is an encouraging result as the amount of cache available for each core in CMPs is likely to be small (Kumar et al., 2003).

20.5.3 Parallel Performance

We evaluated our parallel algorithms on a dual quad-core E5345 Xeon processor system with 6GB RAM, 8MB shared L2, and 1333MHz bus speed (see Figure 20.10a). Our adaptive load balancing strategies achieve near-linear speedups up to 7.85-fold on CS and 7.43-fold on TB, when all eight cores are used. We also considered a 16-node SGI Altix 350 SMP system with 16 1.4GHz Itanium 2 processors and 32GB memory to test the scalability of our techniques. As shown in Figure 20.10b, the speedup continues to increase with the number of processors, giving a 15.5-fold speedup with all 16 processors.

An important observation from Figure 20.10b is that *the need for fine-grained strategies increases as one increases the number of processors*. For CS-600, the performance of hybrid strategy (HyP) reaches its plateau at 12 processors ("CS-600 Hybrid" in Figure 20.10b) because of a 6-node pattern that has up to 33 million matches in a single database tree, whose mining took about 45 seconds. Amdahl's law suggests that HyP can never perform better than 45 seconds since it is limited by the job of mining a single tree. Thereafter, the efficiency can be improved only by employing more fine-grained strategies such as the one in Section 20.4.3. Similarly for TB-35K, the speedup from HyP saturates at 16 processors.

The average number of context switches taken over 10 runs of TB-35K is shown in Table 20.2. For a given granularity g, $\sum_S N(g, S)$ is denoted as N_g in the table. The number of context switches at the fine-grained level increases with $|C|$, indicating that our strategies *adaptively and automatically* exploit the parallelism. It is worth

Table 20.2. *Cost analysis of TB-45K, $|FS| = 451$.*

Cores ($|C|$)	1	2	4	8	16
N_t	0	4	7	26	48
N_d	0	2	2	10	11
N_c	0	0	0	9	19

Table 20.3. *Parallel performance of TreeMiner.*

on TB-$45K$	Cores	1	2	4	6	8
TreeMiner	EqP	1.00	1.61	1.94	1.95	2.01
	AdP	1.00	1.77	2.23	2.25	2.30

noting that these numbers are much lower than their theoretical upper bounds from Section 20.4.4: $N_t = 48 \ll |FS| = 451$; $N_d = 11 \ll 451$; and $N_c = 19 \ll 451*(|C|\text{-}1)$. We observed similar results for CS-600 (Tatikonda, 2010).

Parallel speedups of TreeMiner algorithm using our task-level methods are shown in Table 20.3. Inherent dependency structure in scope-lists makes it difficult to apply more fine-grained strategies to TreeMiner. Further, dynamic data structures in TreeMiner serialize the heap accesses, affecting the parallel efficiency. Techniques such as memory pooling are ineffective here as these data structures grow arbitrarily in size. These results re-emphasize the following mantra for good parallel efficiency: *reduce the memory footprints*; *reduce the use of dynamic data structures*; and *reorganize the computation*, so that more fine-grained strategies can be applied.

We next discuss the broader outcomes of our study and directions for future research and highlight key results.

20.6 Discussion

Memory Optimizations: Improving locality (spatial or temporal) continues to be important, but in addition, bandwidth must also be considered when designing data-intensive algorithms for emerging CMPs. The traditional trade-off between time and space and its implications for parallelism need to be examined carefully in this light. All our memory optimizations target the foregoing challenges. They yield significant savings – L1 misses reduced by up to 1,442 times, memory footprints reduced by a factor of 366, memory bandwidth pressure decreased significantly, and the overall runtime improved by a factor of 4 on sequential execution.

Our optimizations have a broader applicability in many domains. The fundamental idea behind NOEM can be used in mining other types of patterns, including graphs and sequences, and in searching bioinformatic databases and XML repositories (Zezula et al., 2003). Optimizations similar to LF, DOM, and SIMUL are useful to reduce the overhead in dynamic programming-based methods – time series analysis (Berndt and Clifford, 1996); code generation techniques (Aho, Ganapathi, and Tjiang, 1989); (multiple) sequence alignment (Needleman and Wunsch, 1970); and consensus phylogenetic tree computation (Steel and Warnow, 1993).

Chunking refers to the notion of dividing the computation into smaller pieces so that they can be handled efficiently. Such an approach has general-purpose utility in database query processing (Qiao et al., 2008) and in mining graphs, DAGs, induced subtrees and so on. When applied to induced subtree mining, our optimizations exhibited a speedup of 15-fold against FreqT (Tatikonda, 2010).

Applications, especially in the context of CMPs, must focus on the *achieved* memory bandwidth. The approximate method we described in Section 20.5.2 provides an easy and quick way to study the memory behavior of algorithms. We believe that this lightweight mechanism to measure the bandwidth is widely applicable to several other data mining and database applications (Qiao et al., 2008).

Parallel Algorithms and Scheduling Service: With regard to task scheduling, algorithms that can adapt and mold are essential to achieve performance commensurate with the number of cores in emerging CMP systems. Coarse-grained strategies are usually not sufficient since systemic, parametric, and data-driven constraints make the workload estimation a challenging task. In such scenarios, the ability of an algorithm to adaptively modulate between coarse- and fine-grained strategies is critical to parallel efficiency. In fact, how much an algorithm can adapt essentially dictates when the performance plateau is reached, as we observed in our study. Our adaptive strategy demonstrated near-perfect parallel efficiency on both a recent CMP and a modern SMP system. A key outcome here is the realization of a general-purpose scheduling service that supports the development of adaptive algorithms for database and mining tasks.

Acknowledgments

This work is supported in part by grants from the National Science Foundation CAREER-IIS-0347662, RI-CNS-0403342, CCF-0702587, and IIS-0917070.

References

Aho, A. V., Ganapathi, M., and Tjiang, S. W. K. 1989. Code Generation Using Tree Matching and Dynamic Programming. *ACM Transactions on Programming Languages and Systems*, **11**(4), 491–516.

Asai, T., Abe, K., Kawasoe, S., Arimura, H., Satamoto, H., and Arikawa, S. 2002. Efficient Substructure Discovery from Large Semi-structured Data. Pages 158–174 of: *Proceedings of the SIAM International Conference on Data Mining (SDM)*.

Baxter, I. D., Yahin, A., Moura, L., Sant¢Anna, M., and Bier, L. 1998. Clone Detection Using Abstract Syntax Trees. Pages 368–377 of: *Proceedings of the International Conference on Software Maintenance (ICSM)*.

Berndt, D. J., and Clifford, J. 1996. Finding Patterns in Time Series: A Dynamic Programming Approach. Pages 229–248 of: *Advances in Knowledge Discovery and Data Mining*.

Buehrer, G., Parthasarathy, S., and Chen, Y. 2006. Adaptive Parallel Graph Mining for CMP Architectures. Pages 97–106 of: *Proceedings of the Sixth International Conference on Data Mining*. IEEE Computer Society, Washington, DC.

Charniak, E. 1996. Tree-Bank Grammars. *Proceedings of the Thirteenth National Conference on Artificial Intelligence*, **2**, 1031–1036.

Chi, Y., Yang, Y., Xia, Y., and Muntz, R. R. 2004. CMTreeMiner: Mining Both Closed and Maximal Frequent Subtrees. Pages 63–73 of: *Proceedings of 8th Pacific Asia Conference on Knowledge Discovery and Data Mining (PAKDD)*.

Chi, Y., Muntz, R. R., Nijssen, S., and Kok, N. J. 2005. Frequent Subtree Mining – An Overview. *Fundamenta Informaticae*, **66**(1), 161–198.

Gan, H. H., Pasquali, S., and Schlick, T. 2003. Exploring the Repertoire of RNA Secondary Motifs Using Graph Theory: Implications for RNA Design. *Nucleic Acids Research*, **31**(11), 2926.

Ghoting, A., Buehrer, G., Parthasarathy, S., Kim, D., Nguyen, A., Chen, Y. K., and Dubey, P. 2005. Cache-conscious Frequent Pattern Mining on a Modern Processor. Pages 577–588 of: *Proceedings of the 31st International Conference on Very Large Data Bases (VLDB)*.

Han, J., Pei, J., and Yin, Y. 2000. Mining Frequent Patterns without Candidate Generation. Pages 1–12 of: *Proceedings of the ACM SIGMOD International Conference on Management of Data*.

Kumar, R., Farkas, K. I., Jouppi, N. P., Ranganathan, P., and Tullsen, D. M. 2003. Single-ISA Heterogeneous Multi-core Architectures: The Potential for Processor Power Reduction. Pages 81–92 of: *Proceedings of 36th Annual IEEE/ACM International Symposium on Microarchitecture*.

Le, S. Y., Owens, J., Nussinov, R., Chen, J. H., Shapiro, B., and Maizel, J. V. 1989. RNA Secondary Structures: Comparison and Determination of Frequently Recurring Substructures by Consensus. *Bioinformatics*, **5**(3), 205.

Needleman, S. B., and Wunsch, C. D. 1970. A General Method Applicable to the Search for Similarities in the Amino Acid Sequence of Two Proteins. *Journal of Molecular Biology*, **48**(3), 443–453.

Nijssen, S., and Kok, J. N. 2003. Efficient Discovery of Frequent Unordered Trees. Pages 55–64 of: *First International Workshop on Mining Graphs, Trees and Sequences*.

Olson, C. F. 1995. Parallel Algorithms for Hierarchical Clustering. *Parallel Computing*, **21**(8), 1313–1325.

Parthasarathy, S., Zaki, M. J., Ogihara, M., and Li, W. 2001. Parallel Data Mining for Association Rules on Shared-Memory Systems. *Knowledge and Information Systems*, **3**(1), 1–29.

Parthasarathy, S., Tatikonda, S., Buehrer, G., and Ghoting, A. 2008. *Architecture Conscious Data Mining: Current Directions and Future Outlook*. Boca Raton, FL: Chapman & Hall/CRC.

Qiao, L., Raman, V., Reiss, F., Haas, P. J., and Lohman, G. M. 2008. Main-memory Scan Sharing for Multi-core CPUs. Pages 610–621 of: *Proceedings of 34th International conference on Very Large Data Bases (VLDB)*.

Ruckert, U., and Kramer, S. 2004. Frequent Free Tree Discovery in Graph Data. Pages 564–570 of: *ACM Symposium on Applied Computing*.

Saha, B., *et al.* 2007. Enabling Scalability and Performance in a Large scale CMP Environment. Pages 73–860 of: *Proceedings of the ACM European Conference on Computer Systems (EuroSys)*.

Shapiro, B. A., and Zhang, K. 1990. Comparing Multiple RNA Secondary Structures Using Tree Comparisons. *Bioinformatics*, **6**(4), 309.

Shasha, D. W., and Zhang, J. T. L. S. 2004. Unordered Tree Mining with Applications to Phylogeny. Pages 708–719 of: *Proceedings 20th International Conference on Data Engineering (ICDE)*.

Steel, M., and Warnow, T. 1993. Tree Theorems: Computing the Maximum Agreement Subtree. *Information Processing Letters*, **48**, 77–82.

Tan, H., Dillon, T. S., Hadzic, F., Chang, E., and Feng, L. 2006. IMB3-Miner: Mining Induced/embedded Subtrees by Constraining the Level of Embedding. Pages 450–461: *Proceedings of 8th Pacific Asia Conference on Knowledge Discovery and Data Mining (PAKDD)*.

Tatikonda, S. 2010. *Towards Efficient Data Analysis and Management of Semi-Structured Data*. Ph.D. thesis, The Ohio State University.

Tatikonda, S., and Parthasarathy, S. 2009. Mining Tree-structured Data on Multicore Systems. Pages 694–705 of: *Proceedings of the 35rd International Conference on Very Large Data Bases*.

Tatikonda, S., Parthasarathy, S., and Kurc, T. 2006. TRIPS and TIDES: New Algorithms for Tree mining. Pages 455–464 of: *Proceedings of the 15th ACM International Conference on Information and Knowledge Management (CIKM)*.

Tatikonda, S., Parthasarathy, S., and Goyder, M. 2007. LCS-TRIM: Dynamic Programming Meets XML Indexing and Querying. Pages 63–74 of: *Proceedings of the 33rd international conference on Very Large Data Bases (VLDB)*.

Termier, A., Rousset, M. C., and Sebag, M. 2002. TreeFinder: A First Step Towards XML Data Mining. Page 450 of: *Proceedings of IEEE International Conference on Data Mining (ICDM).*

Termier, A., Rousset, M. C., and Sebag, M. 2004. DRYADE: A New Approach for Discovering Closed Frequent Trees in Heterogeneous Tree Databases. Pages 543–546 of: *Proceedings of 4th IEEE International Conference on Data Mining (ICDM).*

Wagner, R., and Fischer, M. 1974. The String-to-String Correction Problem. *Journal of the ACM (JACM),* **21**(1), 168–173.

Wang, C., Hong, M., Pei, J., Zhou, H., Wang, W., and Shi, B. 2004. Efficient Pattern-growth Methods for Frequent Tree Pattern Mining. Pages 441–451 of: *Proceedings of the Pacific Asia Conference on Knowledge Discovery and Data Mining (PAKDD).*

Yang, L. H., Lee, M. L., and Hsu, W. 2004. Finding Hot Query Patterns Over an XQuery Stream. *The VLDB Journal: The International Journal on Very Large Data Bases,* **13**(4), 318–332.

Zaki, M. J. 1999a. Parallel Sequence Mining on Shared-Memory Machines. *Large-Scale Parallel Data Mining,* 804–804.

Zaki, M. J. 1999b. Parallel and Distributed Association Mining: A Survey. *In IEEE Concurrency,* **7**(4), 14–25.

Zaki, M. J. 2005. Efficiently Mining Frequent Trees in a Forest: Algorithms and Applications. *IEEE Transactions on Knowledge and Data Engineering,* **17**(8), 1021–1035.

Zaki, M.J., and Aggarwal, C.C. 2003. XRules: An Effective Structural Classifier for XML Data. Pages 316–325 of: *Proceedings of the 9th ACM International Conference on Knowledge Discovery and Data Mining (KDD).*

Zezula, P., Amato, G., Debole, F., and Rabitti, F. 2003. Tree Signatures for XML Querying and Navigation. Pages 149–163 of: *Proceedings of 1st XML Database Symposium (XSym).*

Zhang, K. 1998. Computing Similarity between RNA Secondary Structures. Pages 126–132 of: *Proceedings of IEEE International Joint Symposia on Intelligence and Systems.*

CHAPTER 21

Scalable Parallelization of Automatic Speech Recognition

Jike Chong, Ekaterina Gonina, Kisun You, and Kurt Keutzer

Automatic speech recognition (ASR) allows multimedia contents to be transcribed from acoustic waveforms into word sequences. It is an exemplar of a class of machine learning applications where increasing compute capability is enabling new industries such as automatic speech analytics. Speech analytics help customer service call centers search through recorded content, track service quality, and provide early detection of service issues. Fast and efficient ASR enables economic employment of a plethora of text-based data analytics on multimedia contents, opening the door to many possibilities.

In this chapter, we describe our approach for scalable parallelization of the most challenging component of ASR: the speech inference engine. This component takes a sequence of audio features extracted from a speech waveform as input, compares them iteratively to a speech model, and produces the most likely interpretation of the speech waveform as a word sequence. The speech model is a database of acoustic characteristics, word pronunciations, and phrases from a particular language. Speech models for natural languages are represented with large irregular graphs consisting of millions of states and arcs. Referencing these models involves accessing an unpredictable data working set guided by "what was said" in the speech input. The inference process is highly challenging to parallelize efficiently.

We demonstrate that parallelizing an application is much more than recoding the program in another language. It requires careful consideration of data, task, and runtime concerns to successfully exploit the full parallelization potential of an application. By using our approach, we were able to achieve more than 3.4× speedup on an Intel Core i7 multicore processor and more than 11× speedup on an NVIDIA GTX280 manycore processor[1] for the ASR inference engine. This performance improvement opens up many opportunities for latency-limited as well as throughput-limited applications of automatic speech recognition.

---

[1] Manycore processors contain dozens of cores – more than what the traditional multicore architecture can support.

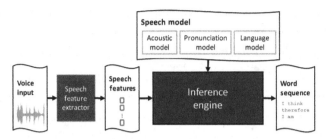

Figure 21.1 System architecture of a large vocabulary continuous speech recognition application.

Automatic Speech Recognition Application Characteristics

Recognition of human speech is a complex task, especially considering the significant variation in the voice quality, speed, and pronunciation among different speakers. Furthermore, differences among languages as well as the speech recording environments pose further challenges to an effective recognition system. After decades of scientific research, many researchers have converged on the hidden Markov model (HMM) "extract and inference" system as a standard setup. In this setup, the acoustic signal is treated as the observed sequence of events, and the sentences to be recognized are considered the "hidden cause" of the acoustic signal. In this chapter, we focus on this setup and discuss approaches to speedup the inference process on both multicore and manycore parallel computing platforms.

As shown in Figure 21.1, ASR first extracts representative features from an input waveform and then decodes the feature sequence to produce a word sequence. The feature extraction process involves a sequence of signal processing steps. It aims to minimize variation among speaker voice quality and room acoustics and preserve features most useful to distinguishing word sequences. A feature vector is extracted per 10-ms segment of the waveform (a time step). A sequence of feature vectors is used in an inference process by iteratively comparing each feature vector to a probabilistic speech model. The speech model contains an acoustic component, a pronunciation component, and a language component. The pronunciation component comes from a typical dictionary. Both the acoustic and language components are trained offline using a set of powerful statistical learning techniques.

The acoustic model is often represented as a multicomponent Gaussian mixture model, which takes into account slight differences in the pronunciations of each phone.[2] The pronunciation model describes each word as a sequence of phones that make up its pronunciation. The language model relates words into phrases and is often represented by unigrams, bigrams, and trigrams, which are the common one-, two-, and three-word phrases and their likelihood of appearance in a language. To recognize a different language in a different environment, only the speech model and the feature extractor need to be changed. The inference engine stays unchanged, producing the most likely interpretation of the input sequence by traversing the speech model for the specified language.

---

[2] Phone is an abstract unit of sound in the phonetic system of a language.

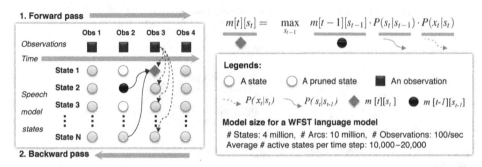

Figure 21.2 Application characteristics: inner working of the performance critical Viterbi forward- and backward-pass steps.

The pronunciation model and the language model can be seen as finite state machines with transition probabilities on the arcs between states. One of the state-of-the-art optimization techniques in automatic speech recognition is to compose the acoustic model with the pronunciation model and the language model offline to produce a weighted finite state transducer (WFST) (Mohri, Pereira, and Riley, 2002), where a single state machine can relate phone sequences to phrases directly. A typical WFST-based recognition network can have millions of states and arcs. The WFST representation could reduce redundancies in the number of state transitions traversal at runtime by $22\times$ (Chong et al., 2010a) and simplify the traversal process to reference only one state machine.

Figure 21.2 shows the inference process of ASR. The inference engine uses the Viterbi dynamic programming algorithm (Ney and Ortmanns, 1999). It performs a forward-pass step to track the more likely interpretations of the feature vector sequence through each increment in the time steps, and a backward-pass step to backtrack the path taken by the most likely outcome at the end of a sequence.

The forward-pass has two main phases to perform the inference. Phase 1 (shown in Figure 21.2 as dashed arrows between observations and states) evaluates the observation probability of the hidden state. It matches the input information to the available acoustic model elements and takes into account only the instantaneous likelihood of a feature matching acoustic model element. Phase 2 (shown in Figure 21.2 as the solid arrows between states of consecutive time steps) references the historic information about what are the most likely alternative interpretations of the utterance heard so far and computes the likelihood of incorporating the current observation given the pronunciation and language models. The computation for each state s_t at time t (with the diamond-shaped state as an example) records the state transition from the prior time step $t-1$ that produced the maximum probability $m[t][s_t]$.

In each time step of the algorithm, the data "working set" involves thousands of active states that are used to keep track of the most likely alternative interpretations of the speech heard so far. We compute the next set of active states by using Phase 2 of the algorithm described earlier. It is found that by tracking less than 1% of the most likely alternative interpretations and pruning away the rest, we perceive negligible differences in recognition accuracy as compared to tracking all alternative interpretations. The process of pruning less likely interpretations is called the beam search technique as described by Ney and Ortmanns (1999).

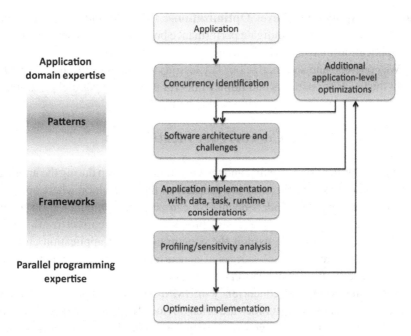

Figure 21.3 Steps in parallelizing an application on a parallel platform.

Our Parallel Programming Methodology

In this chapter, we illustrate our approach for scalable parallelization of a speech inference engine. This process can also be applied to other similar applications in machine learning such as machine translation. Our approach involves a judicious design of a software architecture to efficiently exploit concurrency in an application. We define a software architecture as a hierarchical composition of *patterns*, which are problem–solution pairs to recurring problems that experts in a problem domain gradually learn and "take for granted" (Keutzer and Mattson, 2009). Software architecture is based on a careful analysis of the concurrency sources in the given application.

We illustrate a step-by-step parallelization process in Figure 21.3 and describe the benefits of our approach. Each section of the chapter corresponds to a step in the parallelization process as follows:

Concurrency Identification: Identify a rich source of concurrency that improves application-specific performance metric to obtain continued parallel scalability (see Section 21.1).

Software Architecture and Challenges: Construct a software architecture with software design patterns and use the pattern descriptions to help identify challenges when implementing the application (see Section 21.2).

Application Implementation: Take care of data, task, and runtime efficiency concerns in an implementation for a specific parallel platform (see Section 21.3).

Profiling/Sensitivity Analysis: Analyze the performance by evaluating particular application-specific performance metrics and evaluate sensitivity to changes in implementation styles (see Section 21.6).

Additional Application-Level Optimizations: Examine and apply application-level transformations to mitigate performance bottlenecks that cannot be removed by application-unaware optimizations (see Section 21.7).

We conclude and summarize our key lessons learned in Section 21.8 and highlight the needs for patterns and frameworks for productive parallel programming.

21.1 Concurrency Identification

Concurrency identification is the first and the most important step during the application parallelization process. Concurrency is a property of the application where application modules are identified to be independent. We can perform computation on the independent modules simultaneously and still produce logically correct results. During the parallelization process, we exploit the concurrency in an application and map it onto execution resources. Not all sources of concurrency in an application need to be exploited to achieve efficient execution on a parallel platform.

There are many sources of concurrency in HMM-based automatic speech recognition. These concurrency opportunities are often obvious for domain experts working in the application area. The challenge is to clarify the scalability and benefits of various sources of concurrency and evaluate which ones to exploit during parallelization. First, we enumerate these concurrency opportunities in ASR:

1. **Concurrency Across Sentences:** Each sentence can be recognized independently.
2. **Concurrency Across Phases of the Algorithm:** Different phases of computation can be pipelined to handle multiple time steps of data at the same time.
3. **Concurrency Across Acoustic Model Computation:** Each input feature is compared to thousands of acoustic model elements (or phone models) at a time; the comparison with each phone model is independent.
4. **Concurrency Across Alternative Interpretations of a Sentence:** Many thousands of alternative interpretations are maintained to avoid allowing local noise to cause elimination of the overall most likely interpretation.

Next, we outline the application-specific performance metrics. There are three main performance metrics for ASR: improving accuracy, throughput, and latency (Chong et al., 2010b). Improving recognition accuracy opens up new domains of applications where there is less tolerance for recognition error; improving throughput lowers the cost of existing batch processing usage scenarios; and improving latency can allow more complex processing steps such as language translation to be integrated while still meeting real-time latency constraints.

Table 21.1 illustrates the concurrency identification process for ASR. The table provides a comparison of the different levels of functional concurrency, as well as highlights the benefits in key application domain concerns.

The *concurrency across sentences* is a popular concurrency source to exploit in deploying to today's computing clusters. It is the de facto parallelization approach for speech recognition researchers and developers alike. Each sentence is considered a separate task to be transcribed independently on a cluster node. Assuming an average sentence is approximately 10 seconds long, to transcribe a 60-minute talk, or

Table 21.1. *Available application concurrency and the key application domain concerns being addressed.*

Concurrency sources	Concurrency scalability (# ways)	Improving accuracy	Improving throughput	Improving latency
Across sentences	300–500	Yes*	Yes	No
Across algorithm phases	3–5	Yes*	Yes	No
Across acoustic model computations	500–3,000	Yes*	Yes	Yes
Across alternative interpretations	10,000+	Yes*	Yes	Yes

* Speedup can be used to improve accuracy when the usage scenario is compute-capacity constrained, and the speedup enables more complex processing to be done within the same cost constraints.

3,600 seconds of speech, we would expect 300- to 500-way concurrency, which can be mapped to any number of computers in a cluster. However, this approach does not help in improving the latency of recognizing one particular sentence.

The *concurrency across algorithm phases* involves pipelining the algorithmic phases. For example, Ishikawa et al. (2006) explored this coarse-grained concurrency in implementing a pipeline of tasks on a cellphone-oriented multicore architecture. Although some speedup can be obtained using this approach, it involves significant effort to re-factor an implementation to target every new generation of parallel hardware. The source of concurrency is limited in scalability, and exploiting it with pipelining does not improve recognition latency.

The *concurrency in acoustic model computation* involves estimating the likelihood of an input feature vector matching to particular units (or phones) in an acoustic model. There exists a 500- to 3,000-way concurrency concentrated in a simple Gaussian mixture model computation kernel, representing up to 80% of the total computation time in the inference engine. Research by Dixon, Oonishi, and Furui (2009) and Cardinal et al. (2008) focused on speeding up this part of ASR on manycore accelerators. Both demonstrated moderate (approximately $5\times$) speedups using manycore accelerators and managed the alternative interpretations in the Viterbi search process on the host system. However, this approach introduces significant overhead in copying intermediate results between the host and the manycore accelerator subsystem, which diminishes the benefits of potential speedup.

The *concurrency across alternative interpretations* is the richest among the four choices, as tracking more alternative interpretations increases the likelihood of identifying the overall most likely interpretation and improves accuracy. However, exploiting this level of concurrency involves frequent synchronizations across numerous algorithmic steps. Researchers often exploit the easier source of concurrency in acoustic model computation before attempting to exploit this source of concurrency. Ravishankar (1993) first mapped this fine-grained concurrency onto the PLUS multiprocessor with distributed memory. You, Lee, and Sung (2009b) have proposed an implementation using OpenMP on a multicore system, with later work by You et al. (2009a) using task queues to map tasks to processors. Chong et al. (2009) and You et al. (2009a) have successfully exploited concurrency at this level on manycore accelerators, with thousands of concurrent contexts running at the same time.

Both sources of concurrency in the acoustic model computation and across alternative interpretations are scalable, enabling continued speedup as implementation platforms become more parallel. They can also improve recognition latency, which opens up new application areas in real-time recognition. Thus, we focus on exploiting these two sources of concurrency in this chapter. It is worth noting that the concurrency at the sentence level is orthogonal and can be applied across clusters of multicore and manycore computation nodes to achieve additional improvements in recognition throughput.

Looking back to Figure 21.3, in this section we have presented our approach to concurrency identification; we now continue the flow by examining the software architecture and challenges in Section 21.2.

21.2 Software Architecture and Implementation Challenges

Once the suitable sources of concurrency are identified, a software architecture can be designed to exploit them. We define a software architecture as a hierarchical composition of *patterns*. *Patterns* are solutions to recurring design problems that domain experts learn (Keutzer and Mattson, 2009). Figure 21.4 illustrates one such software architecture constructed to exploit the concurrency both in acoustic model computation and across alternative interpretations.

As shown in Figure 21.4, the inference engine implements the Viterbi search algorithm, which finds the most likely word sequence considered to be the "hidden cause" of the acoustic signal. At the top level, the algorithm employs the *Iterator pattern* – the computation iterates through a sequence of feature vectors extracted from the acoustic signals one time step per iteration. Within each iteration, the algorithm goes through two phases of execution sequentially in a *Pipe & Filter pattern*. The first phase is compute-intensive and estimates the observation probability of the feature vector with respect to a set of acoustic features. The features are represented as sets of Gaussian mixtures in the feature space. The second phase is communication intensive, during which the algorithm manages the likely alternative interpretations of the input feature sequence. In our weighted finite state transducer (WFST)-based speech model, Phase 2 is a traversal through a graph with probabilistic state-to-state transitions. The sources of concurrency being exploited lie inside Phase 1 and Phase 2 in the iteration loop. We exploit this concurrency using the *MapReduce pattern*, where each state-to-state transition is mapped

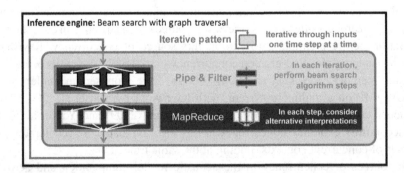

Figure 21.4 Software architecture of the speech recognition inference engine.

to an execution unit and the results are accumulated (i.e., reduced) at the end of the computation.

This software architecture cleanly exploits the target concurrency sources, but its implementation has many challenges. We highlight five areas here:

1. **Frequent Synchronizations:** Phases 1 and 2 of the inference algorithm consist of multiple algorithmic steps that require global synchronization between them. In ASR, for example, one step may be computing likelihood of Gaussian mixtures in the acoustic model, whereas the next step is computing a set of arc traversals based on results from the previous step. This means that all Gaussian mixture computations must complete at a global barrier before any computation in the arc traversal step can begin. Such global synchronization represents an expensive process of data sharing among multiple cores. This synchronization, when occurring frequently, could dominate total execution time. For example, guided by Amdahl's law, if an application has 25% of its execution time taken up by synchronization, the application cannot be sped up by more than $4\times$, even with infinite computational resources.

2. **Large Data Working Set:** During every iteration of the inference algorithm, more than 100 MB of Gaussian mixture model parameters could be referenced in Phase 1. In Phase 2, the range of data that could potentially be accessed exceeds 400MB. This working set size is beyond the scope of on-chip cache hierarchies. Any techniques to reduce the amount of data accessed, or improve the efficiency with which this data is accessed would be beneficial.

3. **Low Computation-to-Communication Ratio**: Many of the algorithm steps involve collecting parameters from various models to infer the likelihood of an observation or manage an alternative interpretation. This process requires few floating-point operations of computation and many data accesses. A low computation-to-communication ratio implies that the application is likely to be bottle necked by the available communication bandwidth rather than the computation throughput. On today's highly parallel platforms, the processing units often have significant processing power but have to share the channel to off-chip memory. Thus, for such platforms a low computation-to-communication ratio indicates that it would be hard to fully exploit the capabilities of the processing unit.

4. **Irregular Data Structure:** The WFST speech model used in Phase 2 is an irregular graph that could contain millions of states and arcs. The number of out-degrees from states in the directed graph ranges from 1 to 897, and the number of in-degrees could be more than 16,000. The distribution of the in-degrees and out-degrees will vary with respect to different vocabulary and languages. This will make it difficult to optimize on platforms with wide vector units, where efficient execution depends on regularity of data accesses and computation.

5. **Unpredictable Workload and Memory Access Pattern:** The traversal through the WFST speech model represents alternative interpretations and is dependent on the acoustic input. This makes the workload size and memory access patterns highly unpredictable.

Having constructed a software architecture and identified challenges in the implementation, we now discuss how to map the software architecture to parallel platforms (following the process in Figure 21.3). In Section 21.3, we demonstrate ASR

Table 21.2. *Parameters for the experimental platforms.*

Type	Multicore	Manycore
Processor	Core i7 920	GTX280 (+Core2 Q9550)
Cores	4 cores (SMT)	30 cores
SIMD width	4 lanes	8 physical, 32 logical
Clock speed	2.66 GHz	1.296 GHz
SP GFLOP/s*	85.1	933
Memory capacity	6GB	1GB (8GB)
Memory BW	32.0 GB/s	141.7 GB/s
Compiler	ICC 10.1.015	NVCC 2.2

*Single-precision giga–floating-point operations per second (SP GFLOP/s).

implementations for a multicore and a manycore platform and address the programming concerns in efficiently exploiting the identified sources of concurrency.

21.3 Multicore and Manycore Parallel Platforms

Nuances in processor microarchitecture components such as memory hierarchy often require the use of different data structure alternatives. Differences in hardware scheduling capabilities could also require different implementations of tasks and different runtime mechanisms to load balance the parallel tasks. An efficient implementation on a parallel platform should be aware of all the resources and limitations of the hardware platform. Depending on the implementation platform, the parallelization approach could be very different.

For ASR, we discuss various data, task, and runtime considerations in implementing efficient solutions on multicore and manycore platforms. Specifically, we use an Intel Core i7 multicore platform and an NVIDIA GTX280 manycore platform, the specifications of which are compared in Table 21.2. We consider multicore processors as processors that devote significant transistor resources to complex features for accelerating single-thread performance. On the other hand, manycore processors use their transistor resources to maximize total instruction throughput at the expense of single-thread performance.

The GTX280 has almost an order of magnitude more cores than the Core i7, but each core runs at half the clock frequency of the Core i7. Leveraging the wider SIMD unit, the theoretical peak single-precision floating-point operation throughput of the GTX280 is over an order of magnitude more than that of the Core i7. However, the microarchitecture of the GTX280 is more restrictive, limiting the achievable throughput to approximately 3 to 6 times the throughput of the Core i7. In terms of access to data in off-chip volatile memory, GTX280 has more than 4 times the bandwidth compared to the Core i7. However, it has a less flexible on-chip cache hierarchy that does not include hardware cache coherency support between cores, which increases the bandwidth pressure on the off-chip memory bus.

These differences in the platform specifications heavily influence the data, task, and runtime considerations in designing efficient implementations of ASR. In the following sections, we describe specific platform characteristics that are driving design decisions and illustrate how the application challenges are met and resolved. Where relevant, we also describe the alternative implementations we experimented with, and why they did not perform as well for ASR.

21.4 Multicore Infrastructure and Mapping

In this section, we discuss various data, task, and runtime considerations in implementing an efficient solution on the Core i7 multicore platform and conclude with the overall flow chart of the implementation.

21.4.1 Data Considerations

The Core i7 multicore processor has four cores, each of which has a dedicated 64KB (32I + 32D) L1 and 256KB L2 cache. There is also a shared unified 8MB L3 cache. The core-specific L1 and L2 caches call for data locality considerations, and frequent data transfers between cache levels make cache alignment important.

Data Locality: Phase 1 Evaluation

Gaussian mixture model (GMM) evaluation in Phase 1 requires a significant number of memory accesses to load Gaussian parameters. Evaluation of the whole GMM would require 10–100MB of Gaussian parameter data to be loaded at each iteration in Figure 21.4. Although the actual number of Gaussian parameters to be utilized in Phase 1 can be reduced by the beam search strategy by as much as 35% in our speech model, the data size is still large enough to hinder the cache locality between consecutive iterations. The working set of GMM evaluation migrates slowly across iterations such that Gaussian parameters utilized in current iterations are likely to be accessed in the next iteration. However, the multicore caches are not large enough to maintain data from one iteration to another, leading to capacity misses. Moreover, this could also displace the working set of Phase 2 in every iteration, eliminating the possibilities of cross-iteration sharing.

For better utilization of the cache, we can load the Gaussian parameters as noncachable streaming data and speculatively evaluate GMM for multiple future iterations. This way, we explicitly manage the temporal locality in Phase 1 across iterations with un-cached data and also allow the Phase 2 working set to reside in the caches across iterations. Although a larger number of future iterations to evaluate brings more data locality, it also increases unnecessary computations due to the migrating working set of GMM. Thus, we need to find the optimal number of future iterations by performing experiments.

Data Alignment: Phase 2 Evaluation

Memory accesses are optimized for 64-byte alignment, which is the size of one cache line. Access to unaligned data is costly both from a memory bandwidth utilization perspective and from an execution efficiency perspective, as unaligned load or store instructions are expanded to multiple micro-ops that reduce the throughput of these types of instructions in the processor execution pipeline.

In ASR, the speech model is represented by a graph, where each state and each arc has properties associated with it. State and arc accesses are input dependent and difficult to pack or align. To avoid unaligned memory access penalties, we choose an array-of-structs data structure for the state. Each state is cache-line-aligned in memory and is stored along with the associated properties in structs that are exactly one cache line in size. For arcs, the information from a source state is stored consecutively in the main memory, in a structs-of-arrays layout. This layout reduces the memory access time of Phase 2, since the outgoing arcs from a source state are accessed consecutively in the same thread.

21.4.2 Task Considerations

Task Granularity

The Core i7 multicore platform has 4-wide vector units that allow one vector instruction to simultaneously operate on four 32-bit data elements. The vector operations are also called SIMD operations for "single instruction multiple data". SIMD efficiency is the ability of all vector lanes to synchronously execute useful instructions. When all lanes are fully utilized for an instruction, we consider the execution "synchronized," and the computation is load balanced at the SIMD level. When operations are not synchronized, we consider the execution "divergent," and the computation becomes unbalanced with some lanes sitting idle while others do useful work. In order to get the best performance of the platform, all vector lanes should execute in a "synchronized" fashion; thus, we should try to assign the same amount of computation to each vector lane.

Phase 1 in the inference process involves computationally intensive Gaussian mixture model (GMM) evaluation. For the evaluation of each Gaussian mixture, we can assign the mixtures to the lanes in the SIMD instruction. As long as the number of mixtures is a multiple of 4, we achieve efficient utilization of Core i7's vector unit.

Phase 2 in the inference process is more complex. As shown in Figure 21.5, a typical implementation is to evaluate each active state in the speech model on a lane in the SIMD instruction. We call this approach *state-based* graph traversal. In this approach, the out-degrees of the states vary widely, which often results in "divergent" execution in the vector unit. On the other hand, we encounter data gather overheads

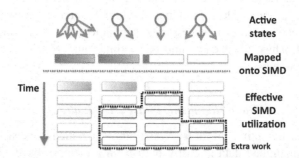

Figure 21.5 SIMD underutilization in a state-based traversal.

if we explicitly collect all the arcs to be evaluated and distribute each arc to a vector lane for evaluation in a "synchronized" fashion. We call this approach *arc-based* graph traversal. Our experiments show that on our speech model, the *state-based* and *arc-based* approaches achieved similar performances on Core i7, with the *state-based* approach being slightly faster. On architectures with wider SIMD instruction sets, however, "divergent" execution will incur higher penalties, and the *arc-based* approach is expected to be faster.

Synchronization Cost

The Core i7 platform supports basic atomic operations by either adding a "LOCK" prefix to integer instructions or directly using special instructions such as compare-and-swap (CMPXCHG) (Intel, 2009). When potential write conflicts arise in the multi-threaded algorithm, we can implement efficient synchronizations between cores using these instructions.

During Phase 2 of the inference process, each core evaluates state-to-state transitions and updates destination states if necessary. The destination state is updated only when a transition provides higher probability than all prior transitions considered. There may be multiple cores trying to update the same destination state during the execution, which results in potential write conflicts. We utilized the compare-and-swap operation to synchronize destination state updates. First, the current value of the destination state is fetched. Then, the evaluated transition probability is compared with the current value. Finally, if the transition probability is higher than the current value, the destination state value is updated by the transition probability with a compare-and-swap instruction.

This *propagation-based* approach, where results are propagated from source states to destination states with atomic operations, can be significantly more efficient compared to software-managed data-parallel write conflict resolution mechanisms. We also experimented with an *aggregation-based* software-managed approach, where unique result buffers are created for each state-to-state transition. The result buffers associated with the same destination state are explicitly reduced at the end of all transition evaluations to obtain the most likely state-to-state transition at each end state. On the Core i7 platform, the *propagation-based* approach was an order of magnitude faster than the *aggregation-based* approach for Phase 2 of the algorithm, as illustrated in Section 21.6.

21.4.3 Runtime Considerations

Task Scheduling and Load Balancing

The Core i7 multicore platform provides a shared memory abstraction that enables a variety of parallel programing abstractions. These include the POSIX Threads (Butenhof, 1997), Cilk (Blumofe et al., 1995), OpenMP (Chandra et al., 2000), or lightweight task queue implementations such as CARBON (Kumar, Hughes, and Nguyen, 2007).

For this parallelization of the ASR application, we have chosen a concurrency source that is most scalable, with fine-grained units of work at each algorithm step that are as short as 10–100 instructions. At this granularity, it is crucial to choose a parallel programming abstraction that is light weight in task generation and execution.

For our multicore implementation, we chose CARBON, a distributed task queue programming framework by Kumar et al. (2007) in which a task is a function that executes in one thread and can be scheduled as a unit. The application creates an array of tasks for arc or state computation, and the framework assigns sections of the task array to available processors. The framework then monitors for idle cores that have completed their tasks early and load balances the system during runtime.

Although the working set of the speech model migrates every iteration depending on input audio features, the working set size, that is, the number of active states/arcs in the speech model, is only 1–2% of the total speech model. Moreover, the working set on average overlaps by 80% between consecutive iterations. Thus, instead of distributing the tasks evenly among the set of task queues, we can assign each task to the thread queue where it was processed in the previous time frame. In this method, the initial workload is inevitably imbalanced when the processors start execution. However, lazy task stealing (stealing more work only when the core runs out of work in its own queue) guarantees eventual load balance. Since the tasks are likely to be processed in the same processor for many iterations, we could achieve approximately 20% speedup in Phase 2 with a notion of affinity between tasks and processors.

To achieve high cache performance, we could also utilize a static scheduling method in which the speech model is partitioned offline and each processor executes on only its designated partition. However, it is difficult to statically partition the irregular graph while maintaining good load balance.

21.4.4 Summary

Given the discussion on data, task, and runtime considerations in implementing an efficient solution on the Core i7 platform, we present the final implementation flow in Figure 21.6a.

In this implementation, all the data structures are stored in main memory and the working set is managed by the hardware cache hierarchy, which is a highly efficient low-latency synchronization mechanism for the *frequent synchonizations*. To efficiently utilize the underlying cache architecture, we speculatively evaluate Gaussian mixtures for multiple future frames for increased temporal locality in Phase 1 and mitigated issues with the *large data working set*. We aligned the data structures with the cache lines to minimize data transfers between cache levels and improved the *low computation-to-communication ratio*. Frequent synchronizations during the graph traversal phase are implemented using efficient hardware-assisted atomic operations. Finally, we adopted task-queue-based dynamic task scheduling to deal with the variable task execution time caused by traversing an *irregular data structure* and achieved good *workload balance* among multiple cores. Additionally, we enhanced the cache utilization and promoted temporal locality by establishing task-to-core affinity.

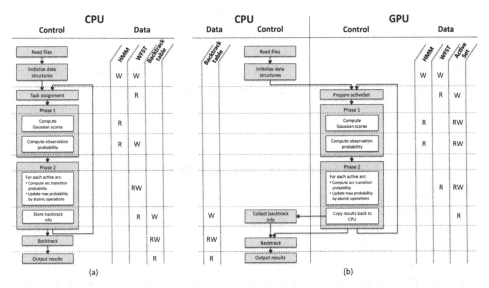

Figure 21.6 Summary of the data structure access and control flow of the inference engine on (a) the multicore platform and (b) the manycore platform.

21.5 The Manycore Implementation

In this section, we discuss various data, task, and runtime considerations in implementing an efficient solution on the GTX280 manycore platform and conclude with the overall flow chart of the implementation.

21.5.1 Data Considerations

Memory Hierarchy

The GTX280 manycore platform has two levels of memory hierarchy for the GPU to access data with orders-of-magnitude differences in the memory throughput. The host-to-device memory accesses have 2.5GB/s data transfer rate, and the device memory bandwidth is about 120GB/s. The graph traversal process of the inference engine has a highly irregular memory access pattern. Thus, it is essential to keep the working set in device memory for high-bandwidth access. The GTX280 provides 1GB of device memory on the GPU board, which can fit the acoustic model (130MB), the language model (400MB), and various temporary graph traversal data structures. The GTX280 architecture has a less flexible memory hierarchy than the traditional cache-based architectures. The GTX280 has a global memory shared by all multiprocessors. Each multiprocessor also has a fast local shared memory space (16KB per multiprocessor) that is software managed. In addition, the memory hierarchy does not include hardware cache coherency support between cores, which increases the bandwidth pressure on the off-chip memory bus.

We architect all graph traversal steps to run exclusively on the GPU with intermediate results stored in the device memory. This avoids the host-device memory transfer bottleneck and allows the CUDA kernels to utilize the high device memory bandwidth. Not all intermediate data can fit in the device memory, however. The traversal history data is copied back to the host system at regular intervals to save space. Since history data is used only at the very end of the traversal process, the data transfer is a one-way, device-to-host copy. This transfer involves around 10MB of data per second, which translates to less than 5 ms of transfer time on a channel with 2.5GB/s bandwidth and thus is a negligible fraction of the overall computation.

Data Structure Regularity and Working Set

Data accesses on manycore platforms need to be extremely regular. Specifically, data accesses can be classified as "coalesced" or "uncoalesced". A "coalesced" memory access loads a consecutive vector of data that directly maps onto the vector lanes of the processing unit of the manycore platform. Such accesses efficiently utilize the available memory bandwidth. "Uncoalesced" accesses, on the other hand, load nonconsecutive data elements to be processed by the vector units, thereby wasting bandwidth. Thus, in order to fully utilize the manycore platform, we must ensure that memory accesses are coalesced by constructing our data structure accordingly.

During the traversal process, we access an arbitrary subset of nonconsecutive states or arcs in the speech model in each iteration, resulting in uncoalesced memory accesses. One solution to this is to explicitly gather all required information into a temporary buffer such that all later accesses to the temporary buffer will be coalesced. Thus, we explicitly manage our working set to contain the current set of active states and arcs, ensuring coalesced memory accesses and data reuse.

21.5.2 Task Considerations

Task Granularity

The GTX280 manycore platform has 8-wide physical, 32-wide logical SIMD vector units. It is essential for an implementation to fully saturate the compute resources of these wide SIMD vector units to obtain good performance on the manycore platform.

We use the *arc-based* approach as discussed in Section 21.4.2, where each SIMD vector lane evaluates one arc transition from state to state during Phase 2 of the algorithm. Each arc evaluation presents a constant amount of work; thus, the evaluation process is "synchronized". This approach requires extra memory storage overhead as well as extra processing overhead to create more fine-grained tasks. For 32-wide SIMD operations, the performance benefit we get from "synchronized" execution including the processing overhead is more significant than the penalty incurred in "divergent" execution.

The alternative approach to mapping execution tasks to SIMD vector units would be to assign each lane to evaluate a state (the *state-based* approach). This approach presents less software overhead. However, as shown in Figure 21.5 for the state-based approach, the control flow diverges, resulting in an unbalanced computation as some lanes are idle while others do useful work. For the GTX280 32-wide SIMD vector unit, the "divergent" control flow results in only 10% SIMD utilization. Using an *arc-based* implementation gives $9\times$ speedup for the same computation, thus nearly gaining back full SIMD efficiency.

Synchronization Cost

The GTX280 provides efficient atomic operations for between-core synchronizations (NVIDIA, 2009). Its atomic support goes beyond the standard CompareAndSwap operations and includes some simple arithmetic and logic operations such as *atomicMax*. When used properly, these atomic operations can merge multiple high-latency operations into a single atomic access, significantly improving application efficiency.

During Phase 2, the task for each core is to evaluate state-to-state transitions. Multiple transitions can end in the same state. This creates a potential write conflict in reading, comparing, and saving the end state properties and eventually in maintaining the highest state-to-state transition probability. By using the *atomicMax*, we solve all these issues by atomically updating the value of the end state only if the probability of the new transition is higher. The efficient atomic support on GTX280 reduces synchronization cost to a theoretical minimum: only one operation per parallel task.

The *propagation-based* approach described earlier propagates results from source states to destination states with atomic operations. It is significantly more efficient compared to software-managed data-parallel write conflict resolution mechanisms. We also experimented with an *aggregation-based* approach as discussed in Section 21.4.2 and observed a 2-ms overhead for using the *aggregation-based* write conflict resolution compared with a 0.05-ms overhead for using the *propagation-based* approach. Leveraging hardware-assisted atomic operations on the GTX280 resulted in an almost two orders of magnitude performance improvement.

21.5.3 Runtime Considerations

Task Scheduling and Load Balancing

We use the CUDA programming framework (NVIDIA, 2009) to implement the inference process. An application is organized into a sequential host program running on the host system(the CPU) and one or more parallel kernels running on the accelerators (the GPU). A kernel executes a set of scalar sequential programs across a set of parallel threads. The programmer can organize these threads into thread blocks, which are mapped onto the multiprocessing units on the GTX280 at runtime. Task scheduling and load balancing are handled by the device driver automatically. In ASR, there is a significant amount of concurrency to allow for good load balance among the many cores at runtime.

21.5.4 Summary

Given the discussions on data, task, and runtime considerations in implementing an efficient solutions on the GTX280 manycore platforms, we present the final implementation on GTX280 in Figure 21.6b.

In this implementation, we offload the entire inference process to the GTX280 platform and take advantage the efficient hardware-assisted atomic operations to facilitate the challenge of having *frequent synchronizations*. The *large data working set* is stored on the 1GB dedicated memory on the GTX280 platform and accessed through a memory bus with 140GB/s peak throughput. We start an iteration by preparing an ActiveSet data structure to gather the necessary operands into a "coalesced" data structure to maximize communication efficiency and *improve computation-to-communication ratio*. We then use an *arc-based* traversal to handle the *irregular data structure* and maximize SIMD efficiency in the evaluation of state-to-state transitions. Finally, we leverage the CUDA runtime to efficiently meet the challenge in scheduling the *unpredictable workload size* with variable runtimes onto the 30 parallel multiprocessors on GTX280.

Following Figure 21.3, after mapping the application to the parallel platform, we need to profile performance and do sensitivity analysis to different trade-offs particular to the specific implementation platform. We describe this process for our ASR inference engine application in Section 21.6.

21.6 Implementation Profiling and Sensitivity Analysis

We have addressed the known performance challenges by examining data, task, and runtime concerns and constructed a functionally correct implementation. Now we can analyze the performance achieved by these implementations.

21.6.1 Speech Models and Test Sets

Our ASR profiling uses speech models from the SRI CALO real-time meeting recognition system (Tur et al., 2008). The front end uses 13 dimensional perceptual linear prediction (PLP) features with first-, second-, and third-order differences, is vocal-track-length normalized, and is projected to 39 dimensions using heteroscedastic linear discriminant analysis (HLDA). The acoustic model is trained on conversational telephone and meeting speech corpora using the discriminative minimum-phone-error (MPE) criterion. The language model is trained on meeting transcripts, conversational telephone speech, and web and broadcast data (Stolcke et al., 2008). The acoustic model includes 52K triphone states that are clustered into 2,613 mixtures of 128 Gaussian components.

The pronunciation model contains 59K words with a total of 80K pronunciations. We use a small back-off bigram language model with 167K bigram transitions. The speech model is an $H \circ C \circ L \circ G$ model compiled using WFST techniques (Mohri et al., 2002) and contains 4.1 million states and 9.8 million arcs.

The test set consisted of excerpts from NIST conference meetings taken from the "individual head-mounted microphone" condition of the 2007 NIST Rich Transcription evaluation. The segmented audio files total 44 minutes in length and comprise 10 speakers. For the experiment, we assumed that the feature extraction is performed offline so that the inference engine can directly access the feature files.

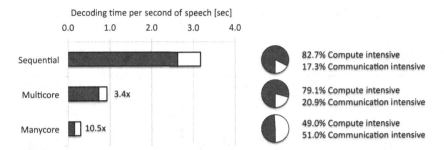

Figure 21.7 Ratio of computation-intensive phase of the algorithm versus communication-intensive phase of the algorithm.

21.6.2 Overall Performance

We analyze the performance of our inference engine implementations on both the Core i7 multicore processor and the GTX280 manycore processor. The sequential baseline is implemented on a single core in a Core i7 quad-core processor, utilizing a SIMD-optimized Phase 1 routine and non–SIMD graph traversal routine for Phase 2. Compared to this highly optimized sequential baseline implementation, we achieve 3.4× speedup using all cores of Core i7 and 10.5× speedup on GTX280.

The performance gain is best illustrated in Figure 21.7 by highlighting the distinction between the compute-intensive phase (black bar) and the communication-intensive phase (white bar). The compute-intensive phase achieves 3.6× speedup on the multicore processor and 17.7× on the manycore processor, while the communication-intensive phase achieves only 2.8× speedup on the multicore processor and 3.7× on the manycore processor.

The speedup numbers indicate that the communication-intensive Phase 2 dominates the runtime as more processors need to be coordinated. In terms of the ratio between the compute- and communication-intensive phases, the pie charts in Figure 21.7 show that 82.7% of the time in the sequential implementation is spent in the compute-intensive phase of the application. As we scale to the manycore implementation, the compute-intensive phase becomes proportionally less dominant, taking only 49.0% of the total runtime. The dominance of the communication-intensive phase motivates further detailed examination of Phase 2 in our inference engine.

21.6.3 Sensitivity Analysis

In order to determine the sensitivity to different styles of the algorithm in the communication-intensive phase, we constructed a series of experiments for both the multicore and the manycore platform. The trade-offs in both task granularity and core synchronization techniques are examined for both platforms. The design space for our experiments as well as the performance results are shown in Figure 21.8. The choice in task granularity has direct implications for load balance and task creation overhead, whereas the choice of the traversal technique determines the cost of the core-level synchronization.

The columns in Figure 21.8 represent different graph traversal techniques and the rows indicate different transition evaluation granularity. The figure provides

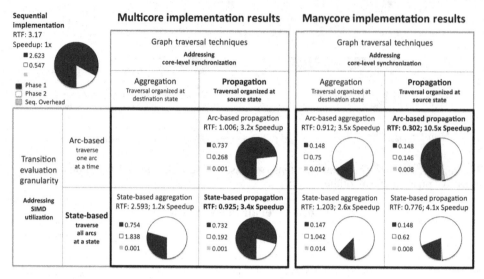

Figure 21.8 Recognition performance normalized for 1 second of speech for different algorithm styles on Intel Core i7 and NVIDIA GTX280.

performance improvement information for Phases 1 and 2 as well as sequential overhead for all parallel implementation styles. The speedup numbers are reported over our fastest sequential version in the *state-based propagation* style. On both of the platforms, the *propagation-based* style achieved better performance. However, the choice of best-performing task granularity differed for the two platforms. For the manycore implementation, the load-balancing benefits of arc-based approaches were much greater than the overhead of creating the finer-grained tasks. On the multicore architecture, the arc-based approach not only presented more overhead in creating finer-grained tasks but also resulted in a larger working set, thus increasing cache capacity misses. On wider SIMD units in future multicore platforms, however, we expect the *arc-based propagation style* will be faster than the *state-based propagation* style.

The figure also illustrates that the sequential overhead in our implementation is less than 2.5% of the total runtime even for the fastest implementations. This demonstrates that we have a scalable software architecture that promises greater potential speedups with more platform parallelism expected in future generations of processors.

After performing the profiling and sensitivity analysis, we end up with a highly optimized implementation of the application on the parallel platform (see Figure 21.3). We can further optimize the implementation by making application-level decisions and trade-offs subject to the constraints and bottlenecks identified in the parallelization process. Section 21.7 describes an example of such optimizations.

21.7 Application-Level Optimization

An efficient implementation is not the end of the parallelization process. For the inference engine on GTX280, for example, we observed that given the challenging algorithm requirements, the dominant kernel has shifted from the compute-intensive Phase 1 to the communication-intensive Phase 2 in the implementation. We have also observed that modifying the inference engine implementation style does not improve the implementation any further. In this situation, we should take an opportunity to re-examine possible application-level transformations to further mitigate parallelization bottlenecks.

21.7.1 Speech Model Alternatives

Phase 2 of the algorithm involves a graph traversal process through an irregular speech model. There are two types of arcs in a WFST-based speech model: arcs with an input label (nonepsilon arcs) and arcs without input labels (epsilon arcs). In order to compute the set of next states in a given time step, we must traverse both the nonepsilon and all the levels of epsilon arcs from the current set of active states. This multi-level traversal can impair performance significantly as each level requires multiple steps of cross-core synchronization. We explore a set of application transformations to modify the speech model to reduce the levels of traversal that are required, while maintaining the WFST invariant of accumulating the same weight (likelihood) for the same input after a traversal. To illustrate this, Figure 21.9 shows a small section of a WFST-based speech model. Each time step starts with a set of currently active states, for example, states 1 and 2 in Figure 21.9, representing the alternative interpretations of the input utterances. It proceeds to evaluate all outgoing nonepsilon arcs to reach a set of destination states, such as states 3 and 4. The traversal then extends through epsilon arcs to reach more states, such as state 5, before the next time step.

The traversal from state 1 and 2 to 3, 4, and 5 can be seen as a process of active state wavefront expansion in a time step. The challenge for data parallel operations is that the expansion from 1 to 3 to 4 to 5 requires multiple levels of traversal. In this case, three-level expansion is required, with one nonepsilon level and two epsilon levels. By flattening the epsilon arcs as shown in Figure 21.9, we arrive at the Two-level WFST model, where by doing one nonepsilon-level expansion and one epsilon expansion we can reach all anticipated states. If we flatten the graph further, we can

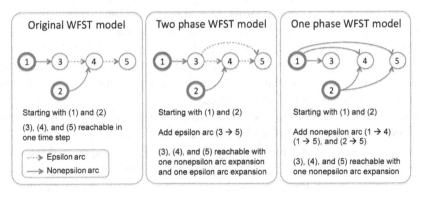

Figure 21.9 Model modification techniques for a data-parallel inference engine.

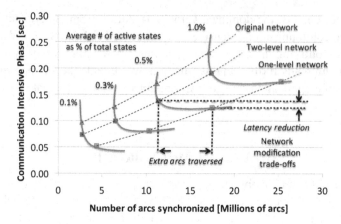

Figure 21.10 Communication-intensive phase runtime in the inference engine (normalized to 1 second of speech).

eliminate all epsilon arcs and achieve the same results with one level of nonepsilon arc expansion.

Although model flattening can help eliminate the overhead of multiple levels of synchronization, it can also increase the total number of arcs traversed. Depending on the specific model topology of the speech model, we may achieve varying amount of improvements in the final application performance metrics.

21.7.2 Evaluation of Alternatives

We constructed all three variations of the speech model and measured both the number of arcs evaluated as well as the execution time of the communication-intensive Phase 2. We varied the number of alternative interpretations, which is shown in Figure 21.10 as a percentage of total states that are active in the speech model.

The "L" shaped curves connect implementations that achieve the same recognition accuracy. At the application level, we are interested in reducing the execution times for the communication-intensive phase. Going from the Original setup to the Two-level setup, we observe a large improvement in execution time, shown as a drop in the execution-time graph of the communication-intensive phase. This execution-time improvement was accompanied by a moderate increase in the number of arcs traversed during decoding, shown as a small shift to the right. Going from the Two-level setup to the One-level setup, we see a relatively smaller improvement in execution time, with a large increase in the number of arcs traversed.

An application domain expert who understands the implications of input formats on performance of the parallel application can make application-level transformations to further improve the application performance. For example, in ASR, for the recognition task that maintains the smallest number of active arcs in this set of experiments, the speech model transformations are able to reduce the execution time of the communication-intensive phase from 97 ms to 75 ms, and further to 53 ms, thus almost doubling the performance for this phase.

21.8 Conclusion and Key Lessons

21.8.1 Process of Parallelization

This chapter describes a process for the scalable parallelization of an inference engine in automatic speech recognition. Looking back at Figure 21.3, we start the parallelization process at the application level and consider the available concurrency sources in an application. The challenge is to identify the richest source of concurrency that improves performance given a particular application constraint such as latency or throughput (see Section 21.1). With the identified concurrency source, we construct the software architecture for the application using design patterns. Design patterns help create software architectures by composing structural and computational patterns (Keutzer and Mattson, 2009), as shown in Section 21.2. The design patterns help identify the application challenges and bottlenecks in a software architecture to be addressed by the implementation.

The detailed implementation of the software architecture is performed with the consideration of three areas of concern (data, task, and runtime) for each particular platform. The most effective parallel implementation strategy must recognize the architecture characteristics of the implementation platform and leverage the available hardware and software infrastructures. Some of the areas of concern are well taken care of by the infrastructure or the runtime system. In other cases, various styles of implementation strategy must be explicitly constructed as a series of experiments to determine the best implementation choice for a particular trade-off, leading to a performance sensitivity analysis.

The performance of an application can be improved by modifying the algorithm based on application domain knowledge. As illustrated in Section 21.6, the speech domain expert can make application-level decisions about the speech model structure while still preserving logical correctness. By identifying bottlenecks in the current implementation of the application, the domain expert can choose to modify the parameters of the application in order to make the application less sensitive to parallelization bottlenecks.

21.8.2 Enabling Efficient Parallel Application Development Using Frameworks

In order to develop a highly optimized implementation, one needs to have strong expertise in all areas of the development stack. Strong application domain expertise is required to identify available application concurrency as well as to propose application-level transformations that can mitigate software architecture challenges. Strong parallel programming expertise is required in developing a parallel implementation, in which one needs to articulate the data, task, and runtime considerations for a software architecture on an implementation platform. This complexity increases the risks in deploying large parallel software projects as the levels of expertise vary across the domains.

Our ongoing work on software design patterns and frameworks at the PALLAS group in the Department of Electrical Engineering and Computer Science at University of California, Berkeley attempts to address this problem by encapsulating the low-level parallel programming constructs into frameworks for domain experts. The PALLAS group believes that the key to the design of parallel programs is software architecture, and the key to efficient implementation of the software architecture is frameworks. Borrowed from civil architecture, the term *design pattern* refers to a solution to a recurring design problem that domain experts learn with time. A software architecture is a hierarchical composition of *architectural* software design patterns, which can be subsequently refined using *implementation* design patterns. The software architecture and its refinement, although useful, are entirely conceptual. To implement the software, we rely on frameworks.

We define a *pattern-oriented software framework* as an environment built on top of a software architecture in which customization is allowed only in harmony with the framework's architecture. For example, if the software architecture is based on the *Pipe & Filter* pattern, the customization involves only modifying pipes or filters. We see application domain experts being serviced by application frameworks. These application frameworks have two advantages: First, the application programmer works within a familiar environment using concepts drawn from the application domain. Second, the frameworks prevent expression of many notoriously hard problems of parallel programming such as nondeterminism, races, deadlock, and starvation.

Specifically for ASR, we have tested and demonstrated this pattern-oriented approach during the process of designing this implementation. Patterns served as a conceptual tool to aid in the architectural design and implementation of the application. Referring back to Figure 21.3, we can use patterns from the software architecture to define a pattern-oriented framework for a speech recognition inference engine application. The framework will be able to encapsulate many data, task, and runtime considerations as well as profiling capabilities and will be able to be extended to related applications. Although this framework is our ongoing research, we believe that these software design patterns and the pattern-oriented frameworks will empower ASR domain experts, as well as other machine learning experts, to quickly construct efficient parallel implementations of their applications.

References

Blumofe, R. D., Joerg, C. F., Kuszmaul, B. C., Leiserson, C. E., Randall, K. H., and Zhou, Y. 1995. Cilk: An Efficient Multithreaded Runtime System. *Journal of Parallel and Distributed Computing*, 207–216.

Butenhof, D. R. 1997. *Programming with POSIX Threads*. Reading, MA: Addison-Wesley.

Cardinal, P., Dumouchel, P., Boulianne, G., and Comeau, M. 2008. GPU Accelerated Acoustic Likelihood Computations. Pages 964–967 of: *Proceeding of the 9th Annual Conference of the International Speech Communication Association (InterSpeech)*.

Chandra, R., Menon, R., Dagum, L., Kohr, D., Maydan, D., and McDonald, J. 2000. *Parallel Programming in OpenMP*. San Francisco, CA: Morgan Kaufmann.

Chong, J., Gonina, E., Yi, Y., and Keutzer, K. 2009 (September). A Fully Data-parallel WFST-based Large Vocabulary Continuous Speech Recognition on a Graphics Processing Unit. Pages 1183–1186 of: *Proceeding of the 10th Annual Conference of the International Speech Communication Association (InterSpeech)*.

Chong, J., Gonina, E., You, K., and Keutzer, K. 2010a (September). Exploring Recognition Network Representations for Efficient Speech Inference on Highly Parallel Platforms. In: *Proceeding of the 11th Annual Conference of the International Speech Communication Association (InterSpeech).*

Chong, J., Friedland, G., Janin, A., Morgan, N., and Oei, C. 2010b (June). Opportunities and Challenges of Parallelizing Speech Recognition. In: *2nd USENIX Workshop on Hot Topics in Parallelism (HotPar'10).*

Dixon, P. R., Oonishi, T., and Furui, S. 2009. Harnessing Graphics Processors for the Fast Computation of Acoustic Likelihoods in Speech Recognition. *Computer Speech and Language*, **23**(4), 510–526.

Intel. 2009. *Intel 64 and IA-32 Architectures Software Developer's Manuals.*

Ishikawa, S., Yamabana, K., Isotani, R., and Okumura, A. 2006 (May). Parallel LVCSR Algorithm for Cellphone-oriented Multicore Processors. Pages 117–180 of: *2006 IEEE International Conference on Acoustics, Speech and Signal Processing. ICASSP 2006 Proceedings.*

Keutzer, K., and Mattson, T. 2009. A Design Pattern Language for Engineering (Parallel) Software. *Intel Technology Journal, Addressing the Challenges of Tera-scale Computing*, **13**(4), 6–19.

Kumar, S., Hughes, C. J., and Nguyen, A. 2007. Carbon: Architectural Support for Fine-grained Parallelism on Chip Multiprocessors. Pages 162–173 of: *In ISCA 07: Proceedings of the 34th Annual International Symposium on Computer Architecture.* ACM.

Mohri, M., Pereira, F., and Riley, M. 2002. Weighted Finite State Transducers in Speech Recognition. *Computer Speech and Language*, **16**, 69–88.

Ney, H., and Ortmanns, S. 1999. Dynamic Programming Search for Continuous Speech Recognition. *IEEE Signal Processing Magazine*, **16**, 64–83.

NVIDIA. 2009 (May). *NVIDIA CUDA Programming Guide.* NVIDIA Corporation. Version 2.2.1.

Ravishankar, M. 1993. *Parallel Implementation of Fast Beam Search for Speaker-Independent Continuous Speech Recognition.* Technical Report, Computer Science and Automation, Indian Institute of Science, Bangalore, India.

Stolcke, A., Anguera, X., Boakye, K., Cetin, O., Janin, A., Magimai-Doss, M., Wooters, C., and Zheng, J. 2008. The SRI-ICSI Spring 2007 Meeting and Lecture Recognition System. *Lecture Notes in Computer Science*, **4625**(2), 450–463.

Tur, G., Stolcke, A., Voss, L., Dowding, J., Favre, B., Fernandez, R., Frampton, M., Frandsen, M., Frederickson, C., Graciarena, M., Hakkani-Tr, D., Kintzing, D., Leveque, K., Mason, S., Niekrasz, J., Peters, S., Purver, M., Riedhammer, K., Shriberg, E., Tien, J., Vergyri, D., and Yang, F. 2008. The CALO Meeting Speech Recognition and Understanding System. Pages 69–72 of: *Proceedings of IEEE Spoken Language Technology Workshop.*

You, K., Chong, J., Yi, Y., Gonina, E., Hughes, C., Chen, Y. K., Sung, W., and Keutzer, K. 2009a (November). Parallel Scalability in Speech Recognition: Inference Engine in Large Vocabulary Continuous Speech Recognition. *IEEE Signal Processing Magazine*, 124–135 .

You, K., Lee, Y., and Sung, W. 2009b (April). OpenMP-based Parallel Implementation of a Continuous Speech Recognizer on a Multicore System. Pages 621–624 of: *IEEE International Conference on Acoustics, Speech and Signal Processing, 2009. ICASSP 2009.*

Subject Index

Printed in the United States
By Bookmasters